ID0918801

62

LIVES OF THE STUART AGE

LIVES BEFORE THE TUDORS

in preparation

LIVES OF THE TUDOR AGE

1485–1603

Compiled by Ann Hoffmann

LIVES OF THE STUART AGE

1603–1714

Compiled by Laurence Urdang Associates

LIVES OF THE GEORGIAN AGE

1714–1837

Compiled by Laurence Urdang Associates

LIVES OF THE VICTORIAN AGE

in preparation

★

Osprey Publishing Limited

Series Editor: ROGER CLEEVE

The biographies presented in these books are those which
during the period covered attained their peak of achievement. Cross-references are given to the relevant volume
where this distinction is not obvious. Further volumes
will be published in due course.

LIVES

OF THE

STUART AGE

1603–1714

Compiled by Laurence Urdang Associates
Editor: Edwin Riddell
Managing Editor: Patrick Hanks

Osprey Publishing Limited

Published in 1976 by Osprey Publishing Limited
12–14 Long Acre, London WC2E 9LP

Member company of the George Philip Group

ISBN 0 85045 087 X

Designed by Frederick Price

Filmset and printed in Great Britain by
BAS Printers Limited, Wallop, Hampshire

PREFACE

This volume contains 322 short biographies of eminent men and women of the Stuart period.

As with other volumes in this series, selection has not been easy. In general, entries have been confined to those people who made a significant impact on the age through their achievements or their abilities. A few foreigners who lived and worked in England and had an influence on English society and tastes have also been included, and a careful selection has been made of some of the founders of the British colonies in North America. Nevertheless, the restricted availability of space has been a constraining factor upon our choice, and omissions are regrettably inevitable.

Entries have been arranged in alphabetical order and each article appears under the surname of the person concerned, with a cross-reference from a title. An exception has been made to this rule in the case of the Duke of Monmouth, whose paternity is doubtful, and whose multiplicity of aliases (Scott, Fitzroy, and Crofts) was felt to be a hindrance to clarity.

A highly selective bibliography is given at the end of most entries. This includes the standard biography and definitive editions of works where applicable. Books of a more general nature have usually been omitted from individual articles for lack of space, but a small number of works having general relevance for the period is provided in the list of sources given below. The place of publication is given only for books published outside the United Kingdom.

In addition to the bibliographies, many entries also carry a selective iconography, listing as far as can be ascertained the principal portraits and their locations, with special emphasis on the accessibility of the portraits to the public. Some care has been taken to ensure that these iconographies are up to date, but total reliability in this respect is not possible. The portrait lists, therefore, are not exhaustive and should be regarded as a guide only.

Sources:

The *Dictionary of National Biography* is of course a major source, although in many respects it has been superseded by more recent research. Information on the lives of the early founders of America may be found in Allen Johnson (ed.), *Dictionary of American Biography* (New York, 1927) although to some extent, this also needs to be revised.

The standard bibliographical work for the Stuart age is Godfrey Davies and Mary Frear Keeler, *Bibliography of British History: Stuart Period 1603–1714* (1970, 2nd ed.), which includes works published well into the 1960s.

G. R. Elton, *Modern Historians on British History, 1485–1945* (1970) is also useful for this period, and lists works up to the end of 1969.

The official papers relating to home affairs for the period 1603–1704 have been published in *Calendars of State Papers*, Domestic series, under the editorship of various scholars (81 vols.; 1857–1947). These include the important *Clarendon State Papers*, preserved in the

Bodleian Library and published in an edition by F. J. Routledge and Sir Charles H. Firth (4 vols.; 1869–76 and 1932), and also Firth and R. J. Rait's edition of the *Acts and Ordinances of the Interregnum, 1642–1660* (3 vols.; 1911). The state papers pertaining to foreign affairs are of perhaps less importance for this crucial era in English history, and have not yet been fully calendared. Of those that are available, the *Calendar of State Papers . . . Venice, 1603–1675* (vols. 10–38 of the series on Venetian affairs), edited by H. F. Brown and A. B. Hinds (1900–40), are interesting not only for their information on Anglo-Venetian relations but also for their frequent allusions to England's domestic situation.

The quantity of literature that has been and continues to be written on Great Britain in the Stuart age is vast indeed, and a mere selection of the most useful general sources available does not even scratch the surface. The following books, however, including as they do some standard authorities, are of particular value.

Maurice Ashley, *The Golden Century 1588–1715* (1968).

Maurice Ashley, *The Glorious Revolution 1688* (1964).

Geoffery Aylmer, *The Struggle for the Constitution, 1603–1689* (1968, 2nd ed.).

Sir George N. Clark, *The Seventeenth Century* (1950, 2nd ed.).

Sir George N. Clark, *The Later Stuarts* (1955, 2nd ed.).

Godfrey Davies, *The Early Stuarts* (1959, 2nd ed.).

Sir Charles Harding Firth, *The Last Years of the Protectorate* (2 vols.; 1909).

Samuel Rawson Gardiner, *History of England, 1603–1642* (10 vols.; 1883–84, rev. ed.).

Samuel Rawson Gardiner, *History of the Great Civil War, 1642–1649* (4 vols.; 1893, rev. ed.).

Samuel Rawson Gardiner, *History of the Commonwealth and Protectorate* (4 vols.; 1903).

Christopher Hill, *The Century of Revolution, 1603–1714* (1961).

D. Matthew, *The Jacobean Age* (1938).

David Ogg, *England in the Reign of Charles II* (1956, 2nd ed.).

David Ogg, *England in the Reigns of James II and William III* (1955).

Sir Charles Petrie, *King Charles, Prince Rupert, and the Civil War* (1975)

Ivan Roots, *The Great Rebellion, 1642–1666* (1966).

G. M. Trevelyan, *England under Queen Anne* (3 vols.; 1930–34).

G. M. Trevelyan, *England under the Stuarts* (1949, 25th ed.).

C. V. Wedgwood, *The King's Peace, 1637–1641* (1955).

C. V. Wedgwood, *The King's War, 1642–1647* (1958).

P. Young and R. Holmes, *The English Civil War* (1974).

Iconographies:

For information on portraits, the chief authority is Roy Strong, *Tudor and Jacobean Portraits* (2 vols.; 1969). Other relevant sources consulted include O. Millar, *Tudor, Stuart and Early Georgian Portraits in the Royal Collection* (1963) and David Piper, *Seventeenth Century Portraits in the National Gallery* (1963).

Abbreviations:

The abbreviations used in this volume are few and mainly to be found in the bibliographies and iconographies.

N.P.G.	National Portrait Gallery, London
R.T.H.	Radio Times Hulton Picture Library, London
Scottish N.P.G.	Scottish National

Portrait Gallery, Edinburgh

V. & A.   Victoria and Albert Museum, London

Dates:

Until September 1752 England employed the Julian or Old Style calendar, some ten days or so behind the Gregorian or New Style calendar in use in the rest of Europe. Moreover, the year was said to begin on 25 March rather than 1 January. In common with most modern historians, we have decided to give dates here according to the Julian calendar but taking the beginning of each historical year as 1 January. Therefore all dates up to and including 24 March will be given, for example, in the form 27 February 1625, and not, as is conventional in some older books, 27 February 1624/5.

Some persons do not fit neatly into one historical period or another. Where such a person made a contribution to the Stuart period but is dealt with in another volume, we have inserted a cross-reference in *Lives of the Stuart Age* directing the reader to, for example, *Lives of the Tudor Age* for Robert Cecil and *Lives of the Georgian Age* for Jonathan Swift.

Finally, it remains for the editor to thank all the contributors to *Lives of the Stuart Age* and all those other helpers who assisted in compiling it.

CONTRIBUTORS

Charles Boyle
Edward R. Brace
Ann Currah
Alan Dingle
William Gould
Patrick Hanks
Catharine Hutton
Alan Isaacs
Amanda Isaacs
Thomas Hill Long

Catharine Limm
Lila Pennant
Valerie Pitt
Edwin Riddell
Michael Scherk
Vera Steiner
Arthur Taylor
Alexa Urdang
Eileen Williams

ILLUSTRATIONS
WITH ACKNOWLEDGEMENTS

Addison, Joseph (1672–1719), essayist, critic, poet, and politician, see *Lives of the Georgian Age*.

Albemarle, 1st Duke of (1608–70), see Monck, George.

Alleyn, Edward (1566–1626), actor, and founder of Dulwich College, see *Lives of the Tudor Age*.

Andros, Sir Edmund (1637–1714), soldier and colonial governor.

Edmund Andros was born on 6 December 1637, the son of Amice Andros, bailiff of Guernsey. He began his long military career in the year 1666 with service in an infantry regiment in the West Indies. In 1672 he became a major of dragoons and received a generous grant of land in Carolina. Two years later he succeeded his father as bailiff of Guernsey. Thus, an experienced soldier, he held administrative office and had a stake in England's colonies, and so was the natural candidate for the Duke of York, his friend and patron, to choose as governor of New York; in that capacity he was sent out to North America in 1674.

Andros proved to be a competent governor, although his autocratic temper led to several clashes with the inhabitants of the colony. He finally overstepped the mark when he arrested the governor of East Jersey in a jurisdictional dispute, and was recalled to England in 1681.

Andros's services were, however, recognized. He was knighted that same year and advanced at court. When the Duke of York became King James II Andros helped crush Monmouth's rebellion, and in 1686 he was appointed governor of the newly-amalgamated Dominion of New England (extended in 1688 to include the Jerseys and New York). This consolidation of the northern colonies had been arranged with an eye to defence needs and in the hope of crushing the hostile Puritan oligarchies of New England – a desire that had already led James to deprive them of their colonial charters. Accordingly, Andros commenced his tasks with a considerable sector of the population bitterly opposed to the régime he represented. Although he fought both Indians and pirates with considerable success, these very activities alienated the landowners, for they had to bear the financial burden for such military exploits. He implemented the Navigation Acts with equal vigour, thereby pinching the merchants. All in all, he was an able practitioner of James's policy of autocratic rule.

In April 1689, when Boston heard that William of Orange had landed in England, the governor and his councillors were seized and bundled off to England to await trial; however, Andros was acquitted and freed.

The hatred he had engendered in New England did not follow him back to England, where his worth was again recognized. In 1692 he was appointed governor of Virginia, where he became both successful and popular. But the Church authorities, with whom he next came into conflict, obtained his recall in 1697. Andros's final post was as governor of Jersey from 1704 to 1706. At the end of this long and varied career he retired to London, where he died in February 1714.

Viola F. Baines, *The Dominion of New England* (New Haven, Conn., 1923).

T. H. Breen, *The Character of the Good Ruler: Puritan Political Ideas in New England 1630–1730* (New Haven, Conn., 1970).

Anne (1665–1714), Queen of Great Britain and Ireland.

Anne was born at St. James's Palace, London, on 6 February 1665, the second daughter of James, Duke of York, later James II (q.v.), and his first wife, Anne Hyde (q.v.), daughter of the Earl of Clarendon. She married on 28 July 1683 Prince George of Denmark (q.v.). Although she had many pregnancies, none of her children survived childhood. The last of the Stuart sovereigns, she succeeded to the throne on 8 March 1702.

Eight children were born to the Duke and Duchess of York, but only Anne

and her elder sister (see Mary II) survived. Their mother died in 1671 and their father later married Mary of Modena (q.v.), whom Anne came to hate and regard as an evil influence on her father. Despite, or perhaps because of the Roman Catholic tenets of their parents, Charles II insisted on the two girls being educated in the Protestant faith, and they were both confirmed by Dr. Lake in 1676. She was delicate and at the age of four was sent to France to consult a specialist about her watering eyes; moreover, she contracted smallpox a few days after Mary's wedding to Prince William of Orange in 1677. The ill health which dogged her all her life thus appears to have manifested itself at a very early age.

Deprived of her mother's affection and finding little in her relationship with her stepmother, Anne found great solace in her early friendship with Sarah Jennings, later Sarah Churchill (q.v.), 1st Duchess of Marlborough. Sarah entered the service of Mary of Modena in 1673 as an attendant to the eight-year-old Princess Anne and the two girls formed a friendship that lasted almost to the end of Anne's life. In 1681 a marriage was proposed for Anne with Prince George of Hanover, but the plans were abandoned and in 1683 Anne married George, Prince of Denmark. It was not a popular union in the country as it was thought to be French-inspired, but it proved to be a very happy and successful marriage, marred only by Anne's failure to produce an heir: most of her pregnancies ended in miscarriages and none of her children survived childhood.

Upon Anne's marriage, Sarah Churchill was made a lady of the bed-chamber, and shortly afterwards Anne made the suggestion to Sarah that in their correspondence they should address each other as Mrs. Morley (Anne) and

Mrs. Freeman (Sarah). They kept up this strange affectation until their friendship broke up.

With the birth of a son to James II and the succession in dispute, Anne, aided by Sarah, took good care to keep out of the way: when William of Orange landed she fled to Nottingham. Sarah advised her to accept her brother-in-law as William III, co-monarch with her sister Mary; and by the Bill of Rights the crown was settled on Anne and her descendants if Mary's line failed. The two sisters had always been good friends, but soon after Mary's accession an estrangement took place, greatly exacerbated by Sarah Churchill and her husband. There were difficulties over Anne's apartments at court, and Anne pressed strongly for a higher annual allowance under the civil list. In addition, William gave away James II's private estate, which Anne, no doubt justifiably, felt she had some claim to. Anne eventually succeeded in obtaining an annuity of £50,000, granted by Parliament, but the whole affair left bad feelings on both sides and relations were cool between the two sisters until Mary's death. The active intervention of the Churchills (now Earl and Countess of Marlborough) did not pass unnoticed by Mary, and when Marlborough was implicated in Jacobite plots Mary made strenuous attempts to induce Anne to dismiss Sarah. Anne refused and was virtually ostracized by the court. She retired to Syon House, taking Sarah with her. After Mary's death from smallpox in 1694, it was in William's interest to effect a reconciliation with his sister-in-law, as she was a natural focus for any plots to depose him. He therefore treated Anne and her husband with every courtesy, eventually granting them St. James's Palace as a residence. In 1695 the Marlboroughs were received by the King and once more Anne's favourites

were in the ascendant. In 1701, being childless, Anne acquiesced to the Act of Settlement, which named Sophia, Electress of Hanover, and her descendants next in line to the throne on the grounds of their descent from James I.

On 8 March 1702 Anne acceded to the throne, and shortly afterwards the Marlboroughs were both given important public offices. Sarah was made mistress of the robes and keeper of the privy purse and Marlborough became captain general of the English forces. Anne did not make her husband co-monarch, but he was given many public offices, such as generalissimo of her majesty's forces, lord high admiral, and warden of the cinque ports. Marlborough was subsequently given a dukedom, although this was apparently against Sarah's wishes.

Anne was not a woman of great intellect and throughout her reign she suffered from conspiracies, persuasion, and less subtle attempts to influence her into following policies contrary to her beliefs. Sarah, Duchess of Marlborough, was not the least of those who attempted to influence the Queen. Anne had always favoured High Church Tory principles and it was largely due to the Marlboroughs' persistent attempts to have her replace Tories with Whigs that there was an estrangement between them.

She was particularly interested in the Church and tried to take the crown patronage of ecclesiastical matters firmly into her own hands. She felt that she should be able to choose her own bishops. In 1704 she announced to the House of Commons that she would grant to the Church crown revenues from tenths and first fruits. These had originally been paid to the pope, but were appropriated by the crown in 1534. This sum amounted to between £16,000 and £17,000 a year and became known as 'Queen Anne's

Bounty'. In 1711 an act was passed on the Queen's recommendation for the building of fifty churches in London.

However, regardless of where Anne's true interests lay, much of her reign was necessarily taken up by the War of the Spanish Succession. In 1703 Anne recognized the Archduke Charles, second son of Emperor Leopold I, as King of Spain, and in the following years English resources and troops were devoted to the defence of his claim. The chief English objectives were to prevent French domination of the Mediterranean or the Netherlands and to ensure that the crowns of Spain and France should not be united under Philip of Spain – the second son of the dauphin. In spite of the many English victories, including the Battle of Blenheim, the war dragged on until 1713, when it was concluded by the Treaty of Utrecht, in which Louis XIV renounced the claims of his grandson, Philip V of Spain, to the French throne and acknowledged the Hanoverian succession to the English throne, while the English abandoned the claims of the Archduke Charles.

The year 1707 was important in Anne's life. It was the year that marked the beginnings of the quarrel with the Duchess of Marlborough and the rise in influence of Sarah's cousin, Abigail Masham (q.v.). Abigail was introduced into Anne's household while Anne was Princess of Denmark, through Sarah's good offices. In 1707 Abigail was secretly married to Samuel Masham and, although Anne was present at the ceremony, Sarah was not informed. When she did find out about the marriage of her protégée, Sarah approached the Queen in an attempt to weaken her relationship with Abigail and re-establish her own position. Although Sarah used all her powers of persuasion, Anne was unresponsive. Apparently this unintel-lectual but obstinate woman had finally come to resist the brilliant Sarah's influence. For the remaining seven years of her life her chief intimates were Abigail Masham and the Duchess of Somerset, a woman of great personal charm. Abigail was a relative of Robert Harley (q.v.) and Harley made much use of her co-operation in influencing the Queen.

In 1708 the Queen's husband, Prince George, died; in the same year Robert Harley resigned his office. Anne turned to Abigail rather than Sarah in her widowhood and Abigail continued to act as a go-between for the Queen and Harley. Harley was thus able to continue as adviser to the Queen while out of office. In 1710 he returned to office as chancellor of the exchequer and head of a solid Tory ministry. Anne was overjoyed, and in 1711 Harley was created 1st Earl of Oxford. When Marlborough returned from his campaigns abroad, he found that his wife's indiscretions had done nothing to further their cause with Anne and that Mrs. Masham was now treated as a woman of authority and influence with the Queen. He made one last attempt to effect a reconciliation between Anne and Sarah, but failed, and in 1711 Harley obtained their dismissal. Mrs. Masham was made keeper of the privy purse and Lady Somerset became Anne's mistress of the wardrobe. In 1712 Anne created twelve Tory peers in order to ensure the acceptance of the Treaty of Utrecht in the House of Lords: Abigail Masham's husband was one of these. Anne's friendship with Lady Masham lasted for the rest of her life. Lady Masham tended her with patient and devoted concern during her last illness. She died on 1 August 1714.

Perhaps the most important constitutional event in Anne's reign was the conclusion of the Act of Union with Scotland in 1707. Anne only visited

Scotland once as a girl but she regarded the Union as 'the greatest glory of our reign'.

It is unfair to attempt any assessment of Anne herself or her reign without taking into account her constant ill health. Her natural weakness, evident in childhood, was worsened by her many pregnancies and miscarriages, which might also have affected her emotional balance at times.

She has been described as having little intellect and great obstinacy of character, and Sarah Churchill was probably accurate when she wrote: 'In matters of ordinary moment her discourse had nothing of brightness of wit, and in weightier matters she never spoke but in a hurry, and had a certain knack of sticking to what had been dictated to her to a degree often very disagreeable, and without the least sign of understanding and judgment.'

Anne had no interest in the arts – her only enthusiasm was for outdoor pursuits. She had a special one-horse carriage constructed for hunting, which was designed to conform to her ample proportions. She was, however, active in matters of state, often presiding at meetings of the Privy Council and attending debates in the House of Lords. But she had little stomach for the day-to-day manœuvring and scheming of political life, which she found distasteful. The trappings of royalty had little attraction for her and her court often looked deserted. In matters of religion Anne was dutiful, perhaps even superstitious. She revived the practice of the royal touch, believed to cure scrofula, and Samuel Johnson was one of the many touched by her.

In appearance, Smollett describes Anne as 'of middle size, well proportioned. Her hair was of a dark brown colour, her complexion ruddy; her features were regular, her countenance was rather round than majestic.' There is no doubt that Anne put on a lot of weight later in life and may have suffered from gout (the medical evidence is scanty); Sarah Churchill described her, with perhaps understandable lack of charity, as exceeding gross and corpulent. When she died, Arbuthnot (her physician since 1705) wrote to Swift: '[Her days] could not exceed certain limits, but these were harrowed by the scene of contention among her servants. I believe sleep was never more welcome to a weary traveller than death was to her.'

A. B. Bathurst (ed.), *Letters of Two Queens* (1924).
B. C. Brown (ed.), *The Letters and Domestic Instructions of Queen Anne* (1935).
David Green, *Queen Anne* (1970).
Geoffrey Holmes, *British Politics in the Age of Anne* (1967).
M. R. Hopkinson, *Anne of England* (rev. ed. 1938).
Herbert Paul, *Queen Anne* (1906).

Portraits: oil, three-quarter length, by W. Wissing, *c.* 1683: St. James's Palace; oil, full-length, by Kneller, *c.* 1705: Windsor Castle; oil, three-quarter length, after Kneller, *c.* 1694: N.P.G.; oil, full-length, attributed to Dahl, *c.* 1690: N.P.G.

Anne of Denmark (1574–1619), Queen consort of James I and mother of Charles I.

Anne was born on 12 December 1574, the daughter of Frederick II of Denmark and Norway and of Sophia, daughter of Ulric III, Duke of Mecklenburg. In 1589, at the age of fourteen, she was married by proxy on 20 August to James VI of Scotland (see James I). James received only a small dowry, but settled his claims to the Orkneys and Shetlands. On her way to Scotland, Anne was caught in a storm that drove her to take refuge in Norway. The raising of the storm was alleged to have been an act of witchcraft and several supposed witches in Denmark and Scotland were

put to death. James was impatient of the delay and travelled to Norway to fetch his bride. The couple were united at Opslo (Oslo) on 23 November. After a visit to Denmark, they sailed back to Scotland in the following spring and reached the port of Leith on 1 May 1590.

Anne was by upbringing a Lutheran. She thus had a much more liberal temperament than the vigorous Calvinists of the Scottish Kirk, and was by nature a pleasure-loving person. She incurred Presbyterian opposition, and as Queen consort became the object of attacks in connection with several scandals and acts of violence in which she probably had no part.

Her position was made more secure by the birth, on 19 February 1594, of a son and heir, the ill-starred Henry Frederick (q.v.). In the following year, however, he was removed from her care, an action which caused her considerable displeasure. Undoubtedly the reason for this was to ensure the prince's upbringing as a Calvinist. There was also a suspicion that, despite her Lutheran

attitudes, she was too much subject to Roman Catholic tendencies. She was subjected to further rebukes by the officials of the Kirk for failing to attend church and for what they called 'vanity' and 'night waking and balling'.

Two years after Henry came the birth of a daughter, Elizabeth (q.v.), and in 1600 Anne's second son, Charles (see Charles I), was born. Three years after that, when Queen Elizabeth I died, Anne was pregnant again. Upon his departure for London in April of that year (1603) James instructed her to follow him to England but ordered her to leave Prince Henry in Stirling, where his guardian, the Earl of Mar, had custody of him. Anne decided that this was her best chance to take back her son and therefore went to Stirling Castle to get him. She was greeted by a 'flat refusal' from the young boy's custodian and became so passionately distraught that in the ensuing trauma she lost the baby she was carrying and almost died. James sent word to Mar that he was to give up the prince to the royal council, who in turn delivered him over to Anne 'to pleasure the queen'.

She finally arrived with Henry at Windsor towards the end of June 1603. She attended James on 24 July at his coronation, at which she gave considerable offence by refusing to take the sacrament according to the Anglican practice. Her clandestine sympathy with Roman Catholicism was confirmed by her acceptance of consecrated objects from Pope Clement VIII. This was a matter of great embarrassment to James in his religious policy, and it affected their marital relationship.

Over the last fourteen or fifteen years of her life, Anne took only a casual interest in affairs of state. She did, however, support attempts to convert Henry to Roman Catholicism as part of the

Spanish marriage negotiations and she also favoured the advancement of Buckingham. Originally well-disposed towards alliance with Spain, she opposed the marriage of her daughter Elizabeth to the Elector Palatine. But she later made a personal appeal to Buckingham on behalf of Sir Walter Ralegh (see *Lives of the Tudor Age*).

Anne took an active role in court life, and loved masques and other entertainments. In these activities, however, her extravagance gave considerable cause for concern. Towards the end of her life, Anne lived apart from her husband and James was not present when, after a protracted illness, she died on 2 March 1619. She was buried in Westminster Abbey.

E. C. Williams, *Anne of Denmark* (1970).

Portraits: oil, half-length, by unknown artist, 1614: Windsor Castle; oil, full-length, by Paul van Somer, 1614: Windsor Castle; oil on panel, quarter-length, by Philip Larkin, *c*. 1612: N.P.G.

Arbuthnot, John (1667–1735), wit, and doctor of medicine, see *Lives of the Georgian Age*.

Argyll, 1st Duke of (?1651–1703), see Campbell, Archibald, 1st Duke of Argyll.

Argyll, 2nd Duke of (1680–1743), soldier and politician, see Campbell, John, in *Lives of the Georgian Age*.

Argyll, 8th Earl of (1598–1661), see Campbell, Archibald, 8th Earl and Marquis of Argyll.

Argyll, 9th Earl of (1629–85), see Campbell, Archibald, 9th Earl of Argyll.

Arlington, 1st Earl of (1616–85), see Bennet, Henry.

Ashley, 1st Baron, of Wimborne (1621–83), see Cooper, Anthony Ashley.

Aubrey, John (1626–97), antiquary and biographer.

John Aubrey was born on 12 March 1626 at Easton Percy, Wiltshire, the son of Richard Aubrey, a wealthy country gentleman with large estates in three counties. A delicate child, he was educated at home by a Malmesbury vicar who had also been Hobbes's tutor. He later attended Blandford Grammar School and in May 1642 entered Trinity College, Oxford, where he inaugurated his antiquarian career by contributing an engraving of Osney Abbey to Dugdale's *Monasticon*. In 1643 Aubrey hurriedly left Oxford because of a smallpox epidemic and the onset of civil war, and for a few years led 'a sad life in the country'. He eventually entered the Middle Temple in 1646, but was never called to the bar, probably because he would keep paying long visits to Oxford, where he later said he had spent the happiest times of his life. He frequently returned to his

Wiltshire home too, where he indulged in long rambles in the neighbouring countryside, jotting down everything he saw and talking to anyone from parsons and schoolmasters to farm labourers and 'the parish clerk's wife'. In 1649 he drew public attention to the magnificent but previously unheeded prehistoric remains at Avebury.

In 1652 Aubrey's father died, leaving his son a great deal of property and endless legal headaches. Aubrey himself did not improve matters by his extravagant way of life. However, he took his scientific interests seriously and in May 1663 was elected a fellow of the Royal Society. In the autobiographical notes he began making at this period, Aubrey glumly states that in 1665 'I made my first address (in an ill hour) to Joane Sumner.' Far from marrying him, the lady in question brought a crippling lawsuit against him.

But there were compensations. In 1667 Aubrey met the Oxford antiquary and recluse Anthony à Wood (q.v.), who persuaded him to contribute his chaotic mass of original observations to a collaborative work, the *Antiquities of Oxford*, published in 1674. The undisciplined Aubrey was always content to have someone else tell him what to do; in these circumstances he could, as he says, 'doe it playingly'. In 1671 he was granted a royal patent to pursue antiquarian inquiries, and he spent much of 1673 perambulating Surrey, making topographical and historical notes. At about this time he also wrote a treatise on the 'druidical' nature of Stonehenge and other prehistoric sites.

Unfortunately, with his 'several love and law suits', Aubrey's descent into penury soon accelerated. By 1670 he had sold every bit of his land, and his journal for 1671 bleakly remarks 'Danger of arrests'. After the sale of his beloved books in 1677 Aubrey had nothing left to lose. But he was well connected and well liked and so, nothing daunted by his circumstances, he descended upon the country houses of all his wealthy friends in succession. His hosts included the Earl of Thanet, 'with whom I was delitescent near a year,' Elias Ashmole, and Thomas Hobbes (q.v.).

In 1680 Aubrey began sending to Anthony à Wood the biographical sketches of famous Englishmen which were eventually gathered together to form his most celebrated work, the *Brief Lives*. Aubrey was a sociable fellow and an incurable gossip who moved in circles where anecdotes about the great could be gathered in abundance. However, his lives of such men as Bacon, Milton, and Ralegh have been criticized for exhibiting unpardonable credulity in that truth, folklore, and blatant fiction seem all alike to him. He amply justifies this apparent lack of method by pointing out that many a curious tale would soon be forgotten, 'did not such idle fellows as me putt them downe', and he was confident that the *Lives* were 'the usefullest pieces I have scribbled'. Aubrey wrote 'tumultuously' but in fits and starts, leaving knotty problems for later editors; it was not until 1813 that a reasonably complete edition of the *Lives* was put together from scattered manuscripts and published. The individual sketches vary considerably in length, probably reflecting Aubrey's personal preferences; his life of Hobbes is the most comprehensive, mainly because the philosopher was a lifelong friend.

Aubrey fell out finally with Anthony à Wood in 1690, when his waspish biography of Chancellor Clarendon involved Wood in a libel case. The aggrieved Wood later described Aubrey as 'a shiftless person, roving and magotie-headed, and sometimes little better than crased'. Aubrey did not seem unduly worried, since he never finished anything anyway. Typically, in 1695 he decided that his history of Wiltshire, on which he had been working since 1659, would never be 'stitched up' because of his advanced years, so he handed it over to the Bishop of St. Asaph to complete.

In 1696 appeared the only book Aubrey published during his lifetime, the *Miscellanies*, grandly subtitled 'a Collection of Hermetic Philosophy', but in reality a motley and entertaining collection of omens, dreams, and ghost stories.

John Aubrey died at Oxford in June 1697, on his way from London to the west country. Despite his apparent lack of even the most basic literary discrimination, his cheerful personality and infinite enthusiasm amply compensate for his chronic inability to see the wood for the trees. Fully aware of his own limitations and wistfully regretting that there were no longer any monasteries he could join, he is among the most attractive of English eccentrics.

A. Clark (ed.), *Brief Lives* (2 vols.; 1898).
O. L. Dick (ed.), *Brief Lives* [a selection] (1958, rev. ed.).
Anthony Powell, *John Aubrey and his Friends* (1963, rev. ed.).
Portrait: engraving, quarter-length, after William Faithorne the elder, after a portrait in the Ashmolean Museum, Oxford, 1666: British Museum.

B

Bacon, Francis (1561–1626), Baron Verulam and Viscount St. Albans, statesman and philosopher, see *Lives of the Tudor Age*.

Baillie, Robert (1599–1662), Scottish Presbyterian theologian and leader of the Covenanter clergy.

Baillie was born in Glasgow, the son of a merchant, and was educated in arts and theology at the University of Glasgow. Around 1622 he was admitted into orders by Archbishop Law of Glasgow; despite this episcopal ordination, he was presented to a Presbyterian congregation in Ayrshire. By and large he showed himself to be a moderate and maintained a friendship with the archbishop, although he refused the latter's request in 1637 to preach a sermon in Glasgow in support of Laud's new prayer book. Baillie was elected to the General Assembly of the Kirk in 1638 that restored strict Presbyterianism; his role was that of a moderate anti-Laudian and, more important for posterity, a careful observer whose letters and journals are a valuable source for the events of this tumultuous gathering.

In 1639 and 1640 Baillie served as a chaplain in the Covenanter armies whose successes forced Charles I to summon Parliament again in England. When the Long Parliament met, it attacked those royal ministers it held responsible for the most hated policies, including Laud. The Scots co-operated in these proceedings, sending a delegation, which included Baillie, to London to frame the charges against the primate. This put Baillie in a position where he could observe events at the centre of activity, and they are faithfully recorded, with staunch Presbyterian bias, in his *Letters and Journals*. He wrote other works in these years as well, publishing in 1641 treatises against episcopacy and Arminianism; these were followed by more tracts and books, many of which were directed against the English sectarians.

By 1642 Baillie's reputation as a theologian stood so high that all the Scottish universities sought his services; he took the chair of divinity at Glasgow. Until 1646, however, he spent much of his time in England, where as a member of the Westminster Assembly, which wrestled with the problem of England's future ecclesiastical structure, he once again witnessed and recorded the great events of his day.

After the execution of Charles I, Baillie was chosen as one of the General Assembly's representatives sent to Holland to offer the young Charles II the Scottish crown if he would accept the Covenant. This agreed with Baillie's ideal of Presbyterian monarchy and, although Charles was defeated at Worcester in 1651, he still had great hopes when the Restoration was achieved in 1660. He soon found that his expectations were to be frustrated, but was appointed principal of Glasgow University after declining a bishopric. He died in Glasgow in July 1662.

D. Laing (ed.), *Letters and Journals of Robert Baillie, 1637–1642* (1841–42).
D. Stevenson, *The Scottish Revolution 1637–1644* (1973).

Baltimore, 1st Baron, see Calvert, George.

Baltimore, 2nd Baron, see Calvert, Cecilius.

Bastwick, John (1593–1654), physician, Puritan pamphleteer, and controversialist.

Bastwick was born at Writtle in Essex; he entered Emmanuel College, Cambridge, in 1614, but stayed only a short time. He then travelled abroad, probably served in the Dutch army briefly, and studied medicine and took an M.D. at Padua.

In 1623 he settled at Colchester, Essex, and practised medicine successfully, but his strong Puritan leanings and his ability to write fluently in the classical Latin style led him to publish highly controversial treatises, at first in Holland. His *Flagellum Pontificis*, a voluble argument in favour of Presbyterianism, came to the notice of the anti-Puritan clergyman William Laud (q.v.). Bastwick was summoned before the high court of commission and convicted of a 'scandalous libel'. He was fined £1,000 with costs and imprisoned in the Gatehouse until he should 'recant his errors'. While in the Gatehouse, Bastwick wrote (1636) a treatise against the high court of commission, and in 1637 he wrote in English his *Letanie of Dr. John Bastwicke*, denouncing bishops as 'God's enemies and the tail of the beast'. For this highly scurrilous publication, which depicted churchmen as gluttonous lechers both brutal and arrogant, Bastwick was summoned before the Star Chamber. This king's council, held in the Palace of Westminster, was more subject to royal (and thus Church) control than the common law courts. Bastwick was tried in company with the Puritan clergyman Henry Burton and the Puritan lawyer

William Prynne (qq.v.). Incorrigible as ever, Bastwick published his defence and was subsequently declared guilty and sentenced to lose his ears in the pillory, to pay a £5,000 fine, and to suffer life imprisonment. The execution of these punishments caused a violent public demonstration of sympathy and the journeys to prison of the three convicted Puritans were practically triumphal progresses, much to the fury of Archbishop Laud.

After the trial, a portrait of Bastwick was published, along with numerous broadsheets which kept his sufferings prominent in the public mind until his release from prison in 1640 by order of the Long Parliament. An order was made too for the reparation of the fines imposed upon him; after his death his widow, Susanna, attempted but failed to collect this money.

In 1642 Bastwick fought on the Parliamentarian side in the Civil War, probably as captain of a Leicestershire trained band or foot company; he was taken prisoner and sent to York, but evidently was released soon after. He continued publishing bitter tracts, most of them for the Presbyterians against the Independents (those Puritans who in the 1640s were the most radical opponents of the King and held extreme individualistic opinions on religious doctrine), until his death, probably in October 1654.

B. Brook, *The Lives of the Puritans, to 1662* (3 vols., 1813).
J. B. Marsden, *Later Puritans, 1642–62* (1852).

Baxter, Richard (1615–91), Puritan divine and political theorist.

Baxter was born in Rowton, Shropshire, in November 1615, the son of Richard Baxter of Eaton Constantine, near Shrewsbury, a gentleman or freeholder of good family. He was educated first by a series of dissolute local ministers; then at the free school in Wroxeter; and later by a private tutor at Ludlow Castle.

The elder Richard Baxter led a wild life until the time of his son's birth, when he underwent a religious conversion. The younger Baxter was strongly influenced by this religious atmosphere, with its leanings towards Puritanism. It awoke in him the desire to enter the ministry, but when he finished his schooling in 1633 his tutor and parents decided he should be launched on a court career. One month of that lax environment repelled him, however, and he returned home determined to study theology. His ill health hindered his progress greatly and he lacked a good education since all his tutors had either lacked interest in or had no aptitude for teaching; his learning, therefore, was largely derived from reading in the library at Ludlow Castle.

During these years of study, Baxter first came into close contact with Puritans. These associations grew closer after 1638, the year of his ordination, when he was appointed headmaster of a new school at Dudley. He continued his reading, especially on the controversial issues of the contemporary Church, such as the use of the surplice, cross, and communion. More and more, he found himself in agreement with the Puritan divines. But on one point he concurred with the High Churchmen: like them, he was disgusted by the prevalence of illiteracy, drunkenness, and neglect of duty among the clergy.

After one year at Dudley, Baxter became the assistant minister at Bridgnorth, Shropshire, where he followed Puritan usages in celebrating divine office, but still remained within the fold of the Established Church. In 1640 Convocation resolved that all members of

the learned professions should take an oath not to attempt to change the existing system of Church government. This – the 'Et Cetera oath' – led to great debates throughout the country. In Shropshire the forces hostile to the oath were led by Richard Baxter. This controversy drove him to further study of episcopacy, and he concluded that the English system was inconsistent with that of the primitive Church.

When the congregation of Kidderminster petitioned against the debauchery of its vicar and curate, Baxter was appointed lecturer to the parish. This position he took up in April 1641 and filled with distinction until 1660.

The Civil War presented Baxter with a dilemma. He saw the weaknesses in the arguments of both sides. As a conservative, a monarchist, and one who had no faith in the judgment of the people, he sympathized with the Royalists, but his religious inclinations proved decisive, and he gave his support to Parliament. After Edgehill he had to leave Kidderminster for a time, since it lay in a Royalist county, and he spent the following years in Parliamentary areas, preaching and serving as a chaplain in the army, where he was horrified by the growth of sectarianism. In 1647 he returned to Kidderminster after a long illness. Politically he was soon in isolation, for on grounds of conscience he found himself compelled to oppose what each party held to be fundamental – the Solemn League and Covenant on one hand and the execution of the King on the other. In 1649 appeared his first book, the beginning of a torrent of publications in which he described his relations with the sectaries. As well as writing, he spent the following years in pastoral duties at Kidderminster and serving on various committees for licensing godly ministers.

Before the Restoration Baxter went to

London, where he was one of those active for the conditional recall of Charles II. Although the Restoration was quite unconditional, Baxter welcomed the King and was appointed a royal chaplain. He was treated with great respect and offered a bishopric, which he turned down. Moreover, the Act of Uniformity (1662) and the restrictions imposed by Nonconformists drove him out of the Church. He retired to Acton in Middlesex, where he wrote, occasionally preached, and was from time to time persecuted, despite powerful patronage.

The accession of James II brought about Baxter's arrest. Judge Jeffreys (q.v.) tried and imprisoned him, but after one and a half years he was released in an attempt to win Dissenter support for the King's anti-Anglican policies. Baxter merely took advantage of the freedom given him, preaching to huge audiences, and he co-operated with the Anglicans in effecting the 'Glorious Revolution' of 1688. He did not long enjoy the fruits of this victory, for he died in London on 8 December 1691.

Politically, Baxter had been in the mainstream of affairs only during the Commonwealth period. He opposed arbitrary rule, whether by the King or by Cromwell, but preferred it without question when presented with the threat of radicalism, the Levellers, and the extreme sectaries. He saw the chief duty of government as the glorification of God and the religious wellbeing of the people, which could be realized only through the maintenance of true religion by one established Church. His tragedy was that he could find no room for himself in the state Church that upheld doctrines he found personally unacceptable.

C. F. Kemp, *Pastoral Triumph* (New York, 1948).
J. M. Lloyd Thomas (ed.), *The Autobiography of Richard Baxter* (1931).
G. F. Nuttall, *Richard Baxter* (1966).
F. J. Powicke, *The Life of the Reverend Richard Baxter, 1615–1691* (2 vols., 1924–7).
Richard Schlatter, *Richard Baxter and Puritan Politics* (New Brunswick, N.J., 1958).

Portraits: oil, half-length, after R. White, 1670: N.P.G.; miniature, after R. White, 1670: N.P.G.

Beaumont, Francis (1584–1616), dramatist.

Francis Beaumont was born in Leicestershire some time in 1584, the third son of Francis Beaumont, a prominent Elizabethan judge. In 1596, at the age of twelve, he entered Pembroke College, Oxford. However, his father died two years later, whereupon Francis and his two elder brothers left Oxford abruptly without taking degrees.

In 1600 he entered the Inner Temple, but does not appear to have studied law very seriously. He probably spent more of his time attending the theatre and the Mermaid Tavern, where he became an intimate of Ben Jonson (q.v.), who is said by Dryden to have had a high regard for his literary judgment, and of the

'charmed circle' of wits and poets who frequented that hostelry. It is likely that Jonson employed Beaumont as an assistant in the writing of his plays of 1603–7, but far more significant for Beaumont's career was the acquaintance that he struck up shortly afterwards with John Fletcher (q.v.). In around 1607 they started a collaboration that was to last until Beaumont's death nine years later. By 1607 both men had already written a few verses and had some dealings with the theatre, but neither was an established dramatist. Their first known joint works (*The Woman-Hater*, 1607, and *Four Plays in One*, ?1608) are of no particular interest, but in 1609 they produced *The Knight of the Burning Pestle*, which was instantly and memorably successful. It is the first English dramatic parody, hitting out in all directions and lampooning at once knight errantry (following Cervantes), heroic domestic drama (as typified by Thomas Heywood's *Four Prentices of London*), heroic blank verse (as typified by Shakespeare's Hotspur in *1 Henry IV*), and the comedy of manners. It also satirizes those members of contemporary audiences who insisted on sitting on the stage and interfering with the action of the play. The plot is slight, but the play's vigour and humour are still impressive; above all, it is immensely actable and shows a remarkably confident grasp of stagecraft by the two apparently inexperienced playwrights.

This play launched the two dramatists on an amazingly successful career of collaboration. In one year alone (1611) they produced three very different works, all of which were and still are highly regarded: *Philaster*, a drama of romantic intrigue and mistaken identity, *The Maid's Tragedy*, a murky concoction of trusts betrayed, murders, and suicide, written in verse that occasionally rises to grandeur in its expression of melancholy and world-weariness, and *A King and No King*, a black comedy based on the contemporary obsession with incest and mistaken identity, which is relieved by a comic subplot and in which all comes right in the end.

Beaumont wrote no plays by himself, so far as is known. Of his works with Fletcher, the breadth of their range is illustrated by the romantic comedy *The Coxcomb* (1612), the tragedy *Cupid's Revenge* (1612), the comedies *The Captain* (1613) and *The Honest Man's Fortune*, the historical tragedy *Bonduca* (1614), and the tragicomedy *The Knight of Malta*, which was probably not acted until after Beaumont's death. The chief impression made on the modern reader by these works is of their competence. On the rather tenuous evidence of Fletcher's surviving works known to have been written without Beaumont, it has been suggested that Beaumont was better at plots than Fletcher, but in fact it is a futile labour to attempt to discern separate contributions in so intimate a partnership. The plays are, above all, good theatre; the plots work well and move steadily to a climax without flagging; the tragic verse, while rarely awe-inspiring, is often grand and arresting; the comic plots and subplots are usually still funny.

If Aubrey (q.v.) is to be believed, there was never so intimate a literary collaboration. Not only did Beaumont and Fletcher write together, live in the same house, visit their respective country homes together, and on occasion share a bed – they even went so far as to dress alike.

About 1613 Beaumont was married to Ursula Isley of Kent. However, the marriage was a brief one, for on 6 March 1616 Francis Beaumont died. He was buried in Westminster Abbey, near

Chaucer and Spenser. The first collected edition of Beaumont and Fletcher's plays appeared in 1647.

A. H. Bullen *et al.* (eds.), *The Works of Francis Beaumont and John Fletcher* (1904–12, unfinished: only four out of projected 12 vols. were completed).

Alexander Dyce (ed.), *Works of Francis Beaumont and John Fletcher* (11 vols.; 1843–46).

Fredson Bowers *et al.* (eds.), *The Dramatic Works in the Beaumont and Fletcher Canon* (10 vols.; 1966–).

E. M. Waith, *The Pattern of Tragicomedy in Beaumont and Fletcher* (1952).

Portrait: engraving, half-length, after George Vertue, 1729: N.P.G.

Behn, Mrs. Aphra, Afra, or Ayfara

(?1640–89), called 'the Incomparable Astrea', playwright and novelist of the Restoration period.

Great confusion surrounds the exact circumstances of her birth, parentage, and early life. Early accounts claimed that she was the daughter of a certain James Johnson, a Canterbury barber, but a later biographical note by Anne Finch (q.v.), Countess of Winchilsea, referred to a record in the parish register at the church of St. Gregory and St. Martin in Wye, Kent, citing the baptism on 10 July 1640 of 'Peter' and 'Ayfara', son and daughter of John and Amy Amis. This reference was taken up by later biographers, who apparently ignored or were not aware of an entry in the Wye burial register a few days later recording the deaths of Peter and Ayfara. The problem is further confused by the dubiousness of Mrs. Behn's own account of her early life, in Gildon's *Histories and Novels of the Late Ingenious Mrs. Behn* (1696). For a fuller discussion of the problems of her biography, readers are referred to the works of Montague Summers and Vita Sackville-West.

It seems true, as Mrs. Behn claimed, that she travelled to Surinam with a couple named Amis. Aphra's childhood experiences there were idealized in her novel *Oroonoko* (not published until 1688), named after a chieftain she met; scandalmongers later maintained that she had been his mistress.

In 1658 Surinam was ceded to the Netherlands, and Aphra returned to London, where she married a wealthy Dutch merchant named Behn. She eventually became known at court, entertaining Charles II with her eloquent conversation. In 1666, during the Dutch war, Mrs. Behn's husband died and she was sent to Amsterdam as a spy. An attractive, bright-eyed woman, she was there surrounded by ardent suitors, one of whom indiscreetly told her of a proposed Dutch naval attack on the Thames; unfortunately, London refused to believe this information. Eventually Mrs. Behn fell in love with a certain van der Aalbert, but before they could both escape to England he died of fever. Heartbroken, Mrs. Behn returned to London, determined to devote her life to pleasure and poetry.

Since her husband had left her nothing, Mrs. Behn had to earn a living, and she became perhaps the first professional woman writer in English literary history. Her first play, *The Young King*, a pallid verse tragedy from the French, no one would stage. She then cultivated playwrights and theatre managers, perhaps becoming Edward Ravenscroft's mistress, and in 1671 managed to get her next play, *The Forc'd Marriage*, produced. A domestic tragicomedy with a rather contrived denouement, it reflects her natural concern for those of her sex trapped in loveless 'marriages of convenience'. However, the play was a flop, since public taste preferred cynicism and coarseness; to hold her own, Mrs. Behn henceforth had to be as obscene as her male contemporaries. In *The Dutch Lover* (1673) she discovered a winning formula: two or three amorous couples become embroiled in a complicated web of intrigue and mistaken identity, interspersed with farcical episodes, until the young men, who are really only interested in sex, are reluctantly dragged to the altar. Admittedly *The Rover* (1677), which first appeared anonymously, has a less tortuous plot, but the men are as coarse as ever, and there are so many affairs going on that the story becomes tedious; however, the play was very popular with fashionable society, which enjoyed speculating on its authorship.

Mrs. Behn next adapted Molière's *Le Malade Imaginaire* as *Sir Patient Fancy* (1678), which has the distinction of being her most salacious play. Even so, she replied spiritedly to the chorus of criticism it provoked. Perhaps her most deplorable efforts were the comedies *The Roundheads* (1682) and *The City Heiress* (1682), adapted from Tatham's *The Rump* and Middleton's *It's A Mad World* respectively; written to divert Tory audiences at the time of the Popish Plot, they raise a schoolboy snigger at the expense of the Whig faction by depicting the outrageous cuckolding of its most prominent members, slenderly disguised.

The Lucky Chance (1687) at least makes a moral point – that an old man who ensnares a young wife must expect to be cuckolded. The play's unconvincingly 'happy' ending does not indicate Mrs. Behn's incompetence, but rather her despair at the difficulty of obtaining divorces and separations in the real world of her time. Her supposed 'obscurity' arose from similar constraints; she wrote like a man because she had to. In fact, being a woman, she had to try even harder; with eighteen plays published or produced, she was one of the period's most prolific dramatists.

Besides plays, Mrs. Behn wrote in the 1680s a great variety of other literary works, including a long allegorical poem, *Voyage to the Island of Love* (1684); an excellent translation from Fontenelle, *A Discovery of New Worlds* (1688); and several rather dull romantic novels with titles like *The Nun* and *The Lucky Mistake*. In a poem that she contributed to Waller's memorial volume (1688), Mrs. Behn complained of 'the toils of sickness', and on 16 April 1689 she died, probably because of her doctor's ineptitude; she lies buried in the cloisters of Westminster Abbey.

Mrs. Behn is now remembered chiefly for her prose romances, particularly *Oroonoko* (1688), and for the fact that she was the first professional English authoress.

Montague Summers (ed.), *The Works of Aphra Behn* (6 vols.; 1915).

F. M. Link, *Aphra Behn* (New York, 1968).

V. Sackville-West, *Aphra Behn* (1927).

G. Woodcock, *The Incomparable Aphra* (1948).

Bennet, Henry (1618–85), 1st Earl of Arlington, politician and courtier, member of the so-called Cabal.

Henry Bennet was born at Saxham, Suffolk, the second son of Sir John Bennet, a lawyer; he was educated at Westminster School and (from 1635) at Christ Church, Oxford. He served Charles I in the court and on the field during the Civil War before departing to spend several years travelling in Europe. He won the favour of the exiled Charles II (q.v.) during the years of the Commonwealth, serving as a close adviser and agent. An accomplished courtier, he demonstrated his talent for bending with the wind by supporting the King in his every design. This ability did him good service in his political career; however, his propensity to make dangerous enemies also came to the fore at an early stage, when he quarrelled during the exile with Charles's brother, the Duke of York (later James II, q.v.).

In 1658 Charles dispatched Bennet to Madrid, where he served as Royalist resident at the court, acquiring experience in foreign affairs and adopting the extremely formal manner that made him an object of ridicule in later life. He returned to Restoration England in 1661, and was made keeper of the privy purse. He supported Charles's decision to issue the ill-fated 1662 Declaration of Indulgence, which suspended the penalties inflicted upon non-Anglicans. Bennet helped manage the King's mistresses and allied himself with one of them, Lady Castlemaine (see Villiers, Barbara), against Charles's chief minister, Lord Clarendon (see Hyde, Edward). In his power struggle with Clarendon, he often worked with the Duke of Buckingham (see Villiers, George, 2nd Duke). Bennet was secretary of state, the dominant minister in the area of foreign affairs, in October 1662, and further undermined Clarendon's position by building up a personal following in the Commons among court supporters, one of whom was Thomas Clifford (q.v.).

Bennet, created Lord Arlington in 1665, supported the policy of war with the Dutch. Responsible for intelligence, he failed to take seriously the threat of intervention by the Netherlands' ally France, which materialized in 1666 to the discomfiture of England. He promoted the dismissal and impeachment of Clarendon in 1667, a manoeuvre that probably helped to divert some of the dissatisfaction felt over the conduct of the war. By now he and Buckingham were leading figures in the government, which his protégé Clifford also joined around this time. Together with Lauderdale (see Maitland, John) and Ashley (see Cooper, Anthony Ashley) they formed

the group of ministers who controlled policy at this time, called the Cabal from the initials of its members, Clifford, Ashley, Buckingham, Arlington, and Lauderdale.

Arlington, who in 1666 had married a daughter of Louis of Nassau, tended towards the Dutch and Spanish camp in European affairs. He sent Sir William Temple (q.v.) to Holland to conclude the Triple Alliance (1668) with the States General and Sweden as part of a plan for a great anti-French league. But by the end of the year, Charles II's grand design for recatholicizing England and making his power independent of Parliament was taking form. For this scheme, an alliance with the wealthy, Catholic Louis XIV seemed most desirable. Arlington and Clifford were let into the secret, and played a large part in the negotiations that culminated in the secret Treaty of Dover (1670), by which Charles and Louis formed an offensive alliance against the Dutch and Louis pledged aid for Charles's plans to reintroduce Catholicism in England. Arlington was privy to these designs, as well as to plans to use Scottish and Irish troops in England in case of resistance. He was cautious enough to refuse gifts – or bribes – from Louis XIV, but he allowed his wife to accept 10,000 crowns.

Charles began putting his plans into operation with the 1672 Declaration of Indulgence and a new war with the Netherlands. He rewarded Arlington with an earldom and the order of the Garter. However, the impecunious Charles was forced in 1673 to summon Parliament, which body then mounted an increasingly formidable assault on his policies. The Cabal, never a harmonious group, began to show signs of a deep disunity and, more seriously, its members began to lose the royal favour. Arlington urged Charles to give way and withdraw the 1672 Declaration. Parliament passed the Test Act, which excluded Catholics from the royal service. It also forced Arlington's erstwhile follower, Clifford, to resign the treasurership, which Arlington had sought for himself the previous year. So great was his jealousy known to be that he was suspected of actually promoting the Test Act and of revealing the contents of the Treaty of Dover to Shaftesbury and Ormonde in order to destroy Clifford.

As Charles's grand strategy crumbled, Arlington advised him to seek peace with the Dutch. Accordingly he was sent with Buckingham to an unsuccessful peace conference in Holland, where his incompetence as a diplomat was clearly displayed. An attempt to impeach him along with Buckingham in January 1674 marked a further decline in power as each accused the other of responsibility for the unpopular policies of the ministry.

The rise of Danby (see Osborne, Thomas), the new treasurer, signified the end of Arlington's power. He re-

signed his secretaryship for £6,000 in September 1674 and received the post of lord chamberlain. In a bid for parliamentary popularity he returned to his earlier pro-Dutch line. As a result, Charles sent him to offer the hand of Princess Mary to William of Orange. This particular mission was a failure, Arlington's arrogance arousing William's animosity.

In Parliament, Arlington co-operated with Shaftesbury against Danby, and joined the attempt to impeach the latter in 1675. Both the King and Sir William Temple unsuccessfully tried to effect a reconciliation between the two men, but Arlington retired to the country in a huff and indulged in his hobby of building. He came out of retirement to participate in Danby's impeachment in 1678. He died, declaring on his deathbed his adherence to Catholicism, on 28 July 1685.

Arlington's lack of principle cost him the confidence of those who worked with him, although it aided his advance to high offices that he was otherwise not sufficiently able to fill.

V. Barbour, *Henry Bennet, Earl of Arlington* (1914). M. C. Lee, *The Cabal* (Urbana, Ill., 1965).

Portrait: oil, three-quarter length, after Lely: N.P.G.

Bentinck, William or Hans Willem (1649–1709), 1st Earl of Portland, politician.

William Bentinck, the son of Bernhard Bentinck, Lord of Diepenheim in Overyssel, a Dutch nobleman, was appointed page of honour to the young William of Orange (see William III) around 1664. The two became close friends and inseparable companions. As William of Orange gradually rose from his position as the closely-guarded, powerless heir of the House of Orange to become effective ruler of the United

Provinces in the last quarter of the century, Bentinck served him and prospered.

During his youth William of Orange travelled to England, ostensibly to collect money owed him by his uncles, Charles II and the Duke of York (1670). Bentinck accompanied him on this trip. Very soon after their return, however, both young men were engaged in the desperate Dutch struggle for survival against the combined English and French forces. Bentinck accompanied William, by now captain general of the Dutch army, and tended him when he fell ill with smallpox, catching the dreaded disease himself (1675).

During the consultations leading up to the Treaty of Nijmegen, Bentinck was sent by William to England, to negotiate a marriage for the young prince with Mary (see Mary II), eldest daughter of the Duke of York. In this he was successful, and the two were married in November 1678.

Bentinck continued to serve William on diplomatic missions. After the collapse of the Rye House Plot (1683) and the defeat of Monmouth (1685), he was sent to convey William's congratulations to the English King. Bentinck also conducted negotiations with Berlin and other north German courts to secure William's continental position as William prepared to make good his claim to the English throne. In the last few months, the preparation became increasingly the responsibility of Bentinck. He corresponded with English supporters, organized the fleet, and sailed with William's force to England in 1688.

By now Bentinck was established as William's closest adviser and confident. Before the coronation he was created Earl of Portland. More honours, rewards, and offices followed. The new Earl took an active part in William's campaigns, fighting at the Boyne and in the Low Countries, but most of his energies went into diplomacy and foreign affairs. William could trust him in his moves to thwart Jacobite plots and in other secret affairs where an Englishman might have proved a correspondent of James.

The favours Portland won and his close relationship with the King aroused extreme hatred. He was blamed for unpopular royal decisions and attacked in the Commons. Nevertheless, he continued to serve the King, especially in the diplomatic field. He contributed to the Treaty of Ryswick (1697) and acted as ambassador at Versailles (January-June 1698), where he began negotiations for the First Partition Treaty. In France he proved popular and competent. But a major reason for this lengthy absence from his master was the sullen jealousy roused in him by the King's new favourite, Arnold van Keppel.

On his return to England, Portland was received with the same warmth by William, but failed to respond; he was, however, still employed on major diplomatic missions, acting, for example, as a signatory to the secret Partition Treaties arranging the Spanish succession. Nevertheless, although he accompanied William on several journeys, he now resigned all his court posts and talked of retiring.

In 1701 Charles II of Spain died, leaving all his domains to Louis XIV's grandson. The French accepted the will rather than the Partition Treaties, and Europe prepared for war. The House of Commons was furious when it discovered the details of the Second Partition Treaty, and proceeded to impeach several ministers, including Portland. But the Lords dismissed the case against him.

On the death of his royal master,

whose deathbed he had attended, Portland withdrew from public life. He was on good terms with Marlborough and supported the latter's war policy; his knowledge of European diplomacy was unrivalled and from time to time he was still called out of retirement for consultation or to undertake negotiations. He died of pleurisy at Bulstrode, Buckinghamshire, on 23 November 1709.

Marion E. Grew, *William Bentinck and William III* (1924).

Portrait: oil, three-quarter length, studio of H. Rigaud, 1698–99: N.P.G.

Bentley, Richard (1662–1742), classical scholar and critic, see *Lives of the Georgian Age.*

Berkeley, Sir William (1606–77), governor of Virginia from 1641 to 1677.

William Berkeley was born near London, the youngest son of Sir Maurice Berkeley. He went to Merton College, Oxford, in 1625 and graduated in 1629. For a year he travelled on the Continent before returning to England, where he was for a time a gentleman of the privy chamber to Charles I. In 1632 he was given a commission empowering him to trade with Canada. He also published a play, *The Lost Lady*, a tragicomedy, in 1638. He was probably knighted around 1639, and in 1641 was appointed governor of Virginia, where he arrived the following year.

As governor, Berkeley soon made himself popular with the colonists. He attempted to diversify the economic activity of the colony from exclusive reliance on tobacco growing, and zealously subdued the Indians. After the execution of Charles I in 1649 he offered Royalists asylum in Virginia, but Parliament dispatched a fleet to subdue the colony and Berkeley was removed from office, although he remained on his plantation in Virginia. When Charles II was restored in 1660 he recommissioned Berkeley as governor.

During his second administration, he met with more problems. Tobacco prices were low in the 1660s and 1670s and this led to much economic distress. Moreover, a group of favourites collected around him, and to these he gave land grants, political office and, in many cases, exemption from taxation. He prevented the airing of grievances against this faction or himself by maintaining the same burgesses in office for fifteen years (1661–76), by the simple device of failing to hold new elections.

A new outbreak of Indian attacks early in 1676 precipitated the major crisis of Berkeley's career. He proposed to erect a chain of defensive forts, but the Virginians were loath to foot the bill for these. A group of settlers led by a newcomer, Nathaniel Bacon, acted against the Indians themselves. After a successful expedition against them, Bacon demanded that Berkeley should authorize him to carry out further punitive expeditions. Berkeley replied by declaring him a rebel, and meanwhile authorized an election. Bacon won a seat, and in June 1676 faced Berkeley with 600 followers, demanding the commission to act against the Indians.

Berkeley acquiesced until Bacon had departed and then again denounced the settler as a rebel. Bacon now turned his forces against the governor; but he died of a fever in October 1676. Berkeley, who in the meantime had fled, gradually regained control. Despite the fact that a new governor was sent from England to replace him, Berkeley remained in Virginia, ignoring a royal amnesty and securing the execution of twenty-three rebel leaders. His reputation suffered severely from this harsh action, although a subsequent investigation found no serious complaints against his conduct or administration before the rebellion began. In the early summer of 1677 he returned to England, where he died within a few weeks, on 9 June, at Twickenham.

Wilcomb E. Washburn, *The Governor and the Rebel* (Chapel Hill, N.C., 1957).

Berry-Godfrey, Sir Edmund (1621–78), see Godfrey, Sir Edmund Berry.

Berwick, 1st Duke of (1670–1734), see FitzJames, James.

Betterton, Thomas (?1635–1710), actor and theatrical manager.

Betterton was born in London in or about 1635. His father was a member of Charles I's kitchen staff. While still very young, he was apprenticed to Sir William Davenant's publisher, and later to John Rhodes, a bookseller who had at one time worked backstage at the theatre in Blackfriars and maintained a great interest in the stage. Betterton gave his début performance at the Cockpit in Drury Lane in 1660 – the year before, Rhodes had been granted a licence for the theatre and organized a company which included Betterton. His performance was well received, and his growing popularity, including Charles II's high regard, soon enabled him to assume leading roles.

In 1661, the year before Betterton married Mary Saunderson, herself a talented actress, Davenant and another manager, Thomas Killigrew (qq.v.), opened a new theatre in Lincoln's Inn Fields. Having secured the patent, they hired most of the established actors of the day, including Betterton. Here he remained until Davenant's death in 1671, after which the company moved to a new theatre in Dorset Garden with Betterton as its manager. It continued there until Betterton's company joined with another at the Theatre Royal in 1682. In 1695, with financial help from well-placed friends, Betterton built the New Playhouse, again in Lincoln's Inn Fields, and moved his company there. However, this new venture ran into financial difficulties within a few years, perhaps because of Betterton's advancing years and illness. He gave his farewell performance on 25 April 1710 in *The Maid's Tragedy*, which was a benefit performance for himself organized by his friends. Three days later he died; he was buried in Westminster Abbey.

Betterton appeared in many Restoration dramas and appears to have been equally successful in tragedy, comedy, and heroic drama, although he was particularly renowned for playing in Shakespearean tragedy. Like most prominent actors and theatre managers of his day, he adapted Elizabethan and Jacobean dramas to suit the new taste of the period, but he displayed little original talent as a writer.

R. W. Lowe, *Thomas Betterton* (1891).
G. C. D. Odell, *Shakespeare from Betterton to Irving*, vol. 1 (1921).

Portrait: oil, half-length, studio of Kneller, c. 1690–1700: N.P.G.

Blake, Robert (1599–1657), Parliamentarian naval commander during the Civil War, who won several naval battles and extensively reorganized the navy under Cromwell.

Blake was born in 1599, and baptized on 27 September that year at Bridgwater, Somerset. The eldest son of a prosperous merchant, he was educated at Bridgwater and at St. Alban Hall and Wadham College, Oxford. He graduated in 1625. It is said that he hoped for a fellowship of Merton College and that his lack of success was due to the Warden's dislike of his short, squat, ungainly figure. For the next fifteen years his life is clouded in obscurity, but it seems possible that he spent some years in the Netherlands, where he may have obtained some nautical experience, and was perhaps engaged in trade.

In 1640 Blake sat in the Short Parliament as M.P. for Bridgwater, but took no part in the Long Parliament until 1645, when he again represented Bridgwater. At the outbreak of the Civil War in 1642 he declared for the Parliamentarian side.

Blake's early success came in serving as a captain in the garrison of Bristol when it was besieged by Prince Rupert. Blake stoutly maintained the defence of his fort until well after the city had been officially surrendered. In the next year he won distinction by his resolute defence of Lyme, Dorset. He took Taunton and held it against two Royalist assaults.

In 1648 a large part of the fleet defected to the Royalist cause and a new one was organized, and in February 1649 Blake was made one of the 'generals-at-sea'. Embarking now on a new phase of his military career, Blake sought to distinguish himself. He blockaded the Royalist ships under Prince Rupert off Kinsale, Ireland, but after six months they eluded him. Pursuing the Prince to the Tagus, Blake again blockaded him near Lisbon, but was forbidden to attack by the King of Portugal. He retaliated by capturing seventeen ships of the Portuguese fleet on its way home from Brazil. After bearing his prizes back to England, he set out again and destroyed most of Rupert's ships at Cartagena in November 1650. In May 1651 he took part in capturing the Scilly Islands from Royalist privateers. For this and for his defeat of Rupert he received the thanks of the Commons

and became a member of the council of state.

In March 1652 Blake received the command of the English fleet against the Dutch in the first Dutch War. His opponent, Maarten Tromp, met him off Dover in May with a fleet twice as numerous as that of the English. In the engagement Tromp was forced to withdraw with the loss of two ships. War was formally declared in July, and in the same month Blake captured the bulk of the Dutch fishing fleet. On 28 September Blake and Sir William Penn (q.v.) encountered and defeated Dutch ships in the Kentish Knock, but in November they suffered a reverse when they met Tromp off Dungeness and had to retreat up the Thames. On this occasion Tromp is alleged to have tied a broom to his mast signifying that he would sweep the English from the seas. At a third battle with Tromp, in the Channel off Portland, Blake was severely wounded, but the Dutchman was forced to retreat. In May 1653 Tromp met the admirals Richard Deane and George Monck (qq.v.) off the Gabbard and pressed them hard until the arrival of Blake turned the scales. Repulsed, the Dutch fleet retreated to the Texel. After a further indecisive battle in August, in which Tromp was killed, Blake was compelled by the effects of his wound to retire from service for some eighteen months.

While away from the sea, Blake took his seat in the Barebones Parliament of 1654. In November he was appointed by Cromwell to carry out operations against the Turkish pirates who constantly threatened English shipping in the Mediterranean. In the battle of Porto Farina he annihilated a pirate force off Tunis and destroyed the two fortresses there.

In 1656 war was declared on Spain,

and Blake, now in declining health, was appointed to take forty-eight ships and cruise off Cadiz, with the objective of capturing Gibraltar if possible. Taking the rock proved an impractical idea, but one of Blake's captains fell upon a Spanish plate fleet and bore off much treasure. By April 1657 Blake's health was failing fast, but his final sea battle was a bold one. Hearing that a second treasure fleet lay at Santa Cruz, Tenerife, he decided to attack, notwithstanding the fact that the Spaniards' position was strong, defended by a fortress and several gun emplacements. Dividing his forces into two, he sent one into the bay against the crescent formation of the enemy's line, and followed himself with the remainder. In a fierce engagement the Spanish ships were routed and even the castle and forts were destroyed.

Blake was now very ill, and the English fleet hastened home. On 10 August 1657, within sight of Plymouth, he died. After lying in state at Greenwich, he was buried in Westminster Abbey. In 1661 Charles II ordered his remains to be disinterred and thrown into a pit. Blake was later reburied at St. Margaret's, Westminster.

Under the Commonwealth and Protectorate, Blake had done much to reform the fighting tactics of the navy, though it was to later men, especially Pepys (q.v.), that administrative reorganization is largely due. A bluff, tenacious general, he was in part responsible for the 'Fighting Instructions' upon which the tactics of the next hundred years were based and for the Articles of War, the framework of naval discipline. A man of sincerity and humility, he did great service for his country and even gained a testimonial from the Royalist, Clarendon, who wrote with less trace of bias than he usually showed that 'though [Blake] hath been very well imitated and followed, he was the first that drew the copy of naval courage.'

Maurice Ashley, *Cromwell's Generals* (1954).
R. H. Beadon, *Robert Blake* (1935).
C. E. Lucas Phillips, *Cromwells Captains* (1938).
J. R. Powell (ed.), *Letters of Blake* (1937).
J. R. Powell, *The Navy in the English Civil War* (1962).
J. R. Powell, *Robert Blake* (1972).

Blood, Colonel Thomas (?1618–80), adventurer and conspirator.

Nothing is known about Blood's birth and early circumstances, but he evidently rendered good service in the Parliamentary forces during the Civil War, for he emerged with the style of colonel and rewards including a magistracy and lands in Ireland, of which he may have been a native. At the Restoration he was dispossessed, and in consequence embarked upon a unique career of conspiracy.

His first essay in this field was as a member of a plot on the part of former Cromwellians in Ireland to reverse their fortunes by seizing Dublin Castle and the person of the lord lieutenant, James Butler (q.v.), 1st Duke of Ormonde, which acts were to be the prelude to a more general insurrection. The *coup* was planned for March 1663. The design was betrayed to Ormonde, but Blood persevered with his arrangements, merely advancing the date by a few days. A well-informed government arrested most of those involved on the eve of the projected attempt, but Blood himself escaped and evaded subsequent capture, despite the offer of a large reward, by assuming various disguises and receiving much help from Irish Cromwellians opposed to the authorities in Dublin. Eventually he was able to escape to Holland.

He reappeared in England among the

extremist Puritan group, the Fifth Monarchy Men, who had troubled the Commonwealth as much as they now troubled the restored monarchy; it is not improbable that Blood was at this time in a new role as an informer. Later he joined the Covenanter rebels in Scotland and remained with them until after their defeat in 1666.

A more personal stroke was his armed rescue of a friend, Captain Mason, who was being taken for trial under escort. Blood and three companions attacked the eight cavalrymen of the escort near Doncaster, killing some of them and snatching off their prisoner, although Blood himself was severely wounded in the process. After this, he took up residence in Kent under an assumed name until November 1670, when he led an attempt to abduct the Duke of Ormonde while he was in London. The six men involved succeeded in taking Ormonde by force from his coach one night in St. James's Street, but failed to carry him off due to the resistance he and his coachman were able to offer. Various explanations were put forward at the time for the attempt – personal revenge for the deaths of Blood's fellow conspirators of 1663 (for which Ormonde was to pay by being hanged on the Tyburn gallows by his kidnappers); simple kidnapping to enable Blood to recover his Irish estate; or an intended political assassination arranged by the Duke of Buckingham. Some colour is given to the last suggestion by Buckingham's emergence as Blood's protector after his ultimate exploit, the theft of the Crown Jewels on 9 May 1671.

To achieve this, Blood insinuated himself into the household of the keeper at the Tower in the guise of a clergyman. With him were three companions. Two of these had been members of the kidnapping gang, one being his own son-in-law; and the other had been the lieutenant of Major-General Harrison, the regicide. They failed to get clear with the jewels, and Blood was saved from the penalty attached to the crime by the influence of Buckingham and the sense of humour of King Charles II, who granted him an audience. Indeed, Blood was given back his estate and for a while was to be found at court, but eventually Buckingham threw him off, and he was sued for slandering the Duke and committed for damages sufficient to ruin him. He was released on bail and returned to his house in Bowling Alley, Westminster. There he fell ill, and died on 24 August 1680.

W. C. Abbott, *Colonel Thomas Blood, Crown-Stealer 1618–1680* (New Haven, Conn., 1911).
W. C. Abbott, *Conflicts with Oblivion* (Cambridge, Mass., 1924).

Blount, Edward (*fl.* 1588–1632), publisher, see *Lives of the Tudor Age*.

Blow, John (1649–1708), composer and musician.

Blow was born early in 1649, and baptized at Newark in Nottinghamshire on 23 February 1649. He probably received his early musical education at the Magnus Song School in Newark, before becoming a choirboy in Charles II's Chapel Royal about 1660. He is almost certain to have taken part in the singing at Charles's coronation (April 1661).

While he was a chorister, or perhaps after his voice broke in 1664, he came under the musical tutelage of Christopher Gibbons (1615–76), son of Orlando Gibbons (q.v.). His first post was organist at Westminster Abbey and dated from the autumn of 1668. A year later he rejoined the service of Charles II as musician of the virginals. In 1674, at the age of 25, he became a gentleman of the Chapel Royal. In July of the same year he succeeded Pelham Humfrey (1647–74), his boyhood contemporary among the Chapel Royal choristers, as master of the children. It must have been at this time, or a little before in his capacity as organist at the Abbey, that he became the teacher of the great Henry Purcell (q.v.). His choristers later included Jeremiah Clarke (?1670–1707), composer of the still popular Trumpet Voluntary.

In 1677 Blow received the title of Doctor of Music from the Dean and Chapter of Canterbury, and two years later he gave up his post as organist at Westminster Abbey and was succeeded by Purcell. He became one of the three organists of the Chapel Royal – it is not known exactly when – and was joined in that post by Purcell in 1682. He added to his duties five years later an appointment as almoner and master of the children of St. Pauls, a post which he held until 1703.

Blow's productivity at this time is marked by a number of fine vocal pieces. From 1684 dates his most important St. Cecilia ode, 'Begin the Song'; for James II's coronation of 1685 he composed the elaborate anthem 'God Spake Sometime in Visions'; and for the crowning of William III four years later he provided another anthem, 'The Lord God is a Sun and Shield'. His only stage work, *Venus and Adonis: a Masque for the Entertainment of the King*, probably dates from 1685.

In 1695, when Purcell died, Blow resumed his post as organist at Westminster Abbey. He commemorated the passing of his colleague and former pupil with a poignant ode setting words by Dryden.

In 1700 Blow published a set of fifty songs under the title *Amphion Anglicus*, dedicated to the future Queen Anne. 1700 also saw the appearance of a *Choice Collection of Ayres for the Harpsichord or Spinet*, to which Blow contributed. Two other volumes followed before his death on 1 October 1708.

Blow's output was enormous, encompassing 110 anthems, thirteen services, and innumerable secular pieces including catches and keyboard compositions. There is greatness in his music, particularly in his church compositions, many of which were incorporated into William Boyce's collection of *Cathedral Musick* (1760–78).

Anthony Lewis (ed.), *Venus and Adonis* (Paris 1939: full score with an introduction).
H. Watkins Shaw, *John Blow, Doctor of Music: a Biography* (1943).

Bolingbroke, 1st Viscount (1678–1715), see St. John, Henry.

Booth, George (1622–84), 1st Baron Delamere or De la Mer; military leader who fought for Parliament during the Civil War, but later led a Royalist uprising against the Commonwealth.

Booth was born in August 1622, the son of William Booth, a member of a distinguished Cheshire family. He entered the Long Parliament as M.P. for Cheshire in 1645. Throughout the Civil War he distinguished himself in the Parliamentarian cause, as did his grandfather, also named George Booth. In 1654 he represented Cheshire in Oliver Cromwell's Parliament, and also sat in the session of 1656. In 1655 he became military commissioner for Cheshire and treasurer-at-war.

It is not quite clear when Booth began to be sympathetic to the Royalists. Perhaps it was after Cromwell's death in 1658. In any event, he was among those excluded from Parliament when it reassembled after Richard Cromwell's failure to gain control over the army in 1659. He then became associated with a group of Presbyterians who favoured the cause of Charles II. In August, when this group collaborated with the Cavaliers, he was the main leader in Lancashire, Cheshire, and North Wales. A demand was put forth by the rebels for a free parliament and a change of government. As yet, however, no mention was made of the restoration of the monarchy. On 19 August Booth took Chester; but elsewhere the plot failed, and he and his men were defeated at Nantwich Bridge by General Lambert (q.v.). He escaped, but was captured at Newport Pagnell four days later. After a short period of imprisonment in the Tower, he was released on bail. He took his seat in Parliament for the 1659–60 session and was among those delegated to go to The Hague and invite Charles II home.

After the Stuart Restoration, Booth was awarded a grant of £10,000 and became keeper of the rolls for Cheshire, a post which he held until 1673. In 1661 he was created Baron Delamere or De la Mer by Charles II at his coronation. He played no further significant role in the country's affairs, and in his later years became highly critical of Charles's government. He died on 8 August 1684.

J. R. Jones, 'Booth's Rising', *Bulletin of the John Rylands Library*, 39 (1956–67).

Boyle, Richard (1566–1643), 1st Earl of Cork, known as 'The Great Earl', Anglo-Irish adventurer, colonizer, landowner, capitalist, and politician.

Boyle was born on 13 October 1566 in Canterbury, the second son of Roger Boyle, a none-too-wealthy gentleman of respectable ancestry. He was educated privately, at King's School, Canterbury, and at Bennett's (Corpus Christi) College, Cambridge.

He then entered the Middle Temple, but soon realized that he was too poor to pursue his legal studies with any hope of success. He took up a post as clerk to the chief baron of the exchequer, but before long recognized that this office held no better prospects for him. Ambitious and greedy for wealth, he decided to try his luck in Ireland.

In 1588 Boyle arrived in Dublin with £27 and a fine suit of clothes. He exerted all his energies in winning introductions and making friends, and as a jovial, clever, and well-dressed young gentleman soon established himself among the Anglo-Irish who controlled Ireland. In 1590 he was appointed assistant to Sir John Crofton, who as excheator-general was in charge of lands forfeited to the crown, wardships, and other lucrative sources of capital and income. By his aggressive pursuit of his own interests in the great Protestant land-grab in Ireland, Boyle made several powerful enemies, and they contrived to have him arrested several times on charges of theft and embezzlement. Nevertheless, they could not prevent him from winning the hand of Joan Appsley, a local heiress, who became his first wife in 1595.

This stage of Boyle's career ended with the great revolt of the native Irish in 1598. Like many other Englishmen he fled from Ireland, his fortunes ruined. The death of his wife compounded his miseries, and he returned to London, where he resumed his legal studies. This peaceable occupation did not last for long. The Earl of Essex, Elizabeth's new viceroy for Ireland, offered Boyle employment – but this advancement again brought upon Boyle the unwelcome attention of his enemies, led by Sir Henry Wallop, lord treasurer of Ireland. Still in London, he was arrested and imprisoned pending an investigation into charges of embezzlement. After two months he was brought before the Star Chamber in the presence of the Queen; he denied all charges, accused Wallop of corruptly obtaining £40,000, and with a stirring speech won the Queen's sympathy. She ordered his immediate release and appointed him clerk to the Council of Munster. At the same time she dismissed Wallop from the treasurership and replaced him with Sir George Carew, lord president of Munster; it was no difficult feat for Boyle to establish good relations with his new superior when he returned to Ireland in 1599.

The new clerk proved his efficiency in helping to suppress the Munster revolt in its last months, and after the decisive victory over the rebels and their Spanish allies at Kinsale in December 1601, Carew chose him to carry the welcome news to the Queen and her new chief minister, Robert Cecil. He was shown great favour in London and in 1602, with Cecil's aid, negotiated the purchase of all the Irish lands of Sir Walter Ralegh – 42,000 acres in Munster for £1,500.

The price of these vast estates was so low because of their condition: ravaged and depopulated, they had cost Ralegh several hundred pounds annually rather than yielding any return. However, Boyle, after marrying again and receiving a knighthood, settled at Youghal and proceeded to develop his estates with skill and energy. He settled them with English colonists who were armed and trained as a militia. Local ore was mined for iron and an ironworks was established. Boyle also developed the woollen industry, built ships, and introduced new manufacturers from England. He constructed roads, bridges, towns, and fortifications, and within a decade had become one of the wealthiest and most powerful men in the island. As a landlord and employer he proved to be a benevolent and generous autocrat, and although he exerted himself to the utmost to crush convents and monasteries,

he showed no interest in persecuting individual Catholics.

Boyle's importance was recognized outside Munster. In 1612 he was appointed to the Privy Council of Ireland. In 1616 he was ennobled and four years later created Earl of Cork, largely through the influence of King James's favourite, Buckingham (see Villiers, George, 1st Duke), to whose brother Edward he gave £4,500. After the accession of Charles I, Cork was made one of the two lord justices of Ireland (1629) and appointed lord high treasurer (1631). He was now at the height of his power. Together with the second lord justice, Lord Chancellor Loftus, he exercised with practically no restraint the royal authority in Ireland. However, in 1633 the vacant position of lord deputy was filled by the appointment of Sir Thomas Wentworth (q.v.). In his implementation of the royal policy of strong, aristocratic rule Wentworth determined to subordinate all notables to his authority and to raise sufficient revenue to maintain a standing army. Cork soon felt the brunt of his plans, for by now he was one of the wealthiest men in the three kingdoms. Wentworth succeeded in humiliating him, stripped him of his power, and extorted vast sums from his estates.

Cork bided his time; in 1638, at the first opportunity, he moved to England, where he was less vulnerable to Wentworth's authority. When the Long Parliament met and turned to attack his enemy, by now Earl of Strafford, Cork provided the most substantial evidence as to misgovernment in Ireland and helped feed the fears of the Commons about Strafford's designs on their liberties. In this he contributed significantly to the attainder and execution (1641) of his once all-powerful enemy.

Cork did not, however, live long to

enjoy his victory. In the autumn of 1641 he returned to Ireland, arriving just before the outbreak of the great native rising in Ulster. He immediately took precautions, and by the time the revolt had spread to Munster, the province was in a state of defence. With his sons and his relatives he held on to Munster, making full use of the aid of his tenants, his money, and the fortifications he had built. But the Great Earl did not live to see the end of this long struggle; he died on 15 September 1643.

Brian FitzGerald, *The Anglo-Irish* (1952).
D. Townshend, *The Life and Letters of the Great Earl of Cork* (1904).

Portrait: miniature, by I. Oliver: N.P.G.

Boyle, The Hon. Robert (1627–91), natural philosopher, father of modern chemistry, and founder member of the Royal Society.

Robert Boyle was born at Lismore Castle, County Cork, Ireland, on 25 January 1627, the fourteenth child and seventh son of Richard Boyle (q.v.), 1st

Earl of Cork. He was educated at Eton, Geneva, and Oxford.

Robert Boyle is remembered for the law that bears his name and for his perceptive experiments that paved the way from medieval alchemy to modern chemistry. Although he spent many hours in futile attempts to convert base metals to gold, he provided an experimental basis for modern atomic theory by distinguishing between elements, compounds, and mixtures. His other great contribution to science was the part he played in the foundation of the Royal Society.

When barely eight years old he was sent by his busy and politically involved parents to Eton. There he displayed a great talent for languages, learning to speak and write fluently in Latin and French. In 1639, accompanied by a tutor, he was sent off to complete his education in France, Italy, and Switzerland (mostly in Geneva). After returning to England in 1645 he spent seven years living quietly on his family's estates at Stallbridge, Dorset. During this period he read widely in natural philosophy and developed his abiding interest in experimental science. This led him to Oxford, where he settled in 1654. Ignoring the strictures of some of the less perspicacious dons, who attempted to persuade him that chemistry was no occupation for a gentleman, he became a prominent member of the group of Oxford thinkers known as the 'Invisible College'. This group formed the basic membership of the Royal Society when it was founded in 1663.

During Boyle's Oxford period, Robert Hooke (q.v.) worked as his assistant, helping him in the development of a vacuum pump constructed on the principle of a pump invented by Otto von Guericke (1602–86). Boyle had heard of this pump as a result of Guericke's famous experiment before the Reichstag at Regensburg on 8 May 1654. In this experiment, Guericke pumped air from a hollow metal sphere made in two halves: sixteen horses, eight harnessed to each half, were unable to pull the two halves apart.

Boyle used his improved version of this vacuum pump to conduct the numerous experiments on gases from which he deduced his law, which states that the pressure of a gas is inversely proportional to its volume. The law was first published in 1662, in an appendix to the second edition of his *New Experiments Physico-Mechanicall*, in reply to criticisms from a Jesuit priest, Franciscus Linus (1595–1675). Although the law goes by Boyle's name in the English-speaking world, in Europe it is named after the French physicist Edmé Mariotte (d. 1684), who published it in 1676. Quite apart from this question of national priorities, some historians have suggested that the law was not discovered by Boyle himself but by his assistant, R. Townley. Boyle's other main publications on the behaviour of gases were *Mechanica Hydraulica-Pneumatica* (1657) and *General History of the Air* (published posthumously in 1692).

Although he carried out transmutation experiments himself, Boyle had very little sympathy with the somewhat nebulous theoretical views of the medieval alchemists. He was a strong advocate of the experimental method of science and believed that chemistry was far too important a subject to be merely a junior branch of medicine. In his famous *Sceptical Chymist* (1662), and later in his *Origin of Forms and Qualities* (1666), he outlined an atomic theory in which most of the properties of matter were attributed to the motions of atoms. As a devout Christian he believed these motions to be a manifestation of the omnipresence of the Almighty.

In 1668 Boyle moved from Oxford to live with his sister, Lady Ranelagh, in London. There, a great deal of his time was devoted to the activities of the recently-founded Royal Society. In recognition of this work and of his eminence as a scientist he was elected President of the Royal Society in 1680, but he declined the honour, partly because of his indifferent health and partly because to accept would have involved him in taking an oath that was unacceptable to him.

During the last years of his life his own poor health encouraged his interest in medicine, especially physiology and pathology. He wrote a number of medical books, including *Memoirs for the Natural History of the Human Blood* (1684), but these are of limited interest, perhaps because he appears to have been too squeamish to carry out dissections.

In the seventeenth century physical scientists reconciled their religious beliefs and their scientific work to an extent that is much less customary today and, like Newton, Boyle had a consuming interest in theology throughout his life. In order to further his biblical studies he made use of his talents as a linguist to learn Hebrew, Greek, and Aramaic. He also used his position as a director of the East India Company to help in the work of spreading the Gospel in the East, spending considerable sums of his own money on translations of the Bible. In his will he left a bequest to finance the Boyle lectures for the defence of Christianity against atheists, Jews, and Mohammedans, with the somewhat specious provision that no controversies among Christians should be mentioned.

After 1688 he shut himself away from public life, and he died in London on 30 December 1691.

T. Birch, *Life of the Hon. Robert Boyle* (1744).

M. B. Hall, *Robert Boyle and Seventeenth Century Chemistry* (1958).

F. Masson, *Robert Boyle, a Biography* (1914).

L. T. More, *Life and Works of the Hon. Robert Boyle* (1944).

Portrait: oil, three-quarter length, by J. Kerseboom, 1689: Kensington Palace.

Boyle, Roger (1621–79), 1st Baron Broghill and 1st Earl of Orrery, Anglo-Irish soldier, politician, courtier, and dramatist.

Roger Boyle was born on 25 April 1621 at Lismore Castle in Waterford, the fifth son of Richard Boyle (q.v.), 1st Earl of Cork. He was created Baron Broghill in 1627, and educated at Trinity College, Dublin, from 1630 to about 1634.

Broghill was sent on the Grand Tour by his father from 1636 to 1639, in the company of an older brother and a Calvinist tutor. Most of their time was spent in Geneva, northern Italy, and France. The young Boyles were taught philosophy, science, and classical literature, but they discovered for themselves the delights of modern drama and romance. Their standing guaranteed admittance to the court in Paris, and they were well received at the English court when they returned home.

Broghill held commands in both wars against the Scots (1639 and 1640), but the campaigns were sufficiently short to enable him to spend a great deal of time at court, where he established something of a reputation as a wit and poet and won the friendship of men like Davenant and Suckling (qq.v.). In 1641 he went to Ireland, arriving on the very day that the rebellion broke out. Immediately he was drawn into his father's service on behalf of the crown, raising cavalry in Munster, where he was soon second only to the Earl of Inchiquin (see O'Brien, Murrough) in the Protestant camp. After Ormonde (see Butler, James, 1st Duke), the King's lord lieutenant, came to terms with the rebels, Inchiquin and Broghill obtained commissions from Parliament to continue the war, which they did with considerable success. Although a Royalist by inclination, Broghill spent the winters of 1644–5 and 1645–6 in London in consultation with Parliamentarian committees. Both jealous and ambitious, he sought to replace Inchiquin as lord president of Munster, and in May 1647 charged his superior with disloyalty, without success. Broghill retired in high dudgeon to Somerset. However, when Inchiquin deserted to the King in April 1648, Parliament gave the Munster presidency to Broghill – who now declined to take it up. Spurred on by the execution of Charles I in January 1649, he determined to aid the new king, Charles II, and began to correspond with him. Some of his letters were intercepted by Commonwealth agents: Cromwell confronted him with them and offered him the alternative of imprisonment or a commission in the Parliamentarian forces serving in Ireland. Broghill chose the latter, and in October 1649 he crossed over once again to his native land.

Cromwell proved himself wise in his generous offer, for the Boyle interest in Munster was very influential. There Broghill rallied the Protestant gentry to his side and soundly defeated both the Royalists under Inchiquin (1650) and the Catholics under Lord Muskerry (1651). A promotion to lieutenant-general in 1651 did not satisfy his ambition, and he was forced to spend two more years campaigning before being awarded a place in Cromwell's cabinet. Each man admired the other's capabilities and a mutual affection developed. Broghill's loyalty was bolstered by his self-interest and ambition, for he recognized in Cromwell the highest fount of patronage.

Broghill sat in the Parliaments of 1654 and 1656 and served for one year (1655–6) as president of the Council of Scotland when he won the respect and esteem of many old Covenanters. Returning to England, he continued as one of Cromwell's closest advisers, and urged him strongly to accept the crown. He was appointed to the new upper chamber in 1657 and, after the death of the Lord Protector, actively supported Richard Cromwell until the latter's downfall in May 1659. Thereupon he withdrew to Ireland to assess the political situation. He entered into correspondence with Monck (q.v.), and in December took control of Munster as Monck's ally. Before the Restoration was agreed upon in England, he invited Charles II to come to Ireland on his own initiative.

Broghill also promoted the Restoration in England, where he was elected to the Convention and Cavalier Parliaments. Charles rewarded him with the earldom of Orrery, a seat in the Privy Councils of England and Ireland, and appointments as an Irish lord justice and as lord president of Munster. For the next decade he was active in the affairs of both England and Ireland. He did good service against privateers and French raiders on the Munster coast in 1666–7, but he yearned after greater things, principally the lord lieutenancy of Ireland. His intrigues against the various incumbents of this position eventually ruined his own career. His alliance with the Cabal brought about a move to impeach him in 1669, and when the Irish presidencies were abolished in 1672 he was given no new office.

Orrery did not devote all his energies to politics. He was one of the stars of the Restoration court, the friend of Charles II and of John Dryden. During the interregnum he had written *Parthenissa*, a long romance in the French style. In 1660–1, as a result of a discussion at court, he wrote *The General, or Altemira*, the first English heroic play. He introduced rhymed heroic drama to England with his *Mustapha, Henry the Fifth*, and other works. These plays proved quite successful in the 1660s, and in 1669 he turned to writing farce. He was also the author of a treatise on warfare, wrote a good deal of poetry, and designed his own castle in Munster.

In the last decade of his life, as his literary powers and his influence declined, Orrery's sense of his own importance increased. His last years were made miserable by gout, and it was from complications arising from this illness that he died on 16 October 1679 in Munster.

K. M. Lynch, *Roger Boyle, First Earl of Orrery* (Knoxville, Tenn., 1965).

William S. Clarke (ed.), *The Dramatic Works of Roger Boyle, First Earl of Orrery* (2 vols.; Cambridge, Mass., 1937).

Bradford, William (1590–1657), a founder of Plymouth colony and its second governor.

He was born in Yorkshire, the eldest son of William Bradford, a prosperous yeoman. Since his father died when he was one year old, the young William Bradford was brought up by his relatives, being trained as a farmer. At the age of 12 or 13 he had some kind of religious experience and began to attend Puritan services and read the Bible. Despite the opposition of his family, he joined a separatist congregation that was soon forced to flee to Holland to escape persecution.

Bradford worked as an apprentice to a silk manufacturer in Amsterdam until, in 1611, he came of age and received his inheritance. This he sold and with his new wealth set up in the fustian trade in Leiden, but did not prosper. More successful were his studies at this time, and he acquired a smattering of theology to complement his general education in Latin, Greek, philosophy, and history.

The exiled Puritans in Leiden wished, however, to live as Englishmen. They determined to found a colony and received a royal patent for a tract of land in North America. This group, grown famous as the Pilgrim Fathers, sailed from Plymouth in the *Mayflower* in September 1620. On 11 November, before landing on the New England coast, they drew up the Mayflower Compact, an agreement of government.

In all these proceedings, Bradford played an important part. However, it was only in 1621, after the death of the first governor, that he became the dominant leader in the colony. He was elected governor annually until his death, except for five years when he begged to be released from the responsibility – and in these years he served as one of the governor's assistants. During his long tenure he established good relations with most of the neighbouring Indian peoples, which, especially in the earlier years, not only reduced a physical threat to the colony's survival but also secured an important source of food. In 1627, with seven other colonists, Bradford bought out the merchant adventurers who owned the settlement and then shared out the wealth. He was instrumental in establishing the colony's constitution, which consolidated power in the hands of those who had signed the Mayflower Compact.

Bradford wrote works on religion and on the colony, his most famous being the *History of Plymouth Plantation*, the most valuable source for the colony's early history, compiled between 1630 and 1650.

Bradford's later years were much saddened by the growing secularism he saw in his settlement, and he died on 9 May 1657.

Samuel E. Morrison (ed.), *Of Plymouth Plantation* (New York, 1952).
Bradford Smith, *Bradford of Plymouth* (Philadelphia, Pa., 1951).

Bradshaw, John (1602–59), lawyer and regicide.

He was baptized on 10 December 1602, the second son of Henry Bradshaw of Marple, Cheshire. His education took place in Cheshire and Lancashire and included a period of study with an attorney at Congleton. In 1620 he entered Gray's Inn and was called to the bar in 1627.

In 1637 he was mayor of Congleton, and was recorder for the borough shortly afterwards. On 21 September 1643, he became judge of the sheriff's court. During the course of the Civil War, he was involved in several court cases. In 1644 he appeared alongside William Prynne in the prosecution of Connor Maguire, 2nd Baron of Enniskillen (1616–45), and Hugh Oge MacMahon (?1606–44) for their parts in the Irish rebellion of 1641; in 1645 he represented John Lilburne in his appeal before the House of Lords against the sentence of the Star Chamber; and in 1647 he conducted the case against the captured Royalist judge, David Jenkins (1582–1665), who in 1643 had issued indictments against Welsh Parliamentarians. 1647 also saw Bradshaw's appointment as a bencher at Gray's Inn, and in the same year he was made chief justice of Chester and a judge in Wales. In the following year he became a serjeant-at-law.

On 2 January 1649, the House of

Lords rejected the ordinance for the trial of Charles I and the 'Rump' of the Commons left after Pride's Purge of the previous month (see Pride, Thomas) took upon themselves the authority for initiating proceedings against the King. Most of the lawyers, Parliamentarian as well as Royalist, refused to be involved in the case and the presidency of the specially established court of justice therefore finally devolved upon Bradshaw. Bradshaw's conduct of the affair was ruthless: upon the King's refusal to make a plea, he overrode all legal objections and even prohibited him from speaking in his own defence. On 27 January Bradshaw pronounced sentence on Charles, and three days later the King was dead.

Subsequently, Bradshaw presided at the trials of other prominent Royalists, including Hamilton, at which he exercised similar ruthlessness. Like the members of the Rump, Bradshaw had the army at his back and carried all before him. In the same year (1649) he was appointed attorney general for Cheshire and North Wales, president of the Council of State, and chancellor of the duchy of Lancaster. A supporter of Cromwell during the early part of the Commonwealth, Bradshaw became violently hostile to the gradual institution of one-man rule. After the establishment of Cromwell as Lord Protector, the breach between them was complete. In 1654 Bradshaw refused to sign the document supporting the Protectorate and withdrew from the House of Commons. He remained secluded from public life until after Cromwell was dead.

He returned to Parliament following Richard Cromwell's abdication, but his health was poor and he was by now well advanced into his fifties. He died on 31 October 1659, and was buried in Westminster Abbey.

At the Restoration, Bradshaw's remains suffered the indignities of other regicides who had died during the Interregnum. He was posthumously attainted, and his body was dug up and hanged alongside those of Cromwell and Ireton (qq.v.), then cast into an unmarked grave at Tyburn.

C. V. Wedgwood, *The Trial of Charles I* (1964).

Bradstreet, Anne (1612–72), American poet born in England; known as 'America's First Poetess'.

Anne Bradstreet was born, probably in Northampton, the daughter of Thomas Dudley, a steward to the Earl of Lincoln and later governor of Massachusetts. When she was 17 years old, Anne married Simon Bradstreet and accompanied him to Massachusetts in 1630. She was a faithful Puritan wife, although she had read widely and could not always accept the suppression and sternness required by life in New England.

She was obviously aware of the limits to which prose and poetry could go in the Puritan confines of the New World. Nevertheless, occasionally some of her lines reached beyond the limits arbitrarily set in her home town of Ipswich and, later, North Andover in the Massachusetts Bay Colony.

In her *Contemplations*, Bradstreet praised the physical beauty of Massachusetts. In speaking of Elizabeth I, she spoke out with wit and defiant vigour:

Now say, have women worth? or
   have they none?
Or had they some, but with our
   Queen is't gone?
Nay Masculines, you have thus taxt
   us long,
But she, though dead, will vindicate
   our wrong.

Let such as say our Sex is void of
Reason,
Know 'tis a Slander now, but once
was Treason.

In 1650 her volume of poems, *Tenth
Muse Lately Sprung Up in America*, was
published in London. *Works in Prose and
Verse* was published posthumously in
1678.

Anne Bradstreet died on 16 September
1672.

J. H. Ellis (ed.), *Works of Anne Bradstreet* (1678; re-
printed 1962).
J. Hensley (ed.), *Works of Anne Bradstreet* (1967).
J. E. Piercy, *Anne Bradstreet* (1965).
See also M. C. Tyler, *History of American Literature,
1607–1765*, vol. 1 (Ithaca, N.Y., 1949).

Breadalbane, 1st Earl of (1635–1716),
see Campbell, John, 1st Earl of Breadalbane.

Briggs, Henry (1561–1630), mathematician, remembered for his work on
logarithms.

Born at Warley Wood, near Halifax,
Yorkshire; graduated from St. John's
College, Cambridge, in 1581, being
made a fellow of the college in 1588.
From 1596 to 1620 he was professor of
geometry at Gresham College, London.

In 1614 John Napier (q.v.) published
his work on logarithms. Logarithms
were acclaimed as an immensely valuable mathematical tool, especially for
astronomical calculations. They were a
remarkable invention, but in their existing form they were awkward to use.
Briggs was considerably impressed by
Napier's work. His careful study of it
led him to propose that the logarithms
could be put into a more convenient
form. After several discussions with him
on the subject, Napier agreed, and in
1617 Briggs published the first thousand
of his new logarithms. Briggs's logarithms were calculated to a base ten, with

the logarithm of ten equal to one. In a
decimal number system this greatly
simplifies the use of logarithms in
calculations.

The common logarithms (or Briggs-
ian logarithms as they are sometimes
called) used today in computation have
a base ten. They are, however, determined in a slightly different and less
laborious way than Briggs's logarithms.
At that time, there was no simple formula for calculating logarithms. They
were determined by repeated multi-
plications and the extraction of square
roots.

In 1619 Briggs became Savilian professor of astronomy at Oxford and a
fellow-commoner at Merton College,
incorporated as an M.A. Much of his
time was spent in the tedious task of calculating logarithms of both numbers
and trigonometric functions to many
places of decimals. In 1624 he published
Arithmetica Logarithmica, which contained the workings of a further 30,000
numbers. His tables of the logarithms of
sines, tangents, and secants, published
after his death in *Trigonometria Britannica*
(1633), were in use up to the early 19th
century.

Although Briggs was primarily a
mathematician, he also wrote works on
astronomy and navigation, including
one on the North-West Passage. He died
at Oxford in 1630.

Broghill, 1st Baron (1621–79), see
Boyle, Roger.

Brooke, 1st Baron (1554–1628), poet
and statesman, see Greville, Fulke in
Lives of the Tudor Age.

Browne, Sir Thomas (1605–82),
author and physician.

Born in London on 19 October 1605,
the son of a mercer, Browne was edu-

cated at Winchester and at Broadgates Hall, Oxford, where he obtained his M.A. degree in 1629. Since medicine was not offered as a subject at Oxford, he probably began his study of it at this time, practising as an assistant to a doctor in Oxfordshire. He continued his studies at Montpellier and Padua, and in 1633 graduated as M.D. at the University of Leiden. Although little is known of his life during his stay on the Continent, the great erudition of *Religio Medici*, written soon after his return to England, suggests how widely he had read during these years. In 1637 he was incorporated M.D. at Oxford and in the same year took up residence to practise medicine in Norwich, where he lived for the rest of his life.

Browne's fame was immediately established with his first work, *Religio Medici*. Written at Shibden Hall near Halifax about 1635, the book was composed as 'a private exercise', a profession of belief in Christianity marked by a tolerant, latitudinarian, occasionally sceptical spirit. In it an enormous number of subjects are treated with characteristic fancifulness and eloquence. Printed without the author's consent in 1642, it was published with his approval the following year, was instantly successful, and was soon translated into several languages. His longest work, *Pseudodoxia Epidemica: Enquiries into Vulgar Errors* (1646), is an examination of superstitions and popular beliefs and an explanation of their causes. The book surveys in a delicately ironic light a multitude of the legends and curiosities that appealed to Browne's antiquarian interests. *Urn Burial, or Hydriotaphia* (1658) contains the author's most elaborate rhetorical prose. Inspired by the discovery of ancient burial urns in Norfolk, the work is both a treatise on various burial customs and a meditation on human mortality. Published with it was a curious work of less importance and of less interest to the modern reader, although it is typical of the author's taste for the odd and fantastic and his habit of examining the allegories which he finds in detail of this kind. *The Garden of Cyrus* concerns the quincunx, the arrangement of five objects in a rectangle, with one at each corner and one in the middle. From a consideration of this figure in the design of gardens, especially Cyrus's garden as described by Xenophon, the author enlarges his theme to a discussion of the mystical attributes of the number five.

Having declared his adherence to the royalist cause during the Civil War, Browne was knighted in 1671. He died on 19 October 1682, a devout Christian; his monument stands in the Church of St. Peter Mancroft, Norwich.

Geoffrey Keynes (ed.), *The Works of Sir Thomas Browne* (4 vols.; 1964, rev. ed.).

Portraits: oil on panel, half-length, attributed to Joan Carlile, *c.* 1641–50: N.P.G.; plumbago on vellum, quarter-length, after R. White: N.P.G.

35

Buckhurst, Lord (1638–1706), see Sackville, Charles.

Buckingham, 1st Duke of (1592–1628), see Villiers, George, 1st Duke of Buckingham.

Buckingham, 2nd Duke of (1628–87), see Villiers, George, 2nd Duke of Buckingham.

Bull, John (1563–1628), organist and composer, see *Lives of the Tudor Age*.

Bunyan, John (1628–88), author of *The Pilgrim's Progress*.

Born at Elstow near Bedford, Bunyan was the son of a travelling brazier or tinker, Thomas Bunyan. Although the family was of yeoman stock, it had declined in prosperity and John Bunyan received only a rudimentary formal education. He attended a local grammar school, where he learned to read and write, but he seems to have left it early to become an apprentice in his father's trade. He wrote of a later period in his

adult life that 'I was never out of the Bible either by reading or meditation', but in fact as a child he must have learned much from the popular culture of his time. His parents belonged to the Church of England, and so he was not cut off from this culture as he probably would have been if he had grown up in a more rigid Puritan environment. He read a wide range of moral tracts and homiletic literature as well as the Bible; the vigorous colloquial qualities of the 17th-century sermon, illustrated with pithy anecdotes and moral parables, seem to have influenced his prose style as much as the Bible.

When he was sixteen, a series of events suddenly separated him from his family. Both his mother and a younger sister died. His father took another wife soon after his mother's death, and shortly after his father's rapid remarriage Bunyan enlisted in the county militia, which was on the Parliamentary side in the Civil War. From 1644 to 1646 he was stationed at Newport Pagnell under the command of Sir Samuel Luke, the Puritan leader whom Samuel Butler (q.v.) probably took as the model of *Hudibras*. While he was in the New Model Army, Bunyan did not see much military action; however, it is thought that his experiences in the army are reflected in incidents in the allegory *The Holy War* (1682), especially in the characterization of the captains Credence and Boanerges.

In 1649 Bunyan married. He wrote of this event that he and his wife were 'as poor as poor might be, not having so much household stuff as a dish or spoon betwixt us both'. Among his wife's possessions were, however, two religious books, Arthur Dent's *The Plain Man's Path-Way to Heaven* and Lewis Bayly's *The Practice of Piety*, popular works of Puritan morality that played a role in his gradual religious conversion. About the time of his marriage, Bunyan underwent a severe spiritual crisis that was to last for several years. He was tormented by a sense of guilt and driven to despair. Temptations seemed to strike him with physical force, and even passages of Scripture seemed to him to have a tangible existence and to 'pinch him very sore'. The intensity of these experiences is almost certainly attributable to the effect of Calvinism on a sensitive imagination. Certainly, Bunyan's struggle with religious despair is related to his meditating on the fearful doctrine of the predestination of all mankind either to salvation or to damnation. It was only gradually that he emerged from this suffering. His recovery was marked by his joining, about 1653, an open-communion Nonconformist meeting in Bedford. There he was baptized by immersion, made a deacon of the church, and soon began to preach. He appears to have been deeply influenced by the pastor of the church, John Gifford, an ex-Royalist officer. His first writings, *Some Gospel Truths opened* (1656) and *A Vindication* (1657), works of religious controversy in which he defends the open-communion group against the Quakers, were written at this time. About 1656 his first wife died, leaving him with four young children; about 1659 he married his second wife, Elizabeth.

With the Restoration of Charles II, the religious freedom of the Nonconformists was restricted and Bunyan soon found himself in conflict with the law. Late in 1660, he was brought before a magistrate in south Bedfordshire and charged with holding a conventicle. On refusing to give assurance that he would desist from preaching without a licence, he was sentenced to imprisonment and, with the exception of brief periods of release, spent the next twelve years in the county jail at Bedford. The imprisonment was not harsh, however, for he was allowed to visit his family and friends on occasion and even to speak at the meeting house. It appears that he might have secured his release at any time during his imprisonment by giving assurance that he would not preach or that he would conform to the practice of the Church of England. But he was now confirmed in his faith and steadfastly refused to compromise his principles. While in prison, he worked at making 'long tagg'd laces', the income from which helped to support his family. His reading consisted of the Bible and Foxe's *Book of Martyrs*. Driven to examine his religious belief in the isolation of prison, he wrote his first major work, *Grace Abounding to the Chief of Sinners: or, A Brief and Faithful Relation of the Exceeding Mercy of God in Christ to his Poor Servant, John Bunyan* (1666).

A spiritual autobiography, *Grace Abounding* deals with his religious conversion, recounting his childhood and youth, his first reading the two moral books owned by his wife, and his finally finding his vocation as a minister. Adopting a plain style, even though he 'could have adorned all things more than here I have seemed to do', the force of the homiletic story derives from the intensity with which he scrutinizes his experiences and relates everything to the state of his soul.

Released from prison in 1672 as a result of Charles II's Declaration of Indulgence, Bunyan was chosen pastor of the Bedford meeting and was given a licence to preach there. Although he was imprisoned again for a brief time in 1675, he was not otherwise troubled by the authorities. He continued to preach in many places and was the most prominent spokesman for the liberal open communion group. He earned the nickname 'Bishop Bunyan' because of his energetic activities on behalf of his church, and it was in the performance of pastoral duties, after a visit to Reading in 1688, that he contracted a fever and died after the journey. He was buried in Bunhill Fields in the City of London.

Bunyan's masterpiece, *The Pilgrim's Progress from This World, To That Which Is to Come; Delivered under the Similitude of a Dream, Wherein is Discovered, The Manner of His Setting Out, His Dangerous Journey, And Safe Arrival at the Desired Country*, was first published in 1678. It was probably written during his first imprisonment, immediately after *Grace Abounding*. An allegory based on the ancient Christian metaphor of life as a journey through this world to the next, the book concerns Christian's journey to the Celestial City. The whole is presented as a dream by the author, who comes to a den – marginally glossed as 'The gaol' – lies down to sleep, and sees Christian, a man bearing a burden on his back, reading from a book. The book tells him that the place in which he lives will be destroyed. Evangelist then appears and tells him to flee from the City of Destruction and the journey commences, Christian having failed to persuade his wife and children to go with him. As he journeys through a number of allegorical places – the Slough of Despond, the Interpreter's House, the Palace Beautiful, Vanity Fair, Doubting Castle, the Delectable Mountains, and the country of Beulah – he meets personifications whose meanings are clearly indicated by their names: Mr. Worldly Wiseman, Faithful, Hopeful, Giant Despair, and many others. The personifications and the dialogue are rendered with great realism, and the episodes, such as Vanity Fair, often involve humour and satire. In 1684 Bunyan published Part II of the book, in which Christian's wife Christiana and her children make the same pilgrimage. The popularity of the book was immediate: 100,000 copies were sold within ten years, and it was eventually translated into most of the major languages of the world. For generations it constituted, together with the Authorized Version of the Bible, the main and often the only reading of many English families. Despite its popularity and the influence of its prose on other writers, the work did not gain full critical acceptance until the 19th century.

Bunyan was a prolific writer and produced many other works after *The Pilgrim's Progress*, but none was so successful. In his next major work, *The Life and Death of Mr. Badman* (1680), he abandoned allegory for a more direct narrative in which Mr. Wiseman, an elderly Puritan, tells the tale to his younger listener, Mr. Attentive. The subject of the story, Mr. Badman, is an exemplum of the many sins about which the older man instructs his friend. In *The Holy War* (1682) Bunyan returned to allegory. The metaphor of a struggle between good and evil for domination of the human soul is again a traditional one and is developed with more complexity than the journey in *The Pilgrim's Progress*, but the narrative lacks the dramatic interest of the earlier work. In the allegory, the scene of the struggle is the city of Mansoul, which is first lost to Diabolus but is finally, after many conflicts, won by Emmanuel, the Saviour.

G. Offor (ed.), *The Works of John Bunyan* (3 vols.; 1853 and 1862).

J. B. Wharey (ed.), *The Pilgrim's Progress*, rev. R. Sharrock (1968).

R. Sharrock (ed.) *Grace Abounding to the Chief of Sinners* (1962).

G. B. Harrison (ed.), *The Life and Death of Mr. Badman* (1928).

J. F. Forrest (ed.), *The Holy War* (Toronto, 1967).

J. Browne, *John Bunyan, His Life, Times and Work*, rev. P. M. Harrison (1928).

O. E. Winslow, *John Bunyan* (New York, 1961).

R. Sharrock, *John Bunyan* (1968, rev. ed.).

R. Greaves, *John Bunyan* (1969).

Portrait: oil, half-length, by T. Sadler, 1684–5 : N.P.G.

Burnet, Gilbert (1643–1715), Scottish historian and Bishop of Salisbury.

Born on 18 September 1643, in Edinburgh, the son of a much-respected advocate, Burnet was apparently a precocious child and at the age of ten entered Marischal College, Aberdeen. At the age of fourteen he received his M.A. and began to study law, but his father wanted him to become a clergyman and Burnet therefore applied himself to the study of divinity. In 1661 he entered the Church but refused the offer of a living and began the practice of extemporary preaching.

In 1663 Burnet visited several English universities and soon afterwards travelled in Holland and France. On his return to England he stayed for a while at court, acquainting himself with the men who were influential in Scottish affairs. He became a close friend of Lauderdale (see Maitland, John) and supported him in his opposition to the repressive anti-Presbyterian policies of the Scottish bishops. In November 1664, Burnet became minister of the parish of Saltoun; here he consistently advocated reconciliation between Presbyterians and Episcopalians.

He kept himself well informed of the politics of the English court and in the late 1660s was on good terms with both the King and the Duke of York. In 1669 he became professor of divinity at Glasgow University. About this time he wrote a *Modest and Free Conference between a Conformist and a Nonconformist*, advocating the liberal principles in church government that he supported

throughout his life. Despite his youth Burnet was offered two bishoprics while he was at Glasgow, but refused them both.

In 1672 Lauderdale began to pursue a changed policy, involving religious persecution, in Scotland and he and Burnet eventually quarrelled. Burnet moved to England and although Lauderdale exerted all his influence to prevent his appointment to a living Burnet became chaplain to the Rolls chapel in 1675. Probably in 1676 he began to write his *History of the Reformation in England* and the first volume, which was published in 1679, appeared at the height of the hysteria over the alleged Popish Plot. Because of the carefully reasoned refutations of Roman Catholic claims embodied within it, the book was enthusiastically received. Both Houses of Parliament passed votes of thanks to Burnet and requested him to complete the work. Yet he spoke against the persecution of Catholics engendered by the revelation of the 'Plot' and during the Exclusion crisis (the move to exclude the Catholic James from succession to the throne) that followed he did his best to conciliate the opposing factions.

Burnet's outspokenness is well illustrated by the advice that he gave to the King in 1680: '. . . permit me to tell you, all the necessities you now are under, all the indignation of Heaven that is upon you, and appears in the defeating of all your counsels, flow from this, that you have not feared nor served God, but have given yourself up to so many sinful pleasures.' The King threw the letter into the fire but apparently bore Burnet no ill will as a result of it.

Towards the end of Charles's reign Burnet was regarded by James with increasing suspicion. His close friendship with Lord William Russell, who was implicated in the Rye House Plot of 1683, and his performance of the last rites for Russell on the scaffold did nothing to dissipate this distrust. On 5 November 1684, he preached a sermon against popery, as a result of which he was deprived of the chaplaincy of the Rolls. When James succeeded to the throne Burnet went abroad, settling first in France but eventually moving to Holland, joining the court of William of Orange and Mary. He was instrumental in persuading Mary that, if they should jointly succeed to the English throne, she should surrender total political power to her husband. Burnet became one of William's most valued advisers, being employed, for example, to draw up the instructions for Dykeveld, William's agent in England. James, infuriated by Burnet's influence at The Hague, initiated his prosecution for treason, but the prosecution was overtaken by events.

On 5 November 1685, Burnet landed with William at Torbay. He had helped to draw up the text of William's declaration on arriving in England and influenced William in allowing James to leave the country peaceably. On 23 December he preached in London on the text, 'It is the Lord's doing and it is marvellous in our eyes.' He was soon appointed to the bishopric of Salisbury. In the House of Lords he consistently supported toleration and he exercised considerable influence over Queen Mary, who had control over church matters. After her death in 1694 his influence at court probably declined, but he was made a member of a commission appointed for dealing with all questions of preferment and he retained his place when a similar commission was named in 1700.

In 1698 Burnet published his *Exposition of the Thirty-nine Articles of the Church of England*, a statement of latitudinarian views that was generally ap-plauded but that caused a storm between the High Church lower house of convocation, who disapproved of it, and the upper house, who refused to ratify the proposed censure of Burnet. In addition to his involvement in affairs of state, Burnet discharged his pastoral duties conscientiously. He tried to raise the standard of clergy in his diocese by careful examination of candidates, waged war against pluralities, and established a divinity school at Salisbury.

In 1696 and 1697 Burnet had proposed to the King that he should transfer the proceeds of the first-fruits and tenths, annexed to the crown at the Reformation, to a fund for clergymen in poor livings. The plan was not enacted by William but became law in 1704, becoming known as Queen Anne's Bounty. During Anne's reign Burnet was less at the centre of affairs than he had previously been, but he continued to be active both in his diocese and in the House of Lords. He spoke for Occasional Conformity in 1703 and against Henry Sacheverell (q.v.) in 1710. He died in London on 17 March 1715, of a cold that turned to pleurisy.

His most important work, the *History of My Own Time*, was published after his death. It is sometimes inaccurate and prejudiced but generally reflects his own liberality of mind and moderation and provides a very valuable source for the history of the period 1660–89.

Osmund Airy (ed.), *A History of My Own Times* (1897).

H. C. Foxcroft (ed.), *A Supplement to Burnet's History of His Own Times* (1902).

M. J. Routh (ed.), *A History of My Own Times* (1833, rev. ed.).

Thomas E. S. Clarke and H. C. Foxcroft, *A Life of Gilbert Burnet, Bishop of Salisbury*, with an introduction by Sir Charles H. Firth. (1907).

Portrait: oil, half-length, after J. Riley, 1690: N.P.G.

Burton, Henry (1578–1648), Puritan clergyman and polemical writer.

Burton was born at Birdsall parish in the East Riding of Yorkshire, and an anecdote told by Sir Robert Carey records that a Mrs. Bowes of Aske predicted, 'this young man will one day be the overthrow of the bishops'. Burton was educated at St. John's College, Cambridge, until 1602, afterwards becoming tutor to the sons of Sir Robert Carey, who helped him to obtain the position of clerk of the closet to Prince Henry (q.v.) in 1612. In this post Burton wrote a treatise on the Antichrist and the manuscript was kept in the Prince's library. On the Prince's death, Burton became clerk of the closet to Prince (later King) Charles. In the year of his appointment, on 14 July, he was incorporated as an M.A. at Oxford and again on 15 July 1617. Then, according to Burton's 'Narration' of his own life, in 1618, at the age of thirty, he decided to enter the ministry.

In 1623 some of Burton's effects were shipped to Spain in preparation for a trip he was to have made with Prince Charles, but he did not make the journey. That year he had completed but could not obtain a licence to publish a book attacking the *Converted Jew*, by the Jesuit John Fisher (q.v.), in which Burton set out to prove the pope to be the Antichrist. When Charles became king, Burton assumed he would become clerk to the royal closet, but Richard Neile, Bishop of Durham, who had been clerk to King James, continued in the post, not surprisingly since Burton had presented a letter to Charles on 23 April 1625 attacking the popery of both Neile and William Laud (q.v.). This indiscretion led Charles to tell Burton 'not to attend more in his office till he should send for him'.

Shortly afterwards, he became rector of St. Matthew's, Friday Street, and used his pulpit in the city to wage a forceful and aggressive campaign against episcopal practices. He was cited before the high commission in 1626 but the proceedings were stopped. In 1627, after voluble attacks on numerous bishops, he published *The Baiting of the Popes Bull &c.*, which had a frontispiece showing Charles assailing the pope's triple crown. Burton was summoned before the Privy Council, but the charge did not stand, despite Archbishop Laud's anger. Burton continued writing and publishing feverish attacks on popery and High Churchmen and preaching radical and inflammatory sermons, which were no doubt highly effective but could hardly be called dignified or convincingly logical. The titles of tracts he wrote at various periods in his life provide examples of his style: *Babel no Bethel, Censure of Simonie, England's Bondage and Hope of Deliverance, Truth Shut Out of Doores, The Grand Imposter Unmasked, or a detection of the notorious hypocrisie and desperate impiety of the late Archbishop (so styled) of Canterbury, cunningly couched in that written copy which he read on the scaffold*. Burton's public oratory ensured the devotion of his congregation, for they were loyal to him throughout his coming ordeals. Among other epithets he called bishops 'caterpillars', playing on 'pillars of the Church', and 'antichristian mushrumps'.

Because of his writings and two special sermons which virtually accused bishops of a popish plot in 1636, he was summoned before an ecclesiastical commissioner to answer on oath a charge of sedition; he refused the oath and appealed to the King. He was then charged before a high commission but did not appear and was suspended; an order for his apprehension was declared. He locked himself in his study, published his sermons, and took up an attitude of general defiance, until finally in February his house was ransacked and he was taken into custody. William Prynne and John Bastwick (qq.v.) joined him in prison, and all three were indicted by the Star Chamber, an offshoot of the King's Council held in Westminster Palace. On 14 June sentence was passed while the defendants cried for justice, Burton declaring 'a minister hath a larger liberty than always to go in a mild strain'. Burton's sentence was harsh: he was to be deprived of his position as rector, to be degraded from the ministry and from his degrees, to be fined £5,000, to be set in the Westminster pillory and to have his ears chopped off, to be imprisoned perpetually in Lancaster Castle with no access to his wife or friends and no use of pen, ink, and paper. Archbishop Laud was satisfied enough to give his 'hearty thanks' to the court.

Burton's parishioners petitioned the King for a pardon; the two who presented the petition were immediately imprisoned. While punishment was being carried out, Burton's ears were sliced off so close to his head that his temporal artery was cut. He later wrote, 'All the while I stood in the pillory, I thought myself to be in heaven and in a state of glory and triumph.' After he was healed, 100,000 sympathizers lined the route as he was taken northwards to prison and 500 friends travelled along as far as St. Albans. Archbishop Laud was infuriated with this public demonstration of support for Burton.

Burton was removed to Castle Cornet in Guernsey in the same year (1636) and later freed by the Long Parliament in November 1640; his sentences were reversed in 1641. He became minister to an Independent, or politically radical, Puritan congregation at St. Matthew's in 1642, and was Tuesday lecturer at St. Mary's Aldermanbury until 1645. Burton continued in his strong beliefs and with his polemical writing until his death in early 1648, probably as a result of the gallstones that he had developed in prison.

B. Brook, *The Lives of the Puritans, to 1662* (3 vols.; 1813).

J. B. Marsden, *Later Puritans, 1642–62* (1852).

Burton, Robert (1577–1640), scholar and author.

Born at Lindley, Leicestershire, probably on 8 February 1577, Burton was educated at schools in Nuneaton and Sutton Coldfield and at Brasenose College, Oxford. In 1599 he was elected a fellow of Christ Church. He took a bachelor of divinity degree some years later and was made the vicar of St. Thomas's, Oxford, and also held a living at Segrave, Leicestershire, but he spent his entire life as a don at Christ Church. He accumulated a sizeable library, which he left to the Bodleian. In *Athenae Oxonienses*, Anthony à Wood describes Burton as 'a general real scholar, a thro' paced philologist'. Apart from *Philosophaster*, a satirical comedy that was performed at Christ Church in 1618, Burton's work as an author was devoted to the writing and extensive revision of the one compendium by which he is known.

The Anatomy of Melancholy (1621; revised and expanded 1624, 1628, 1632, and 1638) is ostensibly a medical treatise. In fact, because of the methods by which Burton develops his exposition of the subject, especially the extreme use of quotation and paraphrase, the book is a vast repository of miscellaneous knowledge and abstruse lore, and indeed it was for this reason that the work had such a great and long-lasting appeal to the writers and poets who borrowed from it. Burton divides his exposition into three parts: the first is concerned with the definition and diagnosis of melancholy, its causes and symptoms; the second, with its cure; and the third, with the melancholy of love and the melancholy of religion. As Burton develops the subject, however, an enormously wide range of topics and a wealth of historical, philosophical, and literary learning are introduced. Authorities and examples, drawn from the Western classics, the Bible and the Church Fathers, from medieval and Elizabethan sources, are quoted copiously, and catalogues and lists abound. The prose style is nevertheless a colloquial one and gives a curious impression of spontaneity.

Although it was most popular in the 17th century, the *Anatomy of Melancholy* was admired or used as a source by writers of many periods, among them Milton, Dr. Johnson, Sterne, Byron, and Lamb.

Little is recorded of Burton's life. Bishop Kennet said that Burton set out to suppress his own melancholy by writing the *Anatomy*, but only succeeded in strengthening his tendency towards despondency. He died at Christ Church on 25 January 1640, at or very near the time he had previously foretold by calculating from his nativity. Some acquaintances even went so far as to suggest that Burton hanged himself so that his prophecy might be fulfilled.

There are three authoritative editions of *Anatomy of Melancholy*: those by A. R. Shilleto (3 vols.; 1893); by Floyd Dell and Paul Jordan-Smith (2 vols.; 1927); and by Holbrook Jackson (3 vols.; 1932).

B. Evans, *The Psychiatry of Robert Burton* (New York, 1944).
M. Mulhauser, *Burton's Anatomy of Melancholy* (1959).

Butler, James (1610–88), 1st Duke of Ormonde; Anglo-Irish aristocrat, general, and administrator.

Born on 19 October 1610, the eldest son of Thomas Butler, Viscount Thurles, and grandson of the 11th Earl of Ormonde, in 1619 Butler became a royal ward on his father's death. In 1629 he married his cousin, also a ward of the crown, Elizabeth Preston, heiress of the Earl of Desmond. He succeeded to the earldom of Ormonde and Ossory in 1631.

The heir to a considerable estate and influence among the Anglo-Irish aristocracy, Butler was tutored as a Protestant under the protection of the English court. He returned to Ireland in 1633 as a loyal supporter of Charles I and used his authority, which was personal as well as titular, to endorse Wentworth's government in Ireland. His own position was a military one; in 1638, having commanded troops of cavalry, he was made lieutenant general of horse, and later the commander-in-chief of all the forces in Ireland, when Wentworth was recalled to England.

In October 1641 the Gaelic Irish (or 'Old Irish') rose against the Protestant colonists in Ulster, and they were joined in rebellion by many of the English of the Pale on the basis of a common Catholicism under threat from the increasingly aggressive Protestantism at Westminster. Ormonde was at once appointed lieutenant general of the army by the King, holding authority under the lord lieutenant. The rivalries within the government of Ireland limited his freedom of action, but nevertheless in January 1642 he defeated a force of 3,000 rebels at Killsalghen and on 15 March won the bloodily contested Battle of Kilrush. He was elevated to the rank of marquis, and in September his situation was eased by a restatement of his appointment, which was to be under the crown and therefore independent of the lord lieutenant. It is not to be assumed, however, that the forces serving under his command were the only ones engaged, for in April 1642 the first contingent of Scottish soldiers landed in Ulster by arrangements made between the English and Scottish Parliaments. Eventually they numbered over 10,000, under the Scottish general Robert Monroe, and co-operated with forces raised by the colonists themselves.

Meanwhile, the rebels had developed a political framework, holding an assembly at Kilkenny and professing loyalty to the person of the monarch while rejecting Westminster-inspired attempts to clamp a Protestant government on them. The attitude of Charles I to this was influenced by the course of the Civil War in England, and Ormonde was empowered to explore the possibilities of a settlement over the heads of the governmental officials. A cessation of hostilities was finally signed on 15 September 1643, at the end of intermittent negotiations that had started in January. During this period fighting had continued and on 18 March Ormonde had won a notable victory over the rebel general Thomas Preston near Ross. With the cessation, there was a return of some 5,000 government troops to assist the Royalist cause in Cheshire, but the erstwhile rebels were unwilling to raise forces from among themselves to serve in England, despite pressure from Ormonde. However, his achievement had been considerable and he was rewarded with the lord lieutenancy of Ireland, a post that he held from 1644 to 1647.

To this Parliament retaliated by nominating Monroe as the commander of all troops, Scottish or English, in Ulster (April 1644) so that fighting was resumed there despite the cessation. The council of Kilkenny offered Ormonde the command of all its forces and urged him to declare the Scots and their Ulster supporters rebels, a course of action which Ormonde declined to take as it offered no prospect of extending the peace in Ireland to a permanent treaty: the Catholic rebels were technically still in revolt, and Monroe was commissioned by an English Parliament in rebellion against the sovereign whose authority Ormonde represented. It was a complicated situation, and Ormonde requested in vain to be relieved of his office and its problems, to which he could see no solution. Forced to persevere by the King's refusal to supersede him, he eventually produced an agreement (28 March 1646) in which the penal laws against Catholics were not repealed, but by exemptions and appointments to positions of trust were to be largely nullified.

Concessions procured from Charles I scarcely mattered at that stage of the English Civil War. The campaign against Monroe was of greater significance for Ireland, and it was vigorously prosecuted under the leadership of Preston and Owen Roe O'Neill; the latter beat Monroe at Benburb (5 June 1646). Ormonde had no choice but to seek help increasingly from the English Parliament, to whose commissioners he formally surrendered his office on 28 July 1647, preferring, as he himself said, 'English rebels to Irish ones'. Having crossed to England to account for his tenure to the captive King, in February 1648 Ormonde retired to the safety of the Continent and the exiled Queen's court.

The Kilkenny assembly were soon paying suit to the exiles in the hope of securing money and arms, and in September Ormonde landed at Cork as the official representative of the Queen and the Prince of Wales, being further confirmed in that capacity by a message from the King. The new Parliamentary commander in Dublin, Colonel Michael Jones, had established a firm hold over Leinster by a considerable victory over the rebels under Preston at Dungan's Hill (8 August 1647), and with the execution of Charles I in January 1649 there was no longer any doubt that the Catholic cause and the royalist cause were one. Ormonde proclaimed Charles II as king and began organizing an Irish army in his name.

In June 1649 he advanced against Dublin with a force of 11,000, which included Preston and the ex-Parliamentarian the Earl of Inchiquin (see O'Brien, Murrough). Only O'Neill and his Ulster army were missing. On 2 August he was beaten by Jones outside Dublin in the Battle of Rathmines, which proved to be the decisive event in the English reconquest of Ireland, for it preserved the base to which Cromwell came with 12,000 men on 15 August. Even with the tardy support of O'Neill, Ormonde could not prevail against these reinforcements. He was not yet permitted to withdraw from Ireland as he wished, for Charles II had come to an agreement with the Scots and commanded him to remain in the hope that the new Scottish alliance might alter the state of affairs in England and consequently Ireland. However, the price for the support of the Presbyterian Scots was the repudiation of that of the Catholic Irish, and at the end of 1650 the King advised Ormonde to leave Ireland.

In exile once more, Ormonde became a member of Charles II's Privy Council, established when the King returned to the Continent after the Battle of Worcester (1651). He was employed in both diplomatic and military capacities and paid a brief visit to England in disguise during the early months of 1658 to investigate the possibilities of a rising. He was closely involved in the negotiations which preceded the Restoration, following which he was showered with court and civil honours, including a dukedom, and some financial recompense for his considerable personal losses in the King's service. He recovered his Irish estates and his official position as lord lieutenant of that country, where his immediate task was the amelioration of the ill feeling among both Catholics and Presbyterians occasioned by the terms of the Restoration settlement. In this he was not altogether unsuccessful, and it is certainly true that his government of Ireland in both political and economic affairs was marked by a sincere concern for the Irish, in the broadest definition of that people, within the limits of a policy laid down in England.

Inevitably, his success attracted the enmity of others less successful, and in 1669 he was removed from office as a result of intrigue against him among the King's councillors in England. He bore the seven years of implied disgrace with

dignity and without reproach, as one against whom no serious criticism could be justifiably made. His return to Ireland in 1677 was generally well received both there and in England, and this second period of government in time of peace was as distinguished by its sincerity as the first. His last act was the proclamation of James II in Dublin, after which he withdrew to England to honoured retirement, dying on 21 July, before the revolution of 1688 occurred.

Thomas Carte, *The Life of James, Duke of Ormonde* (1851).

G. A. Hayes-McCoy, *Irish Battles* (1968).

Portrait: oil, three-quarter length, after Lely, *c.* 1665: N.P.G.; engraving, three-quarter length, by unknown artist, after a portrait by William Wissing in the collection of the Marquess of Ormonde, *c.* 1675.

Butler, James (1665–1745), 2nd Duke of Ormonde; Anglo-Irish aristocrat, politician, and general.

He was born on 29 April 1665, in Dublin Castle, the eldest surviving son of the Earl of Ossory, who was son and heir of James Butler (q.v.), 1st Duke of Ormonde.

The education of the young James Butler was largely directed by the old duke, his grandfather, who decided that his grandson should be educated in France. Accordingly, Butler was sent across the Channel with a tutor in 1675; however, this arrangement did not work out to the satisfaction of the duke, and Butler was recalled and sent to Christ Church, Oxford, where he remained until his father died in 1680.

Now Earl of Ossory, he was sent to the wars to gain military experience in the following years; he returned to England before 1685, when he fought in the royal army against Monmouth. In July 1688 his grandfather died and he succeeded to the vast estates of the Ormonde dukedom. This occurred at a critical time in James II's reign. The seven bishops had been acquitted just three weeks earlier, and the Church of England felt very much under attack from its Catholic sovereign. Ormonde, a High Churchman and a High Tory, was immediately elected to the chancellorship of Oxford University, which had been vacated by his grandfather's death, thus preventing the selection of the King's candidate, Lord Chancellor Jeffreys. James attempted to woo his powerful young subject, but Ormonde joined William of Orange.

Once William had secured the crown, rewards were distributed among his supporters. Ormonde, a generous and popular noble with great influence in Ireland, received the Garter. In the Irish campaign of 1690 he took an active part, commanding William's life guard and fighting at the Battle of the Boyne. He fought in William's wars on the Continent and was present at his royal master's deathbed in 1702. That year he was appointed commander of the land forces which accompanied Sir George Rooke to Cadiz. They failed in their object of taking this ancient city, but fortune brought them a Spanish treasure fleet and they were received as heroes in England.

The following year Ormonde was appointed lord lieutenant of Ireland, a position he held from 1703 to 1707 and from 1710 to 1713. His tenure of that difficult post was less than distinguished, for he proved unable to control his subordinates or to resolve religious conflicts. His one notable achievement was the appointment of Swift as Dean of St. Patrick's. In his last years of office Ormonde was absent from Ireland, for in 1712 he was given Marlborough's post of captain general and commander of the Anglo-Dutch army in the Low Countries. He was prepared to prosecute the war against France with vigour, but the government was determined to secure peace, even though it meant abandoning Britain's allies. Accordingly in secret orders, it forbade him to engage in any major battle without the consent of the ministry. Under these well-nigh impossible conditions, Ormonde struggled through the last year of the war and emerged, remarkably enough, with his honour unscathed.

Although he did not intrigue with the Old Pretender, like Bolingbroke, Ormonde was suspected of Jacobite sympathies and hated by the extreme Whigs for the part he had played in the Tory peace policy. When George I ascended the throne in 1714, and the Whigs returned to power, Ormonde was dismissed from the captain generalship. Defiantly, he associated in public with known Jacobites. With some hesitation the Whigs then impeached him, and he fled to France, where he joined the Pretender's court. Parliament proceeded to attaint him.

In the rebellion of 1715 Ormonde led an abortive rising in southern England, but quickly returned to the Continent. This was the last time he went to Britain, for he retired to Spain and later Avignon, where he died on 16 November 1745.

W. K. Dickson (ed.), *The Jacobite Attempt of 1719: Letters of James Butler, Second Duke of Ormonde . . .* (Scottish Historical Society, 19; 1895).

Portrait: oil, half-length, attributed to Dahl, 1714: N.P.G.

Butler, Samuel (1612–80), satirist.

He was baptized on 8 February 1612, at Strensham, Worcestershire, son of Samuel Butler, a prosperous tenant farmer.

Information about Butler's early life is sparse, but he probably attended the King's School, Worcester, and in about 1627 went up to Cambridge. Shortly afterwards, he became a £20-a-year attendant to the Countess of Kent at Wrest, Bedfordshire. The countess's household also included the antiquary John Selden (q.v.), who filled out Butler's education, and the still unknown Samuel Cooper (q.v.), who taught Butler to paint (he is reputed to have done a portrait of Cromwell from life).

For the next thirty years Butler was employed as secretary to a succession of distinguished country gentlemen, experiences which provided the material for his masterpiece, *Hudibras*. The chief inspiration for the poem's central character was probably Sir Samuel Luke, of Cople Hoo, Bedfordshire, a Parliamentary general and unbending Puritan. However, Butler's first publication was an anonymous Royalist pamphlet, *Mola Asinaria* (1659), which after Charles II's restoration brought him reward in the shape of the stewardship of Ludlow Castle. Within a year Butler had taken a wealthy wife (Miss Herbert or Mrs Morgan, a widow – the identity is uncertain) and resigned his post to live off her money. This was rash; a fall in share prices brought ruin to Butler, who was apparently obliged to become secretary to the Duke of Buckingham.

In 1663 Butler finally published his long-contemplated satire *Hudibras*, which became an immediate and overwhelming success. Charles II was so impressed by it that it was said:

He never ate nor drank nor slept
But *Hudibras* still near him kept.

The poem is a vigorous but basically good-hearted attack on the quirks of Presbyterians, Quakers, and the lower orders, and must have provided much merriment amongst country squires. Viewed objectively, *Hudibras*'s rather obscure topical allusions and galloping verse might now seem monotonous and clumsy, but in fact the work still succeeds, chiefly because Butler is so obviously enjoying the opportunity to stretch his imagination and gift for buffoonery. However, despite the poet's claims to spontaneity, that his verse is but 'a dash thro' thick and thin', it is clear from Butler's notebooks that he worked hard for his effects.

There is a tradition that, despite its enthusiasm for *Hudibras*, English society and in particular the King so neglected Butler himself that he sank into abject poverty. However, Aubrey declares that reports of Butler's poverty are exaggerated, and there is certainly evidence that not only was he drawing a £100 pension but was also employed by Buckingham until at least 1674, accompanying the duke to Europe and helping him to write *The Rehearsal*.

In later life Butler wrote many more satires, sniping at such targets as marriage, the Royal Society, and the mediocrity of fashionable poets, in a manner that combined wit and good sense. These works were not published until 1759. Butler's health eventually declined, and severe gout confined him for many months to his chambers in Covent Garden. He died there of consumption on 25 September 1680, and although his close friend Longueville tried to have him buried in Westminster Abbey, Butler was eventually laid to rest at St. Paul's, Covent Garden.

The evidence as to Butler's character is equally contradictory. Some sources depict him as an obtuse and endlessly critical man, with but a handful of friends, whom he treated abominably. But Aubrey described him as 'a good fellow', and Anthony à Wood said he was 'a boon and witty companion'.

A. R. Waller and Réné Lamar (eds.), *The Complete Works of Samuel Butler* (3 vols.; 1905–28).
John Wilders (ed.), *Hudibras* (1967).
Ian Jack, *Augustan Satire* (1952).

Portraits: oil, three-quarter length, by G. Soest: N.P.G. gouache and pastel on panel, half-length, by E. Lutterel: N.P.G.

Byng, George (1663–1733), admiral, see *Lives of the Georgian Age*.

Byrd, William (?1543–1623), organist and composer, see *Lives of the Tudor Age*.

Byrd, William (1674–1744), colonial planter, public official, and writer.

William Byrd II was born on 28 March 1674, the son of William Byrd, a rich Virginia planter and merchant. His father sent him to England to be educated, and he spent some time in Holland observing mercantile methods and worked in a London tobacco firm before studying law at the Middle Temple. Byrd was admitted to the bar in 1695. In 1696 he was elected a corresponding member of the Royal Society.

Byrd returned to Virginia in 1696 and was elected to a family seat in the House of Burgesses. He went back to England the following year, where he remained until 1704, acting as the colonial agent for Virginia. His father died in that year and Byrd went home as master of the family estate. His wealth, education, and background soon enabled him to assume a position of prominence in the colony, which he retained throughout his life. He became the colony's receiver general and colonel of militia, posts which his father had held before him.

In 1709 he was named a member of the council of state. He was soon involved as spokesman of the council in a struggle against the governor, Alexander Spotswood, who was attempting to curb the planters' monopoly over vast tracts of Virginia land and to withdraw judicial powers from the council. Byrd went to London in 1715 to defend his

Indian trade interests, which had been attacked by Spotswood. He again became colonial agent (until 1726), being successful in his immediate aim of protecting his interests but failing to secure the removal of Spotswood as governor; indeed, his attempts almost led to his own dismissal from the council. However, in 1720, Byrd and Spotswood reached a compromise favourable to the planters' interests.

From 1721 to 1727 Byrd was again in London, where he remarried, his first wife having died in 1716. He returned to Virginia in 1727 and spent much of his time building up his estate, increasing it from 26,000 to 180,000 acres. He had built himself a magnificent mansion on his estate at Westover, and there he collected a library which was the largest in the colony, amounting to 4,000 volumes at his death. He corresponded with literary and scientific friends in England, and in many ways was the typical colonial planter – successful, energetic, elegant, and versatile.

In 1728 Byrd was a boundary commissioner appointed to survey the Virginia–North Carolina border. He recorded some of his observations and experiences in a diary, which was published in 1841 as *History of the Dividing Line*. Similar diaries of his for 1709–12, 1717–21, and 1739–41 have also been published, providing valuable insights into American colonial society of the period. In 1737 Byrd had the future city of Richmond laid out on his land, and from 1743 until his death he acted as president of the Council of State. He died at Westover on 26 August 1744.

L. B. Wright and M. Tinling (eds.), *The Secret Diary of William Byrd of Westover, 1709–1712* (Richmond, Va., 1941).

L. B. Wright and M. Tinling (eds.), *William Byrd of Virginia: the London Diary, 1717–1721, and Other Writings of William Byrd* (1958).

M. H. Woodfin and M. Tinling (eds.), *Another Secret Diary of William Byrd of Westover, 1739–1741, with Letters and Literary Exercises, 1696–1726* (Richmond, Va., 1942).

C

Calvert, Cecilius or Cecil (1605–75), 2nd Baron Baltimore; colonizer of Maryland.

Cecilius Calvert was baptized on 2 March 1605 in Bexley, Kent, the son of George Calvert (q.v.), 1st Baron Baltimore, and educated at Trinity College, Oxford. Little is known of his youth, but the Roman Catholicism of his family must have had a significant effect on his development, and in 1628 he married Anne Arundell, the daughter of the Catholic peer Thomas, 1st Baron Arundell of Wardour.

Calvert was a practical, reserved Catholic, but this made him no less an object of suspicion in the eyes of his Protestant fellow countrymen. In 1632 his father died and Calvert inherited not only his barony but also the newly awarded patent for Maryland. Enemies prevented his emigration to the New World, but in November 1633 the new Lord Baltimore despatched a group of settlers under the governorship of his brother Leonard to colonize his territory. It was in this period that freedom of worship was established for all Trinitarian Christians in Maryland.

Baltimore soon found himself on the defensive once again. Rivals attempted to seize parts of Maryland and Puritans regarded its Catholic overlordship with hostility. After the Civil War Parliament forced him to compound heavily for his estates, although he had not borne arms for the King.

He died in 1675 and was buried on 7 December.

William Hand Browne, *George Calvert and Cecilius Calvert. Barons Baltimore* (New York, 1890).

Clayton C. Hall, *The Lords Baltimore and the Maryland Palatinate* (Baltimore, 1904, 2nd ed.).

Calvert, George (?1580–1632), 1st Baron Baltimore; M.P. and statesman.

Born at Kipling, Bolton, Yorkshire, Calvert matriculated from Trinity College, Oxford, on 12 July 1594, obtained a B.A. in 1597, and was created M.A. in 1605, during the King's visit to Oxford. He travelled for some time, and later became clerk and secretary to Sir Robert Cecil (see *Lives of the Tudor Age*). In 1606 Calvert became clerk of the crown in county Clare, Connaught, in Ireland. He performed various services and duties for the King, and was given a knighthood in 1617. In February 1619 he became secretary of state, having previously entered Parliament as Member for Bossiney (1609).

Calvert held the post of secretary of state until his resignation in 1625. The performance of his duties was difficult; he depended upon Buckingham (see Villiers, George, 1st Duke), the King's favourite, for influence, as he possessed little himself. This is attested to in a letter written by the French ambassador in 1621, describing Calvert as an honourable man of good intentions, respectful and concerned for the welfare of England, but entirely without consideration or influence. Parliament, however, did not trust the secretary, who had to act as intermediary between the King and the House of Commons during many disputes, particularly in the matter of foreign relations, especially those with Spain. Calvert's conduct of foreign affairs was widely thought to be too pro-Catholic, the more so because he himself was a convert to the Roman faith. It was said of him that 'his whole joy and comfort had been to make open profession of his religion.'

After his resignation, he sold his office to Sir Albert Morton for £6,000, and obtained the title of Baron of Baltimore in County Longford, Ireland. The large estates which had been granted to him there were confirmed by a new grant. When Charles I became King, Calvert objected to the oath he had to take to become a privy councillor and so was excluded. He returned to Ireland and took no more part in public life, except on one occasion in February 1627, when he consulted with the King on proposed peace terms for Spain.

For the remainder of his life he was engaged in founding and settling colonies in the New World, a work which a biographer called 'that ancient, primitive, and heroic work of planting the world'. In 1621 Calvert had sent Captain Edward Wynne to establish a settlement named Ferryland in Newfoundland. In 1623 Calvert obtained a charter for the colony to be called the province of Avalon. He travelled to Avalon in July 1627 and again in 1629, when he drove off French privateers. The climate in Newfoundland was hard, and dissension grew after he had brought priests with him, so he applied to the King for a grant of land in a more favourable area. He set sail for Jamestown, Virginia, but was not welcomed there because he would not take oaths of allegiance and supremacy.

Returning to England, he tried to obtain a patent for a new colony, but in 1631 opposition from members of the late Virginia Company forced him to try to obtain a grant for lands northeast of the Potomac River. The patent was further opposed and delayed, and he died on 15 April, before it was granted. He was buried at St. Dunstan-in-the-West, Fleet Street. The charter he had sought was sealed on 20 June 1632, and his son Cecilius founded the new colony, named Maryland in honour of Charles I's Queen.

William Hand Browne, *George Calvert and Cecilius Calvert. Barons Baltimore* (New York, 1890).
Clayton C. Hall, *The Lords Baltimore and the Maryland Palatinate* (Baltimore, 1904, 2nd ed.).

Campbell, Archibald (?1651–1703), 1st Duke of Argyll; one of the three men generally regarded as responsible for the Massacre of Glencoe (1692).

Archibald Campbell was the eldest son of Archibald Campbell (q.v.), 9th Earl of Argyll, by his first wife, Lady Mary Stuart, eldest daughter of James, Earl of Moray. Nothing is known of Campbell's childhood or early life – even the date of his birth is surmise – but it is known that by 1682 he was receiving an allowance out of the estates forfeited when his father was convicted of treason in 1681. In 1685 he was quick to dissociate himself from his father's invasion of Scotland, and even offered to serve against him.

He made every attempt to regain his titles and estates, and tried to win James II's favour by 'converting' to the Roman Catholic faith. All his efforts failed, however; he rapidly changed his allegiance and in 1688 became a supporter of William III. He joined William in Holland, at The Hague, and made the voyage to England with him. This policy soon paid off: in March 1689 he took his place in the Scottish Convention as the Earl of Argyll, with only one member protesting. He was appointed a commissioner deputed to offer the Scottish crown to William and Mary, and indeed administered to them their coronation oath. In May he became a privy councillor and in June all his father's forfeited estates were returned to him.

The restoration of his estates was not popular among the Highland clans, whose support for James II was very largely an expression of their hatred of the Campbells, and Campbell seized the opportunity to make an example of Alexander Macdonald or MacIan, leader of the Glencoe branch of the Macdonald clan. MacIan was the only highland chieftain who had failed to take the oath of submission, and Campbell was largely responsible, along with Sir John Dalrymple and John Campbell (q.v.), 1st Earl of Breadalbane, for the severity with which the Macdonalds were treated. It was his own regiment which took part in the 'massacre' at Glencoe (see Macdonald, Alexander).

Campbell moved from strength to strength: in 1694 he was made an extraordinary lord of session and in 1701 he was created Duke of Argyll. There is no doubt that Campbell's most compelling and perhaps only motivation in all his actions was the restoration of his former titles and possessions and his own personal advancement. He died on 20 September 1703.

Although the date of his marriage is not known, his wife was Elizabeth Talmash, by whom he had one daughter and two sons, John Campbell, 2nd Duke of Argyll (see *Lives of the Georgian Age*), and Archibald Campbell, 3rd Duke of Argyll.

Campbell, Archibald (1607–61), 8th Earl and Marquis of Argyll; Scottish Covenanter executed for high treason; called 'Gillespie Grumach' or 'the glaed-eyed marquis' by reason of his pronounced squint.

Archibald Campbell was probably born in 1607 (not 1598, as was formerly thought), the son of Archibald, 7th Earl of Argyll, and his wife, Lady Anne Douglas. In 1619, as Lord of Lorne, he took over possession of his father's estates, the latter having renounced Protestantism and converted to the Roman faith. In 1626 he was made a privy councillor, and in 1634 an extraordinary lord of session. In 1638 he was summoned to London to advise Charles I concerning the renewal of the Covenant in Scotland, a duty which he apparently carried out with great impartiality and fairness of mind. For some time, in fact, Argyll behaved with great circumspection concerning the Covenanters and refused to commit himself to their cause. However, he finally refused to accept Charles's attempt to enforce the new liturgy in Scotland and found himself in disfavour with the King. By a secret commission, the Earl of Antrim was empowered by Charles to invade Kintyre, part of Argyll's territory. This act of the King came to Argyll's atten-

tion and, although the expedition was a failure, it served to increase Argyll's determination to join with the Covenanters in defence of Presbyterianism. At this time he succeeded to the earldom on the death of his father.

In 1638 the General Assembly of Scotland continued to sit after its dissolution by the King's commissioner and adopted a resolution carrying out the 'National Covenant' by abolishing the episcopacy in Scotland, a move with which Argyll concurred. In 1639 he wrote to Archbishop Laud defending the action of the Assembly. Argyll's power in the Assembly and his increasing opposition to the King brought him into conflict with Montrose (see Graham, James) and his associates, who evolved a plot to discredit Argyll. It misfired, however, and Montrose himself was imprisoned (1641). Charles was obliged to make concessions to the Covenanters and to agree to the transfer of the right to make judicial and political appointments from the King to Parliament. Argyll was created a marquis and granted a pension of £1,000 p.a. (1641).

During the next few years, Argyll was chiefly concerned with maintaining unity among the Presbyterians, and in 1643 helped arrange an alliance with the English Parliament. He was made a member of committees in both Scotland and England. His active participation in the English Civil War began in 1644, when he commanded part of the Scottish army advancing into England. However, he was obliged to return to Scotland before long in order to suppress Royalist uprisings. Scotland was invaded by Irish Royalist troops in the west, and Huntly led a rising in the north, putting Argyll's own territories at risk. He fought inconclusively with Montrose and retired to Inverary castle in December 1644. Montrose followed

him, mounted a surprise attack, and forced Argyll to retreat to his castle at Roseneath, Dumbartonshire. Argyll's lands were devastated by Montrose's troops. In 1645 Montrose again defeated Argyll at Inverlochy (February) and Kilsyth (August), but Argyll was present when Montrose was finally defeated at Philiphaugh (September).

Until now, Argyll had good reason to be satisfied with his policies. Charles I was in prison and Scotland had retained its national liberties and chosen religion. The situation seemed to be further secured by an alliance with the English Parliament. He was therefore strongly opposed to a secret treaty between the King and the Scottish Parliament ('the Engagement') in July, and was satisfied when the Duke of Hamilton and his Engagers were defeated by Cromwell at the battle – or rout – of Preston.

Argyll now joined the extreme Covenanters in establishing a new government in Edinburgh to welcome Cromwell. However, the new alliance of English and Scottish Parliaments was destroyed when news came of Charles I's execution. All Scotland was shocked, and repudiated the action of the English Parliament. The Covenanters, with Argyll's support, invited Prince Charles to Scotland in 1650, and Argyll himself set the crown of Scotland on Charles's head at Scone. Argyll opposed the expedition to England under Charles, but was unable to prevent it. It ended in Charles's defeat at Worcester on 3 September 1651. Scotland now came under strong attack by English forces and in 1652, after holding out at Inverary castle for almost a year, Argyll was forced to submit to the Commonwealth. In 1659 he sat in Parliament as the member for Aberdeenshire.

In 1660, on Charles's restoration as Charles II, Argyll rashly went to the

English court to welcome the King and tender his respects. Charles promptly had him arrested, and he was returned to Edinburgh to stand trial for high treason. He was aquitted of any complicity in the death of Charles I, and it seemed almost certain that he would go free. However, the last minute production of letters by Monck (commander-in-chief in Scotland 1654–60), which demonstrated Argyll's collaboration with Cromwell's government, condemned him. He was sentenced to death and was beheaded at Edinburgh on 27 May 1661.

D. Stevenson, *The Scottish Revolution 1637–1644* (1973).

J. Willcock, *The Great Marquess: Life and Times of Archibald, 8th Earl of Argyll* (1903).

Portrait: engraving, half-length, by unknown artist, after lost original by unknown artist, *c.* 1632.

Campbell, Archibald (1629–85), 9th Earl of Argyll; Scottish nobleman who mounted a rebellion against James II in 1685 in favour of Charles II's illegitimate son, the Duke of Monmouth.

Archibald Campbell was born at Dalkeith on 26 February 1629, the eldest son of Archibald Campbell, the 8th Earl (q.v.), and his wife, Lady Margaret Douglas. He bore the title Lord of Lorne until his father's execution in 1661, when he became the 9th Earl of Argyll. He was educated first at home by his father, and later at various schools and colleges before travelling in France and Italy. He remained abroad until 1650, and upon his return married Lady Mary Stuart, daughter of the Earl of Moray.

From the beginning, Lorne proved to be a far more ardent Royalist than his father. In 1650 he was made captain of Charles II's Scottish lifeguard, and fought for the Royalist cause at Dunbar. He tried to raise his own clan for Charles II, but failed, and in 1653 joined the Highland Royalists. In 1654, however, he quarrelled with their leaders and withdrew, and in the same year was specifically exempted from Cromwell's act of pardon. In 1655 he was directed by Charles II to make his peace with Cromwell, and duly surrendered. He was suspected of involvement with a Royalist plot in 1656 and was imprisoned at Edinburgh (1657–60). He received a warm welcome at Charles II's court on his release in 1660.

Strong efforts were made, particularly by John Middleton, to involve Lorne in his father's downfall in 1661, no doubt at least partly motivated by a desire on Middleton's part to possess the Argyll lands. Lorne was actually sentenced to death and imprisoned, but in 1663 the sentence was suspended and Lorne was restored to the earldom of Argyll.

Argyll's main efforts were now concentrated on restoring the depleted estates of his ancestors. He became involved in a great deal of litigation over debts, but was determined to restore his father's estates, even at the cost of his creditors. He took up residence at Inverary, exercising his hereditary duties. In 1667 he was made a commissioner for quieting the Highlands, and in 1670 raised a militia regiment. From 1671 onwards he was under constant pressure to deal severely with Covenanters, but himself urged gentler measures. Between 1674 and 1680 he was an extraordinary lord of session.

In 1680 James, Duke of York, later James II, was appointed high commissioner in Scotland. Argyll's staunch Protestantism, together with his territorial influence, which made him virtually king of a large part of Scotland, made him suspect to the Catholic James, although Argyll assured him that he would adhere to his interest. Acts of Parliament had been passed with the aim of securing both the observance of the laws against popery and the unalterable succession of the crown. The section referring to popery was omitted in deference to James, but Argyll insisted it should be reinstated, thus further discrediting himself in James's eyes.

In 1681 Argyll was accused on a number of trumped-up charges of treason. He was found guilty and his estates were confiscated. Charles II ordered that the death sentence should be passed but not carried out. However, Argyll, under restraint in jail, was given to understand that his execution was imminent. He was rescued in dramatic fashion by his stepdaughter, Sophia Lindsay, who visited him in the company of a kinsman with his head bound up (as if wounded). The kinsman and Argyll exchanged clothes and Argyll left the jail with Sophia. He took refuge first in Northumberland, then in London, and finally escaped to Holland. No real steps were taken to capture him. In fact, Charles II is thought to have been informed of his whereabouts in London and declined to apprehend him.

His subsequent movements were mysterious. There is evidence that he did not stay abroad for long but returned to London in 1682. Certainly, there is little doubt that he was implicated in the Rye House Plot (1683). A number of letters from Argyll were discovered, but all were in code and could not be deciphered. Later in 1683 he is thought to have been again in Scotland.

In 1685 Charles II died, and the Duke of York succeeded as James II. Argyll mounted an expedition against James in favour of the Duke of Monmouth (q.v.). He sailed from Holland at the beginning of May with only 300 men in three small ships. He landed first at Cariston, in Orkney, where he was soon discovered and rapidly set sail for his own lands. He was forced by contrary winds to go to the Sound of Mull. With a further 300 men collected at Tobermory, he crossed to Kintyre, the stronghold of the Covenanters. He issued his declaration on behalf of Monmouth at Campbeltown. His attempts to advance were ineffectual, his own clan failed to join him, and his troops dwindled away from a maximum of 2000 to under 500. He was captured on 18 June at Inchannan on the Clyde, and was taken first to Renfrew, then, on 20 June, to Edinburgh. On 29 June a letter arrived from James II with instructions for summary punishment. Argyll was, in fact, never brought to trial for his part in the rising. He was executed on 30 June 1685, on the sentence passed in 1681.

He left several children by his marriage to Lady Mary Stuart, including Archibald, 1st Duke of Argyll, two other sons, and three daughters.

J. Maidment (ed.), *The Argyle Papers* (1834).
J. Willcock, *A Scots Earl in Covenanting Times* (1907).

Portrait: oil, three-quarter length, by unknown artist: N.P.G.

Campbell, John (1680–1743), 2nd Duke of Argyll, soldier and politician, see *Lives of the Georgian Age.*

Campbell, John (1635–1716), 1st Earl of Breadalbane; Scottish nobleman who helped William of Orange to gain the submission of the Highlanders and was involved in the Glencoe Massacre.

John Campbell was the only son of Sir John Campbell, tenth laird of Glenorchy. He took part in the rising in support of Charles II that was suppressed by Monck in 1654, and sat as a member for Argyllshire in the first parliament after the Restoration. He soon acquired an intellectual reputation as 'the best headpiece in Scotland'. He was created Earl of Breadalbane in 1681, after failing in a claim on the earldom of Caithness.

After the accession of James II in 1685, he was made a privy councillor, and after his kinsman, the Earl of Argyll, was the most powerful Highland noble. He was notorious for his personal greed, but was regarded with less hostility by the other Highlanders than was Argyll (see Campbell, Archibald, 1st Duke of Argyll). Nominally committed to James in 1689, he soon expressed through Sir John Dalrymple his anxiety to serve William. As a result of these overtures, Breadalbane took advantage of the Act of Indemnity and in September, 1689 took the oath to William and Mary.

William apparently valued Breadalbane's support highly. In 1690 the King's agent, Lord Melville, ordered Breadalbane to negotiate with the High-landers and he was empowered to use a large sum of money (the sum of £20,000 has been suggested) to buy their allegiance. Breadalbane met with many of the chiefs in June 1691 and persuaded them to suspend hostilities against the government for a few months. Although they seem to have been suspicious of his motives and intentions, Breadalbane was largely successful in this, perhaps his only important contribution to Scottish history. The government issued a proclamation offering an indemnity to those who had been at arms, but requiring them to take the oath of allegiance before 1 January 1692. All the Highland leaders submitted, except Alexander Macdonald (q.v.), who refused to do so at first but made strenuous efforts to take the oath when he realized that the other leaders had submitted. Macdonald took the oath five days after the required date.

The Campbells and the Macdonalds had long regarded each other with animosity, since the Macdonalds gained their livelihood chiefly by preying on Lowlanders and Campbells. Breadalbane now had the opportunity for vengeance, although it was probably Dalrymple who devised the scheme to 'extirpate that sect of thieves'. Breadalbane was so cautious in his involvement, however, that no tangible evidence could be found against him by the inquiry of 1695 into the Glencoe Massacre.

Despite his support for William, Breadalbane kept in touch with the court at St. Germain, and engaged to raise 1,200 men for the Pretender if there was a rising in his favour. Yet in 1714, when this occurred, Breadalbane retired to one of his fortresses to avoid commitment. His memory was refreshed by a sum of money, and he sent 300 men to the Pretender's cause, although when his application for more funds was denied these men were soon withdrawn. The feebleness of Breadalbane's support enabled the government to overlook his conduct after the rising had failed. He died in 1716, at the age of eighty-one, and was succeeded by his second son, John. Breadalbane was described by a contemporary as knowing 'neither honour nor religion but where they are mixed with interest.'

William A. Gillies, *In Famed Breadalbane* (1938). John Prebble, *Glencoe* (1966).

Campbell, Robert (1671–1734), see Macgregor, Robert.

Carew, Thomas (?1595–1639), poet.

Carew was born probably at West Wickham in Kent, a younger son of Sir Matthew Carew, a well-known Elizabethan lawyer, and was educated at Merton College, Oxford, where he took a B.A. in 1611.

After leaving Oxford, he entered the Middle Temple, apparently with the intention of following in his father's footsteps as a lawyer. This plan was evidently abandoned, however, for in 1613 he took up an appointment as secretary to Sir Dudley Carleton, whom he accompanied to Italy when his master was ambassador to Venice and Turin, and whom he followed to The Hague when Carleton became ambassador there. A few months later, in the summer of 1616, Carew was summarily dismissed by Carleton on the grounds of making slanderous remarks about him and his wife. He returned to England but found it difficult to get other employment, much to the irritation of his father, who describes him at this time as 'wandering idly about without employment.'

At last, in May 1619, he was offered a secretaryship by Edward Herbert (q.v.), Baron Herbert of Cherbury, who was a friend of long standing and who had just been appointed ambassador to France. Here he remained for five years, living in some splendour, until Herbert was dismissed by James I.

Carew returned to London and to court, which he had already attended in 1616–17. With the accession of Charles I in 1625, he rose in favour and received several court appointments. By the early 1630s he was firmly established as one of the leaders of the group of somewhat disreputable poets and wits at court which included Sir John Suckling and Sir William Davenant (qq.v.). With Suckling, he carried on a frank and bawdy correspondence, which includes poems on their respective sexual exploits. He also wrote a masque, Coelum Britannicum, which was performed in 1634 by no less a person than the King himself, with members of the court.

Carew's best poetry has fastidious elegance of form derived, quite con-sciously, from Ben Jonson, like whom he was a painstaking craftsman. The other major influence on his work was John Donne; Carew's poetry lacks, however, the breathtaking flights of imagination and sense of passion characteristic of Donne, although there are plenty of lines echoic of Donne and plenty containing conceits typical of the period – of Donne himself, for example, Carew writes that his soul 'Committed holy rapes upon our will'.

The subject matter of most of Carew's poems is love or sex in one form or another – The Rapture (his longest poem), To my Inconstant Mistress, Disdain Returned, To a Lady that desired I would love her, etc. There are one or two fine elegies, notably that on Donne, and in the work of his forties, when his health had begun to weaken, a more sombre tone is discernible. Eventually he took to writing metrical versions of the psalms, apparently as an act of repentence for his libidinous youth. Clearly the prospect of death troubled him greatly, for he sent more than once for John Hales of Eton to administer the last rites. He finally died on 22 March 1639, aged forty-three. His poems, which had circulated in manuscript during his lifetime, were published within a few weeks of his death.

Hales made no secret of his low opinion of Carew, but the Earl of Clarendon describes him in his heyday at court as 'a person of pleasant and facetious wit'. If Carew is not the greatest of the Cavalier poets, he may perhaps be described as the most typical.

R. Dunlap (ed.), Poems of Thomas Carew with his Masque Coelum Britannicum (1949).
G. A. Parfitt, 'The Poetry of Carew', Renaissance and Modern Studies 12 (1968).
E. I. Selig, The Flourishing Wreath: a Study of Carew's Poetry (New Haven, Conn., 1958).

Portrait: by Van Dyck, at Windsor Castle.

Carr or Ker, Robert (?1585–1645), Earl of Somerset; court favourite who rose to a position of considerable power under James I.

Carr's birthdate is unknown, but it cannot have been long before 1586, the year in which his father, Thomas Ker of Ferniehurst, Roxburghshire, died.

Carr came of an established Scottish family. In 1603 he came to England in the suite of James I, and after being released from the King's service, spent some time abroad in France. Upon his return to England, he again came to the notice of James. An impressively handsome young man, his looks attracted him to James more than his intellectual capacity, which was meagre. In December 1607, Carr was knighted and became a gentleman of the bedchamber.

Over the next seven years, Carr gradually rose in the King's favour, and attained considerable power. He was an ambitious man and appears not to have had an over-scrupulous moral character. In order to hold his position, he did not even need to be very competent; the

King seems to have been infatuated with him, and Sir Thomas Overbury (q.v.), his adviser at court, tried to ensure that he antagonized as few people as possible.

In 1608 James decided to bestow upon Carr the manor of Sherborne, which had been confiscated from the imprisoned Sir Walter Ralegh. After a legal battle, Carr entered into possession of the property in the following year. His influence over the King was gaining ground rapidly; in the political and financial crisis of 1610 he is credited with having persuaded James to dissolve Parliament, and in 1612, after Salisbury's death, he became the King's secretary.

In March 1611 Carr had been made Viscount Rochester; two years later, on 3 November 1613, James created him Earl of Somerset, and on 23 December of the same year he entered into the lucrative appointment of treasurer of Scotland. An affair that he had started with Frances Devereux, Countess of Essex, was now coming to a head. Lady Essex belonged to the powerful Howard family. In this crucial year of 1613 she divorced her husband Robert (see Devereux, Robert, 3rd Earl of Essex) and married Carr.

The Howards already had the King's confidence. One of the family, Henry Howard, Earl of Northampton (1540–1614), was lord privy seal and a treasury commissioner. The marriage, favoured by the Howards, was thus also acceptable to the King, and the Howard family was attempting to gain influence with James by control of his favourite.

Throughout this period Carr had been under the counselling eye of the ambitious Overbury, who now became troublesome. Carr was persuaded by the Howards to get the King to offer Overbury a foreign commission; Overbury's refusal resulted in his imprisonment in the Tower, where he was said to have been poisoned by agents of Lady Essex.

In 1614 Carr was made lord chamberlain. The Howards, who favoured James's pro-Hispanic policy, continued to exercise their influence through Carr during this period, and it was not until 1615 that the scandal surrounding Overbury's murder finally broke. In the resulting proceedings, Lady Essex's agents were hanged and she and Carr were put on trial for murder. Lady Essex herself confessed, but Carr continually protested his innocence. In the event he was found guilty, but the hold he had over James was sufficient to ensure that neither he nor his wife suffered the full sentence of the court. Nevertheless, Carr's power was broken, though it may be observed that his full part in the murder has never been established. It is probable that he was only an accessory. However that may be, he remained in confinement until he received a pardon from James in 1624. Carr now lapsed into obscurity, taking no further significant role in events. He died in July 1645.

M. A. De Ford, *The Overbury Affair* (Philadelphia, Pa., 1960).

William McElwee, *The Murder of Sir Thomas Overbury* (1952).

Beatrice White, *Cast of Ravens* (1965).

Portraits: oil on panel, quarter-length, after J. Hoskins, *c.* 1620–25: N.P.G.; miniature, in the manner of Hilliard, *c.* 1611: N.P.G.

Cary, Lucius (?1610–43), 2nd Viscount Falkland; politician and secretary of state to Charles I at the outbreak of the Civil War.

Born in Oxfordshire about 1610, the son of Sir Henry Cary, 1st Viscount Falkland, who became lord deputy of Ireland (1622–29), Cary accompanied his parents to Ireland in 1622 and was educated at Trinity College, Dublin.

In 1629 his grandfather died and he inherited the large Oxfordshire estates of Burford and Great Tew. Here he was the focus of a literary and philosophical circle that included Ben Jonson, Edmund Waller, and his immediate contemporary and subsequent political ally, Edward Hyde (qq.v.). He had a good intellect and Hyde later recalled him as the 'incomparable' Falkland. But this period of pleasure was soon disrupted, for after a quarrel with his father he went off for a time with the intention of fighting in the Netherlands. He soon returned, however, succeeding to the family title upon the death of his father in 1633.

Politically, Falkland's principles were less well defined than those of some of his contemporaries. He felt a sense of duty to the sovereign and fought under Essex (see Devereux, Robert) on the King's side in the war with the Scots (1639). But sitting for Newport, Isle of Wight, in the Short and Long Parliaments, in 1640, he inclined enthusiastically towards the Parliamentary opposition to Charles. While at Great Tew he had begun to develop a concept of rationalism in theology. He spoke now against clerical involvement in secular administration and made an attack upon William Laud (q.v.) for the latter's promotion of ceremonies and repressive measures against Puritanism. He denounced ship money and supported the Triennial Bill for prohibiting the dissolution of Parliament without its consent. He also supported Strafford's impeachment and voted for the attainder. His religious views led him to vote in favour of a moderate measure excluding bishops and clergy from non-ecclesiastical posts, but the measure failed early in May 1641. Confronted with the Root and Branch Bill, which called for the complete abolition of episcopacy, Falkland baulked, fearing the establishment of Presbyterianism, which in Scotland had proved so tyrannical.

59

Throughout the summer of 1641, Falkland's change of attitude progressed. Moved by an inclination towards compromise, he took up a standpoint alongside Hyde and voted with him against the Grand Remonstrance. Unprepared to see any irreparable alteration of the relationship between King and Parliament, he accepted under Hyde's persuasion the post of secretary of state in January 1642.

The onrush of events following Charles's attempted arrest of the five members took Falkland to York with the King, where, on 15 June, he was one of the peers who supported the protestation against making war. In September he opened peace negotiations with Parliament. Charles was, he said, prepared to consent to a complete reform of religion. But ensuing events – the failure of the negotiations through unwillingness to compromise on either side, the Battle of Edgehill, where he was present with the King, and the unmasking of Edmund Waller's plot, for which he handled the correspondence – ultimately broke Falkland's spirit. In August 1643 he was with the King at the abortive siege of Gloucester. After this he gave himself up to despair. 'Sitting among his friends,' wrote Hyde, 'often, after a deep silence and frequent sighs, [he] would with a shrill and sad accent ingeminate the word *Peace, peace.*' Victory by either side meant nothing to him any longer. Death was what he sought. On 20 September 1643, at the Battle of Newbury, he deliberately exposed himself to enemy fire and was immediately killed.

Falkland wrote a theological treatise, a *Discourse of Infallibility*, published in 1646. His other writings include a set of poems clearly showing the influence of Jonson.

J. A. R. Marriott, *Life and Times of Lucius Cary, Viscount Falkland* (1907).

Kurt Weber, *Lucius Cary, Second Viscount Falkland* (1940).

Portrait: by an unknown artist in the Bodleian Library, Oxford.

Castlemaine, Countess of (1640–1709), see Villiers, Barbara.

Catesby, Robert (1573–1605), co-conspirator in the Gunpowder Plot of 1605 with Guy Fawkes (q.v.) and Thomas Winter.

Robert Catesby was born in 1573, the only surviving son of Sir William Catesby of Lapworth, Warwickshire, a member of the Catholic gentry. His father suffered severely under the laws against Catholics and was imprisoned for several years as a recusant. Robert entered Gloucester Hall, Oxford (now Worcester College), in 1586, but left without a degree since the oath of supremacy represented a stumbling-block for Catholics. He married in 1592 and came into a considerable estate, which was supplemented in 1593 when his grandmother left him the estate of Chastleton, and in 1598 when his father died.

Catesby was a man of large means, but he was alienated by the relentless cruelty of the anti-Catholic laws. He ardently supported Robert Devereux, 2nd Earl of Essex, when his protest led him to the scaffold in 1601, and was wounded in a street scuffle. He was thrown into prison and pardoned only after a fine of 4,000 marks was exacted, which compelled him to sell the Chastleton estate. Catesby seems to have abandoned himself to thoughts of vengeance and habitually mixed with malcontents. He was committed to prison for a time at the end of Elizabeth's reign.

The forbearance shown to the Catholic gentry during the first few months of James I's reign was soon replaced by renewed enactments against them. The Catholics were even more embittered by this change of attitude and Catesby was willing to undertake any enterprise which he thought likely to lead to the advancement of his holy cause and the glory of God. He seems to have been a man of physical charm and attraction and was said to have exerted a magical influence on those who knew him.

Thomas Winter formulated the plot to blow up the House of Lords while the King was inside in 1604 and apparently communicated the plan first to Guy Fawkes and then to Catesby. The daring of Fawkes and the obstinacy of Catesby carried the plot almost to completion, but Fawkes was arrested on 4 November 1605, the day before it was to have been carried out. Catesby and some of his fellow conspirators fled to Holbeach House, Staffordshire, and prepared to defend themselves. On 8 November, gunpowder intended for the defence of the house mysteriously exploded and scorched Catesby. Soon afterwards a force arrived and demanded the surrender of the conspirators. They refused, and Catesby was fighting back-to-back with Thomas Percy when bullets from the same musket killed them both.

Oswald Tesimond, *The Gunpowder Plot* (1973).
Portrait: engraving, half-length, by unknown artist, after contemporary engraving by unknown artist: British Museum.

Catherine of Braganza (1638–1705), Queen Consort of Charles II.

Catherine was born in November 1638, the daughter of John, Duke of Braganza, who became King of Portugal in 1640. As early as 1645 he proposed her marriage to Charles, Prince of Wales, and as soon as a restoration of the monarchy seemed probable in England the match was suggested to George Monck (q.v.) by the Portuguese ambassador. The marriage took place in 1662 and Catherine brought Tangier and Bombay to Charles as part of her dowry.

Catherine had no preparation for her new role as queen: she was unversed in affairs of state and spoke no French or

English. However, Charles was attracted by her childish simplicity and amused himself by teaching her English. Despite this promising beginning to their marriage Catherine soon had to contend with her husband's mistresses. When Charles introduced Lady Castlemaine at court Catherine was greatly agitated and fainted. Charles employed Clarendon in persuading the Queen of the futility of resistance to his wishes and after several meetings between them her tearful fury gave way to passive acceptance with forbearance, even treating his bastards kindly.

Charles never became an attentive husband but he treated Catherine with kindness and often affection. He remained married to her despite her childlessness (she miscarried three times) and divorce rumours in the late 1660s proved groundless. The Popish Plot of 1678 (see Oates, Titus) presented the gravest danger to the Queen. She was accused of plotting against the King's life, but Charles himself defended her against the charge and declared to Burnet (q.v.) that he would not see an innocent woman wronged. On 17 November in the House of Lords, Shaftesbury proposed a divorce so that the King could marry a Protestant consort, but Charles actively opposed the bill and it was dropped.

In the climate of anti-Catholic feeling, Catherine was also suspected of exercising influence in the interests of her own Catholicism. She did write to the Pope and leading cardinals, but their correspondence seems to have been formal and complimentary in character and chiefly related to the condition of Portugal. Indeed, Catherine had no political influence, perhaps through indifference or perhaps from ignorance. Her only passions seem to have been dancing, masquerades, and games of chance. Place-seekers ignored the Queen and sought the favour of the more powerful mistresses.

When Charles fell ill in 1685, Catherine was anxious for his reconciliation with the Catholic Church and must have been gratified by his deathbed acceptance of the Roman last rites. She must have been aware of his ambivalent religious position, although she was probably not influential in forming it. Catherine went into deep mourning on Charles's death and lived in seclusion, amusing herself only with cards and concerts. In 1692 she returned to Portugal and was received enthusiastically in Lisbon. There she lived quietly but did use her influence towards securing an Anglo-Portuguese alliance, the Treaty of Methuen (1703). Catherine was appointed regent to her brother Pedro in 1704 and under her administration Portugal gained several victories over the Spaniards. She died of a sudden attack of colic on 31 December 1705.

L. C. Davidson, *Catherine of Braganza* (1908).

Portraits: oil, three-quarter length, by Lely, *c.* 1663–65: Windsor Castle; oil, full-length, by Jacob Huysmans, *c.* 1664: Windsor Castle; oil, three-quarter length, by D. Stoop, *c.* 1660–61: N.P.G.

Cavendish, William (1592–1676), Duke of Newcastle; Royalist general in the Civil War.

He was the son of Sir Charles Cavendish and Catherine, heiress of the barony of Ogle in Northumberland. He was educated at St. John's College, Cambridge. In 1610 he was created knight of the Bath and in the same year married Elizabeth, the widow of the Earl of Suffolk.

The Cavendish family seat was at Welbeck in Nottinghamshire, and here William entertained both James I and Charles I, commissioning Ben Jonson to write masques for the latter's visits and sparing no expense. His efforts to please bore fruit, for in 1620 he was created Viscount Mansfield, in 1628 received the earldom of Newcastle, and in 1638 was made governor of the Prince of Wales and a privy councillor. For the Bishops' War of 1639, he lent the King £10,000 and raised a troop of horse consisting entirely of knights and gentlemen. As the opposition to the King mounted at Westminster, Newcastle was canvassed by those involved in the so-called army plot, a plan to secure command of the army for the King, as the potential general, and in 1641 he relinquished his appointment as the Prince's tutor to allay the suspicion of him that this aroused in Parliament.

In January 1642 he was appointed governor of Hull by the King in order to secure the magazine for the Royalists, but the townsfolk would not admit him. Later he joined the King at York, where the court had migrated, and in June he was sent to hold Newcastle and take command of the northern counties, raising troops by means of the Ogle interest, while the possession of the port itself was of considerable value to the Royalist cause. The earl was not without ability, but he leaned heavily upon an experienced Scots soldier, James King, later Lord Eythin, who was his lieutenant general from March 1643.

At the end of November, 1642, Cavendish marched south into Yorkshire in answer to appeals from the county's Royalists, relieving York, which was held for the King by Sir Thomas Glenham. On 6 December he confronted Ferdinando Fairfax (q.v.) at Tadcaster with the advantage of numbers, which enabled him eventually to prevail over stout resistance on the part of the Parliamentarians. He then secured Pontefract Castle and Newark, the

latter place remaining in Royalist hands until the end of the war, covering the Trent crossing and holding Lincolnshire and Nottinghamshire under threat. Thomas Fairfax (q.v.), the son of Ferdinando, made a riposte with the capture of Leeds (23 January 1643), but could not seriously disturb the control which Newcastle now exerted on the county. Yorkshire thus became a safe area for the landing of Queen Henrietta Maria (q.v.), who had been collecting arms and soldiers on the Continent for the royal cause. Cavendish secured Bridlington, concentrating most of his army there to welcome the Queen when she landed (22 February). Her presence hampered his freedom of action, which was not restored until she left York for Oxford (4 June) with some 4,500 men.

At once Newcastle struck at the Fairfaxes, seizing the Parliamentary stronghold of Howley House on 22 June. From there he moved on Bradford, the Fairfaxes marching out to meet him. The Battle of Adwalton Moor (30 June) was the decisive engagement of this campaign, and once again the Royalists had a considerable advantage in numbers which gave them the victory in a hard but not intelligently fought battle. The following day Newcastle assaulted and captured Bradford.

Most military commentators have criticized Newcastle's failure to move south at this juncture, which had important consequences for the future course of the war. A detachment of his army under his cousin Charles Cavendish was indeed operating in Lincolnshire and had laid siege to Gainsborough. In July, however, the town was relieved after a battle in which Charles Cavendish was killed. Almost at once Newcastle was at hand with the rest of his army. Gainsborough capitulated on 30 July after a bombardment which set fire to part of the town, and shortly afterwards Newcastle entered Lincoln. At this point he retraced his steps to besiege Hull. It was to prove a serious mistake, which did not even secure the port, for despite his 15,000 men, he was driven off by a spirited sally on 11 October 1643, directed by the elder Fairfax.

On 19 January 1644, Newcastle's position was further threatened by a force of 20,000 Scottish soldiers crossing the Tweed to support Parliament. He marched north to meet them but they refused battle and he could do little more than harass their lines of communication with his superior cavalry, while falling back slowly in front of them. On 23 March he did provoke the Scots into offering battle at Hilton, near Sunderland, and inflicted some 1,000 casualties on them for the loss of 250 of his own men before the Scots drew off. Any further measures against them were prevented by the capture of Selby by the Fairfaxes (11 April), which cut his communications with the south and threatened York. Accordingly he retired into

York with his 6,000 foot, sending off his cavalry, which could be of little service in a siege.

The city was besieged by the joint Scottish and Parliamentarian armies from 22 April, with a third army, the Earl of Manchester's, arriving at the beginning of June from Lincolnshire. Newcastle settled down to the problems of defence with his usual administrative skill, giving the besiegers no expectation that the place would fall into their hands easily. They were forced to abandon their works by the approach of Prince Rupert's army, which arrived in front of the city on 1 July to the surprise and delight of the besieged, who had no advance notice.

The Prince insisted upon an immediate march to do battle with the allies, against the advice of both Newcastle and Eythin. The result was the decisive Royalist defeat at Marston Moor (2 July 1644), which lost them the North. Newcastle's troops were late in arriving on the field, the foot not coming up until mid-afternoon, which certainly affected Rupert's tactical position in the early stages when opportunities for a successful attack still existed. Newcastle himself was not given a command in the battle but once it started he found himself near the centre of the line, where he placed himself at the head of a troop of gentleman volunteers who had escorted him from York. With these he charged in Blakeston's reserve cavalry brigade, passing through a Scottish foot regiment and himself killing three men. By common consent, the laurels of the day on the Royalist side went to Newcastle's own infantry, the Whitecoats, who stood their ground when the Royalist army was crumbling around them, refusing quarter, until their ammunition was expended and only about thirty were left alive.

Newcastle was so disheartened by the wreck of his army and the loss of previous gains that he left the country, having previously felt himself to be the object of criticism. His wife had died in 1643; he remarried in 1645. Eventually he settled at Antwerp, and in April 1650 was made a member of Charles II's Privy Council, a position in which he exhibited little activity or real influence.

Returning to England at the Restoration, his biggest task was the recovery and rebuilding of his estates, which had been confiscated and dispersed, with considerable plundering and destruction during the Commonwealth. Although he was reinstated in his previous offices and in 1665 created Duke of Newcastle, he took no further part in public affairs. His leisure was devoted to literature and horsemanship, for he was the author of a few mediocre comedies and two good equestrian manuals, one written during his exile. He was also the patron of Descartes and Hobbes. He died on 25 December 1676.

Margaret Cavendish, Duchess of Newcastle, *The Life of William Cavendish, Duke of Newcastle* (1667).

Peter Wenham, *The Great and Close Siege of York* (1970).

Peter Young, *Marston Moor* (1970).

Portrait: engraving, half-length, by George Vertue, 1713: British Museum.

Cecil, Sir Edward (1572–1638), Viscount Wimbledon; military commander.

Edward Cecil was born on 29 February 1572, the third son of Thomas Cecil, 2nd Baron Burghley, 1st Earl of Exeter. In his 25th year, Edward Cecil went to serve in the Low Countries, and by 1599 he had become an infantry captain. In 1601 he was knighted and made his first appearance in Parliament, representing Aldeburgh. His last session in

Parliament was that of 1624, when he sat for Dover.

While serving in the Low Countries, Cecil had risen to the rank of commander of the English contingent (1610). By the 1620s he had gained a fair amount of military experience, but was by no means a competent soldier. Nevertheless, he won the favour of Buckingham (see Villiers, George, 1st Duke), who in 1625 gave him charge of the Spanish expedition. In this year also he was created Baron Cecil of Putney and Viscount Wimbledon.

The most massive demonstration of Cecil's incompetence occurred in the disastrous operation at Cadiz (October, 1625). The failure was complete and Cecil even managed to let slip the treasure ships of the Spaniards.

Yet upon his return he received more commissions. In 1626 Buckingham appointed him lord lieutenant of Surrey. He received the command in Holland from 1627 to 1629. In 1630 he became governor of Portsmouth, a post he held until his death on 15 November 1638.

C. Dalton, *The Life and Times of General Sir Edward Cecil, Viscount Wimbledon (1572–1638)* (2 vols.; 1885).

Portrait: engraving, quarter-length, after Simon van de Passe, 1618: British Museum.

Cecil, Robert (?1563–1612), 1st Earl of Salisbury; statesman, see *Lives of the Tudor Age*.

Chapman, George (?1559–1634), poet, dramatist, and translator, see *Lives of the Tudor Age*.

Charles I (1600–49), King of England, Scotland and Ireland (1625–49).

Charles was born at Dunfermline, Fife, on 11 November 1600, the second son of James VI of Scotland (later James I, q.v.) and Anne of Denmark. He was created Duke of Albany in December 1600 and brought to London in 1604. The details of Charles's earliest years are none too well known. It appears that as a child his health was delicate and this fact accounts for the delay in allowing him to risk the journey to London in

order to join his parents after James's accession to the English throne in March 1603. He was made Duke of York in 1605.

His elder brother Henry, to whom he had been devoted, died in 1612, leaving Charles as heir apparent. The loss saddened him greatly and was made more acute when his sister Elizabeth, for whom he also had affection, left England in 1613 to marry Frederick V, Elector Palatine of the Rhine. Three years later, on 3 November 1616, just before his sixteenth birthday, Charles was made Prince of Wales. In 1618 Charles's brother-in-law Frederick was offered the kingship of Bohemia, hitherto a practically hereditary Hapsburg and therefore Catholic monarchy. Frederick, a prominent German Protestant, accepted the offer, the direct result of his acceptance being the outbreak of the Thirty Years War. As part of James's attempts to mediate between Frederick and the Austro-Spanish alliance that had formed against him, Charles was sent to Madrid in 1623, accompanied by James's favourite, Buckingham (see Villiers, George, 1st Duke), to try to arrange a marriage treaty between himself and the Spanish king's daughter. But his refusal to become converted to Catholicism, together with Spain's unwillingness to use its good offices in restoring Frederick – he had been driven from the Bohemian throne in 1619 – led to humiliating failure.

The last years of James I saw a decline in his powers and effective control therefore lay with Charles and Buckingham, who were bent on war with Spain. The predominantly Puritan English Parliament was also prepared to go to war with the Catholic Spanish and Charles, having pressed James to change his policy, succeeded in 1624 in obtaining war funds from the Commons in return for his consent to the impeachment of Lionel Cranfield (q.v.), Earl of Middlesex, one of James's economic ministers, who opposed war.

After James's death in February, Charles I was crowned on 27 March 1625. Soon afterwards he married Henrietta Maria, sister of Louis XIII of France, under the terms of a treaty arranged in the previous year by Buckingham. In return for this match, England promised to aid France in suppressing a Protestant enclave at La Rochelle and to grant freedom of worship to Catholics in England. This attempt to obtain a French alliance against the Hapsburg-Spanish confederacy inevitably only served to anger the Puritans in Parliament because of the conditions involved. Moreover, Charles had by his actions of 1624 created the constitutional precedent of allowing Parliament to control expenditure and foreign policy and even to displace ministers.

The conflict between King and Parliament manifested itself early on in Charles's reign. The government of the country was becoming increasingly dependent for finance upon the propertied classes, from which Parliament drew most of its members. Added to this was the religious domination of the Puritans, whose opposition to the attempt of Spain and Austria to reverse the Reformation in the Thirty Years War was moulded into a Protestant patriotism of considerable vehemence. The Puritans' zeal for religious reform was almost bound to be inimical to a High Churchman like Charles, who clung to the same high-minded principles that his father had expressed, namely a belief that his own authority was not to be challenged since he ruled by divine right.

In the first two parliaments of 1625 and 1626, Charles was faced with strong hostility towards his foreign policy, which showed itself in an attempt to remove Buckingham, whom he had inherited from his father as a favourite adviser. Buckingham had tried to redeem himself by declaring war on France. This extra burden on expenditure, as well as the fact that the war against Spain was not going well (an expedition sent out by Buckingham in October, 1625, was so poorly organized and equipped that it dispersed before engaging the enemy), almost led to Buckingham's impeachment, which Charles averted by dissolving his second parliament (June 1626). But he failed to get it to vote him any subsidies; in particular, he had not obtained the right to levy tonnage and poundage (customs duties), which had hitherto been granted at the outset of every monarch's reign almost as a matter of form.

In 1627, England, now supporting the Protestants at La Rochelle, sent an expedition to raise the siege laid there by the French. To finance this and the rest of the war effort, Charles levied tonnage and poundage without Parliament's consent and imposed a forced loan upon knights and gentlemen of property. The loan was declared illegal; in response Charles dismissed his chief justice and arrested several persons who refused to contribute. The ensuing test case, the so-called 'five knights' case', upheld the action of the king, declaring that he was within his prerogative, and the defendants were imprisoned.

The failure of the expedition to La Rochelle under Buckingham led to even greater parliamentary hostility, which was embodied in 1628 in the Petition of Right. This document held to be illegal almost all of Charles's actions, especially those of arbitrary imprisonment and levying taxes without the agreement of Parliament. Again Buckingham's removal was called for and again Charles dissolved Parliament to prevent it. Buckingham's subsequent assassination (August 1628) removed a major cause of discontent, but it was now clear that an intractable hostility lay between Charles and the Commons, which left no room for compromise. Thus in 1629, after renewed disputes over tonnage and poundage and other issues, Charles dissolved Parliament and embarked on 11 years of personal government.

The period of his personal administration was characterized by superficial tranquillity. He made peace with both France and Spain almost immediately and continued to levy tonnage and poundage, which together with traditional crown dues, such as fines imposed for the infringement of the statutes against enclosures, helped to balance the budget. Trade was beginning to expand and the country was reasonably prosperous. The King even took over reclamation of the Fens from the Earl of Bedford. His eldest son, the future Charles II, was born on 29 May 1630.

Charles was a cultured man, having a predilection for the visual arts. It was through him that Van Dyck came to England. Though in general courteous, he was none the less shy and failed to mix with ordinary people. Yet though he lacked this common touch, he regarded his duty as a monarch as being that of 'an indulgent nursing father'.

Charles appointed Bishop William Laud (q.v.) as his chief minister in 1629 and his other chief servant, Thomas Wentworth (q.v.), later Earl of Strafford, became his lord deputy in Ireland in 1632, effectively subduing the Irish parliament with tyrannical methods.

Queen Henrietta Maria succeeded Buckingham as Charles's private counsellor and under her aegis Catholicism came back into fashion at court. This, as well as the fact that Charles could offer no aid to the Protestants in the Thirty Years War, strengthened Puritan anger against him, an anger which was acutely exacerbated by the brutal treatment of critics of the established Church like Prynne, Robert Burton, and Bastwick (qq.v.).

Charles's foreign policy was weak for lack of money. Traditional crown revenues were geared to a peacetime economy and only the imposition of ship money (see Hampden, John) served to keep the government solvent. But it met considerable resistance and contributed to the general discontent.

Charles's relationship with Scotland had not been good since his accession. He had alienated the Scottish nobility over land claims by the crown and the Church, and his imposition in 1637 of a new liturgy based on the Book of Common Prayer infuriated them further. The signing of the National Covenant and the ensuing war, in which Charles was defeated by a Scottish army that crossed the border, only served as a prelude to a worse crisis.

On the advice of Laud and Wentworth, Charles summoned a new Parliament in April 1640. He was determined on war with the rebellious and largely Presbyterian Scots and needed Parliament's help. But Parliament, under John Pym (q.v.), opposed him, wishing instead to discuss his conduct of the government. A month later, Charles dissolved this, 'The Short Parliament', achieving nothing. He continued the war with Scotland, financing it through the continued levy of ship money. In August the Scots crossed the border and royal troops were put to flight at Newburn. 'The Long Parliament' was convened in November 1640. In an effort to be outwardly conciliatory, Charles conceded the Triennial Acts, thus guaranteeing the summoning of Parliament every three years. In spite of this, Parliament remained hostile and clamoured for the trial for treason of Strafford, whose Irish policy had been particularly unacceptable. In the event, Charles was finally obliged to grant this and was compelled to sign a bill of attainder that ensured Strafford's execution in 1641.

Charles was slowly but surely losing control. He was compelled to assent to resolutions prohibiting Parliament's dissolution without its consent, making ship money illegal, and abolishing most of the royal prerogative courts. His expedition to Scotland to gain support failed, despite concessions made to Presbyterians and nobles. His reply to the Grand Remonstrance, passed narrowly by Parliament on 23 November 1641, and his proclamation upholding the established Church of England demonstrate an entrenched attitude.

The events of 1642 show the King openly preparing for war. Encouraged by the closeness of the vote on the Grand Remonstrance (159 to 148), Charles speculated that a Royalist party existed in Parliament. His refusal to relinquish his military command and the threatened impeachment of his queen led him to order the arrest of a number of members. Though he personally tried to enforce this order with 400 men, the members escaped and hid in the City. Moving north in January, Charles tried and failed to take over the arsenal at Hull. He settled at York, where his Royalist supporters gradually joined him. After receiving final Parliamentary demands for military, ministerial, and church control, he waited through the summer and on 22 August 1642, raised the royal standard at Nottingham to begin the Civil War.

After Royalist recruitment in Shropshire and the Welsh borderlands and an indecisive battle at Edgehill, Warwickshire (23 October 1642), Charles occupied Oxford. He then advanced on London and was forced to withdraw at Turnham Green, retiring via Reading to Oxford, where he again set up his headquarters.

The first half of 1643 was spent by Charles at Oxford. Henrietta Maria joined him there in July, having returned from Holland, where she had pawned or sold some of her jewels to buy arms. In the autumn, following the capture of Bristol by Prince Rupert, Charles attacked Gloucester but was obliged to withdraw by a Parliamentarian army under the Earl of Essex. He withdrew again to Oxford after an indecisive engagement at Newbury. 1643 was also the year of the Solemn League and Covenant, a pact between the Scots and the English Parliamentarians, and in January 1644 a Scots force again crossed the border.

1644 was the year of Prince Rupert's defeat at Marston Moor and the loss of York. Controlled from Oxford, the west and southwest of England were in Royalist hands. Charles's confidence was boosted somewhat by his defeat of Sir William Waller (Cropredy Bridge, June) and the Earl of Essex (Lostwithiel, Cornwall, August). He was, however, in a mood to make peace and put out feelers to that effect, which the Parliamentarians rejected. Nevertheless, as a result of these feelers he observed dissension among his enemies that must have heartened him temporarily.

In this same year, Henrietta Maria took refuge in France and in the spring of 1645 the young Prince Charles was sent to join her. The Royalists now had to contend with the much more professional New Model Army. Under Thomas Fairfax (q.v.), it completely defeated a force led by the King and Prince

Rupert at Naseby (14 June 1645). Charles was further demoralized by Rupert's loss of Bristol, the defeat of the Marquis of Montrose at Philiphaugh, and his own failure to relieve Chester.

Early 1646 found the King again at Oxford, hemmed in by his enemies. He escaped from the city in disguise and travelled to Newark to treat with the Scots. But under the terms of their alliance with the English, the Scottish army departed for home and delivered Charles over to the Parliamentarian commissioners at Newcastle in 1647.

The squabbles between the Parliamentarians and the New Model Army following Charles's apprehension led to the seizure of the King by an Army force and his removal to and subsequent escape from Hampton Court. His escape was not completely successful, however, and he got only to the Isle of Wight, where he was kept under surveillance by the Parliamentarian supporter, Robert Hammond. Here Charles negotiated separately with the Parliamentarians, the Army, and the Scots. He rejected the demands of Parliament and came to a secret agreement with the Scots, whereby he hoped to regain power. This attempt failed in August 1648, when a Scottish force was defeated at Preston. On the insistence of the Army, Charles was tried for treason 'and other high crimes against the realm' and beheaded on 30 January 1649. He went to his execution with a dignity remarked on by all observers, bravely insisting that he cared for liberty and freedom as much as any man, but that 'a subject and a sovereign are clear different things.' He was buried at Windsor.

Sir Charles Petrie (ed.), *The Letters, Speeches and Proclamations of Charles I* (1935).
F. M. G. Higham, *Charles I, a study* (1932).
M. P. F. Pakenham, *Charles I* (1936).
C. V. Wedgwood *et al.*, *King Charles I, 1649–1949* (1949).
E. Wingfield-Stratford, *Charles, King of England* (3 vols.; 1948–50).

Portraits: oil, by Van Dyck, 1635: Windsor Castle; oil, full length, by Daniel Mytens, 1628: Windsor Castle; oil, full length, by Daniel Mytens, 1631: N.P.G.; oil, half length, after Van Dyck: N.P.G.; miniature, studio of I. Oliver, *c.* 1612: N.P.G.

Charles II (1630–85), King of England, Scotland, and Ireland (1660–85).

Born at St. James's Palace, the son of Charles I and Henrietta Maria (qq.v.), Charles as a child was entrusted to the care first of the Countess of Dorset, then of the Duke of Newcastle, and afterwards of the Marquis of Hertford.

He was present at the Battle of Edgehill when he was twelve, and at fifteen nominally commanded the attempt to hold southwest England for the Royalists against Fairfax. In 1646, his father's forces having been finally defeated, he fled abroad. After his father's execution, Charles was proclaimed King in Edinburgh in January 1649, and in Ireland the following month. In 1650 he accepted the Covenant in order to win Scottish support, and invaded England in 1651 at the head of a Scottish army. However, he was heavily defeated at Worcester and forced to flee once more into exile.

For the next nine years Charles resided in his faction-ridden court in exile. He lived in poverty, dependent on the charity of Louis XIV and English Royalists, in Paris from October 1651 to June 1654, and thereafter travelled around Europe as the influence of the Commonwealth forced him to move on. He may have been converted to Catholicism while in exile, but continued to profess his attachment to the Church of England. He engaged in various half-hearted intrigues with foreign monarchs against the English Commonwealth and, hence, against England. He was formally excluded from succession to the English throne by an Act of Parliament in 1656.

The death of Cromwell in 1658 accelerated the disintegration of the Commonwealth and calls for the restoration of the monarchy began to be heard openly in England. There was a premature Royalist rising in August 1659, in which Charles took no active part, being content to bide his time. Secret negotiations had, however, been opened with Monck (q.v.). Hyde, Charles's chief adviser in exile, had always insisted that the King could not be restored by force, but only by a reaction of public opinion in his favour. On the advice of Monck and Hyde, therefore, Charles issued the Declaration of Breda (April 1660), which stated Charles's position if returned to the throne. He offered an amnesty to all who had opposed him and his father (wisely leaving to Parliament the prosecution of regicides and traitors), the settlement of disputes over land sales resulting from the Civil War, payment of arrears to the army, and liberty of conscience – but all these were to be conditional on the approval of a new Parliament. In May 1660, the negotiations with Monck having been satisfactorily concluded, Charles landed at Dover amid much popular rejoicing. Parliament voted him a revenue of £1,200,000 per annum, largely from customs and excise, but this sum was not produced for a large part of the reign.

For the first seven years of the reign Edward Hyde, whom Charles elevated to be Earl of Clarendon in 1661, was chief minister, although he received only lukewarm support from the King. In 1662 Charles married the Catholic Catherine of Braganza (q.v.), a marriage

that was seen as pro-French and anti-Spanish; however, it proved childless. The King soon made it clear that his wife was of less importance than his current favourite mistress (at that time Barbara Villiers, q.v.), and Catherine was forced to take her as a lady-in-waiting. From 1665 to 1667 England waged war with the Dutch who had the support of France, but this ended in the destruction of English warships anchored in the Medway. Clarendon was used as a scapegoat for the deficiencies of Charles's marriage and the defeats of the war and was removed from office. Charles allowed him to return into exile, despite his long record of loyal service to the King's cause.

From 1667 to 1673 Charles was advised by the group known as the Cabal, but the major act of foreign policy – the secret Treaty of Dover – was largely Charles's own doing. The treaty, negotiated by Charles at Dover in 1670, engaged England to support France in a war against the Dutch, and secret clauses provided for him to declare himself a Catholic and to be paid subsidies by

Louis XIV. The war was duly under-taken in 1672, but Charles was forced to withdraw in 1674 because Parliament refused the funds to continue it. The King kept his Catholicism secret, but in 1672 introduced another Declaration of In-dulgence. Parliament retaliated the next year with a Test Act compelling office-holders under the Crown to take the Anglican sacrament.

The Cabal disintegrated in 1673, and from 1673 to 1677 Danby (see Osborne, Thomas) was chief minister. During most of this time Parliament was pro-rogued, and Charles relied on French subsidies. Despite the marriage of Mary, the Duke of York's daughter, to the Protestant William of Orange in 1677, the country was suspicious of the pro-French and pro-Catholic leanings of the King. The allegations, made by Titus Oates (q.v.) in 1678, of a 'Popish Plot' to kill the King and massacre Protestants confirmed many people's worst fears. The Commons asserted their belief in the plot, and a kind of witchhunt to find the supposed plotters began. Many Catholics were arrested, and some ex-ecuted. Charles made no attempt to defend the Catholic victims until the Queen herself was threatened, although he defended her stoutly.

In 1679 Danby was impeached, partly because of his role in the dealings with France, and a movement began to ex-clude the Catholic Duke of York (see James II) from succession to the throne and to replace him with Charles's illegitimate son Monmouth. Charles showed considerable tactical skill in emerging successfully from the Ex-clusion crisis. He dissolved Parliament and signed a declaration that Monmouth was illegitimate (since Monmouth claimed that his mother, Lucy Walter (q.v.), had been married to Charles). The Duke of York went into voluntary exile,

but returned later in the year and was sent to administer Scotland. Monmouth was exiled in September.

Three Parliaments met and were dissolved in rapid succession. In March 1681, Charles's last Parliament met at the Tory stronghold of Oxford. The Com-mons, however, brought in another Exclusion Bill, but Charles dissolved Parliament after a week when Louis promised him £720,000 over the next three years. This gave the King relative financial independence, and he called no Parliament for the rest of his reign, despite the Triennial Act, which re-quired a Parliament every three years. The Rye House Plot of 1683 enabled him to execute some Whig leaders, and this made his position more secure. Thereafter, Charles attempted to safe-guard the future by remodelling town charters. He died on 6 February 1685, of a stroke; on his deathbed he proclaimed himself a Catholic.

Charles II's court was renowned for its gaiety and splendour, and he retained his personal popularity throughout most of his reign. He was affable and charm-ing, although not always loyal to those who had proved themselves his friends, such as Montrose (see Graham, James) in 1650 and his first chief minister, Clarendon. Charles pursued no very consistent policy, except in being sym-pathetic to France and Catholicism. His foreign policy tended to make Britain a pawn of Louis XIV, whose despotism he envied. He was lazy but politically shrewd, although he employed his tal-ents to only limited ends. His youth having been spent in civil war, exile, and comparative poverty, he was de-termined to avoid 'going on his travels again'.

Charles was tall, dark, and of athletic physical appearance. He played tennis, danced, walked long distances, and rode a winning horse at Newmarket in the year before his death. He had many mistresses, including Lucy Walter, who bore him a son, James Scott, Duke of Monmouth, in 1649, Barbara Villiers, Nell Gwynne, and Louise de Kéroualle (qq.v.). He had at least fourteen illegitimate children. Halifax thought that 'his inclinations to love were the effects of health and a good constitution'. The political influence of his mistresses, except perhaps for Louise de Kéroualle, was small, and Clarendon noted that Charles 'did not in his nature love a busy woman, and had an aversion from speaking with any woman, or hearing them speak, of any business but to that purpose he thought them all made for'.

As a King, absolutism appealed to him, but Burnet thought him too reluctant to run the risk or give himself the trouble of trying to rule despotically, probably an accurate assessment. In any case, his power from the beginning was more constricted than his father's had been. The Commons – though loyal – were aware of their strengthened position in relation to the King and determined to consolidate their authority. The Cavalier element returned in the initial enthusiasm of 1661 was diluted in by-elections, and Charles's pro-French policy alarmed them. However, Charles lacked the idealism of his father and was determined not to sacrifice himself to principle. He was forced to abandon the Declaration of Indulgence that he had made in 1673, and Danby's fall sprang from his part in the unpopular dealings with France. Parliament was demonstrating its interest and ability to act in the previously sacrosanct sphere of foreign policy.

The Treaty of Dover probably represented the policy Charles would ideally have liked to follow – but he was always realistic enough to stop short of real commitment to converting Britain to Catholicism with French help. He survived the crisis of 1678–81 partly because of financial help from France and partly by close collaboration with the Tory Anglican gentry against the newly emerging Whigs. In any event, the Popish Plot and Exclusion threatened not so much himself as the institution of monarchy and the hereditary principle. There was no real alternative to Charles as monarch, and he was realistic enough not to provoke the kind of confrontation that led to the downfall both of his father and of his brother and successor, James II.

Sir Arthur Bryant (ed.), *The Letters, Speeches and Declarations of King Charles II* (1935).
Osmund Airy, *Charles II* (1901).
Maurice Ashley, *Charles II* (1971).
Sir Arthur Bryant, *King Charles II* (1955, rev. ed.).
Godfrey Davies, *The Restoration of Charles II, 1658–1660* (1955).
C. H. Hartmann, *The King My Brother* (1954).

Portraits: oil, full-length, by J. M. Wright, after 1661: St. James's Palace; oil on plaster, quarter-length, by Verrio, *c.* 1677: Windsor Castle; oil, half-length, studio of J. Riley: N.P.G.; oil, three-quarter length, by Willem Wissing, *c.* 1683: Windsor Castle; oil, half-length, after Lely: N.P.G.

Churchill, John (1650–1722), 1st Duke of Marlborough; courtier, politician, diplomat, and one of England's greatest generals.

John Churchill was born at his maternal grandmother's home of Ashe House, Devonshire, probably on 26 May 1650, and was brought up there in genteel poverty. He was the son of Sir Winston Churchill, an impoverished Dorset Royalist, and Elizabeth, née Drake, daughter of a Parliamentarian gentleman, and was educated at the City Free School, Dublin, while his father held a post in that city (1662–63), and at St. Paul's School (1663–65).

In 1666 the young Churchill obtained

a position as page to James, Duke of York (see James II), probably through the influence of his sister Arabella, the Duke's mistress. Once in the court, his charm and good looks brought him advancement. The Duke of York had him commissioned as ensign in the Foot Guards in 1667, and the next year he joined the Tangier garrison as a volunteer, possibly serving against the Moors and the Algerian pirates.

Churchill returned to England in 1671, where his reputation as an amorous courtier grew. His greatest conquest was Charles II's mistress, the Duchess of Cleveland (see Villiers, Barbara), who gave him £4,500, with which he promptly bought an annuity.

During the Third Dutch War, Churchill saw service in the Duke of York's flagship at Solebay (1672) and was promoted to captain. It is probable that he acquired his understanding of naval strategy in this campaign. He gained valuable experience on land in 1673–74, serving in the English regiments of Louis XIV under the Duke of

Monmouth (q.v.) and the great Marshal Turenne, both of whom were impressed by his courage and brilliance as an officer. As a result, he held command of a regiment by the time he returned to England.

Churchill continued to rise in the Duke of York's service, obtaining a household post and going on a mission for the Duke. In 1678 the Duchess aided his love marriage to the hot-tempered Sarah Jennings (see Churchill, Sarah), despite the opposition of their families.

When the Catholic Duke was compelled to leave England in 1679 on account of the Exclusion crisis. Churchill, by now a brigadier general, accompanied him to Brussels and then to Scotland. Churchill was trusted enough to serve as an emissary to Charles II and Louis XIV.

On their return from Scotland in 1682 occurred an incident that probably initiated the break between Churchill and the Duke. Their ship began to sink, but the Duke refused to allow them to take to the boats, despite the advice of his companions, until it was too late to save the lives of the crew. That same year Churchill was made a baron. Meanwhile the Churchills' links with Princess Anne (see Anne), the Duke's daughter and Sarah Churchill's close friend, were strengthening.

In 1685 the Duke of York ascended the throne as James II. The new King sent Churchill to bear the news to Paris. There he is reported to have expressed his growing unease over James's policies: 'If the King should attempt to change our religion, I will instantly quit his service.' Nevertheless, later that year he distinguished himself in defeating Monmouth's rebellion, serving as second-in-command at Sedgemoor.

Churchill's anxieties increased, however, as James continued his attack upon the Church of England. He drew closer to Princess Anne and began to correspond with William of Orange (see William III). James made Churchill a lieutenant general in 1688, but when William invaded England later that year at the invitation of nobles of all parties, Churchill led part of the royal forces over to William. He asserted that religion and conscience had caused him to desert his king and benefactor, but a certain element of opportunism cannot be ignored.

William rewarded him the next year with the earldom of Marlborough and other posts and sent him to the Netherlands to command the British contingent under the Prince of Waldeck in a successful campaign against the French. Although William's wife and co-ruler, Mary II (q.v.), distrusted Marlborough, he was made commander-in-chief in England when William sailed to Ireland in 1690. Later that year he himself led a successful attack on Cork and Kinsale. Nevertheless, like most powerful Tories, Marlborough was conducting a correspondence with the exiled James II at the same time as he was serving William, in this way trying to insure his future in a highly unstable situation. The atmosphere of suspicion certainly contributed to Marlborough's downfall. In January 1692 he was dismissed and in May imprisoned in the Tower on suspicion of plotting to restore James. He was released soon after, when the evidence against him was proved to be a forgery, but he remained out of favour until 1698. This, however, was due to his support for Anne against William and his opposition to the King's Dutch favourites.

In 1698 Marlborough obtained the significant post of governor to the young Duke of Gloucester, Anne's only son. Three years later, in 1701, the ailing William appointed him commander of the British troops in the Netherlands, a crucial post at this time, as the War of the Spanish Succession was slowly beginning. A few months earlier William had appointed a Tory ministry that included Marlborough's closest ally, Lord Godolphin (see Godolphin, Sidney).

The death of William and ascent of Anne in 1702 brought further fortune to the Churchills. Marlborough was made captain general of all British forces, while his wife Sarah, Anne's confidante, became mistress of the robes. Godolphin became lord treasurer.

In May Marlborough sailed to Holland to take up his post. The Dutch accepted him as supreme commander of the allies on that front. In this first campaign, Marlborough demonstrated his brilliance as a general and skilfully continued William's work of forging a Grand Alliance against Louis XIV. Throughout 1702 and 1703, Marlborough advanced slowly in the Spanish Netherlands, taking one French-held fortress after another. The success of his first campaign was rewarded with a dukedom. But Marlborough fumed at the caution of the Dutch, whose field deputies forbade several bold attacks that in Marlborough's opinion could have resulted in great victories.

The success of the French and their Bavarian allies further south posed a direct threat by 1704 to the Holy Roman Emperor, Leopold I, in Austria. Marlborough threatened to attack along the Moselle and into Alsace, but then quickly marched across Germany to unite with the Imperial commander, Prince Eugène of Savoy. The combined force found the French and Bavarians at Blenheim near the Danube and defeated them overwhelmingly. Marlborough had destroyed the French threat to

Vienna, and a grateful Emperor made him Prince of Mindelheim. Parliament voted funds so that he could construct Blenheim Palace near Woodstock.

Marlborough's campaigns were all successful. He defeated the French in pitched battles at Ramillies (1706), Oudenarde (1708), and Malplaquet (1709), and every year from 1702 to 1711 saw successful sieges. The French were forced back to their borders. In 1711, Marlborough conducted what was perhaps his most brilliant campaign. With numerically inferior forces he outmanœuvred Marshal Villars and gained the strong line of defences guarding the northeastern frontier of France.

At home, Marlborough, although a moderate Tory, had been forced increasingly to rely on Whig support for his war policies. Fewer and fewer Tories were holding office. The Whigs were no friends of Marlborough and proved themselves incapable of negotiating a peace as the war dragged on, but his advocacy of their advancement estranged relations with the Queen, who favoured the Tories. At the same time, his wife's relationship with Anne weakened. Thus Marlborough found himself isolated when the Tories regained power in 1710.

As a result, Marlborough was dismissed from his command in December 1711 and charged with corruption. Although the prosecution was dropped for want of a case, he was now without power in England. In 1712 he went to the Continent, where he corresponded with the Emperor and Anne's heirs, the house of Hanover. At Anne's death in 1714 Marlborough returned to England. He was reinstated as captain general by George I, but lived in retirement until his death on 16 June 1722. He was buried in Westminster Abbey, and his remains were later removed to Blenheim Palace.

Marlborough was long the subject of violent controversy. He made enemies who were quick to note his opportunism and miserliness, products of his early career as an impoverished courtier. His betrayal of James II stains his reputation, but one now knows that in his private life he was a loving husband and father. He has always been recognized as one of the great commanders of history, a general who won the love of his troops and proved to be a brilliant administrator and diplomat.

William Coxe (ed.), *Memoirs* (6 vols.; 1820).

Maurice Ashley, *Marlborough* (1939).

C. T. Atkinson, *Marlborough and the Rise of the British Army* (New York, 1921).

Bryan Bevan, *Marlborough the Man* (1975).

I. F. Burton, *The Captain-General: the Career of John Churchill, Duke of Marlborough, from 1702 to 1711* (1968).

D. G. Chandler, *Marlborough as Military Commander* (1973).

Winston S. Churchill, *Marlborough: His Life and Times* (4 vols.; 1933–38).

M. Foot, *The Pen and the Sword* (1957).

A. L. Rowse, *The Early Churchills* (1956).

Portraits: oil, half-length, attributed to J. Closterman: N.P.G.; oil, three-quarter length, after Kneller: N.P.G.; oil, full-length, by Kneller, *c.* 1706: N.P.G.; bust, studio of Rysbrack, *c.* 1730: N.P.G.

Churchill, Sarah (1660–1744), Duchess of Marlborough, wife of John Churchill (q.v.), 1st Duke of Marlborough, and influential friend and counsellor of Queen Anne (q.v.).

Sarah was born at Sandridge, on 29 May 1660, the daughter of Richard Jennings. In 1673 Sarah Jennings entered the service of Mary of Modena, second wife of James, Duke of York, later James II (q.v.), as an attendant to the Duchess's younger stepdaughter, Princess Anne. The two girls formed an early and strong attachment, which was to last for most of Anne's life. The young Sarah was exceptionally beautiful, but she was also headstrong and the

possessor of a fiery temper. She captivated the heart of a young courtier and
soldier, John Churchill, and they were
secretly married (although with the
knowledge and approval of the Duchess
of York) in 1678.

In 1683 Anne married Prince George
of Denmark and Sarah entered her new
household as a lady of the bedchamber.
It was after Anne's marriage that they
began a curious personal correspondence, addressing each other as Mrs.
Morley (Anne) and Mrs. Freeman
(Sarah). By now, John Churchill was a
baron and Sarah had thus become Lady
Churchill.

In 1688 Anne allowed herself to be
guided by Sarah when the succession
was in doubt. Sarah organized Anne's
flight to Nottingham and advised her to
recognize her brother-in-law, the Prince
of Orange, as William III (q.v.). In 1689
Sarah actively concerned herself with
Anne's fight to increase her annual pension under the civil list and Anne was
eventually awarded £50,000 p.a. by
Parliament. Sarah immediately received
a pension of £1,000 p.a. from Anne.

In 1692 Sarah's husband was implicated in Jacobite plots and actually spent
some time in the Tower. Anne resisted
the strong pressure put upon her by her
sister, Queen Mary, to dismiss Sarah, and
despite virtual ostracism by the court
kept Sarah with her at Syon House. After
Mary's death, William and Anne were
reconciled and the Marlboroughs returned to favour. When Anne acceded
to the throne in 1702, the Marlboroughs
received immediate honours from their
Queen. Sarah became mistress of the
robes and keeper of the privy purse,
while her husband was made captain
general of the English forces and later
received a dukedom.

It is not known exactly when the
relationship between Anne and Sarah

began to become strained. There is no
doubt that Sarah went too far in her
overbearing manners with the Queen.
She exhibited a lack of discretion and an
almost continual state of ill temper, and
she gave increasing support to the
Whigs and attempted to influence Anne
in the creation of Whig ministers. She
thought this course necessary for the
successful progress of the War of the
Spanish Succession, in which her husband was actively involved, but it was
unfortunately in direct conflict with
Anne's High Church Tory views.

In 1707 Sarah was made aware of the
fact that she had a rival, Abigail Masham
(q.v.), her cousin, whom she had introduced into the Queen's household. Anne
had attended Abigail's private wedding
while Sarah was kept in ignorance of
the event. Sarah rapidly took stock of
the situation, 'and in less than a week's
time I discovered that my cousin was
absolute favourite with the queen; that
Mrs. Masham came often to the queen . . .
and was generally two hours a day in
private with her. And I likewise then

discovered beyond all dispute Mr. Harley's correspondence and interest at court by means of this woman.'

Robert Harley (q.v.) was a relative of Abigail Masham and a favourite of Queen Anne. He held Tory views that were sympathetic to the Queen's and after his resignation in 1708 Abigail acted as go-between, enabling him to function as the Queen's unofficial adviser. Sarah did nothing to counteract the combined influence of Mrs. Masham and Harley by a series of reproachful outbursts and violent quarrels with the Queen and in 1711 both Sarah and her husband were forced to resign their offices. Jonathan Swift, a virulent enemy of Sarah, accused her in the *Examiner* of misappropriating money from the privy purse. Sarah said that this was arrears of pension due to her. Anne found this, in all fairness, to be true and refused to take any action against her former favourite. The Marlboroughs left the country and lived abroad until the end of Anne's reign.

After George I's accession, they returned to England, to Woodstock, where they had formerly been granted the old palace of Woodstock and funds to build Blenheim Palace. After her husband's death in 1722, Sarah devoted herself to the completion of Blenheim, quarrelling violently with the architect, Sir John Vanbrugh. She also had rows with her surviving children and conducted a bitter feud with Sir Robert Walpole. In 1742 she published her memoirs; she died at Marlborough House in London on 18 October 1744, leaving a large fortune.

Private Correspondence (2 vols.; 1838).
Kathleen Campbell, *Sarah Duchess of Marlborough* (1932).
David Green, *Sarah, Duchess of Marlborough* (1967).
L. Kronenberger, *Marlborough's Duchess* (1958).
A. L. Rowse, *The Early Churchills* (1956).

Portraits oil, three-quarter length, after Kneller, *c.* 1700: N.P.G.; oil, half-length, by Dahl, 1695–1700: N.P.G.

Cibber, Caius Gabriel (1630–1700),

sculptor; Danish by birth, and the father of the actor and dramatist Colley Cibber (see *Lives of the Georgian Age*).

Cibber's father was employed as cabinet-maker to the King of Denmark, and as a young man Caius travelled at the royal expense to Italy to study. He was employed as foreman by John Stone, an English sculptor working on the Continent, and when in 1659 Stone became ill Cibber was appointed to accompany him back to England. Cibber continued to work as foreman for Stone for several years, and in 1667 was appointed to a minor post ('carver to the King's closet') in the royal household. By the 1670s Cibber was receiving numerous personal commissions, which greatly increased his income.

Cibber's first important work was the large relief on the monument near London Bridge erected in memory of the Great Fire. This work was executed in 1672; it portrays in allegorical form 'Charles II succouring the City of London after the Great Fire', and its baroque style shows the influence of Cibber's studies in Italy. Others among Cibber's works in London include a statue in Soho Square and a pair of statues, 'Raving Madness and Melancholy Madness', executed in 1680 for the gate of Bedlam Hospital, now in the Guildhall Museum.

Between 1688 and 1691 Cibber was employed at Chatsworth House in Derbyshire, the country house of the 1st Duke of Devonshire. Here Cibber carried out much garden sculpture, as well as an altar for the chapel and several interior statues. His next major commission was at Hampton Court, where he carved the pediment over on the east park front which shows Hercules triumphing over Envy, and it was probably due to his association with Sir Christopher Wren (q.v.) on this project that he was also commissioned to carve the figure of the phoenix in bas-relief above the south door of St. Paul's Cathedral.

Though not distinctively original, Cibber's work was consistently competent, and it remains of interest for its reflection of both Dutch and Italian influences. Cibber was married twice; his second wife, Jane Colley, whom he married in November 1670, came from a wealthy Rutlandshire family, and her dowry, coupled with his income from commissions, enabled Cibber to live the latter part of his life in considerable prosperity. Cibber died in 1700, and was buried in the Danish and Norwegian church in Wellclose Square, which he himself had designed.

Cibber, Colley (1671–1757), actor, dramatist, theatre manager, and poet, see *Lives of the Georgian Age*.

Clarendon, 1st Earl of (1609–74), see Hyde, Edward.

Claverhouse, John Graham of (?1649–89), see Graham, John.

Cleveland, Duchess of (1640–1709), see Villiers, Barbara.

Cleveland, John (1613–58), poet and satirist.

John Cleveland was born in Leicestershire in humble circumstances and brought up by Richard Vynes, a Presbyterian divine. He went to Christ's College, Cambridge, in 1627, and when that town was occupied by a Parliamentary garrison in 1643 he left for Oxford and the Royalists. After taking his B.A. (1631) and M.A. (1635) at Cambridge, he was made a fellow of St. John's College. He was father of the Cambridge revels, like Milton, and was twice chosen to give Latin orations for distinguished visitors.

After the surrender of Oxford, he came destitute to London in 1647 and was for a time closely involved with Royalist publications. In 1655 he went to Norwich, where he was arrested as a Royalist, but after three months imprisonment was released after writing a personal appeal to Cromwell, admitting that he was a Royalist (and poor), but denying that he was therefore a criminal. He went to Gray's Inn, where he died in 1658.

Cleveland was a Royalist, but not a cavalier poet. He had an energetic quality suitable for a witty and vigorous satirist, not for a dilettante of the court. He was widely popular in his century, but unfortunately the abundance of close topical allusions in his work makes him hard to follow now. He was a zestful imitator of Donne's conceits; their daring enthusiasm is marred now by our sense of the ludicrous and of their impropriety.

The Rebel Scot is one of his best poems, not least because of its direct simplicity – he could write forceful isolated couplets in the manner of Dryden, and like Dryden could create strong satirical portraits of individuals.

J. M. Berdan (ed.), *The Poems of John Cleveland* (1911).
Brian Morris and Eleanor Withington (eds.), *The Poems of John Cleveland* (1967).

Clifford, Thomas (1630–73), 1st Baron Clifford of Chudleigh; politician, member of the Cabal ministry.

Clifford was born on 1 August 1630, near Exeter, the son of Hugh Clifford, an officer in Charles I's army and a member of the cadet branch of the great family of Clifford (Earls of Cumberland. He was educated at Exeter College, Oxford (1647–50), and the Middle Temple.

It is from Clifford's Oxford days that we have the first evidence of his intense interest in religion. This passion was almost certainly inflamed when he served in the Convention and the Cavalier Parliaments as the M.P. for Totnes, for religious issues were hotly discussed in these assemblies and Clifford was not a man to remain silent or unmoved when a subject dear to his heart was being debated. His aggressive energy won him prominence among Henry Bennet's (q.v.) 'King's friends', a young court party.

Clifford showed his zeal in promoting war with the Netherlands, a cause favoured by Bennet. As a convinced royalist Clifford nurtured a deep-rooted antipathy for the Dutch republic, and he saw the Dutch as his natural enemies. Reward came his way in 1664 with an appointment to the 'commission for the care of sick and wounded seamen'; he eagerly took up his post as the commission's representative with the fleet at sea, and distinguished himself in naval actions in 1665 and 1666. In 1665 he was appointed a commissioner of prizes, and financial offices at court followed. His advancement was largely obtained by Bennet, now Lord Arlington, with whom he constantly corresponded. He served on a mission to Copenhagen in 1665 and was sworn into the Privy Council in December 1666.

Clarendon fell from office in 1667, and the new group of royal advisers was composed of his young enemies – the 'Cabal' which included Clifford. In the same year Clifford also obtained a seat on the commission of the treasury.

He proved himself a loyal court man in the Commons, opposing the Triennial Bill and other measures objectionable to the crown.

Charles II found a sincere ally in Clifford for his pro-French and pro-Catholic policy, as well as an opportunistic follower in Arlington, for not only was Clifford an enemy of the Dutch, but his religious interests were bringing him ever closer to Rome, and he longed for a reunion of the Anglican and Catholic churches. In these plans he found a warm ally in the Duke of York (see James II).

Charles entrusted part of the negotiations that led to the secret Treaty of Dover (1670) with France to Clifford and Arlington, who were also involved in producing and negotiating the simulated treaty needed to gull the Protestant members of the Cabal. Clifford's health began to fail under the strain of overwork, but new duties were constantly added as he gained stature as a royal counsellor. To obtain more supplies for the desired war with the Netherlands, he advised Charles in January 1672 to impose a year's stop on all payments out of the exchequer. He was the chief promoter of the royal Declaration of Indulgence in March, which eased the laws against Catholics. The next month he was ennobled, and in November, despite competition from Arlington, he was appointed to the newly re-created post of lord treasurer of England.

Clifford was now at the peak of his power. However, in February 1673, the government, short of money, had to summon Parliament. The Commons were suspicious of Charles's designs and immediately moved to the attack. Clifford urged the King to be firm and dissolve Parliament, but Charles, always the wiser tactician, backed down and withdrew the Declaration of Indulgence, which had aroused the old fears of popery. The Commons pressed on with the Test Bill, which excluded Catholics from office, possibly on the instigation of the jealous Arlington. Clifford made such a violent speech in the Lords against the measure that he effectively prevented a compromise; the bill became law. This conflict, which demonstrated the impossibility of reconciling the Anglicans with Rome, was probably the spark that drove Clifford into the arms of the Catholic church. In June he resigned from the Treasury and Privy Council and retired to Tunbridge Wells. The failure of his policies affected him deeply. He died in September 1673, possibly by his own hand.

Despite his meteoric rise, Clifford was regarded as honest and incorruptible by his contemporaries. His career was aided by his financial ability, but his ruin was encompassed by his lack of political intuition.

Cyril H. Hartmann, *Clifford of the Cabal* (1937).
M. C. Lee, *The Cabal* (Urbana, Ill., 1965).

Portrait: oil, half-length, after Lely: N.P.G.

Cokayne, Sir William (?1561–1626), lord mayor of London; merchant and entrepreneur who was responsible for organizing the Cokayne Project.

Born in 1560 or 1561, the son of William Cokayne, also a London merchant. Cokayne took over the family business when his father died in 1599. He was made sheriff of London in 1609 and became an alderman in the same year. In 1612 he was appointed the first governor of the newly founded colony in Ulster. During his tenure of this post he supervised the establishment of the city of Londonderry.

In 1614 James I entrusted to Cokayne the control of a newly formed company,

the King's Merchant Adventurers. This organization, under royal control and in opposition to the ordinary merchant adventurers whose privileges had been withdrawn, was to be the only channel of export for Britain's most profitable industry, the cloth trade. The object of the new company was to re-establish English dominance in exporting cloth to the Baltic. By the early 17th century, the Dutch had taken over the lead in this area. The ordinary merchant adventurers, however, had made a good trade from sending undressed cloth to the Netherlands for dyeing and re-export to the Baltic. Dyeing was the most lucrative process, and it was the profit from this that the crown was hoping to tap. Thus, the King's Merchant Adventurers Company was granted a licence to export only cloth that had been dressed and dyed. Rural cloths were sent unfinished to the towns and the towns themselves prepared and dyed both the country-made material and their own products. Profits were expected to be as high as £700,000 a year, £300,000 of which would go to the King's desperately impoverished exchequer. In 1615 Cokayne did make a profit, and obtained a knighthood from James.

However, Cokayne had grossly undercapitalized the dyeing process and underestimated the problems in the export procedure. The Cokayne Project was a spectacular failure. The Dutch banned all imports of English cloth, finished or not, and because of Cokayne's shortsightedness the King's Merchant Adventurers lacked the necessary shipping for direct export to the Baltic. The company was left with an enormous amount of unsaleable cloth on its hands, and the preparation of the cloth could not be carried out on an economical scale. The result was that weavers' riots broke out in Gloucestershire and Wiltshire. The government took measures to force clothiers to keep their weavers in work, which led to further overproduction. By 1617 the Cokayne Project had broken down totally. The fiasco gave a tremendous advantage to the Dutch in cloth export and the whole economy of England suffered its effects for about thirty years.

Cokayne obviously did not hold himself responsible for the failure. He continued his speculative ventures, financing such exploring enterprises as those of William Baffin, after whom Baffin Island and Baffin Bay in the Canadian Arctic are named. Cokayne also came to own extensive areas of land in several English counties. In 1619 he was elected lord mayor of London for the year. He died at the age of sixty-five at Kingston, Surrey, on 20 October 1626.

A. Friis, *Alderman Cokayne's project and the cloth trade* (1927).

Coke, Sir Edward (1552–1634), judge, M.P., and noted writer on English law.

Born at Mileham, Norfolk, 1 February 1552, and educated at Norwich and Trinity College, Cambridge. Having entered Lincoln's Inn in 1572, Coke was called to the bar in 1578 and became reader of Lyon's Inn during the following year. In the succeeding period, under the patronage of William Cecil, Elizabeth I's chief minister (see *Lives of the Tudor Age*), Coke's career advanced well. He speedily gained the reputation of being the finest and most learned lawyer of his time, becoming the recorder of Coventry (1585), Norwich (1586), and London (1592). He entered Parliament as the Member for Aldeburgh in 1589, and by 1592 he had obtained the office of solicitor general. Appointed speaker of the House of Commons in 1593, Coke exercised considerable control, following Elizabeth's policy of keeping ecclesiastical matters out of Parliamentary discussion.

At this time Coke encountered the rivalry of Francis Bacon (see *Lives of the Tudor Age*), who competed with him for the post of attorney general in 1594. Coke won the appointment and Bacon's enmity.

In 1582 Coke had made a wise and wealthy marriage, taking a Suffolk woman of good family, Bridget Paston, as his bride. In 1598 Bridget died and Coke sued for the hand of Elizabeth Hatton, William Cecil's granddaughter. Bacon was again his rival, and was again disappointed. Yet though Coke won her as his second wife, the marriage was a stormy one.

At the close of the decade Coke was a powerful and successful lawyer. As a judge he reacted with great prejudice and severity against those arraigned before him. His brutality was excessive even by the harsh standards prevailing during his own day. He presided over the trials of Essex (1601) and Ralegh (1603) and of those concerned in the Gunpowder Plot (1605). His celebrated outburst against Ralegh is indicative of his overbearing personality and unfairness: 'Thou has an English face, but a Spanish heart.'

In 1600 Coke published the first volume of his *Reports*, compilations of his own legal notes that were later to be used against him in his fall from judicial power. Yet it was with his appointment as chief justice of the Common pleas in 1606 that his conflicts with the King began in earnest. Serious clashes came over attempts to remove ecclesiastical cases from the jurisdiction of the common-law courts. Such attempts were supported by James I and Coke's resistance infuriated him. In 1610 Coke disputed the King's right to change the common law by proclamation, making into an offence something that had not been an offence before. He also challenged the claim of the court of high commission to judge a case of adultery.

In 1613, probably at the suggestion of Bacon, James elevated Coke to the office of chief justice of the king's bench, no doubt in an effort to quieten his opposition. Coke was also appointed to the Privy Council. Yet the conflict continued and culminated in 1615 in James's order to delay proceedings in a case concerning the royal grant of commendams (ecclesiastical livings held in plurality), while he sought to canvass the individual judges outside the court. Coke ignored the royal injunction, declaring such a practice to be illegal. When called before the King, the other judges rescinded their support of Coke and expressed their readiness to comply with the sovereign's command. Coke, however, said that he would act in a manner becoming an honest and just judge. In 1616 charges were brought against Coke and he was dismissed from

his offices and instructed to remove 'errors' (opinions contrary to the King's prerogative) from his legal reports.

Having thus been cast down from his judicial posts, Coke also found himself friendless at the royal court. His unwelcome interest in the mystery surrounding the death of Sir Thomas Overbury (q.v.) had been an ulterior reason for his removal. In an effort to return to favour, therefore, he attempted to marry his daughter Frances, then fourteen years old, to John Villiers, brother of James's new favourite, the future Duke of Buckingham (see Villiers, George, 1st Duke). His wife, supported by her former suitor Bacon, opposed the marriage and hid Frances away. Coke discovered the place of concealment, however, and, having abducted his daughter, forced the marriage through. The quarrel between him and his wife incurred by this brutal diplomacy led to a separation between them.

Yet his machinations did secure his recall to the privy council in 1617. After serving on several commissions connected with that office, Coke was returned to Parliament in 1620 by the Cornish borough of Liskeard. A new career for him had begun.

In James's parliament of 1621 Coke allied himself firmly with the popular party opposing the King. He spoke against monopolies; he denounced popery and especially threw his weight against the plan to marry Prince Charles (see Charles I) to the Spanish Infanta; and he supported wholeheartedly freedom of discussion in the Commons. For this he was sent to the Tower. He was released in August 1622 and kept under house arrest at his home in Stoke Poges. The detention did not last long, however, and by 1624 Coke was again in Parliament, this time representing Coventry. He served in the first three parliaments of Charles I, representing Norfolk and then Buckinghamshire. He was a vigorous opponent of Charles and in 1628 he was one of those chiefly concerned in presenting the Petition of Right. He also delivered a heartfelt attack on the Duke of Buckingham during the same session.

Coke retired when the third parliament was dissolved. He devoted his last years, spent at Stoke Poges, to his legal writings. He died there, aged eighty-two, on 3 September 1634.

An undeniably brilliant and eminent lawyer, Coke was an expert in manipulating the medieval precedents in which he was so learned to arrive at his interpretations of common law in 17th-century England. He upheld common law against the Church as well as the royal prerogative and though he was savage he was in the main just and was violently opposed to the illegal exercise of authority. His writings include a set of law reports for the period 1600–15, published in thirteen parts (incomplete) and containing compilations of laws pertaining to certain contemporary cases, together with personal comments and remarks, four volumes of *Institutes*, the first part of which (1628) is also called 'Coke on Littleton', and various other treatises. Upon his death, Coke's papers were confiscated and kept by Charles until 1641. Some of them were never recovered.

S. E. Thorne, *Sir Edward Coke 1552–1952* (1957).

Portrait: engraving, half-length by Robert White, after portrait in Middle Temple, London, 1669: British Museum.

Colepeper or Culpepper, John (d.? 1660), 1st Baron Colepeper; politician and close adviser of Charles I during the first phase of the Civil War and of the Prince of Wales (later Charles II) during his exile.

For the early life of Colepeper direct evidence is lacking, and we must rely upon information from his later colleague, Edward Hyde (q.v.), 1st Earl of Clarendon, who tells us that he was the son of Sir John Colepeper of Wigsell, Sussex, and that in his youth he spent some time abroad, gaining military experience.

When he was first received at court, Clarendon says that 'he might very well be thought a man of no good breeding, having never sacrificed to the Muses or conversed in any polite company'. If Clarendon is suggesting that Colepeper was not considered a cultured man, this may account for the subsequent attitudes shown towards him. His knowledge of country affairs was valued at this time, however, and he often appeared before the council board on such matters.

Colepeper received a knighthood from Charles I and in April 1640 entered the Short Parliament as Member for Rye. In the Long Parliament of the following November he represented Kent, and on 9 November 1640, he delivered a speech against monopolies. Colepeper was attracted to the Parliamentary grouping under John Pym (q.v.); he was appointed to manage the impeachment of the lawyer Robert Berkley, supported the prosecution of Strafford (see Wentworth, Thomas), and voted in favour of Strafford's attainder.

Like Hyde and Falkland, however, he was not in sympathy with the more revolutionary policies of the Puritan faction. The split came in 1641, over the religious question. In February Colepeper opposed the London Petition against episcopacy and in May he put forward an obstructive amendment to the Root and Branch Bill. He put himself further out of countenance with the radical members of the House of Commons by voting in November against the Militia Bill of Hesilrige (q.v.) and against the Grand Remonstrance.

On 2 January 1642, Colepeper finally defected to the King, who gave him the chancellorship of the exchequer, having already offered it to Pym as an empty conciliatory gesture. With Hyde and Falkland, he now joined Charles's most intimate advisers. The disaster of the Five Members (see Pym, John) incident, about which neither he nor his two colleagues were consulted or had any knowledge, followed on 4 January. In February, Colepeper persuaded Charles to make some minor concessions in the hope of splitting the Parliamentary opposition. On his advice, Charles therefore gave the royal assent to a bill abolishing the temporal power of the bishops and also moved his troops out of the Tower of London. Colepeper is also credited with having suggested the design of taking Hull. On 25 August, standing at the bar of the House of Commons, he delivered the King's final terms for peace. In the following October he fought with Rupert's forces at Edgehill and joined the King's court at Oxford, being created master of the rolls in December.

In the Oxford parliament, Colepeper was a prominent speaker and opposed the less able of Charles's counsellors, such as George Digby, who supported the continuation of the war. Colepeper was inclined towards peace and proposed that the King should grant generous concessions to obtain it. His influence in military matters opened a serious rift between himself and Prince Rupert (q.v.) and his relations with Hyde also became cool because of his slowness to give up the post of chancellor of the exchequer. His general unpopularity was increased when, on 21 October 1644 he was created Baron Colepeper of Thoresway.

In March 1645 Colepeper left Oxford with Hyde to accompany the Prince of Wales to the West Country. At Bristol and later at Bath he lent his support to the attempts of the Royalist forces in the West to have the focus of the war shifted there, away from the North and Midlands.

Undoubtedly, this hesitancy and dispersal of the war effort contributed to the final collapse of the King's cause.

On 2 March 1646, he set out with Prince Charles first for the Scilly Isles and then for France. From here he wrote to the King advocating religious concessions to win over the Scots, including the signing of the Covenant, a policy also supported by the Queen. He favoured the attempted negotiations with the army in 1647. In 1648 he accompanied Prince Charles on a futile naval expedition, returning with him to The Hague. Here differences between Colepeper and Prince Rupert led to violent scenes at court followed by a physical attack upon Colepeper by Sir Robert Walsh, a supporter of Rupert.

After Charles I's execution in 1649, Colepeper continued to promote alliance between the Scots and the Royalists. In 1650 Charles II sent him to Russia, where he negotiated a loan of 20,000 roubles from the Tsar, and later to Holland, in order to raise military aid. In 1654, under the terms of an Anglo-French treaty, Colepeper was expelled from France and apparently spent the rest of his exile in Flanders, separated from the King and his other advisers.

Clarendon, often opposed to Colepeper in council, generally praises his colleague, crediting him with an unusual piece of political foresight. On Cromwell's death in 1658, Colepeper wrote a letter advising the Royalists to bide their time and capitalize on dissension among their opponents. General Monck, he said, was the man who would help them most. In 1660, Monck did indeed play his part. The Restoration was effected and Colepeper accompanied the King home to England. He survived for only a few more weeks, however, dying on 11 June 1660.

Edward Hyde, Earl of Clarendon, *History of the Rebellion and Civil Wars in England*, ed. W. Dunn Macray (6 vols.; 1888).

Compton, Henry (1632–1713), Bishop of London and strongest clerical opponent of James II.

Henry Compton was born at Compton Wynyates, Warwickshire, the younger son of Spencer Compton, 2nd Earl of Northampton. His family was strongly Royalist in sympathy and his father was killed fighting for the King at Hopton Heath (1643). Compton was educated at Queen's College, Oxford, and thereafter travelled abroad. He may have served in the army in Flanders and in 1660 was commissioned as a cornet in the Royal Horse Guards. Compton

apparently retained an enthusiasm for military affairs and James II later complained that he was 'more like a colonel than a Bishop'.

In 1666 Compton was ordained, and gained rapid promotion in the church, partly because of his aristocratic background and partly because of his friendship with Danby (see Osborne, Thomas). He became Bishop of Oxford in 1674 and of London in 1675. He was responsible for the spiritual education of the Duke of York's daughters Mary (see Mary II) and Anne (q.v.), and exercised an influence over them. He confirmed and married them both, and did his best to instil them with his own vigorous Protestantism.

Compton became a privy councillor in 1676 but was disappointed in his hopes of appointment to the see of Canterbury by the opposition of James the following year. He opposed the idea of preventing the legal succession to the throne on religious grounds, but when James came to the throne in 1685 Compton was soon in opposition to the King's catholicizing policies. He spoke in the House of Lords against the King's claim that he could dispense with the Test Act by royal prerogative and was consequently dismissed from the privy council. In 1686 he was suspended from his see for refusing to discipline John Sharp, rector of St. Giles-in-the-Fields, whose anti-papal sermons had offended James. In 1687 Compton was in touch with William of Orange's agent, Dykveld, and in 1688 strongly supported the seven bishops who petitioned the King against his Declaration of Indulgence. He was the only ecclesiastic to sign the invitation to William of Orange later that year.

Compton played a prominent part during the crisis of James's abdication. He escorted the Princess Anne from

London at the head of an escort of 200 volunteers and later marched as the colonel of a regiment to Oxford. He apparently experienced no crisis of conscience, such as Sancroft (q.v.) felt, during the debates over the oaths of allegiance to be taken to William; he declared that 'there was not nor could be made an oath to the present government that he would not take'. Compton was reinstated to his see at the end of 1688 and welcomed William to London. He voted for declaring the throne to be vacant in 1689, and was reinstated as a privy councillor and dean of the Chapel Royal.

In April 1689 Compton crowned William and Mary and acted as primate during Sancroft's suspension. He had hopes of being promoted to Canterbury and was bitterly disappointed when John Tillotson was preferred to him in 1691. He was further embittered when he was again passed over in 1695. In the early years of William's reign, Compton supported toleration, but his opinions narrowed as he grew older. In Anne's reign he opposed the idea of occasional conformity, thereby declaring himself in support of Tory policy and against continued toleration. In a sense, Compton's career was an anticlimax after his part in the revolution of 1688. He was a man of action rather than a scholar, and Burnet (q.v.) writes that 'His preaching ... was without much life or learning.' He was always ambitious, and his personal disappointments were capable of influencing his political decisions. Yet his Protestant zeal was genuine and his opposition to James reflected a real concern for the future of Anglicanism.

Compton was also a keen botanist and made an important collection of rare plants, mostly from North America, in the gardens of Fulham Palace. He died there on 7 July 1713.

E. F. Carpenter, *The Protestant Bishop* (1957).

Portrait: oil, half-length, by Kneller, *c*. 1700: N.P.G.

Congreve, William (1670–1729), playwright.

Congreve was born at Bardsey, near Leeds, on 24 January 1670, son of a well-to-do army officer. In 1674 Congreve's father was appointed commandant of the army camp at Youghal in Ireland, and his son was sent to Ireland's best school, Kilkenny, where he began a lifelong friendship with Jonathan Swift (see *Lives of the Georgian Age*), who was two years his senior. In 1686 Congreve followed Swift to Trinity College, Dublin, where the two young men were both tutored by the brilliant St. George Ashe. Meanwhile, the Congreve family in 1688 moved back to their ancestral home, at Stretton in Staffordshire, and in 1690 William's father became land agent to the Earl of Cork.

In 1691 William began to study law at the Middle Temple, but found he could not take it seriously, preferring to write

instead. The following year, under the nom de plume of Cleophil, he published *Incognita*, a rather juvenile parody of fashionable romances, written, so he claimed, 'in the idler hours of a fortnight's time'. Surprisingly, this slight work attracted the attention of Dryden (q.v.), who in 1693 invited Congreve to help him translate some satires of Juvenal and Persius.

In the same year Drury Lane Theatre produced Congreve's first comedy, *The Old Bachelor*, written as early as 1690 to while away a long convalescence. Even during rehearsals, the play's excellence had led the enthusiastic theatre manager to grant Congreve 'privilege of the house'. The public were no less impressed: *The Old Bachelor* ran for a whole fortnight, unusual in those days, and Dryden pronounced it the best first play he had ever seen. However, he made one reservation, that it still needed 'the fashionable Cutt of the Town', and to modern taste its repartee seems somewhat childish in its perpetual search for epigram. Soon after, in November 1693, *The Double Dealer* was staged. Apparently the ladies found this scandalous, until Queen Mary went to see it and approved it. It is a much better play than *The Old Bachelor*, but was far less popular. This may have been because Congreve, in experimental mood, attempted to mix a vein of fantastic satire with his usual straightforward comic realism. But he was temperamentally unsuited to heavy irony, shying away from the portrayal of 'fools so gross, that . . . they should rather disturb than divert'.

In 1695 a group of actors led by Betterton (q.v.) broke away from the Drury Lane company and were given permission to open a new theatre in Lincoln's Inn Fields. Congreve was offered a share in the takings if he be-

came one of its managers, and so it was that the new company's first production, in April of that year, was his *Love for Love*. Congreve here displays an unusual sensitivity to the plight of his individual characters, particularly when the lovers voice their fears that disillusion might set in after their initial infatuation. Such writing went deeper than the customary cynicism of Restoration drama, which was normally written for a resolutely anti-Puritan audience of courtiers and concentrated to a claustrophobic extent on the complex amatory adventures of the fashionable world, peopling it with fanatics, fools, wits, and Frenchified fops.

Love for Love was so enormously popular that Dryden wrote a poem comparing its author with Shakespeare. Congreve himself, flushed with success, rashly promised to write a play a year for the Lincoln's Inn company. He also began to diversify, by writing an essay on dramatic theory, *Letter concerning Humour in Comedy*, and various 'public' poems, including an elegy on Queen Mary and a celebration of the victory at Namur. Charles Montagu (q.v.) secured for him a useful government sinecure, one of the commissionerships for hackney coaches, which added £100 a year to Congreve's already considerable income.

Despite his promise, Congreve's next play did not appear until 1697, *The Mourning Bride*. This was a tragedy, a genre untypical of Congreve, and though its improbable plot has been justly criticized, the play shows considerable poetic force. *The Mourning Bride* ran for a respectable thirteen days and probably saved the Lincoln's Inn company from bankruptcy. But Congreve's reputation soon came under attack; in 1698 Jeremy Collier published his *Short View of the Immorality and Profaneness of the English*

Stage, which, along with numerous wild assertions, made some shrewd observations on the mindless cynicism of much contemporary drama. Though not contentious by nature, Congreve was persuaded to issue his ineffectual *Amendments of Mr. Collier's False and Imperfect Citations*. It was immediately obvious to all that Collier had got the better of him.

Accordingly, when Congreve's *Way of the World* was produced in 1700 with a brilliant cast, he is said to have told the audience not to bother to disapprove of it, since it was to be his last play. It is also his masterpiece, asserting the value of true and mutual affection in the face of the prevailing opinion that 'love' was either gratification of lust or the war between the sexes. But the public did not like *The Way of the World*'s artificial plot, so Congreve all but deserted the theatre, leaving it to the rising star of Vanbrugh (q.v.). However, in 1704 he completed *Squire Trelooby*, a free translation of Molière's *Monsieur de Porceaugnac*, and in 1710 wrote the libretto for the mediocre opera *Semele*.

The disillusioned Congreve spent the remainder of his life in cultural leisure. He was a rich man, thanks to the royalties from his plays and his facility for getting official sinecures; in 1705 he was made commissioner for wines, a job which Swift's intervention allowed him to retain through the 1710 change of government, and in 1714 Congreve not only became an undersearcher of customs, at £600 a year, but also secretary for Jamaica, at £700. He continued to write verse, including slight but polished love lyrics and respectably scholarly translations from the classics. In 1710 he issued a sumptuous three-volume edition of his complete works, poetic and dramatic.

There was a streak of the libertine in Congreve. He carried on a long-lasting and much-discussed affair with the actress Mrs. Bracegirdle, who played the leading lady in most of his productions. She was replaced as Congreve's mistress by no less than the 2nd Duchess of Marlborough, who had a daughter by him, Lady Mary Godolphin, later Duchess of Leeds. In 1726 Congreve's lifelong overindulgence brought on an attack of stomach gout that nearly killed him, adding point to Swift's remark that his friend had 'squandered away a very good constitution in his younger days'.

In 1728 Congreve, in company with Gay and the Duchess of Marlborough, went to Bath to take the waters, but an accident involving an overturned carriage caused him such serious internal injuries that he had to be rushed back to London. He died in his house in the Strand on 19 January 1729, and was buried with great state in Westminster Abbey. The distraught duchess erected a huge monument to him, providing the epitaph herself. When Congreve's will was read, it was found he had left £10,000 to the Duchess of Marlborough and only £200 to Mrs. Bracegirdle.

Montague Summers (ed.), *The Complete Works of William Congreve* (4 vols.; 1923).

Bonamy Dobrée (ed.), *William Congreve* (World's Classics, 2 vols.; 1925–29).

John C. Hodges, *William Congreve, the Man* (New York, 1941).

Kathleen M. Lynch, *A Congreve Gallery* (Cambridge, Mass., 1951).

Portraits: oil, half-length, studio of Kneller, *c*. 1709: N.P.G.; oil, half-length, by Kneller, 1709: N.P.G.

Cooper, Anthony Ashley (1621–83),

1st Baron Ashley of Wimborne and 1st Earl of Shaftesbury, statesman.

He was born on 22 July 1621 at Wimborne St. Giles, the eldest son of Sir John Cooper and Anne, daughter of Sir Anthony Ashley, and educated at Exeter College, Oxford, and Lincoln's Inn.

Cooper was one of the greatest politicians of the late 17th century in England and was virtual founder of the Whig party. Learned and unscrupulous, he was a brilliant organizer, tactician, and demagogue. Although he switched allegiance often, he consistently supported the principles of toleration and moderation until the last decade of his life, when his overriding goal became the reduction of court power and the passage of authority into the hands of the propertied classes as represented in Parliament. It was around this theme that he fought the battles to exclude James from the throne.

Cooper was orphaned at ten, inheriting vast estates that lay chiefly in the West Country. He became a royal ward, suffering a variety of guardians and tutors. As a student he showed great aptitude and displayed a capacity for leadership. Although he was under age, he was returned to both the Short and Long Parliaments of 1640, but since his election to the latter was disputed, he was not seated in that assembly.

In 1643 Cooper joined the King's forces and served in the West Country, where he received several offices. However, in January 1644 he surrendered these posts and in the next month joined the Parliamentarians, in the belief, as he later stated, that Charles sought the destruction of both religion and the state. It is at least possible, however, that Cooper realized that the King's cause was doomed and his change of allegiance may be attributed to self-interest. Cooper fought against the King until April 1646, when he became militarily inactive, for in the dividing Parliamentary camp he took the side of the political Presbyterians in opposition to the New Model Army.

Cooper retired into local affairs, until the wars were over. He re-emerged with the Barebones Parliament to play a role in Cromwellian England as a spokesman for moderation and rule by Parliament. At first a member of the Council of State and an ally of Cromwell, he went into opposition in 1654, when the Lord Protector began to adopt a more personal and dictatorial form of rule. By 1659 he was suspected of working for the restoration of Charles II, probably without grounds. He was, however, definitely corresponding with Monck (q.v.) and he helped to restore the Rump Parliament in 1660, which finally recognized his claim to the seat he had won twenty years earlier. In that body Cooper promoted the readmittance of the purged members and the restoration of the monarchy.

Charles pardoned Cooper for his past actions against the crown, appointed him to the Privy Council, and in April 1661 created him Baron Ashley of Wimborne St. Giles. He earned these rewards by consistently supporting Royalist policies in Parliament, where he spoke and voted for moderation in religious matters and leniency towards former rebels. In 1662 he backed Charles's Declaration of Indulgence, which granted more religious toleration.

Cooper, now Baron Ashley, received his first ministerial post in May 1661, when he became chancellor of the exchequer, a post he ably filled. He was interested in commercial and colonial affairs and became one of the proprietaries of Carolina in 1663; at this time he gravitated naturally into the circle of young politicians who opposed Clarendon (see Hyde, Edward). His trading interests drew him into the anti-Dutch camp, and during the Second Anglo-Dutch War he became treasurer of prizes. When the Treasury was put into commission in 1667, he soon became one of its dominant members. He was a member of the group of advisers employed by Charles II known as the Cabal, after its members' initials. As a Protestant, Ashley was not admitted to the negotiations with Louis XIV that culminated in the secret Treaty of Dover (1670), with its clauses for restoring Catholicism in England; however, like Buckingham, he was duped into participating in the staged meetings at which a dummy treaty was produced that only joined France and England in an offensive alliance against the Netherlands. His consistent support for toleration guaranteed that he would back Charles's second Declaration of Indulgence (March 1672), which he justified on the grounds that the King possessed a dispensing power and could suspend statutes between sessions of Parliament.

Charles rewarded his Cabal, creating Ashley Earl of Shaftesbury in April, president of the council of trade and plantations in September, and lord chancellor in November 1672; Shaftesbury had already demonstrated his interest in law reform while on Cromwell's Council of State. As his secretary he appointed John Locke (q.v.), who had drawn up an aristocratic constitution for Carolina at his behest in 1669.

As chancellor, Shaftesbury issued writs for elections to fill thirty-six vacant seats in the Commons, an action immediately challenged when Parliament met in February, 1673, the result being that the right of the speaker to perform this task was re-established. This did not bode well for the ministry; indeed, Parliament was highly resentful of its conduct in the preceding year and suspicious of Charles's religious designs. Despite a brilliant speech defending toleration, the war with the Dutch, and other government measures, Shaftesbury saw that he too was in danger of impeachment as the Cabal crumbled around him. It was about this time that he began to suspect that Charles and Louis had plans to recatholicize England. Already in 1670 he had become worried about the Catholic and absolutist tendencies of the heir presumptive, the Duke of York (see James II). Accordingly, Shaftesbury supported the Test Act in 1673, although it spelled the end of his hopes of toleration. He began to encourage the enemies of Lauderdale in Scotland and opposed the second marriage of the Duke of York. In November Charles dismissed him from the chancellorship, and Shaftesbury went into opposition.

From this time onwards, he threw all his energies into attacks on the government and its dangerous leanings towards arbitrary rule. He was dismissed from the Privy Council and other offices as he swiftly rose to primacy in the opposition ranks. He fought the Nonresisting Bill, introduced by Danby (see Osborne, Thomas) in 1675, with brilliance and effect; this measure would have muzzled

opposition to the ministry and all prospect of change. Although he generally
took an anti-Catholic line, he did not
hesitate to ally himself with the Duke of
York in seeking a new parliament.

When, after a fifteen-month recess,
Parliament reassembled in February
1677, Shaftesbury argued that a prorogation of more than a year had the
force of a dissolution. This device won
him a term in the Tower along with
Buckingham and his other allies. He was
forced to make a complete submission
to gain freedom after a year's imprisonment, which he spent largely reading
and conspiring against Danby with the
French agents.

Although Shaftesbury did not origin-
ate the Popish Plot – the supposed conspiracy of Catholics to murder the king
and take over the country (see Oates,
Titus) he nevertheless quickly realized its
potential. When Parliament reassembled
in the autumn of 1678 he was quick to
exploit anti-Catholic feeling against his
personal enemies. By December, the
power of Danby was extinguished, and
in January Charles finally dissolved the
Cavalier Parliament.

When the new Parliament met in
March, Shaftesbury was the leading
figure in the Green Ribbon Club, a
formidable anti-Catholic organization
that eventually developed into the first
Whig Party. Charles first attempted
conciliation, and in April 1679 he
adopted the plan of Sir William Temple
(q.v.) for a powerful, expanded privy
council that would include the opposition leaders. But he did not follow the
council's advice, and Shaftesbury continued as opposition leader while serving
as lord president. The introduction of
the first Exclusion Bill, designed to
remove the Duke of York from the
succession to the throne, was backed by
Shaftesbury. In reply, Charles dissolved

Parliament. In the council, Shaftesbury
gave strong support to the Duke of
Monmouth (q.v.), Charles's Protestant
but bastard son, and obtained for him the
command against the Scots rebels.
Charles, disturbed by this increasing
opposition, then negotiated a money
treaty with France and in October felt
strong enough to dismiss Shaftesbury
from office.

Once again without office, the earl
promoted nationwide petitioning for a
new Parliament. London became his
bastion and when in 1680 Charles fell ill
Shaftesbury aroused the City in case the
King were to die and the Duke of York
claim the throne. In the subsequent
elections and parliaments, his party base
grew ever stronger, but he could not
win the necessary support for his Exclusion Bills in the Lords. To the
Oxford parliament of 1681, Shaftesbury
and the Whigs came with high expectations. But Charles had by now
negotiated further subsidies from Louis
XIV to give him the independence he
sought; he dissolved Parliament in
March and Shaftesbury's power began
to evaporate.

Popular support for the Whig cause
dwindled to such an extent that in July
Shaftesbury could with impunity be
arrested and sent to the Tower on a
trumped-up charge of treason. He petitioned the King for his release, promising
to retire to his lands in Carolina, but
Charles persisted in the prosecution.
However, when the government presented its case in November, the grand
jury of Middlesex, picked by Whig
sheriffs, rejected the indictment. London
rejoiced, while Dryden (q.v.) published
his great mock epic, *Absalom and Achitophel*, in which he characterized the fallen
earl as the tempter Achitophel, scheming
adviser to the King's son Absalom
(Monmouth).

The royal reaction proceeded as Charles purged the magistracies and stripped the corporations of their charters. London acquired Tory sheriffs, and Shaftesbury went into hiding. He entered into conspiracies aimed at a rising, but in November 1682 fled to Holland. He died in Amsterdam on 21 January 1683, and was buried at Wimborne St. Giles.

L. F. Brown, *The First Earl of Shaftesbury* (New York, 1933).
K. H. D. Haley, *The First Earl of Shaftesbury* (1968).
J. R. Jones, *The First Whigs* (1961).
M. Lee, *The Cabal* (Urbana, Ill., 1965).

Portrait: oil, three-quarter length, after J. Greenhill, *c.* 1672–73: N.P.G.

Cooper, Samuel (1609–72), miniaturist.

Few details are known of the artist's early life. Together with his brother Alexander, who later worked mainly on the Continent, he learnt the art of limning (the 17th century word for painting in miniature) under his uncle John Hoskins (q.v.); in 1634 they parted, probably owing to Hoskins's jealousy of his nephew's increasing success and popularity.

Before settling in London in a fashionable part of Covent Garden around 1642 Cooper had travelled widely in France and Holland. He was an able linguist and musician, noted for his skill in playing the lute, and among his acquaintances were many of the most distinguished personalities of his time. Samuel Pepys has recorded meeting Cooper and being so impressed by his work that he resolved immediately to commission a portrait of his wife; the portrait cost him £30, plus another £8 for its case.

Cooper was one of the first painters to treat the miniature as a true oil painting rather than as a mere drawing or ornamental pendant. The influence of Van Dyck is seen in his use of rich colours, and an especial characteristic of Cooper's painting is his use of exaggerated lighting: by using candlelight projected from above he was able to define the distinctive features of his sitter's face with absolute clarity. Most of his miniatures are only about two inches high, and his larger portraits of Charles II and the 1st Earl of Shaftesbury are rare exceptions.

In 1663 Cooper was appointed 'His Majesty's Lymner' to Charles II. His work was praised by John Evelyn and John Aubrey, and his portrait of Oliver Cromwell is justly famous. Cooper died in London on 5 May 1672, his prosperity and popularity having steadily increased throughout his career.

Portrait: wash, half-length, after a self-portrait: N.P.G.

Cork, 1st Earl of (1566–1643), see Boyle, Richard.

Cottington, Francis (?1578–1652), Baron Cottington, lord treasurer and ambassador, who supported Roman Catholicism and favoured friendly relations with Spain during the political conflicts that preceded the Civil War.

Born in 1578 or 1579, the fourth son of Philip Cottington of Godmonston in Somerset. Cottington's early advancement was through the diplomat, Sir Edward Stafford, who was, according to Clarendon, a relative of his. Stafford introduced him to Sir Charles Cornwallis, whom he attended on his embassy to Spain from 1605 to 1609.

After Cornwallis's recall to England in 1609, Cottington acted as English agent in Spain. Three years later he was appointed English consul in Seville. In 1613 he returned to England and was made clerk of the council in September of that year. His return approximately coincided with the arrival of the Spanish ambassador to England, Diego Sarmiento, later Count of Gondomar, with whom he became very friendly. Together they helped to foster James I's keenness on a Spanish marriage for Prince Charles, and in 1616 Cottington was sent as English ambassador to Madrid.

In 1618, as the Thirty Years War began to inflame continental Europe, Cottington passed on James's unsuccessful proposal of mediation to the Spanish government in its dispute with Frederick V, the Elector Palatine. In the same year he returned home, subsequently becoming secretary to the Prince of Wales. He still supported the marriage with the Infanta Maria, but he felt that Charles's journey to Madrid would raise more problems than it would solve. Thus he opposed it, but in 1623 he was nevertheless chosen as one of the prince's suite and travelled with him to Spain. While there, Cottington, who had cherished Catholic leanings for years, now received communion in the Roman faith. His opposition to the original expedition and his persistence in a pro-Hispanic attitude after its failure infuriated the royal favourite, Buckingham (see Villiers, George, 1st Duke), and when Charles succeeded to the throne in 1625 Buckingham's animosity kept Cottington out of favour.

It was only after Buckingham's assassination in August 1628 that Cottington was again able to return to court. In November he became a privy councillor and in March 1629 he was made chancellor of the exchequer. He concluded peace with Spain and upon his return to England in July 1631 he was created Baron Cottington of Hanworth.

Throughout the period of Charles I's absolute government Cottington maintained the chancellorship of the exchequer, and together with Queen Henrietta Maria and others he formed the nucleus of a powerful Roman Catholic lobby in Charles's council. In 1635 he and William Laud (q.v.) were appointed commissioners for the Treasury; in the same year he also became master of the court of wards and the fines and exactions levied by him in this capacity exacerbated the political situation.

In the treasury, Cottington and Laud became rivals and Laud succeeded in keeping his opponent out of the post of lord treasurer. But Cottington was not completely excluded from public life; he sat on committees in connection with foreign policy and Scottish and Irish affairs. He was appointed to the Scottish committee in July 1638 and supported the war of the following year, though as chancellor of the exchequer he knew there was no money for it. When the Short Parliament was dissolved in May 1640 without granting supplies, to supplement the continued levy of ship money he tried to raise funds in the City and had to resort to speculating in pepper. He also fortified the Tower in his capacity as constable.

Fearing the mounting opposition of Parliament against him, Cottington resigned from the court of wards in May 1641 and handed back the chancellorship of the exchequer, to be succeeded in this post by Colepeper (q.v.). He joined Charles at Oxford in 1643 and took part in the parliament there. In 1646 he signed the declaration of the surrender of Oxford and was allowed to leave the country. He joined the Prince of Wales at The Hague in 1648 and in the following year he went with Edward Hyde (q.v.) to Spain to raise money for the Royalists. The reception of the commission was cool. Cottington's influence had by now diminished, and no funds were forthcoming. On the failure of the embassy, Cottington decided to stay in Spain. He died shortly afterwards on 19 June 1652, at his residence at Valladolid.

Martin J. Havian, *Caroline Courtier, The Life of Lord Cottington* (1973).

Portrait: oil, quarter-length, by unknown artist, 1634: N.P.G.

Cotton, Charles (1630–87), poet and translator.

Born at Beresford, Staffordshire, on 28 April 1630, only child of Charles Cotton, owner of large estates in Derbyshire and Staffordshire and friend of Donne, Jonson, Herrick, and Walton. Cotton was tutored by Ralph Rawson, Fellow of Brasenose College, Oxford, but probably was not a member of the university. However, he read widely in both classical and modern European literature and, thanks to his family's wealth, travelled in France and Italy. He soon decided to devote himself to writing and in 1649, in company with Dryden, contributed a poem to a memorial volume for Lord Hastings.

Despite his bitter riposte to Waller's eulogy of Cromwell (1654), Cotton did not suffer for his Royalist views. In 1656 he married his cousin Isabella, sister of Colonel Hutchinson. Cotton's father died in 1658, leaving the estate seriously in debt, and in 1665 his son was obliged to sell off large portions of it.

In 1664 Cotton published *Scarronides*, a burlesque of Book I of Virgil's *Aeneid* and the first English example of the classical parodies made fashionable by the French writer Scarron. This barren book, depending on such questionable humour as making Aeneas row the distance "twixt Parson's Dock and Billingsgate', was nevertheless so popular with readers who had been 'lashed into Latin by the stinging rod' that it went

through six editions in Cotton's lifetime. Its coarseness is said to have lost its author a large legacy promised to him by a wealthy kinswoman.

Cotton now translated many worthier French authors, including Corneille, in a style whose colloquial vocabulary makes them read like originals. Increasingly troubled by debt-collectors, he ill-advisedly became an army officer. He was posted to Ireland, nearly drowned en route, and on arrival suffered grievously from being unable to indulge his passion for angling. In between 'drinking good ale' to console himself, he amusingly retold his experiences in *A Voyage to Ireland in Burlesque* (1670).

Cotton's raffish tastes led to his being credited with writing the anonymous *Compleat Gamester* (1674), an unstylish but informative handbook. He was equally a conscientious country gentleman, and his *Planter's Manual* contains commonsense advice on growing fruit trees.

In 1670 Cotton's wife Isabella died, having borne him three sons and five daughters, and in 1675 he married Mary Russell, a well-connected widow with £1,500 a year. Even this was insufficient for Cotton's enormous debts, and he was again obliged to sell some land.

Cotton had always been devoted to the aged Izaak Walton (q.v.), 'the best friend I now or ever knew', and in 1674 he had adorned his newly-built fishing house on the Dove in Derbyshire with a device consisting of his and Walton's monograms intertwined. During ten days in 1676 he wrote a second part to Walton's *Compleat Angler*, dealing with fly-fishing.

Throughout his life Cotton wrote poetry, which was only published posthumously, in 1689, and was long neglected. The unsophisticated freshness of such descriptive poems as *The Wonders of the Peak* (1681) greatly impressed Wordsworth, while Cotton's love poems recall both Herrick and Burns in their directness and their alternation between gloom and gaiety. He liked to begin abruptly, Cavalier fashion:

'Pish! 'tis an idle fond excuse.'

He also had a fantastic strain, best seen in the Rabelaisian *Greater Eater of Gray's Inn*.

Cotton's last major work was a translation of Montaigne's essays (1685) which, though falling short of Florio's version for sheer exuberance, is nevertheless valuable for its lucidity and fidelity. This cheerful man, who according to Lamb 'smacked of the rough magnanimity of the old English vein', died of a fever on 16 February 1687.

J. Beresford (ed.), *Poems* (1923).
J. Buxton (ed.), *Poems* (Muses' Library; 1958).
G. G. P. Heywood, *Cotton and his River* (1928).
E. M. Turner, 'Cotton's Poems', *Times Library Supplement* (29 January 1938).
T. Westwood, *The Chronicle of the 'Compleat Angler' of Izaak Walton and Charles Cotton* (1864).

Courten or Curteene, Sir William

(1572–1636), merchant and creditor of James I and Charles I. Courten was the son of a Protestant tailor who had fled from persecution by the Spaniards to England from Menin in Flanders in 1568.

Courten was born in 1572 and his brother Peter was born in 1581. The family first made French hoods in Abchurch Lane, London, and then traded in silk and linen in Pudding Lane. With his brother Peter and an English relation, the merchant John Moncy, Courten set up a partnership in 1606 to expand the linen and silk business. Courten had then returned from Haarlem, where he had worked from an early age in his father's firm and had married the deaf and dumb daughter of a rich Dutch merchant, who brought him £60,000 as a dowry.

The firm of Courten & Moncy expanded and flourished, and by 1631 their capital was estimated at £150,000, despite the fact that the Star Chamber had levied huge fines against Courten and other foreign merchants for exporting gold. Both brothers were knighted as a result of their prominence in the City of London's financial life, William on 31 May 1622, and Peter on 22 February 1623.

Courten's business dealings led him to build ships and trade far afield – in Guinea, Portugal, Spain, and the West Indies. Sometime around 1624 one of his ships discovered an island which Courten named Barbadoes, and in the next year he petitioned for a grant to all the unknown land in the southern part of the world, which he called 'Terra Australis Incognita'. He did receive letters patent for colonization of Barbados, which he proceeded with on a huge scale, but James Hay, Earl of Carlisle, disputed his claim, and Courten is said to have lost about £44,000 after Carlisle's authority was secured.

Courten, in association with a certain Sir Paul Pindar, lent money to both James I and Charles I – sums which eventually totalled around £200,000. They failed to obtain any consideration in respect of the loans, and litigation was resorted to by both Courten and his descendants.

Although rich and successful, Courten sustained major losses in the East Indies as a result of Dutch interference. At his brother's death a nephew seized all the firm's property in Holland and legal suits, carried on by Courten's heirs, were brought to regain the property.

Courten bought lands in Northamptonshire from the crown, which yielded £6,500 per annum, and continued to pursue a vigorous policy of maritime enterprise. His ships traded with the East Indies again, and he even sent two ships towards China, but they were lost, and the shock proved fatal to Courten. He was buried in the Church of St. Andrew Hubbard after his death in late May or early June 1636, with his claims against Carlisle and the crown unsettled. Seven years later the Courten estates were declared bankrupt, and despite many petitions to Parliament the greater part of Sir William Courten's wealth never reached his descendants.

Cowley, Abraham (1618–67), poet. The son of a London stationer of means, Cowley was educated at Westminster School, where he was a King's scholar, and at Trinity College, Cambridge, where he took his B.A. in 1639, was made a minor fellow in 1640, and became an M.A. in 1643. In 1641 he was ejected from Cambridge because of the Civil War and went first to Oxford and then, in 1646, as cipher-secretary to Queen Henrietta Maria in Paris, where he was employed on diplomatic missions. On his return to England in 1655, he acted as a Royalist spy and was arrested and interrogated by Cromwell. He was, however, released on bail, but remained under suspicion from both sides. He then went to study medicine at Oxford, where he received his M.D. in 1657.

After the Restoration in 1660, he did not receive the mastership of the Savoy as he had expected, but, instead, through the patronage of the Earl of St. Albans and the Duke of Buckingham, he received a grant of the manor of Oldcourt (Nethercot). He retired to the country, where he remained for the rest of his life.

Cowley was considered during his lifetime to be the greatest poet of his age. Milton, who was then himself overshadowed by Cowley, considered him among the three greatest English poets, the other two being Spenser and Shakespeare.

His high reputation, however, did not long outlive him. Pope, who really owed much to him, condemned him thus:

Who now reads Cowley? If he pleases yet
His moral pleases, not his pointed wit.

Cowley was first and foremost an intellectual, passionately interested in the scientific discoveries of his time; he was a founder member of the Royal Society and a friend of Hobbes. His poetry is full of learned allusions and witticisms, but it often lacks passion. Perhaps his greatest achievement was his extreme versatility; he wrote in so many different forms. His most important work is contained in *The Mistress* (1647) and the 1656 volume of *Poems* (for which he wrote a critical preface), the *Miscellanies*, the *Pindaric Odes*, and the *Davideis*.

Cowley introduced the Pindaric ode into English, which, with its irregular verses and irregular rhymes, permitted a greater freedom than heroic couplets and was copied later by Dryden. Cowley's own efforts were not very successful and are really only still readable for their occasional flashes of wit. Like many other poets of his time, Cowley wanted to emulate the great classical epics, a desire which resulted in *Davideis*, intended to have twelve cantos but ending with the fourth.

With his skill in versification, his knowledge and use of the classical tradition, and his rational approach, Cowley forms a part of the English tradition that descends from Ben Jonson through Dryden to the 18th century; today, however, his *Essays* are perhaps more widely read than his verse. He died

97

on a visit to Chertsey, on 28 July 1667, and was buried with great pomp beside Spenser and Chaucer in Westminster Abbey.

A. Grossart (ed.), *The Complete Works in Verse and Prose of Abraham Cowley* (1881).

A. R. Waller (ed.), *The English Writings of Abraham Cowley* (2 vols.; 1905–06).

R. B. Hinman, *Abraham Cowley's World of Order* (Cambridge, Mass., 1960).

Jean Loiseau, *Abraham Cowley: sa vie, son oeuvre* (Paris, 1931).

Arthur H. Nethercot, *Abraham Cowley: the Muses' Hannibal* (1931).

G. Walton, *Metaphysical to Augustan* (1955).

Portraits: oil, half-length, by Lely, *c.* 1600: N.P.G.; oil, three-quarter length, by Lely, 1666–67: N.P.G.

Cranfield, Lionel (1575–1645), 1st Earl of Middlesex and lord treasurer under James I.

Cranfield was born in 1575 of obscure parentage and baptized on 13 March. As a young man, he became apprenticed to Richard Shepherd, a merchant adventurer of London, and soon joined the Company of Mercers, whom he represented before the Privy Council.

Cranfield was an astute and successful merchant and financier, making his mark in the expanding trading world of London, which in 1600 was handling over sixty per cent of England's commerce. His abilities were such that he eventually came to the attention of Henry Howard, Earl of Northampton, who extended to him his patronage and introduced him to King James I. In 1613, Cranfield received a knighthood and was appointed surveyor general of customs.

Northampton's death in 1614 left Cranfield with no influential friend at court. For two years he contented himself with serving the Privy Council in an advisory capacity. In 1616, however, he came into contact with James's new favourite, George Villiers (see Villiers, George, 1st Duke of Buckingham). With this new patron, Cranfield's advancement progressed apace. In 1616 he was made a master of requests; in 1618 he became keeper of the great wardrobe; a year later, he was made master of the court of wards and liveries and chief commissioner of the navy; and in 1620 he was appointed as a member of the Privy Council. In all these positions Cranfield used his skill as a businessman and economist to check wastefulness. The reforms that he instituted to this end, especially in the royal household, the exchequer, and the navy, were not unpopular and no doubt did much to impress James.

Cranfield was returned as Member of Parliament for Arundel in 1621. His popularity with the King was matched by his popularity in the Commons. He was well thought of as a reformer and his generally good reputation recommended him as a valuable mediator between the sovereign and Parliament. James made him a baron in July 1621 and conferred upon him the office of lord high treasurer in October of the same year. In September 1622 he was awarded the first earldom of Middlesex.

As the King's chief financial minister, Cranfield's task was to try to economize in an age of inflation. Not only were prices rising in the everyday lives of ordinary men and women in Britain – there was, for example, a sixfold increase in the price of wheat between 1540 and 1640 – but there was also a general increase in the overheads of the royal government. It is a feature of the early Stuart kings that they were chronically short of money. They needed it not only for their own maintenance and that of their families but also for their court. Royal favourites and other hangers-on expected and got largess from the sovereign and this, together with the bribes they received from those who cherished their influence, made them extremely rich. The government also needed money for the costly business of war. James had tried to avoid war in his reign, having made peace with Spain in 1604. At the outbreak of the Thirty Years War he had preferred to try to intercede peacefully between Frederick and the Habsburgs. Yet he was a personally extravagant man and his lavish treatment of those prepared to take advantage of him depleted his resources. James tried to augment his revenue by several means, from the disastrous Cokayne Project (see Cokayne, Sir William) to the selling of crown lands. In the case of the latter, Cranfield had told him that 'in selling land he did not sell his rent . . . but sold his sovereignty, for it was a greater tie of obedience to be a tenant of the king than to be his subject.' The royal government viewed new industrial developments suspiciously. But they took the opportunity of trying to raise cash by selling monopolies on new manufacturing and refining processes. Far from advancing Britain's backward economy, the Stuarts with their conservative outlook simply wanted to fulfil their perpetual need for money.

Cranfield's business sense may well have advised him to try to capitalize expanding industries out of government funds; but such funds being unavailable, he inevitably had recourse to a policy of retrenchment. He imposed curbs on expenditure and firmly told the King that no grants were to be made nor money spent without his authority. James, however, was no longer in control and when his son and his favourite clamoured for war before a sympathetic Parliament in 1624, Cranfield's opposition to the scheme on financial grounds incurred great hostility. He was impeached by the House of Commons on charges of corruption, heavily fined and deprived of all his offices, and imprisoned in the Tower to await the King's pleasure. He was released after a few days and received a full pardon from Charles I soon after the new King's accession in 1625.

Now at the age of fifty, Cranfield went into retirement. He resumed his seat in the House of Lords in 1640, probably at the suggestion of Charles I, but at the outbreak of the Civil War he endeavoured to remain uninvolved and neutral. He died on 6 August 1645, aged seventy, and was buried at Westminster Abbey.

M. Prestwich, *Cranfield: Politics and Profits under the Early Stuarts* (1966).
R. H. Tawney, *Business and Politics under James I: Lionel Cranfield as Merchant and Minister* (1958).

Crashaw, Richard (?1613–1649), poet.

He was born in London, the son of William Crashaw, a Puritan divine, preacher, and poet. Orphaned as a child, Crashaw was educated at Charterhouse and entered Pembroke College, Cambridge, where he went as an exhibitioner in 1631 and where he was elected to the Greek Scholarship. A large number of the Latin verses in *Epigrammatum Sacrorum Liber* ('Book of Sacred Epigrams'), which he published in 1634, were probably written to satisfy the requirements of the scholarship. He was a fellow of Peterhouse from 1635 to 1643 and in 1639 was appointed curate of Little St. Mary's, the church adjacent to the college. At this time, Peterhouse was the seat of the Cambridge supporters of Archbishop Laud (q.v.). Crashaw was among them, as well as being deeply committed to other High Church principles. He consequently refused to accept the Solemn

League and Covenant when it was concluded in 1643 and left Cambridge to live in exile on the Continent. There he was received into the Roman Catholic Church in 1645. After some time spent in extreme hardship, he was introduced, apparently with the help of his friend Cowley (q.v.), to Henrietta Maria, as a result of which he was eventually given a position in the entourage of Cardinal Palotta of Rome. In 1649 he was appointed a subcanon at the Basilica of Our Lady of Loretto, where he died soon after his arrival.

Crashaw's reputation, like that of George Herbert (q.v.), to whom he is indebted, rests upon one book, a volume of intensely devotional religious verse. *The Steps to the Temple*, to which a section of secular poems, *Delights of the Muses*, was appended, was first published in 1646 and revised and expanded in 1648. A posthumous volume, *Carmen Deo Nostro* (1652), consists chiefly of poems from the earlier book. The extravagantly baroque style, with its rich imagery and often bizarre conceits, owes much to the influence of the Italian poet Giambattista Marino, whose religious poem *La strage degl' innocenti* ('The Massacre of the Innocents') Crashaw adapted. The extremes to which Crashaw developed the style can be illustrated in the famous description of the eyes of Mary Magdalene, in 'The Weeper':

> Two walking baths; two weeping
>   motions;
> Portable, & compendious oceans.

In other poems, however, such as the 'Hymn to the Name and Honour of the Admirable Saint Teresa', the spiritual fervour produces an ecstatic lyricism that is perfectly realized and uniquely Crashaw's.

L. C. Martin (ed.), *Poems English, Latin and Greek, of Richard Crashaw* (1927 and 1957).

G. W. Williams (ed.), *Complete Poetry* (Garden City, N.Y., 1970).
M. Praz, *Richard Crashaw* (Brescia, 1946).
M. Praz, *The Flaming Heart: Crashaw and the Baroque* (Garden City, N.Y., 1958).
A. Warren, *Crashaw: A Study in Baroque Sensibility* (Baton Rouge, Louisiana, 1939).

Crewe or Crew, Sir Randolph or Ranulph (1558–1646), M.P. and judge.

Sir Randolph was born a commoner, but became one of the most respected men in the legal profession in his time. He presided over many important trials, he was eloquent on the bench, and is said to have written one of the very few passages of fine English prose to be found in the Law Reports, a compliment indeed when one considers the dry legalistic language employed in these documents for centuries.

He was the second son of John Crewe, a tanner of Nantwich. The Crewe family was considered to be one of the most ancient families of England, and Sir Randolph's eloquence in several cases involving ancestry and the peerage suggest that he was not unaware of the fact. He was admitted as a member of Lincoln's Inn on 13 November 1577; on 8 November 1584, he was called to the bar. He became Member of Parliament for Brackley, Northamptonshire, in 1597, and in the same year engaged in his first recorded case before the Queen's Bench. In 1600 he was elected a Lincoln's Inn bencher, and in 1602 he was autumn reader. In 1604 the House of Commons asked him to state their objections to the new style of King of Great Britain adopted by James I.

Although his name does not appear in the list of official returns to Parliament after 1597, he was elected Speaker in April 1614. In June of the same year he was knighted. In July 1615 he took the degree of serjeant-at-law, and in 1616 he was a member of the commission which tried Weston for the murder of Sir Thomas Overbury (q.v.) and aided the prosecution of the Earl and Countess of Somerset (see Carr, Robert) as accessories before the fact in the same crime.

Crewe prosecuted numerous officials for corruption in connection with official duties, and he contributed materially to at least one important point in the law of impeachment. This occurred when the House of Commons impeached Edward Floyd for libelling the Princess Palatine and the Lords disputed the right of the Commons to impeach. Crewe settled the matter by establishing that a precedent in the reign of Henry IV supported the Lords' contention.

In 1624 he was appointed king's serjeant, and on 26 January 1625 he was made lord chief justice of the king's bench. Less than two years later, on 9 November 1626, he was removed because he refused to sign a document affirming that forced loans were legal. This was at a time when the taxation policies of James I and Charles I were hotly disputed, leading eventually to civil war and revolution. Although all of Sir Randolph's colleagues seem to have agreed with him in the matter of forced loans, he alone was punished. He tried to seek compensation first through the Duke of Buckingham and later from the King himself. It was not until the judges who had declared the payment of ship money legal, resulting in the test case against John Hampden (q.v.), were themselves impeached that the House of Lords petitioned the King to compensate Crewe.

Crewe spent the rest of his days in retirement at Crewe Hall, his estate at Barthomley, Cheshire, which he had purchased in 1608. During the Civil War, Crewe Hall was garrisoned for Parliament. A letter from Crewe describing his exasperation at what he called 'this plus quam civile bellum' is preserved in the British Museum (Add. MS 15857, f. 193). He died at Westminster in London on 3 January 1646, and was buried on his own estate.

William J. Jones, *Politics and the Bench: the Judges and the Origins of the English Civil War* (1971).

Cromwell, Oliver (1599–1658), Lord Protector of England.

Cromwell was born at Huntingdon on 25 April 1599, the second son of Robert Cromwell, a gentleman, and Elizabeth Steward. He was educated at the free school of Huntingdon and at Sidney Sussex College, Cambridge; both of these institutions were noted centres of Puritanism. After his father's death in 1617 he proceeded to London to acquire some knowledge of the law, as suited a country gentleman. In 1620 he married Elizabeth, the daughter of Sir James Bouchier, a London merchant. Cromwell then returned to Huntingdon to manage the small estate left by his

father. His fortunes were noticeably improved by inheritances he received in 1628 and in 1636, when he moved to Ely, the source of his new income.

In 1628 Cromwell was elected to the House of Commons, to sit for the borough of Huntingdon. His only recorded activity before Parliament was dissolved in 1629 was a speech in which he staunchly upheld Puritan preaching and attacked innovations that smacked of popery.

Back in Huntingdon he became involved in local affairs, supporting the poorer commoners against the aldermen. In 1636 he took the side of the fenmen against the Earl of Bedford and opposed the drainage of the fens. In these incidents the cause of the commoners was probably to the benefit of his own estates as well. In both issues he appears to have demonstrated his talents for organization.

But these were not the only developments affecting Cromwell during the long period of the King's attempted personal rule. Always a Calvinist, he seems to have gone through a period of religious turmoil, emerging with the firm conviction that he was one of the elect, chosen to be saved by God's grace. This absence of doubt as to his predestined fate was complemented further by the belief that he was guided by God Himself and was acting as His agent. Henceforth, he took each of his successes as a sign that he was fulfilling God's will. Not long after this 'conversion' Cromwell was elected to Parliament by the borough of Cambridge (1640), for which he sat both in the Short and Long Parliaments. His fervour on the side of Pym and Hampden was quickly noticed. He was active in committee and brought forward the petition for the release of John Lilburne (q.v.), the anti-prelatist pamphleteer.

This political activity was soon translated into military action when the King began raising an army in the north in 1642. Besides contributing money to the Parliamentary cause, Cromwell secured Cambridge from the outset, disarming the Royalists, capturing the castle, and preventing the college plate from being sent to the King. He raised a troop of cavalry, which was present at the latter part of the Battle of Edgehill (October 1642). Observing the great success of the cavaliers of Prince Rupert against the Parliamentary horse, he insisted to John Hampden that they needed godly men in well-disciplined units to stand against the Royalist gentlemen. In 1643, therefore, he proceeded to raise a double regiment of cavalry on these principles – his famous 'Ironsides' – a formidable force, as it proved itself in battles in the eastern counties and the Midlands in 1643 and 1644. Cromwell was subsequently appointed governor of Ely and chosen a member of the Committee of Both Kingdoms, which joined Parliament to the Scottish Covenanters. In 1644 he became second-in-command to the Earl of Manchester (see Montagu, Edward), the leading magnate in Huntingdonshire. In this capacity he led his regiment north to aid in the sieges of Lincoln and York. On Marston Moor in July 1644 he led the army's left wing to the first great Parliamentary victory of the war, scattering Rupert's cavaliers, but Manchester failed to follow up the success. Similar tardiness by the earl at the Battle of Newbury in October enraged Cromwell, who had already attacked the earl in Parliament for his slow and ineffective command.

Underlying this was a more serious conflict in the army between the Independents, who had begun to look to Cromwell for leadership, and the Presbyterians and their Scottish allies, who wished to tolerate no sectarians. As recently as September, Cromwell had obtained the passage through the Commons of a motion recognizing at least a minimum of toleration for Independents, greatly to the chagrin of the Scots. After Newbury, Cromwell attempted to remove Manchester from his command; in reply, the House of Lords and the Presbyterians attempted to bring Cromwell to trial. Withdrawing his charge, he pressed successfully instead for the establishment of a professional army. Essential to this 'New Model Army' was the Self-Denying Ordinance, by which the members of both Parliamentary chambers were forbidden to hold commissions. Manchester and the other generals had to resign their commands, but Cromwell's commission was specially extended by Parliament and he soon became lieutenant general to Parliament's new commander in chief, Sir Thomas Fairfax (q.v.).

On 14 June 1645, the New Model Army won the decisive victory of the war at Naseby near Leicester. For the next year, Fairfax and Cromwell mopped up the Royalist forces in the south and southwest, ending the First Civil War with the capture of Oxford in June 1646. Earlier that year Parliament had rewarded his services with estates worth £2,500 per annum from sequestrated Royalist lands. With no enemy in the field, the tensions on the Parliamentary side came to the fore. Charles, defeated but still King, was prisoner of the Scots, who were impatient for Parliament to fulfil its promise to impose a strict Presbyterianism in England. Parliament, however, was divided on how to reach a settlement with the King. The majority of the Commons wished to disband most of the army, although the soldiers' pay was in ar-

rears, and send the remainder to crush the Irish rebellion. But the army was dominated by Independents, who desired no Presbyterian settlement and showed increasing suspicion of Parliament and its Presbyterian leaders, such as Denzil Holles (q.v.). There were in addition significant numbers of extreme sectarians, republicans, and Levellers among the troops. Cromwell himself was greatly disturbed by Parliament's attempts to prevent non-Presbyterian worship and to disband the army without paying its arrears. The attempts that he made to bring about a compromise only aroused the fear and suspicion of both Parliament and the army, where radical sentiment was becoming more outspoken. With the situation at a deadlock in May 1647, Cromwell sided with the army. He left London in early June for army headquarters in Newmarket, shortly after an officer of Fairfax's guard had seized Charles and removed him to the army.

The Presbyterians began to arm in London. In August Fairfax and Cromwell moved the army to London and expelled Holles and his allies from the Commons. Meanwhile, a new Army council had been constituted, with two privates and two officers from each regiment sitting alongside the generals. Here Cromwell and his son-in-law Henry Ireton (q.v.) spoke in debates on a political settlement on behalf of those devoted to preserving the social structure. At the same time Cromwell conducted negotiations with Charles for a constitutional settlement.

Charles proved both intractable and devious. The Army grew suspicious of the negotiations with him, while the debate in the council, which moved to Putney in October, grew increasingly bitter. Cromwell's conservative position had grown untenable, when the King unexpectedly provided him with assist-ance – in November he escaped. Quickly recaptured, he was left out of the negotiations, for Cromwell now realized the uselessness of attempting to engage him in an agreement: Charles was in fact in communication both with his Cavaliers and with the Scots. Cromwell could re-establish his position within the army by promising reforms, and when the Royalists and the Scots, linked in the King's cause, began the Second Civil War in May 1648, the army's unity was further strengthened. At a prayer meet-ing at Windsor the officers resolved to bring Charles to trial once the conflict was over. Cromwell crushed the Royal-ists and dissident Parliamentarians before sweeping north to join Major General John Lambert (q.v.). Together they routed the northern Royalists and the Scots under the Duke of Hamilton in battles around Preston. In the south Fairfax triumphed over the Royalists at Colchester.

While the Army was away in the field, however, Holles returned to the Commons and the party hostile to the Army regained control of Parliament. They resumed negotiations with Charles, with a view to settling terms for his restoration. This greatly embittered both the radicals and the more conservative officers in all parts of the Army. They pressed for the punishment of those whom they deemed responsible for this second shedding of blood. Fairfax re-moved the King from Parliament's control. In December his army reached London and Colonel Thomas Pride (q.v.) carried out his famous purge of Parliament, excluding the members who had voted to negotiate with Charles. Shortly thereafter Cromwell arrived in London.

In what was left of the Commons, known as the 'Rump Parliament', he

was relatively quiet, but in the special court composed to try the King he played an active role, pressing for Charles's execution and whipping waverers into line against 'that man of blood', who he felt was responsible for the renewal of the war. Charles I was beheaded on 30 January 1649, following which Cromwell became president of the Council of State and resumed talks with the Levellers, who were pressing for widespread reforms. Although an agreement about reorganizing Parlia-ment was reached, it was rejected by John Lilburne, who denounced Crom-well and Ireton as 'juggling knaves'. He stirred up a mutiny in the Army, which Cromwell and Fairfax quickly crushed.

In March Parliament created Crom-well lord lieutenant of Ireland, ap-pointed to suppress the seven-year-old rebellion. He landed at Dublin in August with 12,000 men and proceeded over the next nine months to put down the rebels and the Royalists with great severity, apparently largely motivated by the hatred and contempt he and his soldiers felt for the Irish as papists and savages who had committed atrocities against English settlers. At the sieges of Drog-heda and Wexford his troops massacred great numbers of the defenders and civilians when the towns fell. Crom-well's army regained much of the coast and he turned inland, taking Kilkenny and Clonmel before being recalled to England in May 1650 to face a threatened Scottish invasion. The Covenanters had recognized the young Charles II as king and an English army was organized to attack the Scots. Fairfax refused the command and resigned his post of Captain General, an office that now passed to Cromwell along with the task of leading 16,000 men against a formid-able Scottish force under David Leslie (q.v.). He entered Scotland in July but could not bring the wily Leslie to battle. Illness deprived him of half his fighting force and in September he fell back towards the port of Dunbar to await supplies and reinforcements from England. Here, Leslie, with 20,000 Scots, cut him off from England, but a bad move on his part and some skilful use of cavalry by Cromwell led to an English victory. Cromwell entered Edinburgh and began to work for a settlement with the Scots.

In the spring he moved out and forced Charles's troops out of their position near Stirling. They then took the road to England, which was now open. Cromwell left George Monck (q.v.) to mop up in Scotland and drove south to catch Charles at Worcester on 3 September 1651. Here, in a 'crowning mercy', he ended the Civil War.

Cromwell was voted an additional income by Parliament and given Hampton Court as a residence. Although living in a royal palace, he still sat as an ordinary M.P. He obtained an amnesty for Royalists but could not move his fellow members to speedy reform of the law and the church or to hold new elections, although only the small Rump remained of the body of the Long Parliament elected eleven years before. The army grew restless, irritated by the corruption of some of the members and by a costly naval war with Holland. Finally, in April 1653, Cromwell led soldiers into the House of Commons and expelled the Rump. He now appointed a new Council of State, which proceeded to nominate the short-lived Parliament of godly men known as the Barebones Parliament. The extreme sectarians quickly gained control and alarmed the moderates into dissolving the body in December, conveying all power over the three kingdoms to Oliver Cromwell.

The council of officers proceeded to draw up a constitution, the Instrument of Government, that vested executive authority in a lord protector and the council of state. A freely elected Parliament was responsible for legislation and supplies. When this body was not sitting, the council could issue ordinances.

Cromwell was invested as the first Lord Protector on 16 December 1653. His constitutional power was quite restricted, but his real power, resting on the army, was greater than that of any Stuart monarch. He abolished anachronistic restrictions in Scots law and began the reform of religion, law, and education in England. He ended the First Dutch War, securing advantageous terms, including the security of British commerce in the East. Treaties had been signed with other maritime states by the time the new Parliament opened in September 1654. It proved to be a fractious body, containing a large contingent of republicans, interested in changing the Instrument of Government, and many members pressing for control over the Army. Cromwell let this Parliament last the constitutionally required five months, before dissolving it in January 1655.

Unrest in the country increased. On the one hand the Levellers were plotting, while on the other the Royalists rose in the spring. This rebellion was quickly defeated and provided Cromwell with the means to finance his new system of government. A levy on Royalists was introduced and England was divided into eleven districts, each under the rule of a major general assisted by the efficient spy network of John Thurloe (q.v.), Cromwell's secretary of state.

The strength of England under Cromwell's personal rule impressed the European powers. France and Spain vied for an alliance with her. Accordingly, when Cromwell's anger was roused by the persecution of the Vaudois in Savoy, his protestations to Cardinal Mazarin brought swift French pressure to bear on the Duke of Savoy. Spain, the more anti-Protestant of the two great Catholic powers, suffered from English raids and from the expedition of William Penn (q.v.), which took Jamaica in 1655. A state of open war existed between England and Spain by the autumn, and an Anglo-French alliance was signed in March 1657. The allies defeated the Spaniards at the Battle of the Dunes (1658) and the English won as their prize Dunkirk, a city of great value in controlling the Straits of Dover. In Cromwell's foreign policy, two themes predominate: the cause of Protestantism and English commercial interest. In this he hearkened back to Elizabeth I – at any rate, as her policies were understood by the Puritans.

Although treaties with Portugal and expeditions to the West Indies benefited English commerce, the vigorous foreign policy and the standing army were great financial burdens. In September 1656 Cromwell was forced to call another Parliament. Even with 100 republicans excluded from the assembly, it continued to show its independence. Not until the New Year did Parliament vote supplies for the Spanish war, and only after refusing funds to the major generals. Without money, their administration ended. In an attempt to resolve the constitutional dilemma, Parliament offered Cromwell the crown in return for the restoration of a more traditional form of government. Although Cromwell himself was probably sympathetic to this conservative ideal, he realized that the Army, the basis of his power and the sole guarantor of order in the realm, was bitterly hostile to the restoration of monarchy. In May 1657 he refused the throne, but accepted the provision of an upper house and the right to appoint a successor as lord protector.

During the summer recess he chose his upper chamber, appointing many of his ablest supporters from the Commons. When Parliament assembled again in January 1658, the 100 excluded republicans took their seats under the new constitution. The Commons expressed the grievances of a large part of the political nation, refused supplies, and attacked the legitimacy of the new 'Lords'. In a temper, Cromwell dissolved Parliament.

Despite his imperious handling of assemblies, Cromwell believed in Parliament, but the legislature insisted upon taking a course that he considered to be against the best interests of the nation, a conclusion reinforced at a spiritual level by his habit of prayer and his firm trust in God's support for his own policies. His conservative nature could not accept the radical changes demanded by Lilburne or Harrison; nor did he support the demands for religious persecution made by all parties in this last Parliament, for he was a compassionate man and a believer in personal liberty. He defended the Quakers, once he had assured himself that they meant no violence, and admitted the Jews into England 350 years after their expulsion by Edward I.

Contrary to the suspicions of the republicans, Cromwell was probably not an ambitious man. He did not favour his sons, neither his heir Richard nor his very capable son-in-law, Henry Ireton, lord deputy in Ireland. Except for his two youngest daughters, he married his children to untitled gentlefolk. He seems to have been a devoted family man in the Puritan tradition. When his favourite daughter died in August 1658 he attended her personally during her last illness. Already a sick man himself, he died on 3 September 1658, the anniversary of his victories at Dunbar and Worcester. After the Restoration, his remains were dug up and posthumously hanged, then thrown into an unmarked grave at Tyburn.

W. C. Abbott (ed.), *The Writings and Speeches of Oliver Cromwell* (4 vols.; Cambridge, Mass., 1937–47).

Maurice Ashley, *The Greatness of Oliver Cromwell* (1957).

Sir Charles H. Firth, *Oliver Cromwell and the Rule of the Puritans in England* (1900).

Christopher Hill, *God's Englishman: Oliver Cromwell and the English Revolution* (1970).

R. S. Paul, *The Lord Protector: Religion and Politics in the Life of Oliver Cromwell* (1955).

Ivan Roots (ed.), *Cromwell: A Profile* (1973).

Peter Young, *Oliver Cromwell* (1962).

Portraits: oil, quarter-length, after S. Cooper, 1656: N.P.G.; oil, three-quarter length, by Robert Walker, *c.* 1649: N.P.G.; oil, quarter-length, by Lely, 1653–54: City Museum & Art Gallery, Birmingham; miniature, by S. Cooper, 1656: N.P.G.; chalk and watercolour, quarter-length, attributed to R. Hutchinson: N.P.G.; bust, by unknown artist: N.P.G.

Cromwell, Richard (1626–1712),

Lord Protector (September 1658 – May 1659), eldest surviving son of Oliver Cromwell, the Lord Protector, and Elizabeth Bouchier.

Born on 4 October 1626, Richard probably briefly served in the Parliamentary army. In May 1649 he married Dorothy Mayor or Major of Hursley, Hampshire. His father took advantage of this occasion to ask Richard's new father-in-law to instil discipline into him. He was always noted as a rather lazy gentleman, more interested in hunting and other sports than in managing either his estates or the country.

He was only brought to the fore of affairs in 1657, when his father was authorized to appoint a successor. Although treated as the ruler's heir in the

country, it was only at his father's deathbed in August or September 1658 that he was actually declared the successor.

Richard Cromwell received numerous addresses of support, but rumblings were soon to be heard in what had been the bulwark of his father's power, the Army, where some demanded that a general should be their commander-in-chief. In retorting to one of these demands, Cromwell astonished his hearers with his ability as a speaker.

His oratorical powers were also admired in the parliament he opened in January 1659. But by then he had shown that although willing to accept advice, he could not dominate the council. Rivalries between the civilians and the military quickly brought about a confrontation between the Army council and Parliament, in which Cromwell was employed to transmit their communications to each other. When he attempted to exert his authority over the generals they gathered the army at St. James's. He gave in, sided with the army, and dissolved Parliament.

The senior officers wished to retain Cromwell as a figurehead, but strong republican sentiment forced them to re-call the Long Parliament on 7 May. Its leaders agreed with the officers to depose Cromwell. The army still took an interest in ensuring that Parliament pro-vide for his debts and his livelihood, but few of its proposed measures were effected. Meanwhile, Cromwell turned down offers of assistance from France and plans for a restoration of the Stuarts. He displayed a complete lack of interest in power and submitted to the new government on 25 May, leaving Whitehall when Parliament gave him six months' immunity from arrest by his creditors.

In the summer of 1660 Cromwell left for France, where he lived under the name of John Clarke. Deemed a danger-ous person by the government, he lived in several European countries before re-turning to England around 1680. Many unsubstantiated stories centre around him, but he appears to have spent the remainder of his life quietly at Cheshunt, still under the name of Clarke, until his death in 1712.

R. W. Ramsey, *Richard Cromwell, Protector of England* (1935).

Portrait: miniature, quarter-length, by unknown artist: N.P.G.

Culpepper, John (d. 1660), see Cole-peper, John.

Curteene, Sir William (1572–1636), see Courten, Sir William.

D

Dahl, Michael (1659–1743), Swedish-born painter who became a leading portraitist in England and for many years was Kneller's chief rival.

Dahl trained in Sweden under Ehrenstrahl, but in 1682 he left his homeland to travel abroad and further his studies. He came first to England where, almost immediately, he became associated with Kneller (q.v.). Three years later, Dahl travelled to France and Italy, staying for a further three years in Rome where he painted the portrait of Queen Christina of Sweden that is now in Grimsthorpe Castle. In 1688 Dahl left Italy to return to England, where he finally settled. He soon secured a number of patrons, including the Duke of Somerset, who in 1696 commissioned Dahl to work at Petworth producing eight full-length portraits of the peeresses there. Although his figures are clumsy and lacking in Kneller's sense of dignity, they are numbered amongst his most successful works and compare well with Kneller's similar studies of the Hampton Court 'beauties'. The works may even have been planned in conscious rivalry.

In Vertue's words, 'the Great busines and high carriage of Kneller gave a lustre to the actions or workes of Mr. Dahl . . . a man of great Modesty and few words.' Dahl was Kneller's most serious rival for public patronage but their political leanings, Dahl being a Tory and Kneller a Whig, made for a natural division in their clientele. Their techniques were greatly contrasting. Dahl's style is softer and less forced than Kneller's, but his works lack Kneller's assurance, especially in female portraiture. His masterpiece is perhaps his self-portrait, painted in 1691 and now in the National Gallery; a striking and carefully constructed work. His light touch and his use of soft pastel-like colours in his larger portraits anticipate the rococo style of the reign of George III.

Dahl was obviously well contented with his situation in England, for in 1698 he refused an offer to take his former tutor Ehrenstrahl's post as painter to the King of Sweden. At this time too, Dahl was patronized by Prince George of Denmark and Princess Anne. In 1702, with the accession of Queen Anne, Dahl, much in her favour, painted many of the presentation portraits. These works are probably more representative of Dahl's honest and gentle style, which made him popular with his more conservative sitters. The portraits of Sir Cloudesley Shovell and Sir James Wishart are perhaps the best examples of Dahl's sympathetic interpretation of character as opposed to Kneller's more forceful and heroic depictions.

Kneller's death in 1723 led to an increased patronage for Dahl and for ten years he enjoyed the largest practice in the country. His increasing age forced him to abandon his career in 1740; he died three years later, on 20 October 1743, leaving his only pupil of note, Hans Hysing, to perpetuate his style for a further decade.

Works at:
Petworth
Gloucester
National Gallery, London

National Maritime Museum, Greenwich
Dulwich
Stockholm

W. Nisser, *Michael Dahl and the Contemporary Swedish School of Painting in England* (Uppsala, 1927).

Portrait: self-portrait, oil, three-quarter length: National Gallery.

Dampier, William (1652–1715), explorer, hydrographer, and buccaneer.

Dampier was born in May or June, 1652, in East Coker, Somerset, the son of a tenant farmer, and attended the local grammar school erratically. He was orphaned in 1668 and went to sea in the care of a Weymouth trader. His first voyage, to Newfoundland, filled him with disgust: his suffering from the cold on this voyage prejudiced him for life against venturing into extreme northern or southern latitudes. Nevertheless, on his return he signed on to the crew of an East Indiaman. He was back in England in time to serve on the *Royal Prince* in battles against the Dutch in 1673; in the next year his father's old landlord appointed him assistant manager of his Jamaican plantation. Dampier soon tired of this occupation and began to sail with traders in this area, a life in which buccaneering was mingled with commerce. Having gained a considerable sum of money, he returned to England in 1678 and married.

In 1679 Dampier returned to Jamaica and resumed his life among the buccaneers. As a member of various pirate bands he attacked the Spanish, crossed the Isthmus of Panama, sacked cities, and enjoyed many other adventures. July 1682 found him in Virginia, where he remained for over a year. Then he joined another crew of buccaneers, which sailed into the Pacific, first stopping at Sierra Leone to steal a new ship. In the Pacific they restocked at the Galapagos Islands and joined a buccaneer fleet that was scourging South America. In 1685 Dampier changed ships, for, as he later stated, the captain he joined was intending to sail into parts he had never visited before. On this voyage they reached Guam, the Philippines, China, and the north shore of Australia. After a disagreement, Dampier and some others were put ashore on Nicobar Island in 1688. With a small boat obtained from natives they made their way to Sumatra. Dampier's adventures continued as he sailed on various trading voyages in the East Indies, finally obtaining a passage back to England on an Indiaman in 1691. He brought with him a native whom he had planned to exhibit, but poverty compelled him to sell his slave.

The subsequent six years of Dampier's life remain a blank. Then, in 1697, he published *A New Voyage Round the World*, which was an immediate success. This tale of his circumnavigation was based on the journal he had been keeping faithfully since at least 1675. In it he had noted with great care and precision all the natural phenomena he had seen; he drew charts and maps and described in great detail geographical features, peoples, peculiarities of the seas and the climate, and anything else worthy of note. As his curiosity and powers of observation were great, his book attracted the interest of the learned world, especially the Royal Society. When, in 1699, he published the second volume of his *Voyage* and *A Discourse on the Winds*, his reputation was still further enhanced. The admiralty commissioned him to plan a voyage of discovery, and he recommended Australia as a goal. He was then placed in charge of the ship *Roebuck* and set sail in January 1699.

Dampier proved himself completely incapable in his first command. He had no idea whatsoever of discipline and succeeded by his actions in alienating his officers and driving his crew to mutiny. But the *Roebuck* did find its goal. Sailing via the Cape of Good Hope, it reached the western coast of Australia but, unable to find good harbours or drinking water, was forced to proceed to New Guinea to replenish its supplies. Dampier explored the coast and reached New Britain, but the terrible state of his crew and ship compelled him to turn about. They refitted at Batavia and sailed as far as the South Atlantic, where the ship gradually sank. Fortunately they were close enough to Ascension to make land safely. Here they waited a month before a homeward-bound convoy passed by and took them aboard. They reached England in the spring of 1700.

A court martial in 1702 found Dampier unfit ever again to command a ship of the crown; nevertheless, in 1703 he was made captain of the privateer *St. George*, given command of its companion vessel, the *Cinque Ports*, and sent to harass the Spanish colonies. Although he made it as far as the Pacific, he proved himself once again an incompetent captain. His officers quarrelled, his crews mutinied, and Dampier failed to capture a single ship. During this voyage Alexander Selkirk (q.v.) was marooned on Juan Fernandez.

In December 1704 this expedition split up while still in the Pacific. Dampier appears to have crossed the Pacific to a Dutch settlement in the East Indies, where he was imprisoned. In 1707 he reached England. By this time, one Funnell, his former mate or steward, had published a highly critical account of this disastrous voyage in the guise of a fourth volume to Dampier's *Voyage*. Dampier responded with a *Vindication*, but his reputation had been sufficiently weakened to prevent any more commands coming his way.

In 1708 he shipped on a privateer as pilot. It rounded Cape Horn into the Pacific and rescued Alexander Selkirk, who almost refused to embark when he heard that Dampier was on board. This vessel enjoyed the best of fortune: it captured one of the Manila ships, and by October 1711 had safely rounded the Cape of Good Hope and reached the Thames. The prize money for this capture was enormous, but Dampier died in London in March 1715 before the shares were paid out.

Dampier kept his extraordinary journal for most of his life, and this is what makes his career so significant. Not only is his *Voyage* an extremely valuable and interesting book, but his treatise on the winds remained the standard reference work on the subject for over a century.

W. Dampier, *A New Voyage Round the World*, ed. A. Gray (1927).
W. H. Bonner, *William Dampier* (1934).
C. Lloyd, *William Dampier* (1966).
J. C. Shipman, *William Dampier: Seaman-Scientist* (Lawrence, Kansas, 1962).

Danby, 1st Earl of (1632–1712), see Osborne, Thomas.

Davenant or D'Avenant, Sir William (1606–68), poet, dramatist, and theatre manager.

He was born in Oxford in February 1606. His putative father was John Davenant, an inn-keeper who was mayor of Oxford by the time he died in 1621. William himself, however, claimed to be Shakespeare's godson (a frequent euphemism at the time for illegitimate son) and in one cryptic passage, which plays on the similarity between the name *D'Avenant* and the River *Avon*, he seems to be claiming direct descent from the Bard of Avon.

Young William attended Lincoln College, Oxford, in about 1620, although he did not stay long enough to acquire a degree. He went to London, where he is said to have written a play, but certainly at around this time he entered the service of the literary courtier, Fulke Greville, Lord Brooke (see *Lives of the Tudor Age*). On Brooke's murder in 1628, Davenant was left as a hanger-on at court and had more time for the theatre. His earliest known plays are *The Cruel Brothers* and *The Tragedy of Albovine, King of the Lombards*, licensed in 1629 but never performed. This was followed by four further dramas, the blank verse of which is hardly distinguishable from prose and none of which appear to have achieved any great success. In January 1633 was enacted *The Wits*, probably Davenant's best play, which together with the tragicomedy *The Platonic Lovers* (1636), was frequently revived for over a century. *The Wits* is the story of three impecunious gentlemen who make their living by using their sharpness and intelligence; it is full of life and vigour and still makes amusing reading. At this time also, he published a collection of poems and wrote masques for the court, on at least one of which he collaborated with Inigo Jones (q.v.), the master of spectacular scenic effects. On the strength of these works and no doubt his connections at court, including the favour of Queen Henrietta Maria, Davenant was in 1638 made poet laureate, an office that had been vacant since Ben Jonson's death the year before.

In 1639 he lost his nose as the result of an illness, presumably syphilis, much to the merriment of his friends, who included Suckling and Denham (qq.v.); Davenant's nose was a favourite satiric subject for occasional verses of the time.

He was a staunch and reckless supporter of the King and as the crisis developed between court and Parliament he did nothing to improve matters. In 1641 he was involved in a plot to bring up an army to secure the safety of the King and to put the Parliamentarians in their place. The plot was bungled disastrously, Davenant was arrested, escaped to Faversham in Kent, arrested again, escaped to Canterbury, arrested, and finally escaped to France. This involvement from the outbreak of the Civil War, coupled with the closure of the theatres, put paid to his theatrical career and to his plans to build a new theatre, for which he had been granted a royal patent in 1639. Once he had made his way to France, he took up gunrunning for the royal cause. In 1643 he was back in England and took part in the siege of Gloucester; it was here that he received his knighthood, apparently for valour in the field. He carried out several commissions for Charles I and for his son after the exile; both nevertheless seem to have regarded him ambivalently, partly because he had an unfortunate habit of ridiculing the Church, and partly because the King's more serious-minded advisers thoroughly disapproved of him. After the execution of Charles I, Davenant again returned to France, but in 1650 he was selected to go to Virginia, ostensibly to help put the colony in order but perhaps also because he was too much of a nuisance at the exiled court.

Whatever the reason, he set sail in the autumn of 1650 and was promptly captured by a Parliamentarian ship. He was confined in Cowes Castle, in the Isle of Wight, from where he wrote to Thomas Hobbes, 'I am pretty certain I shall be hanged next week.' His luck – or influence – held good, however, for he escaped with confinement in the Tower of London. Here he remained for two years (some historians believe for longer), using the time to polish and publish a romantic epic poem, *Gondibert*, on which he had been working for some years.

In 1656 Davenant produced at the Cockpit Theatre, Drury Lane, the first performance of *The Siege of Rhodes*, written by himself. This is a very remarkable work, not by reason of any literary merit, but because it marked a completely new style of theatrical production, a style that was a complete break with the Elizabethan–Jacobean tradition in which Davenant had previously worked. It was the first public production in England since the closure of the theatres sixteen years before; in it for the first time women actors played women's roles, for the first time scenery was used in the theatre (although it had been widely used in masques). Furthermore, the words were not spoken but sung, and by musicians (including Henry Purcell, q.v.) rather than actors. This, then, was the first English opera; the music was by Henry Lawes (q.v.), with some assistance from collaborators.

The next four years were difficult ones for Davenant; he managed to write and produce a miscellany of popular and somewhat sensational plays, with titles like *The Cruelty of the Spaniards in Peru* and *The History of Sir Francis Drake*. He seems to have secured Oliver Cromwell's approval for the continuance of his theatre, although in December 1658 Richard Cromwell called for an account 'by what authority it [opera at the Cockpit] is exposed to publick view'. In the troubles immediately preceding the Restoration Davenant was again imprisoned, but was released before he came to any harm. After the Restoration of Charles II in 1660, he received a royal licence to set up a company of players, but became involved in a long drawn out struggle over rights and powers with Sir Henry Herbert, master of the king's revels. By 1662 Davenant had clearly

won, and the last six years of his life were spent in comparative serenity. He changed the name of his theatre to The Opera and moved to Lincoln's Inn Fields, started several successful actresses on their careers, including Mrs. Betterton, and seems to have made a handsome profit from his productions. He revived some of his own plays and adapted Elizabethan and Jacobean dramas, including Shakespeare's *Tempest*, on which he worked with Dryden (1667). He also wrote several original plays, of which the only survivor is *The Man's the Master*, a comedy. He died at his lodgings in Lincoln's Inn Fields on 7 April 1668, and was buried in Westminster Abbey. His death was the occasion of an amusing poem by Richard Flecknoe, *The Voyage to the Other World, with [Davenant's] Adventures in the Poet's Elysium*, in which Shakespeare is represented as being offended at the mangling of his plays by Davenant.

W. H. Logan and J. Maidment, *The Dramatic Works of Sir William Davenant* (5 vols.; 1872–74).

H. S. Collins, *The Comedy of Davenant* (The Hague, 1967).

C. M. Dowlin, *Sir William Davenant's Gandibert: Its Preface and Hobbes's Answer* (Philadelphia, Pa., 1935).

A. Harbage, *Davenant* (Philadelphia, Pa., 1935).

Arthur H. Nethercot, *Sir William D'Avenant* (Chicago, 1938).

Davenport, John (1597–1670), English Puritan and Congregationalist minister in colonial New England.

John Davenport was born at Coventry in 1597, where his father had been mayor. He went to Oxford in 1613, but there is some doubt as to whether he actually took his degree, and he may have left the university because of lack of money. However, in 1625 Davenport certainly returned to take an M.A. degree from Oxford. In 1615 he was acting as chaplain at Hilton Castle, near

Durham, and afterwards he became vicar of a London church. There, his apparently Nonconformist ideas and activities brought him to the notice of Laud (q.v.) and the High Commission. To escape prosecution, Davenport fled to Holland some time around the end of 1633, where he became co-pastor of the English church at Amsterdam. However, he quarrelled with his colleague there and returned to England in 1635.

In England Davenport came under the influence of John Cotton, another colonial clergyman, and others who intended to emigrate and he was persuaded to sail for New England. He landed at Boston, Massachusetts, in June 1637. Davenport was offered land by the government of Massachusetts, but he and some of his friends went to the territory of the Quinnipiac Indians, where they founded the colony of New Haven in April 1638. He was a leading figure in the organization of the town and colony. His influence is apparent in the constitution of the colony settled on 4 June 1639, which made church membership a precondition of holding civil office or exercising electoral rights. The constitution also provided for a guiding body of seven people called 'The Seven Pillars of State', of whom Davenport was one.

Davenport served as a pastor of New Haven until 1668, and his life was closely linked with the history of the colony, for a colonial minister was almost inevitably a politician. He was noted for his industry and earnestness, attributes which led to his description by the Quinnipiac Indians as 'the big-study man'. In 1661 the regicide judges Whalley and Goffe came to New Haven and Davenport hid them for a month in his own house while royal officers searched for them. The following year he was closely involved in the attempt to maintain New Haven's independent status. Connecticut had applied for a new charter which involved the absorption of New Haven. Davenport was one of ten signatories of a letter to the General Court of Connecticut requesting that New Haven might remain a distinct colony, at least for the time being. He spoke at meetings to denounce the proposed union and helped to write a pamphlet called *New Haven's Case stated.* When the union of the two colonies took place, he apparently felt that Christ's interest was 'miserably lost'.

In 1667, perhaps because of the failure to maintain New Haven's independence, Davenport decided to answer a call to the first church at Boston; he was ordained pastor there in 1668. However, in order for him to go to Boston, church custom required that Davenport should be released by his New Haven church. The church in New Haven opposed his departure, and parts of letters from New Haven reflecting their disapproval were suppressed at Boston, apparently with Davenport's knowledge. This deception soon became generally known and caused a great scandal. This and Davenport's opposition to the Half-Way Covenant precipitated the withdrawal of part of his congregation, who formed a new church, 'the old South Church'. The old and new bodies waged war on each other and Davenport was at the centre of the dispute until his death on 13 March 1670, of apoplexy. He had married in 1663 and had five children.

Deane, Richard (1610–53), Parliamentarian military commander and admiral.

The younger son of Edward Deane of Gloucestershire, he married Mary Grymesditch (1647), by whom he had two daughters. Very little is known about his early life. He appears to have been distantly related to some of the leaders of the Parliamentary opposition to King Charles I, such as Hampden and Cromwell, and to have been associated with merchant shipping interests. Again, while it is clear that he served in the Parliamentarian army from the outset of the Civil War, the precise details of that service are not established. In August 1642 he was in the Gravesend garrison as an artillery volunteer, and exactly two years later he was one of the artillery officers in the army of the Earl of Essex which was forced to surrender in Cornwall after the Battle of Lostwithiel.

With the formation of the New Model Army in 1645, his recorded career really begins, for he was appointed comptroller of the ordnance under Thomas Hammond, the lieutenant general. Captain Deane was responsible for the actual handling of the guns in action, and commanded them in the Battle of Naseby (14 June 1645). When the New Model Army embarked upon the systematic reduction of the Royalist garrisons in the West Country, his role as artillery commander and supervisor of siege engineering was crucial, and he was especially commended for his work at the siege of Bristol (11 September 1645). He assisted in the negotiations for the surrender of the remnants of the Royalist forces at Truro (March 1646) and took part in the siege of Oxford.

Subsequently, he was closely attached to Cromwell, and as a result shared his rising fortunes. In May 1647 there was a move to neutralize Cromwell by sending him to command the army in Ireland, and Deane was nominated as his lieutenant of artillery. Cromwell declined the appointment, and they both remained in England. When Cromwell was placed in charge of that portion of the Army sent to deal with the Royalist insurgents in Wales in 1648, Deane went with him,

now in command of his own regiment. At Preston (17 August), he commanded the right wing of the army. That this was also an attachment of principle is indicated by the facts that Lilburne and Rainsborough (qq.v.) were witnesses at his marriage and that his regiment was among those calling for proceedings against the King and others as instigators of the rising of 1648.

In the events leading up to the execution of the King, Deane played an active, if subordinate, part. When the Army marched on London, Deane's task was to seize the treasuries in the Goldsmiths' and Weavers' Halls, which he accomplished with two regiments of foot and some troops of horse. He was a member of the commission which tried the King, signified his approval of the judgement, signed the death warrant with the others, and was one of the five officers chosen to arrange the execution itself.

A month later (February 1649), Deane was one of the three colonels appointed by a new Council of State to exercise jointly command of the navy, the others being Blake (q.v.) and Edward Popham. Deane's artillery experience was an important element in his selection, since contemporaries drew no clear distinction between the sea and the land services in war, ships being regarded as floating gun platforms. His own area of command was west of Portsmouth, in which position he covered the crossing of Cromwell's army to Ireland in August. In the following year, his naval function shifted to the protection of the army's campaign in Scotland until May 1651, when Cromwell ordered him ashore to duty with the army as a major general.

After the campaign reached its conclusion with the defeat of Charles II at Worcester (3 September 1651), Deane was sent back to participate in the commission for the settlement of Scotland. During 1652 he exercised supreme authority in civil, military, and naval matters, being called back to the navy (December) by the critical situation in the opening months of the Dutch War. Popham had died, and Monck (q.v.) filled the vacancy among the generals-at-sea, much of whose work consisted of naval administration as well as command in action, especially at this juncture. The poor performance of the fleet against Tromp compelled the government to undertake a reorganization of the administrative structure of the navy, and the achievements of the three generals in this field were at least as important as their successes at sea. In February 1653 he sailed with Blake in the latter's flagship, *Triumph*, and took part in the battle of Portland (18 February). The result was a resounding English victory.

On 20 April 1653, Cromwell expelled the Rump Parliament, directing much of his venom against its most able member and his chief critic, Sir Henry Vane the Younger (q.v.), the treasurer of the navy. Vane had been the prime mover of the reforms, and the generals had worked closely with him, but Deane and Monck (Blake was sick) endeavoured to secure the acquiescence of the officers of the fleet in the army's coup by obtaining signatures to a declaration of intent which avoided comment upon the coup while promising a proper discharge of all duties laid upon the navy.

At the beginning of May the news that Tromp was at sea once more caused Deane and Monck to sail in search of him, sweeping the North Sea from the coast of Holland to the Orkneys and back into the Kattegat without success. For his part, Tromp had escorted a merchant fleet out of the North Sea and had returned to offer battle to the English. The two fleets met off The Gabbard on 1 June, battle being joined on the following day between almost exactly equal forces. It was to be the occasion for putting into first practice the new fighting instructions which the two generals had devised during the preceding months with intermittent help from the sick Blake. The basis of the new tactics was to manœuvre the fleet in line by predetermined signals and to use the ships primarily as gun platforms rather than strive to board opponents. The new methods produced another English triumph, but Deane was killed by chain shot as he stood beside Monck on the deck of the latter's flagship, *Resolution*, in the opening stage of the battle.

His body was returned to England and buried in Westminster Abbey, being taken out and thrown in a common pit after the Restoration with those of other regicides.

Sir Charles H. Firth, *Cromwell's Army* (1962, 4th ed.).
See also J. R. Powell, *Robert Blake* (1972).

Defoe, Daniel (?1660–1731), journalist and novelist.

Born in Cripplegate, London, probably in the second half of 1660, Defoe is remembered both as the 'father of modern English journalism' and as the earliest English novelist whose works are still widely read today. His life was stormy and marked by debts, libel suits, and imprisonment, punctuated by periods of popular adulation; his writings are characterized by championship of humane and liberal ideas and political moderation, along with constant opposition to bigotry, prejudice, and intolerance.

His father, James Foe, was a member of the Butchers' Company in London, to which Daniel also belonged at one time. The family were Dissenters, and for this reason Daniel was unable to go to university. He received a good education, however, at the academy kept by Charles Morton, also a Dissenter, at Newington Green, just north of London. This education suggests that he may have been intended for the Presbyterian priesthood, but in 1685 (possibly earlier) he set up on his own account as a merchant, dealing also in insurance. He retained a lifelong interest in trade and commerce, although he seems to have been singularly unsuccessful in the practice of it. In 1692 he went bankrupt, partly through rashness, on his own admission, but mainly through misfortune, the wars with France having ruined him along with eighteen other marine insurers. By 1705 he had paid off £12,000 of the £17,000 he owed. His understanding of the links between commerce and social economics is demonstrated in his *Essay upon Projects* (1698), a radical pamphlet far ahead of its time, containing proposals for a central bank, for savings banks, for reform of the bankruptcy laws, and for personal life and health insurance. Late in life he returned to this interest with many pamphlets and a periodical devoted to trade and commerce.

Defoe's political activities are first heard of in 1685, when, along with many other Dissenters, he joined Monmouth's rebellion against the Catholic James II. He appears to have escaped unscathed after the fiasco of the Battle of Sedgemoor; some anonymous pamphlets attacking James II and his administration are attributed to him. The abdication of James in 1688 clearly came as a relief to Defoe: he rode out to meet William of Orange at Henley, and he became as staunch a supporter of the new king as he had been an opponent of the old. *The*

True-Born Englishman (1701) is a satirical poem written in reply to attacks on William's Dutch origins; it asserts that all Englishmen are mongrels, bred from the scum of Europe through the ages.

1701 saw the start of a flow of pamphlets, journals, articles, and satires from Defoe's pen that continued unabated for twenty-five years. It also saw him reach a position of pre-eminence as a political commentator and agitator. In May of that year a deputation of five gentlemen from Kent presented a petition to Parliament pressing for stronger defences against foreign invasion. They were promptly imprisoned by the Tory majority for their pains. Within twenty-four hours Defoe, who had already written a pamphlet (1697) arguing for a standing army, presented the Speaker, Robert Harley (q.v.), with a pamphlet, the *Legion Memorial* – so called from its claim of authorship, 'Our name is Legion, and we are many' – reminding Parliament that 'Englishmen are no more to be slaves to Parliament than to a King.' The Kentishmen were released and were feasted, along with Defoe, at Mercer's Hall.

One of the chief targets for High Tory politicians at this time was the practice of 'occasional conformity' – the practice among candidates for political or administrative office who happened to be Dissenters of attending just enough Church of England services to secure and hold the position, while maintaining also their chosen forms of worship. Defoe published a satirical pamphlet, *The Shortest Way with Dissenters* (1702), which presented the intolerant and bigoted views of the Tories reduced to absurdity: Defoe suggested that Dissenters should simply be exterminated. Unfortunately, the joke misfired: some of the more extreme Tories are said to have approved the proposal, while some of his Dissenter friends, having perhaps read only the title, took him for a renegade. Moreover, as a result of this pamphlet, Defoe was prosecuted for libelling the Church of England; he went into hiding, was apprehended, fined, pilloried, and imprisoned. He wrote a *Hymn to the Pillory* (1703), a mock-Pindaric ode, with fine scorn for his prosecutors. His popularity with the people was at its height and his pillorying was something of a triumph, the pillory being garlanded with flowers while members of the mob formed a guard of honour and others drank his health.

During his brief stay in Newgate prison, another of his business ventures collapsed and he lost a further £3,500. He had by now five children, and his position was becoming desperate. He was, however, rescued from prison in August 1704 by Harley, who had become secretary of state and who would appear to have been impressed by his previous encounter with Defoe. Harley employed Defoe to inform him on public opinion and in 'several honourable, though secret, services'. Defoe appears to have gained not only his liberty but also a pension from the bargain; in the circumstances he no doubt felt that he could not afford to be too particular in matters of conscience. He has been accused of 'trimming' and it is true that he served both Tory and Whig administrations, sometimes in capacities that would not suit the most fastidious of consciences. Nevertheless, he wrote nothing that is inconsistent with a fundamental passion for tolerance and moderation.

In 1704 he founded a periodical, *A Review of the Affairs of France, with Observations on Transactions at Home*. In spite of the title, most issues were more concerned with the transactions at home than with the affairs of France. This Defoe wrote largely single-handed, edited, and published, producing three issues a week from 1705 to 1713, undeterred by sickness, periodic imprisonment, and absence from home, including a trip to Scotland (1706) to liaise secretly with the party in favour of union. In his practice of devoting a column to his opinions on current political issues of all kinds lies the origin of the modern newspaper leading article; the unbroken sequence of issues for eight years bears tribute to his fluency and his professionalism; the *Review* is couched in characteristically straightforward prose, offering hard facts and commonsensical, readable commentaries. However, the tone changes noticeably with each change of government. Defoe had evidently learned his lesson, and while in 1708 he declared that a Tory Parliament would be the undoing of the nation, in 1710 we find him arguing that all patriots should support the Tory ministry. However, in matters such as foreign policy, where he had a freer hand, he demonstrates considerable insight, drawing attention to the colossal burden of expense of the War of the Spanish Succession and arguing that England's true economic interests lay in her colonies; she should leave Europe alone and concentrate on America.

In 1715 he was in trouble again, this time for libelling Lord Annesley. Although he was found guilty, he escaped sentence by means of a deal with the Whig secretary of state, Lord Townshend (see Townshend, Charles, 2nd Viscount Townshend, in *Lives of the Georgian Age*), according to which Defoe undertook to edit *The News Letter*, a High-Church Tory paper in which he had a share, on the understanding that although 'the style should continue Tory' he would 'take the sting out of it'. Defoe's skill, both as a political commentator and as a parodist, coupled with his perennial impecuniousness and his tendency to be the object of libel suits, made him the ideal tool for both Whig and Tory ministers seeking to control and muffle the press. In 1717 he infiltrated *Mist's Journal*, a Jacobite publication, where he made himself invaluable as managing editor. Eventually, however, his reputation caught up with him: it became common knowledge among proprietors and journalists that Defoe was a government agent; he found it increasingly difficult to get his writings published, and it seems that this as much as anything turned his attention for the time being to the calmer waters of fiction and of historical research.

Thus, in his late fifties, Defoe began writing *The Life and Strange Surprising Adventures of Robinson Crusoe* (1719). Like almost all his narratives, it is written in the first person. As might have been expected from his journalistic background, the style is closer akin to that of a modern newspaper feature article than to that of the 19th-century novel, and it is hardly surprising that the book was at first received as an authentic account. After all, Defoe's fabrications had been taken in earnest before. Evidently the idea originated in the experiences of Alexander Selkirk (q.v.), although there are many differences in detail.

Robinson Crusoe was an instant success and was translated into many languages. Defoe followed it with two sequels – *The Farther Adventures* (1719) and the *Serious Reflections* (1720) of Crusoe. Having discovered his gift for fiction, Defoe in five years produced nine novels, as well as other works. Those of 1720 – *The Life and Adventures of Mr. Duncan Campbell* (a deaf and dumb conjurer), *Memoirs of a Cavalier*, and *The Life of Captain Singleton* – are not particularly memorable; however, in 1722 appeared *The Fortunes and Misfortunes of the Famous Moll Flanders, Colonel Jack*, and *A Journal of the Plague Year*.

The latter work is not a novel; it is a remarkable piece of historical research and a reconstruction of events that took place when Defoe was five years old. With a true journalist's instinct, Defoe took the story of the century and wrote a carefully researched, graphic account in the first person of the events of 1664–65, starting with the gradual, inexorable spread of the plague, with the accompanying growth of terror, and going on to examine the effects on the minds of individuals as they became increasingly isolated by fear, the effects of this isolation on trade, as it came to a virtual standstill, and describing in detail the symptoms of the disease, the measures taken in seeking to stem its spread, the mass burials, and the exodus from London of all who could afford to travel. Here, Defoe's gift for convincing the reader of the authenticity of his account found a legitimate historical purpose.

Moll Flanders is perhaps Defoe's most typical novel. Moll is born in Newgate prison, the daughter of a mother who is transported to Virginia for theft. Brought up by a philanthropic mayor of Colchester, she enters on a remarkable career of seductions, marriages, and sexual liaisons. Visiting America to find her mother, she discovers not only her parent but also that her current marriage is incestuous, her husband being her half-brother. She returns to England and, in destitution, sets up as a pickpocket in concert with one of her former husbands, a highwayman. They make their fortune, set up as planters in America, inherit a further fortune from Moll's mother, and spend the rest of their lives indulging in the luxury of repentance, which they can now afford.

This is a recurring theme in Defoe's novels: his characters are driven, occasionally by choice but more often by force of circumstance, into a life of crime, only wealth allowing them the luxury of repentance at leisure. Captain Singleton is an adventurer, explorer, and pirate, confessing to 'no sense of virtue or religion'; Colonel Jack, abandoned by his parents, falls into evil company, becomes a pickpocket, enlists in the army, deserts, is kidnapped, sold as a slave in Virginia, and, becoming an overseer and eventually being given his freedom, acquires enough wealth to return home to a life of prosperity and penitence. *Roxana, or the Fortunate Mistress* (1724) deserts her husband and five children for a life of prostitution, repenting only after a period of prosperity, although she at least dies in debt as well as penitence. It seems that Defoe found the excitements of a life of crime a much more interesting subject than repentance at leisure; in this he had many followers in this picaresque tradition in the 18th century (see, for example, Smollett in

Lives of the Georgian Age). The novels are tales of events, which tumble over one another; psychological and social insights are very much secondary concerns to that of getting on with the narrative.

Roxana was Defoe's last novel. After 1724, his health began to weaken and although his prodigious output hardly slackened, the sense of urgency and immediacy seems to go out of his writings. Discredited and exposed, he was no longer of use to the government as an agent, while for the same reason he was shunned by his fellow journalists; we find him complaining that he could not get his work published 'without feeing the journalists or publishers'. Historical works and pamphlets on trade, however, he could and did get published.

He produced a *History of the Pirates* (1724–28), *A Tour through the whole Island of Great Britain* in three volumes (1724–27), and a number of interviews with condemned criminals, notably Jack Sheppard, a highwayman who, after repeated escapes from prison, was eventually hanged at Tyburn in 1724, aged twenty-two. He returned also to the subject of trade, writing *The Complete English Tradesman* (1726), *A Plan of the English Commerce* (1728), and *Augusta Triumphans, or the Way to make London the Most Flourishing City in the Universe* (1728).

During the 1720s, Defoe appears to have at last paid off his debts and achieved an interlude of peace and prosperity. He had a substantial house built for him at Stoke Newington, and in 1722 he bought an estate in Essex for his daughter Hannah. However, there is a letter dated 12 August 1730, written to his son-in-law, that shows that Defoe was in hiding, depressed, in fear of death, and that refers to a blow from 'a wicked, perjured, and contemptible enemy'. It has been suggested that this letter shows signs of persecution mania; however, it is more likely that one of Defoe's old enemies or victims had caught up with him, possibly Mist, the Jacobite, who had in 1724 drawn a sword upon him. Mist would probably have been able to make out a case for treason against Defoe, had he felt strongly enough to surrender his Jacobite principles for the sake of revenge.

Whatever the true explanation of this letter, within the year Defoe was dead. He died where he was born, in Cripplegate, London, on 24 April 1731, at the age of seventy.

Novels and Selected Writings (Shakespeare Head edition, 14 vols.; 1927–28).

G. A. Aitken (ed.), *Romances and Narratives* (16 vols.; 1895).

George H. Healey (ed.), *Letters of Daniel Defoe* (1955).

W. L. Payne (ed.), *The Best of Defoe's Review* (New York, 1951).

A. W. Secord (ed.), *A Journal of the Plague Year and Other Pieces* (New York, 1935).

A. W. Secord (ed.), *The Review* (22 vols.; New York, 1938).

G. D. H. Cole (ed.), *A Tour Thro' Great Britain* (1927; rev. ed. in Everyman Library, 1962).

Paul Dottin, *Defoe et ses romans* (3 vols.; Paris, 1924: vol. 1 translated and published as *Daniel Defoe and his Novels*, New York, 1929).

William Lee, *Defoe: his Life and Recently Discovered Writings 1716–1729* (3 vols.; 1869).

John Robert Moore, *Daniel Defoe, Citizen of the Modern World* (Chicago, 1958).

M. Shinagel, *Daniel Defoe and Middle-Class Gentility* (Cambridge, Mass., 1968).

G. A. Starr, *Defoe and Spiritual Autobiography* (Princeton, 1965).

James Sutherland, *Defoe* (rev. ed. 1950).

Portrait: engraving, quarter-length, by M. van der Gucht after Taverner, 1706: N.P.G.

Dekker, Thomas (?1570–?1632), dramatist noted for his lively and good-humoured comedies.

Dekker himself tells us that he was born in London, but beyond that nothing is known of his parentage and childhood. The first indisputable record of his existence occurs in the diary of the theatrical manager Philip Henslowe (see *Lives of the Tudor Age*) in January 1598 – Henslowe paid £4 'to buy a book [i.e. the manuscript of a play] of Mr. Dekker'. Henslowe must have been impressed by the play, for he engaged its author as a writer for his theatre, the Rose. Between 1598 and 1602 Henslowe's diary records Dekker as the sole author of eight plays and as co-author, with such collaborators as Michael Drayton (see *Lives of the Tudor Age*) and Ben Jonson (q.v.), of no less than twenty-five others. Most of these early works are lost. Two that survived, however, are the moral comedy *Old Fortunatus* and the romantic comedy *The Shoemaker's Holiday* (both written 1599, published 1600), the latter being a lively and good-humoured tale set in contemporary London, including in its cast a splendidly eccentric master shoemaker and a young nobleman disguised as a Dutch cobbler, who provides Dekker with the opportunity to poke fun at the Dutch language, which he evidently knew well.

Dekker, in company with Marston (q.v.), was one of the butts of Ben Jonson's satire during the 'war of the theatres' (about 1601–03); he responded by producing *Satiromastix, or the Untrussing of the Humorous Poet* (1602), a caricature of Jonson that is more good-natured than the latter's attacks on Marston and Dekker and is still funny in its own right.

By 1602 Dekker was well established as one of the leading dramatists of his age. Even so, very few details of his personal life are recorded. He continued for the next twenty years or so to write intermittently for the stage, mainly in collaboration with others, but never so prolifically as in those first four years. Massinger, Middleton, Ford, and Webster (qq.v.) now join the ranks of those with whom he worked. In spite of his constant activity, he seems to have suffered from endless poverty and was frequently imprisoned for debt.

Of his later plays that have survived, perhaps the best is *The Honest Whore* (1604, with a second part not published until 1630). The tale of a virtuous and warm-hearted girl married, by a combination of misguided good intentions and force, to a pimp who has seduced her, it is deeply moving by virtue of its deep concern for suffering humanity, with some powerful scenes in Bedlam and Bridewell.

In 1604 Dekker turned to the writing of pamphlets and other prose works. Among these are *The Wonderful Year 1603* (a description of the plague of that year), *The Seven Deadly Sins of London* and *News from Hell* (1606, both in imitation of Nash), *The Bellman of London* (1608, a spirited account of the rogues and cheats to be found in London, with a second part in 1609), and perhaps the most famous of all Jacobean pamphlets, *The Gull's Hornbook* (1609). In this, under the guise of giving instruction to would-be gallants, Dekker provides a vigorous satirical portrait of the fops and 'gulls' of the age. He published at least one devotional tract (*Four Birds of Noah's Ark*, 1609), another plague work (*A Rod for Runaways*, 1625), and also wrote masques and occasional poetry. His last play seems to have been *Match Me in London* (1631), a tragicomedy.

After that he simply disappears from notice, and it is probable that he died in around 1632. His works went on being printed and reprinted for two decades, but surprisingly few of them, compared with those of his contemporaries, were revived and rewritten during the Restoration period. In many ways, with his lively interest in contemporary low life, his concern for the poor and oppressed, and his horror of the suffering not only of humanity but also of animals baited and tortured for idle amusement, he reminds us of the best kind of 20th-century crusading journalist.

Fredson Bowers (ed.), *Dramatic Works* (4 vols.; 1953–61 and 1964–66).

A. B. Grossart (ed.), *Non-Dramatic Works* (5 vols.; 1884–86).

C. Hoy (ed.), *Dramatic Works* [with commentary] (2 vols.; 1974).

F. P. Wilson (ed.), *The Plague Pamphlets of Dekker* (1925).

M. T. Jones-Davies, *Un Peintre de la vie londonienne: T. Dekker* (2 vols.; Paris, 1958).

Delamere or De la Mer, 1st Baron

(1622–84), see Booth, George.

Denham, Sir John (1615–69), poet and translator.

Denham was born in Dublin in 1615, son of Sir John Denham, lord chief justice of the king's bench in Ireland. After school in London, Denham in 1631 went up to Trinity College, Oxford, where he was considered 'a slow, dreaming young man, more addicted to gaming than study'. He soon left, probably without a degree, and took up desultory legal studies at Lincoln's Inn. In 1634 he made a fortunate marriage to Anne Cotton, by whom Aubrey says 'he had £500 per annum, one son, and two daughters'. The couple moved in with Denham's father at Egham, Surrey, but John's increasingly reckless gambling caused a family quarrel. Contrite, he wrote an essay against gaming, dedicated to his father 'to show his detestation of it'. Unfortunately, when in 1638 the elder Denham died his heir John managed to squander several thousand pounds of the family fortune in a renewed gambling spree.

In 1636 Denham translated Book II of Virgil's *Aeneid*, and though in his preface he exhorted translators to eschew 'the servile path' in favour of a free rendering, his book is little more than a terse paraphrase of the original. In 1641 Denham's tragedy *The Sophy* was performed, but though it had an exotic Turkish setting the play suffered from an excessively close adherence to the worn-out Senecan style. Denham's reputation was firmly established by his long poem *Cooper's Hill* (1642). In it he surveys from a hilltop the countryside around his Egham mansion, and prominent landmarks set him musing on weighty themes; Windsor Castle evokes the sanctity of the crown, smoky London the painful conflict between public and private life, and Runnymede the triumph of political liberty. The poem is written with plainness and economy, enlivened with alliteration, and its generalized moral reflections and neoclassical sobriety owe little to the current Metaphysical 'wit', instead looking forward to the rational 'judgment' of Augustan poetry. *Cooper's Hill* was the first of a long line of topographical-philosophical poems in English literature, and was admired and imitated by Dryden and Pope.

At the opening of the Civil War Denham was high sheriff of Surrey and governor of Farnham Castle, where he was captured by Sir William Waller in late 1642. Parliament allowed him to retire to Oxford, where he spent five years amusing his Royalist friends with political doggerel. When in 1644 Denham's property was sold off by Parliament, George Wither the poet, then a Parliamentary captain, petitioned for the mansion at Egham. Soon after Wither was taken prisoner by the Royalists, but Denham interceded with the King to spare his life, on the grounds that while Wither lived he 'should not be the worst poet in England'. Denham

later ran peacemaking errands between the opposing armies, and became intimate with the King, who pointed out to him that politics and poetry did not mix. However, he later stationed Denham and Cowley in London, with instructions to decode all messages coming in for the King from abroad. Parliament became suspicious, and in 1648 Denham fled to Holland, where he made himself generally useful to the exiled royal family, looking after the young Charles II and fund-raising among the Scots in Poland. His gambling was notorious, and it was said that he stayed abroad out of fear, not of English rebels, but English creditors.

Nevertheless Denham did return to England in 1652, placing himself under the patronage of the Earl of Pembroke. His reputation was growing – one contemporary called him 'the state's poet' – and he now mingled with such literary company as Aubrey and Evelyn (qq.v.). However, the authorities eventually forbade him to live in London, so he settled in Suffolk, occasionally going on trips abroad with Pembroke.

After the Restoration Clarendon rewarded Denham's wartime service by appointing him surveyor general of the king's works. Denham was a conscientious surveyor general, supervising much official building and probably designing Burlington House; he later took on a young assistant named Christopher Wren. In 1661 he was one of the organizers of Charles II's coronation, and in 1662 published his waspish political poems in a volume entitled *The Rump*.

In 1665 Denham, now a widower, married eighteen-year-old Margaret Brooke. She soon became the mistress of the Duke of York, who caused a court scandal by openly visiting the Denham household in Scotland Yard. All this provoked in Denham himself a fit of

123

insanity, during which he went to the King and informed him he was the Holy Ghost. In January 1667 Lady Denham died suddenly; Pepys and others claimed that her husband had given her a cup of poisoned chocolate. The public were so outraged with Denham that he had to lock himself in his house, only emerging to give his wife a sumptuous funeral as a placatory gesture. However, Andrew Marvell was convinced that the Duchess of York had administered the 'mortal chocolate', and indeed it was said that the duchess was afterwards 'troubled with the apparition of Lady Denham, and through anxiety bit off a piece of her tongue'. Interestingly enough, the post-mortem found no trace of poison in Lady Denham's body at all.

By now Denham was thoroughly disliked at court, and had 'the name of being mad'. He was a very tall man with stooping shoulders, a slow and stalking gait, and piercing eyes that 'looked into your very thoughts'. His many literary enemies, including Samuel Butler, satirized him as a debauchee, gambler, and cheat, claiming that he had bought *Cooper's Hill* from a vicar for £40. Unperturbed, Denham in 1667 wrote one of his masterpieces, the beautiful elegy on Cowley. He died in London during March 1669 and was buried in Westminster Abbey.

T. H. Banks (ed.), *The Poetical Works of Sir John Denham* (New Haven, Conn., 1928).

Dennis, John (1657–1734), critic.

Born in London, the son of a saddler, and educated at Harrow and Cambridge, Dennis obtained a B.A. from Caius College in 1679 and an M.A. from Trinity Hall in 1683. In 1680 he was rusticated for sword-fighting, this being the first evidence of the belligerent temperament that he brought to the stage and to criticism.

After leaving Cambridge, Dennis travelled in Europe for a while before returning to London to make his living by the pen. He wrote several plays, which were performed without much success, and some poetry. He managed to acquire as a patron the Duke of Marlborough (John Churchill, q.v.), who secured a sinecure for him and in 1705 sent him to Gibraltar on a diplomatic errand.

Dennis's best criticism was published in 1701 (*The Advancement and Reformation of Modern Poetry*) before he became cantankerous, vindictive, and foul-tempered as a result of his failure as a creative writer, coupled with his long quarrels with Pope (see *Lives of the Georgian Age*) and others. His insistence on the importance of passion in literature, and his equation of literature to religion in its moral force seems more appropriate to a Romantic than to a contemporary of the Augustans. 'Poetry', he wrote, 'is poetry, because it is more passionate and sensual than prose ... wherever a discourse is not pathetick, there it is prosaick.' His ideal among English writers was Milton (q.v.), although he also made a notable contribution to the understanding of Shakespeare.

A bombastic tragedy, *Appius and Virginia*, acted at Drury Lane in 1709, was satirized by Pope in his *Essay on Criticism* (iii, 585–588). Dennis replied with *Reflections, Critical and Satirical, upon a late Rhapsody called An Essay in Criticism*, parts of which descend to the level of personal abuse, in which Dennis draws attention among other things to the stature and disabilities of Pope ('a hunch-backed toad'). The battle continued for some years, Dennis becoming increasingly embittered, vituperative, and sour. He launched personal attacks on, among others, Addison, Steele, Swift, Cibber and Savage.

In 1721 he was reconciled temporarily to Pope, but the latter attacked him again in 1728 in the *Dunciad*. Dennis's reply, *A Letter against Mr. Pope at large*, is rather feeble; by this time he was over seventy, going blind, and living in poverty. Pope and other former enemies, including Savage, organized a benefit performance for him in December 1733 of Vanbrugh's *The Provoked Husband*. Pope wrote a prologue specially for the occasion, containing gibes at Dennis which hardly strike the modern reader as good-humoured. Savage wrote a reply, giving thanks on Dennis's behalf. Dennis, on hearing Savage's verses, remarked that the author could be none other than 'that fool Savage'. A few days later, on 6 January 1734, Dennis was dead.

E. M. Hooker (ed.), *The Critical Works of John Dennis* (Baltimore, 1939–43).

H. G. Paul, *Dennis: His Life and Criticism* (New York, 1911).

Derby, 7th Earl of (1607–51), see Stanley, James.

Desborough or Disbrowe, John (1608–80), Parliamentarian soldier.

Born in Eltisley, Cambridgeshire, the second son of James Desborough, a local gentleman, Desborough was trained as a lawyer, but preferred to manage his estates. In 1636 he married Jane Cromwell, the sister of his neighbour Oliver Cromwell. Seven years later he became quartermaster in Cromwell's troop of horse and was promoted to captain when his brother-in-law raised a regiment. He distinguished himself by his ability and courage, and was soon a major in Fairfax's regiment. He fought at the battle of Langport (1645) and the siege of Bristol, and helped crush forces hostile to the New Model Army in the second Civil War. By 1648 he was a colonel, firmly linked to Cromwell's interest, but he refused to have anything to do with the trial of Charles I, although he favoured the deposition of the King. One can perhaps see in this that careful mixture of republican patriotism and self-interest which marked so much of his career.

Desborough was a major general at the Battle of Worcester (1651), and almost succeeded in capturing Charles II in the pursuit. Now the Army and its allies were supreme, and Cromwell was the highest source of patronage in the land: Desborough was among the first to benefit. Honours and offices flowed in his direction, and he proved himself as able an administrator as a soldier, even in the trying post of major general administering the southwest in 1655–56. Politically, however, he was a complete incompetent. Rough and blunt, he always managed to speak his mind in the most tactless manner possible.

Desborough remained loyal to Cromwell until his death, although he was one of the most rabid opponents of the proposal to resurrect the monarchy on his family's behalf. But when the Protector died and Richard Cromwell succeeded, he led the military opposition and cajoled his nephew into dissolving Parliament. The members of the restored Rump appointed him to the Council of State (May 1659), but they too soon became alienated from him and he participated in their expulsion later that year.

Desborough grew ever more violent, and provided an excellent butt for satire, notably in Butler's *Hudibras*. Even his regiment turned against him, and when Monck reinstated the Rump he was banished from London. As the return of the Stuarts grew imminent,

Desborough became alarmed and tried to flee the country, but was caught and imprisoned. At the Restoration, he was exempted from the general Act of Indemnity, but was not made subject to capital punishment, imprisonment, or fine. In fact, he was soon released. He fled to the Netherlands, where he engaged in republican intrigues until, in 1666, he was ordered to return to England or be declared a traitor. This command he meekly obeyed and was promptly jailed. However, he was freed after an examination in 1667 and allowed to live quietly until his death in Hackney in 1680.

M. Ashley, *Cromwell's Generals* (1954).

Devereux, Robert (1591–1646), 3rd Earl of Essex, soldier and commander of the Parliamentary forces during the first phase of the Civil War.

Born in London in January 1591, the son of Robert Devereux, 2nd Earl of Essex (see *Lives of the Tudor Age*), the ill-fated favourite of Elizabeth I, and

Frances Walsingham. In 1601, when Devereux was ten, the inheritance of his title and estates was withheld following the execution of his father. But in 1604, after the succession of James I, the inheritance was restored and he came under the tutelage of the King himself, receiving his education alongside James's son, Henry, Prince of Wales.

On 5 January 1606, under the terms of an arrangement made by James, Essex married Lady Frances Howard. The marriage was, however, no more than a formal agreement, for, having returned from a foreign tour undertaken during the period 1607–09, Essex discovered that his wife was carrying on a passionate affair with Robert Carr (q.v.), James's favourite. A shy, gauche young man lacking in experience, Essex did not inspire the attentions of the ambitious Frances and following her association with Carr, the marriage was eventually dissolved in 1613 by a specially convened divorce commission, the annulment being granted on the grounds that Essex was incapable of cohabiting with his wife.

The next six or seven years were spent in seclusion at his house at Chartley, and Essex did not appear on the stage of history again until 1620, when we encounter him serving with a volunteer force in the Palatinate as part of England's halfhearted support of Frederick V of Bohemia (q.v.). In 1625 he was a vice admiral in the unsuccessful English naval assault on Cadiz. In the following year, after Charles I's financially unproductive second parliament, Essex was one of those who refused to contribute to the forced loan levied to help the war effort, and in 1628 he gave his support to the Petition of Right.

In 1631 Essex married a second time, taking as his wife Elizabeth, daughter of Sir William Paulet. One son was born, who died in infancy, and eventually, after an alleged infidelity on Elizabeth's part, the marriage ended in separation. In 1639 Charles appointed Essex lieutenant general of the army levied to fight the Scots in the First Bishops' War. Yet the swift negotiation of a truce meant that the army never came to battle and was disbanded, Essex himself being discharged 'without ordinary ceremony'. He was further insulted by Charles's refusal to award him an office that had recently fallen vacant.

Throughout 1640 and 1641 the loyalties of Essex were seriously divided, and this tendency to vacillation coloured his whole conduct during the Civil War. In 1640 Charles appointed him one of the commissioners to negotiate with the Scots in Yorkshire. But in the same year Essex was among those who petitioned the King to convene Parliament. In 1641 Charles gave him a seat on the Privy Council, but contrary to Charles's expectations, Essex voted for the condemnation of Strafford (see Wentworth, Thomas). It is probable that shabby treatment on the King's part in 1639 had brought about a change in Essex's attitude. In any event, Essex threw in his lot with the Parliamentarians at the outbreak of the Civil War and, having been made general of the Parliamentarian army in July 1642, he was proclaimed a traitor by Charles.

During the war, as in his earlier military exploits in the Palatinate and at Cadiz, Essex showed himself to be a competent, workmanlike, but unimaginative leader. After the indecisive engagement of Edgehill, in which the Parliamentary force, though master of the field, suffered heavily, Essex went on in 1643 to capture Reading and relieve Gloucester. After the indeterminate Battle of Newbury, Essex in 1644 made an abortive attempt to take Oxford.

His actions were constantly hampered by a diffidence or unwillingness to take on the King in person. This diffidence may have contributed to his defeat at Lostwithiel, Cornwall, at the end of August 1644, but it must also be remembered that the King's forces were on that occasion greatly superior to his own. Essex himself managed to escape, leaving his infantry to surrender. For this and his general vacillation in the conduct of the war, he was strongly criticized in Parliament by Oliver Cromwell (q.v.). A trusted general more than a supporter of the popular cause, Essex opposed the establishment of the New Model Army. In 1645, just as the Self-Denying Ordinance was being passed, by which no M.P. was allowed to hold public office – a manœuvre deliberately designed to get rid of Essex – he resigned his commission.

'Of a rough, proud nature', as Clarendon put it, Essex was also generally popular and had given good service to the Parliamentarians, for which he received an annuity of £10,000 and was made a duke. He died after a period of illness in September 1646 and was buried at Westminster. With his death, the earldom of Essex in the Devereux family became extinct.

W. R. Devereux, *Lives and Letters of the Devereux, Earls of Essex*, vol. 2 (1853).

W. McElwee, *The Murder of Sir Thomas Overbury* (1952).

Vernon F. Snow, *Essex the Rebel: The Life of Robert Devereux, the Third Earl of Essex 1591–1646* (Lincoln, Nebraska, 1970).

Portrait: engraving, quarter-length, by unknown artist, after 1643: British Museum

Digby, Sir Kenelm (1603–65), courtier, diplomat, scientist, and philosopher.

Born 11 July 1603, the son of Sir Everard Digby, who was executed for his share in the Gunpowder Plot in 1606.

After his father's death, Digby was brought up in the Roman Catholic faith by his mother at Gayhurst, Buckinghamshire. After a visit to Spain in 1617 with his cousin John Digby, the future 1st Earl of Bristol, he went in the following year to Gloucester Hall (now Worcester College), Oxford. Digby's abilities impressed his tutor, the mathematician Thomas Allen, who referred to him as the *Mirandula* ('the Little Wonder'). In 1620, however, he left without taking a degree and travelled abroad again, this time to France and Italy. In Florence he must surely have encountered the influence of Galileo, though evidence is lacking. In France, he had been struck by a violent infatuation for Marie de Médicis.

Rejoining his cousin in Spain, he was in Madrid in 1623 when Prince Charles and the Duke of Buckingham arrived there to negotiate for the hand of the Infanta Maria. He ingratiated himself with the royal party and returned with them to England in September 1623, upon which occasion James I favoured him with a knighthood.

In 1625 Digby married Venetia Hanley, a woman renowned for her great beauty and possessed of some intellectual abilities. In eight years of marriage she bore him five children, two of whom survived him.

While at Madrid, Digby's cousin had incurred the hostility of Charles and Buckingham, and as a consequence Digby himself was obstructed in his advancement. Persuaded that he needed to do something positive to win the new King's favour, he set out with Charles I's permission on a privateering expedition in the Mediterranean, which culminated in a victory over French ships in the Venetian harbour of Scanderoon (June 1628). Returning triumphantly to England in February 1629, he was well received. But the threat of reprisals against English traders had hastened his departure from the Mediterranean, and, although the King received him favourably, the government dissociated itself from his action.

The death of his wife in 1633 affected Digby deeply. His demonstration of grief was extravagant, and he went into seclusion at Gresham College, Cambridge, where he concerned himself with experiments in chemistry.

After 1630 Digby had adopted Protestantism, but by 1635, after visiting France, he had been reconverted to the Catholic religion. For this, he was reproved by William Laud (q.v.), but the two remained friends. Digby now became associated with the circle of Roman Catholics around Queen Henrietta Maria (q.v.). In 1639 he appealed on behalf of the King for support from English Catholics against the Scots. The House of Commons censured him for this, demanding his removal from the King's councils. As a consequence, Digby was banished and found himself in France in 1641. Here he was involved in a duel with a French lord who had insulted Charles I. The Frenchman was killed and Digby left France only through the good offices of Louis XIII, who took his part in the affair. Upon returning to England, Digby was imprisoned but soon released. He returned to France in 1643, residing at Paris, where he published two philosophical treatises, *Of Bodies* and *Of the Immortality of Man's Soul* (both 1644). In Paris he also met Descartes.

Digby remained abroad throughout the major part of the Civil War. He was appointed chancellor to the Queen and remained with her in France, except for two visits to Rome in 1645 and 1647 in order to enlist assistance from the Holy See. Pope Innocent X was impressed by his appeal, but Digby failed to give satisfactory assurances that Charles could be brought over to Catholicism – Charles himself had given no guarantee of this – and in the event the Royalists had to be content with a grant of funds rather than more practical support.

Digby made an abortive attempt to return to England in 1649 (he was banished again after only three months), and it was not until 1654 that he was allowed to return without impediment. He now became closely associated with Cromwell, from whom he hoped to win toleration for the Roman Catholics. Cromwell was keen to avoid giving France and Spain the opportunity of uniting against England, and Digby undertook negotiations in Germany and France to ensure this. In 1660 he returned to England and was received well despite his collaboration with the Protectorate. His appointment as chancellor to Henrietta Maria was confirmed.

In 1663 he became a member of the Royal Society. In the same year, however, his peripheral involvement in the attempted impeachment of Clarendon by his cousin, George Digby, the 2nd Earl of Bristol, in which he tried to intercede for Bristol, led to his disgrace. In 1664 he was banished from court. His remaining life was spent in literary and philosophical pursuits. Digby died in London on 11 June 1665, the anniversary of his naval triumph at Scanderoon harbour.

Though intellectually versatile, Digby made little contribution to those fields in which he worked. Given to tremendous exaggeration – John Evelyn refers to him as an 'errant mountebank' and Henry Stubbes called him 'the very Pliny of our age for lying' – Digby as a philosopher is facile and derivative, and as a natural scientist is blessed with too free an imagination. His 'powder of sympathy' is famous: it could, it was claimed, heal a wound by merely being applied to a bandage taken from the wound. Numerous works are attributed to him, including *A Conference with a Lady about Choice of a Religion* (1638) and *Private Memoirs* (edited with an introduction by N. H. Nicholas, 1827).

E. W. Bligh, *Sir Kenelm Digby and his Venetia* (1932).

H. M. Digby, *Sir Kenelm Digby and George Digby, Earl of Bristol* (1912).

R. T. Peterson, *Sir Kenelm Digby, the Ornament of England* (1956).

Portrait: oil, half-length, after Van Dyck: N.P.G.

Disbrowe, John (1608–80), see Desborough, John.

Dobson, William (1610–46), sergeant painter to Charles I.

Born in Holborn, London, in 1610, the son of a gentleman who squandered his estate, Dobson was forced to learn the art of painting to earn his living. He became the most distinguished British painter before Hogarth.

Although apprenticed to Robert Peake, an art dealer and painter, Dobson seemed to have learnt more from Francis Cleyn, the designer for the Mortlake Tapestry Works. Through Cleyn he learnt much of the tradition of the Italian High Renaissance, and it was probably during this period that he saw the royal collection of Venetian paintings. He was also the protégé of Francis Bacon, who employed him to redecorate Gorhambury and Verulam House at St. Albans.

Dobson apparently copied paintings by Titian and Van Dyck as well as a great many other Old Masters. One of these paintings was seen by Van Dyck in a London shop window and he immediately introduced Dobson to the King's notice. In 1641 Charles appointed him sergeant painter and in 1642 he accompanied the monarch and nobles to the wartime court in Oxford. In the four years before his death, Dobson painted over sixty portraits, chiefly of eminent Royalists. He was popular with Charles, though the King never actually sat for him. Dobson was overwhelmed with commissions and in order to lessen the pressure demanded that his sitters pay half the price before he began. Dobson was the first to introduce this practice.

With the surrender of Oxford, Dobson returned to London, but having incurred a great many debts and being 'somewhat loose and irregular in his way of living', was imprisoned. His release was obtained by a sympathetic patron but he died shortly afterwards on 28 October 1646. Married twice, Dobson's personal wit and amiability did much to enhance the popularity of his painting.

Dobson was an excellent draughtsman with a distinctive style and although he lived at a time when Van Dyck was paramount as a society painter, the latter's influence is not evident in his work. His early studies of the Venetian works in the royal collection seem to have been the most important single factor in the formation of his style. The colouring and textures of his canvases are strongly Venetian, while his feeling for mood and character remains uncompromisingly English.

Having closely studied the 'tenebristi' painters, Dobson applied their naturalistic techniques to portraiture in a way no other English painter had yet attempted. His use of enigmatic classical reliefs is not purely decorative as with Van Dyck, but is intended to be of direct relevance to the sitter's personality. Portraits such as those of Sir Charles Lucas, Sir William Fermor, Sir George Carteret, and, perhaps his masterpiece,

Sir William Compton, which is at Castle Ashby, all contain these enigmatic reliefs.

Described by his contemporary Aubrey (q.v.) as the 'most excellent painter England hath yet bred', Dobson shows total mastery of the half-length portrait. Moreover, he shows considerable originality in his group arrangements of half-length figures, in which he introduces a perception of the contrasting psychologies of the sitters not seen before in British portraiture; examples of this are his paintings of 'Prince Rupert, Colonel Murray and Colonel Russell' in Lord Sandys's collection and 'Dobson, Sir Charles Cotterrell, and Sir Balthasar Gerbier', which is at Albury Park.

Works at:
National Portrait Gallery, London.
National Gallery, London.
National Portrait Gallery, Edinburgh.
Birmingham Art Gallery.
Tate Gallery, London.
Hull Gallery.
Liverpool Gallery.
Ashmolean, Oxford.
Duke of Devonshire's Collection.
Duke of Newcastle's Collection.
Earl of Ellesmere's Collection.
Lord Thurlow's Collection.
Hampton Court.

Portrait: oil, half-length, after a self-portrait, c. 1642–46: N.P.G.

Donne, John (1572–1631), poet and ecclesiastic.

Born in London in 1572, in the parish of St. Olave, and recognized in his youth as an accomplished poet and intellect in the court circles he frequented, John Donne later abandoned secular poetry and eventually became the most important preacher of his time. In this century, he has come to be considered one of the greatest English poets.

Both Donne's parents were Roman Catholics, and though his father died when he was young his mother, Elizabeth Heywood, continued to maintain her children in this faith, despite the increasingly strong measures being taken against Roman Catholics in England. In 1593 a brother of Donne's died in prison, where he had been committed for sheltering a priest, and many of Donne's own early poems are mocking satires on the moral laxity of court life and the Anglican Church.

The young Donne was conspicuously precocious, and someone remarked of him that 'he was rather born wise than made so by study'. His grandfather, John Heywood, had been a playwright and epigrammatist, and his mother appeared to recognize his genius for she treated him with great gentleness and care. At the age of twelve, Donne entered Hart Hall, Oxford, where he shared a chamber with Sir Henry Wotton (q.v.), who became a close friend for the rest of Donne's life. Donne left Oxford without taking a degree, probably because this involved swearing loyalty to the reformed Church of England. Izaak Walton reports that he then attended Cambridge, but there is no evidence of this. Before taking up residence at Thavies Inn, a law school, Donne probably travelled on the Continent, possibly taking part in the expedition led by Drake and Norreys and the siege of Corunna in 1589.

At Lincoln's Inn, to which he transferred in 1592, Donne is remembered as being 'not dissolute, but very neat, a great visiter of Ladies, a great frequenter of Playes, a great writer of conceited Verses'. Izaak Walton's account differs, portraying Donne as a serious student perplexed by the theological conflict between Anglican and Catholic doctrines, but in the poems he was now writing both these apparently contradictory aspects of his character are expressed:

often cynical and witty, they manage to combine a severe intellectual toughness with their sensual exuberance. Into the pastoral tradition of Elizabethan poetry Donne injects a new note of realism and intensity. These poems were not published but were circulated widely in manuscript, and contemporary references show that they attracted wide attention. A portrait of this period shows Donne with delicate, rather exquisite features, and an expression that is not without a touch of arrogance.

In 1596 Donne volunteered with other young wits to join Essex's expedition to Spain; he suggests in *The Calme* that one of his motives for military service was to escape from 'the queasy pain/Of being belov'd, and loving'. The fleet returned that year with much booty after the capture of Cadiz and the looting of Faro. Donne joined up again the following year, when new plans were formed for another venture, but the fleet was delayed and then driven back to Plymouth by bad weather. Donne wrote to a friend about the adventure: 'It is true that Jonas was in a whales belly three days but he came not voluntary as I did nor was troubled with the stink of 150 land soldiers as we.' The fleet set sail eventually, but after several mishaps returned home with little achieved.

On his return Donne became secretary to the newly appointed lord keeper, Sir Thomas Egerton; this could have been the start to a successful diplomatic career, for Donne now came into contact with many of the leading statesmen of his time, but any worldly ambitions that Donne may have harboured were wrecked in December 1601 by his secret marriage to Anne More. Anne was Egerton's niece, but her father, Sir George More, was hostile to the marriage, and insisted on Donne's dismissal and imprisonment. He was soon released, but Egerton, having at first been unwilling to dismiss Donne, refused to alter that decision once made, and Donne had to go through a long legal battle before Anne was allowed to join him. All his fortunes were now suddenly reversed; he had little money and no position. He was obliged to leave London with his wife and accept the hospitality of a friend, Sir Francis Wooley, at Pyrford, near Guildford, where they stayed until 1604. Although he made several applications for positions at court, Donne had no success; his abrupt dismissal, and possibly some fear of this independent and sharp-witted young man, seemed to act as a bar against any new appointment.

Anne Donne died in 1617, having borne twelve children, seven of whom survived her. Donne's marriage was undoubtedly the turning point of his life: by it he had forfeited all chance of worldly success, and the only avenue of advancement now left open was the Church. Thomas Morton, a personal friend, urged Donne to take orders, but Donne at first refused; according to Izaak Walton, his reason was his sense of personal unworthiness. There is no firm evidence that Donne was going through a period of crisis, but he was spending much time studying the religious issues between the Catholic and Anglican faiths, and in accordance with James's request wrote *The Pseudo-Martyr* (1610), in which he argued that the Catholics who refused to take the oath of allegiance lacked a genuine cause and were only sham martyrs. Donne's poetry during this period also became increasingly preoccupied with problems of religion, expressing his own spiritual dilemma with the same intensity that his earlier verse had used to express the vitality of the senses. He also wrote *Biathanatos*, a work in which he enquired whether suicide could not under some circumstances be justified.

At last, in 1613, Donne announced to James his willingness to go into the Church, but it was not until 25 January 1615, that he was finally ordained. James I immediately made him his chaplain, with the duty of preaching to the court, and he also accepted livings at Keyston and Sevenoaks. Donne found a deep satisfaction in his work as a minister, performing all his duties with great conscientiousness and sincerity. In 1616 he was appointed divinity reader at Lincoln's Inn, and he preached there so successfully each Sunday that he soon gained the reputation for being one of the ablest preachers of the time. Five years later he received the promised preferment from James I, when he was appointed Dean of St. Paul's. All of his printed sermons were rapidly sold.

In 1623, suffering from a severe attack of spotted fever, Donne wrote the *Devotions upon Emergent Occasions*; he recovered from this illness, but his health again weakened towards the end of the decade, and when he preached before the King on 12 February 1631, his appearance was clearly that of a dying man. Soon after this sermon Donne had his portrait painted in his shroud and composed his own epitaph. When death came, on 31 March 1631, Donne was prepared.

Helen Gardner (ed.), *The Divine Poems* (1952).

Helen Gardner (ed.), *Elegies, and the Songs and Sonnets* (1965).

H. J. C. Grierson (ed.), *Poems by John Donne* (2 vols.; 1912).

J. Hayward (ed.), *John Donne: Complete Poetry and Selected Prose* (1962, rev. ed.).

W. Milgate (ed.), *The Satires, Epigrams and Verse Letters* (1967).

George R. Potter and Evelyn M. Simpson (eds.), *The Complete Sermons of John Donne* (10 vols.; Berkeley and Los Angeles, 1953–61).

Robert C. Bald, *John Donne: a Life*, ed. W. Milgate (1970).

Edmund W. Gosse, *The Life and Letters of John Donne* (2 vols.; 1899).

Frank Kermode, *Discussions of John Donne* (Boston, Mass., 1963).

James B. Leishman, *The Monarch of Wit: An Analytical and Comparative Study of the Poetry of John Donne* (New York, 1965, 7th ed.).

Doniphan Louthan, *The Poetry of Donne: A Study in Explication* (New York, 1951).

Evelyn M. Simpson, *A Study of the Prose Works of John Donne* (1948, rev. ed.).

Portraits: oil, quarter-length, after I. Oliver: N.P.G.; miniature, by I. Oliver, 1616: Royal Collection; oil, attributed to C. Johnson, 1622: V. and A.

Dorset, 6th Earl of (1643–1706), see Sackville, Charles.

Dowland, John (?1563–1626), lutenist and composer, *see Lives of the Tudor Age.*

Drummond, William (1585–1649), known as 'Drummond of Hawthornden', poet and man of letters.

Born at Hawthornden, near Edinburgh, the son of John Drummond, first laird of Hawthornden. Drummond was educated at Edinburgh and took his M.A. degree from the University in 1605. He then travelled to the Continent to study law, attending lectures at Bourges and Paris in 1607 and 1608. Upon the death of his father in 1610, he succeeded to the family estate as laird of Hawthornden, where he retired to devote himself to literature. His grief at the sudden loss of his fiancée, Mary Cunningham, who died in 1615 shortly before the day set for their wedding, is reflected in the melancholy spirit of the madrigals and sonnets that he wrote at this time. He did not marry until 1632, when he wed Elizabeth Logan. Although he led a quiet life, seldom leaving his estate, Drummond corresponded with several prominent men of the day, among them Michael Drayton, and was acquainted with Ben Jonson (q.v.), who visited him in the winter of 1618. Drummond's record of their conversations shows a lively and unrestrained Jonson declaring his opinions on a number of his contemporaries and their works, including the poems of his host, which 'smelled too much of the Schooles, and were not after the fancie of the tyme'.

Drummond's verse, all of which is written in English, is indeed somewhat derivative, being especially indebted to the Italian models that formed a large part of his extensive reading in foreign languages. The sombre style of *Poems* (1616) and *A Cypresse Grove* (1623), a prose meditation on death, contrasts with the more vigorous verse of *Forth Feasting*, a poem written to celebrate James I's visit to Scotland in 1617. In addition to his poems and translations from Italian, French, and Spanish, he wrote a history of Scotland from 1423 to 1524 (published in 1655) and numerous pamphlets in support of the Royalist cause. His collected poems were first published in 1656.

L. E. Kastner (ed.), *Poetical Works* (1913).

C. H. Herford and P. Simpson (eds.), 'Conversations of Ben Jonson with Drummond', *Ben Jonson* vol. 1 (1925).

David Masson, *Drummond* (1873).

Dryden, John (1631–1700), poet, essayist, dramatist, and translator; poet laureate (1668).

John Dryden was born on 9 August 1631, at the vicarage of Aldwinkle All Saints, near Oundle, in Northamptonshire. He was the first of fourteen children born to Erasmus Dryden and his wife, Mary Pickering. The family on both sides supported the Parliamentarian cause during the Civil War and were probably Puritans.

John received his early education at Westminster School under the famous Dr. Busby, and one of his fellow pupils was John Locke (q.v.). He published an elegy upon the death of a schoolfellow, Lord Hastings, in 1649. From 1650 to 1654 he was at Trinity College, Cambridge, where he published complimentary verses to his friend John Hoddesdon (1650) and wrote a love letter to his cousin of eighteen, Honor Dryden (c. 1653). He left Cambridge with his B.A. in January 1654 and in June of the same year his father died, leaving him a modest annual income of

£40. He used the influence of a cousin, Sir Gilbert Pickering, Cromwell's chamberlain, to obtain a clerkship in the Commonwealth government, and composed an elegy, *Heroic Stanzas*, on the death of the Lord Protector in 1658.

Notwithstanding this, Dryden wrote a number of poems, *Astraea Redux*, on the restoration of Charles II in 1660, and addressed verses to Chancellor Clarendon (Edward Hyde, q.v.) and the archaeologist Dr. Charleton. It was on the latter's recommendation that Dryden was elected to the Royal Society in 1662.

Having established his credentials with the new government, an act necessary for the continuing court patronage and notice on which a literary career depended, Dryden tried his hand at his first play, a prose comedy called *The Wild Gallant* (1663). The play was a failure, but attracted the favourable attention of Charles's current favourite mistress, Barbara Villiers (q.v.), Countess of Castlemaine, and Dryden responded to this with a complimentary poem. Later that year (1 December), he married the fairly wealthy Lady Elizabeth Howard. In 1664 his first verse drama, *The Rival Ladies*, was produced, and he collaborated with Sir Robert Howard, his brother-in-law, on *The Indian Queen*. The sequel, *The Indian Emperor*, was put on in 1665 and scored a success, but the outbreak of plague in the spring of that year forced Dryden to leave London for the country.

It was during the Drydens' stay at the country estate of John's father-in-law that their first son, Charles, was born (1666). The following year Dryden published *Annus Mirabilis*, a poem commemorating the Great Fire of September 1666 and the naval war with Holland, with the intention of rallying public support for the monarchy. He also composed *An Essay of Dramatic Poesy*, a supposed dialogue between Dryden, Sir Robert Howard, Charles Sackville (q.v.), and Sir Charles Sedley (q.v.), discussing the new age of theatre that the Restoration had ushered in. It demonstrates that Dryden's attention at this period was almost exclusively concentrated on the theatre. Between 1667 and 1681 he wrote some fourteen plays. The year 1667 saw the tragicomedy *Secret Love*, based on a Molière play, and an adaptation of *The Tempest* carried out in collaboration with the poet laureate Davenant (q.v.). The success of these efforts is evidenced by Dryden being able to lend his monarch Charles II £500 in 1667, a shrewd investment that was to be returned with interest in 1674 and by a warrant being issued to make Dryden poet laureate upon the death of Davenant in April 1668, Dryden renewing his loan to Charles in the same year. This eventful period (1667–69) also saw the production of a comedy, *An Evening's Love* (1668), and the heroic *Tyrannic Love* (1669), in which the part of Valeria was played by Nell Gwynne (q.v.). Two more sons, John (1667 or 1668) and Erasmus Henry (1669), were born, and in June 1668 Dryden received an M.A. from Cambridge 'by the dispensation of Archbishop Sheldon in consequence of a recommendation of King Charles II'.

Among the plays of this period, the most outstanding are *The Conquest of Granada*, produced in 1670 (the year in which he was appointed poet laureate and historiographer royal, with a pension of £200 backdated to 1668), *Amboyna* (1672), an anti-Dutch tragedy about the massacre of some Englishmen by the Dutch in the Moluccas in 1623, *Aureng-Zebe* (1675), his last rhymed heroic tragedy, influenced by Racine and Shakespeare, and the anti-papist tragicomedy *The Spanish Friar* (1680).

Marriage à la Mode (1672) is one of his best comedies. The finest work of this period is, however, *All For Love* (1677), a reworking of the Antony and Cleopatra legend, his best play and his first in blank verse.

In 1672 George Villiers (q.v.), the 2nd Duke of Buckingham, produced *The Rehearsal*, a lively satire on heroic plays, particularly on *The Conquest of Granada*, lampooning Dryden himself as 'Mr. Bayes' (a reference to the laureateship, *Bayes* meaning 'laurel wreath'). This marked the beginning of a disputatious period of Dryden's life, for in 1673–74 he became involved in pamphlet broadsides with one Elkanah Settle, the author of bombastic plays patronized by the nobility. Also in 1676, Dryden wrote *The State of Innocence*, an opera based on Milton's *Paradise Lost*; another adaptation, this time of Shakespeare's *Troilus and Cressida*, appeared in 1679, but neither of these works have the qualities that mark *All for Love*.

There was no doubting that Dryden was now a public figure, however, and one, in the manner of Milton, Pope, and Johnson, who was at the heart of the controversies of the day. Although his first verse satire, the brilliant *Mac Flecknoe*, a lampoon on the Restoration dramatist Thomas Shadwell (q.v.), did not appear in print until pirated in 1682, the manuscript appears to have circulated for some time among Dryden's friends. That he had a tongue to wound, and was feared for it, is the only explanation for a strange episode in 1679, in which Dryden was set upon and beaten by masked thugs hired by John Wilmot (q.v.), 2nd Earl of Rochester, who had been attacked in a passage in the anonymously issued *Essay on Satire*, written by Dryden's friend the Earl of Mulgrave. Rochester suspected Dryden of having contributed the defamatory passage, and a flysheet reporting the outrage can be seen in the Lamb and Flag tavern in Rose Street, Covent Garden, where the attack took place.

Mac Flecknoe marked the beginning of Dryden's new career as a verse satirist, and in 1681 his most famous work, *Absalom and Achitophel*, appeared, running through nine editions in two years. Using the same basic allegorical structure as the earlier work, *Absalom and Achitophel* constructs an elaborate but striking analogy between the Israel of the Old Testament and the England of the middle and latter part of the 17th century. *Israel* is England; *Hebron*, Scotland; *Egypt*, France; *Sanhedrin* is Parliament; *Abbethdins* are judges; *David* is Charles II; *Pharaoh*, Louis XIV; *Absalom*, the Duke of Monmouth; *Achitophel*, Shaftesbury; *Saul*, Cromwell; *Zimri*, Buckingham; *Corah*, Titus Oates; and so on. The poem describes the political situation and tells of the temptation of Absalom by Achitophel, referring of course to Monmouth's Rebellion (see Monmouth, Duke of), with the final assertion of David's superiority. Composed in the form of 'heroic' rhyming couplets, later to be adapted so successfully by Pope (see *Lives of the Georgian Age*), the poem has brilliant sketches of leading political figures of the day, as of Shaftesbury, and exploits Dryden's poetic and satirical gifts in a framework which is all the more impressive for its analysis of power and political motive.

Among Dryden's other poetical works, the most notable are *The Medal* (1682), a further satiric attack on Shaftesbury, and the didactic verse essays *Religio Laici* (1682) and *The Hind and the Panther* (1687). *Religio Laici*, subtitled 'A Layman's Faith', emphasizes the values of tradition and authority in religion, while *The Hind and the Panther* dramatizes the religious and political turmoil in

England during the short reign of James II. Both poems reflect the gradual shift of Dryden's affiliations over the years of confusion that he epitomizes so well in *Absalom and Achitophel*. The culmination of this process was in 1686, after the accession of James, when Dryden was received into the Catholic Church.

Dryden's open espousal of Catholicism placed him in jeopardy when James II was overthrown in the Glorious Revolution of 1688, and after the coronation of William III he was ousted as poet laureate and historiographer royal, with the added irony that the satirical butt of *Mac Flecknoe*, Shadwell, was installed in his place. Dryden's refusal to take the Oath of Allegiance to William also lost him the place in the Customs he had held since 1683, and the rest of his life was marked by a degree of penury that 'Squire Dryden', as his enemies dubbed him, had not been cut out for.

It was the pressure of financial circumstances that drove Dryden to resume his dramatic career, with the opera *Albion and Albanius* and its sequel *King Arthur* (both 1685; *Arthur* not produced until 1691). Among these later works is the tragicomedy *Don Sebastian* (1689), the comedy *Amphitryon* (1690), the tragedy *Cleomenes* (1692), and his last play, the tragicomedy *Love Triumphant* (1694). None of these works can be accounted in the same category as his earlier dramas.

Dryden's last years were devoted mainly to translation, a field in which he excelled. As early as 1680, he had written a preface to an edition of Ovid's *Epistles*. In 1683 he collaborated on a translation of Plutarch's *Lives* and in the following year Jacob Tonson, his publisher, issued *Miscellany Poems*, which included translations from Ovid, Virgil, and Theocritus, as well as Dryden's own major poems. More translations followed in a second part issued in 1685 and in 1692 Dryden translated satires of Juvenal and Persius, with a preface entitled a 'Discourse Concerning the Original and Progress of Satire'. The third part of the *Miscellany Poems* came out in 1693 and in the same year he began his translation of Virgil, which appeared in 1697, containing an essay on the *Georgics* by Addison (see *Lives of the Georgian Age*). The work is calculated to have brought Dryden about £1,200. Among his last works were his much-praised second ode for St. Cecilia's Day, entitled *Alexander's Feast* (1697), and in his final year he published his collection of fables and tales from Ovid, Chaucer, and Boccaccio, brought out shortly before his death on 1 May 1700.

A bare account of the main events of Dryden's life, until his conversion to Catholicism, may give the impression of a somewhat opportunistic man, whose timing of his changes of allegiance seemed to coincide with the shifts in the religious and political climate. But this view is superficial when we consider the import of Dryden's best work, in *Absalom and Achitophel, All For Love,* *The Medal*, and the best didactic verse of *Religio Laici* and *The Hind and the Panther*. Nor should we underestimate the sincerity of his conversion to the Roman Catholic faith, despite his own emphatically Protestant upbringing. His place as the greatest political satirist of the English language is assured. He was buried in Chaucer's grave in Westminster Abbey, and a monument was later erected to him.

G. R. Noyes (ed.), *The Poetical Works of Dryden* (Cambridge, Mass., 1950, rev. ed.).

Sir Walter Scott (ed.), *The Works of John Dryden* (18 vols.; 1808 and 1821: rev. George Saintsbury, 1882–93).

E. N. Hooker (ed.), *Works of John Dryden* (Los Angeles and Berkeley, 1956–).

George Saintsbury, *John Dryden* (New York, 1881).

Charles E. Ward, *The Life of John Dryden* (Los Angeles and Berkeley, 1961).

Portraits: oil on panel, half-length, after Kneller, 1698: N.P.G.; oil, full-length, by J. Maubert: N.P.G.; oil, three-quarter length, by Kneller, 1693: N.P.G.

Dundee, 1st Viscount (?1649–89), see Graham, John.

E

Eliot, Sir John (1592–1632), Puritan parliamentarian and leader of the early opposition to Charles I.

Born on 11 April 1592, in St. Germans, Cornwall, son of Richard Eliot, a wealthy landowner. Eliot was educated at Blundell's School, Tiverton, Exeter College, Oxford, and the Inns of Court. As a young man Eliot showed the passion and impetuosity that were to lead to his death. His excellent education was coupled with a Puritan conscience, rigid on matters of political principle yet flexible when it came to money. To this firm basis for a career were added Continental travels, during which he made the acquaintance of George Villiers (q.v.), the future 1st Duke of Buckingham, who obtained for him in 1619 the post of vice-admiral of Devon. In this capacity Eliot showed great activity, and in 1623 arrested a pirate who enjoyed the patronage of one of the secretaries of state. Eliot was arrested and imprisoned on a trumped-up charge and released several months later only through Buckingham's influence.

In 1624 Eliot was elected to Parliament. He had served in the Commons in 1614, but it was not until this later date that he distinguished himself as a Parliamentarian. He quickly won a reputation for brilliant oratory and independent behaviour, although he supported Buckingham's warlike policy towards Spain. The next year saw him once again an M.P., this time criticizing Charles I's policy of toleration towards Catholics. By the end of the session he was firmly in the opposition, at odds with his former patron Buckingham, who did not wish to accede to the Commons' demands that only men having the confidence of Parliament be appointed councillors.

Before summoning Parliament in 1626, the King appointed the crown's most severe critics in the last House as sheriffs, thereby excluding them from the new assembly. That left Eliot as the foremost leader among opposition members. By this time he was thoroughly disillusioned with Buckingham's leadership and saw treachery where there was merely incompetence. He launched a fiery attack on the duke and called for an inquiry into the failure of the Cadiz expedition. At his urging the Commons resolved that it had the right to question any of the King's subjects, and he managed the impeachment of Buckingham. Charles had Eliot imprisoned, but the Commons immediately forced his release. To save Buckingham, Charles was compelled to dissolve Parliament.

In the aftermath of his session Eliot was stripped of all his posts and in 1627 again jailed, this time for refusing a forced loan. But his freedom was guaranteed by Charles's need to summon a new parliament. In the first session, in 1628, he resumed his leadership of the opposition; with Coke (q.v.), he ensured the passage of the Petition of Right and continued the assault on royal policy. This grew more intense in the next session (1629), when he turned his rhetoric against the Arminian tendencies in the Church. When Charles ordered the Commons to adjourn, Speaker

Finch (see Finch, Sir John) was held in his seat while Eliot read out three resolutions on arbitrary taxation and religious change through the tumult.

Parliament was immediately dissolved and eight of its leaders, including Eliot, were incarcerated in the Tower. When brought before the Court of King's Bench he refused to answer any charges, asserting that he was answerable solely to the House of Commons; nevertheless, he was fined and ordered to be kept in the Tower at the King's pleasure. A confession that he had erred was all that was sought, but Eliot refused to budge.

While in the Tower he spent much time writing, producing a description of the events of Charles I's first parliament and *The Monarchy of Man*, a constitutional treatise advocating government by a strong monarchy relying heavily on the advice of Parliament. Imprisonment ruined his health, and he died in jail from tuberculosis on 28 November 1632. Eliot quickly became a martyr to the Puritan opposition.

J. Forster, *Sir John Eliot* (2 vols.; 1864).
H. Hulme, *The Life of Sir John Eliot* (1957).
H. R. Williamson, *Four Stuart Portraits* (1949).

Elizabeth (1596–1662), Electress Palatine and Queen of Bohemia, called 'the Queen of Hearts'.

Born in August 1596 at Falkland Castle in Fifeshire, eldest daughter of James VI of Scotland (James I of England) and Anne of Denmark (qq.v.), Elizabeth was brought up by the Earl of Linlithgow; after the royal family moved to England, her education was supervised by the Countess of Kildare, and later by Lord and Lady Harington at Combe Abbey in Warwickshire.

From 1608 onwards Elizabeth often appeared at court. Her beauty and charm inspired poets and attracted suitors. In 1612 James I formed an alliance with the

princes of the German Protestant union. For political reasons he supported the marriage between Elizabeth and the Elector Palatine, Frederick V, which took place on 14 February 1613. During their first five years of marriage, the couple resided in Heidelberg, where Elizabeth was renowned for her festive and grand style of living.

On 26 August 1619, Frederick was elected king of Bohemia by the Bohemian estates. Frederick's reign in Prague was short lived. After the disastrous Battle of the White Mountain on 8 November 1620, in which Frederick's Protestant forces were routed by the Catholics under Tilly, he and his family fled into exile. Elizabeth took refuge first in Küstrin, then proceeded to Berlin and Wolfenbüttel. She was finally joined by Frederick at The Hague, where they were received by Maurice of Orange.

Interventions by James I to restore the Palatinate were unsuccessful. The keen help of some of Elizabeth's admirers, among whom were Duke Christian of

Brunswick and the 1st Earl of Craven, achieved nothing. The victories of Gustavus Adolphus of Sweden aroused new hopes, but Frederick's claims were ignored. Frederick died on 29 November 1632, in Mainz, shortly after Gustavus Adolphus, who fell at Lützen.

During her exile in Holland, Elizabeth was dependent partly on the generosity of that state and partly on a pension from the English Parliament. After the Peace of Westphalia in 1648, her son Charles Louis regained the Rhenish Palatinate, but he refused financial help to her. The income from the English Parliament ceased after the execution of Charles I. She was reduced to relative poverty and incurred heavy debts.

With the restoration of her nephew Charles II to the English throne, Elizabeth's fortunes improved in the last year of her life. In 1661 she returned to England, and despite the initial opposition of the King was soon granted a pension. At the beginning of 1662 she moved to Leicester House in Leicester Fields, London, where she died soon afterwards on 8 February.

Elizabeth was an ancestress of the Hanoverian line through her daughter Sophia, who married Ernst Augustus, Elector of Hanover, and was mother of George I of England.

A. Buchan, *A Stuart Princess* (1934).

S. C. Lomas, *Elizabeth Electress Palatine and Queen of Bohemia* (1909).

C. Oman, *Elizabeth of Bohemia* (1938).

C. V. Wedgwood, *The Thirty Years' War* (1938).

Portraits: oil, full-length, by Daniel Mytens, 1626–27: St. James's Palace; oil, full-length, by G. Bonthorst, 1642: N.P.G.; oil on panel, half-length, studio of M. van Miereveldt, c. 1623: N.P.G.

Endecott, John (c. 1589–1665), governor of Massachusetts. The son of Thomas Endecott of Chagford, Devon, the heir of a tin-mining family.

Of the early history of John Endecott very little is known. At some stage he came under the influence of Puritan preachers, and he is thought to have served against the Spanish in the Low Countries.

In 1628, with five other pious men, Endecott bought a patent from the Plymouth council for some land on Massachusetts Bay. That same year, he set off in charge of the vanguard of a larger expedition of Puritan colonists, who followed in 1630. Until that date he governed the small colony, settling at Salem and beginning the clearing of the land. He imposed his strict religious views on the neighbourhood and drove out the inhabitants of Merry Mount, a small settlement that had shown the temerity to raise a maypole. In 1629 Independent congregations were set up in the new colony on the model of Plymouth, and Endecott expelled as 'schismatics' those settlers who wished to remain in the Church of England. The governor's sense of duty was marked neither by humour nor by tolerance.

Endecott surrendered his powers to John Winthrop, whom the General Council had elected governor, when the latter arrived with the main body of colonists in 1630. Endecott remained active, however, in the affairs of Massachusetts, serving as a magistrate and frequently winning the governorship. His army experience secured him military commands, in which he demonstrated an unquestionable mediocrity. Although not devoted to learning in the manner of Winthrop, he helped to establish a free school at Salem and to found Harvard College.

The last years of Endecott's life were spent leading a particularly vicious persecution of the Quakers and struggling to protect the charter and liberties of Massachusetts against the Restoration monarchy. Endecott died, an honest, narrow-minded public servant, on 15 March 1665.

L. S. Mayo, *John Endecott: a biography* (Cambridge, Mass., 1936).

Erskine, John (1675–1732), 6th or 11th Earl of Mar, Jacobite leader, see *Lives of the Georgian Age.*

Essex, 3rd Earl of (1591–1646), see Devereux, Robert.

Etherege, George (?1635–92), dramatist, generally acknowledged as the originator of the Restoration 'comedy of manners' practised by Congreve, Wycherley, Vanbrugh, and Farquhar (qq.v.), among others.

'Gentle George', or 'Easy Etherege', as he was later to be affectionately called, was born in about 1635 of an Oxfordshire family. He was the eldest of seven children; his father, Captain George Etherege, appears to have taken his son abroad during the Civil War, and the young George may well have seen some of the early Molière comedies in Paris. Captain George died in 1650, and in about 1653 George's grandfather, a vintner, apprenticed him to an attorney in Beaconsfield. He studied law at one of the Inns of Court in London.

Etherege's first comedy, *The Comical Revenge, or Love in a Tub,* was performed at Lincoln's Inn Fields theatre in March 1664 and was immediately popular, bringing £1,000 to the company within a month. Its popularity must be seen in relation to the somewhat static heroic verse plays of Dryden (q.v.) and others that were the standard dramatic fare at that time. Although its main plot is written in the usual heroic couplets, its farcical subplot, involving the pursuit of a rich widow by the foppish Sir Frederick Frollick, is entirely new and fresh, exploiting the current vogue for exquisite fop manners among the court and aristocratic circles of Charles II's reign.

The success of this first venture does not appear to have unduly excited Etherege. The facility of his style, always in keeping with his own 'proud laziness' and the current fashionable view of the writer as a gifted gentleman, seemed to be more important to him in gaining him access to the Restoration court, with its famous poetic rakes such as Sir Charles Sedley (q.v.), the Earl of Rochester (see Wilmot, John), and Charles Sackville (q.v.), Earl of Dorset. Like his contemporaries, Etherege managed to get himself involved in a number of scandals and escapades, including a riot at Epsom in 1676 in which a man was killed.

Etherege's second comedy, *She Would If She Could,* was staged at Lincoln's Inn Fields on 6 February 1668, and was a great success in spite of a poor production. Finally abandoning the romantic verse element of heroic drama altogether, the play establishes Etherege's own peculiar terrain of witty persiflage, in which, to use his own words, the object was 'to shoot folly as it flies, And catch the manners living as they rise'. The high spirits and wit of its heroines, Ariana and Gatty, are balanced against the worldly cynicism of their prospective partners, Courtal and Freeman, for whom 'flirtation is the only serious business'. This use of a contrasting pair of lovers, as opposed to the two- or three-tier plots of the Jacobean and later drama, is one of the characteristic features of Restoration comedy.

The world of fops, rakes and wits, of marriages and *mésalliances* is entirely contemporary, and the lives of the gay dogs about whom he wrote are probably much like Etherege's own. One story says that he became the lover of the actress Mrs. Elizabeth Barry and had a daughter by her during this period. At any rate, Etherege's dramatic characters and situations reflect a shrewd, albeit cynical view of a man of the world with a gift for detecting hypocrisy.

In 1668 Etherege was sent to Constantinople as secretary to Sir Daniel Harvey, the English ambassador to Turkey, and he wrote an entertaining account of his time there. After his return, in 1671, he wrote a prologue for the opening of the new Dorset Garden Theatre (9 November), but showed no particular inclination to write any more for the stage himself. For this he is said to have been reproached by Rochester, the result being his last and best play, *The Man of Mode, or Sir Fopling Flutter*, which was produced in 1676. In this play, Etherege cuts out all the extraneous plots and situations, concentrating his focus on the amorous intrigues of the hero, Dorimant, and his final intended, Lady Harriet, and introducing, albeit in a minor role, the character of the title, Sir Fopling, whose lightness and camp is contrasted with the more robust and heartless character of Dorimant. The play is in fact a witty and lucid appraisal of 'affection' and 'affectation' that occasionally reveals a more serious though never disturbed undertow, as when the admirable Harriet reproaches Dorimant for his fear of making a fool of himself by wooing her in public: 'When your love's grown strong enough to make you bear being laughed at, I'll give you leave to trouble me with it: till then, pray forbear, sir'.

After the great success of *The Man of Mode*, Etherege retired from the theatre. He soon spent his fortune, and began to look around for a rich widow, finding

one in Mary Arnold; it is said that the knighthood he received just before 1680 was not unconnected with this project. The marriage was not a happy one, and Etherege escaped it when he was appointed by James II to be resident minister at the imperial German court at Ratisbon (Regensburg). Etherege's manuscript letterbooks, containing both official and personal correspondence, are preserved in the British Museum and add weight to Dryden's estimation of him as 'the undoubted best author' of English prose of the day. The dullness of Germany irked Etherege considerably, and he soon made enemies of the Austrian envoy Windisgratz and his own secretary, Hughes, who reported his many indiscretions back to England. He scandalized the court by an open affair with a travelling actress, and in 1689 he finally left Ratisbon to join the exiled James II in Paris, where he died, probably in late 1691 or early 1692.

H. F. Brett-Smith (ed.), *The Dramatic Works* (2 vols.; 1927).

Sybil Rosenfeld (ed.), *The Letterbook of Sir George Etherege* (1928).

James Thorpe (ed.), *Poems of George Etherege* (Princeton and London, 1963).

A. W. Verity (ed.), *Works of Sir George Etherege: Plays and Poems* (1888).

D. Underwood, *Etherege and the Seventeenth-Century Comedy of Manners* (New Haven, Conn., 1957).

Evelyn, John (1620–1706), diarist and dilettante.

Born on 31 October 1620, at Wotton, Surrey, second son of Richard Evelyn, a wealthy country gentleman, from the age of five Evelyn was brought up at Lewes by his 'too indulgent' grandmother, Mrs. Standsfield, with whom he was so comfortable that he refused to leave her and go to Eton. However, in May 1637 he entered Balliol College, Oxford, where, thanks to a negligent tutor, he seems to have spent much of his time dancing and meeting people. In 1640 Evelyn left Oxford without a degree and took chambers in the Middle Temple, and there he remained 'studying a little, but dancing and fooling more', until the outbreak of the Civil War. On 12 November 1642, just after the battle of Brentford, he joined the King's army, but was politely asked to leave it three days later; he consoled himself with the reflection that had he stayed, he would have been 'exposed to ruin without any advantage to his majesty', and promptly retired to Wotton to cultivate his garden.

Though a staunch Royalist, Evelyn clearly had no taste for civil violence, and in November 1643 he received the King's permission to travel in Europe. After some months in France, in late 1644 he arrived in Italy, where he busied himself variously, buying rare anatomical drawings at Padua, or making etchings at Naples. In April 1646, in company with Edmund Waller, Evelyn set out for France once more. There he became a close friend of Sir Richard Browne, Charles I's ambassador, and in June 1647 he married Sir Richard's twelve-year-old daughter Mary.

Evelyn, worried about the political situation in England, returned home alone in late 1647 and shrewdly converted his considerable fortune into land. He also wrote a decidedly Royalist pamphlet and had talks with the King at Hampton Court, all of which made the Parliamentary authorities suspicious. Accordingly, in July 1649 he had no trouble in getting permission from 'the rebel Bradshaw' to rejoin his wife in Paris.

In 1652, in spite of the victory of the Parliamentarians, he returned to England, settling at Sayes Court, his wife's family home near Greenwich; he was first obliged to redeem the lease from Parliament for £3,500. He now occu-

pied himself with gardening and intelligent company. A letter he sent in 1659 to Robert Boyle contained the first suggestion of a Royal Society, and Evelyn was duly elected to the council when the Society was formally chartered by the King in July 1662. Not all his pastimes were so innocent: in 1659 he corresponded in cipher with the still-exiled Charles II and wrote further Royalist pamphlets, and in January 1660 he tried to persuade the lieutenant of the Tower of London to declare for the King even before General Monck had done so.

At the Restoration Evelyn naturally came into royal favour, but he kept away from the court, since he considered its immorality repugnant and its political intriguing dangerous. Being, however, as public-spirited as he was intellectually inquisitive, he divided his time between sitting on various commissions and writing pamphlets on a great range of topics. In 1661 he published *Fumifugium*, an account of London smog (or the 'hellish and dismal cloude of sea-coale'), with suggestions on how to make the capital a sweet-smelling smokeless zone, including the expulsion of smoke-producing tradesmen and the provision of large public flowerbeds. In 1664 he joined the commission which cared for the wounded of the Dutch War, and was the only commissioner to stay at his post when the plague swept London. Evelyn's years of assiduous gardening at Sayes Court bore fruit in his *magnum opus*, *Sylva* (1664), an extended treatise on tree cultivation, with an appendix concerning cider-making, the whole written in a stately, even pompous, prose full of Latin tags.

James II showed Evelyn as much favour as his brother had done and in 1685 made him a commissioner of the Privy Seal. But Evelyn, a staunch Anglican, disliked the King's religious policy and took to absenting himself every time he was required to vote in favour of concessions to Roman Catholics. He was obviously much happier at the Royal Society, whose presidency he was twice offered, or working in his garden at Sayes Court, or visiting the houses of his many friends, who included Sir Thomas Browne, Samuel Pepys, and Wenceslaus Hollar.

The ageing and Tory Evelyn disapproved of the Glorious Revolution and so in 1688 he went into semi-retirement. In 1694 he moved back to Wotton, where he completed *Numismata* (1697), 'a discourse of medals,

ancient and modern', and *Acetaria* (1699), 'a discourse of sallets [salads]'. His last public office was as treasurer of Greenwich Hospital from 1695 to 1703. In summer 1698 Sayes Court was let to Peter the Great, and that rumbustious monarch amused himself by being trundled in a wheelbarrow all over Evelyn's beloved flowerbeds; the tsar's secretary paid £162 in compensation to the house's disgruntled owner.

John Evelyn died at Wotton on 27 February 1706, and was buried in the village church. His modern fame rests entirely on his *Diary*, covering the period from the early 1640s to his death, and first published in 1818. Unlike Pepys's diary, it is not an intimate journal; Evelyn's cautious temperament meant that he was always an observer of great events rather than a participant, and indeed there is evidence to suggest that he rewrote much of his diary in later life. But it is still valuable as an account of a patriotic and upright life, enlivened by a broad intellectual curiosity and a talent for making friends.

Bohn's Historical Library, *Diary and Correspondence of John Evelyn* (1859, etc.).

E. S. de Beer (ed.), *The Diary of John Evelyn* (1955).

W. G. Hiscock, *John Evelyn and his Family Circle* (1955).

Sir Geoffrey Keynes, *John Evelyn* (1937).

See also articles by E. S. de Beer in vol. 7 of *Notes and Queries* (New Series), Nos. 6–8 (June-Aug., 1960).

Portrait: engraving, quarter-length, by R. Nanteuil, 1650: N.P.G.

F

Fairfax, Ferdinando (1584–1648), 2nd Baron Fairfax of Cameron; Parliamentarian general in the Civil War.

Born on 29 March 1584, the son of Thomas, 1st Baron Fairfax of Denton, Yorkshire, in his youth Fairfax was sent to learn the military arts in the Netherlands, but showed no enthusiasm for them. In 1607 he married Mary, daughter of Lord Sheffield, by whom he had three sons, including Thomas (q.v.), and six daughters. He inherited his title in 1640, having commanded a regiment of Yorkshire trained bands against the Scots during the First Bishops' War (1639). In the Long Parliament he sided with the opposition, being one of the committee charged with the presentation of the Grand Remonstrance and also of the group despatched to Yorkshire to keep the King's activities under observation when he withdrew to York in 1642. Nevertheless, he was not one of the ringleaders and was more characteristically associated with the attempt on the part of the Yorkshire gentry to keep their county neutral by the 'treaty' signed at Rothwell Haigh (28 September). It was promptly repudiated by Parliament and undermined in the county itself by Sir John Hotham and his son, who were local rivals of the Fairfaxes.

Fairfax was M.P. for Boroughbridge (1622–29) and for Yorkshire in the Long Parliament (from 1640). His social position ensured that he would be called upon to raise and lead a force for Parliament within the county, a matter upon which he was engaged even before the 'treaty' was conceived. He drew much of his support from the Puritan clothiers of the West Riding and relied heavily upon his son Thomas for purely military initiatives.

He took the field in October 1643 and was soon confronted by the Duke of Newcastle (see Cavendish, William) moving south with his Royalist army. Fairfax gave a very good account of himself against numerical odds at Tadcaster (6 December). In spite of this, he retreated first to Selby and later to Leeds, so covering the West Riding. It was not until June 1643 that Newcastle was free to concentrate against him and the two armies met at Adwalton Moor (30 June), the Fairfaxes again having to fight with the numerical odds against them and again sustaining the battle with credit. On this occasion, their army eventually broke and, unable to make a stand, the two commanders took refuge in the fortress of Hull, where the elder Fairfax remained as governor during the siege (September–October 1643), which he brought to an end by a well-conducted sortie on 11 October.

In January 1644 a Scottish army crossed into England in support of Parliament, so transforming the strategic balance. On 11 April, the Fairfaxes stormed Selby, capturing the Royalist governor of York, John Belasyse, and obliging Newcastle to abandon his stand against the Scots in Durham by the threat they posed. He retired into York and on 20 April the Scots and the Fairfaxes joined forces at Tadcaster. The siege of York followed and, arising out of it, the Battle of Marston Moor (2

July), in which Fairfax was given command of a brigade of foot on the left of the third line. When the battle appeared to have gone against the allies he quit the field, but was not the only senior commander to do so. Subsequently Fairfax was one of the principal signatories of the terms of the capitulation of York (16 July) and became its governor until his resignation in 1645 as a result of the Self-Denying Ordinance, whereby members of Parliament laid down their commissions. In 1646, his first wife having died, he remarried. He continued to be a member of the committee established at York for the government of the northern counties until his death, on 14 March 1648, as a result of an accident.

G. W. Johnson, *Memorials of the Reign of Charles the First* [*Fairfax Correspondence, 1 and 2, to 1642*] (2 vols.; 1848).

L. P. Wenham, *The Great and Close Siege of York* (1970).

Austin Woolrych, 'Yorkshire's Treaty of Neutrality', *History Today* (Oct. 1956).

Peter Young, *Marston Moor* (1970).

Fairfax, Thomas (1612–71), 3rd Baron Fairfax of Cameron; Parliamentarian general in the Civil War.

Fairfax was born on 17 January 1612, the son of Ferdinando Fairfax (q.v.), and educated at St. John's College, Cambridge, 1626–29.

He married Anne Vere in 1637 and was knighted in 1640. His military education was acquired in the Low Countries, and he commanded a troop of Yorkshire dragoons against the Scots in the First Bishops' War (1639). With his father, he was numbered among the county's moderate Parliamentarians, personally presenting a petition from them to the King on Heyworth Moor (2 June 1642) and participating in the attempt to neutralize Yorkshire by a local treaty. When the fighting began,

he became his father's second-in-command, being involved in the early skirmishes with Newcastle's forces.

Using troops raised in the Bradford area and taking advantage of the Royalists' adherence to the convention of wintering in quarters, he captured Leeds (23 January 1643). In March, while conducting a subsidiary operation to cover his father's retreat to the town, his column was overwhelmed by Goring's (q.v.) cavalry on Seacroft Moor (30 March), and it was to obtain prisoners to exchange against his own soldiers captured on that occasion that he attacked Wakefield (21 May). He took with him only 1,500 troops, sufficient to deal with the reported garrison of 800–900, and took possession after a hard fight. It was now discovered that some 3,000 Royalist infantry held the town, together with several troops of horse. This success, however, was followed by involvement in the defeat of a force commanded by his father at Adwalton Moor (30 June), where Thomas had command of the right wing, which defended itself well during the battle and withdrew in a disciplined manner when the rest of the line had been put to flight. He then covered the retirement by stages into Hull.

As the cavalry could perform no service during the siege which followed, he was sent with twenty-five troops of horse to assist the operations in Lincolnshire under the Earl of Manchester (see Montagu, Edward, 2nd Earl of Manchester). The opposing armies clashed at Winceby (11 October) and the Royalists were routed. Most writers have ascribed the victory to Cromwell, who did indeed lead the first Parliamentary line into the opening attack and was unhorsed during it. The decisive movement, however, was made by the second line under Fairfax, who manœuvred his troops on the field to deliver a flanking attack that broke the Royalists completely. In any case, it was Manchester who drew out the order of battle and received the official credit. On 20 December, Fairfax recaptured Gainsborough.

He was next sent against Sir John Byron, who had been reinforced in Cheshire by troops withdrawn from Ireland and was besieging Nantwich. Collecting 2,500 foot in Manchester, he encountered the besiegers at Acton Church and beat them in a battle that was tactically difficult to handle (29 January 1644). 1,500 prisoners were taken, including Colonel George Monck (q.v.). Fairfax then returned to Yorkshire and took part in the storming of Selby (11 April), his own regiment of horse being the first into the town and responsible for capturing the Royalist commander, Belasyse.

At Marston Moor (2 July), Fairfax commanded the cavalry on the right of the Parliamentary army, personally leading the front line in the action. The troops under his own command drove off and pursued their opponents, but were not well supported. Consequently Fairfax himself was isolated among the enemy, passing through them by the expedient of abandoning his Parliamentary field sign, rejoining the battle on the other wing. He was wounded here and again at the siege of Helmsley Castle in August.

The formation of the New Model Army was initiated in January 1645, and Fairfax was appointed its commander by virtue of his growing reputation and of the Self-Denying Ordinance passed by the Commons, which excluded members of both Houses from military command. The creation of the 22,000-strong army, which was to win the war by its sheer professionalism, occupied

him until April, when it was ready to march. The sequel reflected the utmost credit upon his endeavours. On 14 June he brought the main Royalist army to battle at Naseby and broke it beyond repair. He behaved with his usual courage, fighting in the melée and capturing a colour personally, but tactically it was not a great battle, being merely a formal frontal engagement won by the side that exhibited the better organization.

The subsequent march of the New Model Army into the West Country to deal with Goring's army besieging Taunton and to eliminate the Royalist garrisons there is less often noted, but was a finer display of military ability than Naseby. On 18 June 1645, Fairfax took Leicester. On 10 July he beat Goring at Langport, having relieved Taunton indirectly by drawing the Royalists to battle. Bridgwater was taken on 23 July and Bristol successfully stormed after a three weeks' siege (10 September). The remnants of the King's western army under Hopton were beaten at Torrington on 16 February 1646; Exeter capitulated on 9 April, followed by the Royalist capital, Oxford, on 24 June. The Royalists were now completely defeated; the King himself was handed over by the Scots to Fairfax at Nottingham, to be escorted to London. This journey left both men with a sense of mutual respect. After this, Fairfax took an extended leave to recover his failing health.

The involvement of the Army in the political dissension that followed the end of the war revealed a less decisive strain in Fairfax's personality. The leadership of its internal debates and the control of its external relationships with the King and Parliament passed to others, the Army council usurping his authority and freely using his name to endorse its decisions. Where he could exercise an influence it was usually on the side of moderation, but generally he preferred to busy himself in the details of military organization.

The widespread Royalist risings of 1648 found him still able to impose his authority as the commander of the New Model Army in the field. He was forced to disperse his force to deal with a number of simultaneous threats – revolt in South Wales, Kent, and Essex, a mutinous fleet, and the danger of a Scottish invasion. Fairfax himself retained about 7,000 men to restore order in the southeast, taking action in the capital in March and April and moving out into Kent in the following month. On 1 June he defeated the Royalists under the Earl of Norwich in a fiercely contested assault on Maidstone. Norwich escaped with some 3,000 of the defenders and crossed the Thames into Essex, followed by Fairfax after a delay to deal with the remaining centres of Royalist resistance in Kent. Sir Charles Lucas was in command at Colchester, where the Royalists had concentrated, and he defeated Fairfax's first attack outside the town (11 June) and attempts to storm it during the night. Fairfax was thus forced to commit his men to a formal siege at an inopportune time. It took until 27 August to starve the garrison into surrender, and the treatment of prisoners was severe, Lucas and Sir George Lisle being shot.

Although the New Model Army succeeded everywhere, the effect of the rising was to sharpen the political conflict. Fairfax lapsed into his previous ineffectiveness. He had nothing to do with Pride's Purge, which reduced the Commons to an instrument of the Army's politicians (6 December), nor with the trial and execution of Charles I in January. On the other hand, he did

nothing to prevent them. Nevertheless, it seems that he had now resolved to cover the work of extremists no longer with his name and reputation. Although named as one of the judges in the King's trial, he did not appear after the first preliminary session, and his absence contributed not a little to the difficulties of those who wished to bring about the removal of the King.

Fairfax was nominated to the Council of State and reappointed to the command of the Army (March 1649), but the war with Scotland gave him a reasonable excuse to retire (25 June 1650) on conscientious grounds, since he was now, having inherited the title, a member of the Scottish peerage. Throughout the Protectorate he refrained from political activity, although the object of occasional Royalist hopes and of much suspicion on the part of the government, both without foundation.

The death of Oliver Cromwell and the succession of his son Richard in 1658 forced Fairfax back into public life. He had been M.P. for the West Riding since 1654, and now began to take a more active role. The experiences of the previous twenty years and the threat of anarchy latent in the unresolved situation in the capital convinced him, like many others, that a return to a conditional monarchy was essential to the peace of the state. He was again elected to the Council of State in 1659, but did not act in that capacity. He clearly placed his main hopes on General Monck (q.v.), facilitating his march south through Yorkshire and strongly representing to him local views about the desirability of restoring a free Parliament. Fairfax was included in the interim Council of State (March 1660) and headed the commissioners of the two Houses sent to conclude the formalities of the Restoration with Charles II at The Hague. Under the circumstances, Fairfax could not expect the rewards heaped upon the former Royalist Monck, but he was not subjected to any inconveniences in the remaining years of his life, which were lived in quiet retirement. During this last period, he produced two autobiographical works, *A short Memorial of the Northern Actions, during the War there, from the Year 1642 till 1644* and *Short Memorials of some things to be cleared during my Command in the Army*. He died at Nunappleton on 12 November 1671.

Maurice Ashley, *Cromwell's Generals* (1954).

M. A. Gibbs, *The Lord General* (1938).

C. R. Markham, *A Life of the Great Lord Fairfax* (1870).

Peter Young, *Marston Moor* (1970).

Portrait: engraving, quarter-length, by W. Faithorne after R. Walker: N.P.G.

Falkland, 2nd Viscount (1610–43), see Cary, Lucius.

Farnaby, Giles (?1560–1640), composer, see *Lives of the Tudor Age*.

Farquhar, George (1678–1707), comic dramatist of the late Restoration period; author of *The Recruiting Officer* and *The Beaux' Stratagem*.

Farquhar was born, probably in early 1678, in Londonderry, Ireland, the son of a clergyman. He entered as a sizar at Trinity College, Dublin, in 1694, but did not stay long and probably served as an officer in the Earl of Orrery's regiment before turning to acting. He appeared at the famous Smock Alley Theatre in Dublin, but his career on the stage was curtailed by an accident in which he almost killed a fellow player in a stage fight, having picked up a real sword instead of a foil. On the advice of another actor, Robert Wilks, he gave up acting and went to London to write comedies.

His first play, *Love and a Bottle*, was produced at Drury Lane in 1699. Its high-spirited good humour was well received, and it was followed in the same year by *The Constant Couple*, a farce which was very successful, introducing the exuberant character Sir Harry Wildair. Its sequel, *Sir Harry Wildair* (1701), was less popular. Farquhar adapted Fletcher's *The Wild Goose Chase* in February 1702, calling it *The Inconstant*, and in the following December produced a moral melodrama, *The Twin Rivals*. Neither this nor *The Stage Coach* (1704), a translation of a French farce, is worthy of much attention.

Farquhar may have returned to soldiering for a while after this. At any rate, his experience as a soldier and the comic mistake of his marriage in 1703 to a Yorkshirewoman whom he believed to be wealthy are reflected in his two final plays, on which his reputation rests. The first of these, *The Recruiting Officer* (1706), is a vigorous, warm, and genial comedy with occasional bursts of pungent satire. It is built on a slight plot and deals with the comic situation of recruiting in the provinces for the French wars. It introduces Captain Plume, a genial rake who woos country women in order to seduce their husbands into taking the King's shilling, and his able assistant, Sergeant Kite, who among other ruses disguises himself as an Indian astrologer. *The Beaux' Stratagem* (1706), produced shortly before Farquhar's death, likewise takes us away from the metropolitan setting characteristic of many Restoration comedies, to the freer airs of the country. Its two young blades, Aimwell and Archer, are much more human and attractive than those of Etherege, such as Dorimant, though lacking the latter's febrile, polished wit. Both plays show Farquhar's practical awareness of stagecraft and his gift for dialogue, and both have had many revivals in the 20th century.

Farquhar spent his last days in poverty, *The Beaux' Stratagem* being written, apparently, on the strength of a gift of twenty guineas from his old friend Wilks. He died on 29 April 1707, a few days after it was first performed at the Haymarket Theatre.

Charles A. Stonehill (ed.), *Works* (1930).

W. Archer (ed.), *Best Plays* (1906).

W. C. Connelly, *Young George Farquhar: the Restoration Drama at Twilight* (1949).

See also Bonamy Dobrée, *Restoration Comedy* (1924).

Fawkes, Guy (1570–1606), a leading Catholic conspirator in the Gunpowder Plot of 1605.

Fawkes was born in York of Protestant parents, but when he was nine his father died and his mother remarried. His stepfather, Sidonis Baynbrigge, had connections with many great Catholic families and Guy himself became a zealous Catholic. He inherited property from his father when he came of age, but leased or otherwise disposed of it before going abroad in 1593 to Flanders. There

he enlisted in the Spanish army and was noted – according to one account – for his nobility and virtue.

On the accession of James I in 1603, some English Catholics had hopes of a relaxation in the penal laws against their religion, and for a brief time these hopes appeared to be justified. James's attitude towards Catholics was somewhat ambivalent, and he appears to have flirted with the idea of greater toleration if their loyalty could be firmly secured. However, James failed to conciliate Catholic opinion, despite the temporary remission of recusancy fines, and an abortive Catholic plot against him in 1603 did nothing to sweeten relations. Moreover, James's chief minister, Robert Cecil (see *Lives of the Tudor Age*), shared the common view that Catholics were potential agents of England's enemies abroad, and was uneasy about the idea of extending greater toleration to them. Consequently, the recusancy fines were reimposed with new severity and the disappointment of the hopes of English Catholics led to a plot among a number of them to blow up the House of Lords while the King was inside.

The plot was formulated by Robert Catesby (q.v.) and his friend Thomas Winter, although they apparently hoped that Spanish diplomacy might make it unnecessary. They recruited a number of embittered Catholics, and when Fawkes returned to England in 1604, he was informed of the conspiracy along with another recruit, Thomas Percy. Both approved of the plan and the plotters allegedly withdrew to an upper room, where mass was celebrated. The conspiracy was probably the spontaneous result of long-standing Catholic discontent, although it has been suggested that it may have been engineered by an *agent provocateur* employed by Cecil in order to discredit Catholics and pave the way for further anti-Catholic measures.

In pursuance of the plan, Percy hired a tenement adjoining Parliament, Fawkes posing as his servant. In the cellars of the tenement they hoped to construct a mine. However, in March 1605 they hired a cellar running immediately below the House of Lords and abandoned their mine, which had proved difficult to dig. This cellar was filled with gunpowder and iron bars, and Fawkes was entrusted with firing the powder. He was then to embark for Flanders to spread the news to the Continent.

The conspirators discussed the possibility of warning their friends in the Lords, but a specific warning was forbidden. In spite of this, Francis Tresham, one of three wealthy country gentlemen who had entered the conspiracy to provide armed men to act after the explosion, wrote an ambiguous letter to his brother-in-law, Lord Monteagle, entreating him to stay away from Parliament on 5 November. Monteagle informed Cecil. The conspirators knew of the letter, but concluded that the details of their plan were not known.

Fawkes undertook to watch the cellar by himself. On 4 November, Suffolk (the lord chamberlain) and Monteagle searched Parliament and the surrounding buildings. They saw Fawkes in the cellar but left without speaking to him, afterwards describing him as 'a very bad and desperate fellow'. Fawkes became alarmed, and decided to fire the cellar at the next sign of danger. He left to warn Percy and was captured on his return. He was taken to the Tower, refusing either to name the other plotters or to repent, but after being subjected to the rack he signed a confession and revealed the names of the other conspirators. He was sentenced to death and was executed on 31 January 1606.

Francis Edwards, *Guy Fawkes* (1969).
Henry Garnett, *Guy Fawkes* (1962).
Oswald Tesimond, *The Gunpowder Plot* (1973).
Portrait: engraving, half-length, by unknown artist, 1794, from a contemporary engraving: N.P.G.

Ferrar, Nicholas (1592–1637), founder and leader of the religious community of Little Gidding.

Born 22 February 1592, third son of Nicholas Ferrar, a prominent London merchant, and of Mary Wodenoth, a lady of great piety. Nicholas Ferrar was a religious child whose natural predilection was strengthened by his studies at Clare Hall, Cambridge, which he entered at the age of fourteen, and where he had a tutor noted for his piety. When he was elected a fellow four years later, he selected medicine as a field for further study, but ill health compelled him to leave England in 1613. He spent five years on the Continent, studying history and literature in Germany and Bohemia and medicine in Italy. At the end of this time his health was greatly improved, and upon returning to England he began to take an active part in the family's business affairs, especially in the Virginia Company, on whose council he sat.

Ferrar was active in the defence of the company's privileges, and in 1622 became its deputy treasurer; nevertheless, it lost its patent the following year. Ferrar's association with the company and his efforts on its behalf brought him into political circles. In 1624 he was elected to Parliament, where he helped in the impeachment of the lord treasurer, the Earl of Middlesex, who was responsible for the end of the Virginia Company's patent. A political career lay open to him, but what he had seen of commerce and public life reinforced his desires to live a religious life. In this aspiration he was encouraged by his mother, who bought the manor of Little Gidding in Huntingdonshire as a home for a small Christian community. Ferrar withdrew from business and retired there. In 1626 he was ordained a deacon by Laud, the last occasion on which he left the village.

Ferrar's brother and brother-in-law brought their families, and a small community of about thirty people was organized, each with his separate tasks and all worshipping together three times a day. Members of the family voluntarily kept a prayer vigil all night, and they maintained a school and infirmary for their own and the neighbourhood's children. Despite initial hostility, this small group soon won the esteem of the outside world, and was visited several times by Charles I, who admired their pious way of life, perhaps because Ferrar, the chaplain, conducted the services along Laudian lines. In the long run this proved disastrous; in 1647 supporters of Parliament disbanded the community. But Nicholas Ferrar had already died, on 4 December 1637.

A. L. Maycock, *Nicholas Ferrar of Little Gidding* (1938).

Fiennes, Nathaniel (?1608–69), politician and military commander on the Parliamentarian side during the Civil War.

The second son of William Fiennes (q.v.), 1st Viscount Saye and Sele, he was educated at Winchester and New College, Oxford, where, by virtue of his family's connection with that institution, he became a perpetual fellow in 1624. He left New College in about 1629 without taking a degree and travelled abroad, visiting Geneva, where he came into contact with Calvinist leaders whose influence confirmed in him the Puritan-ism already transmitted from his father. He returned in 1639, going to Scotland, where he opened communications with the Covenanters.

Sitting as M.P. for Banbury in the Short and Long Parliaments of 1640, he took a leading part in attacking the religious policy of William Laud (q.v.). In February 1641, upon reception of the London petition against episcopacy, Fiennes impressed the House of Commons by arguing that episcopacy was both religiously and politically dangerous. He was then placed on a Parliamentary committee responsible for church affairs. In 1642 he was appointed with his father to the Committee of Safety, and when war broke out he immediately raised a troop of cavalry for the Earl of Essex (see Devereux, Robert). After distinguishing himself in the early skirmishes and at the Battle of Edgehill (23 October 1642), Fiennes took his force to the West Country in 1643 and arrested Colonel Essex, the disaffected governor of Bristol. Parliament awarded the governorship to Fiennes in May 1643, but upon the arrival of Prince Rupert two months later, on 22 July, the city was not in a suitable state to withstand an assault and Fiennes surrendered. For this, Parliament tried and convicted him of treachery and cowardice and condemned him to death (December 1643). Fiennes was pardoned, however, and afterwards, when the New Model Army was itself forced to assault Bristol, he was exonerated. The city was simply not capable of withstanding a determined assault or of being defended for long.

In 1648 Fiennes was again a member of the Committee of Safety and was appointed as one of the Parliamentary negotiators who met Charles I on the Isle of Wight. Because he favoured peace with the King, however, he was one of the 130 or so members excluded from the Commons by Pride's Purge (December 1648).

Fiennes was, however, no Presbyterian politician. He favoured Cromwell's party, and after the establishment of the Protectorate he was returned to the 1654 and 1656 parliaments for Oxfordshire and Oxford University respectively. In 1658 he was elevated to Cromwell's House of Lords. Under Cromwell, Fiennes had held several appointments, including that of a commissioner for the custody of the great seal. He was a fervent adherent of the Lord Protector, always stressing the religious basis of his government. In 1657 he tried to persuade him to accept the crown.

Upon resumption of the Long Parliament in 1659, Fiennes was superseded and took no part in the subsequent restoration of the Stuart monarchy. He died in retirement at Newton Toney, Wiltshire, on 16 December 1669.

Fiennes was the author of several tracts, and his four children included the traveller and writer, Celia Fiennes (1662–1741), a remarkably perceptive woman whose journals represent an important source of English social and architectural history.

Fiennes, William (1582–1662), 1st Viscount Saye and Sele; Puritan opponent of James I and Charles I in the House of Lords and administrator of colonial enterprises in America.

Fiennes was born at Broughton Castle, near Banbury, Oxfordshire, 28 May 1582, and educated at New College, Oxford, where he became a fellow in 1600. His father, Richard Fiennes, 7th Baron Saye and Sele, belonged to a family that had been founded by James Fiennes, lord chamberlain and lord treasurer under Henry VI. In 1613 William Fiennes succeeded as 8th Baron.

In Parliament, Fiennes proved himself a firm member of the opposition to the King. In 1622 he earned a six-month spell of imprisonment for objecting to James's imposition of a benevolence. In the brief period of alliance between Prince Charles, Buckingham (see Villiers, George, 1st Duke), and the Parliamentary opponents of James, Fiennes struck up a temporary friendship with Buckingham, and in 1624 he was elevated to a viscountcy by his interest. In Charles I's first two parliaments, however, he opposed the King, and in 1626 he refused to pay the forced loan. Clarendon (see Hyde, Edward) says of him at this period that he was 'the oracle of those who were called Puritans in the worst sense, and steered all their counsels and designs'. He opposed mitigating amendments to the Petition of Right in 1628 and resisted the imposition of ship money.

During the period of Charles's absolute government, Fiennes became involved, along with Pym, Hampden (qq.v.), and others, in the establishment of colonies in America. In 1630 he belonged to the Providence Island Company, and in 1635 he collaborated with Robert Greville, 2nd Baron Brooke, in founding the settlement of Saybrook on the Connecticut River. He also bought a plantation in Cocheco, New Hampshire. As a peer, he went so far as to propose a hereditary aristocracy as part of the government of New England. The idea was rejected by the Massachusetts government.

In 1639 Fiennes reluctantly went with Charles on an expedition against the Scots (the First Bishops' War), but was sent home upon refusing to take the oath to fight for the King 'to the utmost of my power and hazard of my life'. In the gathering storm surrounding the recall of Parliament in 1640, Fiennes again came into conflict with the King. Undoubtedly he was on the list of Puritan leaders to be impeached at the end of that year, and was saved only by Pym's prosecution of Strafford. In 1641 Charles tried to win him over to his own side by making him a privy councillor and commissioner of the Treasury. In 1642, however, he was appointed by Parliament to the Committee of Safety and made lord lieutenant of Oxfordshire, Cheshire, and Gloucestershire. At the outbreak of the Civil War in August, he raised forces for Parliament. A member of the Westminster assembly from 1643, he played a leading part in the passing of the Self-Denying Ordinance of April 1645. In 1647, however, he supported the Army against Parliament, but, motivated by self-interest, he soon became anxious for peace between Charles and Parliament and took part in the negotiations between them at Newport, Isle of Wight, from April to November 1648.

After the execution of Charles, Fiennes retired from public life and took no part in the politics of the Interregnum. His opposition to Charles had not been that of a republican, but rather that of an aristocrat jealously protecting his own interests. The Commonwealth and the Protectorate held nothing for him, and his inactivity saved him from reprisals after the Restoration. In 1660, resuming his seat in Parliament, he was again a privy councillor and also became lord privy seal. Fiennes died at Broughton Castle on 14 April 1662.

Finch, Anne (1661–1720), Countess of Winchilsea; minor poet.

Born in April 1661, the daughter of Sir William Kingsmill of Sidmonton, near Southampton, at the age of twenty-two Anne was one of the maids of

honour to Mary of Modena, who was then Duchess of York. In 1684 she married Col. Heneage Finch.

Anne Finch became a friend of Pope and Rowe, who addressed her in verse as 'Ardelia' and 'Flavia'. Her own work could at times attain to great poignancy, and was always charming, but lacked consistent quality. Her poems were sometimes satirical, sometimes lyrical, and occasionally were marred by sentimentality. She wrote bitingly about society and manners, while other subjects included nature and moral or pious questions. Her poem *The Spleen* appeared in Charles Gildon's *New Miscellany* (1701). In 1713 she published an anthology of her own verse, *Miscellany Poems on Several Occasions Written by a Lady*. She died on 5 August 1720.

Wordsworth thought highly of Anne Finch's work, and gave it a prominent place in an anthology that he prepared for Lady Mary Lowther in 1819.

M. Reynolds (ed.), *The Poems of Anne, Countess of Winchilsea* (Chicago, 1903).
Portrait: miniature, quarter-length, by Lawrence Crosse (1650–1724): N.P.G.

Finch, Daniel (1647–1730), 2nd Earl of Nottingham and 6th Earl of Winchilsea; Tory politician.

He was born on 2 July 1647, eldest son of Sir Heneage Finch (q.v.), later 1st Earl of Nottingham; educated at Westminster School and Christ Church, Oxford.

After Oxford, Finch was sent on the Grand Tour (1665–68). On his return to England, a vacant seat in Parliament was found for him by his relatives, and in February 1673 he entered the House of Commons. Since his father was in the government, it was only to be expected that he should support the court. Furthermore, his Anglican background and natural conservatism made him a staunch upholder of the royal prerogative – so long as it did not disturb the established order. Accordingly, although he saw no reason to persecute other Protestants, in 1673 he opposed the royal claim to suspend the laws against non-Anglicans, and himself attempted to win greater toleration for Dissenters by more legal means in 1674 and 1675. He also opposed the ministry in 1677, when he gave his vote to the Habeas Corpus Bill, but in general the crown could count on his support.

In 1679 Finch was rewarded with a seat on the admiralty commission, where, a novice in affairs of the sea, he contributed to the disintegration of the English fleet; a place on the Privy Council followed in 1680. Politically, he became an ally of Halifax (see Savile, George), and fought the Exclusion Bills, supporting in their stead proposals to limit severely the authority of the Catholic James II when he succeeded to the throne. By the time he had succeeded to his father's earldom in December 1682, the Exclusionists were routed and the Stuart reaction was in full swing. There was little room at court for a moderate Tory such as Nottingham; however, by now he was a comparatively powerful figure, for he not only commanded a political following but also led a powerful group of younger clergymen.

Although Nottingham never conspired against James II, he could not really support a Catholic king; loyalty to his threatened church came first. He was informed of the invitation being prepared for William of Orange to invade England, but declined to be party to it. In 1688–89, after the revolution, he led the unsuccessful parliamentary fight to establish a regency, yet once the dual reign of William and Mary was established he never intrigued against them. He was taken into the ministry as a secretary of state, the recognized leader of the moderate High Churchmen.

Nottingham's concern for Protestant unity continued. Over the next years he struggled successfully for statutory toleration for Dissenters and unsuccessfully for their comprehension in the state Church. At court, he became a close adviser to Queen Mary, but the complicated intrigues surrounding the failure to follow up the naval victory at La Hogue (1692) forced him to resign at the end of 1693. When the Queen died in the following year, another of his links with the court was severed, and he remained in the political wilderness until the accession of Queen Anne (1702).

With Marlborough (see Churchill, John) and Godolphin (q.v.), Nottingham entered Anne's first ministry. The champion of the High Church, he was a leader both of the anti-Jacobite Tories and of the supporters of the Occasional Conformity Bills, measures to prevent Dissenters from breaking the Anglican monopoly on office by occasionally taking communion in the Established Church. These bills embarrassed the government, but not nearly as much as

Nottingham's advocacy of the traditional Tory war strategy – a policy of maritime campaigns rather than the heavy
commitment to the main land theatre as
envisaged by Marlborough. Accordingly, in 1704 Nottingham was manœuvred out of the ministry to make way
for more ardent supporters of Marlborough's war policy.

In the following years Nottingham
drifted away from Anne and his former
Tory associates, for he was hostile to
Harley (q.v.), who was gaining command of the Tory moderates. In 1708
Harley too was ousted from office, and
the ministry became dependent on the
Whigs. When in 1710 it attempted to
impeach the High Church preacher Dr
Henry Sacheverell (q.v.), Nottingham
joined with Harley's supporters in standing by the impetuous divine, doing
damage to the ministry. Nevertheless, in
the next year, when Harley formed a
predominantly Tory government, no
post was offered to Nottingham, who
began to co-operate increasingly with the
lords of the Whig Junto – the real
opposition. They assisted the passage of
the Occasional Conformity Act in return for his assistance in carrying a
motion rejecting any peace settlement
that left Spain to the Bourbons. This
alliance was furthered when, with the
Whigs, he voted against the extreme
Tory Schism Act (1714).

At the accession of George I, the
Whigs took over the government, purg-
ing it of all the Tories, but they gave
office to their ally Nottingham. This
position, however, he did not retain for
long. When he supported a motion asking for clemency for the rebel Jacobite
peers in 1716, he was dropped from the
government. He remained politically
active to fight the Septennial Bill, but
then retired to the country, re-emerging
to vote against the repeal of the Oc-

casional Conformity Act in 1719.

Nottingham wrote a popular theological pamphlet in 1721, which won
him great favour in High Church circles.
Thereafter, he lived quietly in retirement
until his death on 1 January 1730.

H. Horwitz, *Revolution Politicks: The Career of
Daniel Finch, Second Earl of Nottingham, 1647–
1730* (1968).

Portraits: oil, three-quarter length, attributed to
J. Richardson, 1726: N.P.G.; oil, head, by Kneller,
c. 1720: N.P.G.

Finch, Heneage (1621–82), 1st Earl of
Nottingham; lawyer, politician, and
lord chancellor of England.

He was born on 23 December 1621 at
Eastwell, Kent, the eldest son of Sir
Heneage Finch, a judge and Speaker in
the first parliament of Charles I; educated
at Westminster School, Christ Church,
Oxford, and the Inner Temple.

Finch distinguished himself as a legal
scholar and, after being admitted to the
bar in 1645, established a private practice
that soon became profitable. In 1660, in
the last days of the Commonwealth, he
was elected to the Convention Parliament, and at the Restoration was appointed solicitor general, knighted, and
created a baronet. His post was largely
due to his reputation as a constitutional
lawyer, a qualification of some value in a
country that had just experienced turbulent upheavals in its constitution and
government. He soon proved himself a
loyal and persuasive supporter of all
crown policies and a fierce defender of
episcopacy and Anglican intolerance. In
1661 the University of Oxford elected
him to the Cavalier Parliament; during
the long life of this assembly, the only
issue on which he ever differed from the
crown was over toleration for Dissenters, which he strongly opposed.

Such unswerving loyalty to the ministry could have won Finch the enmity

of the Commons or the country, for influential people both within and out of Parliament were growing increasingly disillusioned with the court. However, the solicitor general developed into a valued Parliamentarian – rational, eloquent, if at times florid, and respected as much for his honesty as for his ability to achieve compromises agreeable to all parties. With such talents Finch not only rose in Charles's service, but also managed to earn immunity from Parliamentary attack in an era of mounting hostility between King and Commons. He was elevated to the rank of attorney general (1670), lord keeper (1673), and lord chancellor (1675). He was ennobled in 1674 and created Earl of Nottingham in 1681. A year later, on 18 December 1682, Lord Chancellor Nottingham died in London.

Both during his lifetime and afterwards, Nottingham was recognized as a great lawyer and fair judge, 'the father of equity'.

Portrait: oil on panel, quarter-length, by unknown artist: N.P.G.

Finch, Sir John (1584–1660), Baron Finch of Fordwich; Speaker of the House of Commons, judge in the ship money case, and lord keeper.

John Finch was born on 17 September 1584, the son of Sir Henry Finch, a serjeant-at-law. He became a member of Gray's Inn in 1600 and was called to the bar in 1611. Clarendon observes that he 'set up upon the stock of a good wit and natural parts, without the superstructure of much knowledge in the profession by which he was to grow'. In 1625, when Charles I and Henrietta Maria visited Canterbury, they were addressed in extravagantly loyal terms by Finch, who was recorder of the city. In 1626 he was knighted and made king's counsel and attorney general to the Queen.

Finch was returned to Parliament for Canterbury in 1625, and in the spring of 1628 was elected Speaker of the House of Commons. His speech to the throne was conspicuously loyal, but concluded with three petitions to the King about Parliamentary privilege. For the next few months Finch seems to have acted as mediator between the King and the House of Commons and strenuously tried to prevent harsh criticism of the ministers of state, especially Buckingham. He expressed complete confidence in the King's promise to redress grievances and was praised by one member, Sir Robert Philips, as someone who had 'not only at all times discharged the duty of a good speaker, but of a good man'.

On 25 February 1629, Finch delivered a message from the King commanding the adjournment of the House. However, Members of the House declined to obey the King, and Sir John Eliot read a remonstrance on the subject of tonnage and poundage.

Finch made strenuous attempts to close the debate but was forcibly held in his chair, whereupon he apparently burst into tears protesting that he 'durst not sin against the express command of his sovereign'. Soon after this incident, Parliament was dissolved and did not meet again for eleven years.

Finch then became busily employed in the Star Chamber and in High Commission cases, and took part in the proceedings against Prynne (q.v.), who was accused of a libel on the Queen. In October 1634, Finch became chief justice of the court of common pleas, where he soon became noted for the severity of his sentences and the zealous preservation of royal dignity and prerogative. This is illustrated by his conduct in 1637, when Prynne was again tried. Finch pointed out that although Prynne's ears had already been cropped, part of them remained, and he suggested that his ears be cut close and that the letters S.L. (for 'seditious libeller') be engraved on his cheeks. His proposals were included in Prynne's sentence.

In February, 1637, the King referred the matter of ship money to the judges, who declared in effect that the King had absolute discretion in the matter. Clarendon believed that this judgment stemmed from Finch, who, at the trial of Hampden (q.v.) soon afterwards, reiterated the opinion that the King was entitled to charge his subjects for the defence of the kingdom. Finch became a privy councillor in 1639, and the following year was made lord keeper and created Baron Finch of Fordwich. As lord keeper in the Short Parliament of 1640 he elaborated on the King's magnanimity and his need for immediate supplies. However, the Commons insisted that their grievances must first be heard, and Parliament was dissolved.

When the Long Parliament met later in the year, one of its first acts was the framing of articles of impeachment against Finch on three principal counts – his conduct as Speaker over the tonnage and poundage issue, malpractices on the bench for the purpose of extending the royal forest in Essex, and his conduct during Hampden's trial. Finch appeared once to defend himself, but fled to The Hague on 31 December 1640. He remained at The Hague for many years, although he petitioned the Lords to be allowed to return to England in 1647 without success. In October 1660, Finch was one of the commissioners for the trials of the regicides, but seems to have taken little part. He died the following month, on 27 November 1660. Finch has sometimes been depicted as a very black character, but there seems to be little justification for this. He was apparently free of personal greed and am-

bition and was a conscientious and incorruptible man. What faults Finch had can be attributed to his excessive loyalty to the King and to the preservation of royalty's despotic powers.

W. H. Terry, *The Life and Times of John, Lord Finch* (1936).

Portrait: oil, three-quarter length, after Van Dyck, *c.* 1640: N.P.G.

Fisher or Percy, John (1569–1641), Jesuit priest.

Born on 27 September 1569, at Holmside in County Durham, the son of a yeoman, John Percy. At the age of fourteen, Fisher went to live with a Roman Catholic family, and soon after joined the Church of Rome. He studied classics and rhetoric at the English College in Rheims, and then went on to study at the English College in Rome in September 1589. On 13 March in the year 1593 he was ordained a priest by papal dispensation. Although he was officially too young to be ordained, the Church needed missionary priests. Shortly after defending universal theology at his college, he entered the Society of Jesus (the Jesuits) and began his noviciate in May 1594 at Tournay. After two years' hard study, he was sent to England to recover his health.

Fisher's journey to England marked the beginning of a series of persecutions and imprisonments which were to plague him for most of his life. In the England of James I, being a Roman Catholic was often enough to ensure ill treatment. Fisher suffered because he was a gifted defender, in writing and in speech, of the tenets of the Roman Church. He was also persuasive in converting the doubtful Protestant. His gifts in religious dialectic earned him the enmity of many Anglicans and Protestants, high and low. While travelling through Holland, he was arrested by English soldiers at Flushing and badly mistreated on mere suspicion of being a Roman priest. Then, immediately on reaching London he was arrested and committed to Bridewell prison. After seven months he escaped with nine other Catholics. He was sent to the north of England to begin his pastoral duties; he worked in and around Northamptonshire, and occasionally visited Oxford. There he met the theologian William Chillingworth and eventually persuaded him to convert to the Catholic faith. In 1603, Fisher took the final vows of the Society of Jesus.

He spent the next few years in Stoke Poges and at Harrowden and became chaplain to Sir Everard Digby, who was executed in 1606 for his part in the Gunpowder Plot. In 1610 he was arrested at Harrowden and imprisoned at Gatehouse in London. After a year he was released along with his superior, Father Nicholas Hart, at the insistence of the Spanish ambassador, who literally rescued them from the death sentence. Both priests were banished, and Fisher went to Brussels to become vice-prefect of the English Jesuit mission there. He then became professor of holy scripture at Louvain. Fisher returned to England after some time and was again imprisoned in London. It is believed that during his three years in jail he converted 150 Protestants and was allowed considerable personal freedom.

Among the various controversial disputations that Fisher engaged in were a series of three conferences in 1622 in the presence of James I, when the Countess of Buckingham, mother of James's favourite, was considering the Roman faith. Fisher spoke for the Catholic point of view against Francis White, who later became Bishop of Ely, for the Protestant view. At the third conference, William Laud (q.v.), then Bishop of St. David's and later Archbishop of Canterbury, defended the Protestant viewpoint. The dispute between Laud and Fisher forms the second volume of Laud's own works. Laud was convinced that Fisher's powers of persuasion in religious matters were dangerous. Many other churchmen entered into controversy with the Jesuit too.

In 1625 the French ambassador obtained a free royal pardon for twenty priests, including John Fisher, upon the marriage of the King of France's daughter to Prince Charles (later to become Charles I). Fisher gained almost a decade of liberty, but he was again arrested and brought before the Privy Council in December 1634, and ordered to leave England. He would not find sureties and was imprisoned in Gatehouse until the Queen intervened in August 1635. Fisher suffered from cancer in the last years of his life, and died on 3 December 1641, in London.

FitzJames, James (1670–1734), 1st Duke of Berwick, general and marshal of France.

Born on 21 August 1670, at Moulins in the Bourbonnais, the illegitimate son of James, Duke of York (later James II, q.v.) and Arabella Churchill, elder sister of John Churchill (q.v.), the future Duke of Marlborough, FitzJames was educated in France as a Roman Catholic by Jesuits.

The Duke of York always showed fondness for his bastard son, whose name he had chosen himself, and when he became King of England in 1685, he sent the young FitzJames to acquire a military training in the Imperial army fighting the Turks. As a volunteer, FitzJames displayed great courage in the siege of Buda. He was summoned to England, where in 1686 he was appointed to the lord lieutenancy of Hampshire.

The following year he was created Duke of Berwick and returned for another campaign in Hungary, where he fought in the Battle of Mohacs.

James II recalled Berwick to England, where he was showered with honours and appointed governor of Portsmouth. In this capacity he stood by his father to the end, but when he found that Portsmouth could not be held, crossed the Channel in the wake of the King in 1688. With the French army, Berwick sailed to Ireland, where he raised Catholic troops for the Jacobite cause and fought both at Londonderry and at the Boyne. After the departure of the Earl of Tyrconnel (see Talbot, Richard), he assumed command of the Jacobite army in Ireland, but the situation was hopeless and he eventually returned to France, where he organized Irish regiments for the French army.

Berwick served with the French against the forces of William of Orange (William III of England) in the Netherlands for two years before being promoted to the rank of lieutenant general in 1693, a year in which he was also captured in battle but soon exchanged.

During the War of the Spanish Succession, the allies attempted to re-establish the Hapsburgs in Spain against the opposition of Louis XIV, who sustained his grandson in the position of Philip V of Spain with troops and generals. In this war Berwick travelled south in 1704 to take command of the Bourbon army that faced an Anglo-Portuguese invasion. This advance he thwarted with cautious but excellent generalship; nevertheless, he was recalled to France and sent to Cevennes as governor.

In 1705 Berwick defeated the rebel Protestant Camisards and advanced into the Piedmont to capture Nice. He was rewarded by being raised to the rank of marshal of France in 1706.

The situation in Spain had in the meanwhile deteriorated, and King Philip begged his grandfather to send for Berwick. In 1707 the duke led a small French army into Spain, where he manœuvred with great brilliance until at Almanza he won a crushing victory over the English army of Henri de Ruvigny, Earl of Galway. This is the only battle in which an English general commanding a French army has defeated a French general commanding an English army.

As a result of Almanza Berwick was rewarded generously by the Spaniards, but Louis XIV never gave him another major command. In 1709 and the following years he campaigned skilfully in the southeast of France, where he had to conquer no less an adversary than Prince Eugene. In 1714 he was once again in Spain, where he captured Barcelona for Philip.

Once the war was over, Berwick became a respected military adviser of the French government and supported its policy of alliance with England. He refused to partake in the Jacobite rising of 1715 and would no co-operate with his half-brother, the Old Pretender (see James Francis Edward Stuart in *Lives of the Georgian Age*).

When the War of the Polish Succession broke out in 1733, Berwick was placed in charge of the French army advancing from Strasbourg. He was killed in Germany at the siege of Philippsburg on 12 June 1734.

Sir Charles Petrie, *The Marshal Duke of Berwick* (1953).

C. T. Wilson, *James II and the Duke of Berwick* (1876).

Flamsteed, John (1646–1719), first Astronomer Royal.

Born on 19 August 1646 at Denby,

near Derby, the son of a maltster, Flamsteed was educated at a free school in Derby, and began to study astronomy in 1662 during a long illness. By 1670, following the communication of his observations to the Royal Society and their subsequent publication in the *Philosophical Transactions*, he had gained considerable recognition. At this time he met Sir Isaac Newton, and as a result of this acquaintanceship entered Jesus College, Cambridge, in 1670, where he received the degree of M.A. in 1674. He was ordained in 1675 but did not obtain a living until 1684, when Lord North presented him to Burstow in Sussex.

In 1675 the Royal Observatory was founded at Greenwich by Charles II for the purpose of determining more accurately the positions of the stars. These would be used to improve navigation, of considerable importance to a seafaring nation. The best star catalogue then available, that of Tycho Brahe, was of insufficient accuracy for good navigation. However, with the invention of the telescope at the beginning of the century, accurate studies of celestial objects could be made.

Flamsteed's astronomical studies and observations had gained him sufficient reputation to secure the post of astronomical observator at Greenwich. Since no instruments had been provided at the Observatory, Flamsteed was forced to buy most of those he required at his own expense, out of a salary of £100 p.a., augmented by a small income from the tuition of private pupils. Working single-handed and using instruments that were often inadequate for the job, he toiled for many years at improving existing star catalogues. It was not until 1689, using a small inheritance from his father, that he was able to build more satisfactory equipment and to afford to pay an assistant.

The tens of thousands of observations made by Flamsteed were invaluable to Newton and others in providing evidence for current theories. Newton badgered him for new information and urged him to publish his results. In 1707 the first volume of his observations was printed, at the expense of Prince George of Denmark. This contained the results of his work done between 1676 and 1689. Flamsteed's refusal to publish his later work, which he considered incomplete, resulted in a bitter controversy with Newton. He was eventually obliged to hand over his observations to the Royal Society, of which Newton was then president. These were edited by Edmond Halley (q.v.), and were published in 1712 without Flamsteed's consent.

Objecting strongly to the surreptitious publication of his unfinished work, Flamsteed acquired and destroyed 300 of the 400 copies that had been printed. Some time later he began work on the authorized edition, but died on 31 December 1719, before he had finished it. *Historia Coelestis Britannica* was at last completed in 1725 by his assistant Joseph Crosthwaite. The first two volumes contain all Flamsteed's observations, the third being a catalogue of almost 3,000 stars. This work is still of great value, and formed the basis of the major advances in astronomy made over the next two hundred years.

F. Baily, *Account of the Rev. John Flamsteed* (1835).

Portrait: oil, half-length, by unknown artist, *c.* 1680: N.P.G.

Fleetwood, Charles (?1618–1692), Parliamentarian soldier in the English Civil War.

Fleetwood was the third son of Sir Miles Fleetwood of Aldwinkle, Northamptonshire, receiver of the Court of Wards. He was admitted into Gray's Inn in November 1638; at the outbreak of the Civil War, like other young gentlemen from the Inns of Court, he joined the life guard of the Earl of Essex (see Devereux, Robert), the Parliamentarian commander-in-chief. Fleetwood rose swiftly, and was already a captain when he was wounded at the first Battle of Newbury (1643). The next year Parliament rewarded his services with the receivership of the Court of Wards, which it had taken away from his eldest brother, a Royalist.

Fleetwood commanded a regiment in the Earl of Manchester's army, where he gained a reputation as a protector of Independents, which he carried into the New Model Army, in which he fought at Naseby (1645).

At the end of the First Civil War, he became politically active both in the Army and in Parliament, in which he obtained a seat in May 1646. As tension grew between the two bodies, he consistently supported his military colleagues, as might have been expected of one noted for his loyalty to old friends and comrades and for sympathy with the sectaries. He apparently did little in the Second Civil War and took no part in the trial of Charles I.

In the campaigns of 1650 and 1651 against Charles II, Fleetwood served as lieutenant general of horse to Oliver Cromwell (q.v.), serving at Dunbar and Worcester. He was elected to the Council of State and given command of the Army in England. In 1652 he married Bridget Ireton, the widow of Henry Ireton (q.v.) and the daughter of Cromwell. This brought the two men closer together, and in 1652 Fleetwood was entrusted with the difficult Irish command. In this capacity he showed great ruthlessness, transplanting Catholics to Connaught and settling the vacated regions with discharged soldiers,

especially sectaries. He supported the establishment of the protectorate and, when he returned to England in 1655, became one of the major generals of the horse militia. Fleetwood generally agreed with his father-in-law's point of view, and awaited great things from the 1657 constitution, the Humble Petition and Advice, which raised Cromwell to a semi-regal position and by which he himself was elevated to a seat in the new upper chamber. In these hopes he was to be disappointed, mainly because of Cromwell's death in the following year.

Fleetwood was now the senior officer still serving in the army, but had no clear-cut goals to pursue. Although he supported Richard Cromwell (q.v.) as Protector, he nevertheless played a role in his destruction by forcing Parliament to be dissolved in April 1659 in the interest of the Army. With the other 'Grandees', he recalled the Rump in May and received numerous posts, including a seat on the council and the position of commander-in-chief. But in reality he was losing power, for the more junior officers were acting with greater independence. When Parliament came into conflict with the army, Fleetwood assisted in expelling the assembly once again. In December Monck (q.v.) restored the Rump, which promptly stripped Fleetwood of his military positions.

At the Restoration Fleetwood received only the mild punishment of exclusion from public life, thanks to influential friends and the knowledge that he was politically innocuous. He lived quietly until his death in Stoke Newington on 4 October 1692.

Maurice Ashley, *Cromwell's Generals* (1954).

Fletcher, John (1579–1625), dramatist.
Fletcher was born in December 1579, at Rye in Sussex, a younger son of the

Rev. Richard Fletcher, afterwards Bishop of London. In October 1591 he entered Benet (now Corpus Christi) College, Cambridge, of which his father had once been the president. Several members of the family, among them John's cousin Phineas, achieved note in the Elizabethan and Jacobean literary world.

In spite of his academic and ecclesiastical achievements, John Fletcher's father died a poor man (1596), leaving his sons to divide only his books between them and to seek a living. It is not known how John Fletcher survived the next ten years, but in 1606 he appears again, having become a member of the circle of wits, poets, and dramatists who used to gather at the Mermaid Tavern in London, chief among whom were Ben Jonson and William Shakespeare. It was here in about 1607 that he met Francis Beaumont with whom he was to work and live for some nine years. (For an account of their collaboration see Beaumont, Francis.)

This intimate association became less productive when Beaumont married, in 1613, and finished abruptly with Beaumont's sudden death in March 1616.

Fletcher was throughout his dramatic career extremely productive, finding time even while Beaumont was alive to write plays both in co-operation with other writers and unaided. In many ways he may be regarded as the typical Jacobean dramatist – productive, thoroughly professional, full of stagecraft, devoid of delusions of literary grandeur, willing to collaborate with anyone and everyone, and turning from comedy to tragedy to fantasy according as public taste or his own fancy might dictate.

The earliest work attributed to Fletcher's sole authorship is *The Faithful Shepherdess* (1610), perhaps the best example of the rather mannered tradition

of English pastoral drama. The mode in which he appears to have been happiest was comedy; in this genre perhaps the best examples by his hand alone are *Wit without Money* (?1618), *Monsieur Thomas* (1619), *The Humorous Lieutenant* (1619), *Women Pleased* (?1620), *The Chances* (1620, adapted from Cervantes), *The Wild Goose Chase* (1621), *The Pilgrim* (1621), *The Island Princess* (1621), *The Tamer Tamed* (?1624, answering Shakespeare's *Taming of the Shrew*), *A Wife for A Month* (1623), and *Rule and Wife and have a Wife* (1624). His best unaided tragedy is *Valentinian* (?1619), and his best political drama is *The Loyal Subject* (1618).

Among the playwrights with whom he collaborated, after Beaumont, were Massinger, Middleton, Rowley, Ben Jonson (qq.v.), and possibly, in *The Two Noble Kinsmen* and *Henry VIII*, William Shakespeare. Fletcher and his collaborators wrote for many companies, and enjoyed performances of their works both in the public theatres and at court. With Massinger he wrote *The False One* (a version of the Cleopatra story), *Sir John Van Olden Barnavelt* (1619, a contemporary political melodrama), *The Little French Lawyer* (?1620, a comedy), *The Custom of the Country* (?1620, a bawdy romantic comedy), *The Spanish Curate* (1622, another comedy), and *The Beggar's Bush* (1622, a political drama with scenes containing interesting examples of the thieves' cant of the time).

John Fletcher died of the plague in August 1625, and was buried at St. Saviour's, Southwark. Altogether, he is reckoned to have had a hand in over sixty plays in a period of under twenty years.

See references under Beaumont, Francis.

Portrait: engraving, half-length, by J. H. Robinson, after portrait by John Thurston, in the collection of the Earl of Clarendon, *c*. 1620.

Florio, John (?1553–1625), author and translator, see *Lives of the Tudor Age*.

Ford, John (1586–*c*. 1640), dramatist.

A member of an established landed family and related through his mother to Lord Chief Justice Popham, Ford was baptized at Ilsington, Devon, in April 1586 and probably returned to Devonshire at the end of his life.

The known facts of Ford's life are few. He may have gone to Oxford for a short time before being admitted as a member of the Middle Temple in 1602. In the same year, he was temporarily expelled for debt but readmitted after paying a fine. He seems to have resided there for a long period, perhaps practising law in London. On the death of his father in 1609, he was left the sum of £10, while his brothers received greater consideration in his father's will. In 1616 he was left £20 a year in a brother's will, an income that may well have freed him to pursue his dramatic work. Other details

of his life relate only to his literary and theatrical career. Nothing is heard of him after the publication of his last recorded play, *The Lady's Trial*, in 1639.

Ford considered himself a man of letters rather than merely a writer of plays for the stage, and this attitude, which conceives of dramatic work as having a literary quality suitable for reading as well as for theatrical performance, was probably influenced by the publication of the first folio of Shakespeare's plays in 1623. That event, as well as the earlier publication (1616) of the works of Ben Jonson, seems to have lent a certain literary respectability to the writing of plays. In any case, Ford began his career as a poet and writer, and none of his youthful work was done in the theatre with the exception of a lost play, known to have been acted in 1613. In 1606 he published *Fame's Memorial*, a lengthy and abstract elegy on the death of the Earl of Devonshire, and *Honour Triumphant*, a pamphlet, highly romantic in manner, dealing with a chivalric theme. Appended to this work was a similar poem, *The Monarchs' Meeting*, on the occasion of the King of Denmark's visit to England. He also wrote a lost poem on the life of Sir Thomas Overbury (q.v.) and a didactic prose tract dealing with conduct, but after 1620 all his important work was dramatic.

By an unfortunate accident, some of Ford's plays perished in manuscript; those that survive, however, established him as the major writer of tragedy in the reign of Charles I.

He began his writing for the theatre by collaborating with experienced playwrights, chiefly Dekker (q.v.), with whom he wrote five plays, two of which have survived, *The Witch of Edmonton* (also with William Rowley, about 1621) and a masque, *The Sun's Darling* (1624). The former is remarkable for the sympathy with which the old woman of the title is treated, though the tale of the witch has little to do with the main plot. Ford's major plays, written without a collaborator, all fall between 1627 and 1638. *The Lover's Melancholy* (1628) is the earliest of these, a tragicomedy influenced by *The Anatomy of Melancholy* (see Burton, Robert), especially in the characterization of the hero, who languishes in despair after the death of his father and in the absence of his betrothed. The tragic complications of the characters are developed with considerable delicacy before finally being happily resolved. '*Tis Pity She's a Whore* and *The Broken Heart*, two tragedies, are Ford's masterpieces. The first relates the incestuous passion of a brother and sister, Giovanni and Annabella. Although Ford does not commend the guilty love of the couple, their relationship and predicament is presented with a powerful and moving sympathy rather than in terms of conventional morality. The action involves startling and melodramatic incidents – Giovanni kills Annabella to prevent the vengeance planned by her husband, Soranzo, and then enters with her bleeding heart on his dagger before killing Soranzo and dying himself. Ford's sympathy for the doomed lovers and the more bizarre episodes of the plot have been interpreted as morbid and decadent, but it is more just to note that the centre of Ford's art lies in the full and sympathetic rendering of the mental states and emotions of characters who, with dignity and fortitude, confront their tragic destinies. This is particularly true of *The Broken Heart*, which involves the consequences of a forced marriage and an act of vengeance that again precipitates a tragic chain of events. In the portrayal of the two female characters, Penthea, who is forced to marry although betrothed to another

and consequently is driven mad and dies, and Calantha, who dies broken-hearted at the end of the play, Ford, at the height of his powers, achieved a dramatic poetry of austere magnificence.

Ford's other surviving plays are *Love's Sacrifice*, *Perkin Warbeck*, *The Fancies Chaste and Noble*, and *The Lady's Trial*. The first, despite passages of characteristic power and beauty, is marred by an inconsistent comic subplot. *Perkin Warbeck*, a chronicle play, stands apart from Ford's other work with its variety of characterization, its political subject, and its objective mood. The critical opinion of Ford's contemporaries is perhaps best summed up in a little piece of doggerel that has survived:

Deep in a dump John Ford was gat,
With folded arms, and melancholy
hat.

W. Bang and H. de Vocht (eds.), *Dramatic Works of John Ford* (2 vols.; Louvain, 1908–27).
Clifford Leech, *John Ford and the Drama of His Time* (1957).
H. J. Oliver, *The Problem of John Ford* (1955).

Fox, George (1624–91), founder of the religious Society of Friends (Quakers).

Born at Drayton-in-the-Clay (Fenny Drayton), Leicestershire, the son of Christopher Fox, a Puritan weaver and churchwarden, George Fox was brought up in a pious household in which the Bible was much read. Even as a child he showed the great seriousness and intolerance that marked him in later life. He was apprenticed to a shoemaker and general merchant and soon became his trusted agent.

George Fox was not a happy youth. One night in 1643 he felt a call to leave his friends and acquaintances. He began four years of restlessness and uncertainty, wandering through the country and periodically returning to his native village. Although he sought out sects

and preachers and had many conversations with them, he found no satisfaction. In 1647, in the depths of despair, he heard a voice saying, 'There is one, even Christ Jesus, that can speak to thy condition.' This Fox declared to be the Light Within, or Inner Light, the means by which God spoke directly to people without the mediation of sacraments or priests. He commenced preaching this revelation, attending religious meetings and arguing in churches with powerful stubborn words. In 1649 he was imprisoned for 'brawling' in church.

In these years he developed the simplicity of dress, speech, and manner that became characteristics of the Quakers, as his followers were already being named in 1650: they called themselves the Friends. The movement began to spread in earnest in 1652. While journeying to Yorkshire to meet other unorthodox Christians, Fox had a vision on Pendle Hill of great multitudes approaching him. When he reached the meetings he found large numbers of people and converted many to his belief in Inner Light.

Many of the converts went out too to preach.

Quakers were recruited from all sects and classes, but mainly from the lower middle classes. Fox's enthusiasm, courage, and compassion impressed great numbers, including Margaret Fell of Swarthmoor Hall, Lancashire, the widow of a judge. Her house became the centre of the movement, from which she and Fox administered it; in 1669 they were married. Fox proved to have a genius for organization, gradually instituting a system of meetings that stopped the new sect from disintegrating, and building up a gentle discipline based on such concepts as religious silence, which curbed the wilder excesses of his followers.

Despite persecution by the Commonwealth and, later, the monarchy, Fox did not retire from preaching his revelation. He continued to travel and preach every year until he died, except when he was in prison. By 1675 he had been jailed eight times, during which his health had been broken, but that did not prevent him from taking up the cause of prison reform. Fox was also unusual in that he believed in the equality of the sexes and the abolition of slavery; he abhorred war, and he made his views known in a stream of pamphlets.

Fox's travels took him to Scotland, Ireland, the West Indies, North America, and the Low Countries, and by the time of his death on 13 January 1691, Quakerism was firmly established.

A. N. Brayshaw, *The Personality of George Fox* (1933).
H. E. Wildes, *Voice of the Lord* (Philadelphia, 1965).
Portrait: engraving, half-length, by unknown nineteenth century artist, after an unknown original: N.P.G.

Fraser, Simon (?1667–1747), 12th Baron Lovat; Jacobite organizer, see *Lives of the Georgian Age*.

Frederick V (1596–1632), Elector Palatine and King of Bohemia, called 'the Winter King'.

Born on 26 August 1596, at Amberg in the Upper Palatinate, the son of the Elector Frederick IV and Louisa Juliana, Frederick succeeded his father as elector in September 1610. In 1613 he married Elizabeth (q.v.), daughter of James I. The marriage was regarded as a great political event, since it would connect the English royal family with some of the chief Protestant courts in Europe.

In 1619 the Bohemian Estates revolted against the Hapsburgs and deposed Ferdinand II. On 26 August they elected Frederick, a leading Protestant prince, king of Bohemia. Against the advice of his councillors, he accepted the Bohemian throne and was crowned in Prague on 4 November 1619. The newly acquired power of Frederick was unacceptable to most of the princes of the Protestant union, who declared themselves neutral. Frederick found himself an isolated rebel against the emperor, Ferdinand II. On 8 November 1620, the

Bohemians were crushed by the imperial forces at the Battle of the White Mountain and 'the Winter King' fled into exile in Holland. In 1621 he was put under the ban of the Empire and lost his hereditary estates. In 1623 the Palatinate was given to Maximilian I of Bavaria, who received the title of Elector. Frederick spent the rest of his life as a pensioner of the Dutch States General. He died in Mainz on 29 November 1632.

He was an ancestor of the Hanoverian line through his daughter Sophia, who married Ernest Augustus, elector of Hanover, and became the mother of George I of England.

E. A. Beller, *Caricatures of the Winter King* (1928).
A. Gindely, *Friedrich V von der Pfalz* (Prague, 1884).
C. V. Wedgwood, *The Thirty Years War* (1938).

Portrait: oil, quarter-length, by G. Honthorst: N.P.G.

Fuller, Thomas (1608–61), historian and divine.

Fuller was born in June 1608 at Aldwincle St. Peters, Northamptonshire, son of Thomas Fuller, the local rector. Despite four years at the mediocre village school, he soon developed a 'pregnant wit', and in 1621, aged thirteen, he went up to Queen's College, Cambridge; his fellow undergraduates included Milton and Herbert. Fuller graduated B.A. in 1624, but remained closely associated with Cambridge until 1638. In 1631 he published his first prose work, *David's Hainous Sinne*, full of fantastic conceits. Fuller's father died in 1632, and two years later his influential uncle, Bishop Davenant of Salisbury, gave him the rich livings of Netherbury in Wiltshire and Broadwindsor in Dorset. Fuller's first major book appeared in 1639, *The Holy Warre*, a learned but witty history of the Crusades, which sold well.

Fuller's moderate views almost endangered his ecclesiastical career in 1640, when he had just been elected proctor for the diocese of Bristol. Asked in convocation to approve stern measures against dissenters, he at first refused 'in a commanding and imperious style', but realizing he was heavily outvoted, reluctantly agreed. Later, the Long Parliament fined him £200 for signing. In 1641 Fuller's baby son died, and soon afterwards his wife, whom he had married in 1638. He now resigned both his livings and went to London. He became curate of the Savoy Chapel, and the sermons he gave at the Inns of Court were so popular that crowds would gather outside the open windows of churches to listen to his preaching.

In 1642 appeared Fuller's most popular book, *The Holy and Profane State*. It is a commonsensical primer of Christian conduct, illustrating by means of historical anecdotes the right and wrong behaviour for various walks of life. Despite its pithy maxims, such as 'they that marry where they do not love, will love where they do not marry', *The Holy and Profane State* betrays a prosaic and reactionary mind in its acceptance of a hierarchical society and its reduction of man's noblest impulses to mere domestic duties.

Fuller's comfortable world was now fast being eroded by the Civil War. His well-meaning attempts to preach moderation to both sides were misunderstood; he incurred the Royalists' mistrust for trying to take a petition from Westminster to King Charles at Oxford, and the Puritans' displeasure for refusing to condemn publicly Waller's plot. Eventually he abandoned his job and his belongings and fled to Lincoln College, Oxford. Despite his being allowed to preach before the King, Fuller was attacked by the ultra-Royalists for seeming lukewarm. Lonely and unhappy, in 1643 he became chaplain to the King's

most moderate general, Sir Ralph Hopton (q.v.), and went on campaign with him. Having escaped from the siege of Basing House (1644), Fuller was eventually trapped in Exeter during its long investment by Fairfax (1645–46); he spent his enforced stay writing *Good Thoughts in Bad Times* and acting as chaplain to the recently born Princess Henrietta.

After the Parliamentary victory Fuller, thanks to such influential patrons as Lord Montagu, avoided the persecution suffered by most clergy. Because of this he has been accused of 'complying with the times'. Certainly, his close friends included Sir John Danvers, who signed Charles I's death warrant. It may be that, being more interested in men than principles, he simply did not understand the moral issues at stake. Certainly, he did help less privileged clergy, and was even hauled before a jury of 'triers' for this.

During the Commonwealth Fuller led a somewhat erratic life, at one time serving as Lord Carlisle's chaplain, at another becoming a regular visitor to the Earl of Middlesex's mansion, Copt Hall, and throughout lecturing at various London churches. In 1655 he published his *Church History*, which begins with the Druids and ends in 1649; despite the obvious constraints, Fuller gives a moving account of Charles I's death. As usual, the flow of the narrative is broken up by rambling anecdotes, and the scholar Heylyn violently attacked these 'trencher-jests'. Fuller arranged a meeting with his opponent and so thoroughly disarmed him that they parted the best of friends.

The large number of dedications in the *Church History* reveal how much of a socialite Fuller was. He was a tall, imposing man who dressed untidily, ate sparingly, and apparently took no exercise. His desirability as a dinner guest lay not only in his conversation, but also his prodigious memory; he could walk the breadth of London and remember every street sign he had seen on the way.

In 1658 Fuller became rector of Cranford in Middlesex, and during the 1660 crisis was amongst the loudest in demanding 'better times' after the 'long winter of woe and misery'. The restored Charles II made him a royal chaplain, awarded him a D.D., and gave him back his West Country livings. But Fuller did not long enjoy them; on 16 August 1661, asking 'for his pen and ink to the last', he died of typhus and was buried at Cranford.

Fuller's most characteristic work, *The Worthies of England*, appeared posthumously in 1662. A combination of biographical dictionary, historical gazetteer, and anthology of proverbs, this extraordinary book claims a didactic purpose but persistently diverges into 'delightful stories', concerning marriage customs in Lapland or Ralegh dropping his cloak in the mud. Obviously scholarship was only a hobby for Fuller, since he had too lively a sense of the ridiculous ever to become a pedant or a fanatic. It was this unaffected *joie de vivre* which led Coleridge to exclaim of Fuller, 'God bless thee, dear old man!'

J. Freeman (ed.), *Worthies of England* (1952).
William Addison, *Worthy Dr. Fuller* (1951).

G

Gay, John (1685–1732), poet and dramatist, see *Lives of the Georgian Age*.

George (1653–1708), Prince of Denmark.

Born in Denmark on 21 April 1653, second son of Frederick III, King of Denmark and Norway, by his wife Sophia Amalia, daughter of the Duke of Brunswick-Lüneburg, George was a politically inconspicuous figure in Denmark, where his brother (Christian V) was king. It was perhaps because of rather than in spite of the prince's mediocrity and lack of ambition that Charles II chose him for the husband of his niece, Princess Anne, daughter of James II. On 19 July 1683, at the time of the Rye House Plot, George arrived in England. Within a week his arranged marriage took place, and shortly afterwards the King created him Duke of Cumberland.

George never showed much interest in politics. Throughout the times of the Revolution he was entirely subservient to Anne, who herself was strongly influenced by the Churchills (later Duke and Duchess of Marlborough). After the landing of William III at Torbay, he stayed for a time at court, while other courtiers were deserting James II. Later in the month, George, having previously disapproved of the 'defectors', left the King in order to join William. During William's reign he was not appointed to any important post.

Shortly after Anne was crowned (1702) he was named generalissimo and lord high admiral of England, but had little control over affairs due to his indolence and incapacity. Although George was tolerated by the Tory majority in the Commons, the Whigs grew increasingly dissatisfied and planned to force him out of the admiralty. This never occurred, however, as he died on 28 October 1708, after a lingering illness.

Prince George achieved a somewhat obscure place in history by marrying Anne. His activities were mainly confined to drinking, hunting, and small talk at court. Indeed, it has been reported that Charles II once said of him, 'I have tried him drunk and tried him sober, and there is nothing in him'. He was lazy but good-natured, and it seems that his greatest merit was in not getting in anyone's political way.

Portraits: oil, three-quarter length, after J. Riley, *c.* 1687: N.P.G.; oil, three-quarter length, by or after Dahl, *c.* 1705: N.P.G.

Gibbons, Grinling (1648–1721), woodcarver and sculptor.

The details of Gibbons's early life are not known, beyond the facts that he was born in Rotterdam and came to London as a youth. He had already developed a remarkable facility for soft-wood carving when he was discovered in 1671 by John Evelyn (q.v.), the diarist, by whom he was recommended to both Charles II and Sir Christopher Wren. As a result of the introduction to the King, he was commissioned to undertake carvings in the new suite of royal apartments being built at Windsor Castle. He also received a commission from the Earl of Essex to execute carvings at his country seat, Cassiobury, in Hertfordshire. His work at Windsor Castle and at Cassiobury prompted his appointment in 1693 as Master Carver in Wood to the crown, a position that he held under successive monarchs until his death. In this capacity he carried out some extensive and elaborate work at Kensington Palace and at Hampton Court for William and Mary. He appears to have spent the rest of his life travelling from one great country house or palace to another, carrying out commissions, pausing occasionally to do wood-carving or statues for a country church.

Some of his best work was done for Sir Christopher Wren at St. Paul's Cathedral, notably the choir stalls, organ case, and the bishop's throne. Also in St. Paul's are some of Gibbons's finest stone-carvings – the festoons on the exterior beneath the lower windows and the heraldic panel in the north pediment.

The carved room at Petworth, Sussex, is an impressive display of Gibbons's skill and delicacy as a wood-carver. Horace Walpole declared that it was 'much the finest carving of Gibbons that ever my eyes beheld. There are birds absolutely feathered; and two antique vases with bas-reliefs, as perfect and beautiful as if they were carved by a Grecian master.'

Gibbons was also a very capable sculptor, although he was never as happy in bronze or marble as he was in wood, and he seems to have relied a great deal on his assistants. One of the best bronze statues attributed to him is that of James II, now outside the National Gallery in London, but this may well have been designed by his partner, Arnold Quellin.

There are wood-carvings by Gibbons at Badminton in Gloucestershire, Burghley in Northamptonshire, Hackwood in Hampshire, Kentchurch in Hertfordshire, and Luton Hoo in Bedfordshire.

There are some point-lace cravats in limewood at Chatsworth, Derbyshire, and at Cullen, Banffshire. His marble work can be seen in Westminster Abbey, although this has been criticized as clumsy, and at many country churches, notably Badminton in Gloucestershire and Exton in Rutland.

He also worked on interiors for some Oxford colleges, it is now believed from evidence of the style. In 1708 we encounter him gathering a team of eight assistants to undertake interiors, fireplaces, capitals, cornices, and statues for Blenheim Palace: this work occupied him for at least four years.

His talent for naturalistic carving cannot be exaggerated. He carved in wood with the same eye for detail that his contemporaries in Holland were applying in their painted studies of fruit and flowers in oil. Pendent groups and festoons of flowers, fruit, and other ornaments are all painstakingly copied from nature.

His life appears to have been serene and uneventful, and he continued working until shortly before his death on 3 August 1721.

David Green, *Grinling Gibbons* (1964).
J. N. Summerson, *Architecture in Britain, 1530–1830* (1963, rev. ed.).

Portraits: oil, three-quarter length, after Kneller, *c.* 1690: N.P.G.; oil, by J. D. Watson, 1868: V. & A. Museum; engraving, half-length, by J. Smith, after John Closterman, *c.* 1691: V. & A. Museum.

Gibbons, Orlando (1583–1625), composer and musician, one of the last and best representatives of the English polyphonic school; organist of the Chapel Royal under James I.

Born in 1583, at Oxford, the son of William Gibbons, also a musician, who had been appointed as one of the waits (town bandsmen) at Cambridge in 1567, Orlando was the most famous member of a notable musical family. In addition to his father, three of his brothers were also skilled musicians, and his son Christopher (1615–76) was one of Henry Purcell's most able contemporaries.

Orlando Gibbons's working life as a composer occupies a period of musical

history that is marked by an abrupt transition. In Italy the monodic style was already taking hold and even in England Henry Lawes was already teaching music, in Milton's phrase,

> how to span
> Words with just note and accent.

Yet this great upheaval left Gibbons completely unaffected. His was a musical style taken from a past generation, and especially from his illustrious elder contemporary, Byrd. His artistically refined polyphony represents the last flowering of Tudor music in the Jacobean age.

Gibbons received his education at Cambridge, entering the choir of King's College in 1596, a year after his father's death. His talent was soon demonstrated in the music that he composed for the choir. In the next few years he must have gained a considerable reputation, for in 1604, when he was twenty-one, he was appointed organist of the Chapel Royal.

In 1606 Gibbons obtained the degree of bachelor of music from Cambridge. He evidently gave satisfaction as Chapel Royal organist and throughout James I's reign received from the King several marks of royal favour. In 1619 he was made one of the 'musicians for the virginals, to attend in his highness' privy chamber'. In 1622 Oxford university awarded him an honorary doctorate of music and a year later he became organist at Westminster Abbey. By 1623, the year of William Byrd's death, Gibbons was generally acknowledged as the finest organist in England.

During his time in the Chapel Royal, Gibbons's output consisted of both 'short' and 'great' services and several anthems. These works have an impressive dignity and beauty; in one of his finest pieces is the anthem *O Clap Your Hands*, written in 1622 on the occasion of the award of his doctorate.

But Gibbons was not at all confined to the composition of sacred pieces. His first published work, 'cut in copper [that is, engraved on copper plates], the like not heretofore extant', was the *Fantasies in Three Parts, Composed for Viols* of about 1610. Music for viols was at its height at that time, and during its short ascendancy it found no finer exponent than Gibbons. One of his most inventive viol fantasies is an *In Nomine* that incorporates the tunes of London street cries.

As a brilliant keyboard player, Gibbons contributed many fine pieces for this medium. Better known perhaps than his organ works are his compositions for virginals. In these he joins the ranks of composers like Byrd and Morley (see *Lives of the Tudor Age*) in bringing to artistic perfection the pavan, galliard, and other such musical forms. One of the most celebrated and remarkable of these pieces was *The Lord of Salisbury's Pavan*, included in the *Parhenia* of William Byrd and John Bull (1612). Gibbons also made important contributions in the realm of vocal music. His sacred anthems have already been commented upon, but Gibbons was also a master of the madrigal. In 1612 he published his *Madrigals and Motets of Five Parts*. For the most part, these pieces set moralistic or philosophical texts. Among them are included the melancholy *What is our Life?* and what is perhaps the madrigal par excellence, *The Silver Swan*. This latter piece overflows with sensitivity and personal emotion. The six iambic pentameters of the poem teeter on the brink of sentimentality; however, harnessed to Gibbons's simple yet ravishing music, they seem totally sublime.

In 1625 Gibbons was among those who officiated at the funeral of James I in March. At the beginning of June he travelled in the retinue of Charles I when the latter went to meet his bride, Henrietta Maria, at Dover. At Canterbury he was given the job of preparing the music for the new Queen's reception there, but he fell violently ill, and died on 5 June 1625.

Gibbons's madrigals were edited by E. H. Fellowes and published in vol. v of the *English Madrigal School* in 1921. Vol. iv of *Tudor Church Music*, edited in 1925 by P. C. Buck and others contains the editions of his anthems, while his viol music has been edited by Fellowes (*Viol Music: Orlando Gibbons – 9 Fantasies for Strings in Three Parts*, 1924). Gibbons's *Complete Keyboard Works*, edited by M. H. Glyn, appeared in 1925.

E. H. Fellowes, *Orlando Gibbons* (1925).

Portrait: oil, half-length, copy by unknown artist, after lost original by unknown artist, after 1622: University of Oxford.

Godfrey, Sir Edmund Berry (1621–78), Justice of the Peace and victim of the Popish Plot.

Born on 23 December 1621, the eighth son of Thomas Godfrey, who sat in Parliament in 1614, 1628–29, and 1640, Godfrey was educated at Westminster school and went to Christ Church, Oxford, in 1638, eventually taking the trade of a woodmonger. His prosperity in this trade and his public spirit led to his appointment as justice of the peace for Westminster. Godfrey was active in the affairs of his own parish, St. Martin's in the Fields, and remained there during the plague of 1665, attempting to maintain order and alleviate distress. He was knighted for his services the following year.

In 1669 Godfrey was imprisoned for six days after a clash with King Charles II. A customer of Godfrey's, Sir Alexander Fraizer, the King's physician, was arrested at his instigation for nonpayment of a bill for firewood. The King was furious and ordered the bailiffs concerned to be whipped – Godfrey only narrowly escaped the same fate.

Godfrey was thought by many to be 'the best justice of the peace in England', according to his friend Burnet. He spent much of his money in private charity and, although a firm Protestant, 'had kind thoughts of the nonconformists, and consequently did not strictly enforce the penal laws against either them or the Roman Catholics' (Burnet).

In September of 1678 Titus Oates (q.v.) went to Godfrey with his first allegations of a 'Popish Plot'. Three weeks later, he went to him again and signed further depositions in support of the charges. The revelations made Godfrey increasingly apprehensive and according to one of his friends 'he believed he himself should be knocked on the head'. On Saturday 12 October, Godfrey left home and did not return that night. His body was found a few days later in a ditch on the south side of Primrose Hill. He had been transfixed by his own sword but had died of suffocation beforehand. His money and jewellery were found untouched. An open verdict of wilful murder was returned at Godfrey's inquest. Only later, when his body was taken home, did Burnet notice on Godfrey's clothes 'drops of white wax lights' such as Roman Catholic priests used. The crime was soon popularly ascribed to Roman Catholic priests, and antipapist feeling was rife. Medal portraits of Godfrey with the Pope represented as directing his murder were struck, and ballads and broadsheets were written expressing the same idea.

Eventually, Miles Prance, a Roman Catholic silversmith sometimes employed in the Queen's chapel at Somerset House, was arrested, and after torture confessed to complicity in Godfrey's murder. He declared that Godfrey was strangled in the presence of three priests by Robert Green, Lawrence Hill, and Henry Berry, all occasionally employed at Somerset House. The three were hanged, but many people doubted Prance's story and denounced the hangings as judicial murder. In 1686 Prance pleaded guilty to having perjured himself concerning the murder. The most likely explanation of the event is that Oates or his associates had Godfrey murdered to substantiate their allegations about the plot and to exacerbate anti-Catholic feeling.

J. D. Carr, *The Murder of Sir Edmund Godfrey* (1936).
J. P. Kenyon, *The Popish Plot* (1972).
J. Pollock, *The Popish Plot* (1913).

Portraits: chalk, quarter-length, by unknown artist, *c.* 1678: N.P.G.; oil, quarter-length, by unknown artist, *c.* 1678: N.P.G.

Godolphin, Sidney (1645–1712), 1st Earl of Godolphin; moderate Tory politician; chief minister 1702–10.

He was born at Godolphin Hall, Cornwall, in 1645, the third son of Sir Francis Godolphin, of an old Cornish family. Sidney Godolphin was taken into the royal household at an early age, where he became one of the King's pages (1662). At court he began his long friendship with John Churchill (q.v.), the future Duke of Marlborough. Like Churchill, he obtained an officer's commission in 1667, during the Second Dutch War.

Godolphin's talents, however, were not of a military nature. In 1668 he obtained a seat in the House of Commons. Over the next few years he filled various court posts and participated in the negotiations leading to the Treaty of Nijmegen (1678). He became one of the lords of the Treasury in 1679, at the beginning of the Exclusion crisis. He advised, negotiated, and manœuvred, dealing with all camps and corresponding with William of Orange, but he retained Charles's favour throughout. At the same time he began to acquire that financial expertise with which he later served his country so well. Charles recognized his merits in 1684 when calm was restored, appointing him first lord of the Treasury and creating him Baron Godolphin of Rialton.

Upon the accession of James II, Godolphin lost his Treasury post, but was appointed Chamberlain to the Roman Catholic Queen, whom he accompanied to the chapel door but went no further. He re-entered the Treasury in 1687 and served James to the end, acting as one of the three negotiators sent by the defeated King in December 1688 to William of Orange.

The new King, William III, kept Godolphin at the Treasury until 1696; the last Tory in the ministry, he was then forced out of office, perhaps by Whig threats to reveal the correspondence he had been conducting with the exiled James since 1691.

Two years later, the marriage of Godolphin's heir, Francis, to Marlborough's daughter, Henrietta Churchill, sealed the alliance between the fathers. In 1702, when the Churchills' friend and patroness Anne ascended to the throne, Godolphin benefited as well. He became lord treasurer and effective head of the government for the next eight years. He was a timid person for such a post, easily browbeaten by the tyrannical Duchess of Marlborough (see Churchill, Sarah), but he was possessed of the political skill needed to hold together a ministry and an alliance through treacherous politics during the War of the Spanish Succession, a long and costly struggle.

A moderate Tory, Godolphin was thrown increasingly on the support of

the great Whig lords, for he could not rely on the Tories to back his war policies. But the Whigs, no true friends of Marlborough or Godolphin, were personally distasteful to the Queen. The rift between Anne and the Duchess of Marlborough was exploited by the Tory leader Harley (q.v.) through the person of his relative, Mrs. Abigail Masham (q.v.), Anne's new favourite. Nevertheless, Godolphin not only managed to provide the finances and secure domestic bases essential to Marlborough's campaigns, but also managed the Union with Scotland.

The inability of Godolphin and his Whig colleagues to achieve a peace settlement damaged their position, and the impeachment of Dr. Henry Sacheverell (q.v.) in 1710 further weakened them. Anne began to give posts to High Tories. She rejected Godolphin's advice, but he clung to office until he was summarily dismissed in August. Godolphin retired with his health broken. He died on 15 September 1712.

Godolphin's distinguished tenure at

the Treasury contributed greatly to the continuing development of the power of that institution through a period of marked political turbulence. He stabilized Britain's finances during the long Continental wars.

H. F. H. Elliot, *The Life of Sidney, Earl Godolphin, Lord High Treasurer of England, 1702–1710* (1888). Sir Tresham Lever, *Godolphin, His Life and Times* (1952).

Portrait: oil, half-length, after Kneller, *c.* 1705: N.P.G.

Goring, Lord George (1608–57), soldier and Royalist commander in the Civil War.

George Goring was born on 14 July 1608, the son of the future Earl of Norwich. He early became prominent as a brilliant courtier. In 1629 he married Lettice, daughter of the Earl of Cork, and thereafter made constant demands on his father-in-law for money. After a period abroad, during which he entered the service of the Dutch and was wounded in the leg, he returned to England and was appointed governor of Portsmouth. Disputes between King and Parliament provided him with opportunities to further his career and Clarendon described his ambition as 'unlimited'. He played each side against the other, betraying the Army Plot in 1641, and Parliament seemed convinced of his devotion, but when hostilities broke out he declared for the King (1642).

Goring was soon blockaded at Portsmouth by land and sea and surrendered in September. He then sailed to Holland to assist the Queen, but returned in 1643 and led cavalry raised by local gentry in Yorkshire. He was a skilful and popular commander and he at once achieved a success by routing the younger Fairfax on Seacroft Moor near Leeds. However, two months later Fairfax attacked Wakefield, where Goring was in command,

and he was taken prisoner. He was exchanged almost a year later and joined Prince Rupert.

Goring commanded the left wing of the Royalist army at Marston Moor that routed the opposing cavalry before being thrown into disorder by a counterattack. After the defeat of the Royalists Goring scoured the country to bring in the scattered cavalry. His discipline was bad and his men were allowed to plunder. In August 1644, however, Goring was made lieutenant general of the horse in the King's main army.

In December he was sent to Hampshire. He advanced as far as Farnham but fell back to Salisbury, leaving a bad reputation behind him in the county through which he had passed. He bungled an attempt to intercept Fairfax's forces on their return from the west and his own troops, converging from opposite directions on what they thought to be the enemy, had fought each other for two hours before the mistake was rectified. Lord George, undaunted, described it as 'the most fantastic accident since the war began'. In March 1645 Prince Charles arrived in Bristol and Goring at once began to dispute with the prince's councillors. Prince Rupert, preparing for a decisive battle, sent to Goring urging him to make haste with his cavalry to Market Harborough. Goring took exception to Rupert's orders and failed to answer the summons. He remained near Taunton, alternately promising to improve the discipline of his troops and sinking into debauchery for several days at a time. Desertion steadily thinned his troops and Goring's drinking bouts became notorious.

In July 1645 Fairfax was heading for Taunton and Goring planned to divide his army by a ruse. He drew off 4,000 of Fairfax's cavalry by feigning to move towards Taunton and then entrenching himself at Langport. Goring picked a favourable position at the end of a narrow lane, but Fairfax's forces fought their way through and Goring's troops fled towards Bridgwater. Eventually the Royalists fell back as far as Barnstaple and Goring announced that his men were in no condition to fight again. He remained in north Devon, promising fresh levies but making no attempt to reorganize his men. At the end of November he pleaded ill health and left for France. Goring spent the rest of his life on the Continent, taking military service in the Netherlands and Spain and occasionally attempting to assist Charles II. He was seen by Sir Henry Bennet in Madrid in 1657 looking very ill and very destitute. He died less than a month later.

C. V. Wedgwood, 'George Goring: soldier and rake', *Sussex County Magazine*, 9 (1935), 164–9.

Portrait: oil, half-length, after Van Dyck, *c.* 1635–40: N.P.G.

Graham, James (1612–50), 1st Marquis and 5th Earl of Montrose; Scottish supporter of the Royalist cause in the Civil War.

Educated at St. Andrew's, Glasgow, 1624–26, Graham succeeded to the earldom and the family estates in Stirling, Perth, and Angus in 1626, and in 1629 he married the daughter of Lord Carnegie, Magdalen, by whom he had four sons and a daughter.

His first audience with Charles I, granted during a visit to the court in 1636, was marred by the Marquis of Hamilton (see Hamilton, James), who intended to remain the King's chief adviser on Scottish matters and successfully prejudiced him against this potential rival. Thereafter Montrose encountered suspicion of his motives in court circles,

which he never completely overcame.

In 1637, as a loyal member of the Kirk, he sided with those who opposed the attempt to impose the Prayer Book upon the Scots and was a member of the group of aristocrats who accepted the Covenant in the following year. Unlike some, he was not moved by personal or family advantage but by sincere convictions in religious affairs. His first military actions were thus on behalf of the Covenanters in 1639, breaking up the Marquis of Huntly's attempt to muster his Gordon clansmen for the King, occupying Aberdeen, and defeating Huntly's son Lord Aboyne at Brig of Dee (18 June), the first serious encounter of the Civil War. During the uneasy peace between the two Bishops' Wars he was drawn further into politics as one of the leaders of the moderate Covenanter party against the extremists headed by the self-seeking Earl of Argyll (see Campbell, Archibald, 8th Earl), and after the second war was for a time imprisoned as part of a political plot against himself. In 1640 he served in the army of Alexander Leslie (q.v.). His enthusiasm for the Covenant cause fell short of disloyalty to the monarchy as such, and in March 1643 he travelled to meet Queen Henrietta Maria in the north of England. He warned the court through her that Argyll was working to commit the Scots to the Parliamentary side in the English Civil War, but the influence of Hamilton nullified his warning. In September 1643, by the Solemn League and Covenant, the Scots entered the war, by which time Montrose was in the Royalist capital at Oxford offering his services directly to the King. It was not until February 1644 that Charles commissioned him as lieutenant general of the royal forces in Scotland, the basis of which was to be a force of Irishmen recruited by Lord Antrim.

The Covenanter army was now in England, and Montrose could not persuade the small army he had raised in Cumberland to remain in Dumfries, where he had led it when the Irish failed to appear and their own homes were threatened. His initial role was therefore to defend the northwestern counties against his fellow countrymen, a function which ceased after the Battle of Marston Moor (July 1644), when Prince Rupert took over Montrose's force to make good the losses in his own. He therefore re-entered Scotland with only two companions and the royal standard hidden in a saddle, intending to raise a rebellion in the King's name. In August he at last made contact with Antrim's Irishmen, led in the field by Alasdair MacDonald, who had thus far provoked much hostility and no support in the Highlands. On 28 August Montrose raised the standard at Blair Atholl backed by 2,200 men, half Irish, half Highlanders, with primitive arms and no cavalry.

His subsequent campaign in the Highlands can be better understood as a chapter in the history of clan feuding than as part of the Civil War. Argyll was Montrose's principal opponent, and the traditional attitude adopted towards the Campbell clan, of which Argyll was the head, determined the position of many others. With the numerical odds always against him, Montrose's success rested upon his ability to make best use of the mixed good and bad characteristics of a Highland fighting force – its aptitude for swift movement over rough country coupled with fierce attacks, its powers of endurance in extremes of climate, and its facility for living off a meagre countryside, all qualities which were offset by its disposition to regard loot as the purpose of fighting and its tendency to desert the colours with the proceeds when sufficiently satisfied. It was the nature of the force which undoubtedly provoked a violent reaction against it outside the Highlands, for which Montrose himself was to pay the price. The most important engagements were at Tippermuir (1 September 1644), Aberdeen (13 September), Inverlochy (2 February 1645), Auldern (9 May), Alford (2 July) and Kilsyth (15 August), defeating respectively Lord Elcho, Lord Burleigh, Campbell of Auchinbrech, Sir John Hurry, and in the latter two battles, William Baillie.

After Kilsyth, Montrose was the effective master of Scotland, entering Glasgow and summoning a parliament, but this assembly never met, while as usual the instrument of his power began to shed its rank and file. Meanwhile David Leslie (q.v.) was hastening north from the Scottish army in England with 5,000 mounted men. Montrose moved south to meet him but failed to raise an army in time in the Border area as he had hoped. His 600 were surprised by Leslie at Philiphaugh and overwhelmed

(13 September 1645). He escaped, but the battle was followed by the slaughter of unarmed Irish prisoners and their camp-followers and the judicial executions of his lieutenants. He raised a new force from Atholl, which maintained itself in the field until he was ordered to lay down his arms in July 1646 by Charles I.

He now went into exile on the Continent, refusing an offer to take service in the French army and attempting in vain to interest the court of Queen Henrietta Maria in a Scottish rising. He played no part in the last-minute bid to save Charles I on the part of Hamilton's faction, which ended at Preston (August 1648), but following the execution of the King, Montrose's commission was confirmed by his heir, Charles II. Accordingly, he began organizing an expedition to Scotland in which mercenaries from Denmark were to participate. Unfortunately, the new King continued to negotiate with the Covenanters, giving an implied legality to their position as the *de facto* government of Scotland.

In March 1650 he landed in the Orkneys, crossing to the mainland in the following month with 1,500 islanders and mercenaries. Leslie marched north, but the commander of his advance guard, Colonel Strachan, defeated the invaders at Carbisdale (27 April) with only 220 mounted soldiers and 400 clansmen. Montrose became a fugitive and was betrayed by a Macleod chieftain. He was taken to Edinburgh in a manner calculated to impose the maximum amount of public humiliation, treated with considerable vindictiveness by civil and religious leaders on his arrival, and was hanged without trial as an outlaw (21 May 1650), his body being dismembered and exhibited in the chief towns. At the Restoration, the remains were collected and buried in state in St. Giles's, Edinburgh.

John Buchan, *Montrose* (1928).
Anna A. W. Ramsay, *Challenge to the Highlander* (1933).
C. V. Wedgwood, *Montrose* (1952).

Portrait: oil, half-length, after G. Honthorst: N.P.G.

Graham, John, of Claverhouse

(?1649–89), 1st Viscount Dundee, heir to the Claverhouse branch of the family; Scottish soldier; scourge of the Covenanters and supporter of James II.

On leaving St. Andrews university, Claverhouse proceeded to the Continent to learn the military profession under Turenne, later transferring to the service of William of Orange. In 1677 he was commissioned into the newly raised regiment of horse guards of the Duke of York in Scotland, and was plunged at once into the running contest between the government and the Scottish Covenanters. In the case of Claverhouse, it was a personal crusade in revenge for the death of his kinsman Montrose (see Graham, James) at the hands of the earlier leaders of the sect. With his troop, he was given the responsibility of suppressing conventicles in Dumfries and Annandale and discharged his duty with great energy.

Hard-pressed, the Covenanters reacted with greater determination to resist, and following the murder of the primate of Scotland, Archbishop Sharpe, in May 1679, they planned a mass demonstration in Glasgow. By prompt movement of his troops, Claverhouse prevented their meeting at the original rendezvous, but they assembled instead at Rutherglen. Reconnoitring the area, he encountered the men drawn up in battle array at Drumclog, having sent their woman and children away, and outnumbering his dragoons by about four to one. The resulting battle (11 June

1679) was a triumph for the rebels, who swept the government dragoons from the field by a powerful advance, which routed them and drove the survivors back into Glasgow. Claverhouse was able to defend the town against an attempt of the Covenanters to enter it in force, but it became necessary to call in English troops to restore the situation.

The Duke of Monmouth (q.v.) was given the command, and Claverhouse fought under him at the Battle of Bothwell Bridge (22 June), following up the victory by a punitive ride through Ayr, Dumfriesshire, and Galloway with a mixed column of Scottish and English troops. In the following month, he and the Earl of Linlithgow journeyed to London at the behest of the council to procure a more rigorous policy against the rebels, and in January 1682 he was given a commission by a grant of a series of local appointments to apply such methods to southwestern Scotland. In May he was formally thanked by the council for his diligence; shortly afterwards he narrowly escaped an assassination plot against him prepared by the rebels. In December he was given command of a newly raised regiment.

Throughout this period he had enjoyed the patronage of the Duke of York, and because of this he was entrusted by the principal supporters of Charles II in Scotland with a mission to the court in England (March 1683) to solicit rewards and favours. In this he was successful, and on his return to Scotland, £4,000 the richer, he was admitted to the Privy Council and the area of policy decisions. He was as active as ever in pursuit of rebels, being called out on the very afternoon of his wedding (in 1684, to Jean, daughter of Lord Cochrane), and he attracted both an evil reputation among the Covenanters for his ruthlessness and – inevitably,

in Scotland – jealousy among his fellows. It was on account of the latter that he was removed from the Privy Council for a short time in 1685, being reinstated by the King's command.

The succession of the Duke of York to the throne as James II protected Claverhouse's position in Scotland, but at the same time constrained him to support the King's policies towards Roman Catholicism. He was made a major general in 1686 and provost of Dundee in 1688, in order to strengthen the King's hand in northeast Scotland. When reports of the threatened invasion of England by William of Orange reached Edinburgh, available forces were concentrated near the border under Douglas, with Claverhouse as second-in-command and in charge of the cavalry. They were summoned by the King to his camp at Salisbury, and on arrival Claverhouse was created Viscount Dundee.

When James broke his camp (November) and retired to London, some of the Scottish regiments deserted to the invader, but the mounted regiments under Dundee remained faithful and withdrew with him to Watford. In London he found that the majority of the Scottish Privy Council there were in favour of reaching agreement with William. Only Dundee and Lord Balcarres remained loyal and were prepared to fight. They failed to persuade James to that course, however, and had to make their own terms. Dundee was permitted to return to Scotland upon an undertaking to live as quietly as he could, being allowed a bodyguard of fifty troopers from his own regiment, which was disbanded.

In the confused political atmosphere in Edinburgh, Dundee and Balcarres attempted to rally support for James. They failed to sway the special convention that had been summoned, for it eventually declared for William and Mary (11 April 1689). By that time, fearing for his own life – he had few friends and many active enemies in Scotland – Dundee had ridden towards the Highlands with his dragoons. On 30 March, being technically in arms against the government, the convention declared him a traitor, Major General Hugh Mackay being sent to contain him.

Moving rapidly, he ranged from Inverness southeast to Perth, into Angus, and westwards again to Lochaber, eluding Mackay, who had marched for Inverness. With the support of the Cameron chieftain Lochiel and by now holding a commission from James, Dundee gathered a force of clansmen and hoped for the arrival of the King himself and troops from Ireland. Learning of the march of reinforcements for Mackay under Colonel Ramsay, Dundee moved to intercept, forcing Ramsay to retreat to Perth and in consequence compelling Mackay to retire upon him, his communications being cut.

Confident that the majority of the clans were with him, he attempted to raise the Atholl men, who still stood aloof. In order to forestall him, Mackay marched to seize Blair Castle, the strategic key to the area. Dundee waited for him in a position above the pass of Killiecrankie selected by Lochiel, where the ground favoured the charging tactics of the irregular clan regiments. Mackay thus found that he had marched into a trap, and was forced to defend himself (27 July 1689) in an overextended line below the Highlanders in fading daylight. Although numerically the stronger, many of his regiments broke under the impetus of the clan army's charge. Two regiments, one English (Hastings's) and one Scottish (Leven's) stood firm, and Mackay was able to bring them off in good order. It was this stand that

prompted Dundee to ride into the battle to order forward his cavalry, and at that point he was mortally wounded by a musket ball.

Although Killiecrankie was a severe defeat for the government, the death of Dundee deprived the supporters of James II of their effective leader and put an effective end to any chance that he might have had of recovering the throne.

Baines and Allen, *Uniforms and History of the Scottish Regiments* (1960).
G. Daviot, *Claverhouse* (1937).
M. Napier, *Memorials and Letters illustrative of the Life and Times of John Graham of Claverhouse, Viscount of Dundee* (3 vols.; 1859–62).
A. and H. Tayler, *John Graham of Claverhouse* (1939).

Gregory, James (1638–75), mathematician and astronomer.

James Gregory was born in November 1638 at Drumoak, near Aberdeen, the son of the Rev. John Gregory, and like his elder brother David was gifted with an enquiring mind and an aptitude for natural sciences.

After graduating from Marischal College, Aberdeen, James Gregory published *Optica Promota* in 1663. In this work he describes a design for a telescope in which a curved mirror is used instead of a lens for collecting and focusing the light from a distant object. The light collected by the reflecting mirror was to be focused onto a small converging mirror that reflected the light back through a hole in the centre of the main mirror onto the eyepiece of the telescope. Gregory never actually built such a telescope; this was left to James Short of Edinburgh, who began experiments in telescope design and construction in the 1730s. It was Hooke (q.v.) and Newton (q.v.) who built the earliest reflecting telescopes.

At the time when Gregory published his work, only lenses were used in telescopes and the resulting images suffered from coloured fringes as well as distortion. The reason for these fringes was not known until Newton stated that they were a result of refraction and would therefore always be present (as he thought) in lenticular images. Only in images formed by reflection would there be no chromatic aberration – no coloured fringes. Newton did not start his investigations into optics and colour until about 1667. Gregory's proposal in 1663 is thus remarkable and appears to be a result of inspiration rather than based on theories of the time. He did, however, correspond with Newton some years later, on the subject of the reflecting telescope. The Gregorian telescope is still used today in several astronomical observatories.

From about 1664 to 1668 Gregory lived in Italy. It was there, in Padua, that his mathematical studies began. In 1668 he returned to Scotland and took the chair of mathematics at St. Andrews University, being elected a Fellow of the Royal Society in the same year. In 1674 he moved to Edinburgh University, becoming the first professor of mathematics there.

His studies embraced the fields of geometry, trigonometry, calculus, and algebra, involving work on convergent series, the circular and hyperbolic functions of trigonometry, and formulae used in analysis. He put forward probably the earliest proof of the fundamental theorem of calculus, by which the derivative of a function is related to the definite integral. This proof was contained in *Geometricae Pars Universalis*, which was a supplement to *Vera Circuli et Hyperbolae Quadratura*, published in 1667. This work led to controversy with Christiaan Huygens, the Dutch scientist

who was closely associated with Leibnitz's work on calculus, and who developed a wave theory of light.

In October 1675, Gregory was showing the satellites of the planet Jupiter through a telescope to some students, when he was quite suddenly stricken blind. He died only a few days later. His letters, published posthumously, showed that his discoveries in analysis anticipated work by his contemporaries, such as Newton Brooke and Taylor, and included the Gregory-Newton formula, used in interpolation. Both his and his brother's descendants, especially his nephew David Gregory (1661–1708), who succeeded to his chair in mathematics in 1683 and who in 1691 became professor of mathematics at Oxford, were to continue the tradition of academic accomplishments started by him.

H. W. Turnbull (ed.), *James Gregory: Tercentenary Memorial Volume* (1939).

Greville, Fulke (1554–1628), 1st Baron Brooke; poet and statesman, see *Lives of the Tudor Age*.

Gwynne, Eleanor (1650–87), called 'Nell', actress and mistress of Charles II.

Born 2 February 1650, probably in Hereford, although one account suggests that she was born in Drury Lane. Nell Gwynne's first public occupation was as an orange-seller at the Theatre Royal. She had several lovers, including Charles Hart, the actor, and she probably owed her theatrical training to him. Her first appearance on stage took place in 1665 as Cydaria in Dryden's *The Indian Emperor*. As an actress, she excelled in comedy and was much admired by Pepys, who described her as 'a bold merry slut'. Dryden supplied her with a series of saucy bustling parts well suited to her abilities. Pepys thought her out-standing as Florimel in Dryden's *The Maiden Queen*, which he saw several times. Nell especially enjoyed delivering risqué prologues and epilogues, and according to one tradition, Charles was so taken by her appealing looks as she recited an epilogue in a huge hat the size of a coachwheel that he took her home in his coach and made her his mistress there and then.

His mistress she certainly became, bearing the King one son in 1670, who later became the Duke of St. Albans, and another in 1671. Nell enjoyed great popularity as a royal mistress, probably in contrast to the Duchess of Portsmouth (see Kéroualle, Louise de), who was universally disliked. She accompanied the King when Parliament met at Oxford in 1681 and, when the crowd jostled her coach, Nell is reported to have delighted them by putting her head out of the window and saying 'Pray, good people, be civil; I am the Protestant whore.'

Nell retained the King's favour until the end of his life and received consider-able sums of money from him, although Burnet said 'he never treated her with the decencies of a mistress'. However, Charles's last request to his brother, according to Burnet and Evelyn, was

'let not poor Nelly starve'. James paid her debts and settled an estate near Nottingham on her and the Duke of St. Albans. She died on 13 November 1687, leaving several charitable bequests in her will. In Nell's funeral sermon Dr. Tenison found much to say in her praise.

Bryan Bevan, *Nell Gwyn* (1969).
Arthur Dasent, *Nell Gwynne 1650–1687* (1924).
John H. Wilson, *Nell Gwyn, Royal Mistress* (New York, 1952).

Portrait: oil, three-quarter length, studio of Lely, *c.* 1675: N.P.G.

H

Hale, Sir Matthew (1609–76), lawyer who was noted for his impartiality during the Civil War and who became lord chief justice under Charles II.

Born at Alderley, Gloucestershire, on 1 November 1609, Hale's parents died when he was five years old and he was put by his guardian under the supervision of the vicar of Wotton-under-Edge, an ardent Puritan. At the age of sixteen he entered Magdalen Hall, Oxford, with the intention of reading for the Church. Soon after starting his course of study, however, he underwent a complete change of mind, and, after conceiving a plan to take up a military career, was finally persuaded to study law.

Hale entered Lincoln's Inn in 1628 or 1629. He applied himself vigorously and was eventually called to the bar in 1637. He soon rose to the top of his profession. Though not a fluent speaker, he was nevertheless an extremely learned man. As a student, he had become an authority on English legal records, but his learning was broadly based, for he also devoted much of his time to the study of mathematics and science.

This industry and breadth of intellectualism caused Hale to be widely held in respect. At the outset of the Civil War he was therefore able to hold aloof from the conflict by taking the stand of a moderate. He appeared as defence counsel for several of the prominent figures impeached by the House of Commons, including Archbishop William Laud (q.v.) in 1643. In 1644 he sat with the assembly of divines at Westminster. In 1649 he defended James Hamilton (q.v.), Duke of Hamilton, after the Battle of Preston. He took the oath of loyalty to the Commonwealth required of all lawyers, but in 1651 defended Christopher Love (1618–51), a Presbyterian minister who was alleged to have been involved in Royalist plots.

In 1653, after becoming a serjeant-at-law, Hale became a judge in the court of common pleas. He sat as one of the members for Gloucestershire in Oliver Cromwell's parliament of 1654, but refused to continue as a judge after Cromwell's death. He did, however, sit in Richard Cromwell's Parliament, representing Oxford.

At the Restoration, Charles II treated him well. He was appointed chief baron of the exchequer in 1660 and knighted. The main blemish in modern eyes on what was otherwise a remarkable record of impartiality was his conviction in 1661 or 1662 of two women accused of witchcraft.

In 1671 Hale was made lord chief justice of the court of king's bench. He remained in this office until ill health forced him to resign from it five years later. He died at Alderley on 25 December 1676.

Noted among his contemporaries as a remarkably fair, moderate, and religious judge, Hale was able to hold a neutral position throughout the political upheaval of the mid-17th century. He was a most prolific writer, chiefly on law, his most important work being *Historia Placitorum Coronae* (History of the Pleas of the Crown, first published 1685). He also wrote a treatise on criminal law, and his *History of the Common Law of England* first appeared in 1713. He has also left scientific works, like the *Essay Touching the Gravitation or Non-gravitation of Fluid Bodies* (1673) and theological writings, such as *Contemplations, Moral and Divine* (published 1676–77).

Gerald Hurst, 'Sir Matthew Hale', *Law Quarterly Review*, 70 (1954), 342–52.

Portrait: oil, quarter-length, by J. M. Wright, *c.* 1670: N.P.G.

Halifax, Earl of (1661–1715), see Montagu, Charles.

Halifax, 1st Marquis of (1633–95), see Savile, George.

Hall, Joseph (1574–1656), bishop, controversialist, poet, moralist, and satirist.

Born on 1 July 1574 at Ashby-de-la-Zouch, Hall's father was an employee of the Earl of Huntingdon; his mother was a strict Puritan. In 1589 Hall entered Emmanuel College, Cambridge, where he acquired four degrees (including Doctor of Divinity, 1612) and a high reputation for scholarship. He also gained a name for himself as a poet and satirist with the publication, in 1597, of *Virgidemiarum: First three books of toothless satires*, followed in 1598 by volume two, *Three last books of biting satires*. These are poems on the model of the Latin satirists, notably Juvenal: in 1599 the Archbishop of Canterbury ordered them to be burnt, along with certain other books, on the grounds of scurrilous licentiousness, although the order was not in fact carried out.

In 1599 or 1600 Hall took holy orders: he received the living of Halsted in Suffolk from Sir Robert and Lady Drury, the patrons of John Donne. He married in 1603. His next literary production, *Meditations and Vows* (1605), a collection of Hall's Christian-Senecan aphorisms and reflections, was much more fitting to a clergyman, as was *Characters of Virtues and Vices* (1608). The latter is based on Theophrastus and is avowedly didactic and moralistic, urging that Christians may learn from heathen wisdom. These two works earned him the nickname of 'Our English Seneca'.

Hall remained a prolific writer in both Latin and English throughout his long life, especially on theological controversies. Only the most significant or pioneering of his works are mentioned here.

In 1608 he was appointed chaplain to Prince Henry and received the richer living of Waltham Cross in Essex. In 1616 he became Dean of Worcester and in 1627 was created Bishop of Exeter. His willingness to conciliate the Puritans kept order and harmony within his diocese, but got him into trouble through the spy network of Archbishop Laud (q.v.); three times he was forced to give an account of his conduct and theology to the King and was only left in peace after threatening to resign his see. At the same time he became embroiled in other controversies. In 1625 he wrote *No Peace with Rome* against the Catholics; he also defended the *Divine Right of Episcopacy* (1637) against the more zealous of the Puritans.

In 1640 Hall was translated to the more wealthy see of Norwich, having evidently continued to find royal favour in spite of Archbishop Laud. This good fortune did not, however, last long. Shortly after the outbreak of the Civil War, he was one of the thirteen bishops impeached (1641) and imprisoned (1642), and his episcopal revenues were sequestrated in 1643. In spite of his troubles, Hall attempted for four years to continue his episcopal duties, but he was now an old man and the times were against him; his income was cut off and when, in 1646, the townspeople of Norwich desecrated his cathedral and ejected him from his palace, he gave up the struggle and retired to the village of Higham nearby, where he devoted himself to writing and to religious and charitable works. He published an account of his troubles, *Hard Measure* (1647), and wrote poems, meditations, and expositions of hard passages in the Bible. He died on 8 September 1656, leaving two daughters and six sons, four of whom entered the church.

A. Davenport (ed.), *Collected Poems of Joseph Hall* (1949).

P. Wynter (ed.), *The Collected Works of Joseph Hall*, [*Bishop of Norwich*] (10 vols.; 1863).

T. F. Kinloch, *The Life and Works of Joseph Hall* (1951).

G. Lewis, *The Life of Joseph Hall* (1886).

Halley, Edmond (1656–1742), astronomer and oceanographer; one of the greatest scientists of his age, best known for the comet that bears his name.

Born on 29 October 1656, in London, the son of a soap-maker, Halley's interest in science was aroused when he was still at St. Paul's School, London. While at the Queen's College, Oxford, which he entered in 1673, he studied the theories of planetary orbits and devised a better method for determining their shape, size, and orientation and the position of a planet in its orbit. He published this work in 1676 in the *Philosophical Transactions* of the Royal Society.

The reputation that he gained from his studies led to his meeting and subsequent friendship with John Flamsteed (q.v.), who had been appointed Astronomer Royal at the newly founded Greenwich Observatory. Assisting Flamsteed at Greenwich, Halley was fired with enthusiasm for Flamsteed's appointed task of determining more accurately the positions of the stars. His own work on planetary orbits had already made him aware of the errors and inaccuracies of the existing star guides, which had been prepared without telescopic aid.

Since Flamsteed was observing the stars of the Northern Hemisphere, Halley proposed a similar project for the uncharted Southern Hemisphere. Charles II was persuaded to send him to St. Helena, a small island in the South Atlantic, and for this purpose he set sail in 1676, leaving Oxford without a degree. During his stay there, from 1676 to 1678, he set up a telescope and succeeded in determining the positions of about 360 stars and in observing a transit of Mercury across the sun, which suggested to him a way of calculating the distance of the sun from Earth. The publication of his observations in *Catalogus Stellarum Australium* (1679) brought him great acclaim. By royal mandate Oxford University granted him an M.A. and he was elected an F.R.S.

In 1682 Halley married Mary Tooke, daughter of the auditor of the Royal exchequer. Continuing his astronomical studies, he became interested in the problem of gravity. In the course of his search for further information he met Newton (q.v.) in 1684 at Cambridge and consulted him on the subject. Halley had suspected that it was the force of gravity that controlled the motions of celestial bodies. He learnt at Cambridge that Newton had managed to prove this. Realizing the tremendous importance of not only this work but Newton's other studies, Halley persuaded Newton to publish his theories through the Royal Society, of which he was now assistant secretary and editor. Halley himself financed this work, correcting the proofs, and in 1687 Newton's *Principia* was published. But for Halley, this outstanding work might never have reached the scientific world.

Halley's interests were not restricted to astronomy but also included meteorology, geography, engineering, mathematics, and statistics. He wrote the first detailed description of the trade winds (1686), described the constant circulation of water between ocean and atmosphere (1691), and originated the science of life statistics by publishing the Breslau Table of Mortality (1693), which was the first such table based on fact. He made various expeditions to study and chart the variations in the earth's magnetism in the Atlantic and to survey and chart the coastline and tides of the English Channel. At the request of the Holy Roman Emperor, he twice visited the Adriatic to assist in the marine surveying, building, and repair of harbours, especially Trieste. He discovered that the aurora borealis was magnetic in origin, predicted and observed the solar eclipse of 1715, and recommended that observations of the transit of Venus in 1761 could be used to determine the sun's distance. In 1703 he was appointed Savilian Professor of Geometry at Oxford, where he later had the degree of doctor of laws conferred on him. While at Oxford he edited the work of several Greek mathematicians, including Apollonius of Perga.

Halley published his *Synopus Astronomiae Cometicae* in 1705. This contains his studies on comets, which had begun when he made observations of the comet of 1680. Using information available from previous sightings, he was able to compute the orbits of 24 comets. The similarity of four of these orbits, which had been followed by comets in 1456, 1531, 1607, and 1682, led him to predict that these were all appearances of the same comet and that it would return in 1758. Halley had discovered the periodic

nature of comets. He did not live to see his prediction verified or know that the comet, returning in 1758 and reappearing every 76 years, would later bear his name.

He made a further contribution to astronomy with his discovery of the proper motions of stars, following observations of the stars Sirius, Procyon, and Arcturus in 1718. Up to that time it had been believed that stars never varied in their relative positions.

As assistant secretary and later (1713) as secretary of the Royal Society, Halley was involved in the bitter controversy over the unauthorized publication of Flamsteed's results. Ironically it was Halley who succeeded Flamsteed as Astronomer Royal on Flamsteed's death in 1719. Unlike Flamsteed, he was given sufficient finances to build complex and sensitive instruments, such as a transit telescope. For the next 20 years, usually working without assistance, he carefully observed the motions of the moon through its 18-year period (saros) and discovered that the velocity of the moon around the earth was very gradually increasing. His lunar and planetary tables were published posthumously in 1749.

He died on 14 January 1742, at the age of 85. His prodigious output in many scientific fields and the quality and insight of his work rank him alongside Newton as one of the greatest scientists of the Stuart Age.

E. F. MacPike (ed.), *Correspondence and Papers of Edmond Halley* (1932).

A. Armitage, *Edmond Halley* (1966).

C. A. Ronan, *Edmond Halley: Genius in Eclipse* (1969).

Portrait: oil, half-length, by R. Phillips, before 1721: N.P.G.

Hamilton, James (1606–49), 3rd Marquis and 1st Duke of Hamilton, 2nd

Earl of Cambridge; Scottish supporter of Charles I.

He was born in 1606, the son of the 2nd Marquis, who had been elevated to the English peerage as Earl of Cambridge. In 1620 he was married to Mary, daughter of Lord Fielding. He was educated at Exeter College, Oxford, and in 1625 succeeded as third marquis.

A favourite courtier of Charles I from the very outset of his reign, he exercised a greater influence on Scottish affairs than his political talents warranted. In 1628 he was appointed master of the horse and a privy councillor. An early indication of his mediocrity was the failure of the military expedition he organized in 1631 to assist Gustavus Adolphus in Germany. It had taken him a year to find sufficient recruits in England and Scotland, those he did get being of poor quality, and they were wasted away by famine and plague in static duties, leaving Hamilton to return in 1634 without the military laurels he had sought.

He then assumed the role of principal adviser to the King on Scotland, and in 1638 was sent as commissioner to pacify the country after the violent reaction to the King's attempt to introduce a Prayer Book in the kingdom. Hamilton's title and family carried weight among the self-seeking Scottish nobility, but he lacked the strength of character to impose the royal will, and was more inclined to further his own position by truckling to the malcontents in Scotland and urging compromise with them when in England, since he found it easier to face the King than his own countrymen. The steady deterioration of the situation owed much to his attempts at mediation, although it must be admitted that the King allowed him very little freedom to manœuvre.

In the Bishops' Wars of 1639 and 1640 he was given commands of forces that were as ineffective as the remainder of the English troops, and his reluctance to prosecute serious war was increased by the adverse effect that his presence under arms against the Covenanters was having upon his personal influence in Scotland. He urged peace upon the King on both occasions, but did not earn the approbation of his fellow Scots thereby. His own solution to the King's problems, which had begun to multiply in England also by this time, was for the King to accept Presbyterianism, in return for which the Scots would supply troops for use against the English Parliamentarians. He gave this scheme its first airing in the summer of 1641. It produced no military support for the King, but enabled Hamilton to achieve a short-lived political alliance with the Earl of Argyll (see Campbell, Archibald, 8th Earl), who had used the Covenant to augment his own already powerful influence in Scotland.

With the coming of the Civil War in England, Scottish affairs slipped completely from even the minimal control that the King's court could exert. It became increasingly clear that the Argyll faction was prepared to respond to appeals for help from the English Parliament, but at this juncture Hamilton was more concerned to preserve his own standing at the court by intriguing against the one Scottish leader, Montrose (see Graham, James), anxious to stand by the King and therefore, from Hamilton's viewpoint, a potential rival.

In November 1643 he refused to accept the Solemn League and Covenant, whereby the Scots and the English Parliamentarians bound themselves together, and left Scotland for the King's capital, Oxford. Here the strength of feeling against him was so strong that the King was reluctantly forced to order his imprisonment, and in January 1644 he was sent to Pendennis Castle in Cornwall and later to St. Michael's Mount. He was freed in April 1646 when the army of Sir Thomas Fairfax (q.v.) ended Royalist resistance in the southwest.

In May 1646 Charles I surrendered to the Scots, and Hamilton joined him at Newcastle, producing his 1641 proposals again as the only way of restoring the King's power in England. In August he returned to Scotland to further the project, but made little headway against the influence of Argyll. In the event, the King would not countenance the permanent establishment of Presbyterianism in England and the negotiations foundered.

The seizure of the King by the Army (June 1647) and his subsequent isolation caused a revulsion of feeling in Scotland in his favour, to the personal advantage of Hamilton in his political rivalry with Argyll. In the Scottish parliament that met in March 1648, Hamilton was able to secure a majority in favour of intervention, which prompted widescale Royalist plots in both kingdoms for a conservative alliance of Royalists and Presbyterians to overthrow the ascendancy of the extremist Independents in England.

On 8 July 1648, Hamilton led an army of 20,000 into England. Opposition from Argyll and the more rigorous of the ministers of the Kirk ensured that it was not the best Scottish army that could have been raised, and leaders such as David Leslie (q.v.) were absent. It was beset by bad weather, and its second-in-command, the Earl of Callander, had even less military ability than Hamilton, though greater claims to experience. It had no artillery. Even the adhesion of Sir Marmaduke Langdale and his northern English levies could not redress the weakness of the army, which was brought to battle at Preston (17–18

August) and broken by Cromwell.

What was left of the force disintegrated on the following day, and on 25 August Hamilton himself surrendered at Uttoxeter. The only result of the whole attempt was to pave the way for the execution of King Charles I. Hamilton was held at Windsor, and briefly saw the King when he too was brought there. In February, Hamilton was put on trial and was executed on 9 March 1649.

G. Hamilton, *A History of the House of Hamilton* (1934).
D. Stevenson, *The Scottish Revolution 1637–1644* (1973).

Hampden, John (1594–1643), statesman and Parliamentarian.

Hampden was probably born in London, although his home was at Great Hampden in Buckinghamshire, and he owned many other estates in the county. He was educated at Thame grammar school, matriculated from Magdalen College, Oxford, in 1610, and in 1613 became a member of the Inner Temple. Hampden was acknowledged by friend

and foe to be a learned and highly intelligent man, and praise of his personal integrity, assiduity, good sense, naturally good taste, and fair-mindedness abound in contemporary accounts and historical records. He was also reported to be as subtle as a fox in parliamentary debate and procedure, and there is little doubt that he was one of the most gifted parliamentarians of all time.

Hampden had a large fortune and came of an old and distinguished family. From the beginning of the reign of Charles I he associated himself with the Parliamentarians against the Court. In the first three parliaments during Charles's reign, Hampden sat as member for Wendover; although he did not speak often, he sat on many of the important committees and studied parliamentary law and precedence with special regard to privilege, religion, and supplies.

In 1635 the controversy over the payment of ship money began, and this brought lasting fame in English history to the Buckinghamshire landowner. Charles I had dismissed Parliament in 1629 and, being short of money, determined to raise this ancient tax. The sheriff of Buckinghamshire received a writ on 4 August 1635, demanding that the county raise the sum of £4,500 (the estimated cost of a 450-ton ship). Hampden flatly refused to pay the small sums assessed against his estates in various parishes of the county. Edmund Burke later wrote, 'Would twenty shillings have ruined Mr. Hampden's fortune? No, but the payment of half twenty shillings would have made him a slave.'

The court of the exchequer began trial of Hampden's refusal in 1637; judgment was pronounced in favour of the crown in 1638, leaving, as public opinion saw it, 'no man anything that he could call his own'.

Hampden was prominent in the business of both the Short and Long Parliaments of 1640. As the House was again considering the question of ship money in May 1640, the King dissolved Parliament, and on 6 May Hampden and other leaders were temporarily arrested. In the Long Parliament, the question of ship money was again discussed, and the House declared the judgment against Hampden to be 'against the laws of the realm, the right of property, the liberty of subject, and contrary to former resolutions in Parliament and to the Petition of Right' (7 December 1640). The House of Lords concurred, and the judgment was cancelled. Hampden had won a popular moral victory for the rights of Parliament and the common man over arbitrary taxation by the King.

Hampden did not have an aversion to the monarchy as such, as did some other Parliamentarians, nor was he a fervent Puritan, although he disliked the episcopalian government of the church. Still, in Parliament he remained in active opposition, and on 3 January 1642, the King sent the attorney general to the House of Lords to impeach Hampden and others, while a sergeant-at-arms was despatched to the Commons to arrest them. The charges against Hampden and his colleagues were numerous, but the House authorized them to resist. On 4 January the King himself came to arrest them, but they escaped. When the news reached Buckinghamshire, four thousand men rode to London to present a petition to Parliament promising to defend its rights.

Now Hampden resolved to obtain securities from the King for Parliament's safety in future. War between Parliamentarians and Royalists became inevitable. Hampden raised the Buckinghamshire militia and was active and capable in command of troops during the Civil War. He continued his political activities to keep the Parliamentary side together and to ensure that no peace was concluded on terms unsatisfactory to Parliament. Hampden was fatally wounded in a skirmish with Prince Rupert's troops at Chalgrove Field on 18 June 1643, and he died at an inn at Thame. He was buried in the church of Great Hampden. An obituary notice printed in a newspaper at the end of June 1643 said, 'The loss of Colonel Hampden goeth near the heart of every man that loves the good of his king and country. . . .'

George Grenville, Lord Nugent, *Some Memorials of John Hampden, His Party and His Times* (2 vols.; 1831).
Hugh Ross Williamson, *John Hampden* (1933).

Portrait: oil, quarter-length, attributed to Robert Walker: N.P.G.; engraving, quarter-length, by Jacobus Houbraken, 1740: British Museum.

Harley, Robert (1661–1724), 1st Earl of Oxford; politician.

Born on 5 December 1661 in Covent Garden, the eldest son of Sir Edward Harley, a Presbyterian squire from Herefordshire, Harley was educated at dissenter schools in Oxfordshire and London and at the Inner Temple, although he was never admitted to the bar.

Robert Harley entered politics at the time of the Glorious Revolution of 1688. He helped his father to take and hold Worcester for William III and was afterwards named sheriff of Herefordshire. Like the rest of his family he was deeply religious, and although they conformed to the Established Church, their creed was actually Presbyterianism. This belief drew Robert, as it had drawn his father, into the Country grouping – those gentlemen distrustful of and opposed to the court and its corruption, and hostile to a standing army, high taxation, and government power in the Commons.

In 1689 Robert Harley was first elected to Parliament. His quick mind soon mastered the intricacies of parliamentary procedure and political intrigue. In the Convention Parliament he proved to be a fiery Whig, working closely with the Puritan Foley brothers. In the next Parliament this alliance flourished, and Harley was recognized as a leader of the Country Whigs, at whose centre was the Foley connection. He concentrated his attacks as much against the ruling Court Whigs and the crown as against the High Tories, for he was alarmed by the rapid growth of the government service and the patronage it put in the hands of the ministry. He carried the Triennial Act (1694), requiring new Parliaments to be elected every three years, and accomplished the election of Paul Foley as Speaker.

In these and other designs Harley was aided by the Country Tories, for the two groups found they had much in common. They worked together in the Commission of Public Accounts, a major thorn in the government's side, and Harley relied on their support when he forced reductions in the size of the army in 1697 and 1698.

Harley's role was not entirely negative. During the war with France he carried the vote for supplies in the Commons. His value was recognized by King William, who supported his election to the office of Speaker in 1701.

Gradually, Harley's ties with the opposition weakened. With the shift in politics in the new Queen's reign, he found himself at the centre of power in alliance with Godolphin (q.v.) and Marlborough (see Churchill, John), two moderate Tories. This triumvirate of centre politicians had the Queen's ear and dominated the government. Although they began as an essentially Tory administration, the High Tories' unwillingness to support their war policy compelled the triumvirate to reorganize. The most extreme 'high-flyers' were dropped from the ministry. Harley became secretary of state in 1704 and brought in moderate Tories, such as Henry St. John (q.v.). Moderate Whigs followed, but here a rift opened. Godolphin and Marlborough saw their strategy as a shift from the Tories to reliance on the pro-war Whigs, which necessitated bringing the Whig leadership (the Junto) into their ministry. Harley, with his loathing for party government, sought a ministry of moderates. Furthermore, he was worried by the lack of progress towards peace.

Despite these differences, Harley contributed greatly to the formation and execution of policy in these years, including the achievement of union with Scotland (1707). In this work he built up a formidable intelligence network, which included Daniel Defoe (q.v.), who served him well as both an agent and a propagandist.

Nevertheless, the conflict between Harley and Godolphin grew more bitter. The latter gradually became convinced that Harley was intriguing with the Queen and the High Tories to oust him. In 1708 one of Harley's clerks was found to be in the employ of the French war minister, and the Whigs tried unsuccessfully to implicate Harley in the affair. This did not aid ministerial unity; Godolphin, Marlborough, and the Whigs forced him to resign.

Harley was accompanied into opposition by St. John and other moderate Tories. There they joined forces with the High Tories and disgruntled Whigs. Harley kept in communication with Queen Anne (q.v.), who had now come to favour Abigail Masham (q.v.), Harley's relative, over the Duchess of Marlborough, Sarah Churchill (q.v.). The country was tiring of the war, and it focused its anger on the ministry when Godolphin and the Whig Junto impeached Dr. Henry Sacheverell (q.v.).

In 1710 Anne replaced her leading ministers with Tories and dissident Whigs. Harley became chancellor of the exchequer and effective head of the government. In the subsequent election the Tories became the dominant force in the House of Commons. Unfortunately for Harley, the High Tory element, to which St. John allied himself, was particularly strong. But when a French agent stabbed Harley in an attempted assassination in 1711, popular support rallied to his side. He was able to carry through Parliament a bill for funding the National Debt by establishing the creditors as the South Sea Company, empowered to trade in the Pacific. Anne created him Earl of Oxford and Earl Mortimer and made him lord treasurer of England.

Meanwhile Oxford had initiated peace negotiations with France, which had to be kept secret since they involved abandoning England's allies and giving up the goal of restoring Spain to the Hapsburgs. News about them, however, did leak out and led to a defeat for Oxford in the Lords at the hands of the Whigs. The hard-pressed Oxford persuaded Anne to ennoble a number of government supporters, secured a majority in the upper chamber, and obtained the dismissal of Marlborough from his command. Oxford continued the peace negotiations, bringing them to a conclusion in the Treaty of Utrecht (1713), an agreement that recognized the realities of power in Europe and the colonies.

Unfortunately, the peace terms angered George of Hanover, who was in line for the English throne. Although Oxford had introduced the Act of 1712 which made the entire Hanoverian family heirs after Anne, he was suspected of working for a Jacobite restoration; and indeed, like so many other politicians, he conducted a correspondence with the Old Pretender's court as a form of insurance. But Oxford's religious beliefs made him a natural opponent of Jacobitism.

St. John, now Viscount Bolingbroke, was seeking a Jacobite restoration. He saw it as a means to achieve the power that Oxford had kept out of his hands since 1710. Although in the ministry, he struggled to capture Oxford's primacy and eventually succeeded in alienating Anne and Lady Masham from their old adviser. Oxford went into a rapid decline, both physical and mental, after 1713. Politically, he lost his grip: Bolingbroke forced him into open equivocation, isolation, and defeat over the Schism Bill, by which the High Tories devised new penalties for the Dissenters.

In 1714 Oxford's loss of control was finally accomplished. On 27 July Anne finally dismissed him; five days later she died, and George of Hanover ascended the throne. When the new Parliament of 1715 inquired into the Treaty of Utrecht, the Commons proceeded to impeach Oxford. He was sent to the Tower, where he remained for two years until his trial finally began. After lengthy procedural wrangles he was acquitted, but forbidden the court. Nevertheless, he remained comparatively active in Parliament until 1719 and died in London on 21 May 1724.

Oxford was a brilliant parliamentarian and party leader, although a poor speaker. He was also an avid collector of books, assembling the Harleian library after 1705.

J. H. Davis, *Robert Harley as Secretary of State 1704–8* (Chicago, 1934).

Elizabeth V. Hamilton, *The Backstairs Dragon: A Life of Robert Harley, Earl of Oxford* (1969).

George Holmes, 'Harley, St. John and the Death of the Tory Party', in Geoffrey Holmes (ed.), *Britain after the Glorious Revolution 1689–1714* (1969).

Angus McInnes, *Robert Harley, Puritan Politician* (1970).

A. S. Turberville, *A History of Welbeck Abbey and its Owners* (2 vols.; 1938–39).

Portraits: oil, three-quarter length, after Kneller: N.P.G.; oil, full-length, by Kneller, 1714: N.P.G.

Harrison, Thomas (1616–60), Parliamentarian soldier and Fifth Monarchist.

Born at Newcastle-under-Lyme, the son of Richard Harrison, a wealthy butcher, Harrison was probably educated at the local grammar school before becoming clerk to an attorney at Clifford's Inn. Like many other young lawyers, he joined the life guard of the Earl of Essex (see Devereux, Robert), Parliament's commander-in-chief, at the outbreak of the Civil War. He took part in most of the major engagements of the war, winning a high reputation and rising to the rank of major by early 1644. He also made a name for himself as an Independent – his temperament was warm, emotional, and religious – and established a close relationship with Fleetwood, Thomas Fairfax, and Oliver Cromwell (qq.v.). He served with Cromwell at Marston Moor (1644) and Naseby (1645).

Harrison was elected M.P. for Wendover in 1646. From January to May 1647 he served in Ireland, and when he returned to England he sided with the Army in its quarrel with Parliament, acting as one of the commissioners in the attempts to achieve a reconciliation with Parliament. He was a man of extreme political views, demanding the abolition of the House of Lords and an end to negotiations with the King, whom he denounced as a 'man of blood'.

By this time a colonel, Harrison fought in the Second Civil War on the Parliamentarian side. When the Scots, Royalists, and Presbyterians had been defeated, he was one of those most eager for a compromise with the Levellers, and helped draw up the Agreement of the People. However, when the Leveller troops mutinied, he assisted Cromwell and Ireton (q.v.) in crushing the rebels. He worked with these two men in the trial of Charles I, and was assigned the duty of escorting the King to London. Harrison was convinced of the justice of their actions, believing as he did that the monarchy was responsible to Parliament and that Charles had waged war against the people. Harrison had no doubts about signing the royal death warrant, seeing in it the will of God.

In 1649 he received the command of Wales, where he strengthened his ties with extreme Puritanism, especially the Fifth Monarchy Men, who believed in the imminent return of Christ. When Cromwell led the army against Scotland in 1650, Harrison was made commander of the forces left in England. In February 1651 he was elected to the council of state, and later in that year joined Cromwell's forces fighting the Scots and Charles II. He was present at the Battle of Worcester and was entrusted with the pursuit after this victory. In the council he led the most ardent faction, which desired the disbanding of the Rump, a goal achieved in April 1653. The 'Rule of the Saints' was thus to be ushered in, for Harrison's plan for government by a grand 'Sanhedrin' of God-fearing men took form in the Barebones Parliament, which assembled in July. In this early assembly, Harrison wielded great influence, but his power was short-lived, since he warmly supported its plans to abolish the tithe, drastically alter the law, and otherwise so radically reform the country as to arouse the opposition of Cromwell and the council.

In December the 'Rule of the Saints' came to an end; the Protectorate was established, but Harrison refused to acknowledge it, as a result losing his commission in the army. He was closely watched by the government, since he was suspected of involvement in plots. It is true that the extreme sectaries regarded him as their great general. He was imprisoned several times in the following years, but when the Restoration approached, he refused to flee or beg for mercy. He was arrested and tried as a regicide, but continued to justify his conduct. On 13 October 1660, he was hanged, drawn, and quartered at Charing Cross.

B. S. Capp, *The Fifth Monarchy Men* (1972).

C. H. Firth, *The Life of Thomas Harrison* (Worcester, Mass., 1893).

C. H. Simpkinson, *Thomas Harrison, Regicide and Major-General* (1905).

Hart, Charles (d. 1683), actor.

Charles Hart was the son of William Hart, whose mother was Shakespeare's sister Joan. He made his first theatrical appearances as a boy, playing women's roles during the first years of his apprenticeship. In 1641 Hart played the duchess in Shirley's *The Cardinal*. He was successful in that role, but his theatrical career was interrupted by the outbreak of the Civil War, during which he was a lieutenant of horse in Prince Rupert's regiment. After the defeat of the King's forces in 1646, Hart continued to act occasionally, mainly at the country houses of various noblemen, although he did appear at the Cockpit Theatre at least once, in spite of the fact that the theatres had been officially closed in 1642.

After the Restoration, Hart returned to the stage and played the original Celadon in Dryden's *Secret Love*, to Nell Gwynne's Florimel. He was, moreover, rumoured to have been Nell Gwynne's first lover.

For the rest of his professional career he worked with Thomas Killigrew's company at the Theatre Royal. He was noted mainly for his performances of heroic roles. Thomas Betterton (q.v.) was an admirer of Hart's acting and would not play the role of Hotspur until years after Hart's retirement. Hart's association with the Theatre Royal lasted from the Restoration to 1682, the year that Killigrew's and Betterton's companies merged. It is sometimes thought that after being a principal member of Killigrew's company for so many years, Hart was apprehensive about being part of a larger company and having to compete with Betterton. This is not certain, but Hart did retire from the stage in the year of the merger, leaving an impressive list of original parts he had played. He died at his country home in Stanmore Magna, Middlesex, in August 1683.

Harvey, William (1578–1657), English physician; discovered the circulation of the blood; physician extraordinary to James I and physician in ordinary to Charles I.

He was born at Folkestone, Kent, on 1 April 1578, and educated at King's Grammar School, Canterbury, and Caius College, Cambridge. After obtaining a B.A. from Cambridge in 1597, Harvey went to Padua University to study medicine under Fabricius and Casserius. As the result of observing the work of Fabricius on the valves of the veins, Harvey became interested in the general problem of the blood and its flow throughout the body. In 1602, after four years of intensive study, he received his M.D. degree. He returned to England in the same year and resumed postgraduate studies at Cambridge, where he received his second M.D. degree within a few months. In 1604 he married

Elizabeth, daughter of Lancelot Browne, physician to Queen Elizabeth and James I. At the time of his marriage, Harvey had been practising medicine in London for more than a year.

In 1607 Harvey was elected a fellow of the Royal College of Physicians, and two years later was appointed physician to St. Bartholomew's Hospital, London. In 1615 he began a series of anatomical lectures at the college as the result of being appointed for life to the Lumleian lectureship. His manuscript notes for these lectures show that even by 1615 he had concluded that the blood flows from the arteries to the veins by means of the muscular action of the heart, and that the action of the heart causes 'a perpetual motion of the blood in a circle'.

His practical work in dissecting many different species of animals gave credence to his lectures and supported his theories concerning the action of the heart and the movement of the blood. Up to this time, the general views on the blood were those originally proposed by Galen and some even extended back to Aristotle. Even though a few anatomists in Harvey's time believed that the blood flowed through the lungs (or at least that some of it did), the exact route of this flow was not understood. Additionally, it was supposed by many that the arteries contained air (which was later shown to be partially true, as arterial blood is heavily oxygenated because of its passage through the lungs) and that, by means of hypothetical pores, some of the blood flowed from the right ventricle to the left ventricle of the heart.

It was left to Harvey to unify and correct all previous conceptions, and to demonstrate that blood flows away from the heart through the arteries and returns by way of the veins. He proved that the heart is a giant muscle that acts as a pump

to force the blood through the arterial vessels and that the pulse beat is the result of the pressure exerted on the blood during each ventricular contraction of the heart. Because Harvey had no microscope, he was not able to observe the exact means by which blood passes from the smallest arterial branches to the smallest venous branches, thus permitting a true circulation of the blood. He did, however, deduce the existence of this means – the capillaries – and demonstrated the validity of his logic by means of carefully considered experiments on living animals.

Harvey published the results of his studies in 1628, in a small (72-page quarto) tract that was to influence dramatically the future course of physiological research. The full title of this report is *Exercitatio anatomica de motu cordis et sanguinis in animalibus* ('Anatomical Essay on the Movement of the Heart and Blood in Animals'). It is a remarkable example of clarity, refinement, and scholarly organization of data based on years of research at the dissecting table, experiments with living animals, and scientific reasoning.

In *De motu cordis*, Harvey showed that during each beat of the heart the auricles contract before the ventricles, that all of the blood flows through the lungs, that the valves in the veins act to prevent a backflow of blood, that the pulse beat observed in arteries is caused by muscular contraction of the ventricles and the resulting expansion of the arteries with blood being forced through them, and that arterial blood is returned to the heart through the veins. Because of Harvey's painstaking research, it could no longer be seriously doubted that the heart was in fact a giant muscle that propelled the blood or that the blood – contrary to the previous belief of an ebb and flow within the vessels – was pumped out of the heart into the arteries and returned to the heart by means of the veins.

Harvey was physician to Charles I for 14 years (1632–46), and accompanied the King during his flight from London after the outbreak of the Civil War. He was present, in his capacity as a physician, during the Battle of Edgehill (1642). When Oxford was forced to surrender to Parliament, Harvey returned to London, where he resumed his medical practice. In 1651 he published his second great work, *Exercitationes de generatione animalium* ('Essays on the Generation of Animals'), which summed up many years of observation, study, and thought in the field of embryology. It was primarily focused on the embryonic development of chicks, where Harvey examined and reported on the various stages of development of the hen's egg. This, together with his study of generation in the fallow deer, occupied the last years of his life.

In 1656 he resigned his life appointment as Lumleian lecturer, after more than forty years of teaching human anatomy. Shortly thereafter, Harvey, who had long suffered from gout, became paralysed. He died in London on 3 June 1657, and was buried in the Harvey Chapel of the church at Hempstead, Essex.

Kenneth D. Keele, *William Harvey* (1965).
Sir Geoffrey Keynes, *The Life of William Harvey* (1966).
A. W. Meyer, *An Analysis of the De Generatione Animalium of Harvey* (1936).
W. Pagel, *Harvey's Biological Ideas* (1967).
H. R. Spencer, *William Harvey, Obstetric Physician and Gynaecologist* (1921).
Gweneth Whitteridge, *The Anatomical Lectures of Harvey: Praelectiones* (1964).
Gweneth Whitteridge, *William Harvey and the Circulation of the Blood* (1970).

Portrait: oil, three-quarter length, copy after etching attributed to R. Gaywood: N.P.G.

Haselrig, Sir Arthur (?1610–61), see Hesilrige, Sir Arthur.

Hawksmoor, Nicholas (1661–1736), architect.

Originally from Nottinghamshire, Hawksmoor came down to London at the age of 18 and entered the office of Sir Christopher Wren (q.v.) as a domestic clerk. Within a few years he was already occupying positions of considerable responsibility as Wren's assistant on such works as Chelsea Hospital, St. Paul's and various other City churches, Hampton Court, and Greenwich Hospital. From 1690 onwards, Hawksmoor was probably responsible for the realization of many of Wren's designs.

In 1699 or perhaps slightly earlier, Hawksmoor's connections with Vanbrugh (q.v.) began – an association lasting until Vanbrugh's death 27 years later. Hawksmoor was closely involved in the building of four great Vanbrugh houses, notably Castle Howard and Blenheim Palace. Soon, however, Hawksmoor began to accept his own commissions. In 1706 he completed Easton Neston, his only domestic construction, and by 1712 he had started work on the first of the six churches commissioned from him under the 1711 Act for the building of 50 new churches in the City. Together they form his chief works as an architect in his own right, each being highly original and impressive. They are St. Alphege, Greenwich (1712–14), St. Anne's, Limehouse (1714–24), St.-George-in-the-East (1714–34), St. George's, Bloomsbury (1716–27), Christ Church, Spitalfields (1714–29), and St. Mary Woolnoth (1716–27). Like Vanbrugh, Hawksmoor had a passion for the ornate and heavy, a marked departure from the delicacy of Wren's architectural design. But despite his lengthy associations first with Wren and then with Vanbrugh, Hawksmoor had developed his own very distinct and highly personal style. His designs reveal a sense of stability achieved by a careful balance of solids and voids.

As well as designing churches, Hawksmoor had at the same time undertaken various university projects at both Oxford and Cambridge and it is here that the bulk of his work lies. The Clarendon Building, Oxford (1712–15), with its massive Doric portico, is Hawksmoor's work, as are the extensive rebuilding schemes done at All Souls and Queen's College, not all of which materialized. The Radcliffe Camera, though built by James Gibbs, owes much to Hawksmoor.

Hawksmoor spent the whole of his life in the study of building and architecture and bore a profound respect for the classical styles, which he attempted to imitate in various of his churches. It was perhaps his willingness to play second fiddle to his masters, Wren and Vanbrugh, and his lack of competitiveness or jealousy that meant that he was noticeably deprived of any of the senior and lucrative positions in the works, though certainly worthy of such, having been involved in almost every great building of the time. His genius was allowed to emerge fully only in his six churches and in his university works.

A man of considerable modesty, Hawksmoor died on 25 March 1736, having suffered from gout for ten years, and was buried, according to his own provision, under a plain stone slab.

K. Downes, *Hawksmoor* (1959).
H. S. Goodhart-Rendel, *Nicholas Hawksmoor* (1924).

Portrait: bronze cast, after bust attributed to H. Cheere, 1736: N.P.G.

Heath, Sir Robert (1575–1649), judge.

Born at Brasted, Kent, the son of a member of the Inner Temple, whose name was also Robert Heath, the younger Heath was educated at Tunbridge grammar school, and St. John's College, Cambridge, where he spent three years. He entered Clifford's Inn (1591) and the Inner Temple (1593), and was called to the bar in 1603. For two years he was reader at Clifford's Inn, and in 1607 he obtained a life appointment as clerk of the pleas of the king's bench. In 1617 he was elected bencher of the Inner Temple; in 1618 the King recommended him as recorder of London; he was autumn reader at the Inner Temple in 1619; he became M.P. for the City of London in 1620 and solicitor general in the same year. On 28 January 1621, he was knighted.

Heath sat as M.P. for East Grinstead, Sussex, from 1623 to 1625, when he was appointed attorney general. He was involved in the legal proceedings dealing with the King's attempts to raise forced loans, and also conducted the principal Star Chamber prosecutions of the time (1629–30). He was a distinguished constitutional lawyer, a man of learning and outstanding abilities, and he appears to have been sincerely religious and well disposed towards the clergy even though he was involved in religious prosecutions.

In 1631 he was made serjeant-at-law, and in the same year, on 26 October, became lord chief justice of the court of common pleas. He was one of the concurring judges in the case against William Prynne (q.v.) for publication of the *Histriomastix* (1633). Despite this, Heath was suspected of having Puritan sympathies and was dismissed from office (1634), although he was granted leave to practise as serjeant in all courts except the Star Chamber and was subsequently (1636) appointed king's serjeant. In January 1641 he was appointed a puisne judge in the king's bench, and in May was granted a mastership in the court of wards and liveries. This appointment was cancelled a few days later. However, in 1642 he was appointed chief justice of the king's bench, and in this capacity tried cases of high treason against Parliamentarians, including Lilburne. In retaliation, the House of Commons impeached Heath and several colleagues for high treason (1645), and he was placed on the list of those condemned. Under the terms of the Act of Oblivion, his place was declared vacant and his estates were sequestered. In 1646 he fled to France and on 30 August 1649 died at Calais. He was buried at Brasted Church.

William J. Jones, *Politics and the Bench: the Judges and the Origins of the English Civil War* (1971).

Henrietta Maria (1609–69), wife and queen consort of Charles I of England, Scotland, and Ireland.

She was born on 15 November 1609, the daughter of Henry IV of France (Henry of Navarre) and Marie de Médicis. The assassination of Henrietta Maria's father early in 1610 and the intrigues and generally hostile atmosphere that developed in the relations between her elder brother, Louis XIII, and their mother, culminating in the latter's exile from Paris in 1617, probably inured her to political conflicts.

In 1625, at the age of 16, Henrietta Maria was married by proxy to the newly crowned Charles I. Charles was then 24. The marriage was in the beginning very unhappy. Two factors made it unpopular in England: namely, that the new Queen was a Catholic and that the marriage was the result of an unfavourable treaty between France and England. Charles himself harboured a certain resentment after his humiliating

failure to win the Spanish Infanta in 1623, feeling that this new arrangement was second-best. No doubt the disparity in the ages of the royal pair made for poor relations, as did also the attitude of the King's favourite, Buckingham (see Villiers, George, 1st Duke), who treated the Queen with scant respect, and his reversal of policy regarding France offended her greatly. We may be fairly sure that this animosity served as an obstacle to an understanding between Charles and his bride. In 1626 Charles went so far as to dismiss Henrietta's entourage from Whitehall.

Buckingham's assassination in 1628 led in time to a considerable relaxation of tension between the couple. Charles eventually began to feel love for his Queen and by her he had nine children. Their first-born son died in infancy, but there followed eight more, including the future Charles II (1630) and James II (1633).

Henrietta Maria contented herself at this period with being present at court functions, rather than playing any active political role. A favourite of hers at this time was Walter Montagu, author of the *Shepherd's Pastoral*, in the private rehearsals for which the Queen took part. Her liking for dramatic entertainments was inimical to the Puritans, as was her religion, and she was attacked by such notable antipapists as William Prynne (q.v.). In due course, however, Henrietta Maria began to draw herself into politics. With the lord treasurer, Weston, she became identified as the focus of a circle of Catholicism at the court. Romanism came back into fashion again and the recusancy laws, by which Catholics were fined for not attending Church of English services, were not enforced. Most important, perhaps, was the fact that after Buckingham's death the Queen had become Charles's chief confidante. Her championship of the Catholic cause was in opposition to the work of Laud (q.v.), whose promotion of the Established Church was somewhat undermined. Puritan anger was even more inflamed and the situation was worsened by the reception at court of a papal agent accredited to the Queen in 1637.

Henrietta Maria's taste for politics was developing during Charles's rule without Parliament (1629–40). At the commencement of the Scottish Wars in 1639, she set about the task of raising money among her fellow Catholics in support of Charles's border forces and her subsequent machinations almost led to her impeachment by the Long Parliament in early 1642. Charles's show of force at the House of Commons was caused, among other things, by the mounting Parliamentary opinion against his Queen (see Charles I).

Henrietta Maria threw herself completely into the task of supporting Charles. In 1642 she made her way to Holland, leaving in February and taking some of her jewels, which she pawned to buy arms. She returned to England in 1643, landing at Bridlington, Yorkshire, in February with a shipload of weapons. Leading a force of loyalists across the country, the Queen eventually rejoined Charles at his wartime court in Oxford in July. Throughout her remaining time with him, Henrietta Maria continued to urge ever more uncompromising measures, exhorting him to give way on nothing.

Within less than a year, the Queen had departed from Oxford. In April 1644, she left for the West Country, giving birth to her last child, Henrietta, at Exeter in June, and finally taking refuge in France. She was never to see her husband again. Exiled in her native land, she did not cease to believe in the ultimate success of the Royalist cause. She gave Charles as much encouragement as was possible until his execution in 1649. After this, she took no further part in politics. She lived quietly in France, bringing up her youngest daughter in the Roman faith. But her attempts to educate her son, Henry, Duke of Gloucester, as a Catholic met with hostility from the Prince of Wales. Family relations became strained as a result.

At the Restoration, Henrietta Maria, now the queen mother, was invited back to England. Charles II granted her a pension in addition to one given to her as a compensatory allowance by Parliament. After a brief visit to France to attend the wedding of the young Henrietta to the Duke of Orleans in 1661, from 1662 she resided at Somerset House. Her health was not strong, however, and she returned to the more salubrious climate of France, going there for the last time in 1665. She died at Colombes, near Paris, on 31 August 1669.

Carola Oman, *Henrietta Maria* (1936).

Portraits: oil, half-length, by Van Dyck, 1632: Windsor Castle; oil, quarter-length, by Van Dyck, 1639: Windsor Castle; oil, half-length, after Van Dyck, *c*. 1632–35: N.P.G.

Henry Frederick (1594–1612), Prince of Wales.

He was born at Stirling Castle on 19 February 1594, the first son of James VI of Scotland (later James I of England) and Anne of Denmark (qq.v.). On 25 January 1595 he was removed from his mother's care and put under the guardianship of Alexander Erskine, Earl of Mar. Arabella, the countess-dowager of Mar, who had nursed the King himself, took a special interest in the prince's welfare. Anne was displeased by this, and tried to have the child moved to Edinburgh, but James was adamant that the tendencies towards Catholicism exhibited by Anne should not rub off on Henry. Thus he gave a warrant to Mar in 1595 that Henry was not to be given over to the Queen until he was 18, and even then only at his own wish.

In 1599 Henry came under the tutorship of Adam Newton (d. 1630), though the Earl of Mar still attended on him. In about 1602, Pope Clement VIII offered to grant money to James to help him gain the English throne, provided that control of Henry's education was transferred to the Holy See. This James refused. At the death of Elizabeth I in 1603, Henry became Duke of Cornwall. On leaving for England, James ordered him to remain at Stirling, and instructed the Queen to come in late April to England without him. But Anne eventually did bring him with her, arriving at Windsor on 30 June 1603.

Henry was immediately popular. His 'quick, witty answers, princely carriage, and reverend obeisance at the altar' during his investiture with the Order of the Garter were generally impressive. In 1604 negotiations opened for a marriage between Henry and Anne, eldest daughter of Philip III of Spain. The recurring question of religion, however, again surfaced; the Spaniards laid down the condition that Henry should come to Spain and be educated in the Roman faith; James opposed it, and the negotiations broke down. The question of the marriage cropped up intermittently over the next seven years, but finally petered out in 1611. Anne married someone else, and her sister, Maria, was too young to be considered. Negotiations then entered into for the hands of an Italian and a French princess fared no better.

In 1605 Henry entered Magdalen College, Oxford. He was not a studious type, however, and preferred indulging in outdoor athletic pursuits, especially riding. He sought the company of older boys and was generally popular. His national popularity also grew, and some of his opinions conflicted with those of his father. There was some fear of jealousy, and Salisbury (see Cecil, Robert in *Lives of the Tudor Age*) had misgivings about the prince's influence.

Henry's reputation was founded on decorous behaviour and scrupulous attendance at church. He also showed great general ability, and took an interest in naval and military affairs. He even took Sir Walter Ralegh's part against his father. His mode of living was a welcome contrast to the prodigality of the King. He was far more able than his brother, Charles, though there is plenty of evidence that the younger boy idolized him.

In 1610 Henry became Prince of Wales, and all was set fair for a bright future. But the career, so wonderfully promising, was destined for an abrupt end. In the autumn of 1612, Henry started having violent headaches and periodic high temperatures. In October he took to his bed and on 6 November 1612 he died of typhoid fever, at the age of 18.

E. C. Wilson, *Prince Henry and English Literature* (Ithaca, N.Y., 1946).

Portraits: oil, half-length, after I. Oliver, *c.* 1610: N.P.G.; miniature, studio of I. Oliver, *c.* 1610: N.P.G.; oil, full-length, by R. Peake, *c.* 1610: N.P.G.

Henslowe, Philip (d. 1616), theatrical manager, see *Lives of the Tudor Age*.

Herbert, Edward (1583–1648), Baron Herbert of Cherbury; philosopher, diplomat, and poet.

Born at Eyton in Shropshire on 3 March 1583, Lord Herbert, sometimes called 'the Black Lord Herbert', was a celebrated figure in both the French and English courts. He is known chiefly by his spirited, if self-flaunting, autobiography, but he also wrote some ingenious philosophical treatises and metaphysical poems. The heir of an ancient Welsh family, he showed many of the traits of his independent and frequently warlike ancestors. His father, Richard Herbert, a handsome and courageous man, was twice Sheriff of Montgomery and his mother, Magdalen Herbert, was greatly admired for her charm and kindness, by John Donne among others. George Herbert (q.v.), the poet, was one of his six younger brothers.

Herbert's early education was neglected because he suffered from an ear complaint; there was also a fear that he had inherited epilepsy. At the age of nine, having recovered, he was sent to a tutor in Denbighshire and later to one in Shropshire, and in 1596 he matriculated at University College, Oxford. He was accompanied to Oxford by his mother, who supervised him, and, later, his wife, a distant cousin to whom he was married on 28 February 1599, at the age of 15 by family arrangement, his wife being several years his senior. Soon after he arrived at Oxford, his father died. By his own account, he studied hard at Oxford, being very fond of reading, and acquired a great skill and interest in horsemanship and fencing, as well as modern languages. He lacked high spirits at this age, and claims in his autobiography that he was never unfaithful to his wife in the first ten years of his marriage. He comments that his fellow students were 'young men, in whom I observed . . . much ill example and debauchery.'

When he arrived at court, however, towards the end of Elizabeth I's reign, he was soon drawn into the ways of the court and found himself admired and successful. With a dark complexion, he was considered strikingly handsome and became very conscious of this; he writes, 'I could tell how much my person was commended by the lords and ladies . . . but I shall flatter myself too much, if I believed it.' In 1608, against the wishes of his wife, Herbert set off to travel abroad and began a very restless period in his life. In France he made friends with an elderly beau, the Duke of Montmorency, and was welcomed by Henry IV at the Tuileries. He resented, however, the popularity of a certain M. Balagni at the French court, and this rivalry was taken up again when he returned to France after a brief but undistinguished period of service with an English expedition in Germany. In France again in 1610, he arranged to fight a duel with another English officer, Lord Howard, over an incident at a drinking party, but they were prevented by their seniors. Herbert seems to have been highly sensitive to any form of insult, besides being very fond of duelling and the reputation he thus earned. At this time, Herbert also met the celebrated scholar, Isaac Casaubon, and was much impressed by him.

When he returned to England, he says, 'I was in great esteem both in court and city, many of the greatest desiring my company.' His portraits were in great demand, and he found himself more talked about than he could wish, but despite his general popularity he does not seem to have formed any particularly close or enduring friendships with either men or women. Herbert attended another campaign in Germany led by the Prince of Orange in 1614 and from there he travelled to Italy, boldly introducing himself at the English College, where non-Catholics had never been received before. He was imprisoned in France when on a mission for the Duke of Savoy; characteristically, he challenged the governor responsible to a duel, but was soon released. He returned to England via the Low Countries and Heidelberg, where he stayed with the Prince of Orange, with whom he had become a close drinking companion. In London he returned to his duelling habits, and was on familiar terms with writers such as Donne and Ben Jonson (qq.v.), the latter of whom commended Herbert for his bravery and learning.

In 1619 Herbert was offered the position of English Ambassador in Paris, which he keenly accepted. He took up residence in Paris, where he lived in great style, but also pursued his diplomatic duties with energy and intelligence. He quarrelled, however, with Louis XIII's favourite, the Duke of Luynes, and was recalled to England (1621), but allowed to return to Paris after Luynes's death (February 1622). A few years later, in 1624, he criticized James I's planned marriage alliance for his son Charles with Henrietta Maria and was abruptly dismissed. When he returned to England, he was heavily in debt and found that because of his sudden fall from favour he was unable to find any further employment. He petitioned the King repeatedly for a peerage, membership of the Privy Council, and release from his debts, to which money he claimed he was entitled. He was granted an Irish peerage in 1624 and in 1629 created Baron Herbert of Cherbury.

During the twenty years after his dismissal as ambassador, Herbert retired to Montgomery Castle and wrote a number of works with the hope of regaining favour and recognition; some of these have enough independent merit to survive. His history of Henry VIII was a standard work for two centuries: Wordsworth used and marked his copy of it. He wrote a defence of Buckingham's attack on the Isle of Rhé in an effort to regain official favour.

He admired Donne greatly as a poet and used him as a model for his own poetry, but took the roughness of Donne's style to greater extremes. His poetry tends to be overweighted with ideas. He had more talent and originality as a philosopher, being greatly concerned to resolve the conflict, felt acutely at this time, between faith and reason, and to find a means of reconciling parties with bitterly opposed views. Throughout his life he argued for peace and tolerance as political necessities. In De Religione Laici he also pursues with imagination and originality the problem of ascertaining truth. He rejects the scholastic methods and sets up his own framework, divisions, and subdivisions, which he finds best fitted to his task. Descartes and Hobbes both admired him as a philosopher.

In 1642 he was briefly imprisoned

when he argued for qualification in the Commons resolution that the King had violated his oath by making war on Parliament. Herbert tried to remain neutral in the Civil War. He excused himself from a summons to meet Charles at Oxford, and from another to meet Prince Rupert at Shrewsbury. When Sir Thomas Middleton advanced with a Parliamentarian force on Montgomery Castle on 3 September 1644, Herbert was ordered to surrender. He did so just in time to prevent the confiscation of his property in London, and admitted a small garrison of Parliamentary troops. Montgomery Castle was soon besieged by the Royalists as it was in a key position at the entrance to North Wales. Middleton obtained reinforcements and a battle was fought on 17 September, resulting in a defeat for the Royalists. Herbert then went to London, where he spent most of his remaining four years, until his death on 20 August 1648.

C. H. Herford (ed.), *The Life of Edward, Lord Herbert of Cherbury, written by Himself* (1928).

Sidney Lee (ed.), *The Life of Edward, Lord Herbert of Cherbury, written by Himself* (1906, rev. ed.).

G. C. Moore Smith (ed.), *Poems, English and Latin* (1923).

M. M. Rossi, *La vita, le opere, i tempi di Edoardo Herbert di Cherbury* (3 vols.; Florence, 1947).

Portrait: oil, half-length, perhaps after I. Oliver: N.P.G.

Herbert, George (1593–1633), clergyman and Metaphysical poet.

George Herbert was born at Montgomery Castle on 3 April 1593, fifth son of Sir Richard Herbert by his wife Magdalen, whose 'autumnal beauty' John Donne had praised. From early on, Lady Herbert seems to have wished George to become a clergyman. He was educated at Westminster School and Trinity College, Cambridge, from which he graduated M.A. in 1616. He had already revealed himself as a convinced supporter of the Established Church against Puritanism. Despite his mother's early influence, Herbert now embarked on a worldly career; from being a fellow of Trinity, by dint of patient canvassing he had risen by 1620 to the office of university public orator. This brought him into close contact with the court, where he soon collected some influential friends, and even came to the notice of James I himself. In 1624 he was elected M.P. for Montgomery.

In 1625 Herbert's public career received a severe setback when his two most powerful patrons, the Duke of Richmond and the Marquis of Hamilton, and the King all died within a short space of time. Unhappy about Buckingham's policy, he withdrew to a friend's house to ponder whether he should now take up the priesthood. In July 1626 he was offered the living of Leighton Ecclesia in Huntingdonshire. He accepted, but as his poetry shows, his adoption of the clerical life was not achieved without severe struggles of conscience. Of great comfort to him at this time was the sympathetic friendship of Nicholas Ferrar (q.v.), founder of the nearby religious community of Little Gidding, who encouraged Herbert in his pastoral work and persuaded him to rebuild the dilapidated church. But Herbert was already suffering from the consumption which was to cut short his life.

Nevertheless, his last years must have brought him fulfilment: in 1629 he married Jane Danvers, and in 1630 Charles I presented him with the living of Bemerton, near Salisbury. Many contemporaries speak of his saintly devotion to his parochial duties there. He refurnished his church with pews; he would walk to Salisbury twice a week to hear the cathedral choir; and it was at Bemerton that he wrote his major collection of poems, *The Temple*.

George Herbert died at Bemerton on 3 March 1633. His last request to Nicholas Ferrar was that he should either burn the manuscript of *The Temple* or publish it, whichever he thought fit; fortunately, Ferrar chose the latter course, and within the next few years *The Temple* sold 20,000 copies. It was highly praised by Crashaw, Izaak Walton, and Henry Vaughan; Charles I found it a great consolation during his imprisonment.

The 169 poems of *The Temple* are the record of Herbert's struggle towards faith and spiritual peace. To express this inner conflict he had readily to hand the Metaphysical style of Donne (q.v.), whose works he knew and admired. But Herbert is seldom extreme: although his poems teem with concrete images, these are usually homely, even quaint, rather than bizarre or esoteric. His worst self-indulgence is nothing more than a taste for unusual stanza forms. Ultimately, the most memorable feature of his poetry is its quite conversational tone – as if one were overhearing the poet thinking aloud – and its central conviction that salvation lies alone in submission to God's will:

> But thou shalt answer, Lord, for me.

F. E. Hutchinson (ed.), *The Works of George Herbert* (1941; rev. ed. 1945).

Joan Bennett, *Five Metaphysical Poets* (1964, rev. ed.).

M. Chute, *Two Gentle Men: the Lives of George Herbert and Robert Herrick* (1959).

Portrait: engraving, quarter-length, by Robert White, 1674: British Museum.

Herrick, Robert (1591–1674), poet and clergyman.

Robert Herrick was born in London, fourth son of Nicholas Herrick, a goldsmith from an old Leicestershire family, and Julia (née Stone), a mercer's daughter; he was baptized at St. Vedasts, Foster Lane, on 21 August 1591.

In Herrick's second year his father was killed in a fall from a window of their Cheapside house. Suspicions of suicide threatened confiscation of the estate, but not enough evidence could be found and he duly inherited about £800 and was placed under the guardianship of his uncle, later Sir William Herrick, M.P., a goldsmith and merchant banker. At the age of 17 he was bound to his uncle as an apprentice but, possibly showing signs of more academic talents, was sent to St. John's College, Cambridge in 1613, at the relatively late age of 23. Financial circumstances drove him to request an advance on his estate from his uncle and in 1616 he transferred to Trinity Hall, probably because it was cheaper. There he took Bachelor's and Master's degrees and was subsequently ordained in the diocese of Peterborough in 1623.

Little is known about the middle years

of his life. He was present, as chaplain to the King's favourite, Buckingham (see Villiers, George, 1st Duke), on the fiasco of the 1627 Ile de Rhé expedition. He seems to have been familiar with Ben Jonson's circle and to have produced enough manuscript verses to be compared in 1625 with Jonson and Michael Drayton. Very little of Herrick's work found its way into print in these years and it remains something of a mystery why his vast output of more than 1400 poems was not published until 1648.

In 1629 he was admitted to the living of Dean Prior, near Ashburton in Devon, shortly after the death of his mother, whom he appears to have neglected in her last days. The 'humane' poems of *Hesperides* (published 1648 as *Hesperides or, The Works both Humane and Divine of Robert Herrick Esq.*) may well belong to the period of his life in London before he moved to Devon, at least in their inspiration. In the rising Puritan climate it may have been thought inadvisable for a Royalist clergyman poet to have drawn attention to himself with poems such as 'Upon Julia's Breasts', 'Upon the Nipples of Julia's Breast', and so on. On the other hand, an entry in the Stationer's Register indicates that he considered publishing a good number of poems in 1640. It is not hard to imagine that the quiet years between 1629 and 1640 were relieved by writing amatory verses of the old kind, now superseded in popularity by the Metaphysical school of Donne and Herbert.

If circumspection was the cause of Herrick's reluctance to publish in 1640, by 1648, when *Hesperides* was first offered for sale by Williams & Egglesfield, no such constraint existed, since in 1647 Herrick was deprived of his living by the parliamentary commis-

sioners because of his loyalty to the King. He came to London, having prepared his manuscript for the printers, saw it through the presses, and for the next dozen years or so lived as an ordinary citizen in Westminster.

It is difficult to assess whether Herrick hoped to make money by the work. In the event, public taste had moved away from the old-fashioned type of court verse that Herrick wrote best, and he had little popularity or influence. Though much of his poetry is composed in outdated conventional modes, yet another reason for supposing it to have been written a long time before publication, his best verse has an engaging vigour and liveliness that readily breaks through the standard poetic vehicles, as in 'The Vision':

Her legs were such *Diana* shows,
When tuckt up she a hunting goes;
With Buskins shortened to descrie
The happy dawning of her thigh.

Several of Herrick's verses were set to music by Henry Lawes (q.v.) and other composers and many appeared anonymously in *Witts Recreations* (1650). With the return of the Stuart monarchy, Herrick was restored to the living of Dean Prior (1662), where he died in October 1674 at the age of 83. He wrote little or nothing after the publication of *Hesperides* and his work survives chiefly in collections and extracts. He was largely forgotten until the Romantic revival of the early 19th century, when a selection of his works was published in 1810 and Thomas Maitland edited his *Complete Poems* in 1832.

L. C. Martin (ed.), *The Poetical Works* (1956).
M. Chute, *Two Gentle Men: the Lives of George Herbert and Robert Herrick* (1959).
E. I. M. Easton, *Youth Immortal* (1934).
F. W. Moorman, *Robert Herrick* (1962, rev. ed.).
R. B. Rollin, *Robert Herrick* (New York, 1966).

Hesilrige or Haselrig, Sir Arthur

(?1610–61), 2nd Baronet; politician and Parliamentarian commander during the Civil War.

The son of Sir Thomas Hesilrige, 1st Baronet, of Nosely, Leicestershire, Hesilrige entered Parliament for that county in April 1640. In the Short and Long Parliaments, he made Laud (q.v.) his special target, vehemently condemning his religious reforms. He also took a principal role in introducing the bill of attainder against Strafford (see Wentworth, Thomas), was a promoter of the Root and Branch Bill, and shortly after the Grand Remonstrance (November 1641) he introduced a Militia Bill. He was one of the five members of the Lower House whom Charles I tried to impeach and arrest in January 1642. When hostilities became inevitable, he raised a force of cavalry for the Earl of Essex (see Devereux, Robert), which took part in the engagement at Edgehill (October 23). As Sir William Waller's second-in-command in the west, he distinguished himself at Lansdown and Roundway Down (July 1643), in both of which battles he was wounded fighting at the head of his cuirassiers, 'the lobsters'. His forces were also present in the following March at the Battle of Cheriton.

In Clarendon's phrase, Hesilrige was 'as to religion perfectly Presbyterian', but politically he belonged to the democratic faction in Parliament, the Independents. In the disputes between Cromwell and the more conservative generals Essex and Manchester (see Montagu, Edward, 2nd Earl of Manchester), he supported Cromwell. As a consequence of the Self-Denying Ordinance (April 1645) by which M.P.s were excluded from military command, he resigned his commission. Two years later, Hesilrige became governor of Newcastle and won back Tynemouth from the Royalists in 1648. Although a supporter of the trial and execution of Charles, he declined to act as his judge. In October 1648 he accompanied Cromwell to Scotland and in 1650 supported him there with a reserve force stationed in Newcastle.

Throughout the Commonwealth he remained a supporter of Cromwell, but the dissolution of the Long Parliament in 1653 and the establishment of the Protectorate led to a breach between them. Though returned for Newcastle to Cromwell's first two parliaments, he was excluded from the Commons until January 1658. He refused to pay taxes, and in 1657 he declined the offer of a seat in the Lords, seeing this as an attempt to silence his opposition to the Protectorate.

One of the longest-serving members of Parliament, Hesilrige was unquestionably a republican. Cromwell had bitterly disappointed him, and when the Lord Protector died in 1658 Hesilrige refused to recognize Richard Cromwell (q.v.) as his successor. Intriguing with the military leaders, he played an important part in Richard's downfall and was one of the leaders of the restored Rump Parliament. In this capacity he endeavoured to conduct a republican administration but was cut short in this by the action of John Lambert (q.v.), who in 1659 in a bid for power compelled Parliament to dissolve. Hesilrige supported Monck (q.v.) in thwarting Lambert's attempt. After assisting in the securing of Portsmouth (3 December 1659) he took his forces to London, where he sat on the Council of State and on 11 February 1660, he became a commissioner of the army. He had no suspicion of Monck's real design and the process of restoring the monarchy took him completely by surprise.

Thus, entirely deceived, Hesilrige was

placed under arrest. Saved from execution by Monck's intercession, he nevertheless died soon afterwards as a prisoner in the Tower, on 7 January 1661.

Heywood, Thomas (c. 1574–1641), dramatist.

His early life is uncertain, but it has been suggested that he was the son of Robert Heywood, rector of Rothwell and Ashby-cum-Fenby in Lincolnshire. His claim to have been educated at Cambridge is supported by the classical knowledge displayed in certain of his writings, but he does not appear to have taken a degree there. Later in his life, several of his contemporaries commented on his great erudition. At Cambridge, he writes that he saw 'tragedies, comedies, histories, pastorals and shows publicly acted'. In this way, he probably began his association with the stage.

The first certain evidence of his work in the theatre comes from references to plays by Heywood in Henslowe's diary in 1594. During the next few years, Heywood wrote several plays for the Admiral's Men, and in 1598 he made a two-year contract with Henslowe to act only for that company. His bookseller, Francis Kirkman, later drew attention to Heywood's great industriousness, remarking that he had written and acted every day for several years.

In 1603 Heywood joined the Earl of Worcester's company and appears to have taken a more prominent role in this company than he had with the Admiral's Men. *A Woman killed with Kindness*, Heywood's masterpiece, was put on at this time, together with five other new plays of his. With the accession of James I, Worcester's company became the Queen's company, under royal patronage. Heywood was continuously active in this company in London and on brief visits to the provinces up to

1619. He is also mentioned as taking a prominent part when the Queen's company played at court for royal entertainments, although his company never achieved the importance of its rivals, the King's Men. During this time, several plays and treatises, including his *Apology for Actors* (1612), were published, in spite of Heywood's protest, 'It never was any great ambition in me, to be in this kind voluminously read.' One of the most apparent traits of Heywood's character was his genuine modesty; he refers to himself unaffectedly as one of the least in his profession.

Towards the end of his life, Heywood held the post of city poet, with the duty of writing an annual pageant. Although Heywood was very fond of pageants, his own do not rise above the commonplace, but they do show his great love of London. During these years, he also wrote *The Hierarchie of the Blessed Angels*, an ambitious metaphysical work about man's relations with God, and several more plays. He wrote in 1633 that he had 'either an entire hand, or at least the main finger' in 220 works. Of these, only 23 survive. His output had been prodigious, but in his old age he complains of poverty and that he had neglected his own needs. In 1641, the burial of one 'Tho. Heywood, Poet' is recorded at Clerkenwell.

Gentle and tolerant by nature, Heywood had nevertheless strong moral beliefs. In his *Apology for Actors* he asserts that acting and morality are inseparable and that the actor must be 'clear' in his conduct. The purpose of the theatre is, he claims, among other things to be 'an ornament to the city', to teach history, and 'to persuade men to humanity and good life.'

Heywood's work ranges from history plays, adventure plays, treatises, dialogues and dramas on classical themes, to pageants. He is best known for his domestic plays, which were written at a time when there was a movement from grand to domestic themes in drama. These plays suited Heywood's talent for direct and simple expression. Through them, Heywood conveys his love of ordinary life in London, and often achieves a delicate feeling of pathos in the scenes he creates. His gentle telling of the story of Jane Shore, the King's mistress, in *Edward IV*, was, however, quickly burlesqued by his more cynical contemporaries.

A. W. Verity (ed.), *Thomas Heywood* (1888).
F. S. Boas, *Thomas Heywood* (1950).
A. M. Clark, *Thomas Heywood: Playwright and Miscellanist* (1931).
Michel Grivelet, *Thomas Heywood et le drame domestique élizabéthain* (Paris, 1957).

Hobbes, Thomas (1588–1679), philosopher.

Born on 5 April 1588, at Westport, now a part of Malmesbury, Wiltshire, the second son of the vicar of Westport, Hobbes is said to have had a premature birth as a result of his mother's nervous reaction to rumours about the approaching Spanish Armada. His father appears to have been a violent and irresponsible man, who deserted his family after having assaulted another clergyman at the door of the church. The young Hobbes and his brother and sister were thereafter brought up by their uncle Francis, a man of means who was a glover in Malmesbury. As a schoolboy, Hobbes was precocious, first attending a church school at Westport at the age of four, beginning the study of Latin and Greek two years later, and finally studying at the school of Robert Latimer, who also taught at Westport and, himself a good classical scholar, encouraged the boy's love of learning. When he was 15,

Hobbes was entered by his uncle at Magdalen Hall, Oxford. He received his B.A. in 1608 and entered the service of the Cavendish family as tutor to William, the future 2nd Earl of Devonshire. For much of his life he was closely connected with this family.

At the beginning of his career, Hobbes's interest was still in classical literature. He toured France, Italy, and Germany with his pupil in 1610, when Aristotelian scholasticism was giving way to the new science, but he remained immersed in his classical studies, particularly Thucydides, a translation of which he published in 1629. When the father of his pupil died in 1628, Hobbes was temporarily relieved of his duties and spent some months, mainly at Paris, as the tutor of the son of another gentleman, Sir Gervase Clifton. During this second stay abroad, Hobbes developed a passionate interest in geometry while reading Euclid. He was apparently overwhelmed by the lucidity of the method of demonstration and reportedly exclaimed, 'By God, this is impossible!'

when he came across the 47th Proposition of Book I of the *Elements*. The experience had a lasting effect, and helped to determine the ambitious plan he soon adopted for his philosophical work. In 1631 he was summoned back to his old post with the Cavendish family, this time as tutor to his former pupil's son, who was to become the 3rd Earl of Devonshire. With his new pupil he journeyed abroad a third time (1634–37) and during this trip formulated a plan for a three-part work to consist of treatises entitled *De Corpore*, dealing with first principles and mathematical and physical ideas; *De Homine*, dealing with human nature; and *De Cive*, on politics and religion. These were to embody a comprehensive and systematic philosophy deduced from Hobbes's ideas of matter and motion. When he returned to England, however, the disturbances preliminary to the Civil War compelled him to change his plan and he wrote and circulated in manuscript *The Elements of Law, Natural and Politique* (the dedication of which is dated 9 May 1640; published as two separate volumes, *Human Nature* and *De Corpore Politico*, in 1650). The work contains the first statement of many of the ideas developed later in *Leviathan*. The argument, that anarchy could be avoided only by the agreement of subjects to submit to an absolute sovereign power, was welcomed by neither the Parliamentarian nor the Royalist side, and Hobbes, fearful of consequences that he perhaps exaggerated, fled to Paris, where he remained until 1651.

By this time Hobbes had a wide circle of friends and had come into contact with some of the most influential thinkers, scientists, and men of letters of his day. While touring Italy in 1636, he had met Galileo, whom he greatly admired. Among his countrymen whom he coun-ted as friends were Cowley, Davenant, Lord Herbert of Cherbury, Sir Kenelm Digby, William Harvey, and Edmund Waller (qq.v.). In Paris, he was welcomed to the scientific circle led by Descartes's friend, the mathematician Père Mersenne, who persuaded Hobbes to contribute to the collection of criticisms appended to the second edition of Descartes's *Meditations* (1642). Hobbes was now primarily concerned with the theory of government, however, and, returning to his original scheme, he published *De Cive* in Latin (dedicated to the Earl of Devonshire, 1 November 1641; published 1642). A second, expanded edition was published in Amsterdam in 1647. (An English version, *Philosophical Rudiments Concerning Government and Society*, was finally brought out in 1651.) Hobbes devoted some time to the study of optics and, after the arrival of the Prince of Wales and the court in Paris in 1646, became tutor in mathematics to Charles. In 1651, just after the English version of *De Cive* appeared, *Leviathan*, his major work, was published in London. He presented a copy to Charles. The rationalism of the work, in which religion is given a reduced role and subject to the secular power, aroused strong antagonism both among the clergy of the exiled court and among French Catholics. It was also interpreted by the exiled Royalists as a defence of Cromwell and as an argument that he should be crowned king. Hobbes was told that Charles refused to see him. Again he displayed a characteristic timorousness and, having notified the government of the Commonwealth of his intention to submit, he fled back to England. He settled in London and, without official support but also without interference, was allowed to pursue his writing.

Soon after his return, Hobbes was involved in a controversy with John Bramhall, Bishop of Londonderry, on free will and necessity. More important was the gradual fulfilment of his original scheme for his philosophical work: *De Corpore Politico* appeared in Latin in 1655 (English version 1656) and *De Homine* – as finally realized, primarily a theory of vision – was published in 1658. With these works, Hobbes's philosophical task was complete. Much less to his credit were the controversies that he carried on about this time concerning his geometrical theories; these could not withstand the logical criticism advanced by his opponents, principally Seth Ward and John Wallis, Savilian professors respectively of astronomy and geometry at Oxford.

After the Restoration, Hobbes was received again by Charles II. The King enjoyed his company and his conversation, and Hobbes eventually received a pension of £100 a year as a sign of royal favour. In his later years under the Restoration, Hobbes turned again to the interest of his youth, classical literature. After having published a Latin version of *Leviathan* (1668) and having written a work on the Civil War entitled *Behemoth* (1668; suppressed until 1679), he wrote, in his eighties, an autobiography in Latin verse and verse translations of the *Odyssey* and the *Iliad*. He died on 4 December 1679, at Hardwick Hall in Derbyshire, and was buried at Hault Hucknall.

Hobbes, like Bacon before him, approached philosophy with a regard to practical knowledge. Like John Locke (q.v.), he was influenced by and reacted against the religious unrest of his day. As a result, his most important ideas, embodied in the political philosophy set forth in *Leviathan*, are concerned with a commonwealth in which the sovereign power is unquestioned and religion is subjected to it. Man is seen as basically selfish. In a state of nature, he is capable only of animosity and distrust, and this state is characterized 'by continual fear, and danger of violent death; and the life of man, solitary, poor, nasty, brutish, and short.' It is only by agreeing to submit to a common power, which is sufficient to dominate all men, that men can emerge from this terrifying natural condition into a civilized order in which there is some hope of their self-preservation.

Sir William Molesworth (ed.), *English Works of Thomas Hobbes* (11 vols.) and *Latin Works* (5 vols.) (1839–45; reprinted 1962).
Michael Oakshott (ed.), *Leviathan* (1947; New York, 1960).
Ferdinand Tonnies (ed.), *Behemoth* (1969, 2nd ed.).
W. Förster, *Thomas Hobbes und der Puritanismus* (Berlin, 1969).
David P. Gauthier, *The Logic of Leviathan* (1969).
D. G. James, *The Life of Reason* (1949).
J. Laird, *Hobbes* (1934).
C. B. MacPherson, *The Political Theory of Possessive Individualism* (1962).
Richard S. Peters, *Hobbes* (1967, 2nd ed.).
L. Strauss, *The Political Philosophy of Hobbes* (1936).
Howard Warrender, *The Political Philosophy of Hobbes: his Theory of Obligation* (1951).

Portraits: oil, half-length, after J. M. Wright, *c.* 1669–70: N.P.G.; oil, half-length, by J. M. Wright, *c.* 1669–70: N.P.G.

Hollar, Wenceslaus, Wenzel, or Vaclav (1607–77), illustrator and topographer.

Hollar was born on 13 July 1607 in Prague into, by his own assertions, the Bohemian nobility, but resident in London for the greater part of his adult life. At an early age he studied engraving in Frankfurt. From there he travelled to Strasbourg, Cologne, and Antwerp, constantly drawing, but with moderate success. In 1636 Thomas Howard, Earl of Arundel, saw Hollar's work in Cologne and invited him back to England.

His family having been ruined by the Thirty Years War, Hollar agreed, and arrived in London in 1637. In England his output was prolific and successful. In 1639 he was appointed as tutor to Prince Charles. The sketches by Charles, provided with finishing touches by Hollar, can be seen in the British Museum.

With the outbreak of the Civil War, Hollar chose to remain in England as a Royalist, in the service of the Duke of York. He was captured by the Parliamentarians at the siege of Basing House (1644) but escaped to Antwerp to join his patron Arundel in exile. During the long siege he produced several hundred etchings and drawings. In Antwerp, where he remained for eight years, he was equally productive, etching some of his finest views and a superb portrait of the Duke of York.

In 1652 Hollar returned to England and worked mainly as an illustrator. At about this time he produced illustrated editions of Ogilby's *Virgil*, Stapleton's *Juvenal*, and many other works. However, he earned very little money by his work, being a poor negotiator and being unmercifully imposed on by publishers and booksellers. On the Restoration of Charles II in 1660, he was appointed 'H.M. Scenographer and Designer of Prospects'. The coronation of Charles at Westminster provided the subject matter for one of Hollar's chief works.

He lost his son, who was said to have been as brilliant an artist as his father, in the great plague of 1665. After the Fire of London (1666), he etched a famous series of views of London. However, in 1668, having no ties to bind him to London and being a keen traveller, Hollar joined the suite of Lord Henry Howard on an expedition to Tangier where he remained for a year, drawing the town and the fortifications there. His return journey was nearly disastrous, the ship being attacked by pirates. This adventure inspired an engraving entitled 'Kempthorne's Engagement with the Algerine Pirates'.

Characteristic of his work are the 26 plates collectively entitled 'Ornatus Muliebris Anglicanus, or the Severall Habits of English Women from the Nobilitie to the Country Woman as they are in these times', which he produced in 1640. Similarly, 'Theatrum Mulierum sine Varietas atque Differentia Habituum Foeminei Sexus', dated 1643, was a complete and exact study of female dress throughout Europe. He was equally gifted in his representation of natural objects, such as butterflies, sea-shells, and animal fur.

Hollar is perhaps best remembered as as an engraver, for his total output numbered almost 3,000 plates. These included portraits of the King and Queen and of various contemporary political figures, architectural studies of cathedrals and buildings, maps of England, Scotland, Wales, the Isle of Man, and Hungary, as well as a full map of England surrounded by miniature portraits of kings. All of his works are consistently clean, simple, and economically drawn, and because they provide such accurate documentation on various aspects of 17th-century England, are invaluable to the historian.

In spite of his talent and his huge output, Hollar died in extreme poverty; it is said that his last words were a request to the bailiffs not to carry away the bed on which he was dying. He was buried at St. Margaret's, Westminster, on 28 March 1677.

Collections at:
British Museum
Windsor Castle

Holles, Denzil (1599–1680), 1st Baron Holles of Ifield; Parliamentarian leader.

Born on 31 October 1599 at Houghton, Nottinghamshire, the second son of John Holles, 1st Earl of Clare, Holles was educated at Christ's College, Cambridge, and Gray's Inn. He was elected to the parliaments of 1624 and 1628–29, in which he gravitated naturally into opposition circles. He was a friend of Eliot and brother-in-law to Wentworth, and his father was an enemy of Buckingham, the chief minister. Perhaps an equally formative influence was the keen disgrace that this proud young man felt at the disasters and failures wrought by Buckingham in his foreign policy. He was one of the two members who held the Speaker in his chair at the end of the 1629 session in order to allow Eliot's resolutions denouncing royal policy to be read. As soon as Parliament was dissolved, he was arrested and flung into the Tower. He refused to acknowledge the right of the Court of King's Bench to try him for his actions in Parliament, but the court fined him and ordered him imprisoned at the King's pleasure. Holles was released in 1630 after paying his fine and admitting that he had erred.

For the next decade he lived quietly outside of the political arena, although he refused to pay ship money. However, when the Short Parliament was summoned in 1640, he emerged as a leading critic of royal policy, a role he maintained in the Long Parliament, which annulled the sentence passed on him and restored his fine. The only main point on which he differed from the other opposition leaders was the attack on the King's ministers, for he wished to exempt his brother-in-law, now Earl of Strafford, whose life he vainly hoped to save by persuading Charles to accept the abolition of the episcopacy.

Holles's prominence in Parliament was

attested to in January 1642, when Charles named him as one of the five members whom he wished to arrest. As the struggle between King and Parliament grew more intense, the question of control over the militia became acute. This went to the heart of the royal prerogative, and Holles led the forces in the Commons that demanded parliamentary control over the militia.

When the Civil War broke out, Holles threw himself into the struggle. Although he sat on Parliament's committee of safety, he was also active in the field, raising an infantry regiment, which he led at Edgehill and other major engagements of the first campaign. However, by the end of 1642 he had joined the large number of Parliamentarians who were convinced that a settlement had to be reached with the King. He became a leader of this peace party, as he did also of the political Presbyterians, who were finding an increasing number of differences with their Independent colleagues such as Cromwell and Vane. In December 1644 he tried unsuccessfully

213

to have Cromwell impeached. This development made Holles the natural ally of the Scots and the conservative peers on Parliament's side; accordingly, the war party attempted unsuccessfully in 1645 to convict him of traitorous dealings with the Royalists.

After the first Civil War, the hostility between Holles and the Independents increased. He pressed for an intolerant Presbyterian settlement and the disbanding of the Independent-dominated New Model Army without payment of all the arrears due. The Army naturally saw him as its enemy and impeached him with ten other M.P.s in June 1647; when it occupied London in August, he was forced to flee.

A year later, when the army was busy fighting the second Civil War, Holles re-entered Parliament and led the party that successfully negotiated the treaty of Newport with the King. But his ascendancy was short-lived; the victorious New Model Army drove him to France and executed Charles I.

Charles II offered Holles a post as secretary of state in 1651, but he declined, and was eventually allowed by Cromwell to return to England. For a period during the Commonwealth he sat in prison, and only emerged from obscurity in 1660, when he was readmitted into the full Long Parliament along with the victims of Pride's Purge. He was soon elected to the Council of State, where he actively promoted the summoning of a Convention to recall the Stuarts. The Convention chose Holles as one of its commissioners to Charles II, who rewarded him in 1661 with a barony and a seat on the privy council.

From 1663 to 1667 Holles served his royal master as ambassador in France, where he developed a strong dislike for Louis XIV. Accordingly, he eagerly helped complete the treaty of Breda (1667), which ended the second Anglo-Dutch War. In 1668 he lost favour at court by opposing the banishment of Clarendon. Over the following years he became a respected leader of the more moderate opposition, although he was not often in Parliament since he had become increasingly suspicious of the court. He co-operated with Shaftesbury in the impeachment of Danby in 1678, but separated from his more extreme colleagues on the question of Exclusion. Much as he feared the prospects of the Catholic Duke of York on the throne, he nevertheless preferred the more moderate course of limiting the powers of any Papist monarch. But Holles did not live to see the last stages of the constitutional drama in which he had played such a significant part for over half a century. He died on 17 February 1680.

Gervase Holles, *Memorials of the Holles Family* (1937).

Portrait: oil, quarter-length, by unknown artist: N.P.G.; engraving, quarter-length, after Robert White, 1699: British Museum.

Hooke, Robert (1635–1703), physicist, chemist, inventor, and instrument maker.

Born at Freshwater, Isle of Wight, 18 July 1635, Hooke was the son of a clergyman. His activities in the field of science were both versatile and imaginative, although he appears to have lacked the mathematical expertise and dedication required to pursue many of his ideas to their logical conclusions. He was, however, a highly skilled technician and made improvements to the mechanisms of clocks and watches and developed several valuable astronomical instruments. He is perhaps best known for the law relating to the extension of springs that bears his name.

After completing his schooling at Westminster in 1653 he entered Christ

Church, Oxford, as a chorister, with the intention of studying for the ministry. Owing to poor health, however, he was advised to change to science, then regarded as a less strenuous course of study. While at Oxford he assisted Robert Boyle (q.v.) in the construction of his air pump and in 1662 he was appointed Curator of Experiments to the Royal Society, being elected a Fellow in 1663. By 1660 he had already formulated the well-known Hooke's Law (*ut tensio, sic vis*), that the extension of a spring is proportional to the force applied to it. His work with springs led him into the field of horology and he claimed to have invented the hair spring, now extensively used in watches, though Christian Huygens also claimed this invention. Controversy over priorities was characteristic of several 17th-century scientists and Robert Hooke was no exception. He even claimed to have discovered the law of gravitation before Sir Isaac Newton (q.v.) and there was an extensive ill-humoured exchange between the two men after the publication of Newton's *Principia*.

Hooke proposed a rudimentary form of the wave theory of light in his *Micrographia* (1665) and he later investigated the splitting up of light into the colours of the spectrum. This work was, however, overshadowed by the genius of his great contempory, Newton; in fact, much of the theoretical work attempted by Hooke has been forgotten, either because he failed to give a precise quantitative expression to his ideas or because Newton's work was always more comprehensive, more mathematical, and better formulated. In 1665 Hooke became Professor of Geometry at Gresham College, London, and in 1677 he was elected secretary of the Royal Society, a post that he held until 1683.

It is as an innovator in the field of scientific instruments that Hooke is best remembered. He invented the wheel barometer, the anchor escapement for clocks, a form of Gregorian telescope, and several other astronomical instruments and devices. He was one of the first to use the microscope to examine vegetable matter and in 1667 he verified the existence of cells in a sample of cork.

After the Fire of London (1666) he was appointed city surveyor, in which capacity he was responsible for the design of the new Bethlehem Hospital (Moorfields), Montague House, and the College of Physicians. This position brought him considerable wealth, though he was reputed to be too miserly to enjoy his money. His miserliness may, perhaps, have been a reflection of his persistently poor health. From 1696 until his death in London on 3 March 1703, he was virtually an invalid.

M. d'Espinasse, *Robert Hooke* (1856).
R. T. Gunter, *The Life and Work of Robert Hooke* (4 vols.; 1930–35).

Hooker, Thomas (1586–1647), English Puritan who became a church leader in colonial New England.

Thomas Hooker was born near Leicester, probably in July 1586. He went to Cambridge in 1604, graduating in 1608. In 1620 he became rector of Esher, Surrey, where he lived in Sir Francis Drake's house. While living there Hooker married Lady Drake's waiting-woman, Susanna. He became a lecturer at Chelmsford, Essex, in 1626, and his presentation of Puritan ideas brought him into disfavour with Archbishop Laud (q.v.). He was eventually cited to appear before the High Commission in 1630, but fled to Holland before the case was heard.

Hooker spent some time at Amsterdam, Delft, and at Rotterdam, where he assisted the Calvinist theologian William Ames. In 1633 he sailed for New England, as many of his congregation in Chelmsford had done. At first, Hooker settled at Newtown (now Cambridge), Massachusetts. However, in 1636 he was chosen pastor of the eighth church formed in the colony, and led his congregation from Newtown to Hartford, Connecticut.

Hooker remained as pastor of the church in Hartford for the rest of his life, exercising a considerable influence on the religious and political developments of the colony. He helped to frame the Fundamental Orders of Connecticut in 1639, under which the colony was governed. Hooker has sometimes been seen as an ardent democrat, especially in his emphasis on responsible citizenship, but in the Fundamental Orders he also made it clear that he thought that those chosen to exercise authority in church or state should be able to do so freely.

Thomas Hooker died on 7 July 1647, as a result of an epidemic. He left a good estate and library, and a wealth of essays and tracts. His most important work, *A Survey of the Sum of Church Discipline* (1648), was a defence of the churches of New England and was to prove the main influence on the development of Congregationalism in the United States.

G. L. Walker, *Thomas Hooker* (1891).

Hopton, Ralph (1596–1652), 1st Baron Hopton; Royalist general in the Civil War.

The eldest son of Ralph Hopton of Witham, Somerset, he was educated at Lincoln College, Oxford, and the Middle Temple. In 1623 Hopton married Elizabeth, widow of Sir Justinian Lewin and daughter of Sir Arthur Capel.

Hopton's early military experience was gained in 1620 as one of the volunteers in the English expedition to support the Elector Palatine, in which he rose from ensign to lieutenant colonel's rank by 1624. From this period dated his personal friendship with Sir William Waller and enmity with George Goring (qq.v.), both of whom were on the same service. In 1625 he was granted a discharge and settled into the normal life of a country squire at Evercreech Park in Somerset. As a matter of course, he became a Justice of the Peace, deputy lieutenant of the county, and M.P. when Parliament was occasionally summoned. He was created a Knight of the Bath at Charles I's coronation in 1626.

In 1639 he was recalled to military service in the Bishops' War, commanding a troop of horse in the Earl of Pembroke's regiment, but was more seriously involved in the crisis of the times as an M.P. His membership of the Commons, dating from 1621, commanded the respect accorded to seniority, and his influence was generally exercised on the side of moderation, although he was willing to associate with demands for the reform of specific abuses. He was quite out of sympathy with the party managers of the opposition, however, and in the fury generated by the King's attempt to arrest them, Hopton defended the action. Increasingly critical of the conduct of business in the House, he was confined in the Tower in March 1642 on a Commons vote, and ceased to participate in its affairs on his release. His expulsion followed in August.

By that time he was actively supporting the King in the field, having accompanied the Marquis of Hertford to Somerset to assist him in raising forces in the West Country under the royal Commission of Array. They began their activities in Somerset, where Hopton himself raised a troop of horse, but the Parliamentarians proved the stronger party locally, especially in the clothing districts of the Mendips and Taunton. The Royalists first withdrew into Dorset, and then trekked across Somerset to the harbour of Minehead, Hertford evacuating the foot by sea to Wales and Hopton leading the mounted men into Cornwall (25 September).

The Royalist gentry in the Duchy responded very quickly to his presence, and a 'Cornish army' of volunteer foot regiments came into existence, armed and financed by the sale of minerals and fish on the Continent, supplemented by privateering in the Channel. From November 1642 to April 1643 Hopton made vain attempts to subdue Devon, but at best he encountered apathy for the cause he represented, and more usually hostility to the particular men he led, stemming from long-standing local antagonisms. The Devon Parliamentarians were thus able to confine him for most of the time to the western bank of the Tamar, although he in turn defeated their counter-invasion at Braddock Down (19 January 1643).

The turning point was the Battle of Stratton (16 May 1643), in which his Cornishmen defeated the army of the Earl of Stamford and Major General James Chudleigh. With no force capable of barring his way, Hopton marched through Devon and into Somerset, linking up with Hertford, who had been sent from Oxford with a substantial column of horse, foot, and guns. Sir William Waller concentrated his Parliamentary army from the Severn area at Bath to threaten the flank of the Royalists' march, and the two armies clashed bloodily but indecisively at Lansdown (5 July 1643). Hopton was accidentally and only temporarily blinded, but was still able to exercise command of his Cornish infantry, which took refuge in Devizes while the remains of the cavalry

made for Oxford. They were relieved on 13 July by Wilmot and his Oxford cavalry, which defeated Waller on Roundway Down. In recognition of his services, Charles I now created him Baron Hopton of Stratton.

Hopton's march and the defeat of the Parliamentary field armies paved the way for the capture of Bristol, of which he was made lieutenant governor in September, although he had been unable to take part in the siege itself. The administration and safety of the port occupied him during the autumn, his authority being widened to cover the whole of the southwest in October as Field Marshal of the western Army', with the added responsibility of assembling an army that would march on London in accordance with the planned Royalist strategy. With some foresight, Parliament was simultaneously taking steps to prevent this drive through the southern counties and had placed Waller in charge of its forces in the area. He was much more active in the opening manœuvres, compelling the Royalists not only to reinforce Hopton in March 1644, but in effect to supersede him by sending a senior officer, the Earl of Forth, to assist him. Nevertheless, when the two armies eventually met at Cheriton (29 March), Hopton was really in command and was beaten by a better organized and disciplined army.

It was clear that although Hopton was a good administrator and could hold the loyalty of his soldiers, especially during military reverses, he was too passive to further the King's cause at this juncture. Accordingly, he was employed only in a series of minor administrative tasks, chiefly in the civil government of Bristol. Later, jealousies among the Royalist commanders accounted for his continued inactivity as the war moved towards certain victory for Parliament, for

Hopton lacked the essential connections at the court. It was not until January 1646 that he was invited to take charge of the last disintegrating commands of the King's western satraps, and by then it was too late.

On 16 February, he was beaten by Fairfax at Torrington and the remnants of the Royalist army retired into Cornwall, shedding deserters of all ranks as it went. The final surrender took place there in March. For a year Hopton settled in the Royalist haven of Jersey before moving on to the Low Countries, a respected but not very active exile, largely because he had no taste for intrigue. For a short time in 1649 he commanded a squadron of Channel privateers, with some success. He retired the following year, and died in Bruges in September 1652 after a long period of deteriorating health.

J. Adair, *Cheriton* (1973).
M. Coate, *Cornwall in the Great Civil War* (1963).
F. T. R. Edgar, *Sir Ralph Hopton* (1968).

Portrait: oil, three-quarter length, by unknown artist, *c.* 1637: N.P.G.

Hoskins, John (d. 1665), portrait miniaturist; uncle and teacher of Samuel Cooper (q.v.).

There are few details relating to Hoskins's personal life. He was probably born at the end of the 16th century, since his earliest recorded work is in 1620. At this stage, Hoskins was clearly influenced in style and manner by his predecessors, Hilliard and Oliver (see *Lives of the Tudor Age*). With the arrival of Van Dyck in England, however, his work developed in quite a different manner. He became a specialist in making miniature copies of Van Dyck's portraits and as Sir Kenelm Digby stated, 'By his paintings in little he pleased the public more than Van Dyck.' Hoskins was probably the first 'who gave the strength and freedom of oil to miniature,' although this was apparently actually said of his nephew and pupil, Cooper. A fine example of his copywork is his portrait of the Earl of Dorset in the Victoria and Albert Museum. Besides miniatures, he also made copies of subject pictures after other old masters, notably one of Mercury, Venus, and Cupid after Correggio, now in Burghley House.

His nephew Samuel Cooper trained for a long time under Hoskins and eventually they joined together to work in partnership. This professional relationship soon floundered, however, probably because of Hoskins's jealousy in the face of Cooper's increasing success and popularity. Hoskins's best works were almost as good as Cooper's and his female portraits were often better, though his male portraits are generally preferred.

In 1640 Hoskins was appointed limner to Charles I and given a life annuity. An early biography, De Piles's *Art of Painting* (1699), states that Hoskins was 'a very eminent limner in the reign of Charles I, whom he drew with his queen and most of the court. He was bred a face painter in oil but afterwards taking to miniatures, he far exceeded what he did before.'

Perhaps his masterpiece is the large portrait of Catherine Bruce, Countess of Dysart (1638), in Ham House. His attempts to depict personality led him to concentrate almost exclusively on the exact delineation of his sitters' heads. Finely drawn hair, subdued colouring, and the eyes painted clear with the light reflected, a technique of Hilliard's school, all combine to produce the simple and dignified effect he achieved. The shading of the face, a marked diversion from Hilliard's insistence on portraiture without shadowing, bears close resemblance to the *pointilliste* method.

Despite his loss of his position at court in 1640 to Cooper, Hoskins enjoyed a consistent reputation of being England's leading miniature painter for 15 years. He died in the first few weeks of 1665, being buried at St. Paul's, Covent Garden, on 22 February. It is probable, from references to him as 'Old Hoskins', that he had a son who succeeded him in his trade, but of whom even less is known than of the father.

Works at:
Victoria and Albert Museum.
Ashmolean, Oxford.
Windsor Castle.
Duke of Buccleuch's Collection.
Duke of Portland's Collection.
Duke of Devonshire's Collection.
Duke of Northumberland's Collection.
Wallace Collection.

Hudson, Henry (d. 1611), Arctic navigator and explorer.

The origins of Henry Hudson are obscure. The first reference to him dates from 1607. Middle-aged, with an established reputation as a navigator in northern waters, he was in the employ of the Muscovy Company, searching for an Arctic sea passage to China and the 'spice islands', the East Indies. With his ship, the *Hopewell*, he proceeded to the east coast of Greenland. Adverse conditions forced him eastwards to Spitzbergen, where ice caused him to turn back, but only after collecting information that allowed the development of the Spitzbergen whaleries.

The following year found Hudson once again unsuccessfully seeking the North-East Passage for the Muscovy Company. In 1609 he entered into a contract with the Dutch East India Company to search for the same route. He sailed from Amsterdam with a somewhat rough-and-ready crew in the *Half Moon* and successfully rounded the North Cape. Upon meeting polar ice

off the coast of Novaya Zemlya, the crew mutinied and refused to go on. But rather than give up, Hudson convinced them to cross the Atlantic to search for the route to China in that direction.

Tradition held that a channel to the Pacific was to be found on the North American coast around 40°N latitude. Accordingly, Hudson sailed the *Half Moon* up the Hudson River – as it was subsequently named – almost as far as the site of Albany. Upon his return to England he received a privy council order that forbade him to serve any foreign power.

Hudson's reputation, built on his experience, courage, and vision, soon attracted English patrons for a new expedition. Unfortunately, his inability to lead showed itself in his selection of proven troublemakers for the crew of his new ship, the *Discovery*, in which he set sail on 17 April 1610.

Hudson proceeded to Iceland and by the coast of Greenland, where he entered Davis Strait, for an ice-free sea was thought to lie in polar regions at its northern exit. But strong tides swept his ship south round Resolution Island and westward into Hudson Strait, a body of water well-known to adventurers but unexplored because of its treacherous tides and ice packs.

At this point the crew mutinied, but were calmed and reassured by Hudson. For six weeks he forced his way through the strait. On 3 August he entered the vast expanse of Hudson Bay and thought that he had reached the Pacific. The feat he had accomplished demonstrated no mean skill, and his records were of great navigational value.

Despite the late season, Hudson sailed south, examining the eastern shore of the bay. He revenged himself on his crew, trying and punishing the mutineers, only to apologize to them later. The *Discovery* reached James Bay in October, and in vain sought an outlet to the south. Hudson and his men passed a quarrelsome winter on its southeastern shore. With dangerously low food supplies they began their return voyage on 12 June 1611. Twelve days later a mutiny broke out. Hudson, his son, and six other men were set adrift in a shallop, never to be seen again. The remainder of the crew succeeded in sailing back to England, where the value of their knowledge saved them from the scaffold.

Hudson's Arctic discoveries were of such importance that within five years almost all of the huge inland sea named after him was charted.

Article by L. N. Neatby in *Dictionary of Canadian Biography*, ed. George Brown (1966).
L. N. Neatby, *In Quest of the North-West Passage* (Toronto, 1958).
Llewellyn Powys, *Henry Hudson* (1927).

Humfrey or Humphrey, Pelham

(1647–74), composer and lutenist; one of the leading talents involved in the musical revival that followed the Restoration.

Born in 1647, Humfrey's childhood under the Commonwealth and Protectorate, during which period English music was stifled owing to the domination of Puritanism, is obscure. He is first heard of in 1660 when he became a chorister under Henry Cooke in the Chapel Royal of the newly restored Charles II. In about 1664 he was sent by Charles along with other musicians to the Continent to study. He visited France and Italy, returning to England three years later. In his absence, he had been appointed Royal Lutenist and a Gentleman of the Chapel Royal, later succeeding Cooke as master of the children. In this capacity, Humfrey taught among others the great Henry

Purcell (q.v.). He also held the post of Composer in Ordinary to the King. Tragically death took him early; he died, aged about twenty-seven, at Windsor on 14 July 1674.

Humfrey is now chiefly remembered for his fine anthems and solo songs. He also composed much instrumental music for the King's violins. His untimely death gives us no opportunity to assess his possible genius but his importance lies in the fact that he helped the reawakening of England to the appreciation of music. Continental developments became known in England, whose lengthy isolation during the middle years of the century came to an end with composers like Humfrey, and whose musical life was enriched and brought to perfection by Purcell.

Hyde, Anne

(1637–71), first wife of James, Duke of York (later James II, q.v.), and mother of Queen Mary (see Mary I) and Queen Anne (q.v.).

Anne Hyde, born at Windsor on 12 March 1637, was the eldest daughter of Edward Hyde (q.v.), later the Earl of Clarendon. In May 1649 she went with her family to Antwerp, and in 1654 became maid of honour to the Princess of Orange. She was conspicuous in court gaieties, and although Pepys described her as plain he also thought her witty and lively. She first met the Duke of York in 1656 at Paris, although it is not certain whether they formed a firm attachment then. However, in 1659 they met again at Breda, and became engaged to marry.

When Charles II was restored to the throne in England, Anne and her family returned. There is a suggestion that James now wanted to be released from the engagement, although other accounts assert that he was determined not to give her up. It is certain that her father

now heard of the engagement for the first time, and was firmly opposed to it: in the shock of its discovery he even proposed to send Anne to the Tower and to introduce a bill himself for her execution. By this time, however, Anne was pregnant, and James married her on 3 September 1660. The King later assured Clarendon that the match contented him and that 'his daughter was a woman of great wit and excellent parts'.

Anne was not generally popular, although she did win over her husband's mother, Henrietta Maria (q.v.), who had previously been hostile. She was often accused of parvenue pride, and of being too fond of eating and extravagance. However, the Duchess probably asserted a beneficial influence over her husband in some ways and probably curbed his expenditure. Charles teased his brother for being henpecked, and Pepys declared that 'the Duke of York, in all things but his amours, is led by the nose by his wife'. James's mistresses did cause trouble between them. Anne ap-

parently complained to the King and her father about James's attachment to Lady Chesterfield, and her enemies asserted that when another rival, Lady Denham, died, the duchess had poisoned her. This is very unlikely, but Anne does seem to have retaliated against James's affairs by an attachment to Henry Sidney, the son of the Earl of Leicester.

Anne was a patron of Lely, who painted many portraits of her. She was very accomplished, and had modest literary talents. Her court was smaller but considered more select than that of Queen Catherine. In 1670 she was secretly accepted into the Roman faith, and the King was probably aware of her conversion. Anne died on 31 March 1671, of cancer of the breast. Of her eight children, only two, Mary and Anne, survived infancy.

J. R. Henslowe, *Anne Hyde, Duchess of York* (1915).

Portrait: oil, half-length, after Lely, *c.* 1670: N.P.G.

Hyde, Edward (1609–74), 1st Earl of Clarendon; statesman, historian, and lord chancellor under Charles II.

Edward Hyde was born on 18 February 1609, the eldest son of Henry Hyde of Dinton, Wiltshire; he was educated at Magdalen Hall, Oxford, graduating with a B.A. in 1626. He entered the Middle Temple and was called to the bar in 1633.

Throughout his time at university and at his law studies he fell into an easy congenial way of life, during which industry and studiousness were not particularly evident. He read widely and cultivated the company of such men as Ben Jonson, Edmund Waller, and Lucius Cary (qq.v.), 2nd Viscount Falkland. Falkland was to become Hyde's particular friend and political ally in the approaching strife. But at present Hyde,

somewhat wilful and self-important, was enjoying his idyllic existence as a member of Falkland's intellectual circle centred at Great Tew, Oxfordshire.

During Charles I's period of non-parliamentary government, the 'eleven years' tyranny', Hyde embarked on his public career. His bar practice flourished. The friends he had made at Great Tew included some men of influence, such as the jurist John Selden and Sir Kenelm Digby (qq.v.). Hyde's first marriage in 1631, to Anne Ayliffe, ended only six months later with his wife's death. In 1634 he was married again, this time to Frances, daughter of Sir Thomas Ayles-bury, master of requests. This second marriage led shortly afterwards to his appointment as keeper of the writs and rolls of common pleas.

Hyde's political career began in earn-est with his election as M.P. for Wootton Basset in April 1640; in this, the Short Parliament, he made a vigorous attack on the jurisdiction of the marshal's court, accusing it of perverting the true course of justice. Though a consti-tutionalist, he viewed the period of Charles's absolute rule as one in which the law had been disregarded. Con-sequently, he was driven into the ranks of the Parliamentary opposition. In the Long Parliament (November) he sat for Saltash, and his continued assault upon the marshal's court effectively obtained its abolition.

In 1641 Hyde was prominent in supporting the abolition of the Star Chamber, the Court of Wards, and the Court of High Commission. He sup-ported the impeachment of Strafford and voted in favour of the subsequent bill of attainder, although as his own account shows, despite its inaccuracies of detail, he tried through the Earl of Essex to avert Strafford's execution (*History of the Great Rebellion*, iii, 164). Hyde's lack of political sympathy with Pym and his associates increased during this period. A staunch Anglican and a moderate politician wishing to preserve the bal-anced relationship between the King and his kingdom, he could not support the petition against episcopacy (February 1641), and his vigorous opposition to the Root and Branch Bill (May) led to its failure and caused him to be considered as a supporter of the King. Charles en-couraged this attitude, and in November Hyde was one of the 148 members who voted against the Grand Remonstrance.

By 1 January 1642, Hyde had to all intents made the transfer to the royal service. With Falkland and Sir John Colepeper (q.v.), he became one of Charles's advisers. The King promised to make no move without their counsel but only a few days later, without their knowledge and on the encouragement of Digby and the Queen, he was led into the folly of the 'five members' incident, in which he tried personally to arrest five M.P.s. This unexampled breach of the constitution and of parliamentary privilege almost reduced Hyde to despair. But he persisted in a constructive moderation that attracted several Parliamentarian supporters to the Royalist side. On behalf of Charles, Hyde drafted numerous declarations, including the King's answer to the 'Nineteen Propositions', in which Parliament claimed complete sovereignty and government, including the selection of ministers, control of the army, and the enforcement of the penal laws against Roman Catholics. Hyde's case was based upon 'mixed monarchy' (power-sharing between King and Parliament), preserving the fundamental laws of the constitution. But Pym and his party had long since doubted Charles's sincerity and trustworthiness. Even some Royalists found Hyde's policy feeble. In August, Hyde was formally expelled from the House of Commons and the war began.

Though present at Edgehill, Hyde was a noncombatant throughout the Civil War. He remained in residence at All Souls College, Oxford, from October 1642 to March 1645. In February 1643 Charles made him a privy councillor, and on 3 March he was appointed chancellor of the exchequer. Nominally concerned with directing command of the Royalist forces, his chief task was to raise loans to finance the King's war effort. To preserve some semblance of legality, he urged Charles to call a parliament at Oxford as a counterbalance to the Long Parliament at Westminster and in order that supplies could be seen to be granted constitutionally. But by the end of 1644, the Oxford Parliament's success having been only moderate, he was forced to acknowledge the Westminster assembly as the only legitimate one.

During his time at Oxford, Hyde's advice to the King was undermined by the influence of Henrietta Maria and Lord Digby. He sat upon the Junto, the secret committee that discussed business in advance of its being presented to the council, but it availed him little. Nor could he get on with Charles's militant army leaders. His failure was consummated by his complete ineffectiveness in winning any sort of compromise from the Parliamentarians in negotiations at Uxbridge (January 1645). With no more room left to manœuvre within constitutional terms, Hyde was finally removed and appointed to the guardianship of the Prince of Wales. He left Oxford on 4 March 1645.

Hyde went first to Bristol, and in the spring of 1646 he accompanied Prince Charles to Jersey. While there, he vigorously opposed the Queen's order to remove the Prince to France and the plots to enlist foreign aid on behalf of the Royalists. But apart from successfully thwarting a scheme to sell Jersey to the French, he could do little to influence events and whiled away this period of enforced inactivity by commencing the first draft of his *History of the Great Rebellion*, keeping in touch with affairs through a copious correspondence.

In 1648 he wrote *A Full Answer to an Infamous and Traiterous Pamphlet*, in which he combined a reply to the recent resolution of the Long Parliament to present no more addresses to the King with a vindication of Charles himself. On 27 June 1648, he left Jersey for Paris to join the Queen and the Prince of Wales there. But the prince had gone to join the English fleet in the Thames, and in following him Hyde's ship was attacked and robbed by a privateer out of Ostend. Delayed throughout the summer, he was unable to join Prince Charles until September, when they eventually met at The Hague. The King's concessions made to Parliament on the Isle of Wight, his arraignment by the army, and his execution all had to be endured helplessly.

In acting as adviser to King Charles II, Hyde had as little success as he had had with Charles's father. Disapproving of the Royalist alliance with the Scottish Covenanters, he welcomed the opportunity, in November 1649, to get away from the court and take part in a mission to Spain in the hope of gaining Spanish assistance in the recovery of Ireland. The negotiations in Madrid lasted for a year. They eventually failed after Charles II's defeat at Dunbar. With Cromwell's star in the ascendant, the Spaniards withdrew from the talks and the English mission was ordered out of Madrid in December 1650. In September 1651, Charles escaped from the Battle of Worcester and Hyde, travelling from Antwerp, joined him at Paris. He remained with the King throughout the exile, moving with him to Cologne (1654) and then to Bruges (1656).

During the exile, Hyde worked hard to prevent Charles from deserting the Anglican Church and to bring about a reconciliation between him and his subjects. Keeping a close watch on affairs at home through his correspondence, he entered into intrigue with the Levellers in 1656, and viewed without disapproval their plot to assassinate Cromwell. In 1659 he made strenuous efforts to restrain some impatient Royalists from a premature uprising, realizing that a meaningful settlement could only be obtained by accepting the principle of a free Parliament matching by its own good will the magnanimity of the King. Cleaving to this belief, he had a primary role in drawing up the Declaration of Breda in 1660, by which Charles II acknowledged the rights of Parliament and set out the terms and concessions that made the Restoration acceptable.

Hyde accompanied Charles back to London in triumph upon the restoration of the monarchy. Having been made lord chancellor in 1658, he took his seat in the Lords on 1 June 1660, and did much to promote the atmosphere of reconciliation. He pressed for the disbanding of the army, the passage of an Act of Oblivion, and means of raising money for the crown. Having already received a barony in 1660, he was further honoured by being created, on 20 April 1661, Viscount Cornbury and Earl of Clarendon.

Clarendon's avowed intention was the restoration of the Anglican Church, and his early efforts were moderate in attempting to reconcile the Presbyterians to conformity. He tried to introduce limited episcopacy with a revised prayer-book.

Through Archbishop James Sharp, he attempted to reimpose episcopacy in Scotland. But the predominantly Anglican parliament of 1661 represented a force that his moderation could not control. With little justice has the label 'the Clarendon Code' been appended to the harsh legislation against nonconformists embodied in the Corporation Act, the Act of Uniformity, the Conventicle Act, and the Five Mile Act.

In practice the head of Charles II's administration, Clarendon dominated the Privy Council and many of its subcommittees. He proposed the establishment of an office at Whitehall responsible for Scottish affairs; he supported the moderate and enlightened administration of Ireland by the Duke of Ormonde, becoming unpopular by opposing the prohibition of Irish cattle imports into England; as one of the eight proprietors of the Carolinas he showed tolerance in settling colonial issues. In foreign affairs, however, he was less effective. His pursuit of a peace policy limited his scope of action. In soliciting a French loan he incurred unpopularity at home and was unjustly suspected of accepting a bribe; he organized, but did not initiate, the sale of Dunkirk to France; and the calamities of the Dutch war (1665–67) must with some justification be ascribed to his administrative conservatism.

In 1660, James, Duke of York, married Clarendon's daughter Anne (see James II and Hyde, Anne). Thus, Clarendon attained a special link with the royal family and became the grandfather of two Queens, Mary II and Anne. Yet Clarendon's special relationship with the House of Stuart did not in the event save him from eclipse. Some of his work, such as his support of the Act of Indemnity, angered many Royalists at the very outset. The personal fortune he amassed caused jealousy. His objection to Charles's policy of indulgence, which resulted in its withdrawal, was a source of extreme annoyance to the King. By 1663 Clarendon's power was waning. Charles was listening to other voices at court, especially those of Bennet and Buckingham, who supported his indulgence policy. The impeachment of Clarendon was attempted in July 1663 but gained no support; the King was not yet prepared to overthrow his chief minister.

But the end was approaching. Opposed by younger politicians such as Sir William Coventry and Lord Arlington, and overborne with the disasters of the Dutch war, Clarendon was also on bad terms with the King regarding his extramarital relationships. He was ridiculed by Charles's mistresses and younger courtiers. By 1667 he stood alone against his detractors. Racked with gout and bereft of friends in the government, he could rely only on the Duke of York for support, but it availed him little. In August 1667 Arlington and Coventry obtained his dismissal, and in October

his impeachment was prepared. Clarendon fled.

His last years were spent wandering in exile through France. His life was attended with extreme hardship, and in April 1668 some English sailors who had not been paid and blamed him for it tried to murder him at Evreux. The Act of Banishment prohibited correspondence with him. In 1671, however, he was allowed a visit from his son, Laurence. While in exile, in addition to daily *Contemplations on the Psalms*, Clarendon also wrote his *Life* entirely from memory; but Laurence Hyde's visit provided him with relevant manuscripts that allowed him to take up his *History* again, into which he incorporated his autobiographical material. The result, *The History of the Great Rebellion and Civil Wars in England* (edited in 6 vols. by W. D. Macray, 1888) varies considerably in accuracy, depending on its date of writing. Sometimes less than objective in his distorted characterizations of his opponents, Clarendon nevertheless shows by his work and life an example of the classical conception of using knowledge of the past to guide one's perception of the present and one's vision of the future.

Clarendon never obtained his recall to England. He died at Rouen on 9 December 1674. He is buried at Westminster Abbey.

W. Dunn Macray (ed.), *History of the Great Rebellion and Civil Wars in England* (6 vols.; 1888).

Sir Henry Craik, *The Life of Edward Earl of Clarendon* (2 vols.; 1911).

T. H. Lister, *The Life and Administration of Edward First Earl of Clarendon* (3 vols.; 1838).

F. J. Routledge and Sir Charles H. Firth, *Calendar of the Clarendon State Papers* (4 vols.; 1869–76 and 1932).

B. H. G. Wormald, *Clarendon* (1951).

Portrait: oil, three-quarter length, after Lely, *c.* 1662: Middle Temple, London.

I

Inchiquin, 1st Earl of (1614–74), see O'Brien, Murrough.

Ireton, Henry (1611–51), Parliamentary commander and regicide.

The eldest son of German Ireton of Attenborough, in Nottinghamshire, Henry was baptized on 3 November 1611. He was educated at Trinity College, Oxford (1626–29), followed by a spell at the Middle Temple.

At the outbreak of the Civil War, Ireton took command of a troop of horse raised in Nottingham, which may have been present at Edgehill, and in 1643 he was the major of Thornhagh's Nottinghamshire regiment of horse. In this capacity he fought in the Battle of Gainsborough (28 July), after which he passed into Cromwell's command, an

association which ripened into a close friendship as the war progressed. His first post of authority was as deputy governor to Cromwell in the Isle of Ely, and he was quartermaster general in Manchester's army in the Marston Moor campaign of 1644.

When the New Model Army was formed in 1645, Ireton, who had now entered parliament as M.P. for Appleby, secured the command of a regiment of horse, which he led at Naseby, where he was given charge of the Parliamentary left wing. The cavalry on this wing was broken by Prince Rupert's attack, but Ireton's own regiment performed well and he was able to use them in support of the hard-pressed infantry until he was wounded and for a short time held prisoner. Afterwards, he served at the siege of Bristol (September 1645), the southwestern campaign, and the final blockade of Oxford, the capitulation of which he helped to negotiate (June 1646). During the siege of Oxford, on 16 June 1646, he married Bridget, daughter of Oliver Cromwell. By her he was to have a son and three daughters.

His close association with Cromwell continued into the politics of peace-making, his concern at first being to preserve a just balance between King, Parliament, and the Army. At this stage Parliamentary extremists seemed to him to present the greatest threat to a settlement, and he eventually took his stand with the Army. He was responsible for the outline solution adopted by the council of war, known as the Heads of the Army Proposals (1 August 1647), based broadly upon principles of limited monarchy, regular parliaments elected on a wider franchise, and religious toleration. Its balanced nature can be deduced from the fact that it failed to satisfy the King on the one hand and the Levellers on the other. Ireton was a better political thinker than many of his contemporaries, more concerned with political realities than abstractions; he became the spokesman of the conservative officers in the council.

When the Proposals failed, Ireton was prepared to work for an agreement with the King, but would not countenance the Leveller demands embodied in the 'Agreement of the People' (28 October 1647). It was becoming clear to him, however, that the King's duplicity was now the chief obstacle to a settlement, the King's flight to the Isle of Wight providing the final confirmation. Constitution-making was interrupted by the second Civil War, during which he served under Fairfax in Kent and Essex. Subsequently, he was a member of the inner group of officers that deliberately used the force of the Army in politics with decisive effect.

Pride's Purge of the Commons, the transfer of the King to closer confinement at Windsor, the pressure for his trial, the trial itself, the death warrant, and the execution order – Ireton had a hand in the production of them all. His constitutional views were reflected in the final 'Agreement of the People' (15 January 1649), which represented the mind of the council of war on the future government of the kingless state. As it projected the end of the existing Parliament and the election of a successor on a different basis, lacking even the name of Parliament with its associations with monarchy, it is not surprising that it was largely ignored and Ireton himself was omitted from the list of those nominated for the new Council of State.

In June 1649 he was appointed Cromwell's second-in-command in the army despatched to Ireland, and remained there as his deputy when the latter returned to England in May 1650. By that time, Connaught and parts of Munster and Ulster still remained to be subjugated, which occupied him for the rest of that year and most of the next. Ireton's opinion on the solution to the problem of Ireland was the same as Cromwell's – a replacement of the native Irish by English colonists as far as possible, and no toleration whatever for Catholics. He worked hard at the duties of civil government, with serious effects on his health. He died of a fever on 26 November 1651, and his body was brought back to England for a state funeral and burial in Westminster Abbey. At the Restoration, his remains, along with those of Cromwell, Bradshaw, and other regicides, were disinterred and hanged at Tyburn before being thrown into an unmarked grave.

Maurice Ashley, *Cromwell's Generals* (1954).
R. W. Ramsey, *Henry Ireton* (1949).
C. V. Wedgwood, *The Trial of Charles I* (1964).

Portrait: oil, three-quarter length, attributed to R. Walker after Cooper and Van Dyck: N.P.G.; engraving, quarter-length, by Harding and Gardiner, after Robert Walker, *c.* 1650: N.P.G.

J

James I (1566–1625), King of England and Ireland (1603–25) and James VI of Scotland (1567–1625).

James was born at Edinburgh Castle on 19 June 1566, the son of Mary Queen of Scots and Henry Stewart, Lord Darnley, her second husband. His minority as king was long. He was a sickly baby only thirteen months old when, after the murder of Darnley and the enforced abdication of Mary, he was proclaimed James VI of Scotland. After his coronation on 29 July 1567, he was consigned to the care of John Erskine, Earl of Mar and, after Mar's death in 1572, to that of his brother, Sir Alexander Erskine. James grew up in the violent atmosphere of a still largely feudal Scotland, while successive regents battled for control of the kingdom on

his behalf. Such a situation seems to have had a detrimental effect on his later life; although he eventually overcame the difficulties of his physical weakness by almost fanatical indulgence in riding and the chase, he was always dogged by the residual consequences of the timorousness engendered in him during this period, which clashed with a later over-confidence after he became King of England.

He was brought up a Protestant and, as the ward of Sir Alexander Erskine, he received an excellent education from such teachers as George Buchanan (1506–82). As a consequence, he was intellectual and learned but also pedantic. His earliest literary effort, published in 1584, was *The Essays of a Prentise in the Divine Art of Poesie*. It contained verses and a set of rules concerning the composition of Scottish poetry. It was the first of several works on a wide range of subjects and, although James's gifts as a writer were limited, he exhibited a literary talent rare among princes.

In 1570 his first regent, the Earl of Moray, was murdered. A period of civil war ensued until it was ended in 1573 by his fourth regent, James Douglas, Earl of Morton. Morton's administration was firm. He moved away from alliance with France and attempted to rely on aid from England. In 1578 he was eventually ousted from the regency and James, although only twelve years old, took the government nominally into his own hands.

The boy King was naturally susceptible

to controlling influences. Morton was able to make a brief return to power, but from 1579 onwards was supplanted by Esmé Stuart, the nephew of James's grandfather, Matthew, Earl of Lennox. Stuart, an agent of the French and himself a Catholic, had the task of both converting James and his kingdom to Rome and resuming the Franco-Scottish understanding. After Morton's execution for alleged complicity in Darnley's death (1581), Esmé Stuart, now elevated to the title of Duke of Lennox, had a clear path to his objectives; his plans were disrupted, however, by the kidnapping of the King by a group of Presbyterian supporters, the Ruthven Raiders, led by William Ruthven, Earl of Gowrie.

James was kept in virtual imprisonment for several months, during which time a proclamation was extorted from him assuring the fall of Lennox. In 1583 he managed to escape, and at the age of seventeen he took firm hold of the reins of government. His task in sixteenth-century Scotland was to achieve mastery over two main factions. On the one hand were the nobles, who lived like medieval barons on land appropriated from the Church and who controlled the single chamber of the Scottish Parliament; on the other were the Presbyterians, the popular opposition led by ministers who demanded a say in the administration of the country. There was also the equally important business of asserting his claim to the English throne. In 1584 he wrote to the Holy See requesting support for himself and his mother. He also approved a French scheme for setting Mary free.

The action of Gowrie and his fellows set James against the Presbyterian clergy. Yet he was no Catholic either, having been educated in Calvinistic principles. So, while seeking engagements with the continental Catholic powers, James also adopted an alliance with England; as a consequence, he opened a rift with his mother, who now disinherited him and transferred her claim to Philip II of Spain. Such an action served only to confirm the Anglo-Scottish alliance, and Mary's execution in 1587 drew from James only a nominal protest.

The vacillation of James between Protestant and Catholic interests, which characterized his whole reign, now took a new turn. Originally against the Presbyterians, he was now shocked by the attempted invasion of the Armada (1588) and was driven into their arms by his reaction against the Catholics. Yet although he had already sympathized with their doctrine, he still resented their interference in his personal actions as King.

In 1589 James married Anne of Denmark (q.v.), daughter of the Protestant king, Frederick II of Denmark and Norway. The marriage began inauspiciously. Anne's ship was delayed by a storm on the way to Scotland and James had perforce to travel to Norway in order to meet his bride.

Throughout the 1590s a split developed between the King and the Presbyterian ministers. The clergy were infuriated by the murder of the Earl of Moray by Huntly, a Catholic lord; James's treatment of Huntly seemed far too lenient, for though he drove him from Scotland he did not take away his lands, and soon recalled him. His continued intriguing with the Catholics also infuriated them. James's handling of the situation showed considerable shrewdness, however. In 1596 he banished from Edinburgh four of the Presbyterian ministers and 74 burgesses; he also removed from Edinburgh the courts of justice, blaming the clergy for having created an atmosphere in which they could not peacefully operate. He completed his mastery in February 1597 by asserting his authority over the Kirk at the Perth conference, from which the extremists had been cleverly excluded.

The Presbyterians were cowed, but could not be brought into a constitutional relationship with the nobility who controlled the Scottish Parliament. In 1598 James toyed with the idea of appointing his own nominees to represent the Kirk in Parliament. He reflected upon church interference in state affairs in a book, the *Basilikon Doron* (Kingly Gift, 1599), and in the *True Law of free Monarchies* he asserted the principle of *jus divinum* – the divine right of kings. Presbyterian bitterness reached its peak in 1600 when it was alleged that the Earl of Gowrie's son, deeply resentful of his father's treatment, tried with his brother to capture James again. The two noblemen were slain; the most prominent Presbyterian agitator, Robert Bruce (1554–1631), was expelled, and the recalcitrant clergy finally brought to submission. (For lives of major persons mentioned so far in this article, see *Lives of the Tudor Age*.)

On 24 March 1603, the childless Elizabeth I died, and James succeeded peacefully to the English throne by virtue of his descent from Margaret Tudor, daughter of Henry VII. The contrast between his Scottish and English reigns is almost immediately perceptible. His confidence increased enormously and he vastly overestimated his power. On his way to London in April 1603, he ordered the summary execution of a cutpurse at Newark. Without the authority of the English Parliament he soon proclaimed himself King James I of Great Britain and Ireland. He also overestimated his wealth. Coming from a poverty-stricken land where a commission of eight – the Octavians – had

already failed to balance his budget, James was completely carried away by his new prestige. He made lavish gifts of money and titles and indulged in a lack of economy that continued throughout his reign.

In religion, James early incurred the opposition of Catholics and Protestants alike. With Robert Cecil (see *Lives of the Tudor Age*) as his chief adviser, and with a set of councillors who reflected his own views, he ended the war with Spain (1604) but failed to suspend the recusancy laws against Catholics, one of the results of which was the Gunpowder Plot of 1605 (see Fawkes, Guy). At the Hampton Court Conference of 1604, he rejected the modest terms of the Millenary Petition, by which the Puritans had sought to adapt church government for the accommodation of Puritan clergymen within the existing system. Remembering his previous problems with Scottish Presbyterians, James became more inflexible, and the phrase 'No bishop, no king' now became his watchword. Yet though he threatened to harry the Puritans out of the land, he did commission a new translation of the Bible (published in 1611) and promised to consult Parliament about a new prayerbook. In Scotland he had some limited success. The nobles were now forced to respect his power and his own nominees came to act as permanent moderators in the Presbyterian assemblies. Ordinary people attending the Kirk got used to seeing these permanent officials; in truth, they were James's bishops. Thus, by 1612, Scotland had in effect accepted episcopacy, but James's attempt to impose the Anglican ritual met with hostility.

Another aspect of his overestimation of his new power reveals itself in his legal battles. Riding roughshod over the system of common law that custom and precedent had built up in England, he supported Archbishop Bancroft (see *Lives of the Tudor Age*), who promoted the authority of the ecclesiastical courts. The King came into conflict with Edward Coke (q.v.), who violently opposed church interference in the legal system and staunchly rejected James's attempts to make new laws on his own authority. The conflict was protracted and ended in Coke's dismissal as lord chief justice in 1616, and James's celebrated address to the Star Chamber of the same year: 'It is high presumption and contempt in a subject to dispute what a King can do, or say that a King cannot do this or that; [he must] rest in that which is the King's will revealed in his law.'

James was not a popular king. Although he was a learned man who loved the company of intellectuals, he also loved hunting and his manners and language were considered coarse by his English courtiers. Englishmen also found it hard to accept his broad Scots accent and his weakly appearance. Sir Anthony Weldon, one of his courtiers, writing in 1650, describes him as 'of a middle stature, more corpulent through his clothes than in his body. . . . His beard was very thin, his tongue too large for his mouth. . . . His skin was as soft as taffeta satin . . . his legs were very weak, having had (as was thought) some foul play in his youth.' Added to this was the fact that he dribbled incessantly. His fondness for handsome young men of little merit but considerable ambition who rose to positions of power gave further offence, although the question of whether James was in fact homosexual is open to doubt.

In domestic and foreign politics James fared no better than in the other aspects of his reign. His handling of the English Parliament was unsophisticated and fatally inappropriate. He failed to grasp that Parliament was struggling to assert its own sovereignty at the expense of that of the monarch, and this failure sowed the seeds of dissention that poisoned Charles I's reign and eventually bore fruit in the Civil War. Parliament was occupied by propertied men; it was where the money was, and James was always short of money. He needed it to run his household and court; he also needed it for his foreign policy.

James's first parliament met from 1604 to 1611. In 1606, by the legal action called Bate's Case, the crown's right to levy customs duties without Parliamentary consent was recognized; by 1610, however, James was out of money. Cecil, now Earl of Salisbury, hit upon the idea of wiping out the deficit by bargaining with the Commons. In return for a Parliamentary grant of supply, he offered the assurance that the King would give up his feudal rights. But the Commons, blind to the King's real necessity, could only see his lack of economy. Although prepared to accept the result of Bate's Case, they claimed the right to declare illegal any subsequent crown imposts. In the event, faults on both sides led to the eventual abandonment of Salisbury's Great Contract, and in February 1611 the parliament was dissolved. The 1614 parliament – the 'Addled Parliament' – granted James no supplies either, and he was constrained to ask for a benevolence (a voluntary loan) and sell monopolies, one of which – the Cokayne project – had a disastrous effect on the English cloth industry. He also contemplated the radical step of obtaining money from Spain. Negotiations to marry his son Henry, Prince of Wales (q.v.), had been going on in a dilatory manner since 1604 but had petered out in 1611. Henry's death in 1612 put paid to the idea. But now, in

1614, James was becoming captivated by the Spanish ambassador, Sarmiento (the future Count Gondomar; see under Villiers, George, 1st Duke of Buckingham), and thought of marrying his second son Charles to the Infanta Maria, hoping for a large marriage portion; Gondomar was angling for an Anglo-Spanish alliance and the conversion of England to Rome. James's popularity waned still further, and when finally the project came to an ignominious end in 1623, there was general rejoicing in England. Gondomar's manipulations came to nothing, although his influence was strong with James. In 1618 he successfully demanded the execution of Sir Walter Ralegh (see *Lives of the Tudor Age*), who had been impeached for treason as long ago as 1603.

In 1608 James, in pursuance of his policy of political union with Scotland, had obtained legal status as English subjects for all Scots born after 1603 – the *post-nati*. From the same year was dated the rise of one of the most worthless of his favourites, the Scotsman Robert Carr (q.v.), later Earl of Somerset. In 1612, Salisbury died and Carr succeeded him as the King's secretary. His power was short-lived, however, and he fell in the scandal surrounding the murder of Sir Thomas Overbury (q.v.).

In spite of these danger signals, James both failed to make concessions to Parliament and was unwilling to attend to the details of government business himself; fundamentally he was lazy and found state administration tedious. In 1616 he took up a new favourite, George Villiers (q.v.), later 1st Duke of Buckingham. In the King's declining years, Buckingham's importance became paramount.

James's last years saw the cataclysmic outburst of the Thirty Years War on the continent. A man of peace, he had already tried to mediate in the conflict between Spain and the Netherlands, and in the dispute over the Cleves-Jülich succession. In the Thirty Years War, however, his involvement was more direct. In 1613 his daughter Elizabeth had married Frederick V, the Elector Palatine (qq.v.), who in 1618 stood at the centre of conflict. James failed either to help his son-in-law or mediate effectively with the aggressive Catholic powers. His 1621 parliament was hostile to everything. In particular, it denounced economic monopolies and pandering to Spain and demanded the right of free debate in a protestation that James angrily tore from the journal of the House of Commons. After the final failure of the Spanish marriage negotiations, a disgruntled Charles and Buckingham allied with the Commons, and in 1624 extorted from James a decision to make war on Spain. Control of the government now passed from him. He was no longer the ruler of his country and his death, on 27 March 1625, at his favourite residence of Theobalds in Hertfordshire passed without adverse effect on the country.

James's failure rests on several causes. Primarily, his persistent adherence to the principle of the divine right of kings made him see his authority was unimpeachable. However, even by the end of Elizabeth's reign this concept was already well on the way to being outmoded in England. Secondly, James was not prepared to compromise. His advisers were men who reflected his own views and few of them were in Parliament. James's prodigality and generosity, especially to penniless Scots and handsome young men, thoroughly offended the Commons. Only one minister, Lionel Cranfield (q.v.), came close to making him solvent, and he was disgraced because of his opposition to the

Spanish War favoured by Buckingham and supported by Parliament. James's worst defect was idleness in state affairs. Somerset, Buckingham, and even Gondomar controlled his policy-making; only Salisbury exercised a beneficial influence on him.

James's religious policy cowed the Scottish Presbyterians, but could never have had the same effect on the politically more aware Puritans of England. Like so much else that was fortunate and successful in his Scottish reign, it went against the tide of English political opinion and set the tone for the ensuing revolution.

Political Works (with introduction by C. H. McIlwain; 1918).
Robert Ashton, *James I by his Contemporaries* (1969).
David Mathew, *James I* (1967).
H. G. Stafford, *James VI of Scotland* (1940).
D. Harris Willson, *King James VI and I* (1955).

Portraits: oil, by van Brounckhorst, 1574: Scottish N.P.G.; copies attributed to Lockey: N.P.G. and Hardwick Hall (National Trust); oil, half-length, by unknown artist, *c.* 1587: Royal Collection, Hampton Court; oil, half-length, by unknown artist, Scottish N.P.G.; oil, full-length, attributed to de Critz: Loseley Park (J. R. More-Molyneux); oil, attributed to de Critz: National Maritime Museum, Greenwich; oil, by unknown artist after de Critz: N.P.G.; oil, by unknown artist: N.P.G.; miniature, by Hilliard, *c.* 1603–08: Royal Collection, Windsor; miniature, by Hilliard, *c.* 1609–14: British Museum; oil, full-length, by van Somer, 1618: Royal Collection, Holyroodhouse; oil, full-length, in robes of State, by van Somer, *c.* 1620: Royal Collection, Windsor; oil, in Garter robes, by Mytens, *c.* 1621: N.P.G.; numerous other versions at universities of Oxford, Cambridge, Edinburgh, and in private collections; statue by Colt: Hatfield House (Marquis of Salisbury).

James II (1633–1701), King of England, Scotland and Ireland.

James was born to Henrietta Maria on 15 October 1633 at St. James's Palace, the second son of Charles I. He was created Duke of York in January 1643.

His childhood was obviously clouded

by the Civil War – he was nearly captured at Edgehill, and was taken prisoner when Oxford surrendered to the Parliamentary forces in 1646. In 1648 he escaped to Holland and spent the rest of his youth in exile. He served as a volunteer in the French army from 1652 to 1655 and distinguished himself as a cavalry commander. When Charles's court was driven from France by the influence of the Commonwealth, James took service with Spain (1657). He returned to England with Charles in 1660 and was made lord high admiral.

James was as much influenced by the traumas of the Civil War and exile, as his brother had been, but his attitudes were more fixed and his opinions less flexible as a result. He was much influenced by his mother too, who was unrealistic and unyielding. While he was more idealistic than his brother, James was also politically less shrewd and his inflexibility was to prove disastrous in the future. However, the brothers were very close and James was completely loyal to Charles. Charles teased James about his lack of humour and his stupidity, but admired and respected his loyalty, courage, and industry.

In 1660 James married Anne Hyde (q.v.), who was pregnant by him. Anxious not to upset Anne's father, his chief minister, Charles insisted that James should marry her. Their marriage seems to have been fairly happy and they had two surviving children, Mary (see Mary I) and Anne (q.v.), who were both brought up as Protestants. He had several mistresses, although fewer than Charles, and Charles also thought them a good deal uglier. He once remarked that James must have 'his mistresses found for him by his priests for penance'.

As lord high admiral James showed considerable skill. His abilities in command were demonstrated during the Dutch Wars, when he won a victory at Lowestoft in 1665 and at Southwold Bay in 1672. James was not to blame for the destruction of part of the English fleet in the Medway in 1667, for he had been opposed to laying up the big ships at that time, a course of action that was followed largely because of a shortage of funds. He also supported naval reforms such as those carried out by Pepys (q.v.).

At some time during the 1660s James was converted to Catholicism. His conversion became generally known after about 1668 and thereafter in the public mind James posed the threat of popery. He supported the policy pursued by Charles in the Treaty of Dover (1670) and would probably have preferred to be more zealous in attempting to convert the kingdom to Catholicism. He was compelled to give up his office as lord high admiral in 1673, when the Test Act was passed by Parliament. The reason for the significance of James's religious affiliations was that he was the sole significant heir to the throne, for Charles's marriage to Catherine of Braganza (q.v.) had failed to produce an heir. In 1671 his wife had died, and James's marriage two years later to the 15-year-old Catholic Mary of Modena (q.v.) only served to strengthen general suspicion of him.

In 1678 Titus Oates (q.v.) made his allegations of a 'Popish Plot' to overthrow Charles and put James on the throne. The story gained much popular credence and the House of Commons affirmed belief in the plot. This apparent proof of Catholic machinations on James's behalf was enough to provoke the attempt to exclude him from succession to the throne. In 1679 an Exclusion Bill was introduced to disinherit James and replace him with Charles's illegitimate Protestant son, the Duke of Monmouth (q.v.). James went into voluntary exile for a few months, but soon returned as lord high commissioner of Scotland, a post that he held from 1680 to 1682, occupying himself chiefly with the persecution of the Covenanters. Charles supported his brother's right to succeed and by a series of skilful manœuvres managed to defeat the Exclusion Bill.

James returned to London from Scotland at the end of 1682 and in 1684 was restored to his post at the admiralty. In the last years of Charles's reign public opinion swung in James's favour and this was reinforced when the Whigs were discredited by the Rye House Plot. Consequently, he was able to succeed peacefully to the throne on 6 February 1685. Thanks to the remodelling of borough charters undertaken by Charles, the Parliament that met in May was loyal and liberal with supply. James was voted an income of nearly £2 million p.a. Within a short time two rebellions took place that strengthened James's position: the Earl of Argyll attempted a rising in Scotland and Monmouth landed at Lyme Regis. Both were unsuccessful and the two leaders were executed. These events enabled James to raise a permanent standing army, which was concentrated at Hounslow, just outside London, and served to impose loyalty to the King. However, despite his peaceful succession, loyal Parliament, and growing popularity, James had within three years lost these advantages and was in exile in France. The reasons for this lie almost entirely in James's own character.

From the beginning of his reign, James openly professed his Catholicism and made it plain that he intended to improve the lot of his fellow Catholics. It became increasingly apparent to contemporaries that James's ultimate aim was the reconversion of the country to Rome. He had apparently learnt little from his unpopularity during the Exclusion crisis and felt that opposition would probably yield if he held his ground. James had also remained more extremely Royalist than Charles and was less willing to make concessions or modify his plans. After Monmouth's rebellion, James felt that his enlarged army must be officered by men in whom he had confidence – that is to say Catholics. The Commons presented an address against the employment of Catholic officers and James prorogued Parliament; it never met again during his reign. In October Halifax (see Savile, George) was dismissed for refusing to sanction the repeal of the Test and Corporation Acts and was replaced by the more pliable Sunderland (see Spencer, Robert).

James then began a systematic scheme of replacing civil and military office holders with his own nominees. In 1686 the Catholic Earl of Tyrconnel (see Talbot, Richard) was made lord lieu-

tenant of Ireland and began to form a Catholic army. A Catholic was placed in command of the Navy, and the Jesuit Father Petre (q.v.) became a close adviser of the King. Catholic chapels, schools and friaries began to appear in London. James's right to dispense with the Test Act by use of his prerogative powers was affirmed by the decision of the judges in the legal action of Godden v. Hales (1686), and this moreover demonstrated the King's control of the bench.

James then began a direct attack on the dominant position of the Established Church by instituting a body of ecclesiastical commissioners under Judge Jeffreys (q.v.). This was used to force Oxford and Cambridge colleges to accept Catholics as fellows, and when Magdalen College, Oxford, refused James's nominee as its president the fellows were ejected. James meanwhile issued a Declaration of Indulgence in the hope of gaining the approval of Protestant Non-conformists. To ensure the amenability of his next Parliament, James continued to remodel town charters in an attempt to make local government less Anglican. Many lords lieutenant and J.P.s were removed, and James then questioned remaining justices on their attitude towards repealing the penal laws against Catholics. Their answers were generally hostile.

In May 1688 James issued a second Declaration of Indulgence, and he further declared that it should be read in every church in the kingdom on two successive Sundays. Seven bishops petitioned the King to withdraw the order and were put on trial for seditious libel (see Compton, Henry, and Sancroft, William). However, they were acquitted in June amid much popular rejoicing. James's action in trying the bishops had brought the full weight of the Church of England against him – and significantly it was from the Church that the first effective opposition to the use of his prerogative powers came. The birth of a son to James in the same month as the bishops' acquittal further stimulated the growing conspiracy to remove him. The prospect of a Catholic heir to the throne finally prompted the sending of an invitation in July 1688 to William of Orange to invade England. It was signed by seven leading Englishmen, including the Bishop of London and the Earl of Danby (see Osborne, Thomas).

In September, James attempted too late to restore his situation by making concessions. He abolished the Ecclesiastical Commission, restored the ejected fellows of Magdalen, put a Protestant in command of the fleet, and annulled all municipal charters since 1679. James's concessions were too limited and too obviously inspired by necessity to win a change in public opinion in his favour. William landed at Torbay on 5 November 1688, and much of the peerage and gentry rallied to him, including James's daughter Anne. James had rejected French help until it was no longer available and now wavered disastrously. He sent the Queen and his son from the country and eventually tried to follow himself, but was captured by Kentish fishermen and brought back. He escaped again, with the active connivance of William, and finally landed in France at Christmas.

The first point made in the letter of invitation sent to William of Orange was that there was general dissatisfaction 'with the present conduct of the government in relation to . . . religion, liberties and properties'. To the Anglican gentry, the policies pursued by James seemed to threaten the whole fabric of society. They feared that he would repeal the Test Act – on which the supremacy of the Protestant gentry was built – and

break their control over their local boroughs by placing local administration in the hands of Catholics and Dissenters. Thus James posed a threat not only to their religion but also to their position and influence. James's gravest mistake was that his policy alienated the very section of society from which the staunchest support for the King might be expected to come. Charles was realistic enough to realize that he must work with the Tory Anglican gentry, but James was too idealistic, too devoted to his religion, and perhaps too foolish to temper his policies in order to retain their loyalty. James might have succeeded by forging a Catholic-Nonconformist alliance, but Dissenters were suspicious of a Catholic King who appeared to be using them for his own ends and many of them had only recently supported opponents of the King like Monmouth. The standing army that James had stationed outside London and the Catholic army that he was assembling in Ireland alarmed people of all ranks and opinions; even many Catholic peers seem to have feared that James was advancing towards absolutism.

In exile, James was established at St. Germain by Louis XIV and made appeals for help to various powers. He made one positive effort to regain the throne in 1689, when he landed in Ireland with a French force. James held a parliament in Dublin, which passed a toleration act, transferred tithes to Roman Catholics, and repealed the Act of Settlement. He was present at the Battle of the Boyne in 1690 and after his defeat there by William fled back to France. Various other schemes for invasion were discussed but came to nothing. Louis XIV naturally hoped that James's supporters in England – the Jacobites – would be useful to him during the Seven Years War. However, by the Treaty of

Ryswick (1697) Louis recognised William III as King of England, a final blow to James's hopes of restoration.

In his last years he devoted himself increasingly to his religious devotions and hunting, apparently growing very feeble in mind though remaining physically strong. He died at St. Germain on 17 September 1701, charging his son James Edward to die rather than abandon his faith.

Hilaire Belloc, *James the Second* (1934).
Jock Haswell, *James II, Soldier and Sailor* (1972).
A. Lytton Sells (trans.), *The Memoirs of James II: His Campaigns as Duke of York 1652–1660* (with an introduction by Sir Arthur Bryant; 1962).
F. C. Turner, *James II* (1948).

Portraits: oil, three-quarter length, attributed to C. Wantier, after 1650: St. James's Palace; oil, three-quarter length, by Lely, *c.* 1665: St. James's Palace; oil, quarter-length, by Kneller, *c.* 1683–85: Windsor Castle; oil, full-length, by Kneller, 1684–85: N.P.G.

James Francis Edward Stuart (1688–1766), 'the Old Pretender', see *Lives of the Georgian Age.*

Janssen Vanceulen, Cornelius (1593–1661), see Johnson, Cornelius.

Jeffreys, George (1645–89), 1st Baron Jeffreys of Wem; judge and lord chancellor (1686–88).

Born in Acton, Denbighshire, the son of John Jeffreys, a local gentleman, Jeffreys was educated at the free school in Shrewsbury, St. Paul's (from c. 1659), Westminster School (1661–62), and Trinity College, Cambridge (1662–63). George Jeffreys struck his contemporaries as a man of little learning, despite his years of schooling. Rather, it was his energy and ambition that brought him success in his chosen career, law. He entered the Inner Temple in 1663, where – his enemies later claimed –

he spent more time drinking than studying. There is, however, no question as to the number of useful contacts that he had acquired by 1668, when he was called to the bar.

Jeffreys prospered, aided by his eloquence, loud voice, and talent at cross-examination. His influential friends in the City probably played a greater role in his advancement to the bench. He obtained an introduction to the court, where he cultivated the friendship of the Duchess of Portsmouth, Danby, and other Tories. In 1677 he was rewarded with a knighthood and in 1678 became Recorder of London.

Further advancement came his way during the next year. He proved himself an energetic supporter of the Government in the Popish Plot trials. He demonstrated even greater zeal during the Exclusion crisis and its aftermath, as a partisan of the Stuarts both at the bar and on the bench.

From 1680 to 1683 he was Chief Justice of Chester. He then became Lord Chief Justice of the King's Bench and was concerned in the trials of the Rye House conspirators and in Charles's campaign to deprive municipal corporations of their charters. For these services he was rewarded with the post of lord chief justice and a seat on the Privy Council (1683). On the accession of James II he was raised to the peerage and became a prominent royal adviser, at least during the first part of the reign.

As James's chief justice, Jeffreys has acquired notoriety for the 'Bloody Assizes', which he chaired. At these trials the defeated Monmouth rebels were punished with great severity, several hundred being executed or deported to the West Indies as slaves. James rewarded Jeffreys with the chancellorship, in which position he supported the royal use of the dispensing power and the creation of an ecclesiastical court (1686). He was, as the 2nd Earl of Clarendon related, 'much troubled' over James's decision to bring the seven bishops to trial for misdemeanors in 1688, and also acted for his master in the King's belated attempts to introduce concessions to the Protestant gentry and High Churchmen in the autumn of that year.

As a committed supporter of James II's most hated policies, Jeffreys realized that he had to flee after the Glorious Revolution of 1688. Captured while attempting to do so, he was imprisoned in the Tower, where he died on 18 April 1689, of gallstones, from which he had long suffered and which probably contributed to his notorious ill temper.

Jeffreys was portrayed as an unscrupulous opportunist, a drunkard, and a monster on the bench by his numerous political enemies. This view was immortalized by Macaulay, who elaborated on Jeffreys's partiality and unconstitutional conduct while a judge. Recently, several biographies have appeared that portray Jeffreys as an honest but zealous servant of the crown; they correctly point out that in his day a judge was expected to be a partial political supporter of his royal master, that most sentences were harsh, and that courtroom procedure was quite different from that of the 19th and 20th centuries. As even his detractors admit, Jeffreys was quick to grasp the essentials of a case and was considered an excellent judge in nonpolitical, civil cases. But in the trials that have won Jeffreys infamy, it is hard to believe that what he sought was justice.

P. J. Helm, *Jeffreys* (1966).
H. M. Hyde, *Judge Jeffreys* (1940).
G. W. Keeton, *Lord Chancellor Jeffreys and the Stuart Cause* (1965).
S. Schofield, *Jeffreys of 'The Bloody Assizes'* (1937).

Portrait: oil, three-quarter length, attributed to W. Claret, *c*. 1678–80: N.P.G.

Johnson or Janssen Vanceulen, Cornelius or Cornelis (1593–1661), portrait painter.

Born in London to Dutch parents who had sought refuge in England following religious persecution in Antwerp, Johnson was baptized on 14 October 1593. There is little information on Johnson's early life and training. He may well have studied in Holland, since his early works seem Dutch in both style and content. It is equally probable, however, that he observed and learnt from fellow Dutch painters already in residence in England.

By 1618 he was a practising painter in London and for over twenty years he was to enjoy a flourishing reputation for his fashionable portraits of court nobility and gentry, including both James I and Charles I. His earliest work, done on panel, was meticulous but tentative and insubstantial. His cool and subdued colouring and his sensitivity to personality enabled him to achieve a freer and softer style than that of his predecessors.

Johnson was very sensitive to changes in fashion and to the work of other artists. He initially followed Mytens (q.v.), whose technique he came to copy so exactly that it is sometimes difficult to distinguish their work, as in Johnson's portrait of Charles I, now at Chatsworth. However, even before the arrival of Van Dyck (q.v.) in England in 1632, Johnson's work began to show signs of his influence, and this influence became predominant in the 1630s. Finally, in his later works, his style begins to bear a distinct resemblance to that of Dobson (q.v.).

In 1632, Johnson was appointed 'His Majesty's servant in ye quality of Picture Maker' to Charles I. Until Van Dyck's arrival, Johnson had been England's most successful portraitist. He was certainly the only painter 'in large' who had signed and dated a considerable body of his work. His ability to achieve superb likenesses and his fine draughtsmanship and perfection of heads had made him popular. His concentration on the head of a sitter led him to attempt only rarely a full-figure portrait, and, on the occasions when he did so, notably in his portraits of Thomas, Earl of Elgin, and of the Countess of Redlynch Park, he was not particularly successful.

A characteristic of his portraits is that they are set within a painted oval, often made to look like marble or stone. A fine example of this and also of the silvery facial tone that was characteristic of his work is in his portrait of Susanna Temple, dated 1620. He used this painted stone oval framing unremittingly throughout his career.

In 1636, possibly feeling overshadowed by Van Dyck or having lost part of his patronage to him, Johnson moved from London to Canterbury, where he acquired an altogether different clientele. Here he executed numerous portraits of the neighbouring county families of Kent and Sussex.

With the outbreak of the Civil War in 1643, his fears for the safety of himself and his family, as well as a sharp decline in business, made Johnson decide to leave England altogether and move to Holland. He lived first in Middelburg, then in The Hague, Amsterdam, and finally Utrecht, where he died on 5 August 1661. Throughout these final years he continued to paint without interruption; his portraits of this period, however, are as Dutch in style as his earlier work had been English.

Works at:
Rijksmuseum, Amsterdam.
Holbourne Museum, Bath.
Dublin Gallery.
National Gallery.
National Portrait Gallery.
Tate Gallery.
British Museum.
Victoria and Albert Museum.

Jones, Inigo (1573–1652), sometimes called 'the English Palladio'; architect and stage designer.

Jones was born in London, on 15 July 1573. Architecture in the British Isles at the end of the sixteenth century was developing uncertainly in style from the Gothic to the Flemish-inspired Jacobean. The classical Roman style of Filippo Brunelleschi (1377–1446) was known only by the work of a few foreign, mostly Italian, craftsmen. It was not until Inigo Jones saw the work of Brunelleschi's successor, Andrea di Pietro Palladio (1508–80), that the true Italian Renaissance seriously influenced British architecture. From then on, the work of Jones himself, his pupil John Webb, and above all Sir Christopher Wren (q.v.) transformed the architectural scene in Britain.

Inigo Jones was the son of a London cloth-worker of Welsh descent, who also bore the unfamiliar Spanish name of Inigo. Little is known of his early life and education, but he was probably apprenticed to a joiner in St. Paul's Churchyard. By some lucky chance, his sketches attracted the attention of a rich patron, probably Thomas Howard, Earl of Arundel, and with his backing the young Jones was sent to Italy around the turn of the century to study painting. While in Italy, he acquired a copy of Palladio's *Quattro libri dell'architettura*, which appears to have had such a profound impact on him that he gave up his career as a painter and devoted himself to architecture. His careful annotations on a copy of Palladio's work can be seen at Worcester College, Oxford (though it is possible that these annotations were made on a later visit to Italy).

He probably worked in Venice for some years, having attained sufficient status as an architect to be invited to visit Denmark by King Christian IV in 1604. It is possible that he designed the

two royal palaces at Rosenborg and Frederiksborg during this visit, although there is some doubt about this. He may have been employed only as a draughtsman to Christian, who was himself a keen designer. However, there is no doubt that this royal patronage established his future career. Christian IV's sister, Anne of Denmark, was the wife of James I of England. In 1605 Jones returned to England in the company of Anne and she subsequently appointed him to design the sets and costumes for a series of extravagant court masques written by Ben Jonson (q.v.) and other writers of the day. Many of his drawings for these masques can still be seen at Chatsworth House, Derbyshire. As a stage designer he appears to have invented the proscenium arch to replace the traditional apron stage.

From 1605 to 1610 Jones continued to work under the Queen's patronage, producing his earliest known building, the New Exchange in the Strand (completed about 1608 and destroyed in the 18th century). In 1610, presumably through the Queen's influence, he was appointed surveyor of the works to Henry, Prince of Wales. In itself, this office was of little value to him and Henry died two years later without having commissioned Jones to build anything. However, when the King's surveyor of the works, Simon Basil, died in 1613, the appointment was promised to Jones. Before taking on the responsibilities of this important office he travelled again to Italy, in the company of the Earl of Arundel, to study in more detail the works of the masters of the Italian Renaissance, especially those of Palladio. He returned in 1615 and immediately took up his post as royal surveyor, a career that lasted through the reigns of James and his son Charles I until the outbreak of the Civil War.

In 1616 Jones started work on his first building as royal surveyor, the Queen's House at Greenwich; this was not completed until 1635. At the beginning of 1619 the old Banqueting House in Whitehall was destroyed by fire. Jones's hasty plans for a new hall were completed by the spring of that year and the new Banqueting House was completed by 1622 at a cost of some £15,600. This building made free use of Palladian proportions and elevations, but it was not merely derivative; it represented an audacious and accomplished application of the Italian style to the English environment. This building, together with the Queen's House, set a style for native architects that dominated British buildings for two hundred years. In his own words, buildings should be 'solid, proportional according to the rules, masculine and unaffected.' Perhaps Jones's greatest achievement was to succeed in adapting the more flamboyant Italian style within these sensible British restraints.

The Banqueting House itself formed part of a plan for a magnificent Palace of Whitehall, but in the event it was the only part to be carried out (the plans can be seen at Worcester College, Oxford). Charles I tried to revive this scheme in the 1630s, but unfortunately no funds were available and the King's increasing difficulties meant that the grand plan had to be abandoned. The only surviving royal building of this period is the Queen's Chapel in St. James's Palace, started in 1623 and completed four years later. Nothing now remains of his many other additions to royal palaces or public buildings. Perhaps the greatest loss is the work that he carried out to Old St. Paul's Cathedral (1633–42), especially the massive ten-column Corinthian portico that was added to the west front but destroyed in the rebuilding of the cathedral after the Fire of London (1666). The best that can be said of this loss is that Jones's work on the cathedral had a profound influence on Sir Christopher Wren's reconstruction.

Apart from his royal work, Jones was closely associated with town planning in London. In 1618 he took part in laying out Lincoln's Inn Fields and during the 1630s he planned an Italian-style piazza on the Earl of Bedford's land at Covent Garden. This consisted of a large square (the first in London) surrounded by the Earl of Bedford's garden wall on one side, by arcaded houses above loggias on two sides, and by his Church of St. Paul on the fourth side. Nothing of this now remains except the church; this was damaged by fire in 1795 and later restored by Thomas Hardwick. Its Tuscan portico was a unique feature in England at that time.

The long and successful career of Inigo Jones suffered a severe setback in 1642 with the outbreak of the Civil War. As a Royalist, he was deprived of his public offices in 1643 and he was forced to flee to Basing House in Hampshire, where he remained until the house was taken by Cromwell in 1645. His property was sequestered and in 1646 he was fined £1,045 for being a favourite of the King and a Roman Catholic. However, later in the year he was pardoned by the House of Lords and most of his property was restored. For the remaining years of his life, Jones worked on large country houses rather than public buildings. His designs for the great room at Wilton, the Earl of Pembroke's house, belong to this period. Other examples include Coleshill in Berkshire, The Grange in Hampshire, and a wing at Cranbourne Manor, also in Hampshire.

He died on 21 June 1652, nearly 80 years old; in accordance with his will a monument was constructed to his memory in the Church of St. Benet, Paul's Wharf, where he was buried beside his father. The monument was lost in the Fire of London, but in many respects the whole English Renaissance in architecture is a monument to his work.

W. Kent, *Designs of Inigo Jones* (1727).

J. Lees-Milne, *The Age of Inigo Jones* (1953).

J. N. Summerson, *Inigo Jones* (1965).

J. N. Summerson, *Architecture in Britain, 1530–1830* (1963, rev. ed.).

G. A. Gotch, *Inigo Jones* (1968).

Portraits: oil, quarter-length, after Van Dyck: N.P.G.; wash drawing, three-quarter length, after an etching by R. van Voest: N.P.G.

Jonson, Ben (1573–1637), dramatist and poet.

Jonson was born probably on 11 June 1573, at Westminster, although it is possible he was born as early as the autumn of 1572. Generally considered second only to Shakespeare (see *Lives of the Tudor Age*) as a dramatist of the Jacobean period.

The details of Jonson's early life are

obscure. He claimed descent from a Border family, a claim that is held by some to account for his aggressive and uncompromising character. His father died shortly before his birth and his mother was soon remarried, probably to Robert Brett, a master of the Tylers' and Bricklayers' Company. The family, which lived near Charing Cross, was poor. Jonson was first sent to a school in St. Martin's Church and later to Westminster School, which he entered with the financial assistance of William Camden, the second master of the school. Jonson always acknowledged Camden as his only master, the man responsible for such education as he received; and although he may have had some early connection with St. John's College, Cambridge, he told William Drummond that he was 'taken from school and put to a trade' and that the degrees he later held from both Cambridge and Oxford were 'by their favour, not his study'. It is probable that in about 1588 he was forced to leave Westminster and went to work in his stepfather's trade.

At some time before 1592, Jonson found release from bricklaying by volunteering for military service against the Spanish in Flanders. While there he distinguished himself by an act of traditional valour: with the opposing armies looking on, he joined in single combat with one of the enemy and killed him. After completing his term as a soldier, Jonson again took up his 'wonted studies', presumably literary studies, and married. The marriage is probably that entered in the records of St. Magnus Martyr, London, on 14 November 1594, between Ben Jonson and Anne Lewis. It does not appear to have been a particularly happy union; in Jonson's own words, his wife was 'a shrew, yet honest' and he himself was 'given to venery'. Several children, in whom Jonson seems to have been disappointed, were born; none survived him. At this time Jonson was working as an actor and probably played in Kyd's *The Spanish Tragedy* and Shakespeare's *The Taming of the Shrew*. In 1597 Philip Henslowe (see *Lives of the Tudor Age*) paid him to finish a play by Nashe, *Isle of Dogs*. When performed in the summer of that year, the play was suspected to be seditious, the theatre was closed, and Jonson was arrested together with others involved in the performance. The first of several conflicts between the outspoken playwright and the authorities, this episode may have been the one that Jonson described in the *Conversations* with Drummond of Hawthornden. Freed after being interrogated, Jonson apparently gave a banquet for his friends, among them Camden and John Selden; 'at the midst of the feast his old mother drank to him, and showed him a paper which she had intended (if the sentence had taken execution) to have mixed in the prison among his drink, which was full of lusty strong poison, and that she was no churl, she told, she minded first to have drunk it herself.' It is possible, however, that this incident occurred later, after the first performance of *Eastward Ho!* (1604).

The association with Henslowe continued, but from this time onwards Jonson seems to have stopped acting and devoted himself entirely to writing. Before 1598 he wrote several plays, but all are lost. That his reputation was growing among his contemporaries is certain. Francis Meres in *Palladis Tamia* (1598) curiously ranks Jonson among dramatists 'who are our best for tragedy.' It is possible that he wrote some tragedies that he chose to ignore when he published his *Works*. In any case, it was after the publication of this comment that he began to acquire a reputa-

tion, particularly among the educated, as a writer of comedies. The first of these, *Every Man in His Humour*, was performed by Henslowe's rivals, the Lord Chamberlain's Men, at the Curtain theatre, with Shakespeare in one of the roles (probably Knowell), in September 1598.

On 22 September, Jonson killed an actor, Gabriel Spencer, in a duel. (Henslowe was incensed by this; it is perhaps for this reason that *Every Man in His Humour* was performed by the rival company.) Charged with felony, Jonson was found guilty but, after pleading benefit of clergy, was released from prison. As a felon, he was branded on his left thumb with the Tyburn T and lost all his property. While in prison he became a Roman Catholic, which he remained until he returned to the Church of England in 1610.

Reconciled with Henslowe after his release, Jonson wrote or collaborated on a number of plays both for Henslowe and for other companies. None of these, however, did he later judge worthy of inclusion is his *Works*. In 1599 the so-called 'War of the Theatres' began. (For details, see Marston, John.) Satirical portraits relating to this quarrel appear in Jonson's next three plays, *Every Man Out of His Humour* (1599/1600), *Cynthia's Revels* (1601), in which the characters Hedon and Anaides probably represent Marston and Dekker, and *The Poetaster* (1601). The last play ridiculed not only his fellow playwrights, whom he considered hacks, but actors, soldiers, and lawyers in general. When Jonson appended an 'Apologetic Dialogue' addressed to the insulted professions, he typically succeeded in giving even greater offence and was threatened with prosecution. By this time, however, his reputation was such among the wits and intellectuals of the day that one of them,

243

Richard Martin of the Middle Temple, protected him from legal actions. Probably because of the controversy that his satire inspired, Jonson for a time abandoned writing comedy for the popular stage, 'since the comic muse hath proved so ominous to me.' The tragic muse proved no safer. *Sejanus*, performed by the King's Men at the Globe in 1603, was not only unpopular but also was thought to advocate papacy and sedition. Jonson was summoned before the Privy Council but apparently emerged from the episode unscathed. By this time he numbered among his friends many who were prominent at court. He had visited the house of Sir Robert Townshend and at about this time (1603) or perhaps later (1613–18) spent a lengthy period away from his family as the guest of Esmé Stuart, Lord D'Aubigny. He knew many members of the Sidney family and the Earl of Suffolk, the lord chamberlain. By 1604 he had access to the court. (In January Jonson and Sir John Roe were thrown out of a court entertainment by Suffolk because of unmannerly conduct.) In the spring, Jonson and Dekker wrote speeches to celebrate the entry of James I into London. Jonson also wrote a *Panegyre* to the King at the opening of parliament. His advance in royal favour suffered a temporary setback with *Eastward Ho!* (late 1604), on which he collaborated with Marston and Chapman. Allusions to the Scots caused offence and, according to Jonson, the imprisonment of his two collaborators. He voluntarily joined them in prison. The intercession of powerful friends seems again to have brought their release and prevented prosecution. It is certain that Jonson was soon back in the good graces of the King. He was also trusted by the government and apparently played a part as its agent in discovering the Gunpowder Plot. On 9 October 1605, he dined with Robert Catesby and others connected with the conspiracy and later supplied information to the government on the extent of the plot.

Jonson provided the court masque for Twelfth Night, 1605, the *Masque of Blacknesse*. With this work he entered the most successful period of his career, from 1605 to 1616. Enjoying royal patronage, which was to last until 1625, Jonson produced, with Inigo Jones (q.v.), eight masques that established English supremacy in this form of courtly entertainment. It was now, too, that he wrote his three greatest comedies. *Volpone* (1606) met with enthusiastic approval and was performed at both universities. *The Alchemist* (1610), like much of Jonson's best satire, was the cause of some controversy, but *Bartholomew Fair* (1614) was again an unqualified popular success. Other works written in this period are the plays *Epicœne* (1609), *Catiline* (a tragedy, 1611), and *The Devil is an Ass* (1616), and the masques *Hymenaei* (1606), *The Masque of Beauty* (1608), *The Hue and Cry After Cupid* (1609), and *The Masque of Queens* (1609). For several years after 1606 the writings of Jonson's that survive are masques, probably because of a fire in his apartment in 1623, which destroyed many of his papers. What Jonson wished to preserve to that date was, in any case, published in 1616 and entitled *Works*. The title was considered presumptuous by Jonson's contemporaries, since theatrical writing for the popular stage was not generally regarded as worthy of serious literary status.

In 1612 Jonson journeyed to France as the tutor to the 'knavishly inclined' son of Sir Walter Ralegh. (Jonson had apparently known Ralegh and claimed that he had contributed a section to Ralegh's *History of the World* but had not received acknowledgement.) On one occasion, as reported by Jonson, his charge got him 'dead drunk' and had him drawn about Paris in a cart, 'at every corner showing his governor stretched out and telling them that was a more lively image of the crucifix than any they had.' He was again in England in 1613, when he witnessed the fire that destroyed the Globe theatre. Between 1616 and the death of James I in 1625, Jonson reigned as a literary lion and presided, chiefly in the Apollo room of the Devil's Tavern, over a circle of literary disciples. He had earlier been, with Shakespeare, at the centre of the group of writers and wits who gathered at the Mermaid Tavern. He now became the head of the 'tribe of Ben', which included among others Herrick and Sir Kenelm Digby.

In the summer of 1618 he journeyed on foot to Scotland, where he was made a burgess of Edinburgh. At this time Drummond of Hawthornden, whom he visited, set down his lively *Conversations*, the source of most that is known about his life. On his return trip he received an honorary M.A. degree from the university of Oxford in 1619.

By 1624 the influence at court of Inigo Jones, who had always been a formidable rival of Jonson's, had increased greatly. A quarrel had begun during their collaboration, with Jonson wishing to emphasize the literary and thematic elements of the masque and Jones stubbornly insisting on making the visual, choreographic, and musical elements most prominent. With the accession of Charles I, the favour Jonson had enjoyed was withdrawn. Jonson continued to battle for attention but in 1628 he suffered the first of several strokes that forced him to curtail some of his activities. He was appointed city chronologer with a stipend, but this was withheld after 1631 because of his failure to discharge the formal duties of the post. Two of his masques were produced at court in 1631, but he never regained his central position. In 1634 the King ordered the city to convert Jonson's stipend, which had not been paid, into a pension requiring no duties of him. From then until his death Jonson lived quietly, devoting himself to his reading and writing.

None of the dramatic work of his later years equals that written before 1625. *The Staple of News* (1626) was a failure and *The New Inn* (1629) did not receive the honour of performance at court. *The Magnetic Lady* (1632) was successful, but *The Tale of a Tub* (1633), which attacked Inigo Jones in the character of Vitruvius Hoop, had to undergo the excision of offending passages before it was performed. Jonson's verse was published in *Epigrams* and *The Forest* (1616) and in the posthumous volume *Underwoods* (1640). His nondramatic prose consists of *Timber or Discoveries* (1640), an unoriginal summary of the Renaissance classicism that he practised, and an *English Grammar* (1640).

In his dramatic work Jonson successfully imposed the classical ideals of structure and the unities on his comic material. He also developed the theory of the 'Comedy of Humours', in which each character is drawn according to a single dominant eccentricity or defect, a method that proved useful to such various writers as Congreve and Dickens. His three great comedies have all had successful modern revivals and on these his reputation mainly rests.

Jonson died on 6 August 1637, and was buried at Westminster Abbey, his tomb being inscribed with the simple epitaph, 'O rare Ben Jonson.'

C. H. Herford and Percy and Evelyn M. Simpson (eds.), *Ben Jonson* (11 vols.; 1925–52).

245

William B. Hunter, Jr. (ed.), *The Complete Poems* (New York, 1963).

Bernard H. Newdigate (ed.), *The Complete Poems* (1936).

Stephen Orgel (ed.), *The Complete Masques* (New Haven, Conn., 1969). See also *A Book of Masques in Honour of Allardyce Nicoll* (1967).

F. E. Schelling (ed.), *The Complete Plays* (Everyman's Library, 2 vols.; 1910).

Jonas A. Barish, *Ben Jonson and the Language of Prose Comedy* (Cambridge, Mass., 1960).

Margaret Chute, *Ben Jonson of Westminster* (New York, 1953).

L. C. Knights, *Drama and Society in the Age of Jonson* (1937).

Stephen Orgel, *The Jonsonian Masque* (Cambridge, Mass., 1965).

Edward B. Partridge, *The Broken Compass: A Study of the Major Comedies of Ben Jonson* (1958).

Portrait: oil, by Gerard Honthorst: Knole Park; copy: N.P.G.; oil, quarter-length, by unknown nineteenth-century artist, after Abraham Blyenberch, *c.* 1620: N.P.G.

Juxon, William (1582–1663), prelate and lord treasurer of England.

Born in Chichester, son of Richard Juxon, receiver of the see of Chichester, Juxon was educated at Merchant Taylors' School and St. John's College, Oxford, where he received the degree of bachelor of civil law in 1603. He turned to theology after studying law, and was ordained before 1615. He enjoyed a variety of ecclesiastical livings before being elected president of St. John's College in 1621 on the recommendation of Archbishop Laud (q.v.). Both within and out of the university he demonstrated a disinterested tact and gentle manner that made him much sought after as a mediator, despite his promotion of the Laudian reform of the university statutes after 1630.

Through Laud's patronage, Juxon became Dean of Worcester (1627), Bishop of Hereford (1632), and Bishop of London (1633). In the latter diocese he implemented the Laudian reform of the service with such diplomacy as to win the respect of the London nonconformists. Laud propelled him into still higher office, securing for him in 1636 the lord treasurership of England and a seat on the privy council. Although lacking experience in financial affairs, his integrity and dedication were beyond question, and once in office he displayed great diligence and was soon entrusted with other royal business.

When the Laudian structure crumbled under the attacks of the Long Parliament, Juxon survived unscathed. Even the sharpest critics of 'Thorough' could find no crime in his conduct, and once he had resigned the treasurership (1641) he gradually withdrew from public affairs. His spiritual advice was sought by Charles I, especially in 1648–49; he remained by the King in his last days and attended him to the scaffold.

During the Commonwealth Juxon lived in retirement on his manor at Little Compton, Gloucestershire, where he indulged his passion for hunting and conducted services for local Anglicans. At the Restoration he was appointed Archbishop of Canterbury, but age prevented him from taking an active part in the church settlement. He died on 4 June 1663.

W. H. Marah, *Memoirs of Archbishop Juxon and his Times* (1864).

Portrait: oil, three-quarter length, by unknown artist, *c.* 1640: N.P.G.

K

Kent, William (1685–1748), architect, interior decorator, and landscape gardener, see *Lives of the Georgian Age*.

Ker, Robert (?1585–1645), see Carr, Robert.

Kéroualle, Louise Renée de (1649–1734), Duchess of Portsmouth; mistress of Charles II.

The daughter of a Breton gentleman, Louise first came to England in 1670 as maid of honour to Charles's sister Henrietta, during the negotiation of the Treaty of Dover. When Henrietta died later that year, Louise returned to England and Charles's interest in her, which had previously been apparent, was confirmed when she became a maid of honour to the Queen, Catherine of Braganza (q.v.). By 1671 she was firmly established as Charles's mistress, receiving Louis XIV's congratulations on her success. She gave birth to a son, later the Duke of Richmond, in 1672 and in 1673 was created Duchess of Portsmouth. The next year, Charles persuaded Louis XIV to grant her the fief of Aubigny.

Despite opposition from many quarters and the great dislike she excited in Charles's subjects, Louise's position in his favour never faltered. Her apartment at Whitehall was renowned for its splendour and a contemporary described it as having 'ten times the richness and glory beyond the Queen's'. It was rebuilt two or three times 'to satisfy her prodigal and expensive pleasures'. Sums of money paid to her varied, but in 1681 the total amounted to well over £130,000. During 1682 she visited France and was warmly received at the French court.

Louise's political influence has probably been exaggerated, although she certainly had the power to sway appointments. Politicians like Danby thought it wise to win her favour and Louis XIV and his ambassadors attached considerable importance to her. What influence she had with Charles was certainly used in favour of the French alliance, although he firmly rejected her advice concerning the Exclusion Bill, which she thought, by excluding the Catholic Duke of York (see James II) from the succession, would advance the interests of her own son, the Duke of Richmond.

When Charles fell ill in 1685 Louise was barred from his chamber, but it was

she who obtained a Catholic priest to administer the last rites. After his death Louise received assurance of protection from James and Louis, although her welcome when she crossed to France in 1685 was cold. After 1689 she spent her time chiefly at her estate in Aubigny, struggling against financial difficulties. Among those who saw Louise in old age was Voltaire, who thought her still very beautiful. She died on 14 November 1734, at Paris.

M. Forneron, *Louise de Kéroualle, duchesse de Portsmouth* (Paris, 1886).

J. M. P. J. Lemoine and André Lichtenberger, 'Louise de Kéroualle, duchesse de Portsmouth', *Revue de deux mondes*, 5th series, 14 (1903).

Portraits: oil, three-quarter length, by Philippe Vigrion, *c.* 1673: St. James's Palace; oil, by Lely, Hampton Court.

Killigrew, Thomas (1612–83), dramatist, theatrical producer, and wit.

Born 7 February 1612 in London, Killigrew was the son of Sir Robert Killigrew, a courtier. Already as a child, Thomas Killigrew showed an interest in the theatre, which developed further when, in 1633, he was appointed page to Charles I. He began to write poems and plays, of which two – *Claracilla* and *The Prisoner*, both romantic tragicomedies – were probably performed before 1636 (published 1641). Around 1640 his witty drama *The Parson's Wedding* was first performed; when it was revived 24 years later, Restoration society considered it so obscene that only women were allowed to act in it.

As a courtier, Killigrew naturally took the Royalist part in the Civil War and, as a result, was arrested by Parliament when he appeared in London in September 1642. Eventually he was released, and in 1644 made his way to Oxford, the King's headquarters, before leaving the country to travel on the Continent. In 1647 he joined the Paris court of the Prince of Wales, soon to become Charles II. His wit and debauchery won him a place in this monarch's heart, and in 1651 he was appointed Royalist resident in Venice; however, his recall was demanded the very next year, since his unscrupulous borrowing and general behaviour were not considered suitable for a diplomatic representative. The rest of the Interregnum he spent travelling and writing.

At the Restoration Killigrew returned to England where the King appointed him to several court posts and, as a mark of special favour, granted him a licence along with Davenant (q.v.) to establish two theatres and produce plays without reference to the *de facto* censor, the master of the revels. Killigrew's company was known as the King's Servants and soon established itself as a vehicle for the plays of Shakespeare, Killigrew, and others. For this company he built the first Theatre Royal, Drury Lane, which was opened in 1663. There he developed the use of scenery and music in his productions. In 1673 his position was further enhanced by his appointment as master of the revels.

Killigrew was famed for his wit and permitted an extraordinary freedom with the highest personages. When Louis XIV showed him a picture of the Crucifix hanging between portraits of the pope and himself, Killigrew is reputed to have responded, 'Though I have often heard said that our Saviour was hanged between two thieves, yet I never knew who they were till now.' This dramatist and jester died on 19 March 1683, at Whitehall.

M. Summers, *Restoration Comedies* (1921).

A. Harbage, *Thomas Killigrew* (Philadelphia, Pa., 1930).

King, Henry (1592–1669), poet and Bishop of Chichester.

The eldest son of John King, later Bishop of London, King was baptized on 16 January 1592. He was educated at Westminster School and Christ Church, Oxford, which he entered in 1609. After obtaining his degree he took holy orders and became a parish priest. As a young man he was a friend of Donne, whose executor he became, Jonson, and Izaak Walton. During the thirty years after leaving Oxford he rose slowly in the hierarchy, until in 1642 he was appointed Bishop of Chichester. This appointment coming at the outset of the Civil War, King did not enjoy it for long. On 29 December 1642, Chichester was overrun by the Parliamentarian army and the Bishop was among the prisoners. Being a noncombatant, he was released but, not being permitted to return to his see, was forced to seek refuge with friends in Buckinghamshire.

Here he spent the entire Interregnum. In 1657 he published *Poems, Elegies, Paradoxes, and Sonnets.* In the main unremarkable verses written many years before, this collection contains one poem that is as fine as any other Metaphysical poem. In 1617 King had married a girl called Anne Berkely. In seven years she bore him six children, only two of whom survived infancy; she died in 1624. King's poem *The Exequy: to his Matchless Never to be forgotten Friend* commemorates her death. Were it not for the tone of strongly borne but heartfelt grief that King establishes, the daring Metaphysical conceits and puns would seem coarse and in execrable taste. King pushes punning imagery to its most dangerous limits, relying on his sombre subject and sincere passion to carry him through. The result is that, for example, the pun on 'laid' in the following passage serves to heighten our awareness that King's loss is sexual as well as spiritual:

Mean time, thou has her, Earth: much good
May my harm do thee. . . .
So close the ground and 'bout her shade
Black curtains draw; my bride is laid.
Sleep on, my love, in thy cold bed,
Never to be disquieted!

It has to be recorded that in spite of King's protestation,

Dear Loss, since thy untimely fate
My task hath been to meditate
On thee, on thee. . .
       . . . This, only this
My exercise and business is,

he married again in 1630.

At the Restoration, King was restored to his see at Chichester. The rest of his life passed uneventfully and he died on 30 September 1669.

Margaret Crum (ed.), *The Poems of Henry King* (1965).
R. Berman, *Henry King and the Seventeenth Century* (1964).

Kneller, Sir Godfrey (1646–1723), painter and courtier.

Born Gottfried Kniller at Lübeck, North Germany, on 8 August 1646,

Kneller was the third son of Zacharias Kniller, the city surveyor and a competent portrait painter. After a false start as a military engineer, the young Kneller in 1668 turned to studying painting, first at Amsterdam under the fashionable portraitist Ferdinand Bol, a pupil of Rembrandt. Indeed, Kneller later claimed to have received the occasional lesson from Rembrandt himself; characteristically, he considered that great man's work lacking in 'true proportion and exact design'.

In 1672 Kneller travelled to Italy. In Rome he drew classical statuary, copied Raphael, and worked in the studios of Bernini and the society painter Carlo Maratti, while in Venice he foreshadowed his future career by managing to charm several portrait commissions from the local patrician families. Kneller's few extant early portraits are rather anonymous, merely reflecting the styles of his respective teachers, either Bol's dramatic lighting or Maratti's smudgy technique.

In 1675 Kneller's Dutch patron, Jacob del Böe, gave him a letter of recommendation to a wealthy London merchant, Jonathan Banks. Once arrived in England, Kneller, 'full of fire and ambition', lost no time in making influential contacts: through Banks he met James Vernon, secretary to the Duke of Monmouth, which led quickly to a commission from the Duke himself and eventually to one from Charles II (1678). The confident young Kneller was allowed to share the royal sitting with the aged and venerated Lely, whom he later baited in a rather unseemly way, principally by challenging him to painting competitions. From this moment on, Kneller's fame grew rapidly. He did several more portraits of Charles II and his Queen, and in 1684 went to Paris to paint Louis XIV. On the proceeds, he bought a large house in Covent Garden and began to live the life of a grand courtier. Kneller had no temperamental difficulty in coping with this sudden success: his contemporaries all agree in describing him as a man of immense energy, boundless ambition, and inordinate vanity. It was typical of him that in 1684 he physically assaulted one of the official investigators of the Painter-Stainer's company who had come to inspect his studio.

By the mid-1680s Kneller had matured as a painter. He had started his career in England working very much in the style of Lely. However, the older painter's portraits had contained a fundamental paradox: despite their superficial languidness of posture and lushness of colouring, they generally partook of a rigid overall uniformity of expression. By contrast, although Kneller's poses are apparently 'stiffer' and his paintwork sparser and more monochrome, he allowed himself a much wider range of feeling. This becomes apparent in a comparison of the straight-backed dignity of the portrait of Sir Charles Cotterell (1683) with the asymmetric melancholy of that of Philip, Earl of Leicester (1685).

James II soon showed himself as enthusiastic a patron of Kneller as his brother had been, and by late 1685 Evelyn's *Diary* speaks of Kneller as 'the famous painter'. When, in the autumn of 1688, a scandal arose in which the paternity of Prince James Edward was questioned, Kneller offered himself as an arbiter, claiming that he had painted so many portraits of the King and his family that he was by now expert in the physiognomical peculiarities of the Stuarts.

By the year of the Glorious Revolution, Kneller was the dominant artist of his age. His most serious rivals were recently dead or working abroad. The sovereigns of Europe, as well as almost everyone of any eminence in Britain, seemed uniformly eager to sit for him – during the 1690s he painted both Maximilian of Bavaria and Peter the Great. William and Mary made him their principal painter, to which he responded by producing the noble full-length painting of the two monarchs, now at Windsor. In March 1692 he was knighted and in 1695 granted an annuity of £200 per annum.

At the height of his success, Kneller's workload must have been enormous; he would receive up to fourteen sitters a day, charging on average £50 a head. To cope with all this he evolved something approaching a factory system. Since his distinguished clients were generally disinclined to 'keep the posture' for long, Kneller, always a fluent draughtsman, would simply make a quick chalk drawing of their faces. This he would translate into oils on canvas, then leave the remainder of the painting to his army of assistants, each of whom had a specific talent for depicting hands, hair, drapery, or costume, and so on. The inevitable result of this system was that Kneller's paintings are extremely uneven in quality. Nevertheless, his work is always well constructed, and when 'his fancy was warm', he painted the most vital and varied English portraits since Van Dyck; his portrait of John Dryden of about 1697, almost entirely in calm silver and grey, looks forward to the best of Reynolds, while that of Sir Isaac Newton of 1702 has a disquieting immediacy. He took up from Lely the tradition of painting series of portraits with a unifying theme, and although his initial efforts in this vein suffer from a sameness of posture and expression, in his later years it was to inspire some of his best paintings.

On her accession in 1702 Queen Anne retained Kneller as her principal painter. As his fortune increased, so did the bravura of his life style: in 1703 he bought an elegant house in Lincoln's Inn and began to build himself a sumptuous mansion (today known as Kneller Hall) at Whitton, near Hounslow. He became a J.P. for Middlesex, but tended to interpret the law in a highly personal way; Pope describes him as the magistrate.

Who sent the thief that stole the cash away
And punished him that put it in his way.

In 1711 he was appointed governor of the newly established Academy of Painting in London, where his advice deeply influenced the style of English portraiture for a generation. In 1715 George I, the fifth successive English monarch he had served, created him a baronet.

Perhaps his finest achievement is the Kit Cat portrait series of 1702 to 1717, which depicts the members of a club that was effectively 'the Whig party in its social aspect' and that included some of the finest political, scientific, and artistic minds of the day. The Kit Cat series (now in N.P.G.) is a matchless historical document.

Sir Godfrey Kneller died, rich and respected, on 19 October 1723, and was buried in his country estate. In 1729 a monument to him, carved by Rysbrack and with an epitaph by Pope, was erected in Westminster Abbey.

E. K. Waterhouse, *Painting in Britain, 1530–1790* (1930–55).
M. D. Whinney and O. Millar, *English Art, 1625–1714* (1957).

Portraits: oil, three-quarter length, studio of Kneller: N.P.G.; self-portrait, oil, quarter-length, c. 1680: V. & A. Museum.

L

Lambert, John (1619–84), Parliamentarian commander in the Civil War and one of Cromwell's most powerful generals.

Born into a family of the rising gentry, at Carlton in the West Riding of Yorkshire, he was probably educated at Trinity College, Cambridge, and at one of the Inns of Court. He was related to Sir Thomas Fairfax (q.v.) by marriage, and he entered Fairfax's service as a captain of horse in the Parliamentary forces at the beginning of the Civil War. He was an excellent officer, distinguishing himself in several engagements and reaching the rank of colonel before the end of 1643. He fought under Fairfax at Marston Moor (2 July 1644), and served him as commissary general before taking a commission in the New Model Army.

Although he was not present at the Battle of Naseby (1645), Lambert participated in the pursuit and in the last actions of the first Civil War. He was already being employed in semi-political tasks, such as arranging the surrender of towns, including Oxford, for which he acted as temporary governor. The Army officers chose him as their spokesman in 1647 in negotiations with Parliament, and he assisted Ireton (q.v.) in composing the Heads of the Army Proposals, the conservative scheme proposed as a settlement between the Army, the King, and Parliament. In July he was sent to Yorkshire to restore order in the mutinous northern army, a task he carried out with so much justice as to win the praise of soldier and civilian alike, increasing still further his popularity in the Army.

In the second Civil War, Lambert defeated the first Royalist risings in the north, but was forced to retreat by the superior army of the Scots Engagers, led by the Duke of Hamilton (see Hamilton, James). He joined Oliver Cromwell (q.v.) and helped to defeat the Scots at Preston. Left in command in the north, he was absent from the trial of Charles I, although he had been named a commissioner for the court.

When Charles II joined with the Scots, Lambert served as second-in-command to Cromwell, fighting at the victories of Dunbar (1650) and Worcester (1651). Lambert was by now a power in the state. Wealthy as a result of rewards, land purchases, and speculations, he was close to Cromwell, whose views on toleration, foreign policy, and other matters he shared. After Ireton's death he was the leader and foremost theoretician among the moderate army officers. The Rump Parliament appointed him Ireton's successor as lord deputy of Ireland (1652), but abolished the post a few months later. This action earned Lambert's enmity, and he began to favour the dissolution of the Rump, which finally took place in 1653. He drew up the Instrument of Government, which established the Protectorate, and was conspicuous in the inauguration of Cromwell. This constitution gave executive authority to the Protector with a Council, and Lambert was one of the Council's most powerful members. He was also the second man in the army, the basis of real power. In fact, his position was so strong that he seems to have overruled Cromwell on several important occasions, compelling the dissolution of the Parliament of 1654 and the purge of the Parliament of 1656. His was the idea to rule England by a network of major generals, and when in the spring of 1656 the Army demanded the separation of the posts of protector and general, it called for Lambert's appointment to the latter position.

Cromwell became increasingly estranged from Lambert and his allies. Cromwell's supporters and friends joined with the Presbyterians in Parliament to defeat an attempt by Lambert to institutionalize the hated rule of the major generals, thus clearing the way for the Humble Petition and Advice, which stripped the Council of most of its authority. Cromwell rebuffed Lambert and the officers when they petitioned him in February 1657 to reject this new constitution, although he was eventually persuaded not to take the title of King. Lambert's power was gone, and when he refused to swear an oath of fealty to the Protector, he was dismissed from his posts and retired to Wimbledon.

After Oliver Cromwell's death, Lambert gradually re-entered public life, initially as a supporter of Richard Cromwell (q.v.). In the spring of 1659 he regained command of his regiments, and was soon seated in the Council of State. Parliament gave him command of the expedition against the Royalist rising led by Sir George Booth (q.v.), but when the Army clashed with Parliament, he dissolved that body. The council sent him to oppose the advance of Monck (q.v.) from Scotland, but Lambert delayed engaging the opposing force in the hope of negotiating a settlement, and his army soon melted away.

The restored Parliament stripped him of his commands and imprisoned him.

He escaped, and in an effort to foil the Restoration, attempted to raise a rebellion in conjunction with republicans, but was easily defeated and sent to the Tower. In 1662 the court of king's bench sentenced him to death for his deeds during the Civil War, but Charles granted him a reprieve and banished him to Guernsey. Lambert passed the remainder of his life under surveillance, without being an actual prisoner, and died in March 1684 on St. Nicholas Island off Plymouth. Until his last days his was a name mentioned in rumours of plots, whether republican or papist, for the memory of his military ability and past power lived on.

Maurice Ashley, *Cromwell's Generals* (1954).
W. H. Dawson, *Cromwell's Understudy: General John Lambert* (1938).
George W. Heath, 'Cromwell and Lambert, 1653–57', in *Cromwell: A Profile*, ed. Ivan Roots (1973).
C. E. Lucas Phillips, *Cromwell's Captains* (1938).

Portrait: oil, half-length, after Robert Walker: N.P.G.

Laud, William (1573–1645), High Churchman, Archbishop of Canterbury, and one of the principal government ministers of Charles I.

Born at Reading on 7 October 1573, Laud was the only son of William Laud, a clothier. He was educated at Reading Free School and St. John's College, Oxford, gaining the degrees of B.A. (1594) and D.D. (1608). He was ordained in 1601 and, while still attending his college as a fellow, took up the post of chaplain to Charles Blount, Earl of Devonshire, in 1603.

Confirmed in his opposition to Puritanism even as a student, Laud showed his uncompromising episcopacy by declaring in his thesis for the degree of bachelor of divinity that a 'true church' was impossible without diocesan bishops. For

this and for other 'popish' opinions he was reprimanded by the college authorities.

In 1607 he became vicar of Stanford in Northamptonshire. A year later, he was appointed chaplain to Richard Neile, bishop of Rochester, who considerably boosted his career. In 1610 Laud resigned his fellowship at St. John's and was presented by Neile to the living of Cuxton in Kent, where he remained until 1611. In that year, he was elected president of his old college at Oxford. By 1616 he had become Dean of Gloucester.

Having come to the attention of James I, Laud accompanied him to Scotland in 1617, where he incurred the Presbyterians' anger by wearing the surplice, which they took to be an unequivocal symbol of popery. After his appointment as Bishop of St. David's in 1621, he became involved in the following year at the King's behest in a dispute with the Jesuit John Fisher concerning the conversion to Roman Catholicism of the Countess of Buckingham.

Laud's point of view consisted in accepting the Roman Church as a true church, but he repudiated the concept of papal infallibility. Regarding the Church of England, he asserted that belief should be founded not upon the Thirty-Nine Articles but upon the Bible. 'A lawful and free council, determining according to Scripture, is the best judge on earth.'

Now he met Buckingham (see Villiers, George, 1st Duke), the countess's son and the King's favourite, an association from which he profited. He gained prominence in the establishment of the church and in 1625 the new King, Charles I, made him Dean of the Chapel Royal.

Charles liked Laud because of his High Church orthodoxy and allowed him considerable latitude. Laud was thus in a position to affect directly the prospects of English clergymen. In a list that he drew up for the King, he distinguished the clergy who supported the established forms of religion and were therefore worthy of advancement from the Puritan radicals, who were to be suppressed. In 1626 he was appointed Bishop of Bath and Wells, becoming Bishop of London two years later.

Laud's solidarity with the King against Parliament was staunch. His influence saved Richard Montagu (q.v.) from impeachment by the Commons for his anti-Calvinist publications and he gave assistance on behalf of Buckingham. When Charles commenced his period of nonparliamentary administration in 1629, he chose Laud as one of his chief advisers.

In 1630 Laud was appointed chancellor of Oxford University and in 1633 he became Archbishop of Canterbury. His power was now very considerable. He was a judge in the Star Chamber, a member of the treasury commission, and a privy councillor. Laud showed an uncompromising attitude in pursuing his ministerial duties. In 1633 he wrote to Wentworth saying, 'As for the state, indeed, I am for *Thorough*' – the policy of efficient arbitrary rule by the monarch and his advisers. His support for the catholicity of the English Church manifested itself in his imposition of uniform and mandatory religious ceremonies and customs that alienated not only the already hostile Puritans but other churchmen also. In addition to his ordering of services and conditions of worship, he undertook the renovation of church buildings.

His hostility towards opponents or dissidents was extreme. Those who spoke or acted against the state religion as Laud himself now constituted it were punished with great severity. He exercised a particular cruelty in the punishment of Alexander Leighton, whose pamphlet *Zion's Plea against the Prelacie* constituted an attack on episcopacy, and was a party to the judgment of mutilation and life imprisonment visited upon William Prynne, John Bastwick, and Henry Burton (qq.v.).

The extension of his religious system to Scotland was initiated in 1637 and met with utter hatred on the part of the Presbyterians. The new liturgy based on the Book of Common Prayer was drawn up by the Scottish bishops working in collaboration with Laud and the imposition of this liturgy along with other innovations was seen as an attack both on the Scots' religion and on their independence. The subsequent signing of the National Covenant and the ensuing wars – the Bishops' Wars – were direct results of Laud's attempt to impose uniformity.

Laud was among those who advised Charles I to reconvene Parliament in 1640. In that year, Laud caused to be passed a measure under whose terms all classes of men were to be made to swear an oath of eternal allegiance to 'the government of this church by archbishops, bishops, deans and archdeacons, etc.' – known as the 'Et Cetera oath'.

The failure of the Second Bishops' War in 1640 and the subsequent impeachment of Thomas Wentworth (q.v.), Earl of Strafford, who had led the King's army against Scotland and who was one of Laud's closest associates in pursuance of the policy of *Thorough*, marked the end of Laud's ascendancy. He was attacked on all sides as the chief author of Charles's most hated and divisive policies. He was forced to withdraw the Et Cetera oath and a month later, on 18 December 1640, was impeached by the Long Parliament and confined to the Tower. Here he remained for almost four years. He was granted a royal pardon in 1643, but such a gesture on the part of Charles in the midst of civil war was ineffectual. In the same year William Prynne, entrusted by Parliament with Laud's papers, published a distorted travesty of his diary. In March 1644 a further trial opened. Sentence of death was eventually managed by the passage of an act of attainder and he was beheaded at the age of seventy-one on 10 January 1645.

Laud was a man of consistent but drastically narrow views. His intolerance, forcefulness, and unwillingness to compromise may be seen as a contributory cause of the Civil War.

W. F. Collins (ed.), *Archbishop Laud Commemoration* (1895).

W. H. Hutton, *William Laud* (1895).

H. R. Trevor-Roper, *Archbishop Laud* (1962, 2nd ed.).

Laud's works appear in the *Library of Anglo-Catholic Theology* (7 vols.; 1847–60).

Portrait: oil, three-quarter length, after Van Dyck, *c.* 1636: N.P.G.

Lauderdale, 2nd Earl and 1st Duke of (1616–82), see Maitland, John.

Law, John (1671–1729), Scottish financier and speculator, see *Lives of the Georgian Age*.

Lawes, Henry (1596–1662), English composer.

Born on 5 January 1596, at Dinton in Wiltshire, Lawes received his musical education in London from John Cooper, a noted musician and teacher who had spent many years in Italy. In 1626, when Henry was thirty, he was sworn in as an epistler (one who reads the epistle in the Communion service) and gentleman of the Chapel Royal. Later, he became musician in ordinary to the King and then (about 1633) music master to the Earl of Bridgwater. In 1634 he provided the music for Milton's masque *Comus*, performed at Ludlow Castle, singing the part of the Attendant Spirit himself. Lawes was in fact an accomplished singer and his musical settings of words are remarkable for what Milton called their 'just note and accent' (*To Mr. H. Lawes on his Airs*, included in *Choice Psalms*, 1648).

Whatever his friendship with Milton may have been, he does not seem to have shared the poet's republican attitude. During the Commonwealth, he was deprived of his court appointments, but was restored to them upon the accession of Charles II. For Charles's coronation in 1661 Henry composed a setting of *Zadok the Priest*. He died in London on 21 October 1662, and is buried in Westminster Abbey.

Henry contributed, with his brother William Lawes (q.v.), to *Choice Psalms put into Musick for Three Voices* (1648), and Playford published some of his compositions in *Select Musicall Ayres and Dialogues* (1652, 1653, and 1658) and *The Treasury of Musick* (1669). He also wrote settings of poems by Milton, Herrick, and Davenant.

Willa McClung Evans, *Henry Lawes: Musician and Friend of Poets* (New York, 1941).
R. F. Hart, 'Introduction to Henry Lawes', *Music and Letters* (1951).

Lawes, William (1602–45), English composer and brother of Henry Lawes (q.v.).

Baptized in Salisbury on 1 May 1602, William Lawes studied music with his brother under John Cooper in London. In 1635 he became musician in ordinary in the Chapel Royal of Charles I and joined the King's forces at the outbreak of the Civil War. He died in battle at the siege of Chester in September 1645.

His importance lies in the music that he wrote for some of the court masques of the period, notably James Shirley's *Triumph of Peace* (1634) and Davenant's *The Triumph of the Prince d'Amour* (1635). But his instrumental music is also very important, using as it does bold experimental dissonances. His viol consorts are especially interesting. Of his vocal music, the best remembered is his part-song setting of Herrick's *Gather ye Rosebuds while ye may*.

M. Lefkovitz, *William Lawes* (1960).

Lee, Nathaniel (?1653–92), dramatist; author of many heroic plays of the Restoration period.

Said to have been the son of a clergyman, Lee was educated at Westminster School and Trinity College, Cambridge, where he obtained a B.A. in 1667. He was reportedly a handsome youth, brought to London by the Duke of Buckingham, and instructed in vices by the Earl of Rochester.

Alone in London, he decided to make a living as an actor, but his first appearance, in Davenant's adaptation of *Macbeth* (1668) was a flop. Accordingly he took to the writing of tragedies. His first play, *Nero*, in heroic couplets, was produced in 1675. The following year saw the production of *Gloriana* and *Sophonisba*, but it was not until 1677 that Lee's reputation was established, with *The Rival Queens*, which records in blank verse the jealousy of two wives of Alexander the Great, resulting in the death of both of them. This play was immensely popular, was frequently revived, and is typical of the work of Lee. It is characterized by extravagance of plot and character, cavalier treatment of the sources upon which his work was based, disregard for strains on the audience's credulity, and long ranting speeches, often in rhyme, that are little to the point but were thought stirring stuff by contemporary audiences.

Lee's other 'heroic' tragedies are *Mithridates* (1678), *Caesar Borgia* (1680), *Theodosius* (1680), *Lucius Junius Brutus* (1681), and *Constantine the Great* (1683). With Dryden, he worked on *Oedipus* (1679) and *The Duke of Guise* (1682). He tried his hand at a comedy (*The Princess of Cleve*), but, although bawdy enough for any taste, it was a failure and he wrote no more in that vein.

For all its 'furious fustian and turgid rant' (Colley Cibber), Lee's imagination did have a spark of real poetry in it; a fair picture is perhaps that of Addison: 'Lee's thoughts are ... frequently lost in such a cloud of words that it is hard to see the beauty of them. There is an infinite fire in his works, but so involved in smoke that it does not appear in half its lustre.' He was always of an excitable temperament, and by the middle of 1684 it was apparent to his acquaintances that his excitability was quite abnormal. He was an exceedingly heavy drinker – there is a story that the Earl of Pembroke's butler suspected him of a deliberate effort to drink the cellar dry –

and in a letter written some time before Dryden speaks of 'poor Nat Lee ... upon the verge of madness'. Now it was obvious that he had crossed the verge, and on 11 November 1684, he was confined to Bedlam. Here he remained for five years; in 1689 he was adjudged sober enough and sane enough to be released. He was popular with the actors of the Theatre Royal, who set aside £10 a year as a pension for him. He wrote no more, however, and although he touched up and produced an early work of his, *The Massacre of Paris*, within a year he was back on the bottle.

His wits were failing again when one night in the spring of 1692 he was returning from the Bear and Harrow to his lodgings in Duke Street; the following morning he was found dead in the street. He was buried at St. Clement Danes on 6 May 1692.

T. B. Stroup and A. L. Cooke (eds.), *The Works of Nathaniel Lee* (2 vols.; New Brunswick, N. J., 1954–55).

Roswell G. Ham, *Otway and Lee* (New Haven, Conn., 1931).

Portrait: oil, by Dobson: Garrick Club, London.

Leeds, 1st Duke of (1631–1712), see Osborne, Thomas.

Lely, Sir Peter (1618–80), portrait painter.

He was born Peter van der Faes in Soest, Westphalia, on 14 October 1618, son of Johan van der Faes, a Flemish infantry captain in the service of the Elector of Brandenburg. Lely, the name he always used in England, was taken from a house in The Hague, his father's birthplace, which had a lily as its sign.

Little is known of Lely's early life, except that by 1637 he was apprenticed to Franz de Grebber, a successful Haarlem portrait painter. He probably first came to England for the marriage of Prince William of Orange to Princess Mary, daughter of Charles I, in 1641, the year in which Van Dyck died. At first Lely painted chiefly landscapes and historical pieces rather than portraits. In 1647, however, he met the Duke of Northumberland, whose patronage soon brought him commissions for portraits from other members of the court, as well as a chance to study the Duke's collection of Van Dyck paintings. Northumberland was custodian of the captive Charles I's children, and Lely painted for him the Van Dyckian double portrait, now at Syon, of the King and the Duke of York, and the more original group portrait, now at Petworth, of Charles's three younger children in a wooded park. The latter painting set the fashion of 'a portrait in a landscape' that lasted into the late eighteenth century in English painting. Among Lely's closest friends at this time was the Royalist poet Lovelace (q.v.), who praised 'Pow'r-ful Lilly's' painting of the King for its 'clouded majesty'.

Although Lely's earlier portraits often betray their debt to Van Dyck, they can also show considerable originality and power. His forceful line, bold shapes, and rich palette were unparalleled in England at that time. Even in the many pastoral portraits of the Sidney and Percy families, then his principal sitters, the dreaminess typical of Van Dyck has given way to a more positive feeling; in the painting of Henry Sidney dressed as a shepherd (at Penshurst), the little boy gazes candidly, if a little self-consciously, out of the canvas.

By 1650 Lely was rich enough to afford a house in the Covent Garden piazza and a summer residence at Kew. This was due in part to his skill in adapting to the contemporary political situation. At £6 for a head and £10 for a half-length, he was happy to paint the Royalist aristocracy, depicting its elegant ladies, such as Lady Dering (at Parham), in relaxed poses, dressed in silvery-textured draperies and set in rustic surroundings. The men, for example Sir William Compton (at Ham House), he would render more incisively, in a manner reminiscent of Dobson (q.v.), but perhaps his most original work at this period is the handful of pretty child portraits, such as that of the Duke of Somerset and Lady Elizabeth Seymour. He was equally diligent in seeking the custom of the new men of Parliament, as is shown by his abortive project of 1651 to cover the walls of Whitehall with a pictorial record of their glorious deeds. In 1653 he did a powerful and austere portrait of Cromwell. He also painted at this time numerous 'subject' pieces, apparently very much to the Puritan taste, which were at worst derivative and at best merely decorative. The demand for subject painting fell off after 1655, which provoked Lely's friend Lovelace to castigate the great ones of England for desiring only 'their own dull counterfeits'.

In the spring of 1656 Lely visited Holland, probably to ingratiate himself with the still-exiled Charles II, for at the Restoration Lely was immediately appointed principal court painter and granted the same pension as Van Dyck had received. From this time onwards, a change came over Lely's painting. He launched into mass production of rather monotonous society portraits. His brushwork became thinner and drier, the masses simpler, and the accessories, such as classical busts and columns, often degenerated into mere affectation. By 1671 Lely's prices had gone up to £20 for a head and £60 for a full-length, and he had evolved a rigid studio schedule. He would begin painting at seven sharp and work throughout the day, allotting a fixed amount of time to each sitter, most of whom had booked weeks earlier – latecomers, however eminent, were forced to miss their turn. Details of drapery and background were then filled in by a team of competent minor painters, such as Gaspars and Lankrink. Largillierre worked for a time as Lely's assistant, and took the English portrait style back to France with him.

The best and the worst of Lely can be found in his two great portrait series. The Windsor Beauties, commissioned by the Duchess of York, depicts the great ladies of court in drooping poses, eyes half-closed, and dresses dishevelled in a mildly salacious way. Though brilliant in technique, these fashion-plate portraits lack psychological insight, a shortcoming that did not elude Lely's contemporaries; Pepys said they were 'good, but not like', and Walker insisted they were 'all Brothers & Sisters'. The series of Maids of Honour at Hampton Court is painted in similar style. In contrast, the Greenwich Admirals of 1666–67 combine a sharp interpretation of personality with a crisp technique, and are quite the equal of anything being done in Holland at that time.

Certainly, Lely was the best painter of his day in England; when Lely's brush was free of the unimaginative constraints imposed by his aristocratic sitters, as in his portrait of the foreigner Van Helmont (National Gallery), he approaches genius.

Lely was knighted on 11 January 1680, but died on 7 December of the same year and was buried in St. Paul's, Covent Garden, where he is commemorated by a Grinling Gibbons bust. Although Lely's talent was uneven, it is tribute enough to him that he was a major influence in setting the fashion for every kind of English portraiture throughout the next century.

R. B. Becket, *Lely* (1951).
C. H. Collins Baker, *Lely and the Stuart Portrait Painters* (1912).

Portraits: oil, head, after Lely, *c.* 1670: N.P.G.; self-portrait, oil, three-quarter length, *c.* 1660: N.P.G.

Leslie, Alexander (?1580–1661), 1st Earl of Leven; Scottish military commander in the Civil War.

Son of George Leslie, captain of Blair Atholl castle. Alexander Leslie embarked upon his military career in the Netherlands and in 1605 entered the Swedish service, becoming Gustavus Adolphus's chief officer in 1628, when the King entered the Thirty Years War. Two years later he was attached to Hamilton's contingent as sergeant major general, subsequently returning to the Swedish army until 1638, by which time he had gained immense experience, material rewards, and the rank of field marshal.

The affairs of his native country then claimed his active interest and services. He took the Covenant as a matter of personal conviction and was placed in charge of the military preparations to defend it against attack from England, being appointed lord general of all the Scottish forces on 9 May 1639. Two months earlier, he had seized Edinburgh Castle for the Covenanters by a surprise assault with a handful of men, and when King Charles I approached the border in June, Leslie confronted him with 30,000 horse and foot, enough (with his reputation) to induce a negotiated end to the First Bishops' War. A condition of the settlement was the cancellation of his commission, which the Scots were reluctant to allow, but Leslie resolved the issue by resigning, not really relishing civil war.

He was recalled to office in April 1640 for the Second Bishops' War, and on this occasion his bid for Edinburgh

Castle failed. He did not wait on the defensive, but in August crossed the border, seized Newcastle and the surrounding coalfields after the collapse of the English army at Newburn, and held this district as a bargaining counter for a whole year in defiance of the King at York. When Charles eventually yielded, Leslie escorted him to Scotland, acted as host, and was created Earl of Leven and Lord Balgonie, made a privy councillor, and appointed as captain of Edinburgh Castle. This was supplemented by the Scottish parliament's grant of cash, and he laid down his office once more.

At the end of 1641 he was involved in proposals to raise a Scottish army to assist the Elector Palatine, the King's nephew, in Bohemia, but the rising in Ireland put an end to such Royalist altruism. In 1642 the Scottish army crossed to Ireland instead, and in May Leslie was appointed its general. He took little part in the campaign, spending only the autumn months in that country and leaving the command of the army to Robert Monro. The possibility of a Scottish army being sent to support the English Parliamentarians was under discussion, and in this he played a leading part, despite his earlier protestations of lasting loyalty to the King.

The army was ready by the end of 1643, 22,000 strong with Leslie again in command, and on 19 January 1644, it crossed the Tweed, driving back the Marquis of Newcastle's forces and joining the English Parliamentarians in the siege of York and the Battle of Marston Moor (2 July), in which Leslie had charge of the infantry of the centre, and as the senior general had overall responsibility for the allied dispositions.

When the battle appeared to be going against him, he fled the field, but was not the only senior officer to do so on that day.

The Scottish army remained in England for the rest of the first Civil War, becoming steadily disenchanted with the provision made for it by the English Parliament, being forced to subsist off the country, and enjoying mixed military fortunes. The assault of Newcastle (18 October 1644) was Leslie's crowning act; thereafter, old age inexorably reduced his real capabilities, while it increased his prestige and indispensability. In his headquarters at Newcastle, he acted as host to Charles I once more after the King surrendered to the Scots at Newark (5 May 1646), and in January 1647 Charles was handed over to the English and Leslie led his army home.

In the following year, the dominant faction in Scottish politics led by Hamilton (q.v.) launched a Scottish army into England to rescue the King from the extremists. Leslie was installed in command, but was tactfully relieved of it almost at once, to the subsequent advantage of his own reputation in view of the army's failure. Instead, he was given charge of the home forces, and was called upon to do no more than support the safety of the government and play host to the victorious Cromwell at Edinburgh Castle.

When the Scots declared for Charles II in 1650, Leslie was again (and under protest) charged with the command of the forces prepared to defend Scotland against an invasion from England, but active command in the field devolved upon David Leslie (q.v.). Some were inclined to attribute the disaster at Dunbar (3 September 1650) to the older man, and he was willing to accept responsibility, but the Scots parliament officially and correctly exonerated him.

In August 1651 he and other Scottish leaders were surprised by English cavalry and taken prisoner. He was confined in the Tower, but this was later commuted to restricted residence with his son-in-law, Ralph Delavall, in Northumberland. He was released in 1654 and spent his remaining years on his own estate at Balgonie, Fifeshire, dying in 1661.

William Fraser, *The Melvilles, earls of Melville, and the Leslies, earls of Leven* (3 vols.; 1890).

R. Howell, *Newcastle-upon-Tyne and the Puritan Revolution* (1967).

C. S. Terry, *The Life and Campaigns of Alexander, First Earl of Leven* (1899).

P. Young, *Marston Moor* (1970).

Leslie, Charles (1650–1722), Anglican divine and Nonjuror.

Born in Dublin on 17 July 1650, the sixth son of John Leslie, Bishop of Raphoe and afterwards Clogher, Leslie was educated at Enniskillen school and Trinity College, Dublin, where he took an M.A. in 1673. He studied law in London for some time, but in 1680 took holy orders. In 1686 he was appointed chancellor of Connor through the influence of the Earl of Clarendon.

His loyalty to James II remained unshaken by the 1688 Revolution, and he refused to take oaths of allegiance to William III. (Those clerics who refused were termed 'Nonjurors'.) As a result, he was deprived of his chancellorship. He returned to London, where he became chaplain in the household of the Earl of Clarendon and began writing a series of controversial pamphlets, starting with *An Answer to a Book entitled the State of the Protestants in Ireland under the late King James's Government*, published in London in 1692. In 1693 Leslie went abroad and visited the Pretender at St. Germain. On his return to England, in 1695, he published a virulent attack on William III in a pamphlet entitled *Gallienus Redivivus, or Murther will out*. This publication is a major source for information on the massacre of the Mac-

donalds at Glencoe (see Macdonald, Alexander).

He continued to produce a steady stream of pamphlets attacking Whig clerics such as Burnet, Tillotson, and Sherlock, as well as Quakers and Jews. He brought out the periodical *The Rehearsal* (1704–09) in response to Defoe's *Review*. Leslie's particular brand of ecclesiastical and political commentating flowed on uninterrupted until, in 1710, a warrant was issued for his arrest. He fled to Berkshire and, in 1711, made his escape to St. Germain. Later, he returned to England, but in 1713 accepted a place in the household of the Pretender at Bar-le-Duc, where he continued to produce pamphlets and letters. In the autumn of 1721 he returned to Ireland and died at Glaslough on 13 April 1722.

Charles Leslie, *The Theological Works* (1721: reprinted in 7 vols.; 1832).

Leslie, David (d. 1682), 1st Baron Newark; Scottish military commander in the Civil War.

David Leslie was the son of Sir Patrick Leslie of Pitcairly, Fifeshire. Like his older kinsman, Alexander Leslie (q.v.), he learned his military profession under Gustavus Adolphus, becoming a colonel of horse and returning with other Scots in the Swedish service to assist the Covenanters in 1640. In November 1643 he was appointed major general in the Scottish army that crossed into England in January 1644 to support the Parliamentarians.

At Marston Moor (2 July) he commanded the third line of horse on the left wing in reserve to Cromwell, giving active support in that part of the field where the battle was decided for the allies. After the fall of York, he was sent to assist in the siege of Newcastle, being switched before the assault took place to conduct operations against the Royalists in Cumberland and Westmorland. He besieged Carlisle, which capitulated on 28 June 1645. Subsequently, he moved down into the Midlands until summoned back to Scotland to deal with Montrose (see Graham, James) after the latter's victory at Kilsyth (15 August).

Taking all his 4,000 horse, he re-entered Scotland on the east coast on 6 September and brought Montrose to battle on 13 September at Philiphaugh, taking him by surprise and routing his army completely. Montrose escaped, but when it became clear that he was no longer a threat to the government Leslie returned to the army in England. In January 1647 the army marched back to Scotland and was reduced, the first English Civil War being over. Promoted lieutenant general, Leslie was employed against the last of the rebels in the Highlands among the Gordons and MacDonalds, but stood aside from the army of intervention that Hamilton (q.v.) led into England in July 1648, taking his cue for refusal from the disapproval of the Kirk authorities.

In March 1650, Montrose reappeared in the north of Scotland to raise the country for Charles II, and Leslie deployed scattered forces against him, a single column of which sufficed to break Montrose's small army before its march even began. Montrose was betrayed to Leslie, who escorted him to his death in Edinburgh in a particularly humiliating manner.

When Charles II agreed to accept the Covenant, Leslie became the field commander of the army raised to maintain him against the inevitable English reaction. On 22 July 1650, Cromwell crossed the border from Berwick with the New Model Army, Leslie offering no defence but waiting in a prepared position in front of Edinburgh, having caused the devastation of the countryside between. Cromwell was supplied by sea through Dunbar, but found Leslie too strongly posted to attack, whereupon he withdrew to his port. Leslie followed, and placed his larger force across Cromwell's line of communication with England. Yet it was Cromwell who attacked (3 September 1650) and the Scots who broke.

Leslie abandoned Edinburgh, collecting such troops as he could at Stirling on the orders of the government and providing a rallying point for separate Scottish forces of differing political factions and also for English Royalists. After his coronation on 1 January 1651, Charles took command of the Scottish army, with Leslie as his lieutenant general. Cromwell made attempts to manœuvre him out of his strong position in the midsummer, being unable to attack him directly, and eventually put the bulk of his army across the Firth of Forth and astride Leslie's lines of communication with his areas of support. Leslie would have preferred to have fought to re-establish them, but Charles ordered a march into England, the way being now open.

The march led to a defeat at Worcester (3 September 1651), the English having failed to rise and Cromwell having pursued closely. Leslie appears to have been dispirited by the turn of events, and quite unable to control them. He was captured at Chester on 17 September, fined heavily, and committed to the Tower, remaining confined until 1660.

On 3 August 1661, he was created a baron and granted a pension of £500 a year in recognition of his services to the King. He spent the remainder of his life in retirement, dying in 1682.

Peter Young, *Marston Moor* (1970).

Leven, 1st Earl of (?1580–1661), see Leslie, Alexander.

Lilburne, John (1614–57), Puritan radical and pamphleteer.

John Lilburne was born in Greenwich, the son of Richard Lilburne, a gentleman of Thickley Punchendon, Durham. He was educated in schools in Auckland and Newcastle and around 1630 began an apprenticeship to a London clothier. In his spare time he read the Bible and Protestant works, especially the Puritan writings. This literature probably contributed greatly to his hatred of popery and prelacy and to his elevation of divine law to a position above individual statutes or decrees. It certainly led him to sympathize with Dr. John Bastwick (q.v.), the anti-episcopal writer, whom he met in 1636 in the Gatehouse prison. Lilburne aided the clandestine publication of Bastwick's *Litany*. This action, together with his associations with Puritan pamphleteers, forced him to leave the country for a while.

Returning in December 1637, Lilburne was arrested and brought before the court of Star Chamber. He refused to take the oath and denounced the court's procedures as contrary to the law of the land. He was fined and whipped from the Fleet to Palace Yard, winning the sympathy of the populace by his exhortations and his sufferings for the Puritan cause. Put in the pillory, he distributed copies of Bastwick's tracts and spoke against the bishops until gagged. In prison he wrote pamphlets describing his trials and justifying religious independence.

Lilburne's conduct on this occasion set the pattern for his numerous confrontations with judicial bodies. He refused to be intimidated and rejected offers of a pardon, standing on his rights as a free Englishman to be treated according to the law of the land. Thus his release when the Long Parliament met in 1640 was to be expected. A petition on his behalf was presented by Oliver Cromwell (q.v.), and he received his freedom together with other political prisoners. Lilburne set up as a brewer and married Elizabeth Dewell, with whom he shared a close relationship although never much of a home life. Already in May 1641 he was in trouble again, called before the bar of the House of Lords for words spoken against the King.

When the Civil War began, Lilburne received a captain's commission, fighting at Edgehill and Buntford, where he was taken prisoner. The Royalists removed him to Oxford, tried him for treason, and would certainly have executed him had not threats of Parliamentary reprisals secured his freedom via an exchange in 1643. He entered the Earl of Manchester's army, in which he rose to the rank of lieutenant colonel, and began to work with Cromwell. He acted as one of Cromwell's witnesses in his accusations against Manchester, for he too regarded the latter as lukewarm in his prosecution of the war.

Lilburne's propensity not only to disagree but also to quarrel on grounds of principle blossomed after he left the army in April 1645. An attack on intolerant Presbyterianism aroused the ire of William Prynne (q.v.). This and his pamphlets led to his repeated summoning for examination by the House of Commons. These activities did not speed up parliamentary consideration of financial compensation for his sufferings and services, despite Cromwell's support. Radical pamphlets and refusals to recognize the judicial competence and methods of procedure of parliamentary committees – or the authority of the

Lords – provoked his imprisonment, eventually in the Tower itself (June 1646). From there he wrote pamphlets attacking the monarchy and abuses in city elections, appealing for his release to the full House of Commons as the 'supreme authority in England,' condemning them for their slowness, and finally appealing to the Army. His case was taken up by the radicals among the rank-and-file. He allied himself with these and the Levellers and joined in the call for constitutional change tending towards full republican democracy.

The vicissitudes of politics saw him in and out of prison several times in the next few years. All the while his antagonism to Cromwell and the 'Grandees' was growing. Finally, in October 1649, in the belief that his writings stimulated mutiny, the Council of State put him on trial for high treason in the Guildhall.

By this time John Lilburne was something of a popular hero. Troops had to be stationed around the court when the special commissioner began the proceedings. Lilburne fought on technicalities, denied the jurisdiction of the judges, denounced the laws under which he was charged, and called upon the jurors to judge the law as well as the facts, for in them alone was 'the judicial power of the law'. The jury acquitted him to the joyous demonstrations of the populace.

At liberty for a few years, Lilburne worked as a soap boiler in London and engaged in numerous causes, such as campaigns against monopolies and enclosures. But his intemperate support for his uncle, George Lilburne, in a dispute with Sir Arthur Hesilrige (q.v.) over properties provided the Commons with an excuse to banish him for life in January 1652.

Lilburne now lived in various cities in the Low Countries, constantly writing and attacking the Government. His opposition to the Rump brought him into contact with exiled Royalists, some of whom saw him as a potential ally. However, Cromwell's expulsion of the Rump roused new hope in him, and in June 1653 he returned to London, only to be promptly jailed. In vain he appealed to Cromwell to be set free to live peaceably. Support came once again from the politically active among the common people. Prayers and petitions came forward for 'Free-born John'. A pamphlet expounding his principles was eagerly read.

Lilburne was, however, viewed as a great danger by the Protectorate; hence, in July he was brought to trial at the Old Bailey on the grounds that by returning to England he became a felon subject to the death penalty. He fought this charge in the same manner as his treason trial and was acquitted in August. Great rejoicing followed, in which the soldiers on duty at the court took part.

Despite the decision of the jury, Cromwell kept Lilburne in prison. His health deteriorated as he was moved from the Tower to Jersey, but he still turned down freedom through a pardon and demanded it as his right. His family's plea brought about his removal in 1655 to Dover Castle, where he became a Quaker. His conversion to the way of George Fox led Cromwell to relax his imprisonment and Lilburne was allowed out on parole. He died on 29 August 1657, in Eltham, Kent.

H. N. Brailsford, *The Levellers* (1961).

Joseph Frank, *The Levellers: A History of the Writings of three Seventeenth Century Democrats, John Lilburne, Richard Overton, and William Walwyn* (Cambridge, Mass., 1955).

M. A. Gibb, *John Lilburne the Leveller* (1947).

Pauline Gregg, *Freeborn John* (1961).

Locke, John (1632–1704), the chief English philosopher of the Age of Enlightenment.

Locke was born on 29 August 1632, at Wrington, Somerset, about ten miles from Bristol. His mother, a pious woman, died while he was a child. His father, John Locke, was an attorney who fought as a captain on the Parliamentary side in the Civil War. He also served as clerk to the Somerset Justices of the Peace and acted as agent for one of them, Alexander Popham, whose regiment he joined in the war. The elder Locke did not profit by the war and left a smaller inheritance to his son than that which he himself had inherited. The family nevertheless had property and a comfortable income, and this gave Locke a measure of independence in later life. Relations between father and son were good. Locke wrote that his father 'lived perfectly with him as a friend', asked his advice about matters of business, and in general, it appears, treated his son as an equal.

About 1646 Locke was sent to attend Westminster School, where, with the help of Popham, who had become M.P. for Bath in the Long Parliament, he was placed on the foundation. In 1652 he attended Christ Church, Oxford, where he received his B.A. in 1656 and his M.A. in 1658, thereupon being elected to a studentship. From this time until he joined the Earl of Shaftesbury's household in 1667, Locke resided mainly at Oxford. He seems at first to have intended to take holy orders, which were required for the continuation of his studentship, but in 1666 decided against this step, perhaps because of intellectual reservations, and was granted dispensation by royal mandate in the same year. Reacting against the Aristotelianism that was taught at Oxford, Locke eventually read the works of Descartes and fell

under the influence of Cartesian rationalism. This, together with what he had learnt of the experimental science of men like Robert Boyle (q.v.), whose acquaintance Locke made at Oxford and who remained his friend throughout his life, had a long-lasting effect on his thought. He also attended lectures on chemistry and studied medicine, and in 1674 took an M.B. degree. At that time he transferred to a medical studentship at Christ Church but, although he was for a while a practising physician, he never took an M.D. degree and was clearly not content with medicine as a career.

Apart from a Latin and an English poem that he contributed to a collection of verses, Locke published nothing under his own name while he was at Oxford. He performed various academic duties, however, and was lecturer in Greek and in rhetoric and censor of moral philosophy. In 1661 his father died, leaving him part of his property. Upon the death of his brother soon afterwards, Locke probably inherited all of his father's estate. In the winter of

1665–66 he went as secretary on a diplomatic mission to Frederick William, Elector of Brandenburg. He returned in February and later in the year met his future patron, Anthony Ashley Cooper (q.v.), at this time Lord Ashley, later the 1st Earl of Shaftesbury. Ashley, who was chancellor of the exchequer, required some medicinal water while he was visiting his son at Oxford. Locke was introduced to him, attended to his needs, and the two men were soon friends. The following year, while continuing to hold his studentship at Christ Church, Locke became a member of Ashley's household at Exeter House in the Strand. Although at first he acted as the family physician – he performed an operation on Ashley in 1668 and attended at the birth of his grandson, the 3rd Earl of Shaftesbury, in 1670 – Locke played a more prominent role as Ashley's confidential secretary and was much engaged in the conduct of his public and political affairs. A year after joining Ashley's household, he was elected a fellow of the Royal Society and from time to time took part in the work of committees and the council.

Locke apparently assisted Ashley in drafting the constitution of the colony of Carolina, of which Ashley was one of the lords proprietors. The original draft is in Locke's hand and is dated 21 June 1669. The constitution, which had little actual effect, is chiefly remarkable for guaranteeing religious freedom, a principle that both Locke and Ashley upheld. When they later entered the controversies concerning James II's accession to the throne, both men argued that Roman Catholics, viewed as agents of a foreign power, should be the exception to the rule; however, in the constitution of Carolina any religious practice is tolerated and only atheists are barred. When, in 1672, Ashley (from this time the Earl

of Shaftesbury) became lord chancellor, Locke was appointed secretary for patronage. He also acted as secretary for the council of trade and plantations, of which Shaftesbury was president.

With few interruptions, Locke was in the service of Shaftesbury for 15 years, and his connection with public life and political affairs varied with Shaftesbury's political fortunes. It was while he was actively engaged in Shaftesbury's business that he found time, in 1671, to write two drafts of the *Essay Concerning Human Understanding*, and to this major work he continued to devote himself until its publication in 1690. The inspiration for the *Essay* arose in an intellectual discussion in which Locke participated with his friends in the winter of 1670–71. Finding it impossible to decide some question related to the social and religious topics under discussion, the group approved Locke's suggestion that the first problem was 'to see what objects our understandings were or were not fitted to deal with'. Locke undertook to deal with the problem by himself, and the eventual result was the *Essay*.

When Shaftesbury fell from power in 1675, Locke's public career was temporarily ended, and he made the first of two long visits to the continent. Between 1675 and 1679 he stayed in France, mainly at Paris and Montpellier, a medical centre where he sought treatment for asthma. During his stay, he made numerous friends, among them Thomas Herbert, Earl of Pembroke, to whom he later dedicated the *Essay*. He also carried on an extensive correspondence, describing his investigations into agricultural methods, French institutions, scientific developments, and economic conditions.

In 1679 Locke returned to London at the behest of Shaftesbury who, having regained power, was just entering on the course of conflict with Charles II that would lead to the earl's flight to Holland, where he died in 1683. It is unlikely that Locke was an active party to the intrigues and more desperate schemes initiated by the opponents of the King; on the other hand, he was as a matter of principle opposed to the theory of divine right and doubtless hoped for the emergence of constitutional government. After the fall of Shaftesbury and the discovery of the Rye House Plot (1683), however, Locke found his situation in Oxford, then predominantly Royalist, increasingly difficult. He therefore left for Holland in September 1683. He was deprived of his studentship at Christ Church by royal order the following year. Although he scrupulously avoided having anything to do with plans for Monmouth's rebellion (1685), Locke, who was cautious by nature, lived in hiding for a while, adopting a Dutch pseudonym, Dr. van der Linden. Penn and Lord Pembroke subsequently interceded with James II, who agreed to receive him, but Locke refused to ask for pardon on the grounds that he had done nothing wrong. Having been assured that he was no longer in danger, Locke dropped his disguise and in 1687 settled at Rotterdam in the house of an English Quaker, Benjamin Furly. He became a member of a circle of distinguished men of letters which included Limborch, a leading liberal theologian and remonstrant professor at Amsterdam, and Le Clerc, the most prominent literary figure in Holland at the time. He also came to the attention of William and Mary, who respected him. Locke now devoted himself energetically to his writing. As a contributor to Le Clerc's scholarly periodical, *Bibliotheque universelle*, he published a plan for a commonplace book and an abridgement of the *Essay*. For Limborch he wrote *Epistola de tolerantia* ('On Tolerance') in 1685; this was anonymously published in Holland in 1689, after William and Mary had come to the throne, and soon translated into English by William Popple.

Locke came home to London in 1689 on the same ship that carried the Princess Mary. For the first time in his life he became a public author, and the three major works published in 1689–90, *On Tolerance*, *Two Treatises of Government*, and the *Essay Concerning Human Understanding*, embody the principles of his philosophy. The impact of these works was immediate, and stimulated such discussion and controversy that most of Locke's remaining life as a writer was given to the elaboration and defence of arguments contained in these volumes. In the meantime, he had for reasons of health refused a diplomatic post offered him by William III, but accepted an appointment as commissioner of appeals. In 1696 he was appointed a member of the council of trade, for which he received £1,000 a year. He never abandoned his involvement in public affairs, but his health was impaired, and for the last 14 years of his life he retired from London and, except for regular visits to town, lived at Oates, the house of Sir Francis Masham in Essex. Here he found the tranquillity and leisure necessary for his writing, and with his customary industry set about answering his critics and producing new works. While at Oates, he wrote three further letters *On Tolerance*, replying to various critics of the first letter; *Some Thoughts Concerning Education* (1693), still important for its educational theory; *The Reasonableness of Christianity* (1695), in which he defended the rational part of Scripture with the hope that all might agree on it and avoid dogmatic divisions; two pamphlets on the

267

value of currency, in which he argued against devaluation and in favour of maintaining the standard during the financial crisis of 1695–96; and the tract on *The Conduct of the Understanding*, conceived as an additional chapter of the *Essay* and published posthumously. He died at Oates on 28 October 1704, and was buried in the parish church of High Laver. He left most of his considerable fortune to Sir Francis Masham, whose family had taken affectionate care of him during his final years of declining health.

Informing and giving unity to Locke's diverse interests in the contemporary problems of science and philosophy, religion, government, education, and economics was a philosophical attitude, systematically expounded in the *Essay*, that insisted that knowledge derives from experience and reflection on experience. With the rejection of innate ideas and the argument for sense perception and experience as the source of knowledge, Locke in the *Essay Concerning Human Understanding* delineated a philosophy of empiricism that, especially in the questions it raised and left undecided, influenced the mainstream of European philosophy and such practitioners as Berkeley, Hume, Kant, Comte, and Herbert Spencer. In his writings on religious tolerance and on government, Locke laid the foundations of Whig policy in England for the next century, and presented a model for the constitution of the United States. His refutation of the divine right of kings, his statement of the principle of natural rights with the theory of property rights, and his defence of a constitutional government having a balance of powers, all had an abiding effect on the political thought of the 18th century and later.

J. L. Axtell (ed.), *The Educational Writings* (1968).
A. C. Fraser (ed.), *Essay Concerning Human Understanding* (2 vols.; 1894: reprinted New York, 1959).
P. Laslett (ed.), *Two Treatises of Government* (1967, rev. ed.).
Bishop E. Law (ed.), *The Works of John Locke* (9 vols.; 1777: 12th ed. in ten vols.; 1823: facsimile of this edition, Aachen, 1963).
Richard I. Aaron, *John Locke* (1971, 3rd ed.).
Maurice W. Cranston, *Locke: a Biography* (1957).
J. Gibson, *Locke's Theory of Knowledge and Its Historical Relations* (1917, reissued 1960).
J. W. Gough, *John Locke's Political Philosophy* (1950).
D. G. James, *The Life of Reason: Hobbes, Locke and Bolingbroke* (1949).
Sterling Lamprecht, *The Moral and Political Philosophy of John Locke* (New York, 1918).
D. J. O'Connor, *John Locke* (1952).
J. W. Yolton, *John Locke and the Way of Ideas* (1956).

Portraits: oil, half-length, by Dahl, *c.* 1696: N.P.G.; oil, quarter-length, after Kneller, 1704: N.P.G.; oil, half-length, by H. Verelst, 1689: N.P.G.; oil, quarter-length, by J. Greenhill, *c.* 1672–76: N.P.G.

Locke, Matthew (?1630–77), composer and musician.

Matthew Locke was born at Exeter, Devon. His importance as a composer lies in the boldness and intensity of his vocal writing, yet his instrumental music, especially his *Little Consort of Three Parts* (1656) and his coronation music for the 'king's sackbuts and cornetts', is lively and technically assured. His incidental music for Shadwell's 1674 version of *The Tempest* is remarkable for having dynamic markings in the vernacular. He also wrote an important treatise on thorough-bass technique entitled *Melothesia, or Certain General Rules for Playing upon a Continued Bass* (1674).

Locke was a choirboy at Exeter Cathedral until the coming of the Commonwealth, when all cathedral services were discontinued. Despite the asperity of the Puritan period, Locke spent the next few years pursuing his musical studies. When he was about eighteen, he visited the Low Countries. His attention thereafter centred on the stage and he collaborated in what amounts to the very first English opera, Davenant's *The Siege of Rhodes* (1656). Another example of his stage music for the period appears in Shirley's masque *Cupid and Death* (1653). In 1661 Locke provided processional music for the coronation of Charles II, who appointed him as composer in ordinary in that year. In this capacity he furnished music both for the King's private band and also the Chapel Royal choir. A large number of anthems survive from this period, as well as six suites.

Locke did not, however, forsake the stage. He provided or collaborated in the provision of music for several plays, notably *The Stepmother* of 1664 by Sir Robert Stapleton (died 1669), and some productions by Thomas Shadwell, including *Psyche* (1673; published as an *English Opera* in 1675). The authorship of the music for Davenant's production of *Macbeth* in 1672, attributed erroneously to Locke, remains uncertain.

After the Restoration, Locke was converted to Roman Catholicism and became organist to Queen Catherine. He held his appointment under Charles until his death in London in August 1677, whereupon he was succeeded by Purcell (q.v.).

P. Warlock and A. Mangeot (eds.), *Six Consorts à 4* [the six suites] (1932).

Lovat, 12th Baron (?1667–1747), Jacobite organizer, see Fraser, Simon, in *Lives of the Georgian Age.*

Lovelace, Richard (1618–58), Cavalier poet.

Born at Woolwich some time in 1618, the heir of a large, ancient, and wealthy Kentish family, Lovelace went rapidly through his education at Charterhouse and Gloucester Hall, Oxford, receiving an honorary M.A. in 1636 at the request of one of the Queen's ladies in waiting. Already he had been mixing with wits and courtiers. This was partly because of his background, but also because he was 'the most amiable and beautiful person that eye ever beheld', according to Anthony à Wood. Aubrey confirms this view: 'He was an extra-ordinary handsome man, but proud.' This pride began to show when he left Oxford and 're-paired in great splendour to the court', and then in 1639 fought in the Scottish expeditions. In 1642 Lovelace presented the Kentish Petition (for the retention of bishops and the prayer book) to Parliament, knowing quite well that only a month earlier a similar petition had been ordered to be burnt. As a result, he was imprisoned in the Gatehouse, where he wrote one of his best short poems, *To Althea from Prison:*

Stone walls do not a prison make
Nor iron bars a cage.

He managed to obtain his release on bail 'in order that he might serve against the rebels in Ireland' and on condition that he would not be active against the Parliament. Neither his zeal nor the condition was fulfilled. Instead, he raised men and gave money to his brothers for the King's cause. He also settled down to a lavish existence in London, associating with the wits, painters, and musicians of the time, until 1645, when he joined the King in Oxford.

In the following year, after the surrender of Oxford, Lovelace raised a regiment, which he took to France, serving under the French King against the Spanish. On his return to England in 1648 he was again imprisoned, using his time in jail to prepare *Lucasta* for the press. At the end of 1649 he was released, but the family seat was sold that year and he was ruined in the King's cause.

The last nine years of his life are obscure except for Wood's rather melodramatic picture of total poverty, which has been questioned. In 1659 his *Posthume Poems* were published.

Lovelace is chiefly remembered for poems such as *To Lucasta, Going to the Wars* and *To Althea from Prison*, which have been frequently anthologized, and lyrics such as *Tell me not (Sweet) I am unkind*. There is perhaps more dross in his work than in that of many lesser-known contemporaries. His writings range from comic trivia, epigrams, and songs, to funeral elegies and verse essays. Brilliance and wit make up for and perhaps contribute to his lack of direction and clear form. As a writer he was essentially a dilettante, his poems having a quality of freshness, marred by careless-ness and other limitations. His use of Metaphysical imagery is typical: it is reckless, sometimes collapsing into in-coherence, sometimes achieving its tar-get, but never as impressive as the leaps of imagination typical of Donne.

C. H. Wilkinson (ed., with introduction), *The Poems of Richard Lovelace* (2 vols.; 1925).

Lucan, Earl of (d. 1693), see Sarsfield, Patrick.

Ludlow, Edmund (c. 1617–1692), English soldier and republican; regicide.

Born in Maiden Bradley, Wiltshire, Ludlow was the son of Sir Henry Ludlow of Maiden Bradley; he was educated at Trinity College, Oxford, and the Inner Temple.   .

Sir Henry Ludlow was elected to the Long Parliament for Wiltshire, and soon distinguished himself as one of the most extreme anti-Royalist members. His fiery young son shared these views, and at the outbreak of the Civil War, like numerous other young lawyers, he volunteered for the life guard of Lord Essex, Parliament's general. He fought at Edgehill in 1642, and the next year was commissioned as a cavalry captain in Wiltshire, where he won fame by defending Wardour Castle against a lengthy siege. By the latter part of the war he was a colonel, and devoted most of his efforts to combating the Royalists in his native county, which elected him to Parliament in 1646. There he co-operated with Sir Henry Marten and the extreme republicans, associating also with the Levellers and Anabaptists.

When Parliament and the Army clashed, Ludlow unhesitatingly sup-ported his fellow soldiers. He was an eager promoter of Pride's Purge, and sat on the bench at the King's trial, signing his death warrant. Now that the way was clear to establish a republic, he rose to greater prominence, securing a seat on the Council of State. In 1650, at Cromwell's request, he took up the post of lieutenant general and second-in-command to Ireton (q.v.), the lord deputy of Ireland, which was combined with a commission for the civilian government of the island. When Ireton died in November 1651, Ludlow exer-cised the supreme command in Ireland for a year until his new superior, Fleet-wood (q.v.), arrived. In this time he practically completed the conquest of the country, in which he demonstrated great severity, and actively furthered the policy of transplanting the native Catho-lic Irish to Connaught, settling soldiers on their expropriated lands.

As a republican he opposed the crea-tion of the Protectorate in 1653 and even circulated pamphlets hostile to the new government. When he returned to England in 1655 he was arrested; never-theless, although he refused to give sure-ties for his good conduct, he was allowed to retire to Essex.

Ludlow won a seat in Richard Crom-well's Parliament, in which he actively aided the overthrow of the Protectorate and the recall of the Rump in May 1659, which promptly elected him to the council of state and then sent him to Ireland as commander-in-chief. He only stayed there a few months, reorganizing the Army so as to strengthen the republican elements. When he returned to England in October, he discovered that Lambert (q.v.) and Fleetwood had driven out the Rump. He strove to reconcile these two opposing groups, recognizing the danger that this quarrel presented to the survival of the Commonwealth, but only succeeded in arousing the suspicions of the disbanded Parliament, which impeached him when it was once again restored. Ludlow's position grew even weaker when Monck sided against him, and he began to plot a republican rising when the excluded members were invited back to the Long Parliament. He won a seat in the Convention Parliament and attempted to halt the Restoration. After the return of Charles II in 1660, he surrendered to the Speaker, but, upon learning that his life was in danger, fled abroad.

The crown viewed Ludlow as one of its most dangerous enemies and received the numerous reports of his supposed participation in prospective rebellions with great concern. In fact, however, he was travelling peacefully to Switzerland, where he received permission to stay, settling in Vevey. When the news of his whereabouts filtered back to England, plots against his life began, but he survived them all. During the second Anglo-Dutch War (1664–67) he was offered a high command in the Dutch service and promises of aid in the establishment of an English republic, but he was suspicious of Dutch intentions and refused to co-operate. He remained a keen observer of English affairs and spent his time writing his memoirs, which are a valuable source for the principles of the English republicans and the events of 1659–60.

In 1689, after the Revolution, Ludlow returned to England. His house in London became a hive of republican activity, and his presence infuriated the Tories. A warrant was issued for his arrest on a charge of murdering Charles I and he fled again to Switzerland, where he died on 23 November 1692.

Sir Charles H. Firth (ed.), *Memoirs* (1894).

M

Macdonald (or MacIan), Alexander (d. 1692), of Glencoe; chief of the Clan Ian Abrach branch of the Macdonalds, many of whom, including MacIan, were killed in the Massacre of Glencoe, 13 February 1692.

Alexander Macdonald or MacIan was the chief of a branch of the Macdonalds living in the Glencoe valley on the borders of Argyll and Inverness. The members of this clan were among the most notorious robbers and thieves in the Highlands, but since they directed their attentions mainly to Lowlanders and Campbells their stock stood high with other Highland clans. MacIan took part in the uprising under General Buchan in 1689 following the accession of William III.

The Macdonalds had incurred the special enmity of John Campbell (q.v.), Earl of Breadalbane, who, when the government began negotiations for a settlement with the Highlanders, maintained that MacIan should be asked to make reparation for the past depredations of his clan. MacIan therefore had no interest in the settlement and refused to take the oath of allegiance. However, when he realized that he was the only leader who had not taken the oath, he made strenuous attempts to do so before the time limit elapsed.

He presented himself at Fort William on the last day, 31 December 1691, but no civil magistrate could be found to take his oath. Legally, he was undoubtedly in the clear, especially since he trekked on foot to Inverary, where Sir Colin Campbell, sheriff of Argyll, administered the oath on 6 January 1692. The declaration was sent to the council in Edinburgh, but its secretary, Sir Gilbert Elliot, refused to receive it. The matter was not put before the council and the government remained unaware of the true situation.

It had been expected that some Highland chieftains would resist, and it was decided to make an example of the troublesome Macdonalds. The secretary of state for Scotland, Dalrymple, wrote that 'if M'Kean of Glencoe and that tribe can be separated from the rest, it will be a proper vindication of justice to extirpate that sect of thieves.'

A group of 120 men of Argyll's regiment was quartered on the Macdonalds and, assured of their peaceful intent, MacIan gave them full hospitality. However, acting on orders, the Campbells arose at 5 a.m. on 13 February and slaughtered all the Macdonalds they could find. MacIan himself was shot through the head, and his wife died the following day, but their sons escaped. Only part of the clan, 38 people in all, died, the others managing to escape to the hills as the Argylls had failed to block the passes.

When news of the incident became common knowledge, a government enquiry was ordered. It reported in 1695, and although Dalrymple was censured for his 'excess of zeal', none of the active principals in the massacre was ever brought to justice.

P. Hume Brown, *History of Scotland* (1899).
John Prebble, *Glencoe* (1966).

Macgregor or Campbell, Robert (1671–1734), Highland chieftain, commonly called 'Rob Roy' (Gaelic for 'Red Robert' – so called because of his red hair).

From an early age, Robert Macgregor, although nominally a Perthshire grazier, was involved in the practices of cattle stealing and blackmail, and his principal income was derived from what can best be described as a protection racket. In 1693 the penal acts against the Macgregors for their active opposition to the accession of William of Orange in the revolution of 1688 were reinforced and this caused Robert Macgregor to change his name to Campbell to avoid arrest.

In 1712 his cattle-dealing affairs with James Graham, 1st Duke of Montrose, resulted in a court case. Macgregor, greatly in debt to Montrose, had fled to the Western Isles. He was brought to trial as 'a notour bankrupt who by open fraud and violence hath embezzled considerable sums of money and, refusing to come to any account, keeps himself with a guard or company of armed men in defiance of the law.' While Rob Roy was on trial, Montrose seized his lands and evicted and ill-treated his wife and children. Under the protection of John Campbell, Earl of Breadalbane, Rob Roy and his followers embarked on a career of brigandage, chiefly at the expense of Montrose.

Although advocating the Pretender's cause, Rob Roy never joined the army of the Jacobite rebellion. He and his men followed them closely but plundered indiscriminately. He was captured in 1717 by the Duke of Atholl, but soon escaped to continue his vendetta against Montrose.

After being recaptured, he was taken in 1727 to Gravesend to be transported to Barbados. He was pardoned at the last minute and, having been reconciled with Montrose five years earlier, spent the rest of his life peacefully on his farm. He died on 28 December 1734.

A man whose way of life and reputation has been glorified and exaggerated, Rob Roy has come to be held as a legendary figure, Scotland's Robin Hood. Both man and exploits are immortalized in Sir Walter Scott's novel *Rob Roy* (1817), as well as in various passages of Wordsworth's poems.

Authentic details of life in Scott's Introduction to *Rob Roy*.
A. H. Millar, *The History of Rob Roy* (1883).

Maitland, John (1616–82), 2nd Earl and 1st Duke of Lauderdale; Scottish politician and effective ruler of the country for most of Charles II's reign.

Born at Lethington, East Lothian, on 24 May 1616, Maitland was the eldest surviving son of John Maitland, 1st Earl of Lauderdale, and of Isabel Seton, daughter of Alexander, Earl of Dunfermline.

The future Duke of Lauderdale was brought up a Presbyterian and given a good education in the classics and Hebrew. He became a zealous Covenanter and went on missions to the Long Parliament. He won the confidence of the Parliamentary peers, and in February 1644 was appointed to the powerful Committee of Both Kingdoms, an executive on which his rather brutal and unscrupulous will came into its own. He negotiated with Charles I at Uxbridge on behalf of his fellow countrymen in 1645. Out of these conferences grew Lauderdale's links with the Royalist camp. During the next two years he came increasingly into conflict with the Independents and the New Model Army, and advised Charles on the concessions that he should grant to win the support of the Covenanters, most of whom could envisage no alternative to monarchy and sought only the King's support for their liberties and for Presbyterianism in both realms.

In December 1647, at Carisbrooke Castle, the Scottish commissioners led by Lauderdale obtained from Charles the Engagement, a written promise to follow a more pro-Scottish policy. But this could only be implemented if the power of the New Model Army and the Independents was destroyed. Lauderdale rallied the English Royalists and established links with James Hamilton (q.v.), Duke of Hamilton, the King's leading supporter in Scotland. His standing among the Covenanters fell, but he managed to commit them on the King's side in the second Civil War.

On 10 August 1648, before the disastrous Battle of Preston, Lauderdale was in the presence of the Prince of Wales, with an invitation to the royal family from the Scottish estates to come to Scotland on comparatively easy terms. A close relationship developed between the two men. Lauderdale accompanied the prince, King Charles II after his father's execution, to Scotland in 1650 as a companion and adviser. He fought with Charles at Worcester in 1651, was captured, and spent the next nine years in prison, where he pursued his Hebrew studies.

Monck's entry into London in February 1660 occasioned Lauderdale's release. He immediately threw himself into Charles's cause and worked towards the Restoration. He rejoined Charles at Breda, resuming his close relationship with the King. Despite strong opposition, he won the post of secretary for Scotland and within a few years wielded the entire royal authority in that country. Lauderdale showed a total lack of scruple in winning this power. He abandoned Presbyterianism for episcopacy, and purged public offices of his rivals, his

enemies, and all Englishmen. Nevertheless, Lauderdale was not without ability. He possessed a brilliant sense of timing, a vast store of learning, and loyalty to his master, which, coupled with his great resourcefulness and his skill in building and retaining the support of a faction amounting to a political party, enabled him to rule Scotland as *de facto* viceroy for almost twenty years.

Although Lauderdale probably favoured toleration and, indeed, attempted to permit it at first by such measures as the Letter of Indulgence of 1669, he was unable to win Covenanting support and by the early 1670s returned to a policy of persecution, brutally repressing conventicles for the rest of his rule. He was a member of the Cabal – Charles II's cabinet named after the initials of its members – but survived its disintegration and established ties with Danby (see Osborne, Thomas). In 1672 he was made a duke, and two years later granted an English peerage. He was drawn increasingly into English affairs, for Shaftesbury (see Cooper, Anthony Ashley) considered him an enemy and supported the development of a Scottish opposition about the 3rd Duke of Hamilton; indeed, in 1672 Lauderdale had organized the Scottish militia for potential use in England against Charles's enemies. In 1674 and 1675 the Commons sent addresses to the King calling for Lauderdale's dismissal.

In Scotland the unwillingness of local magistrates in the west to repress the conventicles led Lauderdale to form the 'Highland Host', which he loosed on that recalcitrant region in the winter of 1677. The atrocities committed by this soldiery built yet stronger links between Shaftesbury and Hamilton, and in 1678 Charles ordered the Highland troops to be disbanded.

In the face of continued parliamentary

opposition and his own declining health, Lauderdale resigned his secretaryship in October 1680 and was removed from most of his other offices two years later. He died at Tunbridge Wells in August 1682.

Maurice Lee, *The Cabal* (Urbana, Ill., 1965).

W. C. Mackenzie, *John Maitland, Duke of Lauderdale* (1923).

Portraits: oil, three-quarter length, by J. Huysmans, 1665–70: N.P.G.; miniature, by S. Cooper, 1664: N.P.G.

Manchester, 2nd Earl of (1602–71), see Montagu, Edward, 2nd Earl of Manchester.

Mar, 6th or 11th Earl of (1675–1732), Jacobite leader, see Erskine, John in *Lives of the Georgian Age*.

Marlborough, Duchess of (1660–1744), see Churchill, Sarah.

Marlborough, 1st Duke of (1650–1722), see Churchill, John.

Marston, John (1576–1634), satirist and dramatist.

The son of a lawyer who was a member of the Middle Temple, Marston belonged to a prominent Shropshire family. He was probably born at Coventry and received his early education there. He then attended Brasenose College, Oxford, where he graduated in 1594. In the meantime, he had been admitted specially, at the request of his father, to the Middle Temple and seems to have taken up residence there by 1595, probably sharing his father's chambers until the latter's death in 1599. Although Marston continued to be in residence at the Middle Temple on and off until about 1607, there is little doubt that his interest was not really in the study of law. Such, at least, seems to be the meaning of a passage in his father's will in which he leaves his law books to his son, 'whom I hoped would have profited from them in the study of the law, but man proposeth and God disposeth.'

He began his literary career as a poet and satirist, publishing two volumes in 1598. The title poem of the first of these volumes, *The Metamorphosis of Pygmalion's Image, and Certain Satires*, was little more than a conventional erotic poem in the Ovidian vein, although Marston was to argue later on that he intended it as a parody. The mood of the second volume, *The Scourge of Villainy*, however, was savagely satirical. Originally containing nine satires, with a tenth added in the second edition (1599), the book is written in a harsh obscure style characteristic of Marston's early work as a whole. It is a typical example of the fierce Juvenalian temper that was being cultivated by a number of poets in the last decade of the 16th century. Donne (q.v.) and Thomas Lodge (see *Lives of the Tudor Age*) had earlier written verse of this kind, but it was especially Bishop Joseph Hall (q.v.) who had sounded the new Juvenalian note (in a volume published in 1597) and who boasted:

I first adventure: follow me who list, And be the second English satirist.

Marston aggressively challenged Hall with the publication of his book and seems quickly to have gained a reputation: by 1598 he was being referred to as one of the chief English satirists.

By the Order of Conflagration in 1599 the writing of verse satire was suppressed and Marston's poetic works were condemned along with others. He had already entered upon the second stage of his literary career, however, and was soon again embroiled in controversy, this time as a dramatist. His early plays are primarily of interest as part of the stage quarrel known as the 'war of the theatres', in which the protagonists were Marston and Ben Jonson (q.v.), although many of the playwrights of the time, including perhaps Shakespeare, became involved. The history of Marston's quarrel with Jonson is intricate, and it is now difficult to identify the satirical portraits that the antagonists made of each other in their plays. Suffice it to say that in Marston's first two plays, *Histrio-Mastix, or the Player Whipped*, an older play that Marston revised, and *Jack Drum's Entertainment*, largely or wholly the work of Marston, there appear characters that seem to be satirical portraits of Jonson. The plays, both performed by the Boys of Paul's, in any case elicited satirical counterattacks from Jonson in *Every Man out of His Humour*, *Cynthia's Revels*, and *The Poetaster*. In the last play, Marston is ridiculed in the character Crispinus. Marston attacked Jonson once more in his satirical comedy *What You Will* (probably written in 1601), but thereafter the feud quietened and Marston and Jonson were on friendly terms. It is certain that Marston admired Jonson; he dedicated his best play, *The Malcontent* (1604), to him and soon after that the two playwrights worked in collaboration on *Eastward Ho!* (1605).

Marston's association with the Boys of Paul's ended about 1601. Thereafter and for the rest of his career as a dramatist he was associated with another company of child actors, the Children of the Queen's Revels. The next five years mark Marston's most active period as a dramatist. He wrote *Antonio and Mellida* (a tragedy, produced in 1600; Part II, *Antonio's Revenge*, 1600–01), *What You Will* (1601), *The Dutch Courtezan* (1604), *The Malcontent* (1604), *Eastward Ho!* (written in collaboration with Jonson and Chapman, 1605), *The Parasitaster*,

Or The Fawne (written between 1604 and 1606), the tragedy *Sophonisba* (1606), and another tragedy, which he left unfinished, *The Insatiate Countess* (completed by the actor William Barksted in 1611). Some mildly critical references in *Eastward Ho!* to Scottish adventurers who had come to England with James I got Marston and his two collaborators briefly in trouble after the performance of that play. Jonson reported the incident in his *Conversations* with Drummond: 'He was dilated by Sir James Murray to the King, for writing something against the Scots, in a play *Eastward Ho!*, and voluntarily imprisoned himself with Chapman and Marston, who had written it amongst them. The report was, that they should then [have] had their ears cut and noses.' They were released without punishment, however. *Eastward Ho!*, with its vivid portrayal of city life, remains the best of these plays.

Besides plays, Marston wrote occasional entertainments such as the City pageant for James I and Christian of Denmark (1606). By 1606 his literary career was over. He abandoned the drama and probably began to study for holy orders at this time. In 1609 he was ordained priest. He married Mary Wilkes, the daughter of James I's chaplain, and was appointed to the living of Christchurch, Hampshire, in 1616. Little is known of his life once he entered the church. He died in London on 25 June 1634, and was buried beside his father in the Temple church, 'under the stone', according to Anthony à Wood, 'which hath written on it *Oblivioni Sacrum* (sacred to oblivion).'

A. Davenport (ed.), *The Plays of John Marston* (1961).

H. Harvey Wood (ed.), *The Poems of John Marston* (3 vols.; 1934–39).

A. Capati, *John Marston, Satirist* (Ithaca, N. Y., 1961).

Marvell, Andrew (1621–78), Metaphysical poet.

Marvell was born on 31 March 1621, at Winestead in Holderness, a quiet village outside Hull. His father, described as 'facetious yet Calvinistical', was a devout Anglican clergyman and scholar; he probably taught at Hull Grammar School, which his son attended. In 1633 the younger Marvell went up to Trinity College, Cambridge, where his contemporaries included Crashaw and Cowley (qq.v.). Here he had a brief flirtation with Catholicism; indeed, it is said that Marvell was induced by Jesuit friends to desert Cambridge for London, and that his father found him by chance in a bookshop and 'rescued' him.

In 1641 he left Cambridge without taking his M.A., and although the history of his next ten years is obscure, he probably spent from 1642 to 1646 travelling in Europe, thus missing most of the Civil War at home and also acquiring a grasp of foreign languages that later impressed Milton. His first published poetry appeared some years after his return, including a contribution to Lovelace's *Lucasta* (1649), and a hostile elegy on Tom May, Royalist historian and playwright who turned Puritan.

Since all but a few of Marvell's poems were published posthumously in 1681, it is difficult to date them precisely, but it seems likely that such polished and elegant love lyrics as *The Fair Singer*, *Eyes and Tears*, and *Clorinda and Damon* also belong to the late 1640s. His keeping of Cavalier company and writing in Cavalier genres might imply that Marvell's early sympathies were Royalist. He was, however, too much of a Christian and humanist ever comfortably to take sides in civil conflict, for whatever cause; in 1672 he wrote of the Civil War: 'upon considering all, I think the

cause was too good to have been fought for.'

Marvell's sensitivity to personalities rather than causes is particularly evident in his *Horatian Ode upon Cromwell's Return from Ireland* (1650). He movingly describes the dignity of Charles I at his execution:

He nothing common did or mean
Upon that memorable scene.

On the other hand, Marvell's admiration for Cromwell is obviously equally genuine; he sees him as a man of destiny, the instrument of 'angry Heaven' for England's moral regeneration.

In early 1651 Marvell returned to Yorkshire, to take up the post of tutor to Mary, daughter of Lord Fairfax (see Fairfax, Thomas) of Nunappleton House. Marvell must have found his employer a sympathetic spirit, since Fairfax had recently resigned his generalship in the Parliamentary army in protest against Cromwell's Irish policy. The peace and seclusion of Nunappleton inspired one of Marvell's most distinctive poems, *The Garden*, which evokes powerfully the tranquillity to be found in withdrawal from society to the ordered solitude of a garden,

> Annihilating all that's made
> To a green thought in a green shade.

In 1653 Marvell became tutor to Cromwell's ward William Dutton; he initially lodged at Eton, in the household of John Oxenbridge, a Puritan preacher recently returned from Bermuda. His host's reminiscences probably inspired Marvell's charming *Bermudas*.

To compare the simplicity of *Bermudas* with the complexities of *To His Coy Mistress*, probably written at about the same time, reveals the breadth of Marvell's genius. *To His Coy Mistress*, perhaps Marvell's finest poem, brilliantly evokes the actuality of sexual desire in a perfect logical structure, with an ironic, almost conversational tone.

In late 1657 Marvell was appointed assistant Latin secretary, probably on the strength of an earlier recommendation by Milton. He was certainly one of those who helped Milton, probably as a scribe and reader, as the latter's encroaching blindness threatened to put an end to his work. He was voted lodgings in Whitehall and frequently employed to receive visiting diplomats. In September 1658 Cromwell died; the confidence and enthusiasm of Marvell's 1655 poem on the first anniversary of the Protector's government now became transformed into the genuine personal grief of the *Poem upon the Death of O.C.*:

> I saw him dead, a leaden slumber lies,
> And mortal sleep over those wakeful eyes.

Marvell's public career progressed further in 1659, when he was elected M.P. for Hull. He became briefly associated with Harrington's ultra-republican group, the Rota, until the restoration of Charles II forced its disbandment. Unlike Dryden and Edmund Waller (qq.v.), Marvell did not turn his coat and write eulogies of the new King. Fortunately, his now potentially embarrassing poems on Cromwell had not been published, and the new regime not only allowed Marvell to retain his seat unpunished but even sent him, in 1663–65, on diplomatic missions to Holland, Russia, Sweden, and Denmark.

Marvell was a conscientious rather than a vociferous M.P.; he kept his constituents well informed by means of frequent newsletters containing concise and businesslike digests of current political issues. However, he was not entirely without influence in the House – in 1660 he achieved a substantial reduction of the crippling fines levied on his old friend Milton. Marvell's most dramatic moment in Parliament came in March 1677, during the debate on the Bill for Securing the Protestant Religion, when he protested so vehemently at the power this would give to the bishops that his furious opponents tried to have him committed to the Tower, claiming that he had assaulted another M.P. and disobeyed the Speaker.

John Aubrey (q.v.) gives a brief but vivid account of Marvell's appearance and habits at this time:

> He was of a middling stature, pretty strong set, roundish faced, cheery cheek'd, hazel eye, brown hair. He was in his conversation very modest, and of very few words: and though he loved wine he would never drink hard in company, and was wont to say that, *he would not play the goodfellow in any man's company in whose hands he would not trust his life.* He kept bottles of wine at his lodging, and many times he would drink liberally by himself, to refresh his spirits, and exalt his muse.

Marvell's private letters during these years reveal his deep disgust at the way the degenerate court and the King's corrupt ministers kept Parliament in fawning subservience: 'we are all venal cowards except some few.' He now turned to writing fierce political satires; for obvious reasons, these were usually anonymous and circulated privately, but one prose work, the two-part *Rehearsal Transpros'd* of 1672–73, which Marvell published under his own name, brought him considerable fame. His target was the heavy-handed ecclesiastical policy of the government, and in particular its most bigoted champion, Samuel Parker, Archdeacon of Canterbury, once a Puritan but since the Restoration the most rigid of prelatists. The public was entirely on Marvell's side; Parker and his party could only respond feebly, then lapsed into silence. The King himself overruled a censor who wished to suppress a second edition of Marvell's satire.

It is said that at about this time Lord Treasurer Danby (see Osborne, Thomas) visited Marvell at his lodging 'up two pairs of stairs in a little court in the Strand' and offered him, on behalf of the King, a place at court. Marvell refused, saying that 'he must be either ungrateful to the King in voting against him, or false to his country in giving in to the measures of the court.' Danby then offered him an immediate gift of £1,000; Marvell responded by sending for his manservant and asking him, 'Pray what had I for dinner yesterday?' 'A shoulder of mutton.' 'And what do you allow me today?' 'The remainder hashed.' Then Marvell said to Danby, 'And tomorrow, my lord, I shall have the sweet bladebone broiled.' Danby retired, defeated by such austerity.

In late 1677 Marvell tackled a more perilous subject for satire in his anonymous pamphlet *An Account of the Growth of Popery and Arbitrary Government in England*. This caused an uproar, and the government offered £100 reward for the discovery of the author – Marvell was suspected, but strangely he was never confronted.

In his own day, and indeed right up to the nineteenth century, Marvell's reputation as a writer rested mainly on his satires. To a modern reader, however, they are of little but historical value – many of the allusions are lost, and the personal abuse is often merely spiteful. Yet there can be no doubting the passionate sincerity of his attachment to these forgotten political and religious causes.

Marvell made many enemies with his satire, and his life had even been threatened – one of his letters speaks of 'the insuperable hatred of my foes to me, and their designs of murdering me.' Hence, his sudden death, on 18 August 1678, immediately provoked the rumour that he had been poisoned – by the Jesuits, Fuller suggested. However, in 1692, Richard Morton revealed that Marvell had died of a tertian fever 'through the ignorance of an old conceited doctor.' The poet was buried in St. Giles-in-the-Fields Church, and though the Hull corporation voted £50 for a memorial, the presumably orthodox vicar refused to let it be erected.

Andrew Marvell was a man of paradox, both in his life and in his literary works. The strongest influences on his early manhood seem to have been his Cavalier poet friends, yet a few years later he became a devoted servant of Cromwell's government. Of his greatest poems, one praises complete withdrawal from society and the other forceful action in public life. His early verse dwelt on profound themes in an elegant and detached tone, yet later he turned to

279

vigorous and forthright political satire.

H. M. Margoliouth (ed.), *The Poems and Letters of Andrew Marvell* (2 vols.; 1971, rev. ed.).

M. C. Bradbrook and M. G. Lloyd Thomas, *Andrew Marvell* (1940).

G. Lord (ed.), *Andrew Marvell: a Collection of Critical Essays* (Englewood Cliffs, N.J., 1968).

Harold E. Toliver, *Marvell's Ironic Vision* (1965).

Portrait: oil, quarter-length, by unknown artist, *c.* 1655–60: N.P.G.

Mary II (1662–94), Queen of England, Scotland, and Ireland.

Born at St. James's Palace, London, on 30 April 1662, Mary was the eldest child of James, Duke of York, later James II, and his first wife, Anne Hyde, daughter of the Earl of Clarendon, Edward Hyde (qq.v.). She was married on 4 November 1677, to her cousin, William, Prince of Orange, who upon his accession as William III (q.v.) reigned jointly with her.

Mary was the first child of the Duke and Duchess of York, and it was hoped that the Duchess's pregnancy would

result in a male heir. Mary's birth, therefore, according to Pepys, 'pleased nobody', and as a baby she was eclipsed by the birth of a brother 15 months later.

In her early childhood Mary lived in Twickenham at the house of her grandfather, Clarendon, but she later moved to Richmond Palace, where she was brought up under the care of Lady Frances Villiers. Her childhood friends included her sister, the Princess Anne, to whom she was greatly attached, the Villiers girls, Sarah Jennings (later Sarah Churchill, Duchess of Marlborough), Anne Trelawny (whose friendship lasted well into adulthood), and Frances Apsley (who was Mary's closest friend until she left England for Holland on her marriage). Mary's upbringing was strictly Protestant, on the express instructions of her uncle, Charles II, although her father, James, would have dearly liked to countermand Charles's wishes and bring his children up in the Roman Catholic faith to which he now adhered. Morley, the Bishop of Winchester, took overall charge of Mary's education, but her religious instructor was Henry Compton (q.v.), Bishop of London who became her close and valued friend and adviser. Not a great deal is known of Mary's childhood, but she seems to have been an attractive and charming child. Pepys saw her when she was six, 'a little child in hanging sleeves, dance most finely, so as almost to ravish one.'

When Mary was nine, her youngest and only surviving brother, Edgar, Duke of Cambridge, died, and she was once more the heiress presumptive. Almost immediately, plans were afoot for her marriage. The choice of a husband for Mary was of vital political importance: it was a question of an alliance with France, or an alliance against France. In 1672, Prince William of Orange was mentioned as a suitor, as were Charles II of Spain and the French Dauphin. Danby (see Osborne, Thomas) revived the Dutch marriage scheme, and in 1677 William arrived in England. The scheme won the approval of Charles II, but was unwelcome to Mary's father, who was bitterly opposed to a Protestant marriage for his eldest daughter. He was forced to give way, however, and the match went ahead. It is said that when her father broke the news to Mary, 'she wept all that afternoon and the following day'. Her correspondence with Frances Apsley shows her to have been an imaginative and romantic girl, and perhaps William, with his slight physique, ill health, and air of great seriousness and reserve, failed to live up to her ideas of a suitable husband.

Despite Mary's unwillingness, the wedding arrangements were made with great speed, and on 4 November 1677, William and Mary were married at her own apartments. A fortnight later, after many delays due to bad weather, they set sail for Holland. Mary was undoubtedly very unhappy and lonely in the early years of her marriage. William, by predilection a soldier, was frequently absent on matters of state and on military campaigns against the encroaching armies of Louis XIV of France, and Mary was often left alone. She is said to have 'felt at liberty to fit up her chapel in her dining room as her husband never dined with her'. The marriage remained childless, Mary's hopes of a child being disappointed in 1678 and 1679.

Among the ladies Mary had taken to Holland with her was Elizabeth Villiers, later Countess of Orkney, who in about 1679 became William's mistress. The liaison lasted until at least a year before Mary's death, and it is known from Mary's own memoirs that she was aware of the relationship and greatly grieved by it.

Mary continued to lead a sheltered and retiring life, taking no interest in matters of state and spending many hours in prayer and meditation. Her life was enlivened by visits from her father and his second wife, Mary of Modena (who now called her stepdaughter 'dear Lemon'), her sister Anne, and Sarah Churchill, and later by a visit from the Duke of Monmouth, at which time she excited some scandal by her vivacity with him in public, particularly on the occasions when they went skating together. In 1680 Mary was severely ill, and was not expected to live. William took so little interest in her condition that her chaplain resolved to speak to the prince about it. Mary pulled through, however, and her natural sweetness and submissiveness of temper began to show themselves. She won the hearts of the Dutch people, an affection which she warmly returned.

Mary's father acceded to the throne as James II in 1685 after the death of his brother, Charles II. His Roman Catholicism now became increasingly open, and in 1687 he began a correspondence with Mary, urging her to consider conversion to Roman Catholicism. Mary's Anglican faith was so strong that she remained unimpressed by his arguments and replied advocating Anglicanism in the strongest possible terms. The heartbreaking dilemma of Mary's life was now reaching a crisis. She was greatly devoted to her father, but all her religious predilections and instinctive beliefs urged her to loyalty to her Protestant husband. The crisis broke when the Queen, Mary of Modena (q.v.), gave birth to a son, now the heir to the English throne. There were immediate doubts about the authenticity of such a timely birth (almost certainly unfounded), doubts which

Mary shared. She admitted in her memoirs that she would rather have the English crown herself for Protestantism than see it worn by a Roman Catholic half-brother.

The events of 1688 culminated in an invitation to William to invade Britain. Mary stayed in the background, her usual distaste for affairs of state combining with the unhappiness with which she saw her husband succeed at the expense of her father, but she joined William in England in 1689. She refused all plans to make her sole monarch, and she and William were proclaimed joint sovereigns and crowned on 11 April 1689.

Mary's short reign in England was not a happy one. William was frequently absent on continental campaigns and dealing with Jacobite rebellions in Ireland. In his absences Mary reigned in her own right, but she was not happy in a prominent role. She underestimated her own capacity for understanding and administering affairs of state, and always gratefully relinquished control to her husband on his return. One aspect of government alone was left to Mary: the right of making church appointments. Mary was a dutiful and pious Anglican, and it was more appropriate for her to handle affairs of the Church than the Calvinistic William.

Mary had looked forward to resuming her happy relationship with her sister Anne on her return to England, but Anne was by now under the strong influence of the domineering Sarah Churchill (q.v.) and her husband, the Duke of Marlborough (see Churchill, John). By 1692 William and Mary could no longer ignore Marlborough's complicity with the Jacobites, and their treatment of the Marlboroughs (Marlborough was for some time in the Tower) estranged them from Anne. This was a source of great

distress to the lonely Mary, who was now without parents, children, her sister, and for most of the time, her husband. Her popularity in the country suffered too, quite unjustly.

Late in 1694 Mary contracted an illness which proved to be smallpox. She clearly knew that her illness might prove fatal, and made an attempt to put her affairs in order, destroying letters and leaving a written account of her wishes as to burial ceremonies, etc. Her condition worsened, and on 28 December 1694, she died, at the age of thirty-two. She was mourned most deeply by the King and the nation. Although William had not been a faithful husband he exhibited genuine grief at the loss of his wife, and when he died eight years later he was found to be wearing a ring containing a lock of her hair beneath his clothes on his left arm. Mary was buried with great splendour in Henry VII's chapel at Westminster. Her own wishes for a simple burial were not discovered until long after her funeral was over.

A. B. Bathurst (ed.), *Letters of Two Queens* (1924).
Marjorie Bowen (pseudonym of G. M. V. Long), *The Third Mary Stuart* (1929).
Hester W. Chapman, *Mary II, Queen of England* (1953).
Elizabeth Hamilton, *William's Mary* (1972).
N. M. Waterson, *Mary II* (Durham, N.C., 1928).

Portraits: oil, three-quarter length, by Lely, 1677: Kensington Palace; oil, three-quarter-length, by W. Wissing, 1685: Windsor Castle; oil, full-length, by Kneller, 1691: Windsor Castle.

Mary Beatrice of Modena (1658–1718), second wife of James II (q.v.) and mother of James Francis Edward Stuart, 'the Old Pretender'.

Mary of Modena was the only daughter of Alfonso IV, Duke of Modena. She was brought up in Italy, in strict observance of the Catholic faith, and intended becoming a nun. However, in

1673, mainly as a result of French diplomacy, Mary married James, Duke of York. She was only fifteen, and was described at the time as 'so innocently bred that till then she had never heard of such a place as England, nor of such a person as the Duke of York'. Their marriage was unpopular in England because of her Catholicism, and this factor contributed to the hysteria caused by the alleged Popish Plot in 1678 (see Oates, Titus).

Mary acquired a reputation for haughtiness, although she was apparently gracious and quick-witted. She became fond of James's children, Mary (see Mary I) and Anne (q.v.), and bore five children between 1675 and 1682, all of whom died. She gained a great deal of influence over James, and probably strengthened his devotion to the Catholic faith, although she, like his first wife Anne Hyde (q.v.), still had to tolerate James's infidelities.

James came to the throne in 1685, but within two years had thrown away the goodwill initially felt towards him. The birth of a son, a Catholic heir, to Mary in 1688 only served to exacerbate the situation. The news of his birth gave rise to considerable scepticism and to the legend that he was smuggled into the Queen's room in a warming pan, although there is in fact no doubt that the birth was genuine. As James's position grew more precarious, Mary and the baby prince fled to France, and James soon followed them. They lived at the palace of St. Germain, from where Mary strongly supported schemes to invade England and begin a religious war. She received with James a pension of 50,000 crowns a month from Louis XIV, and after James's death in 1701, received an annuity of 100,000 francs. In exile, Mary remained proud and dignified, and made a favourable impression at the French court, in contrast to James, who became increasingly feeble-minded. She became even more devout, and spent more and more of her time at a nunnery at Chaillot. Mary died in 1718, outliving James by seventeen years, and was buried at Chaillot.

M. Harte, *Queen Mary of Modena. Her life and letters* (1905).
M. Hopkirk, *Queen over the water* (1953).
Carola Oman, *Mary of Modena* (1962).

Portraits: oil, full-length, by Lely, *c.* 1677: Hampton Court; oil, three-quarter length, by William Wissing, *c.* 1685: N.P.G.

Masham, Abigail (d. 1734), favourite of Queen Anne.

Born Abigail Hill, elder daughter of Francis and Mary Hill. Abigail was a cousin of Sarah Churchill (q.v.), 1st Duchess of Marlborough, whom she supplanted in Queen Anne's affections after about 1707, remaining the royal favourite until the Queen's death in 1714.

Abigail Hill was one of four children born to Francis Hill, a Levant merchant, and his wife Mary, who was one of the twenty-two children of Sir John Jennings and an aunt of Sarah Jennings, later Sarah Churchill. Little is known of Abigail's early years, but in later life she was described as a woman of good education and cultivated tastes. Her family being reduced to poverty by her father's unwise speculation, she entered the service of Lady Rivers, wife of Sir John Rivers of Chafford, Kent, early in life, and was later invited into Sarah Churchill's household at St. Albans. Sarah later recalled, 'I treated her with great kindness as if she had been my sister'. Through Sarah's influence, Abigail was in 1704 appointed a bedchamber woman to Queen Anne while Anne was still Princess of Denmark.

Sarah Churchill had enjoyed a close relationship with Anne almost from childhood, but Abigail gradually supplanted her. Temperament certainly entered into this change: Sarah was brilliant and gifted, but her uncertain temper and domineering personality gradually became less acceptable to the Queen. Abigail was less domineering, and although of unprepossessing appearance (she had a plain face and large red nose), was a woman of education and sense. In addition, Sarah identified herself more and more with the Whigs, while Abigail held views similar to Anne's own High Church Tory predilections.

In 1707 Abigail was married to Samuel Masham, a groom of the bedchamber to Prince George of Denmark (q.v.), the Queen's husband. Anne was present at the wedding, but Sarah was kept in ignorance of it. When Sarah became aware of Abigail's growing influence with the Queen, she did all she could to achieve Abigail's dismissal. Her attempts only further alienated the Queen.

Abigail was a close associate – possibly a cousin – of the Tory chief minister, Robert Harley (q.v.), later 1st Earl of Oxford, and after his dismissal in 1708 she acted as go-between for him and the Queen. In this way, Harley remained the Queen's secret adviser and Sarah Churchill never regained her ascendancy. In 1711 the Marlboroughs finally fell from favour and were forced to relinquish all public office, Abigail replacing Sarah as keeper of the privy purse. When Anne created twelve peers to reduce Whig influence in the House of Lords, Abigail's husband was included in their number.

Lady Masham remained in the Queen's service until the end of her reign. She became an intimate of Swift during these years and encouraged him as an adviser to the Queen. Practically her last influential act was to ensure the dismissal of Harley in 1714. Harley had returned to office in 1710, but in 1713 he quarrelled with Lady Masham, who transferred her allegiance to Bolingbroke (see St. John, Henry), with whom Harley had also quarrelled. Five days before her death, Queen Anne replaced Harley as chief minister by Bolingbroke.

Lady Masham was a constant and faithful friend to Anne and treated her with unceasing care and compassion during her last illness. After the Queen's death, Lady Masham left court and lived in retirement with her husband. She died after a long illness on 6 December 1734, and was buried at High Laver, Essex.

Jonathan Swift said of her that she was 'a person of plain, sound understanding, of great truth and sincerity, without the least mixture of falsehood or disguise; of an honest boldness and courage superior to her sex, firm and disinterested in her friendship and full of love, duty and veneration for the Queen, her mistress.'

Massinger, Philip (1583–1640), dramatist.

Massinger was born at Salisbury, Wiltshire, and baptized on 24 November 1583. After the death of John Fletcher (q.v.) in 1625, Massinger, whose writing until then had been mainly done as Fletcher's collaborator, became one of the chief playwrights of the day. It is almost certain that he became chief writer to the King's Men, a position once occupied by Shakespeare.

Massinger's father had had a university education and was a member of the household of Henry Herbert, 2nd Earl of Pembroke, at Wilton. Massinger was thus brought up in one of the most cultured houses of the time. At the age of eighteen he attended St. Alban's Hall, Oxford. Conflicting accounts are given about whether he pursued his studies diligently. Anthony à Wood claims that 'he applied his mind more to poetry and romances'. Massinger did not take a degree and the date on which he left Oxford is uncertain – probably before 1606, the date given by some writers.

Massinger came to London and soon became involved in the theatre. The first certain evidence of his association with other playwrights comes in a letter, written by himself and two other playwrights, Nathaniel Field and Thomas Daborne, to Philip Henslowe (see *Lives of the Tudor Age*), in which the three beg for financial assistance to secure their release from prison. Massinger adds, 'I have ever found you a true loving friend to me and in so small a suit it being honest I hope you will not fail us.' This letter has been tentatively dated 1613. In the next few years Massinger's close association with Henslowe, the financier of the Admiral's Men, is shown by further letters and contracts.

During these years, Massinger was collaborating with others in the production of plays, although the extent of his part is not clear. In about 1616 he began to write for the King's Men and soon became Fletcher's chief assistant. Massinger's name is not mentioned on the title page of any of Fletcher's plays published during his lifetime, but a friend, Sir Aston Cokaine, protested to the publishers of the 1647 Folio of Fletcher's plays:

In the large book of Playes you late did print
(In Beaumont's and in Fletcher's name) why in't
Did you not justice? give to each his due?
For Beaumont of those many writ in few:
And Massinger in other few . . .

Sir Aston Cokaine claims further that Fletcher and Massinger had been great friends and written often together.

Massinger had possibly written plays on his own before 1620, when he was recognized by John Taylor (q.v.) as one of those playwrights 'which do on paper their true worth display'. If these early plays survive, they are among the hundreds of anonymous Jacobean plays. He did not receive credit for authorship until 1620, when *The Virgin Martyr* appeared under his name jointly with that of Dekker (q.v.). At the end of 1623 Massinger left the King's Men and joined the Cockpit Company, for which he wrote *The Parliament of Love* (1624) and *The Bondman* (1624). Later he supplied this company with *The Renegado* (1630).

On Fletcher's death in 1625, Massinger rejoined the King's Men, for whom he probably became the chief playwright. All his known plays but one from this date onwards were produced for the King's Men. Massinger wrote one play a year regularly, and in several years two. His reputation and popularity, however, did not rival that of Fletcher, and in a list of 1641 the King's Men had carefully preserved Fletcher's works, while several of Massinger's are not mentioned.

Massinger had many patrons, and it appears that he was more dependent on an income from them than some of his contemporaries, who made more income from their work.

Massinger's character, though poorly recorded, emerges clearly in his plays. He held strong opinions and tended to rhetorical discourse in his works. He was a great lover of liberty and an opponent of all forms of tyranny. He was bold in his political opinions and many of his characters are believed to be satires of contemporary noblemen and political figures. At a time when Catholics were generally feared and suspected, their connection with the Gunpowder Plot being widely remembered, Massinger was not afraid to depict a sympathetic Jesuit in *The Renegado*. Another play, *Believe as you list*, was refused a licence in 1631 because of the 'dangerous matter' it contained, and was not published until 1653.

Massinger was vigorous and quick in defence of the theatre when the Puritans submitted a request for plays to 'be restrained for ever after'. He promptly wrote his play *The Roman Actor* (1629), in which the principal character Paris, an actor, is a man of exceptionally sound morals and a firm supporter of the monarchy. Acting, Massinger argues through Paris, is a means of showing men their moral choices.

In expressing the author's own opinions, the characters in Massinger's plays lose their own convincing quality. The manifestations of their characters are external, and little is suggested of their inner being. As the characters lack weight, so do Massinger's arguments, which appear somewhat aimless. His morality in fact seems to bring about confusion as virtues and vices are treated almost as separable elements, with the result that they hang in limbo and fail to inspire either approval or disgust. His writing reflects the confusion and dissatisfaction prevalent at this time in the theatre and elsewhere.

Massinger continued to write plays regularly until his death just before the closure of the theatres. He lived all his working life in London, the latter part in a house near the Globe Theatre, where he died suddenly, being buried on 18 March 1640 at St. Saviour's, Southwark.

W. Gifford (ed.), *The Complete Plays of Philip Massinger* (1805, 1813).

D. S. Lawless (ed.), *Poems of Philip Massinger* (Muncie, Ind., 1968).

L. A. Sherman (ed.), *Philip Massinger* (New York, 1912).

A. Symons (ed.), *Philip Massinger* (2 vols.; 1887–89).

A. H. Cruickshank, *Philip Massinger* (1920).

T. A. Dunn, *Massinger: the Man and the Playwright* (1957).

Mather, Cotton (1663–1728), American Puritan clergyman and writer.

Born on 12 February 1663, in Boston, the son of Increase Mather (q.v.). Mather was a precocious child who entered Harvard at the age of twelve and graduated at fifteen. After studying theology he became an assistant minister in his father's church, the Second Church of Boston. He was ordained in 1685. After his father left for England in 1688, Mather was entrusted with the spiritual guidance of the congregation – the largest in New England at that time. He remained in this post for the rest of his life.

During the Salem witch trials, the prosecuting officials asked advice of the

Boston clergy. It was Mather, the most influential among them, who drafted the reply. In 1689 he had written of the evil influences of the Devil in his *Memorable Providences Relating to Witchcraft and Possessions*. He firmly believed that the colonies had become a breeding ground of satanical forces, and that witches were a manifestation of this spiritual disease. His arguments were in large measure responsible for the growing hysterical fear and hatred of those unfortunate persons thought to be witches. In later years, when the hysteria began to abate, he was the object of much criticism for his part in the persecutions.

In other matters, Mather displayed a reasonable and nearly scientific objectivity. During an epidemic of smallpox, in 1721, he preached and wrote in favour of treatment by means of inoculation. At the time, this practice was considered highly suspicious by most of the colonists, in spite of Jenner's success in England. He wrote *An Account of the Method and Further Success of Inoculating for the Small Pox in London* (1721), but unfortunately this reasonable medical treatment did not stir the popular imagination as had his belief in witchcraft. He kept his interest in this subject, and in 1693 wrote *The Wonders of the Invisible World*, which treated of witches and the supernatural. At times Mather thought that his own ideas concerning witches were sown by Satan, and he spent hours in prayer and fasting to rid himself of the dark forces he thought were trying to capture his soul.

Mather's writing style ranged from lucid and straightforward prose to the conceits and rhetorical eccentricities popular in his day. He filled many of his works with pedantic word play, allusions, and quotations. During the years 1693–97, he worked on his ecclesiastical history of New England, *Magnalia Christi Americana*, which was published in London in 1702. It was full of erudition, and sprinkled liberally with inaccuracies, but was nevertheless widely read by the learned. He published over 400 sermons, which were the antithesis of his more formal writing in being at once understandable. In 1721 Mather published *The Christian Philosopher*, a work in which he attempted to reconcile religion with the growing interest and influence of science.

He died on 13 February 1728, in Boston.

R. P. and L. Boas, *Cotton Mather* (1929).
Robert Middlekauff, *The Mathers: Three Generations of Puritan Intellectuals, 1596–1728* (New York, 1971).

Mather, Increase (1639–1723), American Puritan clergyman active in political affairs; president of Harvard (1685–1701); father of Cotton Mather (q.v.).

Born on 21 June 1639, in Dorchester, Massachusetts, the son of Richard Mather, an American Congregational clergyman from Liverpool. Mather entered Harvard in 1651, and took his degree with honours at the age of seventeen. He afterwards visited England, studied at Trinity College in Dublin, and became chaplain to the governor of Guernsey in 1659. On his return to America he was elected pastor of the South Church of Boston in 1664, in which post he remained until his death.

In the American colonial society of his time, the clergy were looked upon as an important source of guidance in civil affairs. Because his church was the largest in New England at that time, Mather was naturally entrusted with the task of helping to solve many political problems, and he gradually obtained great political influence.

When Charles II attempted to deprive the colony of Massachusetts of its charter, Mather took a prominent part in the public meetings of his townsmen. When they passed a resolution against the surrender of their privileges, it was Mather who was appointed to carry their remonstrances to England. His various meetings with James II, during the last year of his reign (1688), were not productive. On the accession of William III, Mather was able to present his position to a more favourable ear. Later in 1689, the Commons voted to approve restoration of the charter.

By the time Mather returned to Boston with the charter, in 1692, he had left behind several political pamphlets that one must surmise had some effect on his successful mission. Among them were *A Narrative of the Miseries of New England* (1688) and *A Brief Relation for the Confirmation of Charter Privileges* (1691). His position with the British government was undoubtedly enhanced not only by his being a prominent religious leader in the Boston community, but also by his post as president of Harvard, of which he was appointed acting president from 1681 to 1682 and president from 1685 to 1701.

Among his published works, numbering nearly 150, one, *Causes of Conscience Concerning Witchcraft* (1693), had a particularly important effect in exerting a restraining influence on the wild frenzy surrounding the persecution of persons accused of being witches. In it, Mather sought to prove that the Devil might appear in the shape of an innocent man. This sobering thought enabled many convicted of witchcraft to escape death. Unlike his son Cotton, who fanned the flames during the Salem witch trials, Increase was basically conservative and moderate in his approach to religious and social problems. His voice in the pulpit was gentle and soothing, and his sermons were a model of clarity and straightforward spiritual guidance, especially considering the over-zealous Puritanism that was then common.

Increase Mather is considered by many historians to be one of the most important and influential proponents of American liberty prior to the War of Independence. He died in Boston on 23 August 1723.

Robert Middlekauff, *The Mathers: Three Generations of Puritan Intellectuals, 1596–1728* (New York, 1971).

Maurice, Prince (1620–1652), Royalist soldier and faithful follower of his brother, Prince Rupert (q.v.).

Born at the castle of Küstrin (now in western Poland) on 25 December 1620, the fourth son of Frederick V, Elector Palatine and King of Bohemia, and Elizabeth, daughter of James I of England; attended university in France and later studied at Leyden, Holland. At the age of seventeen Maurice, together with his elder brother Rupert, joined the army of Frederick Henry, Prince of Orange, under whom he fought with great courage at the siege of Breda (1638). After two years of studying, he resumed his military activities and served in Baner's Swedish army in the Thirty Years War until his reunion with Rupert in 1641. Immediately before the outbreak of the Civil War the two brothers went to England and offered their services to Charles I.

In the initial stages of the war they traversed the north, raising troops and money for the King. Maurice accompanied Rupert in his successful campaigns until March 1643, when he was given independent command, being commissioned to protect Gloucestershire against Waller. In April 1643 he defeated Waller and Massey at Ripple Field. Three months later, acting in the capacity of lieutenant general under the Marquis of Hertford, Maurice successfully made his way to Oxford. Sent to the southwest, he first captured Exeter and Dartmouth and then proceeded to besiege Plymouth, but fell ill and later abandoned the plan to seize the port.

In 1644 he was commissioned lieutenant general of the southern counties but enjoyed no major success on his own account, playing a chief role in the bloody but inconclusive second Battle of Newbury in October 1644. In December of that year Maurice resigned his position in the west and became major general in charge of the defence of Worcestershire, Shropshire, Herefordshire, and Monmouthshire. From Worcester he directed the plundering of these counties; instead of imposing order on them he aggravated the discontent among the population.

In February 1645 Maurice moved towards Shrewsbury, which, however, he lost to the Parliamentarians. A few days later he marched to Chester, where his position became seriously threatened; he was, however, relieved by Rupert. In May Maurice reached Oxford and remained for some time with the King there; he participated in the taking of Leicester and at Naseby (14 June 1645) fought with Rupert on the right wing.

After the surrender of Oxford in June 1646, Rupert and Maurice left England. Maurice spent two years in the service of the Prince of Orange in Flanders. After that he spent the rest of his life at sea, accompanying his brother. On a piratical voyage to the West Indies, Maurice was lost in a storm off the Canary Islands on 14 September 1652.

Unlike his brother, Maurice had no military genius. He was not a particularly capable commander and his knowledge of strategy was negligible. Like Rupert, he had little regard for the civil and political aspects of the English Civil War.

Middlesex, 1st Earl of (1575–1645), see Cranfield, Lionel.

Middlesex, 1st Earl of, of the second creation (1638–1706), see Sackville, Charles.

Middleton, Charles (?1640–1719), 2nd Earl of Middleton; Scottish Jacobite leader, the eldest son of John Middleton (q.v.), 1st Earl of Middleton.

Charles Middleton was caught up in the turmoil of Commonwealth Scotland as a youth, accompanying his father in the campaign against Cromwell in the Highlands (1653–54) and to exile in France (1656–60). After the Restoration, he gravitated towards court circles and was appointed envoy to Vienna. Political prominence eluded him, however, until the Exclusion crisis, the attempt to exclude the Catholic Duke of York (later James II, q.v.) from succession to the throne. Middleton became a firm supporter and friend of James and had accompanied him to Scotland in 1680 when James was sent there as the the King's representative. He was appointed to the Scottish Privy Council and to the joint secretaryship for Scotland in 1682.

The Stuarts triumphed over the English opposition, and in 1684 Middleton became an English privy councillor and secretary of state. In 1685, when York ascended the throne as James II, Middleton was elected to the English House of Commons, where he became one of the government's managers, striving with all his charm and intelligence to win support for a standing army and to soothe the fears roused when James ignored the anti-Catholic Test Act. In private, Middleton attempted to moderate the King's purpose, and refused all the King's attempts to convert him: it is thought that he rejected Catholicism not so much because of Protestant convictions but from religious scepticism.

Although such conduct weakened his standing at court, Middleton's position was secured by his Catholic wife, Lady Catherine Brudenell (daughter of Robert Brudenell, 2nd Earl of Cardigan), who had great influence with the Queen. When the crisis of the reign came, in 1688, he proved his loyalty to James. He did not flee the country after the Glorious Revolution, but stayed behind and became the centre of the more moderate Jacobites, who sought to restore James II on terms acceptable to the bulk of the political nation. Nevertheless, after suffering one sojourn in the Tower, he finally fled to France in 1693 and joined the exiled court at St. Germain.

Middleton applied his energies towards directing James into more moderate paths, and attempted to secure a declaration from him renouncing absolutism and all intention of re-Catholicizing England. In token of this change of course, James appointed him secretary of state. At his death (1701), he appointed Middleton one of the guardians of his son and begged him to join the Catholic Church. Realizing fully how his position had weakened, the Earl complied with this request, thereby regaining some influence at this most Catholic of courts. In 1707 Middleton played a major part in the abortive expedition of the Jacobites to Scotland, in which his sons were captured by government forces.

In 1713 he resigned the secretaryship and became chamberlain to the exiled

Queen, Mary of Modena. Esteemed by all for his pleasant manners, ability, and wit, he died in exile in 1719.

A. C. Biscoe, *The Earls of Middleton* (1876).
George H. Jones, *Charles Middleton: The Life and Times of a Restoration Politician* (Chicago, 1968).

Middleton or Myddelton, Sir Hugh

(?1560–1631), 1st Baronet; entrepreneur who was responsible for the New River Project.

He was born at Galch Hill, in the parish of Henllan, Denbighshire, North Wales, in 1559 or 1560. His father was a Member of Parliament and the governor of Denbigh Castle. As a young man Middleton came to London to be apprenticed to a goldsmith. The trade at this time also included banking, and he soon became a successful financier. His dealings involved overseas ventures, and he became an intimate of Sir Walter Ralegh (see *Lives of the Tudor Age*). His brother, William Middleton, was a sea captain, a fact which must have been of further aid to him in his early career.

In 1603 Hugh Middleton took his seat in Parliament as Member for Denbigh. He served in the House of Commons up to the dissolution of 1629 and gained a considerable reputation, participating in several committees of inquiry into trade and financial matters.

The enterprise for which Middleton is most famous – the New River Project – was commenced in 1609. This was the construction of a canal to convey water from the springs of Chadwell and Amwell in Hertfordshire into London, where the rising population had outstripped its water supply. The project had been under consideration for some time, and the corporation was only too happy to hand over the matter to Middleton when he offered to take on the construction work. Undoubtedly, the activity of another brother of his, Sir Thomas Middleton, in the civic affairs of London also had some effect on the corporation's decision, though they did attach the condition that the job had to be completed in four years. Despite difficulties raised by landowners whose property had to be crossed by the canal, Middleton succeeded in completing the so-called New River by 1613. During the course of the job he had managed successfully to get back half his capital outlay from the crown in return for half the profits. Coincidentally, Michaelmas Day, 1613, the day on which the task was completed, was also the day upon which Thomas Middleton entered into the office of Lord Mayor of London.

The new canal was some ten feet wide and about four feet deep, and traversed a winding course of almost 39 miles from its sources near Ware in Hertfordshire to a reservoir in Islington. To supervise the project, Middleton took up residence at Edmonton.

His capital was totally tied up in the project, and the financial aid granted him by James I did not alleviate his personal monetary problems. In 1614 he managed to get a loan of £3,000 from the corporation of London, which money was apparently never repaid during his lifetime. He was forced to sell some of his shares in the recently formed New River Company, though he subsequently managed to buy a few of them back. In 1619 the company was incorporated under letters patent, and Middleton became its governor.

After the New River Project, Middleton turned his attention to mining. In 1617 he leased from the Company of Mines Royal some lead and silver mines in Cardiganshire, between the rivers Dovey and Ystwyth, which had fallen into disuse and were flooded with water.

After partially clearing the mines, he was able to work them again and succeeded in making a large profit. In 1625 he was even given permission to conscript workers from among the poverty-stricken rural labourers of Cardiganshire.

Another of his ventures was the reclamation of land on the Isle of Wight that had been overrun by the sea. The project was abandoned, however, after Middleton discontinued his association with it in 1624. It was not taken up again until the 19th century, being finally completed in 1882.

Some time after the completion of the New River Project, Middleton was knighted, and in 1622 James awarded him a baronetcy. This title, normally bought from the crown, was given free to Middleton in recognition of the beneficial work he had done in creating the New River. He also received confirmation of his lease of the Cardiganshire mines and was exempted from paying royalties on any metal he discovered. Middleton died in London on 10 December 1631.

Portrait: oil, three-quarter length, after C. Johnson, 1628: N.P.G.

Middleton, John (1619–1674), 1st Earl of Middleton; Scottish military leader in the Civil War.

Middleton was the eldest son of Robert Middleton of Caldhame, Kincardineshire. He married Grizel, daughter of Sir James Durham, and subsequently Lady Martha Carey, daughter of the 2nd Earl of Monmouth.

He began his military career in about 1637 in Hepburn's regiment of Scottish mercenaries, serving as a pikeman. The regiment was 'on loan' to the French King, and in 1639 Middleton returned to join the Covenanters' army, serving as a major under Montrose (see Graham, James) in the first Bishops' War. He took service in the Parliamentary forces at the outbreak of the Civil War as colonel of a regiment of dragoons, fought at Edgehill, and was given command of a regiment of horse. He served under Sir William Waller (q.v.) at Winchester in 1642 and in the Cheriton campaign of 1644, later becoming his lieutenant general of horse. He declined an appointment in the New Model Army, and joined the Scottish army in England.

Middleton was second-in-command to David Leslie (q.v.) at Philiphaugh (13 September 1645), where Montrose was routed, and after Leslie returned to England Middleton remained to harry the indomitable Montrose farther north. In July 1646 the two met in conference in Angus, Charles I having ordered Montrose to disband, with Middleton himself offering magnanimous terms of exile for the leaders and pardon for the ranks. This rebellion ended, in 1647 he put down another under Huntly; yet in the following year Middleton was the lieutenant general of horse in the army of intervention that Hamilton (q.v.) led into England to rescue the King. Middleton himself was taken prisoner at Preston, having personally performed with great energy and gallantry in an otherwise poor army, and for a while was held in custody at Newcastle.

In 1649 he made a vain attempt to raise the Highlands for Charles II, but was not punished other than by censure of the Kirk, and when the King landed in Scotland in 1650 Middleton joined him and subsequently organized an independent force in the north to support the royal cause. The Covenanter government sent Leslie against him; Middleton yielded on the King's orders and endured a humiliating penance imposed by the Kirk. After Cromwell's

defeat of the Scots at Dunbar, Middleton took command of the cavalry in the King's army, again under Leslie, and was wounded and taken prisoner at the Battle of Worcester (3 September 1651). He was confined in the Tower with the prospect of a trial and death sentence, but he escaped in his wife's clothes and reached the exiled court in Paris.

Middleton made one more attempt on the King's behalf, being appointed captain general of a Highland rebel force at the end of 1653. In the following July, Monck (q.v.) scattered it, Middleton escaping and returning to quasi-official employment in the King's entourage on the Continent, being given a peerage in 1656 that was confirmed at the Restoration.

As lord high commissioner, he presided over the Restoration parliaments in Scotland (1661–63) and the processes that swept away the legislation of the Covenanter years, showing more royalist zeal than political wisdom. On the instigation of Lauderdale, he was deprived of his offices in 1663; thereafter, he lived in bibulous retirement until Charles made him governor of Tangier, where he died after a drunken fall.

J. Adair, *Cheriton, 1644* (1973).
A. C. Biscoe, *The Earls of Middleton* (1876).

Middleton, Thomas (1580–1627), dramatist, noted chiefly for his satirical comedies.

Born in London, the son of a well-to-do bricklayer, little is known of Middleton's life. In 1598 he matriculated from the Queen's College, Oxford, and about 1602 became active as a dramatist in London. He had earlier published two youthful pieces, *The Wisdom of Solomon Paraphrased* (1597) and *Micro-Cynicon, or Six Snarling Satires* (1599), neither having much literary merit or giving any indication of his dramatic talent. Two satirical pamphlets published in 1604, *Father Hubbard's Tales* and *The Black Book*, constitute his only other non-dramatic work. The latter, which shows the influence of Nash (see *Lives of the Tudor Age*), does give some evidence of a developing satirical gift. In 1603 he married a daughter of one of the clerks in chancery and had a son the following year.

Between 1602 and 1613 Middleton wrote, often in collaboration with Dekker (q.v.) and others, a group of farcical and satirical comedies of great range and brilliance. Among the best of his early comedies are *A Trick to Catch the Old One* (about 1605), *Michaelmas Term* and *A Mad World, My Masters* (both 1604). They are brilliantly plotted and rapid-paced plays in which the shrewd and inventive villains are always finally outwitted by the young men whom they attempt to cheat. The deceptions and follies of the characters are acutely observed and rendered in a rich colloquial speech.

From about 1613, the date of *A Chaste Maid in Cheapside*, his plays become more serious in mood, with an increasing admixture of the tragic. The satire of the teeming variety of rogues, hypocrites, and cheats that populated the London streets, pawn shops, and brothels of the plays continues, but it is often unmitigated by the cheerful tolerance and merriness characteristic of his earlier comedies. Among his later plays are two tragedies written in collaboration with the playwright William Rowley, *Women Beware Women* (about 1621) and *The Changeling* (1622), notable for the discerning portrayal of the tragic heroines. His final work for the stage and probably the most enthusiastically received of all Jacobean plays was *A*

Game at Chess (1624), a comedy treating allegorically the political rivalry between England and Spain (the White House and the Black House of the play). The success of the play, due largely to the popular dislike of James I's plan to marry Prince Charles to a Spanish infanta, caused offence to the Spanish ambassador, Gondomar, and Middleton and the actors were summoned before the Privy Council. The play was prohibited but Middleton, who seems to have disappeared during the proceedings, his place being taken by his son, was given only a reprimand and otherwise went unpunished.

Other plays by Middleton are *The Roaring Girl* (with Dekker, 1607), *More Dissemblers Besides Women* (about 1615), *No Wit, No Help, Like a Woman's* (1615), *A Fair Quarrel* (with Rowley, 1615), *The World Tossed at Tennis* (1619), *Anything for a Quiet Life* (1621), and *The Spanish Gypsy* (with Rowley, 1623). In addition to his work in the theatre, Middleton wrote an enormous number of pageants and civic entertainments in fulfilling his post as city chronologer, a position that he held from 1620 to his death. He died in London and was buried at Newington Butts on 4 July 1627.

A. H. Bullen (ed.), *The Works of Thomas Middleton* (8 vols.; 1885–86).

R. H. Barker, *Middleton* (New York, 1958).

T. S. Eliot, 'Thomas Middleton', in *For Lancelot Andrewes* (1928: reprinted in *Selected Essays*, 1932).

For editions of *The Changeling*, see under Rowley, William.

Milton, John (1608–74), poet, author of the great epic of English poetry, *Paradise Lost*.

He was born on 9 December 1608 at Bread Street, London, the son of John Milton, a prosperous scrivener and

amateur composer. Milton was given a good education by his father, who taught him to play the organ and hired as his tutor Thomas Young, a brilliant Presbyterian divine. In 1620 John entered St. Paul's school, where he took to studying voraciously until midnight almost every night, bringing on severe headaches. By the age of 15 he knew Latin, Greek, French, Italian, and some Hebrew. He had also developed a deep love and understanding of poetry, Spenser and Du Bartas in particular, and had written some psalm paraphrases; indeed, Aubrey states that Milton was a poet from the age of ten. In 1625 he went up to Christ's College, Cambridge, where he soon fell foul of his tutor, William Chappell, who had him rusticated briefly and even, according to Aubrey, 'whipped him.' Milton's fellow students nicknamed him 'the lady' because of his delicate features and his austere and chaste life, which caused him to scorn their coarser pleasures. He was already convinced of his destiny to be a great poet, and maintained that he who would

'write well hereafter, in laudable things ought himself to be a true poem.'

In his early days at Cambridge Milton had written much Latin verse, often sensuous celebrations of love and spring inspired by Ovid. But all this was swept aside by his first important poem in English, *On The Morning of Christ's Nativity* (1629), in which the amoral glamour of the pagan classical gods is represented as succumbing before the universal serenity accompanying Christ's birth. So began Milton's life-long preoccupation with expressing his own idealistic and deeply felt Christian humanism in noble verse. The rich and fluid poetic language Milton had learnt from Spenser (see *Lives of the Tudor Age*) is used in *L'Allegro* and *Il Penseroso* (1631) to reconcile a formidably scholarly range of motifs, taken from romance, religion, folklore, and the classics, into poems of great technical assurance and lightness of touch. Throughout this early period, Milton's poetry is little affected by the then fashionable Metaphysical mode, instead drawing its inspiration directly from the mainstream of Renaissance literature.

In 1632 Milton left Cambridge, to confront an uncertain future. Originally destined for holy orders, he now found he could not 'subscribe slave' to the prelatist policies of Archbishop Laud (q.v.). Instead, his mission as a poet claimed him, and in preparation he went to live at his father's house in Horton, Buckinghamshire, to embark on a reading programme in religion and the classics. His loneliness is forcefully conveyed in a sonnet written on his 24th birthday, 'How soon hath Time...,' which contrasts the wordly success of his college contemporaries with his own obscure toil. But when Milton eloquently compares the world's transitory corruptness with heaven's eternal purity, this indicates his final conversion to the concept of serving only God with his poetry.

Milton did not, however, eschew the world entirely, for soon after, in collaboration with the composer Henry Lawes (q.v.), he wrote his first masque, *Arcades*, for the aged dowager Countess of Derby. This slight but melodious work outlines Milton's Platonic concept of chastity, considerably expanded in his next masque, *Comus* (1634), written, again in collaboration with Lawes, for the Earl of Bridgwater, and first performed by the Earl's family and friends at Ludlow Castle. The poetry is again compounded from extraordinarily varied sources, but now with a much firmer direction, the celebration of chastity; comparison of successive drafts indicates that Milton is now far more concerned with moral force than mere sensuous evocation. He manages to make the character Comus seem vital and repellent at the same time, an effective irony that he later used in portraying Satan in *Paradise Lost*.

Milton's hitherto confident idealism was shaken by the drowning of his young and gifted friend Edward King, and in the elegy *Lycidas* (1637) he reflects not only on his own dissatisfaction, with nothing achieved after five years of intense labour, but also, by his customary complexity of reference, on the position of all creative artists. Brilliantly employing the hackneyed pastoral form as the arena for his struggle, Milton concludes that true fame lives only in heaven and, abandoning references to Jove in favour of the language of Revelation, he ends the poem with an affirmation of religious faith. The spirited attacks on corrupt clergy in *Lycidas* foreshadow Milton's later exposures of abuses in church and state.

In April 1638 Milton's rural solitude ended when his father sent him off on a tour of Europe. He first visited Paris, whose 'manners and genius' he heartily disliked, and went on to Rome, where he upset everybody with his lofty moral stance and outspoken attacks on the papacy. Nevertheless, he seems to have been as sought after in Italy as he was ignored in England, and in Florence he visited Galileo and lectured to all the literary academies. Uncharacteristically, he also wrote five sonnets in Italian to an unknown lady of Bologna. In his Latin poem *Mansus*, a tribute to his Neapolitan host Baptista Manso, Milton first mentions his plan to write a great epic poem.

Returning to London in late 1639, Milton began a practical propagation of his views on morality by starting a school in Aldersgate, whose curriculum combined a thorough training in ethics with a daunting reading list of the classics. But by now English political life had become 'a troubl'd sea of noises and hoars [sic] disputes,' moving inevitably towards civil conflict. Although Milton enjoyed peace and quiet, he was by no means a hermit; he had attacked the abuses of the age ever since his Cambridge days, and he openly despised 'fugitive and cloistered virtue'. His idealism demanded that he take an active part in bringing about the Christian humanist millenium, and so for the next twenty years he produced a succession of prose works commenting forcefully on the issues of the times.

He first joined battle over church government. Bishop Hall of Exeter (see Hall, Joseph), the defender of episcopacy, had begun a complicated controversy with a group of five Presbyterian-minded clergy nicknamed 'Smectymnuus'. Amongst them was Thomas Young, Milton's old tutor, on whose behalf he wrote several pamphlets, most notably *The Reason of Church*

Government (1642), all of which counter Hall's 'spruce fastidious oratory' with an amazingly undisciplined prose, full of reckless vehemence and biting satirical wit. The supposedly philosophical Milton could speak as harshly as anyone when his feelings were aroused.

At the outbreak of the Civil War soon after, Milton did not join the Parliamentary army, asserting that his mind was stronger than his body; the sonnet *Captain or Colonel, or Knight in Arms*, written when the King's army was at Brentford, proclaims Milton's desire not to be disturbed. He was working hard on his plan for a heroic epic; his notebook of that time lists 99 likely themes, the favourites being a long poem about King Arthur and a Greek drama about the Fall of Man.

In May 1643 Milton made a mysterious trip into Oxfordshire, the heart of Royalist territory, and came back with a seventeen-year-old bride, Mary Powell. Apparently, her father had owed Milton £312 since 1627. Unfortunately, Mary found 'the philosophical life' dull, and Milton found his child-wife not only stupid but also frigid. Within a month she was back with her family, who refused to let her cohabit again with a dangerous Puritan. Soon afterwards, Milton published his *Doctrine and Discipline of Divorce*. The pamphlet states that 'the marriage of true minds' is the only valid kind, and that incompatibility, or 'contrariety of mind', constitutes perfectly logical grounds for divorce. This produced a violent public reaction: the Presbyterian clergy attacked such a monstrous publication, members of the Westminster Assembly demanded that it be publicly burnt, and a Mrs. Attaway, who had left her 'unsanctified' husband and run away with a preacher, blamed Milton for her conduct.

This and similar controversies provoked the Presbyterian-controlled Commons to pass an ordinance in late 1644 imposing strict control of the press. Milton protested against this in his most celebrated pamphlet, *Areopagitica* (1644), which pleads for freedom of speech in measured, noble language quite unlike his earlier rugged prose style. Significantly, Milton does not advocate total freedom, but recognizes the need for some judicious censorship. However, from now on he increasingly diverged from orthodox Presbyterianism, as he had from orthodox Anglicanism, and followed a personal doctrine, to the point where people tended to say that Milton '*was* a sect'.

The poet's next few years were filled with domestic upheavals. In 1645 the Powell family, ruined by the Royalist defeat, asked Milton to take Mary back. He relented, and took her to live at a house in the Barbican, where during the next few years she presented him with three daughters. Shortly after Mary's return her father died, whereupon Mrs. Powell descended on the Milton household, bringing Mary's eight brothers and sisters with her. The publication of his collected poems in 1647 must have relieved the gloom for Milton. Later that year his father died, leaving his son enough money to open a new school in High Holborn.

Strangely, Milton's opinions now began to find favour with the authorities. In 1648 he wrote a sonnet in praise of Thomas Fairfax (q.v.), and in 1649 his pamphlet *Tenure of Kings and Magistrates* supported the execution of Charles I and condemned public emotionalism over the fate of a mere tyrant. Later that year he was appointed Latin secretary to the government, in effect a public relations job. He replied to *Eikon Basilike*, a maudlin but best-selling account of Charles's martyrdom, with the biting *Eikonoklastes* (1649), and when the French scholar Salmasius entered the dispute Milton worked so hard composing his counterblast, *Pro Populo Anglo Defensio* (1650), that he began to go blind from glaucoma. He drafted the letter that Cromwell sent to Europe's rulers protesting at the massacre of the Vaudois Protestants, and privately expressed his grief and anger in the sonnet 'Avenge, O Lord, thy slaughtered saints.'

Again Milton's luck changed. In 1652 his wife died, and by 1655 his blindness was so hindering his work that he had to be given considerable assistance by Andrew Marvell (q.v.). He led a quiet life, his lofty principles always precluding him from having many intimate friends. In 1656 Milton married Catherine Woodcock, whose death in childbirth in 1658 he commemorated in the moving sonnet 'Methought I saw my late espoused saint.' During the turmoil of Richard Cromwell's protectorate Milton published a prose work on republicanism, *The Ready and Easy Way*, which showed he was no democrat, but was prepared to support enlightened oligarchy.

The Restoration of 1660 must have seemed to Milton the negation of all that he had fought for. Not only had he lost his faith in England, but also most of his worldly goods. His very life was now in danger, and he hid at a friend's house while the public hangman burnt his pamphlets. Though he was eventually arrested, he miraculously managed to buy his freedom for £150. His saviour was Andrew Marvell, who used his considerable influence with General Monck and the Commons on the poet's behalf. Wisely, Milton retired to his family circle. Unfortunately, his motherless daughters were seriously mismanaging the household; in 1663 he therefore

married the 24-year-old Elizabeth Minshull and took her to live in the modest house in Bunhill Fields where he spent the rest of his life. He fled from the plague in 1665 to a 'pretty box' in Chalfont St. Giles, Buckinghamshire, found for him by his young Quaker friend Ellwood.

The dashing of his worldly hopes brought a corresponding broadening of Milton's poetic vision, for in 1667 appeared his long-contemplated heroic epic, *Paradise Lost*. By now he had so much to say about God and man that his original plan of an Arthurian tale seemed insubstantial beside the story of the Fall. *Paradise Lost* had its literary precedents, including Vondel's *Lucifer* (1654) and Grotius's *Adamus Exul* (1601), but to fill out the much mightier structure of his epic Milton drew inspiration from an unprecedented range of sources, not only the Bible and the *Aeneid*, but also Ovid, Plutarch, and Renaissance writers.

Milton's use of blank verse in an English epic was a successful innovation; his basic metrical unit is the verse paragraph rather than individual lines, which are varied by careful adjustments of stress. *Paradise Lost*'s language, much criticized for its 'artificiality', is probably no more remote from colloquial usage than that of the *Aeneid*.

Milton and his descendants made precisely £18 from the copyright of *Paradise Lost*, which sold moderately well, some 1300 copies in 18 months. Its fame grew slowly but steadily; Denham called it the noblest poem ever written, while Dryden said, 'this man cuts us all out, and the ancients too.' None of this materially affected Milton's quiet way of life. He would rise at four in summer, five in winter, put on his customary black clothes, and have one of his daughters read the Bible to him in Hebrew before breakfast. The mornings were given over to writing, and after lunch he would take exercise, often swinging on his garden swing. Afternoons were devoted to music, and at six Milton would put on plain grey to receive his increasing number of distinguished visitors. Sitting with his leg slung familiarly over the arm of his chair, he would dictate a dozen or so lines of poetry to anyone who happened to be in the house. He had long since ceased to attend church services, but he admired the Quakers. This life-style was rather hard on Milton's long-suffering children. Understandably, they did not like having to read to him for hours in languages they did not understand, or to take dictation in the middle of the night. Not until 1670 did Milton at last allow them to go out and pursue lives of their own.

In 1671 appeared *Paradise Regained* and *Samson Agonistes*, Milton's last major works and his most autobiographical. Despite the disappointments of his public life, Milton still firmly believed in the value of private experience, 'the paradise within'. Hence *Paradise Regained* goes beyond the epic mode to celebrate 'the better fortitude of Patience and Heroic Martyrdom'. Its theme is the interior drama of Christ's temptation rather than the more obviously tragic Crucifixion. Apart from the sumptuous eulogies of Rome and Athenian culture, the language of *Paradise Regained* is far more austere than that of *Paradise Lost*, as befits its more subdued theme. However, it has been justifiably compared with the Authorized Version for the beauty of its 'perfect statement'.

In contrast to the quiet resignation of *Paradise Regained*, the verse drama *Samson Agonistes* is shot through with bitterness and conflict. Like Milton, Samson is a man once active in public affairs who has now lost everything. Once again,

the action is minimal; the drama is all contained in Samson's agonized soliloquies. As each protagonist accosts him, comforting, taunting, or condemning, his moods change, from hurt pride, through penitence, to crushing guilt. At his lowest ebb he longs for death, whilst the ever-present chorus questions God's providence:

Just or unjust, alike seem miserable.

Samson Agonistes reflects Milton's lifelong saturation in Sophocles, Aeschylus, and Euripides. Probably because he had put so much of himself into them, Milton was particularly attached to these two late works, and he disliked hearing them compared unfavourably with *Paradise Lost*.

Crippled with gout, his marriage failing, the still-defiant Milton in 1673 published his last pamphlet, *True Religion*, attacking the toleration of popery. On 8 November 1674 he died peacefully and was buried next to his father at St. Giles, Cripplegate.

F. A. Patterson *et al.* (eds.), *The Complete Works* (Columbia University Edition, 20 vols.; 1931–40).

D. M. Wolfe *et al.* (eds.), *Complete Prose* (Yale Edition, 8 vols.; New Haven, Conn., 1953–).

H. F. Fletcher (ed.), *Complete Poetical Works* (Boston, Mass., 1941).

Merritt Y. Hughes (ed.), *Complete Poems and Major Prose* (New York, 1957).

Helen Darbishire (ed.), *Poetical Works* (2 vols.; 1952–55).

Merritt Y. Hughes (ed.), *Paradise Lost* (New York, 1935).

C. Ricks (ed.), *Paradise Lost* (1968).

E. M. Pope (ed.), *Paradise Regain'd* (Baltimore, 1947).

F. T. Prince (ed.), *Samson Agonistes* (1957).

F. T. Prince (ed.), *Comus* (1968).

C. A. Patrides (ed.), *Lycidas* (New York, 1961).

B. A. Wright (ed.), *Poems* (Everyman's Library; 1956).

David Mason, *The Life of John Milton* (7 vols.; 1859–94: reprinted New York, 1946).

H. F. Fletcher, *The Intellectual Development of*

John Milton (Urbana, Ill., 1956–61).

J. Milton French, *The Life Records of Milton* (5 vols.; New Brunswick, N.J., 1946–58).

James H. Hanford, *John Milton, Englishman* (New York, 1949).

C. S. Lewis, *A Preface to Paradise Lost* (1942).

E. M. W. Tillyard, *Milton* (1966, rev. ed.).

Portraits: engraving, half-length, by W. Faithorne, 1670: N.P.G.; oil, quarter-length, by unknown artist, *c*. 1629: N.P.G.; plaster cast of bust, attributed to E. Pierce, *c*. 1660: N.P.G.

Mompesson, Sir Giles (1584–?1651), M.P. and monopolist.

Born at Bathampton, Wiltshire, Mompesson matriculated at Hart Hall, Oxford, on 24 October 1600, but seems not to have taken a degree. In 1612 Mompesson married a daughter of Sir John St. John, whose elder daughter was the wife of Sir Edward Villiers, half-brother of George Villiers (q.v.), 1st Duke of Buckingham. Thereafter, Villiers seems to have taken an interest in Mompesson and to have helped him in his career.

Mompesson was elected M.P. for Great Bedwin in 1614 and in Parliament he quickly emerged as an ally of the court. Two years later, with Villiers's help, Mompesson successfully urged the creation of a commission to grant licences to innkeepers and alehouses; in October he himself was appointed as a commissioner with two others, the patent for this being sealed in March 1617 under great pressure from the King, as the granting of licences would benefit the impoverished royal exchequer as well as the commissioners' pockets. Four-fifths of the money obtained was to be paid into the exchequer, the commissioners' fees for licensing being left to their own discretion. Mompesson was granted a knighthood at Newmarket (18 November 1616) to add dignity to his new office.

Mompesson was exceedingly reckless in his new duties. He charged outrageous fees, increased the number of inns by re-licensing those which had been closed as disorderly houses, and charged heavy fines for minor neglect of outdated laws. He acquired an evil reputation as a result, although his friendships with Bacon and Villiers did not suffer. Additionally, Mompesson became a commissioner empowered to impose fines and penalties on manufacturers of gold and silver threads operating without licences. Again he was reckless in the energetic execution of these duties and threatened numerous goldsmiths and silver producers with imprisonment. In 1620 Mompesson was granted a further licence, this time for the conversion of fuels into charcoal; in the same year he became surveyor of the profits of the New River Company and received an annual income of £200 from the profits.

Although he was re-elected M.P. in 1620, public feeling was outraged. On 20 February 1620, the House of Commons began investigating the patent for licensing inns. Witnesses' testimony against Mompesson was highly damaging, and he threw himself upon the House's mercy, but his appeal was received in total silence. After much deliberation, the lord chief justice pronounced against him in the Lords: he was to lose his knighthood, to be fined £10,000, to be paraded along the Strand, to be imprisoned, and to be forever after acknowledged an infamous person. Perpetual banishment was added later. Mompesson became the butt for public abuse and satire in the press and the theatre.

Although supposedly banished, Mompesson came in and out of England for the rest of his life on various private business matters, trying to put his affairs in order. On these protracted visits he lived with relations in Wiltshire in retirement. His property was sequestered by Parliament, as he was a Royalist, though he did not engage in the fighting. After 1651, he was not heard of.

Mompesson, William (1639–1709), clergyman, rector of Eyam, the 'plague village'.

Mompesson was educated at Peterhouse, Cambridge, where he took an M.A. in 1662.

Mompesson entered the service of George Savile (q.v.), Marquis of Halifax, as chaplain, and in 1664 was presented to the rectory of Eyam, Derbyshire, a living of which Lord Halifax held the patronage. At that time, Eyam was a village of some 350 people and a flourishing local centre of the lead-mining industry.

On 7 September 1665, a box of cloths arrived in Eyam from London: they proved to be carriers of the plague. Between that day and 11 October 1666, 259 out of the 350 inhabitants died (this figure is given in Mompesson's letters; the parish records actually give 267 deaths).

Mompesson and his wife Catherine did not leave Eyam, but remained to do all they could for their parishioners, although they appear to have sent their infant children to safety.

Between June and August of 1666 the plague was at its height and Mompesson persuaded the villagers to put themselves into voluntary isolation in order to contain the disease. He had the full support and assistance of a former (Puritan) rector of Eyam, Thomas Stanley, who still lived in the village after his dismissal in 1662. The villagers received food and other necessities from the Earl of Devonshire and from nearby villages. They paid for the goods with money placed in troughs of running water, designed to prevent the spread of infection: these became known as 'Mompesson's Well'. Mompesson conducted simple services of prayer on Sundays in a small valley on the outskirts of the village known as the Delf, and preached from a rocky outcrop. On 25 August 1666, Catherine Mompesson died and, believing he was close to death himself, Mompesson wrote farewell letters to his small children and his patron, Lord Halifax. He also wrote to a friend, John Beilby of York. These letters form the basis of what is known of the events in Eyam during the plague years and there is no doubt that Mompesson wrote them as a record for posterity.

There was subsequent discussion as to whether Mompesson's precautions were necessary, but the fact remains that the plague was contained in Eyam and spread no further in Derbyshire. Mompesson himself survived the plague and later (1669) became the rector of Eakring, near Ollerton, Nottinghamshire. However, his new parishioners were afraid of the plague and he was at first refused entry to the village. For some time he lived in a hut in Rufford Park.

Mompesson subsequently married again and was made prebendary of Southwell (1676) and York. He died in 1709.

C. Daniel, *The Plague Village: a History of Eyam* (1938, new ed.).
William Wood, *The History and Antiquities of Eyam* (1865, 4th ed.).

Monck, George (1608–70), 1st Duke of Albemarle; general and admiral.

He was born on 6 December 1608, the son of Sir Thomas Monck, an impoverished Devonshire gentleman. Although Monck's competence as a general, an admiral, and an administrator in Scotland alone would have secured him a place in history, his chief claim to fame is that of all the moderate-minded men who suffered from conflicts of loyalty and opinion through the Civil War and Protectorate, he was the one chiefly instrumental in healing the wounds and divisions by securing the peaceful Restoration of Charles II in 1660.

In 1625 Monck volunteered for the Cadiz expedition to escape legal proceedings following his assault on an under-sheriff in a family feud. He entered the Dutch service in 1629 and became a very competent officer with a reputation for personal bravery and good discipline. He returned to serve in the Bishops' Wars against Scotland (1639–40) as a lieutenant colonel, and was invited by his kinsman the Earl of Leicester, then lord lieutenant of Ireland, to command his own regiment when the Irish rebellion broke out in 1641. In that capacity he served with distinction in the early campaigns against Thomas Preston and Owen Roe O'Neill. He was appointed the governor of Dublin by Leicester in 1643, but the appointment was rescinded by the King in favour of his own nominee, a certain Lord Lambert.

The cessation negotiated by Ormonde (see Butler, James, 1st Duke) brought this period of service to an end in September 1643 under circumstances in which Monck's personal loyalties were placed in question. He was approached by the Parliamentarians with an offer of service, and was confined on suspicion by Ormonde. Being allowed to take his case to the King at Oxford, he justified himself and severely criticized the organization of the Royalist army. He then rejoined the 'Irish' regiments in Cheshire, where they had been sent to assist Lord John Byron in the English Civil War, and was captured at the Battle of Nantwich (25 January 1644),

fighting as a volunteer at the head of his old regiment against the troops of Sir Thomas Fairfax (q.v.). He was charged with high treason before the House of Commons (technically the 'Irish' regiments had been authorized in Parliament before the war and were supposed therefore not to be part of the Royalist army), and spent two years in the Tower.

At the end of that period the situation in both kingdoms had altered, and Parliament had assumed control of the continuing war in Ireland by virtue of its success in the war in England. As an experienced 'Irish' officer, Monck's ability was being wasted, and he himself was prepared to make a distinction between serving against Irish rebels and serving under English ones, the new lord lieutenant, Lord Lisle, using his influence to bring him to this point of view. In February 1647 he crossed to Ireland with the rank of adjutant general, and when Lisle's term of office ended in April and the civil government was divided, Monck was given the administration of Ulster.

The shifting politics of England continued to trouble the Irish scene. In 1648 the Scottish army that had been assisting operations in Ulster since 1642 defected, and Monck had to take action against them, imprisoning their general, Robert Monroe. The execution of Charles I in January 1649 caused the 'Old Scots' – the Ulster colonists of James I – also to declare against the politicians of Westminster, making Monck's military position precarious. The other Parliamentarian commander, Michael Jones in Dublin, could spare him no aid, so that Monck was forced to buy off the original rebels, the 'Old Irish' – the native Catholics of Ulster under O'Neill. Full details of the truce that he negotiated with O'Neill (8 May 1649) were sent to Cromwell, but the move had sown considerable doubts about their general's intentions among Monck's own men. Consequently, they offered no resistance to the Royalist force sent against him by Ormonde and he was forced to surrender Dundalk, the fortress where he had been with difficulty maintaining himself. Upon his return to England in July, he appeared before the Commons and his action in making the treaty was disowned, but the House accepted that it had been forced upon him by the circumstances.

In July 1650 Monck's ability was further acknowledged by his inclusion in Cromwell's army invading Scotland, a regiment being formed for him by detaching companies from those commanded by Fenwick and Hesilrige, which regiment has enjoyed a continuous existence to the present day as the Coldstream Guards. At Cromwell's victory at Dunbar (3 September 1650) he commanded the foot in the centre of the line, and participated in smaller engagements in the following months, being appointed lieutenant general of ord-

nance in May 1651. Upon Cromwell's return to England in pursuit of Charles II, he nominated Monck as the commander-in-chief in Scotland, and as such he was responsible for the capture of Stirling (14 August) and Dundee (1 September). At the end of the year the civil government was vested in commissioners, of whom Monck was one, but early in 1652 he took leave to recover his health.

The aggressive commercial policy adopted by the Commonwealth involved it in war with the Dutch, hostilities opening in May 1652. In November Monck was appointed as one of the three generals of the fleet, the others, Blake and Deane (qq.v.), already having maritime experience. The appointment coincided with the first serious defeat of the English navy in the Dutch wars, the action off Dungeness in which Blake was beaten by Tromp. As a result Parliament established a committee of four M.P.s, the three generals, and two other persons to work under Sir Henry Vane the Younger (q.v.), treasurer of the Navy, to reorganize its administration and methods. Blake and Monck co-operated closely in this work, and the results were seen in the following year in the three battles that induced the Dutch to make peace, Portland (18–20 February), The Gabbard (2–3 June), and Scheveningen (29–31 July). In the first, Blake commanded overall, with Monck handling the lee division as Admiral of the White, coming into action against adverse winds at a critical moment to save the weather division from being overwhelmed. Blake was wounded in the battle, so that Monck commanded off The Gabbard after Deane had been killed by the opening broadside. Again it was the absence of Blake, this time through illness, that left Monck as the responsible general in the third engagement, which also marked the death in action of Tromp, the Dutch commander.

In the spring of 1654 Monck returned to the army in Scotland to deal with a Royalist rising, which had been continuing unchecked since the previous summer. Before the autumn it was suppressed, leaving Monck free to meet the next crisis, discontent among his own soldiers arising from arrears of pay and political agitation aimed at the overthrow of the Protectorate.

His civil administration of Scotland, in which he had the assistance of an able council, maintained order with firmness and strict loyalty to Cromwell in England, which reinforced the trust that existed between the two men. Generally, his rule was exercised in favour of conservative interests and was therefore as popular with them as could be expected under the burden of heavy taxation. After Oliver Cromwell's death in 1658, Monck offered the same support to Richard Cromwell in his turn, but markedly did not move from Scotland as the political turmoil in London dissolved the Protectorate. Yet however reluctant to become involved he may have been, with his proven loyalty at separate times to the monarchy, to the moderate parliamentarianism of the Presbyterians, and to the Army itself, he became the unexpected key to the situation. As the Rump Parliament and the Army leaders failed to achieve a coexistence, appeals reached him from both Royalists and Parliamentarians alike. On 24 November 1659, members of the old Council of State designated him the commander-in-chief of all the forces in the two kingdoms, thus giving a quasi-legal cover to any action he might take to assert his authority over the Army commanders in England.

On 2 January 1660, he crossed the Tweed with the greater part of his own army, gathering impressive evidence of support as he marched on London, which he entered on 3 February with his intentions still undisclosed. He detected a strong feeling among conservative Presbyterians in favour of a return to monarchy, given some concessions on the part of the Stuarts, and this coincided with his own views. The first step was to permit the members excluded by Pride's Purge to resume their seats in Parliament (21 February), having first explained to them what was expected of them. The next was to extract from his own officers a promise of obedience to whatever solution the civil authorities determined. The Declaration of Breda was issued by Charles II (4 April), based upon Monck's proposals; a newly elected parliament in proper succession to the self-dissolved Long Parliament met three weeks later and on 1 May voted the restoration of the monarchy—all this under the protection of Monck's military power. On 25 May he welcomed the King ashore at Dover.

Honours and material rewards, including an earldom, a barony, and a dukedom, were heaped upon him, but his political activity in the immediate post-Restoration period was limited in most matters to endorsement of the policies of others, especially Clarendon (see Hyde, Edward) by his presence. With the Declaration of Breda, Charles II had sent him a commission as captain general, and this was now confirmed for life. His military ability was therefore still at the service of the state. The second Dutch war began in 1665 and the Duke of York took command of the fleet, deputing his office of lord high admiral to Monck, who was thus involved once again in the shore administration of the naval service. He remained at his post in London during the plague, and in November the King decided to give him a sea command.

In the mistaken belief that the French intended to assist the Dutch, the fleet was divided, Prince Rupert sailing to block the French with one third of the ships in May 1666 while Monck remained in the North Sea with the remainder. The Dutch under de Ruyter arrived off the North Foreland on 1 June, and Monck gave battle with a numerically inferior fleet, sustaining the fight unsupported until Rupert arrived at the end of the third day. On the fourth day the Dutch withdrew, having inflicted heavy losses on the English navy. The two British admirals were at sea again within two months and inflicted a severe defeat on de Ruyter on 24/25 July.

The Great Fire of London caused Monck's recall to his shore duties on 8 September, and despite his energetic efforts to establish defence works, he was unable to prevent the Dutch entering the Medway in the following year to destroy the ships laid up by an impecunious royal government. In 1667–68 he served briefly as first lord of the Treasury, but ill-health increasingly reduced his capacity to perform his duties. After his death, on 3 January 1670, Charles II took personal charge of his state funeral and burial in Westminster Abbey.

J. R. Powell and E. K. Timings (eds.), *The Rupert and Monck Letter Book, 1666* (1969).
Maurice Ashley, *Cromwell's Generals* (1954).
J. S. Corbett, *Monck* (1889).
J. D. G. Davies, *Honest George Monck* (1936).
D. M. W. Warner, *Hero of One Restoration* (1936).

Portraits: oil, quarter-length, after S. Cooper, *c.* 1660: N.P.G.; oil, three-quarter length, studio of Lely: N.P.G.

Monmouth, Duke of (1649–85), leader of an unsuccessful rebellion in 1685.

The illegitimate son of Lucy Walter (q.v.), he was born on 9 April 1649, in Rotterdam. There is some doubt about his paternity, although Charles II acknowledged him as his son and doted on him. He was also variously known as James Scott, Fitzroy, or Crofts.

The young James grew up in the Low Countries and France, where he enjoyed little by way of education, until in 1662 he was brought to England. Already very handsome, he quickly became both the centre of scandal and the object of his putative father's favour. But the shrewdest observers at court soon recognized his lack of intelligence.

In 1663 Charles made him Duke of Monmouth and a knight of the Garter. The new duke was married that same year to Anne Scott, the wealthy Countess of Buccleuch, and adopted her surname.

Monmouth proved to be a popular figure, active in court life, the darling of the people, and the recipient of princely honours. His military career began in 1665, when he served at the naval Battle of Solebay as a volunteer under his uncle, the Duke of York (the future James II, q.v.). The next year he received a commission as a cavalry captain. His life at court came to be marked by escapades of an increasingly coarse and violent nature, culminating in the murder of a watchman in 1670.

Nevertheless, he succeeded George Monck as captain general of the army. He was sent to the Continent to command the English contingent under Louis XIV and Marshal Turenne in 1672 and 1673, where his courage was noted. Five years later, he served with the Dutch against Louis in the Low Countries. In the autumn of 1678 he returned to England, and was immediately caught up in the politics of the Popish Plot and the Exclusion crisis. Shaftesbury (see Cooper, Anthony Ashley) and the Whigs saw Monmouth as a possible asset – the 'Protestant Duke' to be put forward as their candidate for the succession in opposition to Charles II's brother and heir presumptive, the Catholic Duke of York.

In spite of his intriguing, Monmouth was sent to Scotland in 1679 to crush a Covenanter revolt. He accomplished this task at Bothwell Bridge and further enhanced his popularity by the clemency with which he treated these Protestant rebels. But his campaign for the succession to the throne led Charles to exile him at the end of the year. To counteract popular rumours, the King was twice forced to deny to the Privy Council that he had ever married Lucy Walter.

Early in 1680, Monmouth returned to England without the King's permission. Charles stripped him of all his offices. Monmouth responded by making progresses through the southwest, where he received much acclaim. He became involved in the Rye House Plot, the unsuccessful conspiracy developed in 1682 and 1683 to overthrow the King and his brother, but the degree of his involvement remains unclear. Charles pardoned him, but remained cold. Monmouth retired to the Netherlands in 1684, where the news of his father's death found him the next year.

In concert with other exiles, Monmouth planned a rebellion. The Earl of Argyll (see Campbell, Archibald, 9th Earl) sailed in May to raise Scotland. Soon after, Monmouth set out with three ships and an assortment of incompetent and quarrelsome officers. They landed at Lyme Regis on 11 June 1685, and the common people quickly rallied to their cause. But James II had not yet alienated the gentry, who generally stayed aloof or raised the militia for the King.

Monmouth led his ill-equipped peasant army irresolutely towards Bristol and

then away again, without daring to attack the city. On the night of 6 July he attempted a desperate surprise attack on the royal forces, encamped on Sedgemoor behind numerous trenches. Caught in front of regular soldiers, but separated from them by a last ditch, the rebel army was slaughtered.

Monmouth fled the field before the battle was over, but was later captured. He begged for mercy from his uncle but was executed on 15 July on Tower Hill.

E. D'Oyley, *James, Duke of Monmouth* (1938).
W. R. Emerson, *Monmouth's Rebellion* (1951).
Allan Fea, *King Monmouth* (1902).
B. Little, *The Monmouth Episode* (1956).
Derrick J. Porrit, *The Duke of Monmouth* (1953).
G. Roberts, *The Life, Progresses and Rebellion of James Duke of Monmouth* (2 vols.; 1844).

Portraits: oil, half-length, copy after Wissing, *c.* 1683: N.P.G.; oil, by Lely: N.P.G.

Monmouth, 1st Earl of, of the second creation (1658–1735), see Mordaunt, Charles.

Montagu, Charles (1661–1715), Earl of Halifax; politician and economist; a member of the Whig Junto.

Born on 16 April 1661 in Horton, Northamptonshire, the fourth son of George Montagu, a country gentleman and younger brother of the 2nd Earl of Manchester, Montagu was educated at Westminster School and Trinity College, Cambridge.

At an early age Montagu made his mark as a writer of witty epigrams and poems. As a student he achieved distinction and won the friendship of Newton. He was awarded an M.A., became a fellow of Trinity College, Cambridge, and set about to become a clergyman. However, verses he composed on the death of Charles II (1685) attracted the attention of the Earl of Dorset (see Sackville, Charles), who introduced him to London literary circles. His reputation as a man of letters was further enhanced when, with Matthew Prior (q.v.), he published a popular burlesque of Dryden's *The Hind and the Panther* (1687).

As the reign of James II continued, Montagu joined other notables in resistance of the King's arbitrary measures and signed the famous letter inviting William of Orange to come to England. And when this champion of the Protestant cause arrived, Montagu joined the anti-Stuart rebellion in Northamptonshire. In 1689 he was elected to the Convention Parliament and obtained his first government post as a clerk of the Privy Council. He was a brilliant speaker and a skilled parliamentary manager, and although his arrogance and vanity won him numerous enemies, he advanced quickly. In 1691 he became a commissioner of the Treasury, and in that capacity established the National Debt (1692) and the Bank of England (1694). His financial and political services warranted further promotion, and

in 1694 he became chancellor of the exchequer and a privy councillor. With Newton's assistance he produced the Recoinage Act (1695), which put an end to clipping and counterfeiting by a recall and reissue of all coins; from now on new coins were issued with milled edges. (This move was paid for by a window tax.) He further expanded the money supply by issuing the first exchequer bills that same year. In 1696 he established the Consolidated Fund and in 1697 became first lord of the Treasury.

Montagu adopted these successful measures to finance King William's wars. In the next reign they served Marlborough equally well and have since functioned as the basic structure of British public finance. Because of Montagu's new institutions, creditors could for the first time feel secure when lending money to the state.

By this time Montagu was firmly established as one of the Whig leaders along with Edward Russell, John Somers, and Thomas Wharton (qq.v.), who together made up the so-called Junto. However, as a member of this Junto, Montagu's position was badly weakened when the Whigs suffered losses in the 1698 elections. Attacks on his personal financial integrity, which was indeed open to question, mounted, and in 1699 he resigned his Treasury posts. In December 1700 William created him Baron Halifax.

This elevation to the peerage proved of considerable value to him when, in 1701, the Commons – by now dominated by Tory and Country M.P.s – impeached him for corruption and for his share in the Partition Treaties; as a peer he was tried in the Lords and the Lords threw the charges out. Although Halifax remained a Whig leader, he never held office under Anne, even when the ministry had to rely on Whig support for its war policies; his tendency to antagonize others ensured that he was passed over. During these years he joined the successful attack on the Occasional Conformity Bills (1702, 1704), thereby reinforcing the enmity of the extreme High Tories. In 1706 he brought the insignia of the Garter to the electoral prince of Hanover, the future George I (see *Lives of the Georgian Age*), with whom he established a good relationship. That same year he was appointed a commissioner for the Union with Scotland.

On Anne's death in 1714, Halifax was appointed one of the regents by King George until he arrived from Germany. For his loyalty to the Hanoverian cause he received his old post of first lord of the Treasury, the order of the Garter, and an earldom. However, he did not survive long to enjoy these honours, for he died in London on 19 May 1715.

Portrait: half-length, by Kneller: Trinity College, Cambridge.

Montagu, Edward (1602–71), 2nd Earl of Manchester; Parliamentarian commander in the Civil War.

Edward Montagu was born in 1602, the eldest son of Sir Henry Montagu, 1st Earl of Manchester. He went to Sidney Sussex College, Cambridge, in 1618, and represented the county of Huntingdon in Parliament in 1623–26. In 1626 he was elevated to the upper house as Baron Montagu of Kimbolton, largely through the influence of the Duke of Buckingham (see Villiers, George, 1st Duke). His father was then created Earl of Manchester and Edward received the courtesy title of Viscount Mandeville.

In 1626, Montagu married for the second time. His father-in-law was the Earl of Warwick, and through the influence of his wife's relations he seems

to have begun to lean towards the Puritan party. He was one of the twelve peers who signed a petition asking the King to call a parliament in August 1640 and was acknowledged leader of the Puritan party in the early sittings of the Long Parliament. He was one of those accused by the King of high treason in January 1642, but was cleared of the accusation by both houses in March.

In September, Montagu took command of a foot regiment in Essex's army, and was soon made lord lieutenant of Huntingdonshire and Northamptonshire by Parliament. He succeeded to his father's title that autumn. In 1643, he was appointed major general of the eastern counties in order to quell local squabbles. After several successes, Lincolnshire was added to his command in January 1644 and he was directed to 'regulate' the University of Cambridge.

Manchester fought at Marston Moor in 1644, but after the surrender of York by the Royalists his army parted from Fairfax's. He returned to Lincoln and inactivity. Manchester was directed to march against Prince Rupert's army from Lincoln but was reluctant to undertake 'so large a commission, and a work so difficult'. He made no move to follow out the command, and although he took part in the second Battle of Newbury his disinclination to fight was obvious. He disliked the idea of a protracted war, which he now saw developing, and held the view that 'If we beat the King 99 times .. he is King still, and so will his posterity be after him; but if the King beat us once, we shall be all hanged, and our posterity be made slaves.' His religious views were sincerely held, and he was by nature generous and gentle. Manchester favoured peace, a constitutional monarchy, and Puritanism.

A break with Cromwell was inevitable, and in November Cromwell accused Manchester of neglect and incompetence in the pursuit of the war before the House of Commons. Cromwell cited 'his Lordship's continued backwardness to all action, his averseness to engagement or what tends thereto, his neglecting of opportunities and declining to take or pursue advantages upon the enemy. . . .' Manchester was a civilian at heart, and believed that a lasting end to the war would only be achieved by conciliation, not by the sword. A committee of inquiry was appointed to investigate the charges, but they were forgotten as the bill for remodelling the army came before Parliament. He resigned his commission on the day before the Self-Denying Ordinance passed the Lords.

Manchester remained in Parliament, frequently acting as Speaker of the House of Lords. He actively worked for peace during this time, and was one of those to whom Charles, in December 1645, was willing to entrust the militia. Manchester was one of the commissioners engaged in working out a treaty between England and Scotland in 1646, and early in 1647, with other Presbyterian peers, he sought to frame a peace that would gain royal approval. However, when Parliament was attacked by a mob in 1647 Manchester fled to the army and signed an engagement to stand by the Army for the freedom of Parliament. Fairfax escorted him back to London, where he resumed his duties as Speaker of the Lords. He opposed the ordinance for the King's trial in 1649 and retired from public life when the Commonwealth became inevitable.

Cromwell summoned Manchester to sit in his Upper House of Parliament in 1657, but he disobeyed and took an active part in bringing about the Restoration. As Speaker of the Lords, he welcomed Charles II when he returned, and was invested with many honours. In 1660 Manchester was appointed one of the commissioners of the great seal, restored to the lord lieutenancy of Northamptonshire and Huntingdonshire, and to the chancellorship of Cambridge University. He was also made lord chamberlain of the household, privy councillor, and chamberlain of South Wales. In October of that year he was engaged in the trial of the regicides, towards whom he seems to have favoured leniency. Manchester bore the sword of state at Charles II's coronation in 1661 and was made a knight of the Garter. From 1667 until his death he was a fellow of the Royal Society. He died on 5 May, 1671, and was buried in Kimbolton Church, Huntingdonshire.

Peter Young, *Marston Moor* (1970).

Portrait: oil, three-quarter length, by Sir Peter Lely, 1661–5: N.P.G.

Montagu, Edward (1625–72), 1st Earl of Sandwich; military and naval commander.

He was born on 27 July 1625, in Barnwell, Northamptonshire, the son of Sir Sydney Montagu, a Royalist member of the Long Parliament. Despite his father's leanings, Edward Montagu joined the Parliamentary forces at an early age. His attitude was probably influenced by his cousin Edward Montagu, Earl of Manchester (q.v.). In 1643 he raised an infantry regiment in Cambridgeshire and joined Manchester's army, in which he fought at Marston Moor (1644). He was given command of a regiment in the New Model Army and fought courageously at Naseby (1645) and at the siege of Bristol (1645).

Although a close friend of Oliver Cromwell, and by now a Member of Parliament, Montagu did not play an active role in the turbulent years surrounding the execution of Charles I. He emerged in 1653 as a member of the Barebones Parliament and was appointed to the Council of State. More government posts followed, including a seat on the treasury commission (1654), and in 1656 he was made joint commander of the fleet along with Blake (q.v.). Montagu had no experience of the sea, but he could be relied upon as a loyal supporter of Cromwell.

As a Commonwealth admiral Montagu led an uneventful life, but in the political world he gained prominence as a staunch upholder of Cromwell's policies, and was appointed to the new upper chamber in 1657. When the old Lord Protector died (1658), Montagu threw his weight behind Richard Cromwell, who sent him with the fleet to make peace between Denmark and Sweden. While away from England, he received word that the younger Cromwell had fallen; his bond of loyalty to the Commonwealth broken, he took up communications with the exiled Charles II. The complicated manœuvres and in-trigues that Montagu now indulged in are described by his secretary, Samuel Pepys (q.v.); finally, in 1660, he found himself in a strong enough position to purge the navy of republicans and to transport Charles II, whom the Convention had recognized as king, back to his native land.

Montagu was rewarded with the Garter, the earldom of Sandwich, and a string of offices, including that of lieutenant admiral to the Duke of York (later James II), England's new lord high admiral. In this capacity Sandwich took the fleet to the Mediterranean, where he arranged the transfer of Tangier to the English crown. This was part of the dowry of Catherine of Braganza, whom he brought back to become England's queen.

When the Second Anglo-Dutch War broke out, Sandwich took command of a squadron in York's fleet, and at the Battle of Lowestoft (1665), led the ships that broke the Dutch line. Later that year he captured several ships of the Dutch East India Company and led or co-operated with his officers in plundering these valuable prizes. A great outcry arose, eagerly furthered by his enemy and rival Albemarle (see Monck, George), and Sandwich was forced to resign his command. Charles then appointed him ambassador to Madrid, a post that he filled with distinction from 1666 to 1668, during which time he concluded a commercial treaty much to the advantage of English merchants and contributed to the peace between Spain and Portugal.

In the third Anglo-Dutch War, Sandwich once again led a squadron in York's fleet. On 28 May 1672, the Dutch and English joined battle at Solebay, off Lowestoft, in one of the bloodiest naval engagements of the century. The ships under Sandwich fought with great tenacity, bearing the brunt of the Dutch attack until, suddenly, his flagship caught fire and exploded. His body was later found at sea and buried in Westminster Abbey.

R. C. Anderson (ed.), *The Journal of Edward Montagu, first Earl of Sandwich, Admiral and General at Sea 1659–1665* (1928).
F. Harris, *The Life of Edward Montagu* (1912).

Portrait: oil, quarter-length, after Lely, *c.* 1660: N.P.G.

Montagu, Ralph (?1638–1709), 1st Duke of Montagu; politician who held a variety of appointments under Charles II and achieved a dukedom under Queen Anne.

Ralph Montagu was the second son of Edward, 2nd Baron Montagu of Boughton. His exact birth date is not known, but he was baptized on 24 December, 1638. He was educated at Westminster School. Very early on he gained a reputation for gallantry, and it is thought that his early appointments were a result of feminine influence. He was master of horse to the Duchess of York (see Hyde, Anne) and, on the death of his elder brother, became master of horse to Queen Catherine. In 1666 and 1669 he was sent to France as ambassador extraordinary. However, these posts did not meet his financial expectations and he made several unsuccessful attempts to get a Treasury appointment.

In 1671 he purchased the mastership of the wardrobe, and in 1673 he made the first of his two financially advantageous marriages. He married Elizabeth Wriothesley, daughter of the late lord treasurer and widow of the Earl of Northumberland. Her income was alleged to be in the region of £6,000 p.a. In 1672 Montagu was made a privy councillor, and in 1676 he was again ambassador to France. Once more Montagu involved himself in intrigues

to obtain a more influential and more rewarding post, this time that of secretary of state. He plotted with the Duchess of Cleveland (Barbara Villiers, q.v.), mistress of Charles II. However, when she became aware of the full ramifications of his deviousness, she denounced him to the King. He returned from France to find himself dismissed from his posts and out of the Privy Council (1678).

Montagu plotted his revenge. He negotiated with the French ambassador, promising to secure the downfall of Danby (see Osborne, Thomas). In the same year as his own dismissal, Montagu managed to procure two compromising letters that proved that Danby was conducting secret negotiations with Louis XIV. This was enough to ensure Danby's impeachment, a serious political crisis, and the dissolution of Parliament.

Montagu was now in the pay of France, where he lived for five years (1680–85). He was also actively scheming on behalf of the Duke of Monmouth (q.v.). In 1684 he succeeded his father as Lord Montagu of Boughton, and in 1685 he returned to England, but despite approaches to James II on his accession, was given no office. He transferred his allegiance to William of Orange as soon as it became certain that William would become king, and in 1689 he was created Earl of Montagu and Viscount Monthermer. His mastership of the wardrobe was also restored.

In 1692 Montagu married again, his first wife having died two years earlier. His bride was Elizabeth Cavendish, widow of Christopher Monck, 2nd Duke of Albemarle. She was allegedly mad, but undoubtedly wealthy. In Queen Anne's reign, Montagu's position was further strengthened by the marriage of his son John to a daughter of the Duke of Marlborough, and in

1705 he was elevated to the dukedom of Montagu and was made Marquis of Monthermer.

On 9 March 1709, he died in London. The title became extinct after the death of his son John in 1749.

Montagu was a man of little principle, both in public and private life, and there is no reason to disagree with Swift's opinion that Montagu was 'as arrant a knave as any in his time.' However, he did have a keen interest in building, both at Boughton, in Northamptonshire, and on his London property. Montagu House, Bloomsbury, was built (1675–80) to designs by Robert Hooke (q.v.) and contained some of the finest frescoes of Antonio Verrio. The house burned down in 1686, but was rebuilt on the original plan. In 1753 it was bought to house the national collection of antiquities, and subsequently became the site of the British Museum.

Montagu, Richard (1577–1641), bishop and theologian, whose controversial writings inflamed the Puritans and almost caused his impeachment.

Born at Dorney, Buckinghamshire, Montagu was educated at Eton and King's College, Cambridge, where he obtained his M.A. in 1602 and his B.D. in 1609. Montagu was made a fellow of Eton in 1613, and took up the deanery of Hereford in 1616. In the following year, he became canon of Windsor, rector of Petworth, Sussex, and chaplain to King James I.

In religion, Montagu inclined to episcopacy, following William Laud (q.v.), upholding Catholicity in the Anglican Church. Like Laud, he had no time for the extremes of Calvinism, nor yet did he advocate wholehearted Roman Catholicism. As a result, he came under attack from both the Puritans and the Catholics. In about 1619 he came into

conflict with some Roman Catholics in his own parish, and in 1623 Matthew Kellison, president of the English College at Douai, published a pamphlet against him called *The Gag of the Reformed Gospel*. Montagu's reply came in 1624 with *A Gag for the New Gospel? No, A New Gag for an old Goose*. He came under attack from the Puritans in the same year for his publication of *An Immediate Address unto God Alone*, a tirade against Calvinism. Early in 1625, John Pym (q.v.) was given the job of organizing his impeachment, but Laud used his influence at court and Montagu was protected by Charles I. 1625 also saw the appearance of his famous work *Appello Caesarem*, in which he vindicated himself from charges of Arminianism and popery laid against him by opponents on both sides.

In 1628 Charles made him Bishop of Chichester, and he became Bishop of Rochester ten years later. He remained a controversial figure for the rest of his life, continuing to incur Parliamentary hostility, but he held his ground under the protection of Laud and the King.

Montagu died on 13 April 1641.

Montrose, 1st Marquis and 5th Earl of (1612–50), see Graham, James.

Mordaunt, Charles (1658–1735), 3rd Earl of Peterborough and 1st Earl of Monmouth of the second creation (1689); admiral.

The eldest son of John, Viscount Mordaunt, he was educated at Eton and at Christ Church, Oxford; in 1675 he succeeded to the viscountcy and in 1678 married Carey, daughter of Sir Alexander Fraser.

In 1674 Mordaunt entered the Royal Navy as a volunteer, under the aegis of his kinsman Arthur Herbert, later Earl of Torrington, sailing in several commissions until taking his seat in the House of Lords in 1680 as a member of Shaftesbury's faction. This involvement in the politics of opposition to the court caused him to withdraw to Holland after the accession of James II, where he attached himself to William of Orange. In 1687 he was given command of a Dutch squadron in the West Indies.

When William landed at Torbay in 1688, Mordaunt was in his entourage and was despatched ahead of the main body to raise a regiment of horse. He occupied Exeter and secured Dorset and Wiltshire for the Prince, and for this and for his part in the intrigues which preceded the coup he was showered with favours after its success. His brief and purely nominal tenure of the Treasury enabled him to pass some of this patronage on, for instance to John Locke (q.v.), the philosopher, whom he had befriended in Holland.

Although invited to do so, the new Earl of Monmouth did not accompany William on his Irish campaign, preferring to remain in the capital and indulge his propensity for political intrigue in the Queen's Council, at the cost of any trust the Queen and others may have been prepared to repose in him. It is significant that William took him to Holland in 1691 and 1692, but even he withdrew his confidence in Monmouth at the end of the latter year, when the earl associated himself with peers critical of the conduct of the war against Louis XIV. Continuing upon his course of opposition to such ministers as Russell and Marlborough, who continued in royal favour, he was in 1697 struck off the Council and committed to the Tower for a brief period. In June of that year he inherited the earldom of Peterborough from his uncle.

The accession of Queen Anne in 1702 brought about his restoration to the court circle, the first manifestation of which was his reappointment to the lord lieutenancy of Northamptonshire. He was nominated as the civil and military governor of Jamaica in the expectation of a combined Anglo-Dutch expedition in the Caribbean, but in the end the force did not materialize and his appointment was cancelled. He was not employed until March 1705, when he was made joint commander with Sir Cloudesley Shovel (q.v.) of a maritime expedition to Spain in support of the Archduke Charles, claimant to the throne. The force arrived at Lisbon in June, where it was joined by the archduke and the Huguenot Earl of Galway, commander of the British forces already in the Peninsula.

After initial indecision, the expedition assisted in the capture of Barcelona (28 September), some credit for this going to Peterborough, who was made the governor of the town. His authority was extended by Charles in the following January to include the town and province of Valencia, but already he was displaying an unfitness for sustained administrative work, neglecting his military security, quarrelling with colleagues, and demanding from the home government the sole command of all the forces in Spain. That the gains were not lost to the French at this time was due entirely to Sir John Leake, commanding the fleet in the absence of his two superiors. Peterborough's incompetence was even more marked in the events leading up to the capture of Madrid by Galway and his Portuguese allies: Peterborough merely frustrated by ill advice and inactivity the designs of Charles himself to march on the city from Valencia. He attempted to cover this up by recriminations against other commanders and by elaborate schemes to attack the Balearic islands or Turin. In February 1707 he was recalled to England to render account, Galway being appointed commander-in-chief of all the forces in Spain.

Peterborough did not arrive in England until August, having disregarded the first order to return and having travelled through central Europe to call on the Emperor, on Charles XII of Sweden, on the Electress Sophia of Hanover, and on the Duke of Marlborough, airing to each his views on their respective state policies. On arrival, he took care to put in circulation his own version of his part in the Spanish campaign, which afterwards became difficult to dislodge. An investigation into his conduct began before the Lords in January 1708, but the Tory majority used the occasion to embarrass the Whig ministers, to Peterborough's complete advantage. The government was therefore reduced to a prolonged examination of his financial management of the expedition, which was such that it took two years to accomplish satisfactorily. Yet his political strength could still command favours: in November 1710 he was made captain general of the marines on salary, and in February 1711, having emerged triumphant from another process against him in the Lords by default, due to the political turmoil in the House, he was appointed ambassador extraordinary to Vienna.

The purpose of the appointment was to remove him from London, disguised as a mission to work for cordial relations between the courts of Vienna and Turin, to which latter he was appointed in the same capacity in November 1713. By his intrigue and disregard of instructions, he muddied the waters of true diplomacy. He established no trust in himself but managed to gather up the colonelcy of The Blues, the order of Garter, and, in Vienna, the singer Anastasia Robinson,

whom he is said to have married in 1722.

The death of Queen Anne and the accession of George I, bringing with it a permanent ascendancy of Whig ministers supported by the King and, after the customary election, a Commons majority, brought Peterborough's career to an abrupt end. He was recalled, and after a cold reception at court was forbidden to reappear. He was deprived of his colonelcy soon afterwards, although surprisingly his title and authority over the marines was extended – even though with the end of the war against France the marines were reduced to four Invalid Companies.

Peterborough continued to use the Lords as a personal platform and to practise intrigue on occasional private visits to the Continent. His normal state of indebtedness he was wont to explain as the result of having used his private estate on public service in Spain. He was never again employed, and passed the final years of his life as a popular host and guest, which had always been characteristic of him, and in writing his memoirs, which were burnt by Anastasia Robinson while still in manuscript.

W. Stebbing, *Peterborough* (1890).

Myddelton, Sir Hugh (?1560–1631), see Middleton, Sir Hugh.

Mytens, Daniel (?1590–c. 1645), Dutch portrait painter; court painter to James I and Charles I.

Born at Delft and trained in Holland, Mytens matriculated in 1610 from the guild at The Hague, and it is supposed that he studied under Miereveldt and modelled his early style on that of Rubens. In 1618 he arrived in England, where he was soon acknowledged by the court and nobility. In 1619 he was introduced to James I; in 1621 he succeeded

Paul Van Somer as the court painter, finding himself especially popular with Prince Charles. In 1624 he received a grant of a house and a life pension, with the attached proviso that he might never leave the country without first obtaining royal permission. This condition was felt to be necessary after the court's experience of Van Dyck (q.v.), who had accepted a position at court in 1620, only to disappear a year later and refuse to return for eleven years.

On the death of James and the accession of Charles in 1625, Mytens was appointed 'Picture Drawer to the King', and soon after was sent to Holland, his task there being to study the current fashions in court portraiture. His most notable works were produced as a direct result of this trip, specifically portraits of the Duke of Buckingham, Lord Baltimore, and the full-length Duke of Hamilton (1629). The latter has been acclaimed as the masterpiece of pre-Vandyckian portraiture in England. Mytens's work was typical of that of his contemporaries in that greater emphasis was placed on setting and accessories and on elegance of costume than on any attempt to convey the personality of the sitter.

Unfortunately for Mytens, in 1631 Van Dyck reappeared in England, after an absence of eleven years. In this artist Charles found everything he had been searching for and had found lacking in Mytens. Aware of Van Dyck's artistic superiority, Mytens asked permission to leave the English court and was refused. Both the King and Van Dyck persuaded him to remain and, from all accounts, there seems to have been little if any antagonism between the two painters. Indeed, there is, in Woburn Abbey, a portrait of Mytens and his wife painted by Van Dyck at this time. In or before 1635, however, Mytens did return to Holland, where he passed the remainder of his life in obscurity. The exact date of his death is not known, but he was certainly no longer alive in 1648.

Works:
Charles I with Henrietta Maria (Buckingham Palace)
Earl of Arundel and family (Duke of Norfolk's Coll.)
Marquis of Hamilton and others (Hampton Court)
Marquis of Hamilton (Earl of Hopetoun's Coll.)
Earl of Portland (Duke of Bedford's Coll.)
Charles I and Henrietta Maria (Earl of Dunsmore's Coll.)
Sir Randolph Crewe (N.P.G.)
Charles I and Henrietta Maria, 1637 (Dresden Gallery)
Charles as Prince of Wales, 1624 (Copenhagen Gallery)
Charles, 1627 (Turin Gallery)
and others at New York (Metropolitan Museum), Ottawa, and St. Louis.

Portrait: self-portrait, oil on panel, half-length, *c.* 1630: Hampton Court.

N

Napier or Neper, John (1550–1617), 8th Laird of Merchiston; mathematician, distinguished particularly for his invention of logarithms.

Born at Merchiston Castle, near Edinburgh, Napier attended the University of St. Andrews but left without taking a degree. In 1571 he was granted possession of the baronies of Edenbellie-Napier and Merchiston, remaining in Scotland for the rest of his life. He succeeded to the lairdship of Merchiston on the death of his father in 1608. He was twice married, his first wife dying in 1579.

Napier devoted a considerable part of his life to the study of mathematics. At that time, there was no short cut to multiplication, division, and the extraction of the roots of numbers. Computations were often long and complicated, especially those involved in astronomical measurements. There was good reason to search for a method to simplify computation. One result of that search was Napier's system of logarithms.

Napier's first work on the subject, published in 1614, was *Mirifici Logarithmorum Canonis descriptio*. This was the culmination of about forty years of study, and contained tables of logarithms that had taken twenty years to compile, canons for their use, and an explanation of their nature. Napier's work was based on the correspondence that he had established between arithmetic and geometric sequences of numbers. For the geometric sequence 1, 10, 100, 1000, the logarithms of these numbers, 0, 1, 2, 3, form an arithmetic sequence when the base of the logarithms is taken as 10.

How Napier arrived at his result is obscure. There had been no previous work on the subject for him to study. The laws of exponents, so vital to the theory of logarithms, had not yet been formulated. His invention, landing like a bombshell on the scientific world, was quickly acclaimed as a remarkable and immensely valuable tool. Logarithms, although modified in form, were used in large-scale calculations up to the end of the nineteenth century, when they were gradually replaced, first by electric calculating machines and later by electronic computers.

Napier's second work on the subject, *Mirifici Logarithmorum Canonis constructio*, published in 1617 (two years after his death), explained how logarithms were calculated. In this work, Napier pioneered the use of the decimal point to separate the integral from the decimal part of the logarithm. The exact process of evolution of logarithms, however, was not revealed.

The system known today as Napierian or natural logarithms is not identical with but is related to Napier's logarithms. It was after discussion with Henry Briggs (q.v.) that Napier agreed that logarithms could be put into a more convenient form using a base 10 rather than the number later identified with the transcendental number e. Although common logarithms (base 10) are usually used in computation, Napierian logarithms are of considerable importance in advanced mathematics, especially calculus.

Napier not only invented the means to simplify astronomical computation, but also formulated certain rules and analogies for solving spherical triangles. The angles of spherical triangles are important elements in astronomical measurements. In addition to this work, he published in 1617 his *Rabdologia*, in which he describes how graduated rods ('Napier's bones') could be used for multiplication and division and how the same operations could be performed by moving counters on a chess board.

Napier's mathematical studies were interrupted throughout his life by religious controversies. He was an ardent and uncompromising Protestant and was involved in several representations to King James concerning the wellbeing of the Scottish Church. His publication, *A Plaine Discovery of the Whole Revelation of St. John* (1593), was the earliest Scottish work on the interpretation of the Scriptures. The dedication, addressed to the King, warned of the infiltration of papists and atheists into the country, especially into the King's own household. Not content with having expressed his suspicions, he actually invented devices, including burning mirrors, for the defence of his country.

Napier, renowned for his doggedness in both his mathematics and his Calvinism, died at Merchiston on 4 April 1617.

C. G. Knott (ed.), *Napier Tercentenary Memorial Volume* (1915).

Newark, 1st Baron (d. 1682), see Leslie, David.

Newcastle, Duke of (1592–1676), see Cavendish, William.

Newcomen, Thomas (1663–1724), engineer; inventor of the first practical steam engine.

Newcomen was born at Dartmouth, Devonshire, and christened on 24 February 1663. During the early years of the eighteenth century, the scene was being set for the impending Industrial Revolution. Coal was being mined extensively for use in the production of iron (about eight tons of coal were needed for each ton of iron) and the mining of non-ferrous metals, especially tin, was active in Devonshire and Cornwall. As all mining operations are beset with the problem of removing water from underground workings, there was an urgent need for a cheap mechanical pump that would operate automatically day and night. This need was filled by Thomas Newcomen.

Not much is known of his early life. He appears to have come from a family of local merchants and to have been a devout Baptist throughout his life, probably receiving his education from a Baptist scholar called John Favell. He was probably apprenticed to a toolsmith in Exeter and when he set up on his own he was assisted by a brother Baptist, John Calley.

To solve the problem of pumping water from the local tin mines Newcomen, with the help of Calley, devised a simple and reliable steam-operated pump. Essentially, it consisted of a heavy centrally pivoted horizontal beam, one end of which was attached to a vertical pump rod; the other end was connected to a piston, which was free to move up and down within a cylinder. One side of the cylinder was open to the atmosphere, the other was supplied with steam from a boiler. Steam entering the cylinder pushed the piston up, cold water subsequently injected into this side of the piston condensed the steam, allowing the weight of the atmosphere on the open side to push the cylinder down. The reciprocating motion of the beam so created operated the pump rods. As the necessary valves were all operated by the movement of the beam, the whole machine was entirely automatic. It is not known exactly when the first of these machines was put to work in the Cornish mines; the first authenticated record of a Newcomen engine refers to an engine built in 1712 in Dudley, Worcestershire.

Unfortunately for Newcomen, even in the early eighteenth century patent laws were strictly enforced in Britain and his application for a patent fell foul of an earlier patent by Thomas Savery (1650–1715). Savery had devised a similar but more primitive water-pumping engine in 1698, which was patented by Act of Parliament in 1699 for a period of thirty-five years. The machine was not sufficiently reliable to be used in the mines and there are no records of its application for this purpose. However, the patent covered the use of 'the Impellent Force of Fire' to operate an engine and there was no doubt that Newcomen's engine did indeed rely on this principle. Newcomen was therefore obliged to allow Savery to share in the exploitation of his brainchild. After Savery's death in 1715, Newcomen seems to have been excluded from the benefits of the patent rights altogether, but he continued to construct and install his engines. By the middle of the century Newcomen's 'fire-engines', as they were then called, were in constant use in many mines.

If the Industrial Revolution relied heavily on the use of steam, Newcomen must be counted as one of its instigators. For not only did his engine cheapen the mining of coal and non-ferrous metals, but he also provided the rudiments of the engine that Watt developed to power the machinery in the factories. Indeed, it was while repairing a model of a Newcomen engine at Glasgow University in 1764–65 that Watt perceived the improvements that were to make Newcomen's engine an efficient industrial machine.

Newcomen died in Southwark, London, on 5 August 1729.

L. T. C. Rolt, *Thomas Newcomen: The Prehistory of the Steam Engine* (1963).

H. W. Dickinson, *A Short History of the Steam Engine* (1963, 2nd ed.).

Newton, Sir Isaac (1642–1727), mathematician and natural philosopher. Lucasian Professor of Mathematics in the University of Cambridge (1669–1701), president of the Royal Society (1703–27), Master of the Mint (1699–1727).

Born 25 December 1642, in Woolsthorpe, Lincolnshire, and educated at King's School, Grantham, and Trinity College, Cambridge, Isaac Newton was probably one of the greatest scientists of all time. Albert Einstein said of him: 'In one person he combined the experimenter, the theorist, the mechanic and, not least, the artist in exposition.' This un-

doubted genius was not, however, a gentle and unworldly academic. Indeed, he appears to have been, especially in his later years, something of a querulous, intolerant, and jealous tyrant. It is possible that this aspect of the man was related to the disturbances of his early childhood and particularly to the preoccupation of his mother with her second husband. Whether or not this interpretation is correct, the facts are undisputed. His father, Isaac Newton, a small-freehold farmer, died two months before he was born and his mother, Hanna (née Ayscough), married the Rev. Barnabas Smith some three years later. The Rev. Smith took his new bride to live in his rectory in North Witham but the three-year-old Isaac was left in Woolsthorpe with his maternal grandmother. This arrangement lasted for eleven years – until Newton's mother became a widow for the second time. Shortly after her husband's death, she returned to her native Woolsthorpe and in 1658 brought her son home from school to help on the family farm.

Newton was then sixteen and but for two factors he might have remained a small country farmer for the rest of his life. The first was his ineptness as a farmer and the second was the intervention of his mother's brother, William Ayscough, who was a member of Trinity College, Cambridge. It was on his advice that Newton was sent back to King's School, Grantham, to prepare for entry to his uncle's college. Although there are no records to suggest that Newton was an exceptionally gifted pupil either at school or as under-graduate, he entered Trinity College in 1661 as a subsizar and graduated with a B.A. degree in 1665. As a result of the Great Plague, the University of Cambridge closed shortly after his graduation and Newton returned to his home

in Lincolnshire. For eighteen months he worked in the peaceful countryside and produced some of his most original work. When the university opened again in the spring of 1667 he was elected a Fellow of his college, succeed-ing to the Lucasian Chair of Mathe-matics in 1669.

Newton remained at Cambridge for the twenty-seven most productive years of his life, leaving in 1696 to become Warden of the Mint. This appointment was obtained for him by his Cambridge friend, Charles Montagu (later Lord Halifax). In 1699 he became Master of the Mint and in 1701 he relinquished his Fellowship and Chair at Cambridge. He remained at, the Mint until his death in Kensington on 20 March 1727, having played a major part in the revision of the coinage in the closing years of the seventeenth century.

During his years at Cambridge he took an active part in university politics and was elected Member of Parliament for the university in 1689 until the dissolution in 1690. He was elected again in 1701, but made very little im-pact either in the House of Commons or in politics generally. He was knighted by Queen Anne in 1705, during a visit to Cambridge, and was president of the Royal Society from 1703 until his death.

Newton's scientific work has had a profound influence on several branches of physical science, and even during his lifetime his name and achievements were known throughout Europe. His first contributions were made immedi-ately after graduation, during the closure of Cambridge University. Working at home in Woolsthorpe, without access to fellow scientists, experimental facili-ties, or an adequate library, he made three extremely important discoveries. Perhaps the most far-reaching of these was the universal law of gravitation. The story that he was led to this theory by observing an apple falling from a tree may well be apocryphal. It was first told by Voltaire, who heard it from Newton's niece, a Mrs. Catherine Barton Conduitt. Apocryphal or not, it well illustrates the kind of insight that enables a genius to formulate a universal law by associating the causes of apparently unconnected effects. It took a man of Newton's great perception to understand that the force pulling the apple towards the earth is the same as the force that holds the moon in orbit round the earth. Using Kepler's observations of planetary orbits, he was able to show that the gravitational force between the sun and planets held each of the planets in its orbit and that the magnitude of the force depends directly on the product of the masses of the bodies involved and inversely upon the square of the distance between them. This law is still accepted today, subject to certain refinements arising from Einstein's general theory of relativity.

The concept of gravitation required a precise definition of a force and its relation to mass: this was provided by Newton in his second law of motion, in which the force acting upon a body is defined as the product of the mass of the body and the acceleration it produces. Newton, continuing the work of Galileo a generation earlier, perceived that Aristotle's concept of motion was false. In Aristotelian mechanics no motion can occur without a force to cause it. Newton realized that, in fact, a body does require a force to set it in motion but that once moving it will continue in motion unless another force acts on it to stop it. Thus, according to Newton's first law of motion, a body continues in a state of rest or uniform motion unless acted upon by an external force. The moon and man-made satellites continue to orbit the earth because there are no friction forces in space to stop them. Moreover, without Newton's laws there would be no rockets to launch man-made satellites, for the thrust of a rocket is the reaction to the force of expansion of the burning gases. It was Newton who saw that for every force there has to be an equal and opposite reaction – this is his third law of motion.

The second of Newton's great discoveries, made in Woolsthorpe during the time of the plague, was the method of fluxions, the mathematic tool by which all problems connected with motion are solved. This work formed the basis of the differential and integral calculus and it is a matter of some regret that his acrimonious and unbecoming bickering with Leibniz over who invented the method should have clouded his later years. It is now generally accepted that Newton's claim that Leibniz had plagiarized his work is unfounded; Leibniz almost certainly invented the method independently of Newton.

The third major contribution to human knowledge made by the young Newton concerned the nature of light. He discovered that white light (daylight) is composed of thousands of individual colours, which can be grouped into the six colours of the spectrum, familiar to us in the form of a rainbow. When white light is passed through a glass prism, each colour is diffracted (bent) to a different degree. Newton incorrectly assumed that this splitting-up of white light into coloured fringes at the edge of an image produced by a lens (chromatic aberration) could not be corrected. This led him to invent the reflecting telescope, which uses a concave mirror rather than a lens to collect the light. Many of the world's most powerful telescopes still use this principle.

Newton's greatest published work,

319

Philosophiae Naturalis Principia Mathematica (Mathematical Principles of Natural Philosophy), was a collection of all his scientific work. It was started in 1684 and first published in 1687. As the Royal Society was at that time short of funds, the whole cost and responsibility of production was accepted by Edmond Halley (q.v.). After publication, Robert Hooke (q.v.) claimed that Newton had used some of his original work, but Halley managed to pacify the irascible Newton. *Principia* has remained for nearly 300 years a milestone in scientific exposition.

His other major published work, *Optics*, was first brought out in 1704. In it he postulated a combination of the wave and corpuscular theories of light that is not dissimilar to the present view. During the nineteenth century light was regarded as a pure wave and Newton's theory became unfashionable. It was not revived until the beginning of this century, when Einstein's work on photochemistry required an explanation in terms of light quanta (photons).

Two aspects of Newton's life have not been widely publicized. They concern his views on religion and the occult. A considerable amount of this great scientist's time was spent delving into alchemical and astrological researches that now seem very unscientific. Even though this dichotomy of interest was not as clear cut in the seventeenth century as it is today, Newton was very secretive about his activities in the occult. He was equally guarded on his religious views. Although a professing Christian, it appears that he was never able to accept the concept of the Trinity and this may account for the fact that he never held Holy Orders and had to be granted a special dispensation to hold his professorship. Nevertheless, he was honoured with the most prestigious form of

Christian burial – on 28 March 1727, his remains were interred in Westminster Abbey.

I. Bernard Cohen (ed.), *Isaac Newton's Papers and Letters on Natural Philosophy and Related Documents* (Cambridge, Mass., 1958).
A. R. and M. B. Hall (eds.), *Unpublished Scientific Papers of Isaac Newton* (New York, 1962).
H. W. Turnbull and J. F. Scott (eds.), *The Correspondence of Isaac Newton* (4 vols.; 1959–   ).
D. T. Whiteside (ed.), *The Mathematical Papers of Isaac Newton* (5 vols.; 1967–   ).
David Brewster (ed.), *Memoirs of the Life, Writings and Discoveries of Sir Isaac Newton* (2 vols.; 1855, 2nd ed.).
I. Bernard Cohen, *Franklin and Newton* (Philadelphia, Pa., 1956).
Alexandre Koyré, *Newtonian Studies* (1965).
Frank Manuel, *A Portrait of Isaac Newton* (1968).
Louis T. More, *Isaac Newton: A Biography* (New York, 1934).

Portrait: oil, quarter-length, by Sir Godfrey Kneller, 1702: N.P.G.

Nicholas, Sir Edward (1593–1669), politician and secretary of state under Charles I during the Civil War and under Charles II while he was in exile.

Born on 4 April 1593, at Winterbourne Earls, Wiltshire, Nicholas was educated at Salisbury, Winchester, and Queen's College, Oxford. In 1612 he entered the Middle Temple and studied law intermittently for about the next six years. He left in 1618 to become secretary to Lord Zouch, warden and admiral of the Cinque Ports, and continued in the same capacity to Buckingham, who succeeded Zouch in 1624. M.P. for Winchelsea in 1621 and 1624, he served for Dover in the parliament of 1628 and lost his seat after the passage of the Petition of Right. An extraordinary clerkship was created for him on the Privy Council in 1625, in connection with admiralty affairs, and Charles I created him clerk in ordinary in 1635. In this employment, Nicholas had much to do with administering the levy of ship money.

In the summer of 1641 Charles went to Scotland to try to enlist Royalist support. While he was away, Nicholas had the responsibility of keeping him informed of events in London, an office that he found irksome. In November Charles returned, and Nicholas was raised to the office of secretary of state. He joined the King at Oxford, and throughout the hostilities of the Civil War acted as one of his ablest advisers. Nicholas was one of the Uxbridge negotiators who had unsuccessful talks with the Parliamentarians in February 1645. In the following year, he arranged the details of Charles's surrender to the Scots at Newcastle, and signed the terms of the surrender of Oxford in June 1646.

Nicholas was given leave to depart from the city. He took his family out of England and eventually got to France, where he was recommended to the Prince of Wales by letter from the King. After Charles I's execution in January 1649, he continued to work on behalf of the new King, Charles II, in close consultation with Edward Hyde and his other colleagues. But he incurred the hostility of Queen Henrietta Maria, and consequently lost influence with her son. During the interregnum he lived at The Hague and elsewhere in extreme poverty, which Charles II did little to alleviate, and although he had resumed the rank of secretary of state, more and more of his duties were taken over by Hyde. He returned with Charles at the Restoration in 1660, and after two years was persuaded to give up his post. He retired on a grant of money from the crown and died at his country estate at West Horsley, Surrey, on 1 September 1669.

David Nicholas, *Mr. Secretary Nicholas 1597–1669* (1953).

Nottingham, 1st Earl of (1621–82), see Finch, Heneage.

Nottingham, 2nd Earl of (1647–1730), see Finch, Daniel.

Noye or Noy, William (1577–1634), M.P. and judge.

Noye was born in Carnanton, Mawgan-in-Pyder, Cornwall. On 27 April 1593, he matriculated at Exeter College, Oxford, and in 1594 was admitted to Lincoln's Inn. He was called to the bar in 1602, was autumn reader (1622), and from 1618 until his death was a bencher; in 1632 he was treasurer.

In his lifetime Noye had no peer more learned in the finer points of law; he spoke clearly and well, and had a sharp, dry wit. Contemporaries acknowledged that he was scholarly, meticulous, and somewhat cynical, with a deep curiosity which reached beyond the law. His career progressed steadily, although slowly.

In 1614 Francis Bacon recommended him for the post of official law reporter. Noye was M.P. for Grampound, Cornwall, in James I's first two parliaments. Subsequently, he was Member of Parliament for various other constituencies in the county – Helston, Fowey, St. Ives, and Helston again (1628–29). At first he supported the popular party, attacking monopolies, proposing a habeas corpus act, resisting the royal prerogative clause in the Petition of Right (1628), and proposing that the right of the King to levies on tonnage and poundage be negated.

It therefore caused some surprise when he was appointed attorney general on 27 October 1631, but he himself wittily translated 'Attornatus Domini Regis' as 'one that must serve the King's turn'. From this time on, Noye's performance of his official legal duties earned him great public hatred. It is probable that he had always had High Church sympathies; Archbishop Laud (q.v.) counted him as a 'dear friend'. Noye's vast knowledge of law was now prostituted in support of royal tyranny. He supported the royal prerogative, revived the forest laws, issued the writ of ship money, and legalized the soap monopoly, which became infamous.

In the Star Chamber he prosecuted two members of his own inn: Henry Sherfield, who had defaced a window in St. Edmund's Church, Salisbury, where he was recorder, was treated with moderation (1629); William Prynne (q.v.), however, was tried with great zeal in 1634, and Noye unsympathetically witnessed Prynne's suffering in Westminster pillory, later denouncing him as 'past grace' and shocking Laud by suggesting that Prynne should be debarred from attending divine service. Noye's judgments against Prynne seem to belie his reputation for a moderate temperament, but then Prynne's vicious attacks against Laud and the King might well have driven any sensible man of the law to zealous prosecution.

After Noye had succeeded in obtaining an order for Prynne's close confinement, when the Star Chamber lords were out of town, he retired to Tunbridge Wells to drink the waters. He was seized by vesical haemorrhaging (an illness that had first occurred after watching Prynne's sufferings), and died at his house in New Brentford on 9 August 1634. On both occasions, Puritans saw the hand of God in Noye's afflictions.

O

Oates, Titus (1649–1705), perjurer and conspirator, fabricator of the Popish Plot of 1678.

Titus Oates was born at Oakham, the son of a Norfolk rector. He was expelled from Merchant Taylors' School, London, in 1665, during his first year. In 1667 he went to Cambridge, where, his tutor wrote, 'He was a great dunce, ran into debt, and, being sent away for want of money, never took a degree.' Nevertheless, he then took religious orders, and after a time in Kent joined his father as a curate in Hastings. There Titus and his father trumped up a charge against a local schoolmaster, which was discovered to be false. Titus was arrested in 1675; he escaped from prison and obtained a berth as chaplain on a King's ship, but was soon dismissed.

In 1676 Oates encountered Israel Tonge (q.v.), a rector who was writing anti-Jesuit literature. Oates joined him in this work, but their books had little effect. By this time Oates had conceived the idea of ingratiating himself into Jesuit circles in order to betray them for profit. He entered a college of the society at Valladolid, but was expelled for scandalous behaviour. His subsequent stay in an English seminary at St. Omer was similarly cut short, but Oates had gathered enough information from them and the Catholics he had met in London for his purpose.

The infamous Popish Plot was then fabricated by Oates and Tonge, and Titus prepared a paper purporting to give details of the plot. In September 1678 they visited Sir Edmund Berry Godfrey (q.v.), a local justice of the peace, and announced the alleged plot to him. It supposedly involved a plan to assassinate the King and his councillors, to be followed by a massacre of Protestants, a French invasion of Ireland, and the setting up of a Catholic government under the Duke of York (see James II). Oates was flamboyant and inventive as he repeated his story to the Privy Council, and he knew just enough about the London Jesuits to supply a mass of circumstantial detail. The story leaked to the town and was accepted by the credulous mob.

In October, Sir Edmund Berry Godfrey was found dead in mysterious circumstances and the Catholics were popularly credited with his murder. The House of Commons called Oates before

them to affirm belief in the existence of the 'hellish plot', as did the House of Lords. Many people, including Catholic priests, were arrested. Oates was the chief witness at a series of trials in which his fabrications became more transparent. Despite this, public confidence in him was sustained until 1681, and at the highest point in his fortunes few dared challenge him. During this period he directly or indirectly contrived the deaths of more than thirty men.

Public credulity waned thereafter, and Oates was arrested in 1684 for accusing the Duke of York of treachery. When the latter came to the throne as James II in 1685, Oates was tried for perjury, resulting in his being fined, pilloried, whipped, and imprisoned. However, on the accession of the Protestant William of Orange he was released and granted a pension. In 1693 Oates married a wealthy widow, although her money proved inadequate to satisfy his extravagant tastes. Sometime around 1698 he was admitted to a Baptist sect in Wapping and frequently officiated in the pulpit. He was discovered in an intrigue to gain money from a wealthy devotee and expelled from the sect as 'a disorderly person and a hypocrite.' Oates died on 12 July 1705. A contemporary, Roger North, described Oates as 'a most consummate cheat, blasphemer, vicious, perjured, impudent, and saucy, foulmouthed wretch, and, were it not for the truth of history and the great emotions in the public he was the cause of, not fit to be remembered.'

E. Dakers (J. Lane, pseudonym), *Titus Oates* (1949).
J. P. Kenyon, *The Popish Plot* (1972).
J. Pollock, *The Popish Plot* (1913).

Portrait: engraving, quarter-length by R. Thompson, after Thomas Hawirer, *c.* 1680: British Museum.

O'Brien, Murrough (1614–74), 1st Earl of Inchiquin; Irish soldier and statesman, known as 'Murrough of the Conflagrations'.

O'Brien was the eldest son of Dermod, 5th Baron Inchiquin, and married Elizabeth, daughter of Sir William St. Leger. He served his military apprenticeship in the Spanish army in Italy, returning to Ireland in 1639 and saving his estates by co-operating with Wentworth's colonization plans. In 1640 he was made vice-president of Munster, and in the following year, when the Irish rebellion began, he took the field in Leinster as the lord president's subordinate. In July 1642 he succeeded to the duties of the office of lord president on the death of the holder, Sir William St. Leger, and on 20 August defeated the rebel General Barry at Liscarrol. The difficulty of properly supporting an army and the lack of assistance from England prevented him from exploiting the victory, so that he could do little more than hold his own.

The cessation that Ormonde (see Butler, James, 1st Duke) negotiated with the Kilkenny confederates in September 1643 was endorsed by Inchiquin, whose force was subsequently reduced by the transfer of some of his regiments to the royal armies in England. In February 1644 he journeyed to Oxford to secure the title of president, but Charles I had promised it elsewhere. An important consequence of his visit was his realization that the Royalists were in no condition to afford reliable aid to the Protestant colonists in Ireland and that he would fare better with the Parliamentarians.

Accordingly, he obtained a confirmation of his title from Parliament and continued to defend his province with scratch garrisons until Lord Lisle arrived in March 1647 with Parliamentary authority extending over the whole country and with men, arms, and money. Lisle's commission, already over a year old, expired the following month, so that in practice Inchiquin was not displaced. He proceeded to recover territory lost to the rebels in the previous two years, and by the end of the year he was master of southwest Ireland, his culminating victory being at Knocknannus (13 November).

The level of support from the Parliamentarians did not match his hopes and, after protesting, in the spring of 1648 he declared for the King, thenceforward co-operating with Ormonde, from September the official representative in Ireland of the exiled English court. He was appointed lieutenant general of Ormonde's Royalist army of reconciled Irish factions, and in the summer of 1649 conducted subsidiary operations to recover Drogheda, Dundalk, Newry, and Trim from Parliamentary hands before rejoining the main army. He was not present at the decisive defeat of the Irish army at Rathmines (2 August), having been detached again with a column of horse into Munster to guard against a possible landing by Cromwell and the New Model regiments, which landing now took place in Dublin.

Inchiquin could not defend Munster against this new element in the confused military situation in Ireland, the garrisons being only too willing to recognize the inevitability of defeat after the storm of Drogheda (12 September) and to defect. Additionally, Cromwell appeared as a better guardian of the Protestant minority than Inchiquin, who had compromised with the Catholics in the Royalist interest, whatever his past services had been. By the summer of 1650 he had been driven across the Shannon into Clare, and at the end of the year he left Ireland in company with Ormonde.

In May 1652 he was made a member of the Privy Council of Charles II in exile, a position he himself undermined when he subsequently adhered to the Church of Rome. From time to time he found employment in the French service in Catalonia, and became the high steward of Queen Henrietta Maria's household. In 1662 he was general-in-chief of the expedition sent by Charles II to Lisbon to assist the Portuguese against the Spaniards, a campaign which produced no battle and much pointless marching. In 1663 he returned to Ireland, prevented by his Catholic profession from achieving the presidency of Munster, but receiving the vice-presidency again in 1664, together with a measure of financial compensation for his losses on behalf of Protestant ascendancy in Ireland.

He spent the remainder of his life quietly in Ireland and died on 9 September 1674.

Ogilby, John (1600–76), writer, translator, printer, and cartographer.

Ogilby was born in Edinburgh in November 1600; because his father was for a long time in prison for debt Ogilby received little formal education, and he had to rely on his personal industriousness and ingenuity for his own advancement. With money gained from a small investment in a plantation in Virginia Ogilby was able to obtain his father's release and also to secure for himself an apprenticeship with a dancing master in Gray's Inn Lane, London; his early reputation as one of the best dancers of his time was confirmed when he was invited by the Duke of Buckingham to dance at the court of Charles I.

In 1633 Ogilby travelled to Ireland as tutor to the children of Thomas Wentworth, Earl of Strafford, the newly appointed lord deputy. He built a theatre in Dublin and for a few years enjoyed the patronage of many of the nobility, but the outbreak of the Civil War in 1641 brought an end to his personal good fortune. Shipwrecked on his voyage from Ireland in 1646, Ogilby arrived in England completely destitute: his personal energies were once more his only remaining resources.

After travelling on foot to Cambridge, Ogilby was able to learn enough Latin from sympathetic scholars to enable him to translate Virgil into English verse (1649–50). This work sold well, and encouraged by its success Ogilby then took lessons in Greek from David Whitford, an usher employed by the dramatist James Shirley. Because of the ridicule of Dryden in *Mac Flecknoe* and Pope in the *Dunciad* Ogilby's name has become proverbial as that of a bad poet, but in fact his verse translations of the *Iliad* (1660) and of the *Odyssey* (1665) were both skilful and accurate, and the success of these works gave new impetus to Ogilby's social advancement. At the Restoration of Charles II in 1660 Ogilby presented the King with a fine edition of the Bible, which he himself had printed at Cambridge, and for the ceremony of the coronation Ogilby was commissioned as the official artistic adviser.

In the next six years Ogilby established a prosperous career as a translator and publisher, and even the destruction of all his property in the Great Fire of London in 1666 could not impede his progress. In 1664 he established a lottery in which the prizes were to be his own books, and in the following year he obtained from the King a proclamation forbidding the reprinting of his own books by rival companies for a period of fifteen years, an early example of copyright protection. After the Great Fire Ogilby rebuilt his house at Whitefriars and set up his own large printing press,

from which he produced a great variety of books, mostly in folio editions and illustrated by distinguished engravers. He now took up cartography, styling himself 'His Majesty's Cosmographer and Geographic Printer'. His survey of the whole city of London, a commission on which he worked from 1666 until his death, took up much of his remaining energy, but Ogilby was also able to produce during his final years many other books on geography and topography remarkable for their range and accuracy. Notable among these was *Britannia*, a survey of all the post roads of England and Wales, carefully laid out on a scale of one inch to the mile, for the surveying of which Ogilby invented the odometer. It was the first proper admeasurement of the country's roads ever to take place, introduced the statute mile of 1,760 yards, and influenced British cartography to the extent that no further survey was carried out until Cary's at the end of the following century.

At an unknown stage during his busy life Ogilby found time to marry a widow, Christian Knight, by whom he had one daughter; he died in London on 4 September 1676, and was buried in St. Bride's Church, Fleet Street.

John Ogilby, *Britannia, or an Illustration of the Kingdom of England and the Dominion of Wales by a Geographical and Historical Description of the Principal Roads, 1675* (1973, facsimile ed.).

R. H. Hill, 'The King's Map-maker (John Ogilby)', *Blackwoods* 236 (1934).

Orford, Earl of (1653–1727), see Russell, Edward.

Orford, 1st Earl of, of the second creation (1676–1745), Whig politician and statesman, see Walpole, Sir Robert, in *Lives of the Georgian Age*.

Ormonde, 1st Duke of (1616–1688), see Butler, James, 1st Duke of Ormonde.

Ormonde, 2nd Duke of (1665–1745), see Butler, James, 2nd Duke of Ormonde.

Orrery, 1st Earl of (1621–79), see Boyle, Roger.

Osborne, Thomas (1631–1712), 1st Earl of Danby, Marquis of Carmarthen, and 1st Duke of Leeds; statesman, leading minister under Charles II and William III.

Thomas Osborne was the great-grandson of Sir Edward Osborne, a former Lord Mayor of London, his father being a Yorkshire Royalist and vice-president of the Council of the North under Wentworth. As a boy Thomas reflected his father's strong Royalist sentiment. He succeeded to the baronetcy and his father's Yorkshire estates in 1647, and in 1653 married Lady Bridget Bertie, daughter of the Earl of Lindsey.

He appears not to have suffered undue loss under Cromwell's Protectorate, in spite of his Royalist sympathies. One of his near neighbours was the Duke of Buckingham (see Villiers, George, 2nd Duke), who introduced him at court shortly after the Restoration. Osborne became high sheriff of Yorkshire in 1661 and M.P. for York in 1665. In Parliament he readily aided his patron Buckingham, especially by attacks on Clarendon (see Hyde, Edward), and was soon given office. In 1668 he was appointed joint treasurer of the navy, a post in which he displayed considerable financial and administrative ability. In 1671 he became sole treasurer of the navy, and other distinctions were soon conferred on him – he became a privy councillor, was raised to the Scottish peerage, and in 1673 became lord treasurer of England. He had a clear head and soon improved the financial position of the government. He reduced the interest rate on government loans, regulated the abuses of customs and excise farmers, and increased the yield of hereditary crown revenues. These policies were highly acceptable to the King, whose aim was always greater financial independence, and Osborne was rewarded with the English titles of Baron Osborne of Kiveton and Viscount Latimer in 1673 and Earl of Danby in 1674. Danby also replaced Buckingham as lord lieutenant of the West Riding of Yorkshire, and by 1675 was firmly established as Charles II's chief minister.

Danby was not particularly rich, and his circumstances were straitened when he became lord treasurer. He was greedy for wealth and honours, and this aspect of his character was one reason for the intense dislike he inspired in many of his contemporaries. From 1674 Danby set about building a parliamentary majority by using the patronage system of the crown. Offices and pensions were distributed to secure the support of M.P.s, and their holders were systematically

327

organized as a political party in Parliament. Danby accepted the necessity of support in the House of Commons, and by 1679 214 members were allegedly receiving government money in one form or another. However, according to Burnet (q.v.), Danby confined his bribes or gifts to less prominent M.P.s, fearing that men of ability might usurp his position or replace him in his influence with the King.

Despite his management of Parliament by dubious means, Danby had consistent political principles, although he had to work within clearly defined limits. His policies were always tempered by deference to the King's views and he exercised great diplomacy to give effect to any of his own aims. He strongly supported the authority of the King and in 1675 introduced a bill requiring office holders and M.P.s to swear an oath declaring resistance to the sovereign's authority to be criminal, although this was heavily defeated. Danby wanted a strong monarchy based on traditional Cavalier loyalty and Anglicanism. He was a zealous Protestant himself and favoured strict enforcement of the penal laws against Catholics and Dissenters. Danby was also anti-French and wished to counteract the power of France by increasing the influence of England in European affairs. To this end and in order to reinforce internal stability, he also wished to maintain national credit and the financial independence of the King.

The ending of the Dutch war in 1674 reflected Danby's aim of curbing the predominance of France, and this was further confirmed in 1677 when he strenuously promoted the marriage of Mary, daughter of the Duke of York, to the Protestant William of Orange. This marriage was probably the most important action of Danby's political career. Charles, however, differed from his chief minister in his attitude towards Catholics – whom he wanted to treat more tolerantly – and towards France. Danby was involved against his own better judgment in secret negotiations with Louis XIV on behalf of the King. Charles received a series of subsidies from Louis as the price of English neutrality or support, and Danby was compelled to press for payment through the English ambassador in Paris, Ralph Montagu (q.v.). Danby complied with the King's wishes, mainly because he wanted to retain power, although in his defence it should be said that he probably did feel a duty to serve the monarch and believed that his sovereign will should be respected.

In 1678 Titus Oates (q.v.) made his allegations about an alleged Popish Plot to kill the King and replace him with the Catholic Duke of York. Danby met Oates, but was very sceptical about his revelations. However, the story engendered an atmosphere of rampant anti-Catholicism and the House of Commons affirmed belief in the plot. Linked with this anti-Catholic feeling was a growing hostility to France, and Ralph Montagu, now returned to England after being dismissed from his post, revealed his correspondence with Danby over the financial dealings with Louis XIV. Danby reflected the views of the gentry, who supported him in disliking the acceptance of money from Catholic France, and the Commons now proceeded to impeach him. Since he had built his position on a parliamentary majority, he could not survive once he had lost the confidence of the House of Commons. Danby was impeached on several charges, including the accusations that he was a papist sympathizer and had suppressed evidence concerning the Popish Plot. His enemies linked Danby with the plot solely because he had not fallen prey to the general anti-Catholic hysteria and had doubted the charlatan Oates.

Charles prorogued and then dissolved parliament, which did not please Danby because he believed he could frustrate the attempts to impeach him. However, the new House of Commons at once revived the impeachment charge. The King regarded Danby with friendship – in 1678 one of his illegitimate sons had married Danby's daughter, but it was neither in Charles's nature nor politically expedient for him to assert himself too much on his minister's behalf. Burnet said that Danby was 'the most hated minister that had ever been about the King', and he was lampooned for his corruption, personal aggrandisement, pale appearance, and supposed dependence on his wife. Charles announced that he had pardoned Danby under the Great Seal, but the Commons voted the pardon illegal and sent him to the Tower. No serious attempt was made to bring Danby to trial, but he was refused bail and remained in prison for five years. His wife and family probably had free access to him, but he was often ill.

Danby was released in 1685, but his political career appeared to be over. He spent much of his time in seclusion in his mansion at Wimbledon and in Yorkshire. However, when Halifax (see Montagu, Charles) was dismissed from office in 1685, Danby began to speak openly against the Catholicizing policies pursued by James II. By 1687 he was in touch with William of Orange through the latter's agent Dykvelt. Danby was respected at The Hague and his affiliations were important since he had been the architect of the marriage that enabled William to succeed to the English throne jointly with his wife. He

was one of the seven leading Englishmen who signed the letter inviting William to England, and when the latter landed he speedily secured York and brought the north of England to William's side.

Danby would have preferred Mary as queen, but accepted the idea of joint sovereignty. He was now richly rewarded for his support by William, being made Marquis of Carmarthen and lord president of the Council in 1689. He was temporarily reconciled with the Whig leaders, although he soon quarrelled with them and with Halifax. Danby was discontented with his office and would have preferred to return as treasurer, but William's confidence in him grew and by 1690 Danby was again chief minister. He was responsible for government during William's absences in Ireland and Flanders. Danby's position, however, was precarious, and his unpopularity soon revived. After his quarrel with Halifax he was lampooned as 'Tom the Tyrant', and rumours spread that he was secretly communicating with James, although there appears to have been no foundation in this charge. James in any case clearly recognized Danby's role in the events that led to his downfall and in 1692 included Danby among the few men he would not pardon if he recovered his throne.

In 1694 Danby supported the Triennial Bill against the King's wishes, and his power began to wane. The next year he was impeached by the Commons on the charge of accepting a bribe to obtain a new charter for the East India Company. The charge came to nothing, but Danby thereafter lost all influence on public affairs. He had argued in his defence that to receive bribes was a custom characteristic of the age – certainly he had used it to the full throughout his career. Danby retained the lord presidency of the Council until 1699, but

329

never regained much influence. He appeared in the Lords occasionally, attacking Halifax in 1702 and speaking in the debate on the Sacheverell affair in 1710, when he was nearly eighty. Also in 1710, he published a defence of his conduct under Charles II. Danby died of convulsions on 26 July 1712, leaving a princely fortune.

In 1694 Danby had been made Duke of Leeds, thus adding another title to his name. His enthusiasm for outward honour had made him much disliked, and in a sense both parts of his career had ended in failure. Yet Danby's career was very important. Under Charles II he had been a new kind of minister. He was a financial administrator, relying on a blend of corruption and the support of the Tory-Anglican gentry to give him a firm majority in the House of Commons. His success in the craft of political management foreshadowed a firmer control over party allegiance in Parliament. Above all, Danby's support of the House of Orange in 1677 and 1688 was decisive, and despite the infertility of William and Mary's marriage, the political consequences of this policy were immense for the future of Great Britain.

Andrew Browning, *Thomas Osborne, Earl of Danby and Duke of Leeds 1632–1712* (3 vols.; 1944–51).

Portrait: oil, by Lely.

Otway, Thomas (1652–85), dramatist, noted for his tragedies, the best of which at least partly transcend the somewhat mannered style of the heroic tragedies of the period.

He was born near Midhurst in Sussex on 3 March 1652, the son of an impoverished curate. His father managed to scrape together enough money to have him educated at Winchester School, and in 1670 or 1671 he went up to Christ Church, Oxford. In the autumn of 1672 he left, however, without taking a degree, having become infatuated with the stage and having met Mrs. Aphra Behn (q.v.), who promised him a part in one of her productions.

This, in fact, was Otway's first and only appearance on the stage; he was so nervous that he fluffed his lines and ruined the play. He turned to writing for the stage and in 1675 his first tragedy, *Alcibiades*, was produced. This play is not particularly talented and was not very successful at the time. It did, however, have the effect of adding to Otway's stagestruck frame of mind a passion for Elizabeth Barry, who played one of the leading roles in *Alcibiades*. Both obsessions were to last for the rest of his short life, although his love was never requited and his writing did not make him rich. Elizabeth Barry was Lord Rochester's mistress and, whether she disdained Otway or was fearful of losing the earl's favours, she took little notice of the dramatist's importunings. The next two years brought him some success, however, with his writing, starting with the production in 1676 of *Don Carlos*, a tragedy in rhymed verse. In the following year he turned to the French dramatists for models, adapting *Titus and Berenice* from Racine and *The Cheats of Scapin* from Molière. The success of the latter encouraged him to try his hand at writing original comedies, and in 1678 the Dorset Garden Theatre presented *Friendship in a Fashion*, a species of bedroom farce that was considered 'very diverting' by contemporary audiences.

In spite of his growing success as a dramatist, Otway became more and more restless and miserable – probably the effect of his continuing rejection by Mrs. Barry – and in the summer of 1678 he ran away and joined the army. He served in Holland, where he received a commission, but apparently did not enjoy military life, although it was to provide him with the background for a future comedy, *The Soldier's Fortune* (1681). At all events, by the end of 1679 he was back in London and writing again.

It was now that he wrote what are, in the opinion both of his contemporaries and of modern critics, his finest tragedies. Like all nine of his plays, *The Orphan* (1680) and *Venice Preserved* (1682) were first produced by Thomas Betterton (q.v.). Both were frequently revived throughout the following century. In them, Otway abandoned rhyme in favour of blank verse and he seems to have given serious thought to the problem that to modern critics seems the besetting shortcoming of Restoration tragedy, namely that its writers 'continually confront us with emotional conflicts in which we are either not interested or in which we cannot believe' (James Sutherland). *Venice Preserved* is considered by Sutherland 'both credible and distressingly actual'; it was noted by contemporary critics and by Dr. Johnson for its dignity and restraint – as compared, for example, with the extravagant rantings of Nathaniel Lee (q.v.) – while at the same time portraying real emotion.

Otway's last play, *The Atheist* (1684), is a comedy; it is a competent effort, but is no better than his other comedies and is not up to the standard of *Venice Preserved*.

Whether his health was always weak, whether he drank too much, or whether he was just worn out with disappointment is not known; he died quite suddenly, however, still impoverished and unrequited, in April 1685, at the age of 33, in a house on Tower Hill. Some accounts say that he died in a public house; others, that it was a sponging house.

J. C. Ghosh (ed.), *The Works of Thomas Otway* (2 vols.; 1932).

R. G. Ham, *Otway and Lee* (New Haven, Conn., 1931).

Portrait: miniature, by Thomas Flatman: V. & A.

Overbury, Sir Thomas (1581–1613), victim of a murder plot by Frances Howard and Robert Carr.

Born in 1581 at Compton Scorpion, Warwickshire, Overbury was educated at the Queen's College, Oxford, and the Middle Temple, London. In 1601 Overbury travelled on holiday to Scotland, where he met the young Robert Carr (q.v.), later Earl of Somerset. On his return to London he secured a post in London under Robert Cecil, Earl of Salisbury (see *Lives of the Tudor Age*), who was eager for connections among the followers of the heir to the throne, James VI of Scotland. Overbury appears to have served Cecil well, being sent on at least one diplomatic mission to the Continent, but when in 1607 Carr became James's favourite, Overbury quickly established himself as Carr's adviser and confidant. From this relationship he soon profited, becoming servitor to the King, gaining a knighthood in 1608, and sharing in the financial spoils of a post in the administration.

Overbury took great pains to ensure that the King's new favourite should antagonize as few powerful people as possible, but then, in 1611, Carr began an affair with Frances Howard, Countess of Essex. There are conflicting accounts of the events of the next two years and the attitudes of the protagonists, but it seems that from the first Overbury opposed the liaison, which the Howards saw as a means of gaining control over Carr – a project to which Overbury was an obstacle, for it was popularly said that 'Overbury governed Carr and Carr governed the King.' In spite of the disreputable liaison with Lady Essex, Carr's power continued to increase, especially when the death of Robert Cecil in 1612 left the conduct of foreign affairs and the control of various lucrative appointments, such as the treasurership of Scotland, in Carr's hands, which in practice meant Overbury's. The latter had grown arrogant and boastful and, although politicians as powerful as Sir Francis Bacon had to curry his favour, he had succeeded in alienating some of the most influential men at court.

In the autumn of 1612 Carr and Lady Essex decided to marry, although this would first entail a divorce between Lady Essex and her husband. This, it seems, led to a quarrel between Carr and Overbury, and in April 1613 Carr induced the King to offer Overbury a foreign mission. He refused and was sent to the Tower. Here, Lady Essex is alleged to have arranged for him to be slowly poisoned by jailers who were in her pay, and he died in prison on 15 September 1613.

Over a year went by before the growing tide of rumours and suspicions led to any action. Eventually, a trial took place in which the details of the supposed murder were dramatically revealed. Four of the minor accomplices were hanged, but Carr and Lady Essex, now his wife, escaped with a sentence of imprisonment. Carr himself continually protested his ignorance of the plot, and was eventually pardoned by James I in 1624.

Overbury's writings, which were of little intrinsic worth, enjoyed a wild success after his death, especially a poem called *A Wife* (published in 1614 by an enterprising bookseller as *A Wife now the Widow of Sir T. Overbury*), which catalogues the virtues that a young man should look for in a wife and was popularly supposed to have been written to dissuade Carr from his liaison with Lady Essex.

M. A. De Ford, *The Overbury Affair* (Philadelphia, Pa., 1960).

William McElwee, *The Murder of Sir Thomas Overbury* (1952).

W. J. Paylor (ed.) *The Overburian Characters* (1936).

Beatrice White, *Cast of Ravens* (1965).

Oxford, 1st Earl of (1661–1724), see Harley, Robert.

P

Paterson, William (1658–1719), founder of the Bank of England and promoter of the unsuccessful Darien scheme.

William Paterson was born in April 1658 at Skipmyre Farm in Tinwald parish, Dumfriesshire, son of John Paterson and his wife, Elizabeth. Paterson's early life is something of a mystery, but it is fairly certain that he left Scotland in infancy and was brought up in England. He appears to have lived with a kinswoman of his mother in Bristol, from whom he is said to have received a legacy.

Paterson became a merchant, travelling to the West Indies and New England, and in 1681 was admitted to the Merchant Taylors' Company. By 1691 he was a man of considerable influence and sizable fortune, and joined with several others, including Michael Godfrey, to propose the foundation of the Bank of England. In 1692 he was the principal witness before the Parliamentary committee appointed to receive proposals for raising supplies, and conducted negotiations between the merchants and the government. Paterson became a director of the bank on its foundation in 1694, but resigned in 1695 over a matter of policy.

He busied himself with other schemes: he tried to organize a rival bank but failed, and he pointed out the necessity of restoring the currency, which had become debased. In 1693 he was actively involved with the Hampstead Water Company. However, his energies were now mainly concentrated on the revival of his Darien project. This was a scheme, which he had first conceived in 1684 and had proposed unsuccessfully to James II, to colonize the Darien area of central America. He managed to gain a great deal of support from Scottish merchants, and in 1695 he secured an act in the Scottish parliament establishing a trading company. William III opposed the expedition because of the political situation in Europe. Unfortunately, Paterson was soon forced to resign from his position, as one of his agents had appropriated £25,000 out of the funds. Paterson himself was almost certainly not involved, but felt obliged to make reparation to the tune of £6,000. In spite of this setback, Paterson accompanied the expedition as a private citizen when it set sail on 26 July 1698, and did

what he could to save it from ruin, caused by the squabbling of the seven councillors. He was unsuccessful, however, and after a serious illness returned to Britain, arriving in December 1699. He suffered great financial loss, and great personal loss too, as his wife and only child died at Darien.

William III welcomed Paterson on his return, and Paterson advised him on a number of financial issues, including provision for the management of the national debt and control of the Treasury department. Paterson was also strongly in favour of union between England and Scotland. He published a very able pamphlet advocating the union, and was actively involved in Scottish politics. One of the last acts of the Scottish parliament was to recommend him to Queen Anne 'for his good service'.

After William III's death, Paterson was consulted by Godolphin and continued to advise ministers on financial matters. In 1701 he was already urging measures which became the basis of Walpole's Sinking Fund (1716). He was also an early advocate of free trade.

From 1703 until his death, Paterson lived in Queen Square, Westminster. Towards the end of his life he was apparently in somewhat reduced circumstances, although he still retained an interest in the Hampstead Water Company and received fees from the South Sea Company. He did eventually receive a government indemnity to offset his losses on the Darien scheme, shortly before his death, on 22 January 1719.

Saxe Bannister (ed.), *The Writings of William Paterson* (3 vols.; 1859).

Portrait: sculpture, quarter-length, by Sir Charles Wheeler, *c.* 1934–5: Bank of England.

Penn, Sir William (1621–70), admiral in the First and Second Dutch Wars (1652–54 and 1665–67).

Born at Bristol, 23 April 1621, the son of a naval captain and merchant, with whom Penn served at sea during his youth. When the Civil War broke out, Penn was twenty-one. He fought on the Parliamentarian side in the fleet under Warwick (see Rich, Robert), and in 1647 he was given the position of rear admiral of the Irish seas. In 1648 he was arrested, probably for alleged correspondence with Charles I. He was soon released, however, and resumed his post as rear admiral, taking part in the pursuit of Prince Rupert's ships in the Mediterranean (1650–51).

In 1652, at the outbreak of the first Dutch War, Penn was appointed vice admiral to Blake (q.v.). He was involved in the successful encounter with the Dutch in the Kentish Knock (September 1652) and in the fight off Portland (18 February 1653), in which Blake was injured. He also served in the battles that ended the war. In December he was made a general of the fleet.

The charge of communicating with the Royalists, which had perhaps been brought against Penn in 1648, may have had some grounds at this time. Certainly, such a charge would have been justifiable in 1654: for now Penn secretly offered to deliver up the fleet to Charles II. Apparently a Royalist at heart, he was willing to remain in the service of Parliament and Cromwell as long as it was profitable. Thus, with his colleague Robert Venables, he set sail in December 1654 in command of an expedition to the West Indies. In April 1655 he was forced to withdraw at Santo Domingo, owing to panic among his troops. In May, however, the expedition went on to capture Jamaica. Penn and Venables were blamed for the Santo Domingo incident, and upon their return to England (September 1655), they were confined in the Tower for about three weeks. Upon his release, after making an abject submission, Penn retired to his estates in Munster. Until the end of the Interregnum he continued to correspond with Charles II, and when the Restoration came he received a knighthood and became a navy commissioner.

In the Navy Office he was the superior of Samuel Pepys (q.v.), whose reflections on him in his diary are unfavourable. 'To horse again,' writes Pepys on 1 May 1662, 'and got to Guildford, whereafter I to bed, having this day been offended by Sir W. Penn's foolish talk, and I offending him with my answers.'

Penn saw action in the Second Dutch War, serving as captain of the fleet under James, Duke of York, and being present at the engagement off Lowestoft (Solebay) in June 1665. After the end of the war (1667) he continued to work in the Navy Office until his death at Wanstead on 16 September 1670. He was buried at the church of St. Mary Redcliff, Bristol.

Penn's character seems to have been somewhat unscrupulous. He profited from the Commonwealth and Cromwell and also from the restored King. Pepys called him a 'mean fellow'. It is, however, as a seaman that we should remember him now. He helped to draw up the tactical code that formed the basis for 'The Duke of York's Fighting and Sailing Instructions', long in use after his time. Penn married Margaret Jasper, a Dutch lady. His son was the great Quaker and founder of Pennsylvania, William Penn (q.v.).

G. Penn, *Memorials of the professional Life and Times of Sir William Penn* (1833).
A. Pound, *The Penns of Pennsylvania and England* (1932).

Penn, William (1644–1718), English Quaker and founder of Pennsylvania.

Penn was born in London on 14 October 1644, son of Admiral Sir William Penn (q.v.). The area around Wanstead in Essex where Penn lived during his childhood was a stronghold of Puritanism, and the Puritan teaching that he received at Chigwell school had a strong influence on his early intellectual development. In 1660, during his second year at Oxford University, Penn was expelled for Nonconformity; his father sought to distract him from further intellectual controversies by sending him to the Continent, but in the event the two years that Penn spent in France at the Protestant university of Saumur served only to increase his commitment to Puritan doctrines. On his return to England in 1664 Penn was admitted as a student at Lincoln's Inn, but two years later his formal education was again cut short when his father sent him to Ireland to govern the family estates.

Penn was so impressed by a Quaker meeting that he attended in Cork soon

after his arrival in Ireland that he became a regular attender; he was briefly imprisoned for attending these meetings, but on his return to England in 1667 even his father was forced to admit that he could do no more to divert his son from his convictions. In 1668 Penn published his first pamphlet, *Truth Exalted*, in which he attacked both Anglican and Roman Catholic doctrines; two further pamphlets attacking the traditional doctrine of the Holy Trinity were published in the following two years, and during his consequent imprisonment in the Tower of London Penn wrote his most famous tract, *No Cross, No Crown* (1669), an eloquent and learned dissertation on Quaker morality. Through his father's influence Penn was released from the Tower, but in 1670, after holding an open-air meeting when the Quaker meeting-house in Gracechurch Street was closed by the authorities, he was again imprisoned. At his trial following this latter arrest Penn exposed with both courage and skill the illegality of the proceedings, and indeed it was clearly apparent that mere imprisonment would not be enough to quell his ideals; 'the Tower', he wrote, 'is to me the worst argument in the world.'

On his father's death in 1670 Penn inherited considerable wealth, and for brief periods throughout the next ten years he lived as a country gentleman at Rickmansworth in Hertfordshire and later at Warminghurst in Sussex: his appreciation of material comforts in no way lessened his concern for social justice. In 1671 Penn travelled through Holland and Germany on a preaching mission in support of the Quaker cause, a journey that he repeated six years later in company with George Fox (q.v.). He married Gulielma Stuart, a well-born Quaker, in 1672, and worked ceaselessly both in England and

Ireland as a minister and pamphleteer. At court Penn was friendly with both Charles II and his brother the Duke of York (see James II), in spite of their differences on religion; in politics he campaigned vigorously for the Whigs, often causing much anxiety to those Quakers who held more strict opinions than himself on the proper division between politics and religion.

Alongside all these activities during the 1670s Penn was gradually formulating his plans for the establishment of a Quaker colony in America, and in 1681, after buying the proprietory rights to East New Jersey, he asked for and was granted by the King a vast province on the west bank of Delaware. He named this province Pennsylvania after his father (to whom King Charles had owed a large debt, now cancelled by this grant), and immediately began to draw up the Frame of Government upon which his 'holy experiment' would be constructed. The principles upon which Penn based his constitution were those of the Sermon on the Mount, the text construed by all Quakers as a practical guide to the business of living; religious toleration was to be absolute, and there was an amending clause to allow the laws to be altered as circumstances might necessitate.

Late in 1682 Penn sailed for America; for the next two years he supervised the building of the city of Philadelphia and personally presided over the governing assembly, but in 1684 a dispute with Lord Baltimore concerning the colony's boundaries with Maryland caused him to return to England. On the accession of his friend the Duke of York as James II in 1685 Penn was able to use his influence to have over 1,200 Quakers released from prisons in England, and for several years this renewed political involvement kept him from his colony. In 1696 Penn married Hannah Callowhill of Bristol, his first wife having died in 1694. During the reign of William and Mary after James II's abdication in 1689 Penn was virtually forced into hiding to avoid arrest, but his writings of this period, which include *Some Fruits of Solitude* (1693) and a draft plan for the union of the American colonies, continued to be published.

Penn returned to his colony in 1699; he worked hard to produce a revised constitution, known as the charter of privileges, by which he managed to solve many of the initial administrative difficulties of the colony, but within two years his domestic interests again demanded his presence in England. Penn was well received by Queen Anne, to whom he had made known the gratitude of all Quakers for her support for the Toleration Act, but his final years were troubled by the untrustworthiness of his deputy governors and by the repercussions of his own financial mismanagement. In 1712, having already been compelled to mortgage his American proprietory rights, Penn commenced negotiations to surrender Pennsylvania to the crown, and the completion of these negotiations was prevented only by a sudden stroke of apoplexy, which left Penn paralysed and with his memory and intellect seriously impaired. Fortunately, Penn's secretary in America, James Logan, upheld the principles of his democratic constitution and governed capably for the next half century. Penn himself, now almost completely helpless, lingered on in England for a further six years: it was a hard end for a man who, although strict in his spiritual observance of all the Quaker doctrines, had always dressed well and enjoyed good food and conversation. He died at Jordans in Buckinghamshire on 30 July 1718.

S. M. Janney, *Life of William Penn* (Philadelphia, Pa., 1851).

C. O. Peare, *William Penn: a biography* (Philadelphia and New York, 1957).

Portrait: engraving, quarter-length, by R. Stanier, 1790: British Museum.

Penruddock, John (1619–55), leader of an abortive Royalist insurrection against Oliver Cromwell.

Born in 1619, the second son of Sir John Penruddock of Compton Chamberlayne, Wiltshire, Penruddock was educated at Blandford School and the Queen's College, Oxford; he entered Gray's Inn in 1638.

In 1643, just before the Civil War, Charles I appointed the elder Penruddock high sheriff of Wiltshire. In the ensuing hostilities young Penruddock, with his family, took the Royalist side. He lost two brothers in the war, and both he and his father were fined by the victorious Parliament. He also incurred considerable debts, but resolved to risk the remainder of his fortune in the service of the King.

Thus, in 1655, Penruddock set an uprising in motion. On 12 March he led 200 men into Salisbury, capturing two circuit judges as hostages, and proclaimed Charles II. The expected support of the country people was not forthcoming, however, so Penruddock and his followers made a bid to get into Cornwall, where a similar uprising had been reported. At his quarters in South Molton, Devon, he was surprised and taken prisoner along with sixty of his adherents; the rest succeeded in escaping.

At his trial at Exeter, Penruddock argued in his defence that he was legally not guilty of high treason at all, and had surrendered only on condition that he would not be harmed. But such a condition was denied by the officer who had captured him. Nor was his plea accepted. He was beheaded at Exeter on 16 May 1655.

A. H. Woolrych, *Penruddock's Rising* (Historical Association Pamphlet G. 29; 1955).

Pepusch, John Christopher (1667–1752), German-born composer and music teacher, see *Lives of the Georgian Age*.

Pepys, Samuel (1633–1703), statesman, diarist, and an administrator of the navy department under Charles II.

Born in London on 23 February 1633, the second son of a tailor, Pepys was educated first at Huntingdon, then at St. Paul's School, London, until 1650, when he entered Magdalene College, Cambridge, receiving his B.A. in 1654 at the age of twenty-one.

When Pepys married, in 1655, he was far from wealthy, nor indeed was his bride, Elizabeth Marchand de St. Michel, daughter of an impoverished Huguenot refugee from Anjou. Pepys could, however, rely on the support of Edward Montagu (q.v.), 1st Earl of Sandwich,

his cousin, who helped him. In 1659, the year after he had been 'cut for the stone' (an operation, probably for a gallstone, that he celebrated annually with a solemn dinner), Pepys went as secretary to Montagu on a voyage to the Sound during his intervention between Denmark and Sweden. Upon returning, he was appointed clerk to Edward Downing, one of the four tellers of the exchequer, who later gave his name to Downing Street.

While employed in this capacity, Pepys commenced his *Diary* (1 January 1660). In that same year, he accompanied the party that brought Charles II out of exile, and through the influence of Montagu he was appointed clerk of the acts in the Navy Office at a salary of £300 per annum. In the succeeding years, Pepys's career progressed well: he was appointed a clerk of the Privy Seal (1660); he joined the commission administering the affairs of Tangier, then garrisoned by English troops (1662); and he joined the corporation of the Royal Fishery (1664).

Pepys's industry during this period was prodigious. He learnt everything he needed to know concerning his administrative office, having entered upon it in complete ignorance. Following the outbreak of the second war against the Dutch in 1665, Pepys was in the next year given the added responsibility of administering the victualling office, remaining at his post throughout the Plague and the Fire. He showed himself an able and progressive administrator and his abilities recommended him to James, then Duke of York and lord high admiral (see James II). When the navy came under attack in the Commons after the conclusion of the war, it was Pepys who conducted a vigorous reasoned defence before the House in 1668, acknowledging his department's own shortcomings but laying much of the blame at the door of Parliament also.

1669 marked the end of Pepys's diary because of the increasing weakness of his eyesight. He went abroad for a time, standing as Member of Parliament for Aldborough on his return. But his wife died (10 November) and, having for this reason neglected his canvassing, he failed to win the seat. He was more successful in 1673, however, becoming member for Castle Rising in Norfolk.

By this date, Pepys had begun to make enemies. The unpopularity of the Duke of York's open adherence to Roman Catholicism rubbed off on him also; the Castle Rising result was contested, and Pepys was accused of popery; Charles II's prorogation of Parliament, however, saved him for the moment.

Charles now appointed Pepys as secretary of the Admiralty, thus giving him complete charge of naval administration. He set about his task of reforming both the navy and its organization with great energy. In the next six years he managed to obtain Parliament's consent to the building of thirty new battleships. However, animosity towards him grew, led by Lord Shaftesbury (see Cooper, Anthony Ashley), who in 1678 attempted to implicate him in the alleged murder of Sir Edmund Berry Godfrey (q.v.). Pepys, now the member for Harwich, was sent to the Tower in 1679. Again he was saved by royal intervention, for Charles dissolved Parliament and prevented its being reconvened for eighteen months. Pepys was released on bail in February 1680.

In 1683, in his capacity as one of the Tangier commissioners, Pepys accompanied the Earl of Dartmouth on a voyage to Tangier to evacuate the English garrison. His journal, the *Tangier Papers*, records the events of the journey.

Having lost his government post in 1678, Pepys returned to the secretariat of the Admiralty in 1684. He continued his reorganization, and in 1686 he obtained the appointment of a special commission 'for the recovery of the navy'. In 1689, following the overthrow of James II, Pepys was dismissed and spent his last years in retirement at Clapham, where he died on 25 May 1703.

Pepys's achievements in the navy department were considerable. Associated with it over a period of thirty years, he effectively doubled the navy's fighting power and thoroughly overhauled its inefficient administration. Though not above a little petty corruption himself – the *Diary* records his receiving 'compliments' (gifts) from clients – he nevertheless did much to eradicate the far worse corruption that had for years made England's command of the sea an empty boast. His labours, chronicled by him in *Memoirs of the Navy* (1690), created an effective fighting machine based on systematic organization.

A man of wide cultural interests, Pepys was friendly with such men as Dryden, Evelyn, and Sir Isaac Newton. In 1664 he was elected to the Royal Society, becoming its president twenty years later.

In his lifetime Samuel Pepys achieved honour and wealth as an administrator, but posterity remembers him chiefly for his unique *Diary*. This personal journal of his life from 1 January 1660, to 31 May 1669, kept in a form of shorthand devised by Pepys himself, was bequeathed together with the rest of Pepys's large library to his old college, Magdalene. It remained undeciphered until John Smith's transcription of it appeared in 1825.

The diary chronicles, with a frankness only possible in complete secrecy, the rise of an unknown and impoverished clerk to a position of riches and power by dint of hard work, determined ambition, and astute opportunism. An amiable, colourful, and not too respectable character emerges from these pages, together with a remarkably vivid picture of Restoration society. We see Pepys the efficient clerk:

> To the office, where all the morning, and I find Mr. Coventry is resolved to do much good, and to inquire into all the miscarriages of the office . . .

or Pepys the playgoer:

> . . . then to the King's theatre, where we saw 'Midsummer's Night's Dream', which I have never seen before, nor shall ever again, for it is the most insipid, ridiculous play that ever I saw in my life . . .

or Pepys the amateur astronomer:

> I find Reeves there [at Pepys's house], it being a mighty fine bright night, and so upon my leads, though very sleepy, till one in the morning, looking on the moon and Jupiter with the twelve-foot glass and another of six foot that he hath brought with him tonight.

Disclosed in the diary too are his amorous exploits and numerous infidelities, all recorded honestly and frankly – though he often shifts into a foreign language in describing some of the more bawdy situations. The diary is valuable not only as a portrait of its author, but also for the light it sheds on contemporary events, notably the Plague of 1665 and the Great Fire of London in the following year. What appeals most about it, however, is its sense of immediacy and the impression gained from it that one is there in the 1660s, that one is in fact living Pepys's life:

> As I was writing of this very line the bellman passed and cried, 'Past one of the clock and a cold and a frosty windy morning.'

R. Latham and W. Matthews (eds.), *The Diary of Samuel Pepys* (11 vols.; 1970–   ).

J. R. Tanner (ed.), *Private Correspondence and Miscellaneous Papers of Samuel Pepys, 1679–1703* (2 vols.; 1926).

J. R. Tanner (ed.), *Samuel Pepys's Naval Minutes* (1926).

J. R. Tanner (ed.), *Further Correspondence of Samuel Pepys 1662–1679* (1929).

Edwin Chappell (ed.), *The Tangier Papers of Samuel Pepys* (1935).

Richard Barber, *Samuel Pepys, Esquire* (1970).

Arthur Bryant, *Samuel Pepys* (3 vols.; 1967, rev. ed.).

Edwin Chappell, *Samuel Pepys as a Naval Administrator* (1933).

Cecil Emden, *Pepys Himself* (1963).

Richard Ollard, *Pepys: A Biography* (1974).

J. R. Tanner, *Samuel Pepys and the Royal Navy* (1920).

Portrait: oil, half-length, by John Closterman, *c*. 1690–1700: N.P.G.

Percy, John (1569–1641), see Fisher, John.

Peter or Peters, Hugh (1598–1660), English Puritan preacher, executed as a regicide.

Peter's baptism is recorded on 29 June 1598. He was born into a well-to-do merchant family of Fowey, Cornwall, and at the age of fourteen went up to Trinity College, Cambridge. In 1623 he was ordained and for a time lived and preached in Essex, where he married in 1624.

After returning to London in 1624 or 1625, he gained a reputation as a converting preacher and his orthodoxy began to be suspected. An attack on Queen Henrietta Maria for popish practices apparently led to his suspension from preaching and he left England for Holland around 1629.

Peter spent some time with the Dutch troops fighting against Spain and with the army of Gustavus Adolphus before settling as a minister of the English church at Rotterdam. Among his congregation were many exiled Puritans, including John Winthrop (q.v.), who became a close friend. Under his guidance the church progressed along Puritan lines and this came to the notice of Archbishop Laud (q.v.) in England, who was attempting to gain the conformity of the British churches in Holland to the doctrine and ceremonies of the Anglican Church. In the face of this renewed scrutiny of his activities Peter decided to emigrate to New England, where many of his acquaintances and members of his wife's family had already settled. He arrived at Boston in October 1635.

In 1636 Peter became minister of the church at Salem, Massachusetts, and soon began to take a prominent part in the affairs of the colony. He was engaged in the founding of the new colony at the mouth of the Connecticut River and of Harvard College. He was also much concerned in the economic development of the colony. In religious matters Peter was less tolerant than he later became and zealously enforced the narrow Congregationalist orthodoxy.

In 1641 the fortunes of the colony were adversely affected by the political situation in England; Peter was one of three agents sent home to seek financial and other support. However he soon became involved in the political and religious upheaval at home and never returned to New England. When the Civil War broke out he quickly established himself as a valuable exponent of the Parliamentary cause. His sermons were effective both in winning recruits for the army and in inspiring Parliamentary soldiers before and after battle. He served as chaplain to Fairfax and the New Model Army and played an important part in the campaigns of 1645 and 1646, especially at Naseby and Langport.

Peter also acted as a confidential agent

of the general and as a kind of war correspondent – his accounts of battles and sieges were eagerly read, and on several occasions he was invited to narrate his accounts to the House of Commons. After the outbreak of the Second Civil War in 1648 he strongly supported bringing the King to trial. Although he later denied playing any active part in the death of the King, his sermons during Charles's trial were undoubtedly inflammatory. In one of them he took as his text the words 'To bind their kings in chains and their nobles with fetters of iron,' and on the eve of Charles's execution he preached in St. James's Chapel on the denunciation of the King of Babylon in Isaiah (xiv 18–20). His violence of speech and manner and occasional buffoonery at this time earned Peter a reputation as a rabble-rouser and was at least partly responsible for his later condemnation and execution as a regicide. However, ironically enough, Peter's views at this time seem to have moderated considerably: he strongly advocated religious toleration and suggested that if ministers of different views dined together more often their mutual animosities would disappear. After the establishment of the republic Peter intended to return to New England but at first ill health and then continued involvement in public affairs prevented him from doing so. He accompanied Cromwell to Ireland in 1649 and towards the end of that year he received from Parliament a grant of £200 per annum. In 1650 he became one of the chaplains of the Council of State and soon became permanently established as one of the preachers at Whitehall. Throughout the 1650s he interested himself – or meddled, as many contemporaries thought – in all the important issues of the day. In 1651 he advocated extensive social and administrative reform in such publications as *Good Work for a Good Magistrate, Or, a short cut to great quiet*. During the war with the Dutch in 1652 and 1653 he attempted to heal the breach between the two countries by his personal influence and even wrote to Sir George Ayscue asking him to desist from fighting his co-religionists. In 1654 he became one of the 'Triers', whose business it was to examine and license all candidates for livings.

Towards the end of the Protectorate and during the troubled period following Oliver Cromwell's death Peter was in poor health and took little active part in public affairs. When the Restoration of Charles II appeared certain he wrote to Monck (q.v.) stressing his peaceableness and present inactivity. Nevertheless he was exempted on 18 June 1660 from the Act of Oblivion and Indemnity and was tried as a regicide. Despite his denials of any share in the King's death and the proof he was able to offer of his kindnesses to individual Royalists, Peter was found guilty and condemned to death. He was executed at Charing Cross on 16 October 1660.

R. P. Stearns, *The Strenuous Puritan, Hugh Peters, 1598–1660* (Urbana, Ill., 1954).

Peterborough, 3rd Earl of (1658–1735), see Mordaunt, Charles.

Petre, Father Edward (1631–99), English Jesuit and adviser of James II.

Edward Petre was born in Paris in 1631, the second son of Sir Francis Petre, who belonged to the Essex branch of a prominent Roman Catholic family. He was sent in 1649 to study at the Catholic seminary of St. Omer and joined the Society of Jesus in 1652. In 1679 Petre succeeded to his father's title and about the same time was sent on a mission to England. During Charles II's reign he was imprisoned twice. He was committed to Newgate at the time of the Popish Plot, but no charges were proved against him. In 1681 Petre became vice-president of the English Jesuits and was promptly arrested again and imprisoned until 1683.

Petre had attracted notice at St. Omer for his boldness and plausible tongue, and his religious zeal had been noted by James, Duke of York. When York came to the throne in 1685 as James II, Petre was soon welcomed at court. James placed him in charge of his royal chapel and installed him in the palace of Whitehall. Petre became an ally of Sunderland (see Spencer, Robert) and a member of the King's informal inner council. James saw Petre as 'a resolute and undertaking man', and in 1687 appointed him a member of the Privy Council. James also sought some preferment for him from Rome, and Sunderland even suggested that he might be made a cardinal. However, the Pope had no great liking for Jesuits, nor for Petre's ambition, and firmly refused to notice him.

The admission of Petre as one of his closest advisers did James much harm, and was later admitted by James to have been imprudent. Petre himself declared that he accepted office with reluctance, and he may have been persuaded by Sunderland. Public suspicion of James was strengthened by this move, which reinforced the belief that the King placed his trust only in Catholics. With Sunderland, Petre was active in catholicizing the municipal corporations and in the replacement of the ejected fellows of Magdalen College, Oxford.

When a son was born to James in 1688, many scurrilous tales began to circulate, some suggesting that Petre was the father and others that he had had a hand in smuggling a baby to the Queen's bed. During the crisis of 1688 Petre advised the King to remain in England, but secretly escaped to St. Omer himself. In 1693, after a visit to Rome, he became rector of St. Omer, and he died on 15 May 1699 at Walten in Flanders. Petre was much hated in England, as much for what he represented as for any advice he actually gave the King. He was burned every year in effigy on Guy Fawkes's Day and Queen Elizabeth's birthday until the end of Queen Anne's reign.

Pope, Alexander (1688–1744), poet and satirist, see *Lives of the Georgian Age.*

Portland, 1st Earl of (1649–1709), see Bentinck, William.

Portsmouth, Duchess of (1649–1734), see Kéroualle, Louise Renée de.

Pratt, Sir Roger (1620–84), architect.
Born into the Norfolk gentry and baptized on 2 November 1620, Pratt received his education at Magdalen College, Oxford, where he matriculated in 1637. In 1639 he entered the Inner Temple. The civil unrest in England in the 1640s caused him to go abroad, and from 1643–49 he travelled widely in Europe. While in Rome he met and be-friended John Evelyn (q.v.), the diarist. His interest in architecture seems to have been developing at this time, for he made copious scholarly notebook studies of French and Italian architecture throughout this trip.

His first architectural work on his return to England was to assist his cousin in the rebuilding of his house at Coleshill. The experience he had gleaned from abroad, together with what he learnt from Inigo Jones (q.v.), who on occasions visited Coleshill during its construction, contrived to produce a remarkable building, combining a mix-ture of Italian and French themes of design. It has a massive structure, totally lacking in unnecessary affectation.

Between 1663 and 1665 Pratt built two more large houses: Horseheath, which was destroyed in 1777, and Kingston Lacy, built in a manner similar to Coleshill. In 1663 Pratt was chosen as a member of the committee responsible for the restoration of St. Paul's Cathedral. According to Evelyn's records, Pratt's views as to the preservation of the steeple were totally opposed to those of Wren and others. By the summer of 1666 Pratt's suggestions had been over-ruled and a scheme of action devised. Several days later the Great Fire began and the cathedral perished. Pratt was made a royal commissioner for the design and rebuilding of the City after the fire, and for his services he received a knighthood.

From 1664 to 1667 Pratt was engaged on the building of his greatest house – Clarendon House, Piccadilly, for the lord chancellor, Edward Hyde, 1st Earl of Clarendon. In Evelyn's words it was 'without hyperbolies, the best contriv'd, the most usefull, gracefull, and magnificent house in England.'

This was one of the first classical houses to be built in London, and its position of prominence led it to be widely imitated, most closely perhaps by Belton House, Lincolnshire. Clarendon House itself was demolished after only 18 years of existence, however, and it is only from an engraving of the house that we know anything of its plans. Facets of its design are directly reminiscent of Pratt's earlier works. The roof rises to a balustraded flat top with a domed lantern in the centre and the wings projecting forwards. The two main floors are of almost equal height, with a pedimented frontispiece and rustic quoins. Altogether it is a striking work, its importance diminished by its brief life.

After coming into his own inheritance in 1667 Pratt undertook no further important commissions. Apart from one or two brief appearances in his official capacity as a royal commissioner Pratt lived in comfortable retirement on his family estates at West Ryston in Norfolk; the only work that he performed during these years was the rebuilding of his own house in a novel style much influenced by his Continental sympathies, and it was in this house that he died on 20 February 1684.

Pretender, The Old (1688–1766), see James Francis Edward Stuart in *Lives of the Georgian Age.*

Pride, Colonel Thomas (d. 1658), Parliamentary commander in the Civil War and leader of Pride's Purge of 1648.

The origins of Thomas Pride are obscure. Born somewhere in southern England, he married Elizabeth, the niece of George Monck (q.v.). In the Civil War he entered the Parliamentary army as a captain or an ensign and was a major in the Earl of Essex's infantry that surrendered in Cornwall in 1644. He became a lieutenant colonel of foot when the New Model Army was organized and commanded his regiment with distinction at Naseby, Bristol, and Dartmouth.

After the First Civil War, Pride espoused the cause of the Army against Parliament, and in the Second Civil War he served under Cromwell in Wales and at Preston. His regiment petitioned for the punishment of the King when this war was over and was one of the units with which Fairfax occupied London in December 1648. During the Second Civil War, the groups hostile to the Army, led by the Pres-

byterians, had regained control of Parliament while the Army was absent from London. Now that the soldiers were back, they proceeded to deal summarily with their parliamentary enemies.

On 6 December 1648, Pride took a guard to the Commons. There he excluded about ninety members and arrested over forty others. This action became known as 'Pride's Purge', and reduced the Long Parliament to a Rump dominated by the political Independents.

Pride served as one of the commissioners at the trial of Charles I and signed the death warrant. In 1651–52 he campaigned with Cromwell against the Scots, receiving as a reward from Parliament confiscated lands.

He grew quite wealthy and during the Protectorate abstained from most political activity, although a republican. Knighted by Cromwell in 1656, Pride was one of the officers actively hostile to plans to crown him in 1657. Subsequently he did, however, take a place in Cromwell's 'House of Lords'.

Pride did not long survive his commander, and died on 23 October 1658.

Mark Noble, *Lives of the English Regicides* (1798).

Prior, Matthew (1664–1721), diplomat, wit, and poet.

Prior was born on 21 July 1664 at Wimborne in Dorset, where his father was a joiner. As a child Prior seems to have been somewhat precocious, for in spite of his humble origins he impressed the Earl of Dorset (Charles Sackville, q.v.), by turning passages from Horace and Ovid into faultless English verse, to such an extent that that nobleman undertook the expense of his education. Accordingly, Prior was sent off to Westminster School and then to St. John's College, Cambridge, where he received the degree of B.A. in 1686, becoming a fellow in 1688.

While at Cambridge Prior had begun to write verse, including a political satire answering Dryden's *The Hind and the Panther*. The verse of Prior's reply is mediocre, but the political sentiments expressed were sufficient, when coupled with the patronage of the Earl of Dorset, to win him an appointment in 1689 as secretary to the ambassador to The Hague, Lord Dursley. He spent several years in Holland, and in 1697 was active in the negotiations for the Treaty of Ryswick. His skill in negotiation was noticed; he received a gratuity payment of 200 guineas, and there followed a hectic period of increasingly responsible appointments in Paris, Ireland, and eventually London. In 1701 he served for a short time as M.P. for East Grinstead. Up to this time his political masters had been Whigs, but on the accession of Queen Anne in 1702, Prior joined the Tories. For nine years he remained comparatively inactive. However, in 1711 he found employment again, being sent on a secret mission to Paris. This appears to have been a preliminary to the Treaty of Utrecht (1713), which was negotiated largely by Prior, to the extent that the treaty was widely known among his contemporaries as 'Matt's Peace'.

Following the death of Queen Anne in 1714, Prior was recalled from Paris and, in 1715, when Walpole impeached Bolingbroke, Oxford, and other leading Tories on the grounds that the Treaty of Utrecht was a 'treasonable misconduct', Prior, the chief negotiator of that treaty, was thrown into prison. He appears to have accepted his fate philosophically, contenting himself by continuing to write verse of a characteristically whimsical, but amusing style.

Prior was released from prison in 1717, but was never again active in public life. In 1719 a folio edition of his poems was brought out by his admirers, earning him the astonishing sum of 4,000 guineas. His friend and patron, Robert Harley (q.v.), Earl of Oxford, put up a further sum for the purchase of Down Hall in Essex, to which Prior retired to pass the rest of his life. In prison he had written:

Great Mother, let me once be able
To have a garden, house, and stable;
That I may read and ride and plant,
Superior to desire or want;
And, as health fails, and years increase
Sit down, and think, and die in peace.

Down Hall was the fulfilment of all these wishes; Matthew Prior died there, in peace, on 18 September 1721.

A. R. Waller (ed.), *The Writings of Matthew Prior* (2 vols.; 1905–07).

H. Bunker Wright and M. K. Spears (eds.), *The Literary Works of Matthew Prior* (2 vols.; 1956).

C. K. Eves, *Matthew Prior: Poet and Diplomatist* (New York, 1939).

R. W. Ketton-Cremer, *Matthew Prior* (1957).

L. G. Wickham Legg, *Matthew Prior* (1921).

Portraits: oil, three-quarter length, by T. Wright after J. Richardson, *c.* 1718: N.P.G.; oil, three-quarter length, by T. Hudson after J. Richardson, *c.* 1718: N.P.G.; oil, half-length, attributed to Dahl, 1713: N.P.G.; oil, by Kneller: V. & A. Museum.

Prynne, William (1600–69), lawyer, Puritan pamphleteer, and controversialist.

William Prynne was born at Swanswick in Somerset, the son of Thomas Prynne, who farmed lands there belonging to Oriel College, Oxford. His family probably originated in Shropshire; his great-grandfather was sheriff of Bristol (1549). Prynne was educated at Bath grammar school and later at Oriel College, Oxford, graduating with a B.A. in 1621 and becoming a Lincoln's Inn student in the same year. In 1628 he was called to the bar.

As a student at Lincoln's Inn, Prynne

came under the influence of Dr. John Preston, a militant Puritan lecturer there, and from this time Prynne combined studies of law, theology, and church antiquities. A year before he was called to the bar he published the first of his books on theology, *The Perpetuity of a Regenerate Man's Estate*, followed by three attacks on Arminianism, the Dutch school of Protestantism, which was anti-Calvinistic and whose theology was taken up by English Wesleyans. In one tract, Prynne appealed to Parliament to suppress publications that were anti-Calvinistic, and at the same time began his self-appointed task of trying to reform the fashions and manners of the day by attacking them as evil vices.

The scurrility and virulence of Prynne's attacks on society and his strong defence of Calvinism from this time on earned him popular notoriety and the implacable hatred of church authorities. His religious fervour and vituperative pen combined to produce a stream of controversial and malicious documents on theological topics. In addition, his legal training enabled him to present seemingly convincing 'proof' of his charges against churchmen like Archbishop Laud (q.v.), which certainly damaged reputations and lent credence to Prynne's views.

In November 1632 he published the *Histrio-Mastix*, an indexed volume of plays showing that theatrical productions were unlawful, encouraged immorality, were condemned by the Holy Scriptures, the Church Fathers, the wise pagan philosophers, and modern Christian writers. In January 1633 the Queen and some of her court performed in *The Shepherd's Paradise*, and a passage from Prynne's book was then considered a direct attack on the Queen, on audiences, and on magistrates who allowed plays to be put on. Proceedings against Prynne were begun in the Star Chamber; he was imprisoned in the Tower on 1 February 1633, and a year later was sentenced to life imprisonment, to a fine of £5,000, to be expelled from Lincoln's Inn, to be deprived of his Oxford degree, and to have his ears clipped in the pillory. Sentence was carried out and Prynne wrote to Archbishop Laud charging him with unlawful and unjust persecution.

From the Tower, Prynne continued to write, mostly anonymously, although his works were almost always correctly attributed to him as soon as they were published. He attacked episcopacy, sabbath breakers, prelates in general, and particularly the Bishop of Norwich. This attack again brought him before the Star Chamber, and on 14 June 1637, he was further sentenced to a fine of £5,000 and to lose the remainder of his ears. Chief Justice Finch (see Finch, Sir John) proposed that Prynne be branded on the cheeks S.L., standing for 'seditious libeller'. On 30 June Prynne again stood in the pillory, in company with Henry

Burton and John Bastwick (qq.v.), and his ears were cropped so close that an artery was severed. He survived, however, to announce that the initials of the branding stood for 'Stigmata Laudis'. Upon his return to prison, a much closer watch was set upon him and he was deprived of pens, ink, and paper. He was taken to Caernarvon Castle in 1637, and later to Orgueil Castle in Jersey, where the governor, Sir Philip Carteret, treated him kindly and allowed him to write on non-theological topics.

A petition for redress on his behalf was presented to the Long Parliament, and he and Henry Burton made a triumphal entry into London. On 20 April 1641, the House of Commons declared the Star Chamber sentences against him unlawful, restoring his degree and membership of Lincoln's Inn. However, by October 1648 the amount of financial recompense for his troubles had still not been settled, although the Commons had voted for reparations in principle.

Upon the outbreak of the Civil War, Prynne became Parliament's defender in the press, and showed historical precedents for Parliament's case against the King, contending that citizens had the right to defend themselves against infringement of their basic rights by a monarch. Once he had taken up politics, Prynne again became embroiled in numerous controversies, notably attacking the Army from 1647, when its breach with Parliament occurred. He was imprisoned by army officers, but kept writing, and later denounced the proposed trial of the King. In January 1649 he was freed, and immediately began to attack the new government. He was imprisoned in 1650 for a period of three years by the government and was offered release on condition that he

cease attacking the government and pay a surety of £1,000. He refused, but was finally released without conditions on 18 February 1653, whereupon he began a fresh attack with modified virulence, although his writing now received little notice. When the Long Parliament was finally re-established, Prynne began attempts to get his seat back; he managed to sit for a whole session, but was excluded thereafter. He continued pamphleteering on behalf of the 'excluded members', finally rousing popular opinion, and on 21 February 1660, he marched at the head of a cheering crowd to Westminster. Prynne accelerated the Restoration, and later, as M.P. for Ludgershall and for Bath, he continued a stream of pamphlets on all manner of controversial theological and political problems of the day. Several times he was reprimanded and in danger of punishment for sedition. After the Restoration, Prynne became keeper of the records of the Tower.

Altogether, Prynne published about two hundred pamphlets and books. He died on 24 October 1669, unmarried, and was buried at Lincoln's Inn chapel. He left his manuscripts to Lincoln's Inn and a set of his works to Oriel College, Oxford.

E. W. Kirby, *William Prynne* (Cambridge, Mass., 1931).

Portrait: engraving, quarter-length, by W. P. Benoist, 1757: British Museum.

Purcell, Henry (?1659–1695), composer and musician.

Purcell was born probably in London. It is now generally accepted that he was the son of Thomas Purcell, a gentleman of the Chapel Royal at Westminster. It has been said that Henry Purcell was a natural genius. Undoubtedly, he is the most outstanding composer of seventeenth-century England. He must cer-

tainly have been something of a prodigy, for he wrote a song, *Sweet Tyranness*, in 1667, when he was only eight. Two years later, in 1669, he joined the Chapel Royal as a choirboy. In the Chapel choir Purcell's life was comfortable and like all the boys he was well cared for. In addition to his ordinary school work, which consisted chiefly of Latin and writing, he received lessons on the organ, violin, and lute.

In 1673 his voice broke and he was given an allowance of £30 a year and appointed assistant keeper of the King's instruments under John Hingston. In the next year he was given the regular post of organ tuner at Westminster Abbey, where John Blow (q.v.) was organist. Whether Purcell had received organ lessons from Blow before this appointment is uncertain. Undoubtedly he received them during his tenure of the post and much impressed the older musician.

In 1677 Matthew Locke (q.v.) died and his office as composer in ordinary to King Charles II fell to Purcell. This brought the young composer into contact with the King's private band, a

string orchestra for which he was called upon to write a large amount of occasional and diverting music, none of which has survived. Among his serious works for this period are an elegy on the death of Matthew Locke (published 1697) and his set of fantasias for strings (1680).

In 1679 Purcell replaced Blow as organist at Westminster Abbey, a post to which the latter was to return upon Purcell's death. It is possible that Blow may have given up the post voluntarily in favour of his brilliant former pupil.

The following year, 1680, saw the composition not only of his string fantasias but also of his incidental music for Nathaniel Lee's play, *Theodosius, or the Force of Love*, and the first of his twenty-nine celebration odes for state occasions, *A Song to Welcome Home the King from Windsor*. The fact that in this and many of the other odes Purcell married some of his finest music to the most unutterable doggerel is seen by many as a gross misapplication of his talent and genius.

In about 1681 Purcell married. The maiden name of his bride Frances is in doubt. Evidence indicates that it was most probably Peters. By her Purcell had four sons, three of whom died in infancy, and two daughters. In 1682 Purcell was appointed one of the three organists in the Chapel Royal, a post that required him also to take part in the services as a chorister. In the same month that this appointment was conferred his father, Thomas Purcell, died.

1683 was an eventful year for Purcell. It saw the publication of his treatise *The Art of Descant* in the tenth edition of Playford's *Brief Introduction of the Skill of Music*; it saw the appearance of his two *Odes to St. Cecilia*; it saw his appointment as keeper of the King's instruments upon the death of Hingston, who had held it since the Restoration; and, most importantly perhaps, it saw the appearance of his first chamber music, *Sonatas of III Parts: two violins and bass: to the organ or harpsichord*, in which he determinedly broke with the current French vogue in music in favour of Italianate influences.

With the accession of James II and the consequent reassertion of Catholicism, Purcell was at pains to keep his place at Westminster. His post as keeper of the instruments afforded him no salary, but he wrote one of his finest anthems, *My Heart is Inditing*, for the coronation of 1685 and a petition he made to James for the sum of £81, £56 of which was to be his first year's salary, was favourably received.

When William III came to the throne in 1689, Purcell had only six more years to live. Into this short span he crammed an impressively prolific output, including the first real opera in English, *Dido and Aeneas*, composed in 1689 for a girls' boarding school in Chelsea. Other stage works included *King Arthur, or the British Worthy* (1691), *The Fairy Queen* (1692), *The Indian Queen* (1695), and an abundance of incidental music. His sacred works included the *Te Deum* and *Jubilate* in D of 1694 and, also in that year, the poignant funeral music composed for the burial of Queen Mary. The English composer Thomas Tudway (1650–1726), who was present at the funeral, wrote afterwards that Purcell's composition showed 'the power of music, when 'tis rightly fitted and adapted to devotional purposes.'

Purcell died at the tragically young age of thirty-six, on 21 November 1695. He was buried in Westminster Abbey five days later, to the accompaniment of the very music that he had composed for the Queen.

The *Te Deum* of 1694 remained in use at Westminster until 1743, when it was replaced by Handel's *Dettingen Te Deum*. This is a measure of the esteem in which Purcell was held by his contemporaries and the immediately succeeding generation. But Purcell had to wait long for a detached evaluation of his greatness. Not until 1876 was the Purcell Society formed to make his works available. However, in modern times, with the revival of old music, his reputation as one of England's greatest composers has become well established.

A. K. Holland, *Henry Purcell: The English Musical Tradition* (1932).
Imogen Holst (ed.) *Henry Purcell: Essays on His Music* (1959).
R. E. Moore, *Henry Purcell and the Restoration Theatre* (1961).
J. A. Westrup, *Purcell* (1973, 7th ed.).
F. B. Zimmerman, *Henry Purcell, 1659–1695: An Analytical Catalogue of His Music* (1963).
F. B. Zimmerman, *Henry Purcell, 1659–1695: His Life and Times* (1967).

Portraits: oil, half-length, by or after J. Closterman, 1695: N.P.G.; oil, head, by unknown artist: N.P.G.

Purchas, Samuel (?1575–1626), ecclesiastic and compiler of travel books.

Purchas was born in Thaxted, Essex. After graduating from St. John's College, Cambridge, he became curate of Purleigh in Essex in 1601. In 1604 he moved to Eastwood, also in Essex; in 1614 he was appointed chaplain to George Abbott, Archbishop of Canterbury, and from this year until his death in 1626 he was rector of St. Martin's, Ludgate. In 1601 he married Jane Lease, the daughter of a Suffolk yeoman.

Purchas his Pilgrimage, an account of all known religions throughout the world 'from the Creation unto this present,' was first published in 1613 and quickly went into several editions. This work was followed in 1619 by *Purchas his Pilgrim: Microcosmus, or the History of Man*, another historical work of little difference from the first save that it was longer.

Purchas's most famous work, *Hakluytus Posthumus, or Purchas his Pilgrimes*, was published in four volumes in 1625. The material for this book is taken from the manuscripts of Richard Hakluyt (see *Lives of the Tudor Age*) and from narrative accounts by Will Adams of a journey to Japan and by William Hawkins of a visit to the court of the Great Mogul at Agra. A comparison between the surviving original sources and the actual text as published by Purchas shows that he possessed little skill as an editor, and indeed the real value of this book lies in its preservation of some otherwise unknown records rather than in any literary originality.

Although the accusation that many of his original sources were lost because of Purchas's own carelessness is probably true, he was successful in his aim of compiling popular works to satisfy his contemporary public. He died in London in the autumn of 1626, his will being read on 21 October of that year.

Pym, John (1583–1643), statesman and political leader, who came to head the Parliamentary opposition to Charles I.

Pym was born in 1583 at Brymore, Somerset, where his family had been established since the thirteenth century. His father died while he was still a child and his mother married Sir Anthony Rous of Halton St. Dominic, Cornwall, where he was brought up in a highly Puritan atmosphere. In 1599 Pym matriculated as a commoner at Broadgate Hall (now Pembroke College), Oxford, and three years later he entered the Middle Temple.

Through his stepfather, Pym came to know Edward Russell, Earl of Bedford, by whose influence he obtained the position of receiver general of the King's revenue for the counties of Gloucestershire, Wiltshire, and Hampshire. In this capacity, he gained valuable business and financial experience.

Pym entered Parliament in 1614 as M.P. for Calne. He represented Calne again in 1621, and it was in this year that he began to make his name. During this, the third sitting of Parliament convened by James I, Pym made a speech proposing the enforcement of the penal laws against Catholics. Commonly considered now as a Puritan because of his upbringing, Pym was actually at the very outset of his career a moderate. His speech shows that it was not the religion of Catholics that he opposed but their politics. Such a standpoint went back to Elizabethan times and for Pym, who had been a child at the time of the Armada, the old concept that Catholics were potential rebels still had meaning. His other important act in the 1621 sitting was his support of Edward Coke (q.v.) and others whose protestation asserting Parliament's freedom of discussion so enraged James that he tore from the House of Commons' journal the record of the proceedings relating to it and instantly dissolved the session. Pym, like Coke, felt the King's anger and was detained under house arrest for three months, first at his London home and then at Brymore.

In the parliament of 1624, in which he took little active part, Pym sat for Tavistock, a constituency that he continued to represent for the rest of his life. After the accession of Charles I, Pym showed himself to be an assiduous opponent of monarchical absolutism. He continued his campaign against Catholicism and in 1626 was one of the main promoters of the prosecution of Richard Montagu (q.v.). In the same year he organized the impeachment of

Buckingham (see Villiers, George, 1st Duke). Neither enterprise was successful – Montagu was saved by the influence of Laud, while Charles himself rescued his favourite Buckingham by proroguing Parliament – but Pym's involvement set him alongside Sir John Eliot (q.v.) at the head of the Parliamentary forces now ranging themselves against Charles. As a politician, Pym stands apart from Eliot, a man of stern principles who believed in Parliamentary rights and died a martyr's death imprisoned in the Tower, and from Thomas Wentworth (q.v.), whose early support of parliamentary freedom was not so wholehearted that it would allow him to sanction any real diminution of the sovereign's power. In 1628 Eliot, Pym, Wentworth, and Coke all had important parts to play in the formulation and passage of the Petition of Right. After this the Parliamentary attack on Buckingham got under way again, but Pym did not join it straight away, being first concerned with managing the impeachment of Roger Manwaring, the King's chaplain. In 1627 Manwaring had delivered a sermon preaching 'peril of damnation' upon those who resisted the sovereign, especially in his right to levy taxes. Bringing the impeachment before the House of Lords (June 1628), Pym delivered his famous speech in which he asserted that history was 'full of the calamities of whole states and nations . . . (when) one part seeks to uphold the old form of government and the other part to introduce a new.'

In Charles's next parliament (1629), Pym was again present. In the previous year he had prevailed upon Eliot to concentrate on passing the Petition of Right rather than on attacking Buckingham immediately, which had been Eliot's original design. Once again he was at variance with his colleague, for

while Eliot was concerned with challenging the exaction by Charles of tonnage and poundage on the grounds of Parliamentary privilege, Pym wanted to consider it in the wider context of a breach of the law. 'The liberties of this house', he said, 'are inferior to the liberties of the kingdom.' In the event, Eliot had his way. His resolutions against Charles's religious policy and against the imposition of customs duties were passed amid uproar, after Charles had ordered the adjournment.

Pym was not involved in these disturbances and in the ensuing period of non-parliamentary monarchical government he devoted himself to business enterprises in the American colonies. As a patentee of Connecticut and Providence and as treasurer of the Providence Company, he put his business experience to good use. His associates – John Hampden, Oliver Cromwell, William Fiennes, and Robert Rich, the Earl of Warwick – were all prominent Puritans. It is possible that they may have all contemplated emigration to the New

World. At any rate, they all became thoroughly used to working in concert and when Charles called his fifth parliament in 1640 he had to deal with a much more cohesive opposition in these men than he had hitherto encountered.

The last four years of Pym's life were characterized by enormous political activity. Now in his late fifties, he was about to attain an ascendancy that was to give him more effective power than Charles himself. With some justification, the Royalists were to dub him contemptuously 'King Pym'.

In April 1640 Charles convened the Short Parliament. In a two-hour speech, Pym, now undisputed leader of the opposition to Charles, catalogued the general grievances that had accrued during the eleven-year period of personal government. Co-operating with several others, he brought in a petition that the King should treat with the Scots. Rejecting this, Charles dissolved Parliament early in May. During the summer the Scots invaded the northern counties and the disastrous defeat of Newburn ensued. In August, Pym brought in another petition signed by twelve peers, including the Earl of Essex (see Devereux, Robert), calling for the redress of grievances and peace with the Scots. Eventually, Charles was constrained to recall Parliament. After a vigorous campaign, in which Pym, according to Anthony à Wood, 'rode about the country to promote election of the Puritanical brethren to serve in Parliament,' the Long Parliament met on 3 November 1640.

Wentworth, now Earl of Strafford, attempted to impeach Pym and the other popular leaders for alleged treasonable correspondence with the Scots. Whether Pym was guilty of this or not is academic. Having foreknowledge of Strafford's intention, he himself took the

Earl's own impeachment up to the Lords on 11 November. How much matters had changed between them since Wentworth's acceptance of a barony in July 1628 and his subsequent 'defection' to the royal service is indicated by the vehemence of the impeachment proceedings when they finally got under way, in late March 1641. For Pym was now prosecuting Strafford, the late lord deputy of Ireland, the ruthless ruler who had undermined English authority in Ireland and had introduced Laudian reforms there. Pym's case, resting on his use of Vane's notes of a conference between Strafford and the King, was circumstantial and Strafford was adept in defending himself. Yet in the situation then prevailing Pym thought he could win, pinning his case on the deliberate misapprehension that Strafford was preparing to use his Irish army to reduce Charles's English opponents rather than his Scottish ones (see Wentworth, Thomas). There was also the constitutional question of whether or not the leader of an administration could be held responsible for his misdeeds. When the bill of attainder was finally introduced, Pym was reluctant to drop the impeachment, preferring the more procedural approach. But getting wind of Charles's plot to free Strafford, he immediately went ahead with the bill.

In the meantime the court tried to be conciliatory. Pym was offered the post of chancellor of the exchequer. Twice more he was to be offered it, and on each occasion he refused. Pym could not be bought as Strafford had been.

Overshadowed by the prosecution of Strafford, the impeachment of William Laud (q.v.), which Pym initiated in December 1640, was no less significant. An adherent of the orthodox church before it had been subjected to Laud's reforms, Pym was, by his political rather than his religious interest, forced into the position of voting with the Puritans. After the institution of proceedings against Laud, a London petition to abolish episcopacy was in February 1641 referred to a religious committee for report. Though supporting the Puritans, Pym had on this occasion 'thought it was not the intention of the House to abolish either Episcopacy or the Book of Common Prayer, but to reform both, wherein offence was given to the people.' But Pym was too much of a politician not to realize the fact that the bishops were simply Charles's nominees for the making of 'innovations in religion'. In May 1641 he voted for the abolition of episcopacy in the so-called Root and Branch Bill.

With the removal of Strafford and Laud, Charles was forced to make concessions, including one whereby Parliament could not be dissolved without its own consent. But though outwardly willing to compromise, the King still schemed in private. His plans were monitored by Pym through his friend at Court, Lady Carlisle, and in October he disclosed the King's intention to bring troops into London, a plot that had been on foot since June. This, coupled with news of an uprising in Ulster, panicked the Commons into moving the Grand Remonstrance (November 1641). The passage of this protestation by only eleven votes encouraged Charles to take advantage of suspected parliamentary disunity and make a desperate bid to regain control of the situation. Pym was now his target along with four other members from the Commons and one from the Lords. Charles instituted impeachment proceedings against them and in the famous incident of the 'Five Members' tried to arrest them himself, entering the Commons on 5 January 1642, with a band of armed soldiers.

Forewarned of the King's intentions, Pym and his associates had escaped to safety. As Charles ruefully observed, 'the birds are flown', but the birds returned in triumph, escorted back to the Commons six days later. Charles had completely failed and Pym was again the victor. War was now inevitable.

On 20 May 1642, a resolution was passed in the House of Commons declaring that 'the King intends to make war against the Parliament.' Pym was enough of a constitutionalist to cause the words 'seduced by wicked counsel' to be added to it. In July he was placed in control of the supply and maintenance of the Parliamentarian army in the field. A month later the war had started.

The first battle, an indecisive engagement at Edgehill, occurred in late October. On 9 November 1642, Pym urged the initiation of peace negotiations with the King. But when it became clear that Charles was not prepared to enter with any seriousness into such negotiations, Pym went all out for victory.

Into the achievement of this Pym threw all his efforts throughout 1643. He proposed and eventually got the imposition of an excise on the sale of all goods, in addition to the heavy taxes already levied. Chiding Essex for inaction, he urged on the war to the extent that he incurred the hatred of those who wanted peace. In August, a mob of women surrounded the House of Commons clamouring for Pym's execution.

In March 1643 Pym published his *Declaration and Vindication*, in which he claimed, 'I am, and ever was, and so will die a faithful son of the Protestant religion.' In this pamphlet, he also asserted his constitutionalist principles.

One of Pym's last acts in the Parliamentary cause was to help bring about the Anglo-Scottish alliance. One of the architects of the Solemn League and Covenant, Pym was one of the first to sign it in September. The promise to establish Presbyterianism at the end of the war was exacted by the Scots as the price of the alliance. For Pym, such a price was disagreeable but essential.

On 7 November 1643, Pym became master of the ordnance, looking after the weapons kept in the Tower. Only a month later, however, on 8 December, he died of cancer. A moderate but firm man of consistent principles, John Pym left behind him a gap in the Parliamentarian administration that was to be filled not by a constitutionalist but by a dictator – Oliver Cromwell.

S. R. Brett, *John Pym* (1940).

J. H. Hexter, *The Reign of King Pym* (Cambridge, Mass., 1941).

E. Wingfield-Stratford, *King Charles and King Pym 1637–1643* (1940).

C. E. Wade, *John Pym* (1912).

Portrait: woodcut, quarter-length, after E. Bower, 1641: N.P.G.

R

Radcliffe, John (1650–1714), English physician.

Born at Wakefield, Yorkshire, in 1650, Radcliffe was educated at Wakefield grammar school and University College, Oxford, After obtaining his B.A. (1669) and M.A. (1672) from Oxford, Radcliffe devoted himself to the study of medicine. He was elected a fellow of Lincoln College in 1669 and obtained his first medical degree, an M.B., on 1 July 1675. He then began immediately to practise medicine in Oxford. Shortly afterwards he received his M.D. degree (5 July 1682), and then moved to London, where his reputation in successfully treating many cases of smallpox had preceded him. He was richly rewarded and enjoyed a large following at his surgery in Bow Street, Covent Garden. His success was due in part to his pleasant personality and wit, and it has been said that 'patients feigned themselves ill in order to enjoy a few minutes conversation with the humorous doctor.' In 1686 he was appointed physician to Princess Anne of Denmark, and in the following year was elected fellow of the Royal College of Physicians. In 1690 he was elected M.P. for Bramber, but appears not to have played an active role in the House of Commons.

Radcliffe's humour was not always appreciated by royalty. Although he frequently attended William III, in 1699 he offended the King. William had returned from Holland and sent for Radcliffe to examine his swollen ankles, which contrasted with the generally emaciated condition of the rest of his body. When the King asked Radcliffe's opinion, he received the reply, 'Why truly, I would not have your majesty's two legs for your three kingdoms.' The King never forgave him.

In 1713 Radcliffe was elected M.P. for Buckingham. His career as member for this constituency was short, however, as he died of apoplexy just over a year later (1 November 1714) at his home in Carshalton, near London. He was buried at St. Mary's Church, Oxford.

In his will he left a substantial part of his fortune to the University of Oxford. This was used to set up medical fellowships and to expand the buildings of the university, notably the Radcliffe Infirmary, the Radcliffe Observatory, and the Radcliffe Camera (an extension to the Bodleian Library).

Rainsborough, Thomas (?1610–48), naval officer, soldier, and radical politician.

Rainsborough was the son of Captain William Rainsborough, who served King Charles I as a naval officer and adviser, was M.P. for Aldborough in the Long Parliament, and died in 1642.

When the Civil War broke out, Thomas was serving in the Royal fleet and was given command of the thirty-four-gun *Swallow* when her Royalist captain was removed, the navy having declared for Parliament. Shortly afterwards, he was appointed vice admiral, with the special task of preventing Irish recruits reaching the King's forces in northern England, flying his flag in the *Lion* (forty guns). In June 1643 he captured a vessel containing 200 such recruits bound for Newcastle and travelled to Westminster to report his success personally to Parliament. He was ordered to Hull with his ship when the port was besieged in September 1643, going ashore with 100 of his crew to assist the defenders and being given a commission as a colonel in the army for that purpose. Early in the following month he was captured during a determined sortie by the garrison, which caused the Royalists to break up the siege.

A subsequent exchange of prisoners enabled him to resume his soldier's career in command of a newly raised regiment of foot forming part of the garrison of Cambridge. In December 1644 Rainsborough and his regiment were sent against the Royalist stronghold at Crowland Abbey. By using a fleet of longboats in which he had mounted ordnance, he was able to overcome the waterlogged fenland that constituted the chief defence of the place, and to seize the outworks and establish a blockade, so starving the defenders into surrender. The episode firmly established his reputation and guaranteed him a colonelcy in the New Model Army, which Parliament formed in February 1645.

With his new regiment, he was in action at Naseby (14 June), and at the capture of Bridgwater (23 July) and of Sherborne Castle (15 August). At the storming of Bristol (10 September), he was responsible for the assault on the strongest point in the line, Prior's Hill fort, which Robert Blake (q.v.) had successfully defended when the Royalists had taken the city in 1643. Rainsborough carried it after two hours of fierce fighting, and put its garrison to the sword. The city itself was consequently untenable, and he was one of the

three plenipotentiaries who negotiated its surrender with its commander, Prince Rupert (q.v.).

An independent action followed, the subjugation of Berkeley Castle, which capitulated to Rainsborough's force of four regiments on 23 September after a brief siege, and as the First Civil War drew to its end he was employed in the elimination of other Royalist garrisons – Corfe Castle, Oxford, Woodstock, Worcester, and Raglan Castle.

After the fall of Worcester (19 July 1646), he was made governor of the city at the wish of the Army's commander, Sir Thomas Fairfax (q.v.), and he entered Parliament as M.P. for Droitwich. In the Commons he quickly made his mark among the small group of extreme republicans who wanted no negotiations with the King and a wider participation in politics than the constitution had hitherto permitted. Preparations for an expedition to capture Jersey, which he had proposed and was to command sidetracked him during the spring of 1647, but they were halted by the revolt of the Army rank and file in April and May. His own regiment was one of those involved, and his opponents in Parliament suspected Rainsborough's motives. Nevertheless, he was now accepted as a leading figure in the Army's politics and was one of the officers appointed to treat with Parliament on the one hand and the King on the other. When it was decided to march on London in August, he commanded the advance guard, which seized London Bridge by a well-organized coup and gained an entry for the main body.

During the subsequent debates at Putney, in which the Army sought to reach unanimity on constitutional questions, a conflict emerged between Cromwell and Rainsborough, who represented the two poles of opinion, the latter backing the egalitarian demands of the Levellers against the exclusive notions of the 'Grandees'. An open breach was averted by the pressure brought to bear upon Rainsborough, through Commons resolutions, to take up the vice admiral's appointment in the fleet in the Channel, which had been his since the retirement of Batten in September.

His last sea command (January–May 1648) was not conspicuously successful and was brought to an end by the Royalist rising in Kent and elsewhere. Rainsborough went ashore to put Deal Castle into a state of defence, and in his absence several ships mutinied. He was not allowed to reboard his own vessel and Parliament did not attempt to restore him to effective authority. Instead he rejoined his regiment, which was among those attempting to reduce the Royalists in Colchester. He played his usual active part in the operations of the siege and in the negotiations that brought about the surrender of the Royalist garrison on 28 August, and he had the additional duty of presiding over the execution by firing squad of the Royalist commanders, Lucas and Lisle. This earned him the particular hatred of all Royalists. An attempt to assassinate him was made in September.

His political opponents were still concerned to keep him away from Westminster, and he was sent north to take over the ill-conducted siege of Pontefract Castle. While waiting in lodgings in Doncaster for his predecessor to give up the command, Rainsborough was attacked by a party of Cavaliers from Pontefract and in the ensuing struggle was killed (29 October). It appears that the intention was to take him as a hostage against further executions of Royalist leaders, particularly Sir Marmaduke Langdale, who was held in Nottingham Castle. Although his body was given an impressive military funeral at the family home in Wapping, his death in fact conveniently removed one of the many problems facing those in control of events in the capital.

H. Ross Williamson, *Four Stuart Portraits* (1949).

Ralegh, Sir Walter (?1552–1618), courtier, explorer, and author, see *Lives of the Tudor Age*.

Ray or Wray, John (1628–1705), biologist and botanist, known as 'the Father of English Natural History', noted for his system of natural classification; until 1670 he spelled his name Wray.

Born at Black Notley, near Braintree, Essex, on 29 November 1628, the son of a blacksmith, Ray was educated at Catherine Hall and Trinity College, Cambridge. After obtaining a B.A. degree (1648), Ray was appointed a fellow of Trinity College (1649) and obtained an M.A. in 1651. As a tutor, Ray explored his diverse interests in several

academic areas, being appointed lecturer in both Greek and mathematics, among other academic posts. Although he was ordained in the Church of England by the Bishop of Lincoln (1660), Ray's interests throughout his life were primarily secular and scientific rather than clerical. He was elected a fellow of the Royal Society in 1667.

In 1660, Ray published (in Latin) *A Catalogue of the Flora of Cambridge*, the first systematic study of all the plants of a specific area. The book marks a considerable advance in descriptive scientific precision, although it is marred by Ray's misguided attempt to distinguish trees from herbs on a scientific basis.

During his period as a tutor, Ray guided the progress of many men destined to make significant contributions in their own fields. Chief among these was Francis Willughby, who was to become a close friend and lifetime companion. In 1662 Ray resigned his fellowship, being unwilling in conscience to subscribe to the Act of Uniformity. With Willughby, he set out on several tours to explore the flora and fauna of Britain and Europe. They returned from their most extensive tour (1663–66) with a vast collection of notes and preserved plants and animals, which they planned to use as the basis of a complete system of descriptive classification. Originally, Ray was to have classified the plants and Willughby the animals. Willughby died, however, in 1672, after completing only a draft descriptive classification in the fields of ornithology and ichthyology. Ray was left to edit and complete this work and to continue with his own projects in the field of botany. He was partially assisted by the annuity of £60 left to him by Willughby with the stipulation that Ray was to oversee the education of his two sons.

In 1682 he published *Methodus plantarum nova* ('A New System of Plants'), using as a basis the collection of plants obtained during his tours with Willughby. It was in this work that Ray first suggested a system for the natural classification of all plants based on the grouping of individual specimens. He assigned the term 'species' to a specific kind of plant. As a result of this and later work, Ray is considered to have contributed equally with Linnaeus in proposing a workable and systematic method of biological taxonomy.

His greatest work was *Historia generalis plantarum* ('A General History of Plants'), published in three volumes (1686, 1688, 1704). In it, he clearly described and classified over 18,000 separate plants.

After Willughby's death in 1672, Ray had moved from place to place several times, finally settling at his birthplace, Black Notley, in 1679. Here he lived, in spite of poor health, for twenty-five years, keeping up a wide correspondence on the sciences with many of the leading thinkers of his day. He died at Black Notley on 17 January 1705.

E. Lankester (ed.), *Memorials of John Ray* (1846).
C. E. Raven, *John Ray* (1950, 2nd ed.).

Portrait: oil, half-length, by unknown artist: N.P.G.; engraving, quarter-length, by Abraham de Blois, after William Faithorne, 1694: Science Museum, London.

Rich, Robert (1587–1658), 2nd Earl of Warwick; colonial administrator and admiral on the Parliamentarian side during the Civil War.

Rich was born in 1587, the eldest son of Robert Rich, 1st Earl of Warwick, and Penelope, daughter of Walter Devereux, 1st Earl of Essex. Educated at Emmanuel College, Cambridge. After a period at the Inner Temple, he became M.P. for Malden in 1610 and again in 1614. He succeeded to his father's title upon the latter's death in 1619.

Warwick had early become associated with colonial enterprises. While still a young man he joined the Bermudas, Guinea, Amazon River, New England, and Virginia Companies. His connections with the last-named were characterized by disagreements with his associates and in 1624 the company was suppressed. During the 1620s Warwick was involved in privateering expeditions, and contended with the merchant companies. He was concerned with the founding of New Plymouth, and in 1628 became indirectly the patentee of the Massachusetts Bay Colony. In 1632 he granted the patent for the colonization in 1635 of Saybrook, Connecticut. Also in 1632, he was forced to resign as president of the New England Company. He continued to manage the Bermudas Company and also the Providence Company, which was founded in 1630 and administered Old Providence on the Mosquito Coast of Central America.

With Warwick's colonial interests there went also Puritan sympathies, which caused a gradual estrangement between him and the court. He was one of those who refused to contribute to Charles I's forced loan in 1626. During the period of Charles's absolute government (1629–40) his associates in administering colonial companies included Pym and Hampden (qq.v.), and like them he opposed ship money. He was also an opponent of the religious innovations of William Laud (q.v.), and with his brother, Henry Rich, Earl of Holland, he became a figurehead for the Puritans in the eastern counties.

Upon the dissolution of the Short Parliament (May 1640), Warwick was arrested and his papers were examined. In March 1642 the Long Parliament, in defiance of Charles's veto, appointed him admiral of the fleet, and in July he brought the whole navy over to the Parliamentarian side. In 1643 he was made lord high admiral and worked assiduously throughout the First Civil War in intercepting the King's supply ships and relieving ports vulnerable to Royalist attacks. He continued at his post until 1645.

Throughout this period Warwick also continued his colonial activities. In 1643 he was made nominal head of a commission to govern the colonies, which in 1644 incorporated Providence Plantations (later Rhode Island). His administration at this time was notable for the perseverance with which he strove to obtain guarantees of religious freedom.

In May 1648 he was reappointed as lord high admiral to win back ships that had lately defected to the King. He had little success in this, but managed in the event to raise another fleet against the defectors. In the following year, however, he was deprived of his office upon the abolition of the House of Lords.

Warwick's last years were spent in retirement. He was intimate with Cromwell and in 1657 his grandson married the Protector's daughter. Warwick died on 19 April 1658.

Rob Roy (1671–1734), see Macgregor, Robert.

Rochester, 2nd Earl of (1647–80), see Wilmot, John.

Rooke, Sir George (1650–1709), admiral who captured Gibraltar.

George Rooke was born near Canterbury some time in 1650, the second son of Sir William Rooke, sheriff of Kent. He served as a volunteer in the navy during the second Anglo-Dutch War. When the next conflict between these maritime powers erupted he was a lieutenant, and in that capacity fought at the battle of Solebay (1672) and other actions, in which he displayed competence and tenacity. In November 1673 he was given post rank and his first ship, and over the following years commanded a variety of vessels both in home waters and in the Mediterranean.

Rooke was always counted a Tory, but, like the rest of the navy, supported the 'Glorious' Revolution of 1688. In the wars of William's reign he fought at Bantry Bay (1689), led ships to the relief of Londonderry, and commanded a squadron at Beachy Head (1690) as rear admiral of the Red. At the great victory of Barfleur (1692) he commanded a squadron and afterwards led the boats that burned those French ships that had taken refuge in the bay of La Hogue. For these services he was knighted, and in 1693 received command of a small squadron to escort 400 merchant vessels to the Mediterranean. England's main fleet accompanied the convoy for the first stage of its voyage until, as the admirals thought, they were well past the French navy, which was thought to be in northern ports. Rooke's squadron and its charges were then allowed to sail on alone, but suddenly they were attacked by the whole of the French fleet, which had been lying in wait for the convoy. The result was chaos; Rooke and his warships managed to escape, but many of the merchantmen were seized. Nevertheless, no blame for this misadventure was assigned to Rooke because of the vast superiority in numbers of the French, and next year he was made admiral of the Blue and given a seat on the admiralty commission.

In 1695 Rooke was promoted to the rank of admiral of the White and placed in command of the Mediterranean fleet. Subsequent years saw him active in the Admiralty and in command of the Channel fleet, and from 1698 he also sat as an M.P. at Westminster.

When the War of the Spanish Succession broke out, Rooke was appointed to the chief command of an expedition against Cadiz. With the Duke of Ormonde (see Butler, James, 2nd Duke) in charge of the soldiers, he sailed to Spain in 1702, but was unable to effect anything. Then news arrived that a treasure fleet with a convoy of French and Spanish warships was in the neighbourhood, and in Vigo Bay Rooke fell upon them, capturing some of the bullion and destroying the enemy fleet. For this victory he received the thanks of the House of Commons.

In 1704 Rooke once again led a fleet to Spain, this time with Archduke Charles, the Austrian claimant to the throne, on board. They wished to capture Barcelona, Cadiz, or any other outpost that would give the Hapsburgs a base from which to establish their claim to Spain. But no city appeared to be a practical proposition. The situation gradually changed, and when reinforcements reached him in July, Rooke turned his attention to Gibraltar, which he quickly captured (21 July 1704). He set to sea again, and a month later encountered a French fleet near Malaga (13 August 1704). The two forces fought all day, but the battle was inconclusive. Nevertheless, it was celebrated in England as a great victory by those Tories hostile to Marlborough, and held to be of equal importance to Blenheim. The result, however, was that Marlborough's supporters ensured that Rooke received no further commands until his death on 24 January 1709; he retired from active service in February 1705.

J. Ehrman, *The Navy in the War of William III, 1689–1697* (1953).

J. H. Owen, *War at Sea under Queen Anne, 1702–1708* (1938).

Edward B. Powley, *The Naval Side of King William's War* (1972).

Rowley, William (?1585–?1624), English actor and dramatist.

Rowley's exact birth and death dates are not known, but the year of his birth is generally estimated as being 1585. Virtually nothing is known of his early life, up to the time when he joined the Duke of York's company as an actor, sometime before 1610. This company joined with Lady Elizabeth's to form Prince Charles's Men in 1614. It was probably as a result of this merger that Rowley first met Thomas Middleton (q.v.). Rowley had by now achieved a fair reputation as a comic actor, and had probably already written or contributed to some plays for his company.

Rowley continued to appear on the stage throughout his life, but he is now noted mainly as a dramatist. Very few of his plays were produced by solitary effort. Of those that were, *All's Lost by Lust* (?1619), a characteristic Jacobean tale of rape and murder to save the heroine from 'a fate worse than death' (marriage to a Muslim), is generally considered the most important. His best work, however, was done in collaboration with other dramatists, notably Middleton, with whom he wrote *The Old Law* (?1618) and *The Changeling* (1622). His role in this latter work, another classic Jacobean tale of murder, lust, rape, and suicide, is thought to have been mainly in the construction of the ironic subplot. His collaborator in *The Birth of Merlin* (no date – not printed until 1662) was once thought to have been Shakespeare, whose name appeared on the title page, but this is now disproved. The collaborator is now thought to be one of the many dramatists Rowley is known to have worked

with – Middleton, Dekker, John Ford, Webster, Beaumont, or Fletcher. It is known that Rowley worked on about fifty plays, but very few of them are now extant.

It was previously thought that Rowley died around 1642, but evidence put forward by C. J. Sisson in *The Lost Plays of Shakespeare's Age* (1936) indicates that he did not outlive Middleton, but died in 1624.

C. W. Stork (ed.), *All's Lost by Lust and A Shoemaker a Gentleman* (Philadelphia, Pa., 1910).

P. Thomson (ed.), *The Changeling* (1964).

Roy, Rob (1671–1734), see Macgregor, Robert.

Rupert, Prince (1619–1682), later Duke of Cumberland and Earl of Holderness; Royalist commander in the Civil War, known as 'the Mad Cavalier'.

Born in Prague on 17 December 1619, Prince Rupert was the third son of Frederick V, Elector Palatine and King of Bohemia, and Elizabeth, daughter of James I of England.

Frederick's short-lived reign in Bohemia was terminated in November 1620 by the Battle of the White Mountain, after which the whole family fled into exile. Rupert's childhood was spent in Holland, where his parents took refuge. Little is known about his life and education during this period. His first military experience came in 1633 when he accompanied Frederick Henry, Prince of Orange, at the siege of Rheinberg. Two years later, Rupert served in the same army during the invasion of Brabant. In 1636 he left for England, where he was received with great favour by his uncle, Charles I. A scheme to establish Rupert as the governor of a proposed English colony in Madagascar never materialized, and the prince returned to Holland. In the subsequent two years he served in the Palatinate wars, taking part in the invasion of Westphalia, but his military career was interrupted when he was taken prisoner at Vlotho in 1638 and kept imprisoned at Linz for three years. Soon after his release from captivity in 1641 Rupert returned to England, where the Civil War was imminent. He landed at Tynemouth in July 1642.

The King welcomed the prince's arrival and made him immediately a general of horse, his command being independent of that of Lord Lindsey, the nominal commander in chief. Rupert almost at once became involved in skirmishes with the Parliamentarian troops and soon built up a reputation as a skilful and courageous cavalry commander. He gained his first victory of the war defeating a body of Essex's cavalry at Worcester. His military zeal, however, sometimes amounted to recklessness that did not always escape retribution. At Edgehill (1642), Rupert, in command of the right wing of the King's cavalry, threw away victory by pursuing the enemy cavalry at the expense of supporting the infantry of his own side. During the winter of 1642–43 he concentrated on extending the King's territory round Oxford and supporting the Royalists of the west. He captured Cirencester, stormed Birmingham, and recaptured Lichfield. The King, however, soon recalled him to Oxford to take part in the main campaign. In June 1643 Rupert distinguished himself against Essex's army at Chalgrove field, where the Parliamentarian commander Hampden was mortally wounded. Joined by his brother Maurice (q.v.), he conquered Bristol after a short siege in July 1643 and two months later put up a stubborn fight against Essex at the first battle of Newbury, but could not prevent him returning to London. Rupert's last successes of the First Civil War included brilliant expeditions to relieve Newark (March 1644) and York (June 1644). At Marston Moor, in July 1644, his cavalry suffered its first defeat, and the Royalist army was almost annihilated by Cromwell's forces. The enemies met again at Naseby in July 1645, and although the Royalists lost and their cause in the north collapsed, Rupert's cavalry once again was triumphant. The prince returned to his governorship of Bristol and prepared to meet Fairfax's impending attack, but after a parley with Fairfax decided to surrender. It seems that Rupert realized that the town, which he himself had taken with comparative ease, was indefensible against a large army. Charles, however, who had made his nephew the general of the Royalist forces in 1644, accused Rupert of dereliction of duty and dismissed him. A court martial, however, cleared him, and he joined the King in Oxford, which was to capitulate to Fairfax in June 1646, afterwards receiving permission from Parliament to leave the country.

Rupert entered the French service in July 1646 and became a commander of a contingent of exiled English troops. A year later, he took part in the siege of La Bassée, where he was wounded in the head. Having accepted command of the Royalist fleet, he sailed to Ireland in order to assist Ormonde (see Butler, James, 1st Duke) in the reconquest of Ireland. His aid proved to be ineffective and Rupert turned his ships towards Portugal, capturing English merchantmen on the way. In 1650 Blake accused him of piracy, attacked his squadron, and burnt or sank most of his ships. With the remnant, Rupert made his way to Toulon, refitted his fleet, and undertook a piratical cruise to the West Indies, sailing via the Azores, Guinea, and the Cape Verde Islands. He finally reached Barbados in the summer of 1652. In March 1653 he returned to France, but after a quarrel with the council of the exiled court of Charles II went to Germany, where he lived in obscurity for the following six years.

At the Restoration, he returned to England and was well received by Charles II, who made him a privy councillor. On the outbreak of the Second Dutch War he was appointed admiral of the White under the Duke of York, subsequently participating in the victory at Lowestoft (1665) and, in association with Monck (q.v.), in other naval actions.

Back in England, Rupert, in conjunction with Monck and others, formed a scheme for discovering the supposed passage through the Great Lakes of Canada to the South Seas. In 1670 he became the first governor of the Hudson's Bay Company and the territory granted to it was named 'Rupert's land' in his honour.

In March 1672, at the start of the third Dutch War, Rupert was appointed vice admiral of England. In the following year he became general on sea and land; later he was promoted to admiral of the fleet. Success seems to have deserted him, however: he lost battles at Schoneveldt and Texel to the Dutch fleet. Between 1673 and 1679 Rupert was the first commissioner of the Admiralty. He died on 29 November 1682, in Spring Gardens, Westminster.

Apart from being a dominant figure of the Civil War and renowned for his military skill and courage, Rupert had widespread interests in the arts and sciences. He claimed to have invented the process of mezzotint, a method of copperplate engraving. He also experimented with the production of gunpowder and the boring of guns.

Prince Rupert never married, but left two illegitimate children – a daughter, who married General Emmanuel Scrope Howe, and a son, who was killed in 1686 at the siege of Buda.

J. R. Powell and E. K. Timings (eds.), *The Rupert and Monck Letter Book, 1666* (1969).
James Cleugh, *Prince Rupert* (1934).
Bernard E. Fergusson, *Rupert of the Rhine* (1952).
E. Scott, *Rupert, Prince Palatine* (1899).
E. G. Warburton, *Memoirs of Prince Rupert and the Cavaliers* (3 vols.; 1849).

Portraits: oil, three-quarter length, by Lely: Windsor Castle; miniature, after Lely, *c.* 1665–70: N.P.G.; oil on panel, attributed to Honthorst, *c.* 1641–42: N.P.G.

Russell, Edward (1653–1727), Earl of Orford; admiral and politician; a member of the Whig Junto.

Russell was born in 1653, the son of Edward Russell, a gentleman. He spent the first half of his life as a sailor. In 1671 he was commissioned lieutenant on the *Advice* and saw action against the Dutch at Solebay in May 1672. He became a captain in June and received a variety of commands over the next decade, serving under several distinguished admirals, including Prince

Rupert (q.v.), Sir John Narborough, and Arthur Herbert. A Whig like most of his family, he gave up his commission in 1683, when his famous cousin, Lord William Russell (q.v.), was executed. He gravitated to the cause of William of Orange and in 1688 not only signed the letter inviting the prince to come to England but also accompanied him on the invasion that brought about the Glorious Revolution.

Russell was elected to Parliament, became treasurer of the navy (April 1689), and admiral of the Blue (July). His services and connections also won him a place in the Junto, that small circle of Whig leaders who dominated their party for the next 20 years. Although he was supposed to be at sea under the command of Arthur Herbert, now Earl of Torrington, he apparently spent most of the time in London, intriguing against Torrington and contributing to the latter's defeat at Beachy Head (1690). Russell now received command of the fleet, and from this important position, like most other English politicians, he probably communicated with the exiled James II. Nevertheless in May 1692 he led a combined Anglo-Dutch fleet down upon the French off Cape Barfleur and won the great Battle of La Hogue. But the feeling was widespread that he had not properly followed up his victory and a public outcry necessitated his removal. A series of naval setbacks, however, led to his reinstatement just over a year later, in November 1693.

As first lord of the Admiralty (1694–99), Russell served only once more at sea. In 1694 he took the fleet to the Mediterranean, where it wintered and where its presence blocked any likelihood of French offensives. In 1697 he was made Earl of Orford, and in 1701 suffered an unsuccessful attempt by the Tories to impeach him for his part in the Partition Treaties. Under Anne he was appointed a commissioner for the Union with Scotland (1706) and served again briefly as first lord of the Admiralty (1709–10). On her death he acted as one of the regents until George I arrived from Germany, when he was once again appointed to his old Admiralty post (1714–17). His last ten years were spent quietly in retirement and he died on 27 November 1727.

J. Ehrman, *The Navy in the War of William III, 1689–1697* (1953).

Edward B. Powley, *The Naval Side of King William's War* (1972).

Portrait: by R. Bockman: Greenwich.

Russell, Lord William (1639–83),

Whig politician, executed for his share in the alleged Rye House Plot.

Born 29 September 1639, the third son of Francis Russell, 5th Earl and 1st Duke of Bedford, Russell was educated privately by a Puritan tutor and at Cambridge. After leaving Cambridge, William Russell was sent on the Grand Tour for three or four years, returning to England in 1659. He was soon after elected to the Cavalier Parliament. In this body he was long inactive, but suspicions about the Catholic leanings of the court and disgust at its corruption and waste drove him, along with many other M.P.s, into the 'country' party opposition. This political awakening was aided by his marriage in 1669 to Rachel Wriothesley, daughter of the Earl of Southampton and member of a family of similar political leanings. One of her relatives was the Earl of Shaftesbury, the opposition leader (see Cooper, Anthony Ashley).

By the early 1670s the Cavalier Parliament was no longer the docile Royalist assembly it had been a decade before. It pursued the Cabal – Charles II's advisers, of which Shaftesbury was a member – with venom, and, having achieved the disintegration of that body, moved on to attack Charles II's new chief minister, Danby (see Osborne, Thomas). Russell moved to the fore in 1674 with a scathing attack on the Duke of Buckingham (see Villiers, George, 2nd Duke) and the King's policies, and in the next year initiated an unsuccessful attempt to impeach Danby. By 1678 he was effectively Shaftesbury's deputy and leader of the country party in the House of Commons. With the other opposition leaders, he co-operated with Louis XIV's ambassador to destroy Danby, their common enemy. By the end of the year this strange alliance was no longer necessary: the Popish Plot had begun.

Russell evidently believed the adventurers and liars (see Oates, Titus) who declared that a plot existed to murder the King and establish a Catholic tyranny over Protestant England. But like his more sceptical colleagues, he also used the plot to further the country party's interest. In November 1678 he called for the removal from the royal presence of the Catholic Duke of York, the King's brother and heir (see James II). Charles was forced to bow before the storm: Danby was dismissed and imprisoned, a new Parliament was summoned, and the Opposition leaders, including Russell, were appointed to an enlarged privy council (April 1679). Russell and his friends used these new opportunities to continue their campaign against arbitrary rule, Catholicism, and the Duke of York. At first, Russell was apparently willing to accept the prospect of a Catholic King, provided that legislation was enacted securing the liberties and the religion of the realm, but gradually he came over to the idea of Exclusion: York should never ascend the throne. In 1680 Russell kept Shaftesbury company when he resigned from the privy council. He accompanied the crafty earl in June to Westminster to indict the Duke of York as a papist recusant, and led the campaign for the Exclusion Bill in the Commons. When the bill failed in the Lords and Parliament was dissolved, Russell was again prominent among the Whig magnates who helped return a Whiggish Parliament to Oxford in 1681. But here, too, Exclusion failed.

As the Stuart reaction set in, Russell retired to the country, only to emerge in July when William of Orange visited London. His house became a meeting place for prominent Whigs, where they discussed proposals that became increasingly drastic and violent. In October 1682 he accompanied the Duke of Monmouth, the Earl of Essex, and others to a meeting at which government informers were present. Out of this visit the government concocted the Rye House Plot, an alleged conspiracy to murder the King and the Duke of York.

On 21 June 1683, Russell was arrested. The following month he was tried for treason. He denied, probably truthfully, that he had ever taken part in such a plot or had ever been present at discussions of an assassination. He also denied that talk of resisting the King's authority was treason. But perjured witnesses and the suicide of his fellow victim, Essex, ensured his conviction. He was sentenced to death, and despite pleas by his friends and relatives, executed on 21 July at Lincoln's Inn Fields.

Although not in the ranks of great statesmen, Russell's integrity and other personal qualities caused him to be remembered almost as a martyr by the later Whigs.

H. Armitage, *Russell and the Rye House Plot* (1948).
J. R. Jones, *The First Whigs* (1961).
Lord John Russell, *The Life of William Lord Russell* (2 vols.; 1820).

Portrait: oil, by Mary Beale: V. & A.

Rymer, Thomas (1641–1713), archivist, critic, and versifier.

Thomas Rymer was the son of Ralph Rymer, lord of the manor of Brafferton, Yorkshire, who was an ardent Parliamentarian, joined the Presbyterian rising of 1663, and was arrested and executed for treason.

Thomas went up to Cambridge in 1658, but left without taking a degree. He turned next to the law, becoming a member of Gray's Inn in 1666 and being called to the bar in 1673. In 1677 he wrote a tragedy, *Edgar, or the English Monarch*. According to the *Dictionary of National Biography*, 'The only service that this piece rendered to art was to show how a play might faithfully observe all the classical laws without betraying any dramatic quality.'

Rymer's criticism was equally disastrous. Ferociously bombastic, it won some attention at the time by its energy, but is now largely forgotten. Rymer condemned *Othello* as 'a bloody farce, without salt or savour' in *A Short View of Tragedy* (1692), and in *The Tragedies of the Last Age Considered* (1678) he attacks *Paradise Lost*, 'which some are pleased to call a poem'.

It was not until 1693, at the age of fifty-two, that he began the work for which he has a claim to fame, namely *Foedera, Conventiones, et cuiuscunque generis Acta Publica*, a collection of public records and treaties from 1100 A.D. to 1654, undertaken by the government without any great enthusiasm, but edited by Rymer until his death in 1713 and completed thereafter by his assistant, Robert Sanderson. The collection is in twenty volumes, the first of which was published in 1704 and the last in 1735; it made accessible for the first time a foundation of facts upon which historical judgments might be based.

C. A. Zimansky (ed.), *Critical Works of Thomas Rymer* (New Haven, Conn., 1956).

D. Douglas, *English Scholars* (1951, rev. ed.).

S

Sacheverell, Henry (?1674–1724),
High Church clergyman and controversial political preacher.

Henry Sacheverell was one of several
children of Joshua Sacheverell, the impoverished rector of St. Peter's church,
Marlborough, in Wiltshire. In view of
his father's large family and small
income, Henry was adopted by his
godfather, Edward Hearst, an apothecary
who paid for his education at Marlborough School. After Hearst's death,
his wife Katherine provided for the boy
and sent him, at the age of fifteen, to
Magdalen College, Oxford. Here he
shared rooms with Addison (see *Lives of
the Georgian Age*). He gained his B.A. in
1693, his M.A. in 1695, and became a
fellow of the college in 1701. In 1708 he
gained his doctorate in divinity, becoming a bursar of the college in 1709.
He appears to have held the living of
Cannock, Staffordshire, and in 1705 was
made chaplain of St. Saviour's, Southwark.

In 1701 Sacheverell published *The
Character of Low Churchmen*, denouncing
Nonconformists and Dissenters and
arguing that they should be deprived of
all political rights. In 1705 he preached a
fiery sermon at Oxford attacking all
Whigs, moderate Tories, and Dissenters,
and suggesting that the Church of
England was endangered by the neglect
of self-interested politicians. This seems
to have passed without arousing too
much comment at the time, but he repeated the substance of his sermon twice
in 1709, four years later. He claimed as a
relative George Sacheverell, high sheriff

of Derbyshire, although the family
connection has not been verified, and
was invited to preach the assize sermon
at Derby. Here he reiterated the bulk of
his 1705 sermon and repeated this
address at St. Paul's Cathedral, London,
later in the year. He was an energetic
speaker and his sermons were extremely
virulent in language. He attacked the
Whig ministers, referring to them as
'Volpones' ('Volpone' was the nickname
of Godolphin (q.v.), a reference to Ben
Jonson's comedy *Volpone, or the Fox*).
This assault from the pulpit of St. Paul's
was too much for the Whig Junto and
impeachment proceedings were started
against Sacheverell in order to silence
him before the election of 1710.

However, the Whigs had greatly mis-
judged the mood of the country. There
was widespread public support for Sacheverell and riots broke out in London in
his favour. Many dissenting meeting
houses were attacked and ransacked and
troops had to be called in to restore
order.

The verdict was a disaster for the
government. Sacheverell was condemned by only sixty-nine votes to
fifty-two and was sentenced to three
years' suspension from preaching. His
freedom to carry out all other clerical
duties was untouched. This was tanta-
mount to a Tory victory and brought
about the dismissal of Godolphin and
the downfall of the Whig government.
Sacheverell was regarded by the Tories
as a martyr and a hero.

During his trial, Sacheverell was
appointed to the living of Selattyn in

Shropshire. His journeys to and from Shropshire, through Oxford, Banbury, Warwick, and Shrewsbury, were like royal progresses. In 1713, when his period of suspension expired, he was presented by the Queen to the rich living of St. Andrew's, Holborn. In 1715 George Sacheverell of Derbyshire died, leaving Henry a valuable estate, and in the following year Henry married George's widow, thus becoming a rich man. He quarrelled with a number of his Holborn parishioners and on 5 June 1724, he died at his residence in Highgate.

Sacheverell was an indifferent scholar who had little regard for learning, but he dressed well and had a commanding presence. He was inordinately vain; his overweening sense of his own importance was probably a direct result of the Whig reaction to him in 1709. If Godolphin had ignored him, Sacheverell would have been a figure of little or no significance. As it was, his coming into prominence brought down a government and politicians of all parties, though they might despise the man, were forced to heed his influence with the mob.

F. Madan, *A Bibliography of Dr. Henry Sacheverell* (1884).

A. T. Scudi, *The Sacheverell Affair* (1939).

Sacheverell, William (1638–91), Whig politician.

He was born in 1638, the son of Henry Sacheverell and his wife, Joyce Mansfield, of Morley, Derbyshire, and Barton, Nottinghamshire. He came from an ancient and prosperous landed family. In 1667 he entered Gray's Inn – nothing is known of his earlier education. In 1670 he was returned to Parliament as member for Derbyshire. He immediately became one of the leaders of the anti-court party, concentrating his attacks mainly on Roman Catholic and French influences at Charles II's court. In February 1673 he opened a debate on a motion to debar Roman Catholics from military office; this was later extended to include civil office as well. This proved to be a preliminary to the Test Act, whereby office-holders had to take the Anglican Communion. Sacheverell played a major part in preparing the bill and guiding it through in 1673. This bill was largely responsible for the overthrow of Charles's Cabal ministry.

By now Sacheverell had embarked on an intensely active political career, and took part in almost every debate. He constantly opposed 'popery', expressed the view that the security of the crown should rest on the love of the people, not on a standing army, and advocated an alliance between England and Holland. He showed strength and readiness of wit as a debater, legal knowledge, and familiarity with parliamentary history. He also advocated a return to the policy of the Triple Alliance.

In 1678 Sacheverell was closely involved in the proceedings following the revelation by Titus Oates (q.v.) of an alleged Popish Plot. Sacheverell appears to have been honestly convinced of the reality of the plot: he served on a number of committees, and for some time presided over the Committee of Secrecy. He became firmly convinced that James, Duke of York, later James II (q.v.), was a threat to the peace of the country, demanded in Parliament that he should be removed from the royal presence, and was one of the first to suggest his exclusion from the throne. In 1679 he actively pursued this design by his parliamentary management of the Exclusion Bill. However, the bill failed in the House of Lords. Sacheverell also lent his active support to the successful demands for the impeachment of Danby (see Osborne, Thomas).

For a while, he retired from parliamentary life, but in 1682 he led opposition to the surrender of the old charter of the city of Nottingham, and was tried and fined by Judge Jeffreys (q.v.) for his part in the riots that followed.

Although a supporter of Protestantism, Sacheverell took no active part in the Glorious Revolution of 1688, but in 1689 he was returned as the member for Heytesbury in Wiltshire in the Convention Parliament, and was a member of the committee which drew up the Declaration of Right. In the first administration of William III, Sacheverell was made a lord of the admiralty, but was not very successful in this post, resigning in December 1689. He involved himself in a bill to prevent Tories from controlling elections, and was the author of a clause designed to preserve the charters and liberties of municipal boroughs. William III declined to commit himself, and in an attempt to unite his kingdom prorogued Parliament before the bill could go any further.

In the autumn of 1691 Sacheverell was elected member for Nottinghamshire, but was in failing health and died at his home in Barton, Nottinghamshire, as Parliament was about to meet. He was buried at Morley, Derbyshire, on 12 October 1691.

Sacheverell was married twice: first to Mary Staunton; then to Jane, daughter of Sir John Newton. He had children by both marriages.

Sacheverell has been called 'the First Whig', and Mr. Speaker Onslow regarded him as the 'ablest parliament man' of Charles II's reign. He influenced the policy of his party, but never had the opportunity of showing whether he possessed the higher qualities of statesmanship, since – except for one year – he was always in opposition.

G. Sitwell, *The First Whig* (1894).

Sackville, Charles (1638–1706), Lord Buckhurst, later 6th Earl of Dorset and 1st Earl of Middlesex of the second creation; poet and wit at the Restoration court of Charles II.

Sackville was born on 24 January 1638, the son of Richard Sackville, 5th Earl of Dorset, and Frances, sister of Lionel Cranfield (q.v.), 1st Earl of Middlesex. In his youth he was educated by a private tutor and travelled in Italy, the usual grounding of young men of fashion and means. In 1660 he became M.P. for East Grinstead, but had no taste for politics and soon gravitated to the court of Charles II. There he joined in the life of dissipation with enthusiasm, and became one of the 'merry gang', according to Marvell, of wits and writers that included George Villiers and Sir Charles Sedley, who gathered round the restored monarch. Apart from his share in the escapades of Sedley and Rochester, in 1662 Sackville and his brother Edward were charged along with three other gentlemen with the murder and robbery of a tanner called Hoppy. They were somehow acquitted, but within a year he was arraigned again, this time with Sedley, for his part in an outrageous exploit in Covent Garden where they exposed themselves to the mob (see Sedley, Sir Charles).

He volunteered to serve in the fleet prepared for action against the Dutch in 1665, and took part in the engagement of 3 June off Harwich. He inherited his uncle's titles in 1675, becoming Baron Cranfield and Earl of Middlesex. During the short reign of the Catholic James II he withdrew from the court, but after the Glorious Revolution of 1688 he became lord chamberlain of William and Mary's household, a post that he held from 1689 to 1697. He acted as regent on three occasions during William III's absence on Dutch affairs, and his services were recognized by an award of the Order of the Garter in 1691. His poems appeared jointly with Sedley's in a collection of 1701, perhaps the best-known being the ballad *To all you ladies now at land*. He was a patron of other writers, and the ambitious Dryden (q.v.) dedicated several poems to him. He died on 29 January 1706, in Bath, and was interred in the family vault at Withyham, Sussex.

To Pope, he was one of that 'mob of gentlemen who wrote with ease', and shared with his fellow literary courtiers the merits and failings that are characteristic of the mode. The superficial ease of writing does not disguise a primitive technique, and the prevailing light-heartedness and cavalier satiric manner covers a more fundamental deficiency.

See *The Works of the Earls of Rochester, Roscommon, Dorset etc.* (1714, 1st ed.).
Brice Harris, *Charles Sackville, Sixth Earl of Dorset: Patron and Poet of the Restoration* (Urbana, Ill., 1940).

St. John, Henry (1678–1751), 1st Viscount Bolingbroke; politician and political philosopher.

Henry St. John was the son of Sir Henry St. John, a Royalist gentleman, and his wife, who was the daughter of the Parliamentarian Earl of Warwick (see Rich, Robert). He was baptized in Battersea on 10 October 1678 and was educated at Eton.

St. John spent two years on the Grand Tour in 1698 and 1699, drinking his way from orgy to orgy round Europe in a manner that surprised even his most hardened contemporaries. The next year he made a wealthy marriage (to Frances Winchcombe), which provided him with the means to engage actively in politics, although he neglected his first wife for most of her life. In 1701 he took the family seat of Wootton Bassett in the House of Com-

mons and swiftly distinguished himself as a brilliant orator in the High Tory cause. He supported the impeachment of the Whig ministers responsible for the Partition treaties and in the Tory cause managed the Act of Settlement (1701), with its clauses hostile to King William. In 1702 and 1704 he also worked on the Occasional Conformity bills, which were directed against Nonconformists and Dissenters.

In spite of these actions, which would seem to identify St. John as an extreme High Tory, he now began to associate with the more moderate Robert Harley (q.v.), whose parliamentary skill he admired and whom he took to addressing as 'Dear master'. In 1704 Harley brought him into the ministry as secretary for war, after forcing out several extreme high-flyers; St. John proved his reliability in several major clashes with his former associates and was soon counted among Harley's closest supporters. As secretary for war he also developed close links with Marlborough, who showed considerable regard for the younger man.

When Harley was forced to resign in 1708 by Godolphin and his Whig allies, St. John followed him into the political wilderness and lost his seat in the subsequent election. During the next two years St. John lived in the country, employing his enforced leisure to read widely in history and philosophy. He gradually became aware of the growing strength of anti-war and anti-Whig feelings in the country and moved again into the High Tory camp.

In 1710 the country voted Tory. St. John re-entered Parliament as member for Berkshire and obtained the post of secretary of state from Harley, now leader of the government, although the latter was none too eager to employ him. Harley's fears were given substance by the actions of St. John, whose ambition was only whetted, not satisfied, by his new appointment. The High Tories demanded a more partisan, anti-Whig policy of Harley; St. John adopted this cause as his own. In 1711 he promoted a military expedition to Canada, against Harley's urgings, in pursuance of the High Tory policy of carrying on the war chiefly at sea and in the colonies, to exploit Britain's maritime advantage. St. John's support for this expedition won the favour of Abigail Masham (q.v.), whose brother was given command of it, and secured St. John a handsome profit on contracts, even though the expedition itself was a failure.

St. John also played a role in the secret peace negotiations with France that began in April 1711, but Harley kept him on a tight rein. During one visit to Paris in 1712 he attended the same theatre as the Old Pretender – an act of indiscretion that greatly annoyed Harley. St. John, for his part, was angered when he was created Viscount Bolingbroke and not raised to an earldom like Harley, now Earl of Oxford. Although the two men worked actively together in and out of Parliament on behalf of the peace that was finally signed at Utrecht (1713), the friendship between them had now been completely replaced by distrust, and Bolingbroke campaigned more or less openly to undermine Oxford's postion. One of his most effective strokes was the Schism Bill (1714) against Dissenter schools, which succeeded in isolating Oxford both from the Whigs and from the Tories. On 27 July 1714, Oxford was dismissed and Bolingbroke emerged as leader of the ministry, but five days later Queen Anne died and was succeeded by George I (see *Lives of the Georgian Age*).

George had objected to the Utrecht treaties and distrusted their author. Moreover Bolingbroke was said to favour a Jacobite restoration; he had unsuccessfully urged the Pretender to become a Protestant, or at least simulate a conversion, and had planned to use his power after Oxford's overthrow to install sympathetic Tories into key military and governmental posts. But five days were not long enough. The succession machinery moved into operation; George was proclaimed King and dismissed Bolingbroke.

As the threat of impeachment by the new Whig ministry loomed ever nearer, Bolingbroke fled in March 1715 to France, where he joined the Old Pretender and was made his secretary of state. Parliament responded by passing an Act of Attainder. Bolingbroke was quick to realize that fantasy dominated Jacobite strategy and urged a more cautious and realistic approach. He advised against the 1715 rising and clashed with James's priests. Early in 1716 he was dismissed.

Bolingbroke turned again to England and sought the favour of the government. The occasion seemed propitious, for his father was raised to the peerage around this time. He began by writing his anti-Jacobite *Letter to Sir William Wyndham* (1717, first published 1753). But the ministry failed to respond favourably.

Bolingbroke bought an estate near Orléans, where he settled and spent the next few years studying philosophy and mathematics and enjoying the company of learned men, such as Montesquieu and Voltaire. After his first wife's death (1718) he married (1720) the Marquise de Villette, with whom he had a close and happy relationship for the remainder of his life.

In May 1723 Bolingbroke was pardoned and, in 1725, restored to his estates after his wife had paid a sizeable bribe to George I's mistress, the Duchess of Kendal. He returned to England, settling at Dawley near Uxbridge, where he lived the life of a country gentleman, entertaining many of the leading poets, wits, and intellectuals of the day, among them Pope, Swift, and Voltaire. He is said to have made a contribution to Pope's *Essay on Man*.

Although Bolingbroke had worked secretly for the ministry while in exile, Robert Walpole (see *Lives of the Georgian Age*) had repeatedly blocked his restoration; even now he was forbidden to take his seat in the House of Lords. Bolingbroke joined the opposition forces of Pope, Swift, and William Pulteney and wrote scathing attacks on the ministry in *The Craftsman*, a journal with which he was associated from its foundation in December 1726. A sizeable party, consisting of miscellaneous Tories and a group of discontented Whigs led by William Pulteney, now gathered around him. It has been suggested that he was only prevented from replacing Walpole as chief minister by the death of George I, but this would seem to be an overestimation of his political power in 1727.

He continued to attempt to overthrow Walpole throughout the first years of George II's reign. However, although he won occasional skirmishes, Bolingbroke never succeeded in seriously threatening Walpole; the latter's electoral victory in 1735 sounded the death knell to his ambitions.

His writings in this period (published mainly in *The Craftsman* under various pseudonyms, such as 'John Trot') comprise first and foremost an attack on Walpole, his policies, and his system of government. Bolingbroke voiced the opinion that the latter, being founded on bribery, party, and self-interested connection, was inimical to clear thinking and free speech, and declared that the Glorious Revolution of 1688 had rendered the bases of both Whiggery and Toryism obsolete and that the real division now lay between Court and Country.

After Walpole's electoral victory of 1735, Bolingbroke again withdrew to France, where he continued his historical and philosophical studies. His political influence declined. His association with the Leicester House Opposition around the Prince of Wales (1738–39) resulted not in shifts of power but in the composition of *The Idea of the Patriot King*, his most famous work. In this treatise on statecraft he sets out to demonstrate that limited, hereditary monarchy is the best form of government and calls upon the king to rule on behalf of the people and not for any particular party. The influence of his writings on his contemporaries and the succeeding generation has sometimes been overestimated. Bute and George III certainly paid lipservice to his ideas, though that monarch had rather different ideas from Bolingbroke about what constituted a 'limited' monarchy. As for his supposed influence on Voltaire, Gibbon, and Edmund Burke, there is little evidence for it. In the words of Burke, 'Who now reads Bolingbroke, who ever read him through?'

In 1744 he returned to England, settling at the home in Battersea of his friend Hugh Hume, Earl of Marchmont. He passed his remaining years writing and plotting, a quarrelsome and increasingly irrelevant old man. His writings display a perceptive and learned political thinker, whereas in action he was devious and unscrupulous in the pursuit of his ambitions. He was a notorious libertine, but proved a devoted husband to his second wife. The enemy of partisan politics, he destroyed his mentor, Oxford, by the use of party. He died of cancer on 12 December 1751.

Isaac Kramnick (ed.), *The Historical Writings* (1972).
H. T. Dickinson, *Bolingbroke* (1970).
H. T. Dickinson, 'Henry St. John: a Reappraisal of the Young Bolingbroke', *Journal of British Studies* 8 (May 1968).
Geoffrey Holmes, 'Harley, St. John and the Death of the Tory Party' in *Britain after the Glorious Revolution 1689–1714*, ed. Geoffrey Holmes (1969).
Isaac Kramnick, *Bolingbroke and His Circle* (1968).
W. S. Sichel, *Bolingbroke and His Times* (2 vols.; 1901–02).

Portraits: oil, quarter-length, attributed to J. Richardson: N.P.G.; oil, three-quarter length, attributed to A. S. Belle: N.P.G.; enamel, quarter-length, by unknown artist: N.P.G.

St. John, Oliver (?1598–1673), Parliamentarian leader and judge.

The son of Oliver St. John, a gentleman of Bedfordshire, St. John was educated at Queen's College, Cambridge (1615–19), and Lincoln's Inn (1619–26). St. John was admitted to the bar in 1626. He prospered under the patronage of the 4th Earl of Bedford, in whose service he spent a short term in the Tower on a charge of publishing seditious libel. Clarendon declares that this experience was responsible for a hatred that St. John bore the royal court in later years. This is perhaps partisan comment, but St. John was undoubtedly a proud and reserved man. He became associated with leading Puritans such as Pym (q.v.) and the Earl of Warwick (see Rich, Robert) in their colonial adventures and married a cousin of Oliver Cromwell. His involvement with the opposition to Charles I intensified, and in 1637 he acted as counsel for Lord Saye and Sele (see Fiennes, William) and John Hampden (q.v.) in the court cases arising from their refusal to pay ship money; he now achieved sudden fame through his brilliant defence of Hampden.

In 1640 St. John was elected to the Short Parliament and Long Parliament, in both of which he emerged as an Opposition leader, working in close co-operation with Pym and Hampden. Charles tried to win him over with the post of solicitor general (January 1641), but this new honour did not deter him from continuing in Opposition. He played a major role in the destruction of Strafford (see Wentworth, Thomas) and in the preparation of the Militia Bill, which sought to deprive the King of control over the army. Charles could not find a replacement for his insubordinate solicitor general until October 1643, at which time Parliament promptly appointed him one of the commissioners of their Great Seal.

During the First Civil War, St. John co-operated closely with Sir Henry Vane the Younger (q.v.). Together they inherited the mantle of Pym, led the war party and the political Independents in the Commons, established and sat on the Committee of Both Kingdoms (the Anglo-Scottish war executive), supported the New Model Army, and became leading supporters of Oliver Cromwell as more and more power fell into the latter's hands. After the war St. John supported the Army in its quarrel with Parliament (1647), but himself receded from the foreground of political activity. This change was facilitated when, in October 1648, he was appointed chief justice of the Court of Common Pleas, a post that traditionally incapacitated its holder from attending Parliament. Thus he avoided the debates on the King's trial, and when he was appointed a commissioner for the trial, he refused to serve.

He is generally reckoned to have been a fair judge; he occupied himself with his legal duties during the first years of the Commonwealth, but gradually became active on the Council of State and in general government business. In 1657 he was one of the prominent men who urged Cromwell to take the throne.

Two years later, after the Protector's death and the fall of his son, St. John played a moderate, conciliatory role, striving to achieve peace between Army, Parliament, and London, and finally co-operated with Monck (q.v.). This served him in good stead after the Restoration. He also published a defence of his conduct over the previous decades, *The Case of Oliver St. John*, and his sole punishment was to be barred from public office. He retired to the country and in 1662 went to the Continent, where he passed into obscurity. He died on 31 December 1673.

Portrait: watercolour, quarter-length, by G. P. Harding after A. Van Brounckhorst, 1578: N.P.G.

Salisbury, 1st Earl of (?1563–1612), statesman, see Cecil, Robert, in *Lives of the Tudor Age*.

Sancroft, William (1617–93), Archbishop of Canterbury; leader of the seven bishops who opposed James II's Declaration of Indulgence in 1688.

William Sancroft was born at Fressingfield, Suffolk, on 30 January 1617, of yeoman stock. He went to Bury St. Edmunds grammar school and in 1634 to Emmanuel College, Cambridge. He became a fellow of the college in 1642 but was ejected in 1651 for refusing to take an oath of loyalty to the existing government (the Commonwealth). He remained in England until 1657, when he crossed to Holland, spending eighteen months at Utrecht and later visiting Geneva, Venice, and Rome.

On the Restoration in 1660, Sancroft returned to England and became chaplain to his friend John Cosin, Bishop of Durham. His subsequent advancement was fairly swift, and he became a chaplain to the King and rector of Houghton-le-Spring in 1661, and prebendary of Durham and master of Emmanuel College in 1662. In 1664 Sancroft became Dean of St. Paul's Cathedral, where he remained until 1677. He did much to speed the rebuilding of the cathedral after the Great Fire of 1666 and himself contributed £1,400 towards the rebuilding. He became Archbishop of Canterbury in 1678 and made considerable efforts to reconvert James, Duke of York, to Anglicanism. When Charles II died in 1685 Sancroft was present at his deathbed and is said to have chided the King about his past life.

James's accession placed Sancroft in an awkward position. He may have served for a short time on James's ecclesiastical commission in 1686, but soon declared that he could not be a party to a commission dealing with spiritual matters of which a layman – Judge Jeffreys (q.v.) – was the head. In the following year Sancroft felt compelled to dispute openly with James when the latter decreed that a Declaration of Indulgence, permitting freedom of worship specifically to Roman Catholics, be read in every Anglican church in the land. He headed the seven bishops who petitioned James to withdraw the order, and with them was imprisoned in the Tower. At their trial for seditious libel, Sancroft maintained that his opposition to the King was on the grounds that the Declaration itself was illegal. Among Sancroft's fears was the possibility that James would use this precedent of his dispensing power to set aside any ecclesiastical or civil law that he disliked. The Prince and Princess of Orange (William III and Mary II, qq.v.) congratulated Sancroft on his firmness, and there was great public enthusiasm when he and the other six bishops were acquitted.

After his acquittal, Sancroft continued to urge moderation on James and tried to persuade him to call a free Parliament. After James's abdication at the end of 1688, he retired to his palace at Lambeth and did not intervene in the ensuing political manœuvres. He played no part in welcoming William of Orange and was not present when the Convention of 1689 declared the throne be vacant. He was in favour of appointing William 'custos regni' but made no effort to secure this compromise. Sancroft thereafter maintained that no one who had taken an oath of allegiance to James could honestly take one to William. William and Mary made considerable efforts to secure his support and overcome his qualms of conscience, but Sancroft would not compromise. He was accordingly suspended from office by Act of Parliament on 1 August 1689, but would not leave Lambeth Palace until he was ejected by law in 1691.

Sancroft then retired to Fressingfield, the exercise of his authority being delegated to the nonjuring Bishop Lloyd of Norwich. Until his death on 24 November 1693, he continued to pray for James II as King of England, and declined to take communion with people who had sworn loyalty to William. Sancroft can be accused of trying to perpetuate a schism in the Church of England, although his sincerity cannot be doubted. Burnet (q.v.), who disliked him, described him as 'a dry, cold man, reserved and peevish, so that none loved him, and few esteemed him'. However, a friend, Needham, who lived with Sancroft for several years, thought him 'the most pious, humble, good Christian I ever knew'.

Sancroft may have been unyielding, but his integrity was unquestionable,

and unlike other ecclesiastics of the time, such as Compton (q.v.), he seems to have been totally lacking in personal ambition. Dryden notes this in *Absalom and Achitophel*, where he writes of him as

> Zadock the priest, whom, shunning power and place,
> His lowly mind advanced to David's grace.

For Sancroft, the political implications of his actions were always secondary. What he was concerned with was the spiritual independence and integrity of the Church.

G. D'Oyley, *The Life of William Sancroft, Archbishop of Canterbury* (2 vols.; 1821).

Portrait: chalks, half-length, by E. Lutterel, *c.* 1688: N.P.G.

Sandwich, 1st Earl of (1625–72), see Montagu, Edward, 1st Earl of Sandwich.

Sandys, Sir Edwin (1561–1629), a leader of the Parliamentary opposition to James I and one of the founders of Virginia.

Born in Worcestershire, 9 December 1561, the son of Edwin Sandys, later Archbishop of York, Sandys was educated at Merchant Taylors' School, London, and Corpus Christi College, Oxford. He studied at Corpus Christi for some twelve years (1577–89), and he was still a student when he entered Parliament for Andover in 1586, subsequently sitting for Plympton, Devonshire, in 1589. On leaving college, he entered the Middle Temple, where he continued his close contact with the Anglican theological writer, Richard Hooker (see *Lives of the Tudor Age*), who had been his tutor at Corpus Christi and became master of the Temple in 1585. He travelled on the Continent between 1593 and 1599, during which time he wrote an analysis of the state of religion in Europe, *Europae Speculum* ('A Mirror of Europe'). This treatise was pirated in 1605 under the title 'A Relation of the State of Religion'.

Upon the succession of James I in 1603, Sandys received a knighthood. In the period before the death of Elizabeth I he had paid some court to James, for which the knighthood had been a reward, but in parliament, in which he now sat for Stockbridge, he soon found himself at odds with the crown. Leading the opposition, he criticized the King's economic policy, speaking against monopolies. He also sat on Parliamentary committees to discuss Cecil's Great Contract in 1610 and the question of crown imposts in 1613. He also became involved in several overseas ventures: he joined the Virginia Company in 1607; by 1611 he was a member of the East India Company; and in 1615 he took up membership of the Somers Islands Company. By 1619 he had obtained a directorship in all three organizations.

By 1619 also, Sandys had gained control of the Virginia Company, being both its director and treasurer. Under his government, a period of prosperity began in the colony. Many settlers, including the Pilgrim Fathers of 1620, went out over the Atlantic. But at home the suspicion was fostered that he planned to make Virginia a Puritan republic, and in 1621 he was accused of maladministration of funds. He spent some time in prison, and the Virginia Company finally folded in 1624.

Sandys sat in three more parliaments, the last two of James I (1621 and 1624) and the first of Charles I (1625). He represented Sandwich, Kent, and Penrhyn respectively. He continued to be ranked with the opposition members, though he now played the role of elder statesman, while younger men like Eliot and Pym (qq.v.) came forward to challenge the sovereignty of the crown. He died in October 1629.

W. M. Wallace, *Sir Edwin Sandys and the First Parliament of James I* (Philadelphia, Pa., 1940).

Portrait: oil, quarter-length, by unknown artist: N.P.G.

Sarsfield, Patrick (d. 1693), Earl of Lucan; Anglo-Irish soldier and supporter of James II.

Patrick Sarsfield was born at Lucan, near Dublin, probably in the early 1650s, the grandson of Rory O'More, who had led an Irish Catholic uprising against the English in 1641. He was educated at a French military college and served in the army of Louis XIV of France from 1671 to 1678. In 1678 he went to England, where he received a commission as captain in a regiment of foot. He soon earned himself a reputation as a fiery champion of Ireland; in 1681, for example he challenged Lord Grey to a duel for making derogatory remarks about some Irish witnesses in a trial. After the accession of the Catholic

James II to the throne in 1685, Sarsfield fought at Sedgemoor and was made a colonel. He assisted James's commander in Ireland, Tyrconnel (see Talbot, Richard), in the Catholicizing reorganization of the Irish army. During the final months of James's reign, Sarsfield was put in command of these Catholic troops. It is possible that James intended to use this army in a last effort to preserve his throne. However, he was overtaken by events – in the form of William of Orange's landing at Torbay – and in November 1688 was forced to flee to France. Here he was joined by Sarsfield.

In March 1689, Sarsfield accompanied James to Ireland, where he was made a privy councillor and colonel of horse. He now distinguished himself as a cavalry commander, especially in securing Connaught for James, and was promoted to the rank of major general. On 1 July 1690, however, when William of Orange heavily defeated the Jacobites at the Battle of the Boyne, Sarsfield was so badly placed during the battle that his cavalry could do nothing. Nevertheless, he managed to rally the beaten army, and defended Limerick with great success against William's forces for several months, making a spectacular attack on William's artillery train on the road between Limerick and Cashel.

James and Tyrconnel now returned to France and, although Sarsfield was not given supreme military command in Ireland, apparently all the Irish soldiers and officers were unwilling to obey anyone but him. Tyrconnel returned to Ireland in January 1691, bearing a patent creating Sarsfield Earl of Lucan, although the title was recognized only by the Jacobites. Sarsfield consistently opposed the idea of another pitched battle against William's forces, but his opinions were overruled by James's new commander-in-chief, St. Ruth,

who accordingly joined battle with William's general, Ginkel, at Aughrim on 12 July 1691. St. Ruth was killed and Sarsfield, though second in command, was unaware of his general's plans and had received no orders. All he could do was to retreat with his force intact to Limerick. When further resistance was obviously futile he negotiated a surrender at Limerick in October. He left Ireland for France on 22 December 1691, taking about 12,000 Irish troops with him. Thereafter Sarsfield fought for France and joined Louis XIV's army in the Spanish Netherlands, where he was mortally wounded on 19 August 1693, fighting the English at Neerwinden. He died a few days later.

J. Todhunter, *Life of Patrick Sarsfield* (1895).

Savile, George (1633–95), 1st Marquis of Halifax, statesman and political writer; a powerful advocate of moderation, who became known as 'the Trimmer'.

George Savile was born at Thornhill, Yorkshire, on 11 November 1633, the

son of Sir William Savile. He was too young to play any part in the Civil War, but his father was Royalist governor first of Sheffield and then of York. He was educated at Shrewsbury, subsequently travelling with a private tutor in France and Italy. In 1660 he became Member for Pontefract in the Convention that recalled Charles II as King. This was his sole appearance in the House of Commons, and in 1668 Savile was created Baron Savile of Eland and Viscount Halifax.

His promotion was partly due to his extensive estates and family connections and perhaps also to the influence on his behalf of the powerful Duke of Buckingham (see Villiers, George, 2nd Duke). Halifax became a privy councillor in 1672 and was sent on a mission to Louis XIV in connection with Anglo-French co-operation against the Dutch. However, he remained faithful to the principles of the Triple Alliance and had previously drawn away from Buckingham and his pro-Catholic policies. When Danby (see Osborne, Thomas) came to power in 1674, Halifax was equally critical of the new chief minister's policies and vigorously opposed Danby's attempt to require all office holders and M.P.s to swear that opposition to the King's authority was illegal. Halifax was also critical of the continuation in being of a parliament that no longer reflected public opinion, and in 1676 was dismissed from the Privy Council.

In 1679, following the fall of Danby, Halifax was reinstated as a privy councillor and now enjoyed a period in the King's favour. He was created Earl of Halifax in that year, and was active in almost every major parliamentary debate in 1679–80. He strongly supported Charles II in his determination to defeat the proposals to exclude his brother James from the succession. Halifax was concerned for the continuation of Protestant supremacy in England, but he saw no solution in the shallow Monmouth (q.v.) and preferred the idea of imposing limitations on James, Duke of York, when he became king. Halifax's greatest personal feat was the defeat of the Exclusion Bill in the House of Lords on 15 November 1680, which was generally attributed chiefly to his powers of oratory. After this crisis, Halifax enjoyed considerable political authority, being created Marquis of Halifax and lord privy seal in 1682. His ambition was to secure moderate government, but the defeat of exclusion did not necessarily pave the way for this, and James remained as doctrinaire a Catholic as he had ever been. The latter's return to England in 1682 resulted in a decline in Halifax's influence, for he had supported a scheme for limiting James's powers if he were to succeed to the throne while still adhering to Catholicism, and James found him too clever for comfort.

Halifax resumed his customary role of detached critic, committed to no faction and opposing the execution of the Rye House 'plotters' Algernon Sidney and Lord William Russell (qq.v.). At about this time, he privately circulated his pamphlet, *The Character of a Trimmer*, which advocated a moderate middle path in politics. In the preface, Halifax asked 'Why – after we have played the fool with throwing Whig and Tory at one another, as boys do snowballs – do we grow angry at a new name, which by its true signification might do as much to put us into our wits as the other hath done to put us out of them?' There was a reaction in favour of his views towards the end of Charles's reign and he was appointed lord president of the council by James. However, he was soon dismissed for refusing to support the repeal of the Test and Habeas Corpus Acts.

Halifax spent the next three years in retirement at his mansion at Rufford, criticizing James in various political pamphlets. His *Letter to a Dissenter* (1687) warned Nonconformists of the dangers involved in trusting James's promises of toleration, and in *Anatomy of an Equivalent* (1688), he argued that there was no substitute for the safeguards provided by the existing established religion. Halifax kept in touch with moderate opposition to the King and apparently felt that James would be sure to fail in time. He did not encourage approaches from William of Orange's agent Dykveld and declined to sign the invitation to William. He preserved his neutrality during the crisis of 1688 and was therefore ideally placed to mediate between James and William. He tried to persuade James to call a free Parliament, and only after they had failed to agree and James had fled did he abandon his neutrality and declare support for William.

Halifax became speaker of the peers in the Convention Parliament and largely through his efforts the idea of a regency was defeated and William and Mary were offered the crown. Halifax was reappointed to his old office of lord privy seal and became William's chief minister. This was not solely because of his services to William but also because of the similarity of their political outlook. William was anxious for a balance between the political parties to be achieved and hoped through Halifax to form a broadly based government. However, Halifax was disliked by Whig and Tory factions at either extreme and it soon became clear that such a government would not work in practice. He resigned in February 1690 and spent the rest of his life in opposition to each administration of the moment. Like many of his contemporaries, Halifax also remained in contact with the Jacobite court in France. He took part in debates in the Lords occasionally, and wrote several more pamphlets. By the end of 1694, his health was failing, and he died on 5 April 1695. He was buried in Westminster Abbey.

Halifax had many outstanding attributes: he was intelligent, witty, courageous, and a fine orator; politically he was the outstanding moderate of his age. Dryden writes of him in *Absalom and Achitophel* as:

Jotham of piercing wit and pregnant thought,
Endued by nature and by learning taught
To move assemblies.

Yet Halifax was a somewhat ineffective politician and had remarkably little influence on the political events of his time. Perhaps his ability to see both sides, and his personal inclination to act as a mediator in any situation, made him incapable of taking resolute action. Burnet (q.v.) wrote that 'With relation to the public, he went backwards and forwards, and changed sides so often, that in conclusion no side trusted him.' His contemporaries did not appreciate Halifax's critical stance and independent judgment, and he was either incapable of or disinclined to organize a band of followers in support of his principles. Halifax made many enemies and was thought treacherous by many of his contemporaries, but his incorruptibility and disinterestedness were genuine, and he remained faithful to his political principles despite the fact that they met with little favour in his time.

J. P. Kenyon (ed.), *Works of George Savile* (1969).
J. H. Wilson (ed.), *The Rochester-Savile Letters* (Columbus, Ohio, 1941).
Joseph S. Fletcher, *Yorkshiremen of the Restoration* (1921).

H. C. Foxcroft, *The Life and Letters of Sir George Savile, Bart., First Marquis of Halifax* (2 vols.; 1898).

H. C. Foxcroft, *A Character of the Trimmer* (1946).

Portrait: oil, three-quarter length, attributed to Mary Beale, *c.* 1674–76: N.P.G.

Savile, Sir Henry (1549–1622), scholar; provost of Eton and warden of Merton College, Oxford, noted for his knowledge of Roman antiquities and his contribution to the Authorized Version of the Bible.

He was born on 30 November 1549 at Bradley, near Halifax, Yorkshire. Savile's family was rich and well established in the county. His parents, therefore, were well able to afford him a good education, and he entered Brasenose College, Oxford, in 1561 at the age of ten, becoming a fellow of Merton College four years later and gaining the degree of M.A. in 1570.

Savile began to make his scholarly reputation over the next few years on the strength of his lectures in mathematics and on Ptolemy's astronomical treatise *The Almagest*. After a journey abroad collecting manuscripts, during which time he visited the Netherlands and was resident there on behalf of Queen Elizabeth for a short period, he returned to England and became the Queen's tutor in Greek. In 1585 he was appointed warden of Merton College.

Besides his advantages of birth and background, Savile was in any case a brilliant scholar. In 1591 he brought out a translation of Tacitus's *Histories*. He was held in high esteem by the Queen, who now made him her Latin secretary, and his friendship with the Earl of Essex secured him other favours. By skilful manœuvring, he obtained in 1595 the provostship of Eton in spite of the fact that he was a layman, without having to give up his position as warden of Merton. These posts he held for the rest of his life. His reign over both colleges was dictatorial but beneficial, for he was determined to appoint fellows and scholars who possessed real knowledge of their subjects, without regard to rank or influence.

In 1601 some of the repercussions accompanying the fall of Essex affected Savile also and he was imprisoned for a short time. By the end of Elizabeth's reign in 1603, however, he was once again in good odour at court and received a knighthood from James I in 1604.

When James commissioned a new translation of the Bible as part of his religious policy, Savile was one of the scholars involved on the project, and the Acts of the Apostles, as well as a section of the Gospels, appears in the Authorized Version of 1611 in his translation. That he did not neglect his own personal scholarly interests is shown in the production between 1610 and 1613 of what is generally regarded as his masterpiece, an edition in eight volumes of the complete writings of St. John Chrysostom. This scholarly work is still reckoned by some modern authorities to be the best available edition. Other works include an edition of Xenophon's *Education of Cyrus*, editions of several little-known medieval historians, and one of the fourteenth-century philosopher, Thoman Bradwardine, into whose work Savile, by virtue of his own mathematical interests, was able to bring a special insight.

Savile as a patron of learning and of learned institutions is probably best remembered for his establishment of two Oxford professorships, which bore his name, one in geometry, the other in astronomy. He also gave generous assistance towards the founding of the Bodleian Library, to which he left several valuable manuscripts. Savile's contribution to the advancement of learning was a major one; his reputation continued without diminution up to his death at Eton on 19 February 1622.

M. H. Curtis, *Oxford and Cambridge in Transition 1558–1642* (1959).

Saye and Sele, 1st Viscount (1582–1662), see Fiennes, William.

Scott, James (1649–85), see Monmouth, Duke of.

Sedley, Sir Charles (?1639–1701), Restoration poet and wit; one of the 'mob of gentlemen who write with ease' (according to Pope), who gathered around the court of Charles II, and who included Buckingham (George Villiers, 2nd Duke), Dorset (Charles Sackville), Etherege, Rochester (John Wilmot), and Wycherley (qq.v.).

He was born, probably in 1639, at Aylesford in Kent, being the youngest and posthumous son of Sir John Sedley, Bart. His mother was the daughter of Sir Henry Savile. He went up to Wadham College, Oxford, but left without taking a degree. After the Restoration of Charles II he entered Parliament as one of the members for New Romney in Kent. He is said to have taken his duties seriously, in spite of his reputation as a man of wit and a thoroughgoing profligate. The first of these characteristics is attested to by a story concerning James II, who had seduced Sedley's daughter and made her Countess of Dorchester; Sedley commented that as he hated ingratitude he would try to make the King's daughter a queen. His reputation as one of the 'merry gang' of courtier rakes possibly has more substance. Perhaps the most outrageous of his exploits was the incident when he,

Dorset, and Rochester showed their contempt for the townsmen of Covent Garden, after an orgy at the Cock tavern, by exposing themselves in indecent postures, a piece of fine contempt for which they were almost lynched. Yet another detail of his rake's progress is a note by Samuel Pepys (q.v.) in 1667 bemoaning the fact that Sedley and Dorset had lured Nell Gwynne (q.v.) away from the theatre to Epsom, where they kept 'merry house'.

Sedley was well known as a patron of literature and is the 'Lisideius' of Dryden's *Essay of Dramatic Poesy*. Of his own literary output, his three comedies and two tragedies are hardly worth remarking; his best and most successful work was in poetry, particularly in love lyrics that have a certain gaiety and transparency, and a careful diction that sometimes approaches those of Dryden (q.v.). Among the best known are *Phyllis is my only joy*, *Constancy*, *To Clovis*, and *Not Celia that I juster am*. Of his comedies, perhaps the best is *Bellamira* (1687), an adaptation of Terence, while *The Mulberry Garden* (1668) is taken from Molière's *L'école des maris* and *The Grumbler* (1702) is a somewhat heavy-handed adaptation of another French model. In this, Sedley was typical of the dramatists of his time, for whom originality seemed to have no meaning. His tragedies, if such they can be called, were *Antony and Cleopatra* (1667) and *The Tyrant King of Crete* (1702).

The lyrics by which alone he is worth remembering as a literary talent, rather than as the *vainqueur du vainqueur du monde* of Restoration rakes, were collected in *A New Miscellany* and in a *Collection of Poems* of 1701, the year in which he died on 20 August.

V. de Sola Pinto (ed.), *The Poetical and Dramatic Works* [with bibliography] (2 vols.; 1928).
V. de Sola Pinto, *Sir Charles Sedley* (1927).

Selden, John (1584–1654), parliamentarian, jurist, authority on legal history and antiquities, and orientalist.

Born at Salvington, Sussex, on 16 December 1584, the son of John Selden, a small farmer whose family 'flourished honourably' in that area, Selden was educated at Chichester Grammar School and Hart Hall, Oxford. He left the latter institution without a degree and in 1602 entered Clifford Inn, moving to the Inner Temple in 1604. He was called to the bar in 1612 and in 1633 he became a bencher.

Selden's legal practice seems to have been quite lucrative. It was, however, not so much as a lawyer but more as a scholar that he made his reputation. In 1605 he met Ben Jonson (q.v.) and through him became involved in a circle that included the antiquary, Sir Robert Cotton, and later the Irish cleric, James Ussher. Selden's acquaintance with Cotton was decisive in that Cotton brought the young lawyer to live at his London home for a time and placed at his disposal his vast library. In 1607 Selden contributed a preface to Jonson's play *Volpone* and at about the same time completed his *Analecton Anglo-Britannicon*, a history of Britain down to the Norman Conquest, which was not published until 1615.

In 1610 he brought out three weighty works on legal history. Two were substantially the same work, one version, *England's Epinomis*, being an English translation, with differences, of the other. These two treatises dealt with the history of English law from Anglo-Saxon times to the reign of Henry II. His third *opus* traced the history of the 'duello', or trial by single combat, from the Norman period.

In 1614 Selden published his *Titles of Honour*, still regarded by some as a standard authority, despite its obvious shortcomings. Other works on legal history followed, and it was also at this time that he established his reputation as an orientalist with the publication in 1617 of *De Diis Syriis* ('Concerning the Syrian Gods'). This work, still valuable in the field of Semitic mythology, appeared in the same year as a treatise on the Jews in England, and Selden was acclaimed as a prominent Hebraic scholar.

In 1618 appeared his most controversial work, *A History of Tithes*. This, like his *Analecton*, was dedicated to Sir Robert Cotton, and dealt with the history of tithe payments from ancient times to his own day. The bulk of the essay was concerned with the English tithe system and posed, through skilfully evaded answering, the question whether tithes were levied by divine right or in accordance with natural human law. The work brought down a storm of reproof from clerics and culminated in the intervention of James I, who banned the book and prohibited Selden from replying to any of its attackers.

This controversy opened the way for Selden into the political arena. In 1621, though not a member of the House of Commons, he played an important part behind the scenes in the formulation of the protestation on freedom of debate that caused James indignantly to suspend the session in December. Selden suffered the fate of Sir Edward Coke, John Pym (qq.v.), and others in being confined for several months in the Tower.

He sat in the 1624 parliament for the borough of Lancaster. In the same year, he was fined and disqualified for a time from his law practice for refusing the readership of Lyon's Inn. No record exists of his having sat in Charles I's first parliament of 1625, but he was M.P. for Great Bedwin, Wiltshire, in 1626, and he was appointed one of the organizers of the impeachment of Buckingham (see Villiers, George, 1st Duke). In 1627 Sir Edmund Hampden, one of those imprisoned for refusing to contribute to Charles's forced loan, sued for a writ of habeas corpus in the court of king's bench. In November, a case was brought over the doubtful legality of the imprisonment, and Selden appeared for Hampden. His defence speech was sympathetically received, but the King's prerogative was upheld. In 1628 he took up the matter of imprisonment without trial in the Commons. He also played an active role in the formulation and passage of the Petition of Right and joined in the resumed attack on Buckingham.

In 1629 Selden brought out *Marmora Arundeliana*, a catalogue of the Arundel Marbles. His political activities in Charles's fourth parliament were stormy. A supporter of Sir John Eliot (q.v.) in the matter of tonnage and poundage, he was involved in the uproar that terminated the session in March and, with Eliot, Holles, Strode (qq.v.), and others, he was arrested and imprisoned. Early on in his confinement he was denied books and papers, and even when this interdict was removed he was allowed access to them only with irksome restrictions. Selden refused to give assurances for his good behaviour and his release was delayed until 1631. In that year he was paroled on the petition of the Earls of Arundel and Pembroke, who required his services in some litigation. In 1635 he received his unconditional discharge.

Selden's release in 1631 was not due solely to the good offices of Arundel and Pembroke, however; Laud (q.v.) also interceded for him, and rumour alleged that Selden entertained the idea of defecting to the royal court. In 1635 he took up at Charles's behest a work that had been commenced in 1618

but laid aside by order of James, who had thought it politically unwise. This was his *Mare clausum* ('A closed sea'), a defence of England's claim to the rule of the sea, written in reply to the Dutch author Grotius's earlier *Mare liberum* ('A free sea').

Selden apparently did not sit in the Short Parliament of April 1640, but took his seat for Oxford University in the Long Parliament of the following November. His position was very much that of a moderate. Like his contemporary Pym, a constitutionalist with great respect for the law, he was nevertheless shy of the bold step needed to assert parliamentary sovereignty. By no means an extremist then, he helped prepare the articles of impeachment against Strafford (see Wentworth, Thomas), but refrained from supporting the prosecution proceedings. He opposed ship money, but also the abolition of episcopacy. He signed the declaration of adherence to the Church of England, and in the following month was placed on the committee to organize the impeachment of Laud. This same year (1641) also saw his appointment to a committee investigating Charles's breaches of parliamentary privilege, to which he subsequently presented his *Privileges of the Baronage of England, when they Sit in Parliament* (1642).

1642 began as a year of personal crisis for Selden. On 4 February, he was with others the subject of an order requiring continued attendance in the service of Parliament. Obviously teetering on the brink of defection, he was approached indirectly by the King, who tried to induce him to join the Royalists at York. Subsequent events, however, made up Selden's mind for him.

In 1643 he sat in the assembly of divines, where his knowledge of Hebrew and Greek often proved embarrassing to the more dogmatic members. In 1645 he joined the committee for the admiralty. In 1646 he signed the Solemn League and Covenant and was· prominent in speaking for the abolition of the Court of Wards. Following Charles's execution in 1649, he sat on a committee called by the Council of State to consider the dignity and precedence of ambassadors. After this he retired from public life and devoted his remaining years to his last publications. As a young man, Selden had become steward to Henry Grey, 9th Earl of Kent, and he continued in this office to Grey's widow. He may even have married her. At any rate, when she died in 1649, her London mansion at Whitefriars came to him; here he lived in some comfort until his own death on 30 November 1654.

Selden left a prolific output of written material. His thoroughgoing erudition is clear in all his work, but most of all perhaps in his treatises on the Jews and their legal system, especially his treatise *De Synedriis et Prefecturis Iuridicis Veterum Ebraeorum* ('Concerning the Counsels and Judicial Offices of the Ancient Hebrews'; 1650, 1653, and 1655). In 1647 he edited the first printed version of the ancient English law book *Fleta*, and his last piece of writing was a preface in 1653 for Sir Roger Twysden's *Historiae Anglicanae Scriptores Decem* ('Ten English Historians'), for which he also collated some of the manuscripts.

In 1689 Selden's secretary, Richard Milward, published *Table Talk*, a collection of Selden's sayings. His biography was written by Anthony à Wood (q.v.) in *Athenae Oxonienses* (1691–92). His complete works, edited by D. Wilkins, appeared in 1726.

Sir F. Pollock (ed.), *The Table Talk* (1927: Everyman's Library; 1934).
S. H. Reynolds (ed.), *The Table Talk* (1892).

J. Aikin, *The Lives of John Selden and Archbishop Ussher* (1812).
G. W. Johnson, *Memoirs of John Selden, etc.* (1835).

Selkirk, Alexander (1676–1721), sailor, stranded for four years on an uninhabited island, model for Defoe's *Robinson Crusoe*.

Selkirk was born at Largo, Fife, the seventh son of John Selcraig, shoemaker. In 1695 he ran away to sea to escape trouble at home, having been summoned for 'indecent behaviour' in church. It appears that he had wished from childhood to go to sea, but although he was encouraged by his mother, his father strongly opposed him. Little is known of Selkirk's first voyages; he reappeared in Largo in 1701. Again he found himself in trouble, quarrelling violently with his brothers, and in 1703 he sailed with an expedition to the South Seas. He must have attained a fairly high standard of seamanship by then, for he shipped as sailing master of the galley *Cinque Ports*, captained by Charles Pickering. By this time he had changed his name from Selcraig, his father's name, and was known as Selkirk. The expedition was led by William Dampier (q.v.), captain of the *St. George*. After a successful buccaneering expedition, the ships arrived in September 1704 at the island of Juan Fernandez, about 400 miles west of Valparaiso, Chile. Here Selkirk apparently quarrelled with his captain, Thomas Stradling, who had succeeded as captain of the *Cinque Ports* after the death of Pickering. He asked to be set down on Juan Fernandez and was put ashore with all his belongings. Once ashore, he changed his mind, but Stradling was adamant and refused to take him back on board. Selkirk remained alone on the otherwise uninhabited island for four years and four months. He apparently adapted well to his lonely life: he built two huts as living accommodation, fashioned knives from old iron hoops, and enthusiastically hunted the wild goats with which the island abounded, making clothes out of goatskin. He later tamed wild cats and goats as companions. He sighted two ships in his four years as a castaway, but only one spotted him. It proved to be a Spanish ship and contented itself with firing a volley of shots at him before passing on.

In 1709 Selkirk was discovered by an expedition led by Captain Woodes Rogers, which sighted his beacon. The pilot of this expedition was the same William Dampier with whom Selkirk had sailed earlier. Selkirk was taken aboard the *Duke* and was appointed mate under Woodes Rogers. In March he took command of the prize ship *Increase*. In 1710 he became sailing master of a new prize ship commanded by Captain Dover, and in 1711 the expedition finally returned home and reached the Thames. Selkirk's share of the booty came to £800.

His story was written by Woodes Rogers (*A Cruising Voyage round the World*) and Captain Edward Cooke (*A Voyage to the South Seas and round the World*). Selkirk also met the essayist Richard Steele (see *Lives of the Georgian Age*), who wrote up his adventures in *The Englishman*. Steele described Selkirk as a man of good sense with a strong and serious but cheerful disposition. A second edition of this essay (1718) was almost certainly the direct inspiration for Daniel Defoe's *Robinson Crusoe*.

When Selkirk return to Largo in 1712, he took up a hermit-like existence in a kind of cave constructed in his father's garden. This period of meditation did not last long, however, for in 1713 Selkirk eloped with Sophia Bruce, first to Bristol and thence to London. Records show that while he was in Bristol, proceedings were taken against one 'Alexander Selkirke' for an assault on Richard Nettle, a shipwright.

By 1720 Selkirk appears to have resumed his life as a sailor and to have married a widow called Frances Candis, whom he made sole beneficiary and executrix of his estate in a will of that year. In 1721 Selkirk died at sea, while serving as master's mate on a man-of-war, H.M.S. *Weymouth*. After his death, both Sophia and Frances claimed to be his legal widow, but only Frances could produce evidence of her marriage. She successfully claimed the house in Largo, which had been left to Alexander by his father. Selkirk appears to have left no children.

J. Howell, *Life and Adventures of Alexander Selkirk* (1829).

Isaac James, *Providence Displayed, or the Remarkable Adventures of Alexander Selkirk* (1800).

P. K. Kemp and C. C. Lloyd, *The Brethren of the Coast* (1960).

Sewall, Samuel (1652–1730), American colonial magistrate, merchant, and writer.

Born on 28 March 1652, in Bishopstoke, Hampshire, the son of Henry Sewall, a merchant, Samuel Sewall was educated at the grammar school, Romsey, a private school in Massachusetts, and Harvard College. At the age of nine he travelled to America with his parents and settled in Boston. After further education he was sent to Harvard, where he was awarded a B.A. (1671) and an M.A. (1674), and appointed a tutor (1673). Further studies led to his ordination as a minister, but then he married and turned to politics and business, becoming a freeman of the colony in 1679. His father helped him become established as a printer, and being conservatively inclined, Sewall experienced little difficulty in winning election to the General Court and obtaining a seat on the council.

In 1692 Sewall was appointed one of the judges at the infamous Salem witch trials, which condemned nineteen people to death. Of the judges, he was the only one ever to admit that he had erred, and in later years he appeared greatly burdened by a sense of guilt for this episode, confessing publicly in church in 1697. Nevertheless, he later became a regular member of the bench, in spite of his lack of legal training.

Sewall was involved in furthering missions among the Indians. He was also one of the first to protest against the enslavement of Blacks and in 1700 published an anti-slavery tract. His writings include poetry, works on public affairs, and his diary, which covers the years 1674–1729, with one eight-year gap. This journal provides us with valuable insights into the social and political history of contemporary New England.

Samuel Sewall died on 1 January 1730.

'The Diary of Samuel Sewall', in *Massachusetts Historical Society Collections*, 5 ser. V-VII (1878–82).

Sexby, Edward (d. 1658), Parliamentarian soldier and anti-Cromwellian plotter.

Sexby is known to have come from Suffolk, but was otherwise of obscure origin. Around 1643 Sexby was serving as a trooper in Cromwell's cavalry regiment. He was still a private soldier at the end of the First Civil War; as such he played a leading role in opposing Parliament's attempts to disband the New Model Army in 1647; he was one of three common soldiers deputed to state to the generals the demands of the rank and file. Thus it was natural that he should become an 'agitator' and spokesman for the ordinary soldiers in the debates of the Army council at Putney in October 1647, demanding a drastic extension of the franchise and opposing any compromise with the King.

Sexby apparently left the army towards the end of 1647. He was present at the Battle of Preston (1648) as a civilian, and then seems to have launched on a career as a military-political officer, serving for example as governor of Portland. In 1650 he raised a cavalry regiment and commanded it in Scotland, but the next year he was court martialled and deprived of his colonelcy for withholding his soldiers' pay. Despite this conviction, the Council of State sent him on an intelligence mission to France, where he contacted Huguenots and the *Frondeurs*.

In 1653 Sexby returned to England, where he soon fell out with Cromwell and the new Protectorate. He set himself the task of uniting the Royalist and republican opposition and soon had Cromwell's agents hot on his heels. In 1655 he fled to Flanders, where he was welcomed by the Spanish authorities as well as the Royalists. The former pledged support for a revolt in England, and Sexby began negotiating with the Royalists and plotting the assassination of Cromwell. But the efficient spy service of John Thurloe (q.v.) kept the Protectorate well informed about all these intrigues.

In 1657 Sexby wrote *Killing no Murder*, defending tyrannicide, and smuggled copies into England. To co-ordinate the proposed assassination he went to England, but was discovered and arrested. He died in the Tower on 13 January 1658.

Shadwell, Thomas (?1642–92), dramatist, poet, and miscellaneous writer, author of seventeen plays; now best remembered as the butt of Dryden's satire, *Mac Flecknoe* (published 1682, but written in 1678).

Shadwell was born, probably in the year 1642, at Stanton Hall, Norfolk, by his own son's account. He was himself the son of John Shadwell, a Justice of the Peace. His early education took place at home, though he spent one year at Bury St. Edmunds' School. He was entered, on 17 December 1656, at Caius College, Cambridge, but left the university without taking a degree. He joined the Middle Temple for a time and was subsequently abroad.

His assault on the portals of literature opened in 1688 with his first prose comedy, *The Sullen Lovers* (subtitled *The Impertinents*), based on Molière's *Les fâcheux* but essentially modelled on the drama of contrasting 'humours' of Ben Jonson, whom he thought 'all dramatic poets ought to imitate' (Preface to *The Sullen Lovers*). After this first success, for the next fourteen years he produced a play virtually every season. He wrote in various dramatic forms besides the Jonsonian humour comedy, including an operatic adaptation of Shakespeare's *Tempest*, entitled *The Enchanted Island*. His best plays are the gay and bawdy *Epsom Wells* (1672), the didactic *Bury Fair* (1689), and *The Squire of Alsatia* (1688), a lively portrayal of the contemporary London underworld. They share a vigorous and picturesque quality, capturing Restoration life at the level of ordinary society, that is absent from the plays of his greater contemporaries, Dryden, Congreve, and Etherege.

The origins of Shadwell's feud with Dryden lie in the peculiar conditions of London literary and theatrical life in the 1660s and 1670s. Like Dryden, Shadwell was a professional at a time when the greatest successes in drama were being made by the gifted gentleman amateurs – Etherege, Vanbrugh, Wycherley, Congreve, and Farquhar. To make a living out of writing, it was necessary to find a rich patron and this usually meant following also the patron's political line. Where Dryden gravitated towards Mulgrave and the Tories, becoming poet laureate in 1669, Shadwell, 'the True-Blue Protestant Poet' as Dryden calls him, leaned towards the Duke of Newcastle, the Earl of Shaftesbury (Anthony Ashley Cooper, q.v.) and the Whigs. Until 1678, however, personal relations between the two were cordial enough, although there had been some sniping in prefaces. The spark that lit the fuse in 1678 was Shadwell's praise of the Duke of Buckingham's *Rehearsal* (1672) (see Villiers, George, 2nd Duke), in which Buckingham had satirized Dryden's *Conquest of Granada*.

Dryden's answer, *Mac Flecknoe*, appears to have been written in 1678 and circulated in manuscript, though it did not appear in print until 1682, after which Dryden and Shadwell were in open feud. Shadwell's *The Medal of John Bayes: A Satire against Folly and Knavery* (1682) was essentially a reply to *MacFlecknoe*, though in name it purported to attack Dryden's satire (*The Medal*) on the Whig leader, Shaftesbury. The first authorized version of *Mac Flecknoe* appeared in 1684. The central idea of the poem derives from Shadwell's delusion that the mantle of the great Jonson had descended upon him. Dryden hit upon the idea of substituting for Jonson a wretched minor poet of the time, Richard Flecknoe, who bequeaths to his son ('Mac') Shadwell the empire of bad writing. Dryden portrays Shadwell as large and fat and an opium addict:

Thy tragic muse gives smile, thy comic, sleep.

With due allowance for bias, Dryden's picture of Shadwell is probably fairly accurate, and certainly vastly entertaining, producing some of his most pungent lines:

> His brows thick fogs, instead of glories, grace,
> And lambent dullness plays around his face.

It may be said of Shadwell that if he never actually wrote a masterpiece he at least inspired one. It was with true irony that in 1688 he replaced Dryden as poet laureate and historiographer royal. He died suddenly on 19 November 1692, and was buried five days later at Chelsea.

Montague Summers (ed.), *The Complete Works of Thomas Shadwell* (5 vols.; 1927).

A. S. Borgman, *Thomas Shadwell* (New York, 1928).

Portrait: oil, half-length, by unknown artist, 1690: N.P.G.

Shaftesbury, 1st Earl of (1621–83), see Cooper, Anthony Ashley.

Shakespeare, William (1564–1616), poet and dramatist, see *Lives of the Tudor Age*.

Shirley, James (1596–1666), poet and dramatist.

Born in London in September 1596, Shirley was educated at Merchant Taylors' school and then probably at St. John's College, Oxford, where, according to Anthony à Wood, Archbishop Laud showed much interest in him but advised him not to take orders because of a disfiguring mole on his left cheek. In 1615 he went to Catherine Hall, Cambridge. In 1618 Shirley printed his earliest poem, *Eccho, or the Unfortunate Lovers*, although there is no copy extant now. A few years later he took orders, but was then converted to the Church of Rome, afterwards becoming a teacher at Edward VI's Grammar School near St. Albans, a post that he held from 1623 to 1625.

In 1625 Shirley abandoned scholastic life and returned to London, where, according to Wood, he 'set up for a play-maker', at which he proved to be most prolific. He wrote some forty plays, most of which are still extant. For about ten years he wrote almost exclusively for the Cockpit Theatre and then, in 1636, during a plague, he went with Thomas Wentworth, Earl of Strafford, to Dublin and for four years wrote for the Werburgh Street Theatre. In 1640 he returned to London and became the principal dramatist with the most famous company of the time, the King's Men, replacing Philip Massinger.

When the theatres closed in 1642, it is probable that he returned to teaching, and in 1646 he published another volume of verse, but the theatre still held a strong attraction for him and from 1653 he published three further collections of plays. He died in 1666, reputedly from terror and exposure during the Great Fire of London; he was buried at St. Giles's in the Fields on 29 October of that year.

Shirley's tragedies, typical examples of which are *The Maid's Revenge* (?1626), *The Traitor* (1631), and *Love's Cruelty* (1631), reflect the taste of his time, but lack any sense of true tragedy and rely totally on conventional gestures of tragic drama. They are, therefore, too derivative to be important in themselves. In 1641, for example, he wrote a revenge tragedy called *The Cardinal*, which is a slavish replica of Kyd's *Spanish Tragedy*, written in about 1587. His comedies, however, are much more important, as here he was developing his own style. His audience, which mostly consisted of cavaliers and courtiers, wanted a new style in comedy; something more intellectual than Shakespeare, who now seemed old-fashioned, but more refined than Jonson, who seemed now too coarse for their taste.

His best-known comedies, such as *Hyde Park* (1632), *The Witty Fair One* (1633), *The Gamester* (1637), and *The Lady of Pleasure* (1635), foreshadow in many ways the mood and style of Restoration comedies. Much importance is given to contemporary codes of behaviour; intellect is of prime importance and the dialogue abounds with *bon mots* and witticisms.

When the theatres were reopened in 1660 Shirley's plays were performed again and continued to be extremely popular. One in particular, *The Gamester*, the plot of which is said to have been suggested by Charles I, was later adapted by Garrick and continued to be performed throughout the eighteenth century.

Shirley's plays, however, are not revived for the theatre today and are now really of interest only to the student of drama.

W. Gifford and Alexander Dyce (eds.), *Dramatic Works and Poems* (6 vols.; 1833).

Edmund Gosse (ed.), *James Shirley* (1888).

S. J. Radke, *Shirley: His Catholic Philosophy of Life* (Washington, 1929).

A. W. Green, *The Inns of Court and Early English Drama* (1931).

E. Welsford, *Court Masque* (1927).

Shovel or Shovell, Sir Cloudesley or Clowdisley (1650–1707), admiral of the fleet.

He was born at Cockthorpe, Norfolk (baptized 25 November 1650), the son of John Shovel, a gentleman of the neighbourhood. Cloudesley Shovel went to sea in 1664, under the care of first one relation, Sir Christopher Myngs, and

then of another, Sir John Narborough. He was probably present at battles during the second Dutch War, and won quick promotion through his courage and his competence at navigation, which was largely self-taught. In 1673 he became second lieutenant on one of Narborough's ships in the Mediterranean. Here he served on a number of vessels, and in 1675–76 led a force that burnt four pirate ships under the walls of Tripoli. He was promoted captain in 1677 and spent most of the following ten years harassing the Mediterranean pirates.

Shovel was given a command in the fleet formed to oppose the crossing of William of Orange (1688), but like most sailors felt no qualms about supporting the Protestant prince after the success of the Glorious Revolution. At the inconclusive Battle of Bantry Bay (1689) he commanded the ship-of-the-line *Edgar*, and was knighted on his return to England. He was given a squadron in the Irish Sea, and in the next year was promoted to rear admiral of the Blue. Under Admiral Edward Russell (q.v.) he served as rear admiral of the Red and played a major part in winning the Battle of La Hogue (1692). He was made vice-admiral of the Red and sent as second-in-command on several expeditions against the French in the following years.

Shovel was promoted to admiral of the Blue in 1696 and put in command of the Channel and Biscay fleets until the end of the war (1697). Under King William, he accumulated various offices and sinecures and won a seat in Parliament (1698), which he kept until his death. On the accession of Anne (1702), he was made admiral of the White and sent to Spain, where he joined Sir George Rooke (q.v.) in time to bring back to England the prizes from the battle of Vigo Bay. He served chiefly with Rooke in the Mediterranean for the next two years, fighting at Malaga and Gibraltar and in other actions. At the end of 1704 he was created rear admiral of England, and the next year, admiral of the fleet. He shared command of the joint expedition to Spain in 1705 with the Earl of Peterborough (see Mordaunt, Charles) and took part in the capture of Barcelona in the same year.

In 1707 Shovel commanded the fleet that blockaded Toulon and assisted Prince Eugène and the Duke of Savoy in their unsuccessful attempt to take the city; however, the attack did result in the complete destruction of the French Mediterranean fleet. On the return voyage to England, an error in navigation led the fleet in among the rocks of the Scilly Isles, and three ships, including his flagship *Association*, sank (22 October 1707). According to tradition, the admiral was still alive when he was swept ashore but was buried in the sand by a local woman for the sake of an emerald ring on his finger. His body was recovered and is buried in Westminster Abbey.

J. Campbell, *Naval History of Great Britain* (8 vols.; 1818).

Edward B. Powley, *The Naval Side of King William's War* (1972).

T. H. Cooke, *The Shipwreck of Sir Cloudesley Shovel* (1883).

J. Ehrman, *The Navy in the War of William III, 1689–1697* (1953).

Sidney or Sydney, Algernon (1622–83), politician; executed for treason and supposed implication in the Rye House Plot.

Algernon Sidney was born in 1622, probably at Penshurst Place. He was the second son of Robert Sidney, 2nd Earl of Leicester, and great nephew of Sir Philip Sidney, the Elizabethan soldier-poet (see *Lives of the Tudor Age*).

Between 1641 and 1643 Sidney served in Ireland under his brother, Lord Lisle, fighting the Irish rebels. He was already attached to the constitutional cause, however, and when he returned to England he joined the Parliamentarians. In 1644 he fought as a lieutenant colonel at Marston Moor against Charles I and received very serious injuries. In 1645 he was given command of a cavalry regiment under Oliver Cromwell in Fairfax's army and was made governor of Colchester. In 1646 he entered the House of Commons as member for Cardiff, and the following year returned to Ireland as lieutenant general of the horse, subsequently being appointed governor of Dublin. He was almost immediately superseded, as his appointments gave rise to jealousy, so he returned to England and from 1648 to 1650 was governor of Dover.

In 1648 Sidney was appointed as a commissioner for the trial of Charles I, but he opposed the proceedings and the subsequent 'engagement' as invalid, and refused to take part. He retired to Holland for some months. However, in 1652 he was appointed to the Council of State, but consistently opposed Cromwell after he became Lord Protector (1653), as Cromwell's assumption of power was against Sidney's principles and political persuasions. In 1659, with the restoration of the Rump of the Long Parliament, Sidney was again made a member of the Council of State.

The Restoration of Charles II in 1660 found Sidney on a diplomatic mission to Sweden. He did not return to England straight away, but instead went to Rome, where in spite of a quarrel with his father over money, he spent his time studying. In 1663 he left Rome and took up residence in Brussels, afterwards moving to The Hague. He was closely watched by the English government and his attempts to obtain foreign military employment were thwarted by English intervention. So great was the enmity that he inspired in the English government that an attempt was made on his life at Augsburg. In 1666 Sidney was in France, negotiating with Louis XIV over the possibility of raising a revolt in England. He quarrelled with that monarch, however, and returned to the south of France.

Sidney finally returned to England in 1677. His father was in failing health and died in November of that year. Sidney remained in England and became the focus of liberal aspirations and anti-government plots, although he was unable to find a seat in Parliament. He was himself charged with complicity in a Nonconformist plot, but vindicated himself in a personal interview with Charles II. Throughout 1679 and 1680 Sidney, along with others, is said to have received regular bribes from the French ambassador, Paul Barillon, to assist in bringing about the downfall of Charles II's government. Throughout this period the government appears to have regarded Sidney as a dangerous opponent, but not to have been able to find any convincing evidence against him. Finally, in June 1683, Sidney was implicated, along with Lord William Russell (q.v.) and others, in the Rye House Plot (June) to assassinate the Catholic Duke of York (later James II) and replace him as heir with the Protestant Duke of Monmouth. Sidney was arrested and sent to the Tower, and was tried before Judge Jeffreys on three charges of treason (November). He defended himself ably, but the rules of evidence were weighted against him, the jury was packed, and he was convicted. He was beheaded at Tower Hill on 7 December 1683, and his remains were buried at Penshurst.

Sidney was never very effectual as a politician, but he was seen as a leader of popular opposition to Charles II and his government. In the years leading up to his death, Sidney worked on his *Discourses Concerning Government*, published posthumously in 1698. He was not, strictly speaking, a republican, but advocated a limited monarchy governed by a voluntary civil contract.

Sidney was a friend of the younger Penn (q.v.), and possibly helped to frame the Pennsylvanian constitution: its enlightened clauses, including universal suffrage by ballot, freedom of worship, and the abolition of capital punishment except for the crimes of murder and treason, chime with Sidney's known views.

Alexander C. Ewald, *The Life and Times of the Hon. Algernon Sydney* (2 vols.; 1873).
J. R. Jones, *The First Whigs* (1961).

Portrait: oil, half-length, after J. van Egmont: N.P.G.

Skippon, Philip (d. 1660), professional soldier, Puritan, and Parliamentarian commander; known as 'Daddy Skippon'.

Little is known of his early life. He was born at West Lexham, Norfolk, probably in about 1605. His military career started as a volunteer with Sir Horace Vere in Germany, under the flag of the Elector Palatine. From 1623 he served for thirteen years in Holland against the Spanish.

He returned to England in 1639 after twenty years of soldiering, with the rank of captain and considerable reputation. After Charles's raid on the House of Commons in 1642, Parliament began more active preparations to defend itself and Skippon was appointed major general in command of the drilling of the City trained bands. These bands or militia were the most reliable Parlia-

mentary troops in the early stages of the war. Since it was Skippon's duty to ensure the security of London, he was not involved in the Battle of Edgehill in October 1642, but Skippon and his bands repulsed the southward advance of Charles's victorious army at Turnham Green the following month. In 1643 he was placed in charge of the approach works at the siege of Reading under Essex (see Devereux, Robert), but it was at the inconclusive first Battle of Newbury later the same year that Skippon's trained bands proved their worth, bearing the brunt of some of the heaviest fighting.

Skippon was second in command to Essex during the latter's Cornish campaign of 1644. When Essex surrendered at Lostwithiel in September, Skippon was left in an impossible position. He attempted to hold out for a few days, but eventually, realizing the hopelessness of his position with a tired, dispirited, and hungry army, surrendered too, bearing this adversity calmly and stoically.

He rejoined his own side as part of an exchange of prisoners, and fought bravely at the indecisive but bloody second Battle of Newbury (27 October 1644), recapturing some of the artillery he had lost at Lostwithiel.

In 1645 the New Model Army was created, and the organization and training was left chiefly to Skippon. At the victorious Battle of Naseby (14 June 1645), in which Skippon was in command of the infantry, he suffered a serious injury and for several weeks his condition was critical.

In the following year the New Model Army was in a state of virtual mutiny. Their pay was greatly in arrears and Parliament proposed to enrol volunteers for service in Ireland and disband the rest. Skippon reluctantly accepted the appointment to command an expedition to Ireland, but even his own soldiers were unwilling to serve under Skippon until their grievances were redressed. Representatives from the army urged Skippon to press their case in Parliament, which he now did, and for several months acted as one of the representatives of the Army in its conflicts with Parliament. At the time of the outbreak of the Second Civil War, Skippon was once more in command of the London militia.

Skippon was in 1648 named a judge of Charles I but, like Thomas Fairfax (q.v.), he refused to support Charles's execution. He was, however, created a member of the Council of State, which governed the country after the King's death. As a Member of Parliament for King's Lynn, Skippon rarely played an active political role. He was, however, sufficiently enraged by the blasphemy of one James Naylor, a Quaker who had impersonated Christ, to speak out in the House, declaring, 'If this be liberty, God deliver us from such liberty . . . I was always of opinion the more liberty the greater mischief.'

After the death of Oliver Cromwell in 1658 and during the fall of Richard Cromwell in 1659, Skippon was once again in charge of the London militia. Old age and illness, however, now prevented him from playing any very active role in events. He died in March 1660, shortly before the Restoration.

'Stout Skippon', 'Honest Skippon', and 'Daddy Skippon', as he was known, was both loved and respected as a commander, a loyal and courageous soldier, and a man of conscience. A deeply religious man, he was the author of devotional works for soldiers, with titles such as *A Salve for every Sore* and *The Christian Centurion's Observations, Advices, and Resolutions.*

Maurice Ashley, *Cromwell's Generals* (1954).
C. E. Lucas Phillips, *Cromwell's Captains* (1938).

Portrait: engraving, quarter-length, by unknown artist, 1647: British Museum.

Smith, Captain John (1580–1631), soldier, colonist, explorer, and writer.

Born in Willoughby, Lincolnshire, the son of George Smith, a prosperous farmer, John Smith was educated at a local grammar school, and entered into an apprenticeship that he left in 1596 to become a soldier of fortune. After serving with French and Dutch forces, he returned to England for a short while to study military science, before setting off again in 1600 to begin a series of adventures that probably took him to the Mediterranean, Turkey, and Hungary. He was back in England by 1604 or 1605, and set sail as a planter with the first Virginia colonists, who arrived at Chesapeake Bay in April 1607, where they founded Jamestown. They were extremely ill-prepared for the privations of a life completely cut off from

supplies and civilization. They had no concept of self-sufficiency, nor of how to grow crops for survival on virgin soil. Most of them were adventurers rather than farmers, and they spent much of their time quarrelling. At one point an attempt was made to hang Smith, who in fact did much to save them from themselves. From the outset, Smith had been a member of the colony's council, and he gradually asserted his leadership over his fellow settlers, proving especially effective in such practical matters as organizing expeditions to secure food. On one such journey, in December 1607, he was captured by Indians and his life only saved, according to tradition, by the intervention of the Indian princess Pocahontas.

Smith's account of the colony's first year was sent to England for publication in June 1608. In September he became president of the colony, and under his vigorous guidance the construction of houses and fortifications was pressed ahead and a strong start was given to farming and fishing. Smith took time to explore the region around the settlement and established peaceful relations with the neighbouring Indians.

The arrival of new colonists in August 1609 led to struggles against Smith's authority. Conditions in Jamestown deteriorated: Smith was severely wounded in an accident, and in October he returned to England, where he took up the cause of colonization. In 1612 he published a good map of the Chesapeake Bay area, along with a description of Virginia. Two years later, on a voyage of exploration to New England, he gave this area its name and drew the first competent map of its coast, published in 1616.

On his next trip, in 1616, Smith was captured by the French and forced to serve against the Spanish before being set free. Although he attempted once more to reach North America, he never again succeeded. He wrote a great deal on the colonies and produced a romantic tale of his early life. He died on 21 June 1631.

Philip L. Barbour, *The Three Worlds of Captain John Smith* (Boston, Mass., 1964).
Everett Emerson, *Captain John Smith* (1971).

Somers or Sommers, John (1651–1716), Baron Somers of Evesham; lawyer, politician, and leader of the Whig Junto.

Born on 4 March 1651 near Worcester, Somers was the son of John Somers, a prosperous attorney, landowner, and Parliamentarian officer, who became administrator of the estates of the Earl of Shrewsbury. He was educated in private schools, at Worcester Cathedral School, at Trinity College, Oxford, and at the Middle Temple, where he was admitted to the bar in 1676.

He was exceptionally widely read, especially in the realms of European literature, philosophy, and theology, and was considered an authority on civil and constitutional law. His patron, the Earl of Shrewsbury, introduced him to Lord William Russell, Algernon Sidney (qq.v.), the Earl of Essex, and other leaders of the country opposition. He made his mark in June 1688 when he served as junior counsel in the defence of the 'Seven Bishops' who had defied James II's orders that the Declaration of Indulgence be read in churches. He based his case on precedents that upheld the principle that no statute could be suspended without the consent of Parliament.

After the Glorious Revolution of 1688, Somers was elected to Parliament, where he quickly won influence and position. In 1689 he managed the passage through the Commons of the all-important proposition that James II had vacated the throne by fleeing; hence William and Mary could be given the crown. He also played an important role in formulating the Bill of Rights. Recognition came swiftly in the form of the solicitorship general and a knighthood, and the next year he was appointed attorney general. Politically he was associated with the other leading Whigs, Charles Montagu, Edward Russell, and Thomas Wharton (qq.v.), who with him became known as the Junto.

Somers was active in most important legislation and trials of this period and gradually established a good relationship with William, who trusted him. At the same time he was an active patron of the arts and literature. Soon the older politicians of James's reign lost their power, and Somers emerged as chief minister and leader of the Junto, was appointed lord chancellor in 1697, and became Baron Somers of Evesham. His pleasant manner and reputation for honesty had brought him to the height of his authority when, in 1698, the Tories greatly increased their strength in the Commons. They turned on him, harrying him especially for granting a privateering licence to the notorious pirate, Captain Kidd. At the same time his relations with William began to decline and in 1700 the King asked for his resignation.

Somers now directed his energies to the work of the Royal Society, of which he had been president since 1699. But the attacks on him continued in Parliament, and in 1701 he was impeached, unsuccessfully, for his share in the Partition Treaties of 1698. The King now wished him to build a new ministry, but these plans came to nothing when William died and Anne came to the throne.

Anne disliked the Whigs and they held few offices during her reign. But

Somers and the Junto loyally supported the war policy of Marlborough (see Churchill, John) and Godolphin (q.v.), as well as Union with Scotland. The ministry came to rely increasingly on their support, and as a result Somers was made president of the Council in 1708. He opposed the disastrous impeachment of Dr. Henry Sacheverell (q.v.), which did the government so much harm, but fell from power with his ministerial colleagues in 1710. With increasing age Somers became less active. George I recognized his services by appointing him a privy councillor in 1714. He died in Hertfordshire on 26 April 1716.

Portraits: oil, half-length, by Kneller, *c.* 1700–10: N.P.G.; miniature, by unknown artist, 1690–1700: N.P.G.

Somerset, Earl of (?1585–1645), see Carr, Robert.

Spencer, Charles (1674–1722), 3rd Earl of Sunderland; politician and connoisseur of rare books, see *Lives of the Georgian Age.*

Spencer, Robert (1640–1702), 2nd Earl of Sunderland; statesman, who held high office under Charles II and James II and was a close adviser of William III.

Robert Spencer was born in Paris in the autumn of 1640, the only son of Henry Spencer, 1st Earl of Sunderland, and his wife Dorothy, daughter of Robert Sidney, 2nd Earl of Leicester. He succeeded to his father's titles in 1643, when the latter was killed at the First Battle of Newbury. Sunderland showed great promise as a child. His tutor was the famous Calvinist, Dr. Thomas Pierce, chosen by his mother to ensure that her child would be brought up in the Protestant faith. Sunderland studied languages abroad and spent nearly two years in the south of France.

In 1661 he went up to Christ Church, Oxford, but left before completing his studies.

Sunderland's influential connections ensured that he started his career in a strong position. He was closely related to the Sidneys through his mother and was more distantly related to the Saviles, the Coventrys, and Lord Shaftesbury. In 1665 he married Anne Digby, daughter and heiress of the 3rd Earl of Bristol, and considerably increased his potential influence as well as his future wealth.

Sunderland's earliest political activity involved entertaining the King's mistresses, and he made a useful ally in Louise Renée de Kéroualle (q.v.), later Duchess of Portsmouth. As a result, he was appointed ambassador to Madrid (1671–72) and to Paris (1672–73). In 1674 he became a privy councillor and gentleman of the bedchamber to Charles II.

In 1678 Sunderland was again appointed ambassador extraordinary to Paris, but returned to England in 1679, at the beginning of the Exclusion crisis, being appointed secretary of state. At first Sunderland did not support the proposed exclusion from succession to the throne of the Catholic James, Duke of York (see James II), but soon an inner group began to emerge in the Privy Council; this included Sunderland, Essex, Halifax, Temple, and Sunderland's uncle Henry Sidney, later Earl of Romney. This group supported the claim of William and Mary of Orange to the throne and rejected that of Monmouth. By 1680 Sunderland had become one of Charles's chief ministers, but he decided that it was necessary to sacrifice James, Duke of York, in order to contain the threat of Monmouth and the Whig opposition, and he voted for the Exclusion Bill in November 1680. As a result, he was dismissed from his offices by Charles in 1681.

Sunderland spent the remainder of Charles II's reign trying to regain his former offices and status. In 1682, with the aid of the Duchess of Portsmouth, he was reconciled with the King and the Duke of York and was readmitted to the Privy Council. In the years 1683–88 Sunderland associated himself with the pro-French, pro-Catholic policies of the period and was in the pay of Barillon, the French ambassador. When James II came to the throne, it was generally thought that Sunderland would be ruined, as his past behaviour would hardly recommend him to the new King. However, James rapidly – and pragmatically – recognized Sunderland's ability and usefulness, and in 1685 appointed him lord president and principal secretary of state. With the dismissal of Lawrence Hyde, Earl of Rochester (1687), he was left James's chief minister.

It does now appear that Sunderland did what he could to ameliorate some of James's more extreme policies towards the end of his reign, but there is probably no truth in the widely held belief that he betrayed James to William of Orange. In 1688 Sunderland actually became a Roman Catholic, and on the arrival of William in England he fled abroad. In 1690 he returned to England and renounced Roman Catholicism, and within two years had established himself as one of William's most valued advisers and the principal intermediary between William and his parliamentary leaders.

It was William's belief that he would achieve maximum stability by balancing the two parties, but he allowed himself to be persuaded by Sunderland that much greater stability would be achieved by showing a marked preference to one party, and Sunderland's advice was that William should favour the Whigs.

Sunderland was thus largely responsible for the ascendancy of the Whig Junto, and can be said to have influenced William into encouraging the growth of the two-party system, which began to emerge in his reign.

In 1697 Sunderland accepted the post of lord chamberlain, but his chequered career of changing loyalties had made him so mistrusted and unpopular in the Commons that he felt obliged to resign. William is said to have regarded this as desertion, but Sunderland nevertheless continued to act as his adviser and was consulted in 1700 and 1701 on the formation of new ministries. He died at Althorp, Northamptonshire, on 28 September 1702.

Sunderland was undoubtedly a schemer and intriguer, and eventually became detested by his contemporaries. His political adroitness and practical intelligence is equally evident. Little is known of his personal character, but his love of gambling, particularly at cards, was notorious. He was said to have conducted a great deal of his business over the gaming tables.

Sunderland's only surviving son married Anne Churchill, daughter of the Duke of Marlborough, and his grandson, Charles, 5th Earl of Sunderland, succeeded as the 3rd Duke of Marlborough in 1733, and founded the Spencer-Churchill family.

J. P. Kenyons, *Robert Spencer, Earl of Sunderland* (1958).

Stanhope, James (1675–1721), 1st Earl Stanhope; soldier and Whig statesman, see *Lives of the Georgian Age*.

Stanley, James (1607–51), 7th Earl of Derby, called 'the Martyr Earl'; Royalist commander in the Civil War.

Born at Knowsley, Lancashire, on 31 January 1607, Stanley was the son of

William Stanley, 6th Earl of Derby. The earldom of Derby was an ancient one, having been originally created in the twelfth century. It had come into the Stanley family in 1485.

Much of James Stanley's early life was spent abroad. In 1625 he entered Parliament as the member for Liverpool. Known at this time as Lord Strange, he was elevated to the title of Baron Strange when he took his seat in the Lords in 1628. In 1626 he was made a knight of the Bath and in the same year he married Charlotte de la Trémoille, daughter of the Duke of Thouars and granddaughter of William the Silent, Prince of Orange.

Stanley took no part in the early disputes between Charles I and Parliament. Having been made, with his father, joint lieutenant of Lancashire and Cheshire and chamberlain of Chester, he also co-operated with him in the government of the Isle of Man, whose sovereignty was vested in the Stanley family, and he was subsequently made lord lieutenant of North Wales. He was, apparently, just not interested in life at court. Until 1639 he concerned himself more with country pursuits and looking after his estates than with public affairs. He also showed an artistic bent and gave his patronage to some minor authors and actors.

In 1639 however, Stanley apparently felt it necessary to make his position clear, and in 1639 and 1640 he waited upon the King at York. He did not re-enter Parliament, and in the preliminaries to the Civil War he is supposed to have mustered some 60,000 Royalists in Lancashire and Cheshire. His plan to capture Lancashire for the Royalists at the outset promised to bear some fruit, but Charles was not amenable to it. It has been alleged that the King was jealous of Stanley's lineage. A far more

likely reason, however, was that Lancashire was an inconvenient base from which to attack London; and after failing to get into Hull, the King must have hit upon Nottingham as the most suitable alternative. Stanley therefore joined the mustering of the Royalists at Nottingham in the summer of 1642. But the necessity of holding the north was not totally lost on Charles, and he soon dispatched Stanley thither with the initial task of recovering Manchester. Meanwhile, the Commons impeached Stanley for treason.

By his father's death, on 29 September 1642, Stanley succeeded as 7th Earl of Derby. Throughout the following months he concentrated on trying to win back the advantage lost by his enforced attendance on the King. He failed to capture Manchester and suffered defeats at Chowbent and Lowton Moor. Although he captured Preston and successfully beat off a Parliamentarian assault upon Warrington, his success was devalued by his failure to gain Lancaster and Bolton Castles and he was forced to abandon Warrington after being defeated at Whalley. He was compelled to retire to York, whence he departed in 1643 for the Isle of Man, to secure it for the King.

Summoned back to the mainland in 1644, Derby assisted Prince Rupert (q.v.) in his northern campaigns and was present at the capture of Bolton by the Royalists, the relief of his own besieged property, Lathom House, and finally at the disastrous Battle of Marston Moor. This last catastrophe meant that the Royalist cause in northern England was completely lost. Stanley withdrew again to the Isle of Man, where for over five years he maintained control on behalf of the King, offering refuge to Royalist fugitives. Derby ruled like a despot. He curbed some abuses, especially by the church, and encouraged trade and commerce. But he preserved law and order with iron control, and his treatment of opponents was ruthless. He left an account of his administration in *A Discourse concerning the Government of the Isle of Man*, still in manuscript at his death.

Derby continued his government of Man after the execution of Charles and refused to come to terms with Parliament, scoffing at the conditions offered to him by Ireton in July 1649. In 1650 he became a knight of the Garter and Charles II made him commander of the Royalist forces in Lancashire and Cheshire. He left the Isle of Man and in August 1651 landed at Wyre Water, Lancashire. On 17 August he linked up with the King and his invading force and proceeded to Warrington. Here, a group of Scottish Presbyterians met him. They were in a co-operative mood, but Derby's refusal to accept the Covenant turned their co-operation to hostility and he failed to win their support. His forces were routed by Robert Lilburne at Wigan on 25 August; he himself suffered severe injury, and his escape was only accomplished with difficulty. After the defeat of Charles's army at Worcester (3 September), he accompanied the King to Boscobel and then continued northwards alone. He was captured by Commonwealth forces at Nantwich and was tried by a court martial at Chester on 29 September. A recently passed Act of the Commonwealth Parliament declared communications with the exiled Charles II to be a crime of treason. The quarter earlier granted him was therefore disallowed. He was sentenced to death and his appeal for pardon rejected, despite the support given to it by Cromwell. After an unsuccessful escape attempt, he was executed on 15 October 1651.

Derby's death earned him the name of 'Martyr Earl', and Clarendon described him as 'a man of great humour and clear courage'. He seems also to have been a man of sincere religious beliefs, rigidly opposed to Presbyterianism. Such inflexibility led to his dislike of the Scots and to an inevitable diminution in his value in political negotiations.

In addition to the *Discourse* mentioned above, Derby wrote a number of volumes of historical anthologies, devotions, and observations, and a commonplace book.

F. R. Raines (ed.), *Private Devotions and Miscellanies* (for the Chetham Society, Manchester, 3 vols.; 1867).

F. Peck, *Desiderata Curiosa* (1732; vol. 2 contains Stanley's *Discourse concerning the Government of the Isle of Man*).

Stanley, Thomas (1625–78), poet, translator, and classical scholar.

Stanley was born at Cumberlow, Hertfordshire, only son of Sir Thomas Stanley, a wealthy descendent of the 3rd Earl of Derby, and his second wife Mary, a cousin of Richard Lovelace (q.v.). Stanley's tutor was William Fairfax, son of the translator of Tasso, and he early on introduced the boy to contemporary European poetry. Thomas entered Pembroke Hall, Cambridge, in 1639, but soon left for a protracted Grand Tour of Europe. He returned at the outbreak of the Civil War, but preferred to return to lodgings in the Middle Temple, and soon after married Dorothy, daughter of the wealthy Sir James Enyon.

Stanley now began to cultivate literary society, especially Lovelace and Edward Phillips, and he used his considerable fortune to help such struggling writers as James Shirley (q.v.), the dramatist. He published a collection of his own amatory poems in 1647; praised as 'smooth and genteel' by Anthony à Wood, they show an unexpected toughness underneath the conventional Cavalier trappings of appeals to an imaginary Doris or Celia. The book also includes graceful 'Englishings' of Tasso, Petrarch, and Lope de Vega, which were followed in 1651 by a volume of translations of Bion, Moschus, and others, as well as of a prose novel by Montalvan. The fluency of Stanley's poems was such that several of them were set to music by Henry Lawes (q.v.).

Probably at the suggestion of his uncle, Sir John Marsham the historian, Stanley now took up a more solemn task, the compiling of a monumental four-volume *History of Philosophy* (1655–62). It consists of reliable biographies, drawn from many sources, of the prominent Greek thinkers, together with careful accounts of the Platonic, Aristotelian, and Stoic doctrines. Although more descriptive than analytical, Stanley's *History* was nevertheless a pioneer attempt at popularization and had been published all over Europe by 1690. Stanley's critical scholarship is most evident in his edition of Aeschylus, published in 1663. This was again an international success, running through many editions, and was not effectively superseded until the early nineteenth century.

Thomas Stanley died in London on 12 April 1678, and was buried in St. Martin-in-the-Fields. His genuine and versatile literary talent, together with his attractive personality, moved Winstanley to describe him as 'the glory and admiration of his time', a worthy representative of the accomplished Caroline gentleman.

L. I. Guiney, *Thomas Stanley* (1907).

Portrait: oil, half-length, by G. Soest, *c.* 1660: N.P.G.

Steele, Richard (1672–1729), essayist, dramatist, and politician, see *Lives of the Georgian Age.*

Stone, Nicholas (?1587–1647), sculptor and architect.

Born at Woodbury, Devon, son of a quarryman. In about 1604 Stone became an apprentice in the Southwark workshop of Isaac James, a Flemish refugee, where he was trained in the conservative and stolid Anglo-Flemish sculptural style. In 1606 Hendrik de Keyser, city architect of Amsterdam, during a visit to James, noticed the talented Stone and took him back to Holland as a journeyman. Stone may perhaps have contributed figures to de Keyser's greatest work, the tomb of William the Silent; certainly, the slightly confused version of French Mannerist sculpture that Stone learnt in Amsterdam profoundly affected his style thereafter. There is a tradition that as a reward for designing a portico for Amsterdam's Westerkerk, Stone not only received the hand of de Keyser's daughter but also a share in his quarry at Portland.

Whatever the truth of this, Stone was back in London by 1613, running his own workshop at Long Acre. His earliest commissions were in collaboration with Isaac James and other sculptors, but by 1615 he was working alone on such monuments as the one to Thomas Bodley at Merton College, Oxford; this exhibits a rather discordant eclecticism, with elongated allegorical figures, derived from the Fontainebleau school, enclosed by heavy pilasters typical of Flemish work. By 1617, however, Stone had developed the individual style seen in Lady Carey's tomb at Stow-Nine-Churches, Northamptonshire. The standard Jacobean monument is here transformed by a new naturalism. The recumbent figure, formerly usually represented as lying rigid with hands in prayer, now sleeps in a relaxed curve, the texture of the embroidered costume is finely reproduced, and contrasting coloured marbles increase the dramatic effect.

Stone soon built up a large and successful tomb-making practice, working usually within the traditional types dictated by his clients but giving his figures a novel and increasing fluency. In 1619 he was made master mason at the Banqueting House and so came into close contact with Inigo Jones's Italianate style. This produced no immediate radical change; although the seated figure of Francis Holles in Roman costume on his Westminster Abbey monument (1622) is derived from Michelangelo's Medici tomb, the slight awkwardness of the pose suggests that Stone gained his knowledge of the original at second hand. Nevertheless, it set a precedent for the future use of isolated seated or standing figures on tombs.

In 1628–29 Stone worked for Charles I at St. James's Palace, and in 1632 he was appointed master mason to the crown. As a result, he would undoubtedly have studied the large collection of classical statuary which the King had lately bought from the Duke of Mantua. Stone's eventual assimilation of the antique style is shown in his Lyttelton monument (1634) at Magdalen College chapel, Oxford; the modelling of the nude is fluid and delicate, and the architectural framework is austerely well-proportioned in an Italian rather than Flemish manner.

Of Stone's various small architectural commissions, the two most outstanding are at Oxford: the gateway to the Botanic Garden, impeccably in the Palladian manner, and the porch of St. Mary the Virgin, perhaps the most florid example of the baroque in England.

As Stone's practice grew, so the quality of his tombs declined, since the majority of the carving came to be done by assistants. The outbreak of the Civil War adversely affected Stone's livelihood, and he died at Long Acre on 24 August 1647. His talent was eclectic rather than original, and perhaps his main achievement was to instil an awareness of European sculptural practice into the insular English tradition.

W. L. Spiers (ed.), *The Note-Book and Account Book of Nicholas Stone* (1918).
See also M. D. Whinney, *Sculpture in Britain, 1530–1830* (1964).

Strafford, 1st Earl of (1593–1641), see Wentworth, Thomas.

Strode, William (?1599–1645), politician actively involved in the Parliamentary opposition to Charles I; one of the five members of the House of Commons whom Charles tried to arrest in 1642.

He was born about 1599, son of Sir William Strode of Newnham, Devonshire. In 1614 Strode entered the Inner Temple, after which he went to Exeter College, Oxford, graduating with the degree of B.A. in 1619.

In 1624 Strode entered Parliament and sat for Bere Alston, Devonshire, a seat which he held for the rest of his life. An assiduous and enthusiastic opponent of Charles I from the very beginning, he was, on 2 March 1629, a major figure in the disturbances that marked the dissolution of Charles's fourth parliament, during which the speaker of the House of Commons was held down in his seat while resolutions attacking the King's arbitrary taxation and religious policy were passed (see Eliot, Sir John). For his part in this, Strode was arrested and imprisoned during the King's pleasure.

Strode's imprisonment, in the Tower and elsewhere, lasted until 1640, when Charles, having come to the end of his personal government, hoped to win support for his campaign against the Scots by a demonstration of magnanimity and released Strode. The latter, however, was racked with bitterness at his past treatment and remained one of Charles's most implacable enemies. In Parliament again, he rose to an undeserved pre-eminence among the members of the opposition group. He advocated parliamentary control of ministerial appointments and the militia and he called for annual parliaments. He was particularly vicious in the prosecution of Strafford, seeking to have his defence counsellors arraigned with him on the same treason charge. In November of the same year (1641) he supported the Grand Remonstrance, and Charles moved against him along with Pym, Hampden, Hesilrige, Holles, and Lord Mandeville in January 1642. When Charles came to arrest the five members of the Lower House, Strode was with difficulty removed to safety.

With this fuel added to the fire of his hostility, Strode opposed all schemes for reconciliation or compromise with the King, and on 23 October 1642, he fought in the first battle of the conflict, at Edgehill. Strode's last major act was to take from the Commons to the Lords a message desiring that proceedings be expedited against Archbishop Laud (q.v.). Strode welcomed Laud's execution but did not long survive him. He died at Tottenham on 9 September 1645, and was buried in accordance with a Parliamentary order at Westminster Abbey. In 1661, after the Restoration, his body was exhumed and buried elsewhere.

Stuart, Arabella (1575–1615), claimant to the English throne, see *Lives of the Tudor Age*.

Stuart, James Francis Edward (1688–1766), 'The Old Pretender', see James Francis Edward Stuart in *Lives of the Georgian Age*.

Suckling, Sir John (1609–42), poet and dramatist.

Suckling was born at Whitton, near Twickenham, Middlesex, a descendant of an ancient Norfolk family. He was educated at Westminster (according to Aubrey) and at Trinity College, Cambridge, where he matriculated as a fellow-commoner in 1623. He then went to Gray's Inn from 1626 to 1627.

His father's death made him an heir to a considerable fortune and this and his family connections served as an introduction to life at court. Aubrey describes him thus: 'He was the greatest gallant of his time, the greatest gamester both of bowling and of cards.' He did, in fact, invent the game cribbage.

In 1628 he travelled abroad and on his return in 1630 he was knighted. He then went abroad again and fought under Gustavus Adolphus. On his return in 1632 he resumed his life at court, where he proved to be a great success – 'he was incomparably ready at reparteeing, and his wit most sparkling.'

He wrote his first play, *Aglaura*, in 1637 and produced it lavishly at his own expense. The King, however, disliked the unhappy ending, so Suckling provided an alternative last act and called it tragicomedy.

He fought for the King in the First Bishops' War of 1639 with his own personal troop of followers. In the Second Bishops' War (1640) he fought as a captain of carbineers. During that winter he wrote his letter of counsel to the King, in which he advised the monarch to give up his passive attitude and 'do something extraordinary' – namely, grant all the popular demands and gain the love of the people.

Suckling was involved in an army plot to liberate Strafford (see Wentworth, Thomas) from the Tower. The plot was discovered, but Suckling had already fled to the Continent. He died in 1642, according to Aubrey by poisoning himself.

Only a small fraction of his work appeared during his lifetime. The rest was published four years after his death. The best of his works appeared in *Fragmenta Aurea* (1646), consisting of poems, plays, letters, and tracts.

His art perfectly matches the life of an exemplary Cavalier. 'Natural, easy Suckling', in Congreve's phrase, was extremely popular during the Restoration and Augustan eras and is now held to be a fine minor poet. His appeal throughout the Augustan age lay in his mixture of mannered grace shot through with an impertinent wit. His short bright poems are constantly quoted in Restoration plays with the same casual ease with which he claimed to have written them – at the same time mocking Carew (q.v.) for trying too hard.

Suckling frequently echoes Donne in his technique, but the desperate anger, intellectualism, and universality of Donne's mood is replaced by one of genial irony. Suckling was, fashionably, a proponent of the French style (he was a close friend of Davenant, the leading importer of French taste) and wrote for a court audience and its 'precious' taste.

Suckling's plays are much more exalted than the poems – much of the dialogue consists of elaborate debate. One of his main influences seems to have been Shakespeare, from whom he quoted extensively and without acknowledg-

ment. The best of the plays, *The Goblins* (1638), gives rise to sharp social and literary criticism and lively dialogue, although the action is extremely complex. *The Tragedy of Brennoralt* (an expanded version of *The Discontented Colonel*, 1639) was less successful, although the protagonist gives an interesting insight into Suckling's own character.

The main value of the plays lies in their lyrics, which were set pieces, the most famous of which is 'Why so pale and wan, fond lover?' from his first play, *Aglaura*.

H. Berry (ed.), *Suckling's Poems and Letters from Manuscript* (London and Ontario, 1960).

T. Clayton and L. A. Beaurline (eds.), *The Works of Sir John Suckling* (2 vols.; 1971).

A. Hamilton Thompson (ed.), *The Works of Sir John Suckling* (New York, 1910: reissued 1964).

Thomas Clayton, 'Sir John Suckling and the Cranfields', *Times Literary Supplement* (29 January 1960).

Portrait: oil on panel, quarter-length, after Van Dyck, *c.* 1640: N.P.G.

Sunderland, 2nd Earl of (1640–1702), see Spencer, Robert.

Sunderland, 3rd Earl of (1674–1722), politician and connoisseur of rare books, see Spencer, Charles, in *Lives of the Georgian Age*.

Swift, Jonathan (1667–1745), writer and cleric, see *Lives of the Georgian Age*.

Sydenham, Thomas (1624–89), English physician, known as 'the Father of English Medicine' and 'the English Hippocrates'.

Born at Wynford Eagle, Dorsetshire, on 10 September 1624, Sydenham was educated at Magdalen College, Oxford. He entered Magdalen College in 1642, but his course of study was temporarily interrupted by service in the Parliamentary forces, in which his brother William was a colonel; he became a captain of horse. With the surrender of Oxford he returned to his studies and obtained an M.B. degree in 1648. At some time during the period between his subsequent medical practice in Oxford and his removal to London, Sydenham undertook postgraduate studies at Montpellier, apparently for the purpose of attending the lectures of the celebrated French physician Charles Barbeyrac. In 1663 he was admitted a licentiate – although never a fellow – of the Royal College of Physicians.

He appears to have been little favoured by the courts of Charles II and James II; nevertheless, in a relatively short time he rose to the top of his profession and enjoyed an extensive medical practice. If not befriended by royalty, Sydenham was known and admired by some of the leading intellectuals of his day, including John Locke and Robert Boyle.

Sydenham's contributions to the science of medicine were many. He stressed, for example, that the symptoms of disease were complex phenomena that must be closely studied and understood before treatment could be prescribed. He was one of the first modern medical practitioners to profess that the body has its own powerful means of dealing with disease, and that 'the recuperative energy which belongs to every organized being ought not to be interfered with.' Sydenham insisted that the physician should assist nature in the healing process, not interfere with it by prescribing 'quack' cures. It is thus not difficult, in light of the known medical practice of the day, to see why many of his professional colleagues viewed him with a degree of suspicion.

Among his various writings, the most significant dealt with the treatment of smallpox, venereal disease, hysteria, gout, fevers, and chorea. He gave classic descriptions of other diseases as well, including scarlet fever (which he named), and was the first English physician to introduce the medicinal use of cinchona bark.

Sydenham died in London on 22 December 1689.

J. D. Comrie (ed.), *Selected Works of Thomas Sydenham, with Short Biography and Explanatory Notes* (1922).
K. Dewhurst, *Dr. Thomas Sydenham* (1966).
J. F. Payne, *Thomas Sydenham* (1900).

Portrait: oil, half-length, by Mary Beale, 1688: N.P.G.

Sydney, Algernon (1622–83), see Sidney, Algernon.

T

Talbot, Richard (1630–91), Earl of Tyrconnel; Irish politician and soldier; supporter of James II.

Richard Talbot was the eighth son of an Irish baronet. At the age of seventeen he was present at the defence of Drogheda (3 September 1647) against Cromwell, where he was wounded and left for dead. He was saved by a friend and escaped dressed as a woman. After the Royalist cause was lost in Ireland Talbot fled to Spain and later joined his brother in Flanders, making a living partly as a casual mercenary. It was in Flanders, in around 1653, that he met the Duke of York (later James II). Clarendon (see Hyde, Edward) writes that Talbot was recommended to him as someone very willing to assassinate Cromwell.

In 1655 Talbot went to England to further the Royalist cause and in November was arrested and was examined by Cromwell himself. He escaped by making his guards drunk. Clarendon thought this escape surprisingly easy and suggests that Talbot may have been in Cromwell's pay. This is not substantiated, however, and did not apparently harm his career. Despite some opposition, he was now given command of the Duke of York's regiment, and at the Restoration he returned to England and was made a gentleman of the Duke's bedchamber. He had a reputation for being blustering and quarrelsome and was very fond of duelling. He twice brushed with Ormonde (see Butler, James, 1st Duke) over Irish affairs and was imprisoned (1661 and 1670). He was also imprisoned for a short time in 1678

for supposed involvement in the Popish Plot, as a result of which his health suffered, but was soon released and allowed to go abroad, where he remained until 1685.

Talbot was a devout Roman Catholic and a nationalistic Irishman and when James came to the throne in 1685, he welcomed the opportunity to further both causes. He had long been an outspoken critic of such measures as the Acts of Settlement, under which Irish Roman Catholics suffered, and now confidently expected some redress under James's rule. Shortly before Charles II's death, Talbot had supposedly boasted the Catholics would soon be in power and would pay off old scores. He had shown himself very loyal to James – probably even helping him procure mistresses – and James now created him Earl of Tyrconnel and gave him command of the army in Ireland. Tyrconnel immediately began military reorganization. The Protestant militia was disbanded and private arms were seized from Protestant householders. Tyrconnel soon made it clear that he planned to neutralize the Act of Settlement and to Catholicize the army and administration in Ireland.

When Henry Hyde, 2nd Earl of Clarendon, was sent to Ireland as viceroy in about 1685, he soon found his position undermined by Tyrconnel, who had the confidence of the King. Changes in the army and judiciary were made without Clarendon's approval, and the Oath of Supremacy in corporations was dispensed with, enabling Catholics to take office. Whole battalions of Protestant soldiers were discharged, and many regiments were instructed to admit none but Roman Catholics. At the end of August 1686 Tyrconnel returned to England, and in October was made a privy councillor. In January he was appointed lord deputy of Ireland without Clarendon's knowledge. Tyrconnel was given almost unlimited discretion, but was especially required to admit Catholics to all corporations and other offices. He now proceeded to pack Irish courts and town corporations with Roman Catholics, and many Protestants left Ireland.

Shortly before James fled to France in 1688 Tyrconnel began to raise a new army. These new troops were often unpaid, and when they took to plundering Tyrconnel began to meet resistance from such towns as Londonderry. In 1689 James landed in Ireland. Tyrconnel carried the sword of state before the King when he entered Dublin and helped to formulate the measures approved by James for his Dublin parliament, including the repeal of the Act of Settlement. Tyrconnel's health was failing during this time, but he continued to organize James's army, although he appears to have thwarted the efforts of his more competent second-in-command, the Earl of Lucan (see Sarsfield, Patrick). After a defeat by the English army in the spring of 1690, Tyrconnel was entrusted with the defence of the passes over the River Boyne. During the Battle of the Boyne in July he was, according to a report of some French officers, lethargic and indecisive through illness, although other accounts declare that he fought bravely. After the retreat from the battle, Tyrconnel advised James to return to France, which he speedily did.

Soon afterwards there was a move among other Irish leaders to remove Tyrconnel from command, but on a visit to France in September he succeeded in retaining the confidence of James and Louis XIV. He returned to Ireland in 1691 as lord lieutenant and commander-in-chief of the army, with arms and money from Louis XIV. After being again defeated at the Battle of Aughrim (12 July), he died suddenly of apoplexy on 14 August 1691.

Sir Charles Petrie, *The Great Tyrconnel* (1972).
P. W. Sergeant, *Little Jennings and Fighting Dick Talbot, a Life of the Duke and Duchess of Tyrconnel* (2 vols.; 1913).

Portrait: oil, three-quarter length, French school, 1690: N.P.G.

Tate, Nahum (1652–1715), poet and dramatist.

Born in Dublin, Tate was the son of Faithful Teate, an Anglo-Irish clergyman. Educated at Trinity College, Dublin (1668–72), in 1677 his first volume of poems was published in London, where he took up residence. The next year saw the appearance of his *Brutus of Alba; or the Enchanted Lovers*, and soon his works began to receive frequent performances. Even more successful were his adaptations of Shakespeare, especially of *King Lear*, which was the usual form in which this play was staged until 1840. In it Tate omits the Fool and allows Cordelia to survive and happily marry Edgar.

Thus it is not surprising that Tate should also have been a staunch warrior in the fight to reform the morals of the theatre – especially as his own contributions to the dramatic arts are distinguished by a mediocrity that finds its climax in *Cuckold's Haven* (1685) and *Island Princess* (1687).

Of a higher quality is the second part of *Absalom and Achitophel*, which Tate composed, possibly with Dryden's assistance, in 1682. Around 1689 he contributed to the libretto of *Dido and Aeneas*. At any rate he was thought to merit high rewards, and in 1692 succeeded Shadwell (q.v.) as poet laureate; he is deemed a strong contender for the rank of 'lowest of the laureates'.

Tate's best poem is considered to be *Panacea: a Poem on Tea*, which he wrote in 1700. But his fame rests on his translations and religious poetry, including a metrical version of the psalms that he published with Nicholas Brady in 1696; it eventually came into universal use. The carol 'While shepherds watched' possibly ranks as one of his works as well.

Tate died on 30 July 1715. Legend has it that he was hiding from his creditors in the mint at Southwark.

Christopher Spencer, *Nahum Tate* (New York, 1972).

Taylor, Brooke (1685–1731), mathematician, physicist, and artist.

Born in Edmonton, London, Taylor graduated as LL.B. from St. John's College, Cambridge, in 1709 and was granted an LL.D. in 1714. Taylor is remembered principally as a mathematician who wrote many papers on pure and applied mathematics. In 1708 he obtained the solution to the problem of the centre of oscillation, although he did not publish this work until 1714. The invention of calculus in the late sixteenth century had produced an outburst of papers describing developments of the subject. Taylor's work, *Methodus Incrementorum directa et inversa*, published in 1715, was the first treatise on the calculus of finite differences. He demonstrated that this treatment could be applied to a variety of problems in physics, such as the pattern of movement of a vibrating string. Taylor's main contribution to

mathematics was the theorem (Taylor's theorem) discussed in this publication. This states how a general mathematical function can be expressed approximately as a power series (Taylor's series), the terms of the series containing derivatives of the function. It took almost sixty years for the theorem to be recognized as a basic principle in differential calculus, many important equations being derived from the series.

In 1712, at the age of twenty-seven, Taylor was elected F.R.S., becoming secretary to the Society in 1714. He wrote several papers that were published in *Philosophical Transactions of the Royal Society* on dynamics, hydrodynamics, heat, and magnetism. As a Fellow of the Society, he strongly defended Newton (q.v.) in the bitter dispute, lasting twenty years, between Newton and Leibnitz as to the originator of calculus.

Taylor was not only a brilliant mathematician, but also a gifted musician and artist. He applied his mathematical mind to the study of perspective and to art in general. *Linear Perspective*, published in 1715, was followed by *New Principles of Linear Perspective* in 1719, which considered the subject of vanishing points. He now became interested in religion and wrote several works in this field, such as *On the Lawfulness of Eating Blood*.

He married twice; both his wives died in childbirth after only a few years of marriage. After the second of these tragedies, Taylor himself fell into a deep depression and, his health never having been strong, he died a year later, on 29 December 1731.

Portrait: miniature, by J. or L. Goupy: N.P.G.

Taylor, Edward (1642–1729), American poet and clergyman.

Taylor was born in England, and is

considered the most important American poet before the nineteenth century. He moved to Massachusetts in 1668, and shortly thereafter entered Harvard. After studying theology he became a clergyman and in 1671 obtained a post as minister in Westfield, Massachusetts – then a frontier town.

His religious duties did not seriously affect his metaphysical sensitivities, although he was definitely categorized as ultraconservative in his theological beliefs, not an uncommon position for his time.

His experiments in poetry followed long after he had started publishing his written work – in the form of pamphlets attacking liberal ideas. It was not until the age of forty, in 1682, that Taylor began to write his series of six-line stanzas, published as a collection of 217 poems under the title *Preparatory Meditations*. About three years later, he began to write his major poem, *God's Determinations Touching His Elect*.

Taylor died in 1729, leaving several manuscripts of sermons and his *Metrical History of Christianity* unpublished. Only about two of Taylor's poems were published in his lifetime. In addition, he left instructions that his other poetry should not be published. The reason for this is fairly clear, for some of his poems were not entirely orthodox and his parishioners might have been shocked to know that a mild degree of sensuousness could flow from the pen of their spiritual leader.

T. H. Johnson (ed.), *Poetical Works* (New York, 1939).

Donald E. Stanford (ed.), *Poems* (New Haven, Conn., 1960).

Norman S. Grabe, *Edward Taylor* (New York, 1962).

Donald E. Stanford, *Edward Taylor* (Minneapolis, Minnesota, 1965).

Taylor, Jeremy (1613–67), Bishop of Down and Connor; preacher and devotional writer.

Born in Cambridge and baptized on 15 August 1613, Taylor was the third son of Nathaniel Taylor, a barber and local churchwarden. After a thorough grounding 'in grammar and mathematics' from his father, Taylor attended the newly opened Perse grammar school in Cambridge. On 18 August 1626, he was admitted to Gonville and Caius College, where he swiftly distinguished himself: he graduated B.A. in 1630, was elected a fellow in 1633, took holy orders soon after, and proceeded to his M.A. in 1634.

A college friend secured Taylor a position as part-time preacher ('lecturer') at St. Paul's Cathedral, where his spirited defence of episcopacy won the approval of Archbishop Laud (q.v.). Laud resolved to send Taylor to Oxford, where the orthodox in religion could breathe more easily; accordingly, despite the warden's objection that Taylor was already a Cambridge fellow, the young preacher was elected a fellow of All Souls on 14 January 1636. The archbishop's favour did not stop here: by 1638 he had arranged that Taylor, not yet twenty-five, become not only his own private chaplain but also Charles I's. At Oxford Taylor was considered a bookish and somewhat sardonic man but a persuasive preacher. His first published work, the Gunpowder Plot sermon of 1638, is primarily an attempt to deny charges that he had leanings towards Rome, but it also asserts the impeccably Establishment view that all recusancy is treasonable.

On 23 March 1638, Taylor became rector of Uppingham in Rutland, where he seems to have taken his parish duties seriously. In May 1639 he married Phoebe Langsdale, a gentlewoman, but their peace was soon broken by the onset of the Civil War. By 1642 Taylor had abandoned his parish and may have been back in Oxford, fulfilling his duties as chaplain to the King. The living of Uppingham was sequestered by Parliament in 1644 and Taylor probably now became an army chaplain, since he was captured in a skirmish at Cardigan Castle in February 1645 and briefly imprisoned.

In late 1645 Taylor found refuge again, as chaplain to Richard Vaughan, 2nd Earl of Carbery, and took his family to live at Golden Grove, the earl's beautiful country house in Carmarthenshire. The ensuing decade of peace in the Welsh countryside inspired Taylor's greatest devotional works. *The Liberty of Prophesying* of 1647 is a heartfelt plea for toleration, 'a latitude of Theologie' in the face of the 'common calamity' of civil war. Taylor asserts that most sectarian differences have arisen from mere theologians' quibbles, and that in fact everyone is basically agreed on the fundamentals of the Christian faith; all that is presently lacking is humility. However, Taylor's ecumenicalism is more apparent than real; he is careful to add that the 'governors of the church' are quite justified in setting reasonable limits to individual freedom, for the sake of 'the public good'. He was after all in a difficult position; a High Anglican trying to be 'liberal' without actually making a case for Presbyterianism.

In his next book, *Holy Living* (1650), Taylor wrote a primer of personal conduct for the good Christian. Sober and comprehensive, it deals with such topics as daily prayers, social duties, and charitable works.

Taylor's reputation as a prose-writer rests chiefly on his *Holy Dying* of 1651. Though not endowed with a particularly profound intellect nor even passionate emotions, he is unsurpassed in dealing with the great commonplaces. In this work he drew not only on the medieval Christian *de contemptu mundi* tradition, but also on such classical moralists as Seneca, Plutarch, and Cicero. His prose is simple and fluent; his imagery is homelier than Donne's. Considering the discomforts of earthly life, he says:

> Here is no place to sit down in, but you must rise as soon as you are set, for we have gnats in our chambers, and worms in our gardens, and spiders and flies in the palaces of the greatest kings.

In 1655 Taylor spent six months in jail for an unspecified offence, and shortly after his release his two young sons died. He then spent a year in London, where he became acquainted with John Evelyn (q.v.), but in 1658 he accepted his friend Lord Conway's gift of a chaplaincy at Lisburn in northern Ireland. This was staunch Presbyterian country and Taylor was soon in trouble locally for his High Church practices. Nevertheless, at the Restoration he was elected Bishop of Down and Connor, an Irish diocese overrun with Nonconformists as well as Catholics; since *The Liberty of Prophesying* Taylor had perhaps been considered doctrinally 'unsafe' for an English see. He sincerely believed that Presbyterians were 'criminally disobedient' and that common sense should lead them towards Anglicanism, which was the only way to 'understand and live'. He was less than courteous to the local Presbyterian ministers, calling them 'anabaptists' and 'Scotch spiders' and refusing to recognize their authority. His obduracy merely succeeded in welding the northern Irish Presbyterians into a coherent and separate political body once and for all.

Continuous strife soon drove Taylor to request another, quieter diocese, but his pleas went unanswered, and on 13 August 1667 he died, worn out, at Lisburn, and was buried in the cathedral that he had built at Dromore.

Bishop Reginald Heber (ed.), *The Whole Works of . . . Jeremy Taylor, with a Life of the Author and a Critical Examination of his Writings* (15 vols.; 1822: rev. ed. by C. P. Eden, 10 vols.; 1847–54: reissued 1968).

L. P. Smith (ed.), *The Golden Grove: Selected Passages of . . . Jeremy Taylor* (1930).

W. J. Brown, *Jeremy Taylor* (1925).

C. J. Stranks, *The Life and Writings of Jeremy Taylor* (1952).

Taylor, John (1580–1653), self-styled 'The Water Poet', eccentric writer and traveller and author of Royalist pamphlets during the Civil War.

Born at Gloucester, 24 August 1580, John Taylor came of humble stock. He attended Gloucester Grammar School, but was, to quote his own words, so 'mired in Latin accidence' that he left off his formal education to become apprenticed to a waterman in London. A victim of the press gang, he served abroad with the navy and saw action at Cadiz in 1596 and Flores in 1597. Upon his return to London, he took up his trade as a Thames waterman, becoming active in the Waterman's Company. For some years, he held a semi-official post as a collector of the perquisites of wine exacted by the lieutenant of the Tower of London.

At the outset of the second decade of the seventeenth century the waterman's trade was somewhat depressed. Theatres had been closed or knocked down along the Surrey side of the Thames and an excessively large number of men were involved in ferrying too few customers. Taylor, like many of his fellows, therefore suffered from diminution in his earnings, and to supplement his income he took to dashing off doggerel verse. He had a coarse ready wit, which manifested itself in lampoons and racy pamphlets. A particular target was the traveller and writer, Thomas Coryate, one of whose works, *The Odcombian Banquet*, was bitingly parodied in Taylor's *Laugh and Be Fat* (about 1613). Coryate was very offended, and succeeded in getting the authorities to have Taylor's parody burnt. Taylor himself was furious, and he kept up his satires against Coryate until 1620. His other literary efforts – though they hardly rank as literature – included an elegy on the death of Prince Henry in 1612 and a celebratory poem on the marriage of Elizabeth to Frederick V in 1613. For this event, he also organized a splendid water pageant.

To draw attention to himself, Taylor hit upon the idea of undertaking a series of eccentric trips and writing short accounts of them to be sold to those who would take out advance subscriptions. The plan may have suggested itself after a journey on the Continent that he made in 1616. The book that resulted was virtually a travesty of Coryate's *Crudities*, an account of travels on foot made by that writer through France, Italy, and other countries in 1608.

Taylor's first notable exploit was a journey on foot to Scotland, undertaken without any money in his pocket and with a prohibition on begging or borrowing either food or coin. The account of it, entitled *The Penniless Pilgrimage . . . of John Taylor . . . on Foot from London to Edinburgh*, appeared shortly after the trip in 1618. Taylor actually went as far as Braemar, and on his way home he met Ben Jonson at Leith, who had undertaken a similar journey to Scotland. Whether or not he believed that Taylor's own effort was not a burlesque aimed at him, Jonson nevertheless was good-natured enough to give him twenty-two shillings to drink his health in England.

This and subsequent journeys made Taylor popular, and he continued to entertain the public for some time. In 1619 he set out with an equally softheaded friend to travel down the river from London to Queenborough in Kent. His means of conveyance was a boat made of brown paper and propelled by two canes with stockfish tied to the ends. After three miles the bottom fell apart and Taylor and his companion almost drowned, but they continued the journey, reaching Queenborough two days later, 'more dead than alive.'

In 1620, in accordance with a bet, Taylor went to Prague, where Elizabeth (q.v.), now Queen of Bohemia, entertained him and gave him one of her baby son's shoes as a memento. In 1622 there appeared *A Very, Merry Wherry-Ferry-Voyage, or York for my Money*, which was an account of how, under the terms of another bet, he travelled with four friends to York by sea. On the way, bad weather forced their wherry to put in at Cromer in Norfolk, where they were arrested on suspicion of being pirates.

Plague broke out virulently in London in 1625 and Taylor withdrew to Oxford for a time. In 1630 he published a collected edition of his entire output, *All the Works of John Taylor, the Water Poet, being 63 in Number* (reprinted by the Spenser Society, 1868–69). The original folio was an immense work and had to be set up on four different presses.

In 1642, at the outbreak of the Civil War, Taylor retired to Oxford again and kept a public house. He wrote a number of tracts and became one of the Royalists' most effective propagandists. His works were the usual hard-hitting

racy lampoons for which he had become famous; turned to political use, his style was devastatingly brutal.

In June 1646 Oxford finally surrendered, and Taylor was allowed to return to London, to the management of another public house, The Crown in Phoenix Alley, off Long Acre, near St. Martin-in-the-Fields. When Charles I was executed, Taylor changed the name of the establishment to The Mourning Crown, thereby giving offence to the authorities. He then substituted his own portrait for the other inn sign and called the place The Poet's Head. The new sign carried the following inscription:

There's many a head stands for a sign,
Then, gentle reader, why not mine?

Taylor kept the establishment for over seven years, until his death. One of the most colourful characters of the seventeenth century, he was buried in the churchyard of St. Martin-in-the-Fields on 5 December 1653.

C. Hindley (ed.), *Works of John Taylor, a Selection* (1872).

C. Hindley (ed.), *Miscellanea Antiqua Anglicana*, vols. ii and iii (1873).

The Spenser Society, *All the Works of John Taylor, the Water-Poet . . . 1630* (3 parts; 1868–69).

The Spenser Society, *Works of John Taylor . . . not included in the folio volume of 1630* (5 parts; 1870–78).

Temple, Sir William (1628–99), statesman, diplomat, and writer.

Born on 25 April 1628, in Blackfriars, the eldest son of Sir John Temple, master of the rolls in Ireland, Temple was educated at Bishop's Stortford school and Emmanuel College, Cambridge (1644–46).

He spent the better part of the Interregnum travelling on the Continent. At the Restoration he sat in the Irish Convention Parliament, and had the good fortune to be introduced at court by the Duke of Ormonde (see Butler, James, 1st Duke), who later used his influence with Henry Bennet (q.v.) to obtain a diplomatic post for Temple. He was sent in 1665 to the Bishop of Munster, England's ally against the Dutch. It was Temple's job to spur the bishop on to more aggressive acts, using promised subsidies as bait and leverage. But the bishop proved too crafty for the fledgeling diplomat and succeeded in avoiding costly military activities.

That same year Temple was posted as English envoy in Brussels and made a baronet. He gained experience at the peace negotiations of Breda (1667) and journeyed to the Netherlands, where he struck up a warm friendship with the grand pensionary, John de Witt. From this basis he played the major role in bringing about the Triple Alliance (1668) of England, the Netherlands, and Sweden, a pact designed to protect the Spanish Netherlands from French designs. With the formation of this alliance Temple won recognition as one of the most honest and skilled diplomats of his age.

However, the treaty was signed against the secret pro-French inclinations of Charles II, who proceeded to establish a secret understanding with Louis XIV. At the same time Temple was appointed ambassador to The Hague, where his well-known friendship for Holland could serve to cloak his sovereign's designs. In spite of the respect in which he was held in Holland, however, Temple's position became untenable as Charles's plans developed. He was summoned to England and, when he discovered how the situation stood in the Council, he withdrew into private life.

While an active diplomat Temple had begun writing, preparing in 1667 a study on Ireland. Now he wrote, in a graceful, fluid style on the origin and nature of government and on the Netherlands.

In 1674 Temple was recalled to help negotiate a peace with the Dutch. He was offered various high posts, including the secretaryship of state, but chose once again to serve as ambassador to The Hague. He strengthened his position by establishing good relations with Danby (see Osborne, Thomas), the King's chief minister, and carefully furthered the marriage of Mary, the King's niece, with William of Orange.

In England the Popish Plot led to the Exclusion crisis, which threatened the rule of the Stuarts. In an attempt to win over the opposition leaders, Charles turned to a scheme designed by Temple, a reformed Privy Council of thirty members, representing all the interests of the country. This body was established in 1679, blessed with the prestige of Temple's name and membership, but it soon proved a failure. The King relied on a small, inner circle of councillors, giving the opposition leaders on the Council only a token hearing. Temple refused to condone the hysterical measures taken to combat the fabricated Popish Plot, but rejected equally the arbitrary actions of Charles. Elected M.P. for the University of Cambridge, he consistently spoke out for moderation; in January 1681 he was dismissed from the Privy Council.

Once again Temple withdrew from public life. He devoted his time to cultivating fruit trees and developing his new estate of Moor Park, near Farnham. He wrote essays on gardening, history, and literature, including *Of Ancient and Modern Learning*, which sparked off the great debate on classical and modern writers that culminated in Swift's *Battle of the Books*. Temple employed Swift in 1689 as his secretary to help prepare his *Letters* and *Memoirs* for publication.

Temple's writings achieved considerable popularity in the eighteenth century.

After the Glorious Revolution of 1688, William of Orange offered the secretaryship once again to Temple, but the ageing diplomat refused. He died on 27 January 1699.

S. H. Monk (ed.), *Five Miscellaneous Essays by Sir William Temple* (Ann Arbor, Mich., 1963).

J. A. Nicklin (ed.), *Essays of Sir William Temple* (1903).

Joel E. Spingarn (ed.), *Essays on Ancient and Modern Learning and on Poetry* (1909).

Jonathan Swift (ed.), *Life and Works of Sir William Temple* (4 vols.; 1814, rev. ed., including the *Letters*).

M. L. R. Beaven, *Life of Sir William Temple* (2 vols.; 1836).

Thomas P. Coustenay, *Sir William Temple: a seventeenth century 'libertin'* (New Haven, Conn., 1932).

Homer E. Woodbridge, *Sir William Temple: the Man and His Work* (New York, 1940).

Portraits: oil, half-length, attributed to Lely, *c.* 1660: N.P.G.; oil, three-quarter length, by C. Netscher, 1675: N.P.G.

Thornhill, Sir James (1675–1734), decorative painter, see *Lives of the Georgian Age.*

Thurloe, John (1616–68), administrator and head of Cromwell's secret service.

The son of Thomas Thurloe, rector of Abbot's Roding, Essex, John Thurloe was baptized on 12 June 1616. He was trained in the law at Lincoln's Inn. On completing his studies he recommended himself to Oliver St. John (q.v.) as a patron. One of the more important posts St. John helped him to obtain was the secretaryship to the Parliamentary Commissioners who went to Uxbridge in January 1645 to treat with Charles I. In 1651 Thurloe was appointed secretary to a diplomatic mission to Holland, and in 1652 he was given the secretaryship of

the Council of State, where he emerged as a reserved but reliable supporter of Cromwell. He played an important role in the establishment of the Protectorate and appears to have been regarded by Cromwell as indispensable.

As part of his new duties, Thurloe had overall control of the intelligence department and, as a natural complement, the department of posts as well. He quickly built up the best spy network in Europe, with agents in all important Royalist and dissident circles and in foreign courts. What they could not ferret out was gathered from the mails, which he had intercepted and opened at will. He was thus able to keep the government informed of foreign plans, Royalist plots, schemes for Anabaptist risings, and to thwart the numerous conspiracies aimed at the Lord Protector's life.

Thurloe was elected as M.P. for Ely to the Parliaments of 1654 and 1656, in which he faithfully supported the government. He was rewarded with a Council seat in 1657, but he was no politician, rather a civil servant high in the trust of Cromwell. He displayed great admiration and affection towards the Protector and was one of those who urged Cromwell to accept the crown.

Thurloe's post allowed him to accumulate great wealth, not all of it by the most scrupulous means. He used the power it gave him to help Richard Cromwell succeed his father in September 1658. He now took a more active role in politics, and by skilful management secured a Cromwellian majority in the Parliament of January–April 1659, in which he was a leading government spokesman. His success was short-lived, however. Parliament was not the only power in the land; the Army was opposed to Richard Cromwell, while having no very constructive alternative to offer. Moreover, Thurloe was now attacked openly by radicals and republicans on the grounds of the arbitrary powers of arrest, imprisonment, torture, and transportation that he had exercised during the Protectorate. He did not succeed in thwarting the Army's insistence on the dissolution of Parliament. The Rump, restored under the Army's supervision in May, immediately stripped Thurloe of his posts, but he was reappointed secretary of state by the full Long Parliament in February 1660.

Although he enjoyed the support of Monck (q.v.), Thurloe was unable to obtain a seat in the Convention Parliament. As the prospects for a return of the Stuarts loomed nearer, he offered his services (somewhat belatedly) to Charles, but at the Restoration he was arrested on a charge of treason. The next month he was released on condition that he assist the new secretaries of state with his expertise in foreign affairs. Stripped of most of his estates, he lived in retirement until his death at Lincoln's Inn on 21 February 1668.

Thurloe was a conventional Puritan, not of a particularly devout frame of mind. In money matters he was no more corrupt than most men in government posts. What distinguished him was his brilliant and faithful service to the Commonwealth in the fields of intelligence and foreign affairs. His state papers and correspondence are a major source for the history of this period.

D. B. Holman, *Cromwell's Master Spy: A Study of John Thurloe* (1961).

Portrait: oil, three-quarter length, by unknown artist: N.P.G.

Tomkins, Thomas (1573–1656), composer.

Tomkins was born at St. David's, Pembrokeshire, where his father, also called Thomas, was choirmaster and organist. Tomkins came of a highly musical family; apart from his father, five brothers of his were also gifted musicians.

The family moved to Gloucester, where Tomkins's father had been appointed a minor canon in the cathedral, later becoming precentor there in 1625.

By about 1596, after receiving tuition from the great William Byrd (see *Lives of the Tudor Age*), the young Tomkins became organist at Worcester cathedral, a post that he held until 1646.

In 1607 he was awarded the degree of Bachelor of Music from Oxford. In 1621, at the relatively late age of forty-seven or forty-eight, he was appointed as one of the organists of the Chapel Royal and contributed music for Charles I's coronation in 1625. As a Royalist he lost his place during the age of the Puritans, and eventually died at Martin Hussingtree, Worcestershire, in June 1656, aged eighty-two or eighty-three.

Tomkins wrote services, anthems, and much music for virginals and viols. Yet it is for his fine madrigals dating from 1622 that he is best remembered today.

S. de B. Taylor, *Thomas Tomkins* (1933).

Denis Stevens, *Thomas Tomkins* (1957).

Definitive editions of works by Edmund H. Fellowes (vol. XVIII of the *English Madrigal School*, Stainer & Bell, 1913–24) and S. D. Tuttle (keyboard music in *Musica Britannica*, vol. 5). The services appear in *Tudor Church Music*, vol. VII.

Tompion, Thomas (1639–1713), English clock-maker, known as 'the father of English watchmaking'.

Tompion was probably born in 1639 at Northhill in Bedfordshire; little is known of his early life, but in 1664 he was apprenticed to a London clockmaker. Seven years later he became a member of the Clockmakers' Company and established his own shop in the district of Blackfriars.

The year 1675 marked the beginning of Tompion's long friendship with Robert Hooke (q.v.), and it was through Hooke's influence that he gained an introduction to John Flamsteed (q.v.), the first Astronomer Royal. Tompion was already a skilled and inventive watchmaker, as is shown by the watch he made for Hooke in 1675, which is one of the first English watches to make use of a balance spring, and in 1676 he was commissioned to construct the clocks for the newly established Royal Observatory at Greenwich. The year timepiece that Tompion produced was originally set into the panelling of the Octagonal Room there and is now in the British Museum.

Tompion's reputation was now established: he became one of Charles II's leading watchmakers, and later was appointed official clockmaker to William III. Developing the theories of his predecessor Edward Barlow, Tompion refined the whole art of clockmaking with his own inventions: he produced clocks with astronomical and perpetual calendar devices, and in 1695 he pioneered the design of the now familiar flat-bodied watch that replaced the earlier bulbous style. Probably the most popular of his inventions was the 'repeating' work, a device attached to the striking mechanism of a clock that enabled the time to be discovered at night by the mere pulling of a cord.

In 1690 Tompion moved his business premises to 67 Fleet Street, and here he remained until his death. Besides clocks and watches Tompion constructed many barometers and sundials; the patronage of William III ensured his constant prosperity, and in 1704 he became master of the Clockmakers' Company. It has been claimed that Tompion was a fellow of the Royal Society, but his name does not appear on any of that society's lists. Tompion died on 20 November 1713, and was buried in Westminster Abbey; not having married, he left his business to another craftsman, George Graham, whom he had taken into partnership in 1711 and who had married his own niece.

R. W. Symonds, *Thomas Tompion: His Life and Works* (1970).

Portrait: by Sir Godfrey Kneller: the Horological Institute.

Tonge or Tongue, Israel or Ezerel

(1621–80), clergyman and author of anti-Catholic literature; associate of Titus Oates (q.v.) in the fabrication of the 'Popish Plot'.

Israel Tonge was born in November 1621, the son of Henry Tonge, a minister of Holtby, Yorkshire. He gained a B.A. degree from University College, Oxford, in 1643. Tonge apparently left Oxford soon afterwards to avoid bearing arms for Charles I, and was described as being 'Puritanically inclined'. He excelled in Latin, Greek, poetry, and alchemy, on which he spent a great deal of time and money.

In 1648 Tonge returned to Oxford and was made a fellow of University College. The following year he became rector of Pluckley, Kent. From 1656 Tonge moved around a great deal, spending some time in Dunkirk and Tangier. When he returned from Tangier in 1669 he began to study anti-Jesuit literature and to turn his hand to producing his own diatribes against Catholics. In 1675 he met one Richard Greene, who told him of a rumour of a Catholic plot to murder the King and replace him with the Duke of York (see James II). Tonge seems to have been very credulous on the subject of Catholic intrigues, and was readily convinced that such a plot existed.

In 1676 Tonge met Titus Oates. He had already convinced himself by various occult researches that a Catholic plot was hanging over the King, and he readily entered into Oates's plans. During July and August of 1678 he incorporated Oates's inventions into a narrative of the 'hellish plot'. This was in documentary form, with forty-three clauses of indictment, and Tonge handed it to Danby (see Osborne, Thomas) in mid-August. Soon afterwards, he called on Gilbert Burnet (q.v.), who wrote that he was 'full of projects and notions . . . . He was a very mean divine, and seemed credulous and simple, but I looked on him as a sincere man.'

Tonge saw the King several times, but Charles was unconvinced of the existence of a plot. In order to gain publicity, Tonge persuaded Sir Edmund Berry Godfrey (q.v.) to take down Oates's depositions on oath on 6 September 1678. At the end of the month Tonge and Oates were summoned before the Privy Council and were assigned rooms together in Whitehall. After a few months Tonge dissociated himself from Oates, but had to appear with him at the bar of the House of Commons in March 1679. Tonge stated that Oates had told him that his (Tonge's) writings had so angered the Jesuits at St. Omer (where Oates had stayed) that they had dispatched Oates to murder their author. Oates was thus able to escape their clutches and to save King and country by his revelations of this and their even more heinous plot. By this time, Tonge probably really believed in the plot himself (for a further account of the plot see Oates, Titus and Godfrey, Sir Edmund Berry).

In 1680 Tonge began to write a defence of his part in revealing the plot. He returned to Oxford and took part in the burning of a huge effigy of the Pope, in the body of which cats and rats were imprisoned to represent devils. Tonge returned to London at the end of the year and died there on 18 December.

J. P. Kenyon, *The Popish Plot* (1972).
J. Pollock, *The Popish Plot* (1913).

Tourneur, Cyril (c. 1575–1626), tragedian and adventurer. Little is known of his life; his reputation rests on two plays ascribed to him, *The Revenger's Tragedy* and *The Atheist's Tragedy*.

Tourneur was born sometime between 1575 and 1580 and may have been the son of Captain Richard Turnor, an English soldier and administrator in the Netherlands. The earliest record of his existence is the publication in 1600 of *The Transformed Metamorphosis*, an allegorical verse satire. In 1609 he published *A Funeral Poem on the death of Sir Francis Vere, Knight* and in 1612 an elegy on the death of Prince Henry. Tourneur served with Vere in the Netherlands, but between 1603 and 1612 spent at least some of his time in London, where he became involved with the theatre. The first of the plays ascribed to him to be published was *The Revenger's Tragedy*, which appeared in 1607; the ascription to Tourneur was not made until 1656 and some scholars think that it was written by Thomas Middleton (q.v.). *The Atheist's Tragedy* is definitely by Tourneur, having been published under his name in 1611. It is to the title page of this play that the spelling *Tourneur* can be traced; in other documents of the time his name is spelt *Turner*, *Tournor*, and *Turnour*. He is known to have written a third play, *The Noble man*, which was published in 1612; however, the manuscript was burned by Warburton's cook in about 1750 and no copies survive.

Both the surviving plays are characterized by a tone of unrelieved moral gloom and cynicism. Both are in the tradition of revenge tragedy or 'tragedy of blood', the first notable English example of which was Thomas Kyd's *The Spanish Tragedy* (see *Lives of the Tudor Age*). Both portray a society that is utterly corrupt and proceed for five acts through a catalogue of rape, treason, and murder in which good, if it triumphs at all, does so seemingly only by chance. The moral anguish of Shakespeare's tragic heroes is not present; the audience's sympathy for the chief characters is not invited. The verse has vitality and a certain ghastly splendour. The plays have been described as 'the sort of plays that Hamlet might have written in his darker moments'; the writer's attitude is that of the moral satirist rather than the tragic dramatist; the deaths of the protagonists invite a cynical laugh more often than not. 'Atheist' in the title of the second play is used in the old sense of a man with no moral code at all rather than one who on philosophical grounds rejects the existence of a deity.

During the early 1600s Tourneur came into the sphere of influence of the Cecil family. In 1613 he was employed to carry letters to Brussels; he served for a time under Sir Edward Cecil (q.v.) in the Netherlands. During this period he also wrote a prose *Character* of Robert Cecil, 1st Earl of Salisbury. In 1617 he appears to have got into trouble, for he was imprisoned by the Privy Council for a time. In 1625 he was appointed by Sir Edward Cecil as secretary to the Council of War. This was a controversial appointment and was cancelled by the Duke of Buckingham; nevertheless, Tourneur sailed with Sir Edward in the same year on a raid on Cadiz. On the return voyage, fever broke out and Tourneur was put ashore with the other sick men at Kinsale in Ireland. He did not recover and died on 28 February 1626.

Allardyce Nicoll (ed.), *Complete Works* (1930).
R. A. Foakes (ed.), *The Revenger's Tragedy* (Revels Plays; 1966).
B. Gibbons (ed.), *The Revenger's Tragedy* (New Mermaid Series; 1967).
P. B. Murray, *A Study of Cyril Tourneur* (1964).
L. G. Salingar, 'Tourneur and the Tragedy of Revenge', in *The Age of Shakespeare*, ed. Boris Ford (1955).
See also Fredson Bowers, *Elizabethan Revenge Tragedy* (Princeton, N.J., 1940).

Townshend, Charles (1674–1738), 2nd Viscount Townshend; Whig statesman and agriculturalist, see *Lives of the Georgian Age*.

Traherne, Thomas (1637–74), clergyman, prose writer, and poet, whose fame rests principally on works discovered by chance in manuscript and first published in 1903.

Born in the West Country (probably at Hereford), Traherne was the son of a shoemaker. His short life was uneventful and serene: his chief concern was the pursuit of religious felicity. He entered Brasenose College, Oxford, in 1653, where he obtained a B.A. degree in 1656. His connection with the University of Oxford continued until 1669, when he received the degree of Bachelor of Divinity. In 1657 he was presented to the living of Credenhill, near Hereford, but did not take it up until 1661, after he had been episcopally ordained. He held this living until his death, but spent only part of his time in Herefordshire, living also in London and Teddington after leaving Oxford. In 1669 he was appointed private chaplain to Sir Orlando Bridgeman, who was lord keeper to Charles II. He held this office until his death on or about 27 September 1674.

Of his writings, only *Roman Forgeries*

was published under his name in his life-time (1673). Published anonymously were *A Serious and Pathetical Contemplation of the Mercies of God* and *Thanksgivings. Christian Ethics* appeared in 1675, and his brother Philip prepared some of his poems ('poems of felicity') for the press, although in the event these were not published until 1910.

Traherne remained virtually unknown until, at the end of the nineteenth century, a collection of manuscripts by him was discovered on a London bookstall. The bookseller Bertram Dobell identified them and published first the *Poetical Works* (1903) and followed it in 1908 with a prose work, interspersed with poems, to which he gave the title *Centuries of Meditations*. This is Traherne's most powerful and characteristic work. It is divided into sections numbered in hundreds ('centuries') and was originally written for Mrs. Susannah Hopton, the leader of a small religious community in Kington, Herefordshire.

Traherne's poems are in the tradition of serene joy of George Herbert; he appears to have been influenced also to some extent by Henry Vaughan. In the *Centuries* he expounds his concept of 'felicity', the concept that every man is 'heir to the world', which he may make a paradise for himself by consciously recognizing his own happiness and acknowledging the relation of the temporal world to the infinite and timeless world of the Spirit, that is, God. In a remarkable passage ('The corn was orient and immortal wheat . . .') he anticipates Wordsworth's view of the child as being still dimly aware of the immortal and spiritual world from which he came, before being trammelled by adult cares and worldly considerations.

Gladys I. Wade (ed.), *Poetical Works of Thomas Traherne* (1932).

H. M. Margoliouth (ed.), *Traherne's Centuries, Poems, and Thanksgivings* (2 vols.; 1958).

Gladys I. Wade, *Thomas Traherne* (Princeton, N.J., 1944).

Tull, Jethro (1674–1741), writer on agriculture and inventor of the seed drill, see *Lives of the Georgian Age*.

Tyrconnel, Earl of (1630–91), see Talbot, Richard.

U

Urquhart, Sir Thomas (1611–60), translator of Rabelais.

Urquhart was born of an ancient Scottish family in Cromarty, eldest son of Sir Thomas Urquhart, a fanatical episcopalian and a favourite of James I. In 1622 Thomas entered King's College, Aberdeen, a loyalist stronghold, where he studied natural philosophy, including optics and geometry; his tastes were influenced by his celebrated and eccentric great-uncle, John Urquhart, the 'Tutor of Cromarty'. Having become fluent in French, Italian, and Spanish, he then set off on the Grand Tour, spending his time vehemently praising Scotland's 'valour, learning, and honesty' to everyone he met.

Soon after his return, in July 1637, Urquhart and his brother were prosecuted for forcibly locking up their spendthrift father in his house, to stop him frittering away his fortune. Naturally the aristocratic Urquhart opposed the 'vulgar Covenant', and the first skirmish of the Scottish Civil War, in 1639, was caused by him trying to rescue some guns that had been seized by an opposing family. He took part in the ill-fated Royalist occupation of Aberdeen, but after the anti-Covenanters' defeat fled to London, where in April 1641 he was knighted by Charles I. While in London he published his first book (1642), a three-volume collection of rather sententious epigrams dedicated to Hamilton, the Scottish Royalist leader.

In August 1642 Urquhart's father died and he hurried back to Cromarty to disentangle the 'crazed estate'. Confident that all was settled, he went abroad for three years, but returned in 1645 to utter chaos. He decided to live in the fifteenth-century Tower of Cromarty, to avoid further 'solicitudinary and luctiferous discouragements'. There he wrote *Trissotetras*, an abstruse work on trigonometry dedicated to 'Cynthia', Urquhart's affectionate name for his spirited mother. He spent much time with his books, 'a compleat nosegay', and despised the 'iron-handed' creditors who forced him to sell them off. For recreation, he would wrangle bitterly with the local Presbyterian ministers.

Charles I's execution in 1649 provoked Urquhart and other Scottish gentlemen to stage an abortive Royalist uprising in Aberdeen. The Edinburgh government pronounced Urquhart a 'malignant' and he was hauled before a Parliamentary commission; they presumably judged him a harmless eccentric, since his only punishment was a reprimand from an Inverness minister. Nevertheless, at Charles II's coronation at Scone he joined the Scottish Royalist army, though he expressed discontent at the number of Presbyterians it contained. He was eventually captured at the Battle of Worcester (1650), when Parliamentary troops sacked his lodgings in the town, destroying by 'the inexorable rage of Vulcan' a hundred of his manuscripts. In September 1651 Urquhart was put in the Tower of London, but after a fortnight was sent to Windsor and finally freed on parole by Cromwell.

He now set out to rewrite his hundred

burnt manuscripts, and in 1642 published a fantastic genealogy, intended to convince Cromwell of his family's worth. He traces the Urquharts back to the 'red earth from which God framed Adam, surnamed the protoplast', and claims that he himself is 143rd in direct line from Adam. Shortly afterwards appeared Urquhart's most eccentric work, *The Jewel*, intended as an introduction to a new 'universal language', but in fact a farrago of anecdote and keen observation, including the story of the original 'Admirable Crichton' and a rhapsody to Scottish history. It apparently took only fourteen days to write and produce; Urquhart and his printer closeted themselves together to see whether the head could think of words faster than the hand could set them in type. What little is described of the universal language, 'the most compendious in the world', shows ingenuity and scholarship, its vocabulary built on the identical principles used a century later for the terminology of modern chemistry.

In 1652 the government allowed Urquhart to return to Scotland, but he found so many creditors waiting for him that he fled straight back to England and his hardly onerous 'imprisonment'. Soon after, he published his masterpiece, a translation of the first part of Rabelais's *Gargantua and Pantagruel*. Urquhart's exuberant diction was stylistically so close to the original that he could have been Rabelais reincarnated. His many mistakes were 'condoned by their magnificence'; for example, when stuck for a word's precise meaning, Urquhart tended to insert a string of all the approximate synonyms he could think of, on one occasion expanding Rabelais original thirteen adjectives to thirty-six, mostly culled from Cotgrave's rather bawdy French dictionary.

The remaining years of Urquhart's life are obscure. He probably spent most of them in London, continuing with the Rabelais translation, which was eventually completed by Richard Motteux. However, he is said to have died abroad, from an attack of uncontrollable mirth on hearing the news of Charles II's restoration.

Urquhart's translation of Rabelais was edited by Charles Whibley (3 vols.; 1900). His other works were edited by T. Maitland (1834). See also F. C. Roe, *Sir Thomas Urquhart and Rabelais* (1957).

Ussher, James (1581–1656), Irish scholar and ecclesiastic; Archbishop of Armagh.

Born on 4 January 1581, Ussher was the son of Arland Ussher, a Dublin lawyer. In 1594 he enrolled as one of the first students at Trinity College, Dublin. This institution, though not limited as to religion by its charter, was in effect a Protestant stronghold and many of its early officials were Puritans. During Ussher's years as a student, one such prominent Puritan, Walter Travers, was provost of Trinity College until 1598. He extensively influenced the young man, who early became interested in theology, chronology, classics, and Semitic languages.

Ussher graduated with a B.A. degree in 1597. In compliance with his father's wishes, he reluctantly prepared to go to London to read for the bar. But his father died the following year and the considerable estate that he thus inherited burdened him with problems of which he eventually rid himself by transferring it to his uncle, to be held in trust for his brother and sisters. He remained at Trinity College, becoming a fellow in 1599, and later being appointed catechist of the university and its first proctor. He was also appointed one of the lay preachers at Christ's Church, Dublin. He obtained his M.A. in 1601.

Ussher was already a prodigious academic. He disputed in theological controversies, notably with the Jesuit Henry Fitzsimon. His success as a disputant, like his later success as a scholar, lay in his brilliant use and mastery of his sources. He became an authority on the early church, and in 1599 he set himself the monumental task of making a systematic reading of patristic writings, which took eighteen years to complete.

In 1601, by a special dispensation, he was ordained deacon and priest, though as yet he was too young, being still only twenty. In that same year, Trinity College received an endowment from the English army to buy books for the college library and Ussher was sent to England – his first visit there – to select them. Upon his return in 1602, he was appointed to lecture on the Roman controversy on Sunday afternoons. But in 1603 the government issued an order allowing freedom of practice to Roman Catholics and his appointment was discontinued.

From 1603 to 1605, the then provost, Henry Alvey, was absent on several occasions for health reasons. During these absences, Ussher and his friend Luke Challoner ran the administration of the college. In 1605 Ussher resigned his fellowship in favour of the chancellorship of St. Patrick's Cathedral and the rectory of Finglas, Co. Dublin. On another book-collecting expedition, he visited Oxford, Cambridge, and London in 1606. In 1607 he obtained his B.D. and in the same year was appointed professor of controversial theology at Dublin; in 1609 he was offered the position of provost, on the resignation of Alvey. Ussher declined it, however, nominating Sir William Temple (q.v.), a much better organizer than himself.

During the next few years Ussher's academic responsibilities increased, cul-minating in his appointment as vice-chancellor of Trinity College in 1615. His first published work was a continuation of a history begun by Jewel, taking the history of the Western Church from the sixth century up to just before 1300. Ussher never completed it. In 1614 he obtained his doctorate of divinity, and in the same year married the daughter of his lately deceased friend Challoner.

In 1615, as vice-chancellor, Ussher was concerned in drafting the articles for the first English-style convocation of the Irish clergy. Extending their number to 104, he produced a code that was highly Calvinist in tone. Having already been criticized for his Puritanical leanings, he was now denounced to King James I, and it was not until 1619 that his career was allowed to advance again.

In 1620 he became rector of Trim and in 1621, after preaching before the members of the House of Commons in St. Margaret's, Westminster, he was consecrated at St. Peter's, Drogheda, as Bishop of Meath and Clonmacnoise. Ussher's diocese was poor, and most of the churches in disrepair. He worked hard in winning over Roman Catholics to Anglicanism, though he was wholly intolerant of Catholic attempts to win converts from among the Protestants. Having by now convinced James of his orthodoxy, he was allowed leave of absence to continue his antiquarian studies in England (1623–26).

On 22 March 1625, Ussher was appointed Archbishop of Armagh. In the same year he fell ill and did not return to Ireland until 1626. In July, just before his return, he was incorporated D.D. at Oxford.

Ussher was hostile to any toleration of popery. His office as archbishop is characterized by this and also by his aversion to the use of Irish in the service as well as the translation of the Bible into that language, as a result of which his relations with his protégé, William Bedell, Bishop of Kilmore and Ardagh, became strained. Yet Ussher was to no small extent a defender of Ireland's religious independence, however ineffectual he may now seem. He co-operated with but was not overshadowed by Thomas Wentworth (q.v.) during the latter's administration, and he by no means totally acquiesced in Wentworth's imposition of the English articles upon the Irish convocation in 1634. He was also anxious to preserve his own more Calvinistic articles and refused to repeal them, enjoining the clergy instead to subscribe to both sets of articles of religion. He was an acknowledged expert on both the language and the early history of his country. He collected several Irish manuscripts, including the Book of Kells.

From 1628 to 1640 he corresponded with William Laud (q.v.). Like Laud, Ussher valued allegiance to authority, but was not so passionately committed to uniformity. Upon Laud's appointment as Archbishop of Canterbury, Ussher secured for him the chancellorship of Trinity College in the following year (1634).

In 1640 Ussher visited England. His stay, intended to be short, was extended owing to the outbreak of the Ulster rebellion (October, 1641), in which he lost everything but his great library. He never returned to Ireland.

In the preliminaries to the Civil War Ussher had some part. He tried to prevail upon Charles I not to accept Strafford's attainder and, having failed in this, he attended Strafford at his execution. The same year, 1641, also saw the appearance under his authorship of a secretly printed document outlining a scheme of compromise between Episcopacy and Presbyterianism. Then, strangely, he tried to suppress it, but it was submitted for consideration to a Parliamentary committee and even the Puritan leaders were disposed to accept it. However, nothing came of the proposal in the end.

By the outset of the war, he had been lately appointed bishop of Carlisle in addition to his other positions. In 1643 he refused a seat at Westminster, denouncing that Parliament as an illegal assembly. Notwithstanding this, he commanded sufficient respect to be awarded a pension by Parliament, although payment of it was deferred until 1647. Moreover, his refusal angered the Parliamentarians, and for a time his library, lodged at Chelsea College, was confiscated. He was in Wales in 1645–46 and, having returned to London, he became preacher to Lincoln's Inn (1647). In 1648 he attended Charles, who was brought round to accepting his 1641 scheme. But the intervention of the army and the King's trial and execution supervened; Charles's acceptance of the compromise came far too late.

Ussher's publication in 1639 of *Britannicarum Ecclesiarum Antiquitates* ('Antiquities of British Churches') had brought him to the notice of Cardinal Richelieu, who after the fall of the English monarchy offered him refuge and religious freedom in France. Ussher did not accept this, however. During the Commonwealth he was consulted by Cromwell and appears to have got onto good terms with him. Ussher died after a bout of pleurisy on 21 March 1656, and was buried in Westminster Abbey.

A man of incomparable learning and great sincerity, Ussher was respected by both Parliamentarians and Royalists, though he was himself a King's man. Totally academic, he seems not to have comprehended fully the political ramifications of his period.

Ussher's best-known work is his biblical chronology, *Annales Veteris et Novi Testamenti* ('Annals of the Old and New Testament', 1650–54), because in it he naïvely dates the Creation to 4004 B.C. It is unfair that with all his other erudition, this fact has come to be the most significant in our remembrance of him.

Upon his death, Ussher's library, which contained manuscripts bought for him in the Levant, was purchased by the state and in 1661 presented to Trinity College, Dublin. His complete works were edited with a biography by C. R. Elrington and J. H. Todd (Dublin 1847–64).

J. A. Carr, *The Life and Times of James Ussher, Archbishop of Armagh* (1895).

R. B. Knox, *James Ussher, Archbishop of Armagh* (1967).

W. B. Wright, *The Ussher Memoirs* (Dublin, 1889).

Portrait: oil, half-length, after Lely: N.P.G.

V

Vanbrugh, Sir John (1664–1726), architect and dramatist, noted for his sparkling comedies and for his designs for great country houses, especially Blenheim Palace.

John Vanbrugh was born in London in January 1644, son of a wealthy sugar-refiner, whose wife was one of Sir Dudley Carleton's daughters and whose father had been a Protestant refugee from religious persecution in Flanders. The Great Plague of 1665 apparently induced the family to move to Chester; it is thought that John attended the grammar school there, but little is known of his early life until 1686, when he was given a commission in the Earl of Huntingdon's foot regiment. However, faced with the prospect of joining the garrison of Guernsey, Vanbrugh soon resigned. In 1690, 'on the information of a Paris woman', he was arrested in Calais on suspicion of spying and spent the next two years in various French jails, ending up in the Bastille, where he was given a spacious chamber and allowed to entertain his friends.

On his release, he briefly became a captain of marines, but it was not long before he abandoned soldiering for a very different career – the theatre. On Boxing Day 1691, *The Relapse*, by 'Captain Vanbrugh', was first performed at Drury Lane. This brilliant comedy of manners, which the prologue claimed was 'Got, conceived, and born in six weeks' space', was a runaway success. Vanbrugh followed this up the next May with the even more popular *Provok'd Wife*, starring Betterton and

Mrs. Barry. But already puritanical minds were complaining publicly about the 'immorality and profaneness' of Vanbrugh's work, and though he defended himself ably, he never again equalled the sparkle of his early comedies. His last half-dozen plays were all adaptations of French or English originals. Even so, he remained a favourite amongst playgoers well into the eighteenth century.

In 1699 Vanbrugh submitted a successful design for a great house in Yorkshire, Castle Howard, to be built for the Earl of Carlisle, who had rejected the design of William Talman as being too expensive. The abruptness of Vanbrugh's transformation from playwright to architect astonished his contemporaries. Swift wrote:

> Van's genius, without thought or
>   lecture,
> Is hugely turned to architecture.

However, architecture was at that time still considered an accomplishment within the reach of gifted amateurs, and it was Vanbrugh's mixing in Whig society that probably led to his coming under Lord Carlisle's patronage. From then on, Carlisle, the influential first lord of the Treasury, spared no pains to advance his protégé's career; in 1702 he had Talman ousted from the comptrollership of the King's works and appointed Vanbrugh, who thereby became the aged Wren's principal colleague and one of the two official leaders of English architecture. Vanbrugh lost no time in

blackening Talman's reputation when-ever possible, and managed to secure for himself the majority of the lucrative architectural commissions offered by the Whig aristocracy.

As if this were not enough, in 1703 Carlisle, then temporarily earl marshal, managed to get Vanbrugh appointed herald extraordinary, and in 1704 Cla-renceux King of Arms. Not only did Vanbrugh know nothing about herald-ry, but he had ridiculed it openly in his plays; the indignant College of Heralds petitioned the King's Council to remove this upstart, but they were overruled.

In the winter of 1704 began the cen-tral tragicomedy of Vanbrugh's life – Blenheim Palace. This mighty mansion was to be a national monument as well as a house, Queen Anne's token of gratitude to the Duke of Marlborough (see Churchill, John) for his humbling of Louis XIV's armies at Blenheim and Ramillies. The Queen's decision was undoubtedly supported by her current favourite, the Duchess of Marlborough, the formidable Sarah Churchill (q.v.).

Vanbrugh eagerly accepted the com-mission, which would give him the chance to erect a truly heroic building, unhampered by limitations of finance; the Queen approved his design and work started in 1705, even though no one had prepared any detailed estimates of cost. Vanbrugh was loyally assisted by Nicho-las Hawksmoor (q.v.), who perhaps provided the much-needed technical expertise for the execution of Van-brugh's huge design. Unfortunately, the whole project depended on royal favour – the Queen had only given verbal agreement to the duke, and Vanbrugh himself did not even have a proper con-tract – so when Abigail Masham (q.v.) displaced Sarah Churchill in Anne's affection, Treasury payment for the building work ceased. The workmen at Blenheim sued the duke for their arrears of wages, but he understandably resented having to 'pay for his own reward', so all work on the palace stopped.

Vanbrugh, however, had enough to keep him busy. In 1705 he designed the Opera House, Haymarket, but this was a financial disaster. In 1707 he recon-structed Kimbolton Castle for Lord Manchester. In 1711 he built Kings Weston, near Bristol, for Sir Edward Southwell, and soon after, for the Duke of Newcastle, the enormous Claremont House in Surrey.

Vanbrugh was a thoroughgoing Whig – friend of the Marlboroughs and a founder member of the Kit-Cat Club – so the coming to power in 1710 of Harley and his Tories, as well as causing the eclipse of the Marlboroughs, dis-rupted his career too. In 1713 an in-discreet letter lost him his job as comp-troller of the King's works, and in 1714 he was defeated in his attempt to become Garter King of Arms. The accession of George I in 1714, however, meant an immediate return to favour for Vanbrugh; he was knighted, reinstated as comptroller, made Garter King of Arms, and in addition surveyor of gardens and waters. In 1716 he succeeded Wren as surveyor to Greenwich Hospital, where he supervised the completion of the Great Hall and the King William block. Indeed, Vanbrugh's prestige was now such that he could have secured the surveyship of the King's works too, but he refrained, out of 'tenderness to Chr. Wren'. George I also rehabilitated the Marlboroughs, which meant that in the summer of 1716 work on Blenheim Palace was restarted. But by now Sarah Churchill was determined to curb what she considered Vanbrugh's 'extravagance', and their frequent and bitter disputes led, in November 1716, to a final break. Vanbrugh completely washed his hands of the project, only pausing to observe that the Duchess would have the pleasure of seeing 'your Glassmaker, Moore, make just such an end of the Duke's Building as . . . Harley did of his victories for which it was erected.' The 'Glassmaker' was the cabinetmaker James Moore, who supervised the building of the palace until 1722, when Hawksmoor was recalled. In 1725, when Vanbrugh came to view the completed structure, he was not even allowed into the grounds.

Vanbrugh's later years were not entirely unhappy, however. He retained the comptrollership until his death, and also designed several more great houses: in 1716 Eastbury in Dorset, for Bubb Dodington; in 1720 Seaton Delaval for Admiral Delaval; and in 1722 Grimsthorpe for the Duke of Ancaster. In January 1719 he married Henrietta Yarborough, who bore him two sons. The only one to survive infancy, Charles, was killed at Fontenoy in 1745. Sir John Vanbrugh himself died at his house in Whitehall on 26 March 1726, and was

buried in the church of St. Stephen Walbrook.

Vanbrugh's architectural style was absolutely individual. He was at his best when working on a large scale; fortunately, he lived at a time when patrons' purses were able to match the grandeur of his conceptions. Unlike European baroque, his effects did not depend overmuch on the external 'grammar' of classical architecture – such surface devices as split pediments and long porticoes – but rather on a skilful balancing of masses and an intuitive understanding of the value of projection and recession in giving 'movement' to even the most massive building. Though he occasionally used such archaic features as castellation, and though the general configuration of some of his houses is arguably influenced by medieval forms, the final effect of Vanbrugh's architectural work is far more than merely 'picturesque'. It is genuinely dramatic.

Bonamy Dobrée and Geoffrey Webb (eds.), *The Complete Works of Sir John Vanbrugh* (4 vols.; 1927–28).
Bonamy Dobrée, *Restoration Comedy* (1924).
Laurence Whistler, *Sir John Vanbrugh, Architect and Dramatist 1664–1726* (1938).

Portraits: oil, three-quarter length, attributed to T. Murray, *c.* 1718: N.P.G.; oil, half-length, by Kneller, *c.* 1704–10: N.P.G.

Van de Velde, Willem (1610–93), the elder, and his son, also Willem (1633–1707), the younger; marine painters and court painters to Charles II and James II. Father and son became the dominant influences on British marine painting.

Van de Velde the elder was born in Leyden, the son of a Flemish sea captain. He began his life as a sailor and before he was twenty he had earned himself a reputation as a marine draughtsman. By 1634 he was being regularly commissioned by the Dutch navy. As official

Dutch war artist in 1652, he was provided with a ship in which to follow the fleet to battle. His son often accompanied him on these trips. During the third Anglo-Dutch war in 1672, with the French invasion of Holland both father and son left for England. On their arrival, they were appointed painters to Charles II, the father's task being the 'taking and making draughts of sea-fights' and the son's 'putting the said draughts into colours'. Although this need not be taken too literally, father and son were in partnership for over thirty years. Their studio was in the Queen's House, Greenwich.

Van de Velde the younger was born in Amsterdam in 1633 and learned the rudiments of his art from his father, though he also trained under the oil painter Simon de Vlieger while still in Holland. His early works were mainly general seascapes, but in England his style developed and his work became much bolder and richer than that of his father.

Both father and son specialized in the official portraiture of ships and in drawn and painted records of naval engagements, but whereas Van de Velde the elder never roamed far from his official role as the recording artist, his son had a greater sense of the picturesque, and would paint a ship in the way that a portrait painter would paint a sitter. An atmosphere of elegance pervades his seascapes and he is at his finest when he paints tranquil marine scenes. The charm of such paintings lies in his masterly handling of colour, light, and atmosphere. His fine drawing and transparency of colour are often lost in his stormy seascapes and become opaque and inky. As well as aerial views of naval battles and portraits of ships, Van de Velde the younger also painted sea pieces for the mere pleasure of the marine subject. Towards the end of his life, he was especially interested in cloud and storm effects and his portrayal of the fury of the elements can be seen in paintings such as 'The Shipwreck'.

Van de Velde the younger was enormously prolific, about 330 paintings being attributed to him. In the period 1778–80, some 8,000 of his drawings were sold at auction.

Van de Velde the elder died in 1693, and was buried at St. James's Church in Piccadilly; his son died at Greenwich on 6 April 1707. Although the formation of their style belongs to Dutch art history rather than English, the influence of both Van de Veldes was enormous on succeeding British marine painters. Throughout the eighteenth century British marine artists directly styled their work on them.

Works:

Van de Velde the elder:
Hampton court (twelve naval battles).
British Museum (thirty-nine drawings).
Greenwich Maritime Museum (thirty-one drawings).
National Gallery of Scotland.

Van de Velde the younger:
British Museum (eighty-nine drawings).
Dulwich Art Gallery.
Glasgow Art Gallery.
Greenwich Maritime Museum (twenty-nine drawings).
National Gallery, London (sixteen drawings).
National Gallery, Scotland.
Wallace Collection.
Bristol Art Gallery.

M. S. Robinson, *Van de Velde drawings in the National Maritime Museum, Greenwich* (1958).
A. Wilson, *A Dictionary of British Marine Painters* (1967).

Van Dyck, Sir Anthony (1599–1641), painter.

Born Anthonis van Dyck in Antwerp on 22 March 1599, seventh son of Frans van Dyck, a wealthy silk mercer. Van

Dyck had the good fortune to be born into a family that was as cultured as it was well-to-do and in a city that was then one of Europe's liveliest centres of the visual arts. His mother, who died when he was seven, was skilled at embroidery and probably first stimulated the boy's interest in the arts. Indeed, he developed into something of a child prodigy: at the age of eleven he was apprenticed to Hendrik van Balen, a painter of considerable local standing and a friend of Rubens. By 1615 young Van Dyck had left home and was sharing a house in Antwerp with Jan Brueghel (the Younger). In 1618, at the unusually tender age of eighteen, he was admitted to the Antwerp painters' guild as a master and even began taking in apprentices himself.

The dominant influence on northern European painting at this time was Rubens. His exuberant style had carried all before it and, since he was given most of the important commissions, he came to exercise a virtual monopoly over art production in the Netherlands. It was fortunate for Van Dyck that around 1618 his series of portraits of Christ and the apostles was noticed in a dealer's window by Rubens. Correspondences between the two painters' styles have prompted the suggestion that Van Dyck was actually a pupil of Rubens. However, there is no evidence for this; a likelier explanation is that it would have been difficult for any young painter then working in Antwerp to escape the all-pervasive influence of Rubens. However, Rubens fully appreciated Van Dyck's precocious talent and in 1619 gave him the important job of making drawings after his own paintings, for use by engravers. By 1620 Van Dyck was practically Rubens's right-hand man, even being allowed to contribute paintings wholly his own work to help fulfil his employer's large-scale commissions. A traditional story tells how a group of Rubens's apprentices, brawling in the studio, accidentally damaged one of the master's paintings; they insisted that Van Dyck repair it, since he was the only one who could get away with the deception.

Van Dyck's reputation was spreading over Europe. In the winter of 1620 the Earl of Arundel, apparently acting as unofficial talent spotter to the English court, persuaded him to settle in London. Van Dyck probably felt concern over his individual artistic development; perhaps continued residence in the same city as Rubens might rob him of his due share of public attention. James I, though not noted for his artistic discrimination, nevertheless took Van Dyck into his service, at £100 a year; what the King got for his money is unclear, unless it be the full-length portrait now at Windsor.

In early 1621 Arundel secured from the King permission for Van Dyck to travel abroad for eight months. But the young painter did not come back for eleven years. In 1622, probably acting on Rubens's advice, he went to Italy, Mecca for all northern painters, and joined a colony of Flemish artists in Genoa.

From now on Van Dyck began to find himself as an artist. He had long been feeling his way towards a personal style that, though indebted to Rubens's robust colouring and brushwork, nevertheless placed more emphasis on reticence and refinement of feeling than the rather boisterous works of his mentor. In the palaces of the Genoese nobility Van Dyck saw the works of Titian and Veronese, and their elegance and rich southern colours irrevocably confirmed his emerging feelings about his art; his Italian sketchbook, now at Chatsworth, shows how deeply Van Dyck studied the Venetian masters. He had been advised by the perceptive Rubens to concentrate on portraiture; accordingly, he now launched into a series of paintings of the Genoese aristocracy that demonstrate his genius for depicting his sitters as both individuals and as symbols of their social class. The face shows us the sitter's personality and the richly-painted robes and trappings show us restrainedly but precisely his place in the wider scheme of things.

Having visited Florence, Mantua, and Venice, Van Dyck was by 1623 in Rome, where he painted the local worthies, in particular a brilliant portrait of Cardinal Bentivoglio. The Flemish artists' community in Rome took to calling him *il pittore cavalleresco* ('the chivalrous painter'), since his sober diffidence and elegant manners prevented him from sharing their rumbustious way of life. Van Dyck's wanderings had not caused him to lose touch with England; he had painted Nicholas Lanier, then in Italy buying pictures for Charles I, and it is said that the Lanier portrait finally decided the King to try to entice Van Dyck back to London.

However, for the time being the painter's movements are uncertain, but he was probably back in Antwerp by 1626, to enjoy his new-found fame as the foremost portraitist in Europe. Furthermore, he now responded to his father's death (in 1622) by producing a series of austere but powerful religious pictures, demonstrating an individual synthesis of the styles of Rubens and the Venetians. He painted portraits of all levels of society, from the exiled Queen Marie de Médicis down to homely Flemish burghers, in a manner which had lost a little of the warmth of the Genoese period but had gained considerably in subtlety. He finally confirmed his artistic pre-eminence by engraving a brilliant series of one hundred etched portraits, the *Centum Icones*.

By 1631 the English court was once more beckoning him. Traditions conflict as to who was responsible for finally persuading Van Dyck to settle in London, whether it be Arundel, Kenelm Digby, or the Duke of Buckingham. George Vertue claims that Charles I asked Van Dyck over to draw Henrietta Maria, and that when the King showed the portrait to his court painter, Mytens, he immediately gave in his notice, asserting that the King had found a better painter. Whatever the exact circumstances, Van Dyck was certainly warmly welcomed; his defection of 1621 was forgiven. He was given a house in Blackfriars (next door to Cornelius Johnson) and a pension of £200 a year, and on 5 July 1632, he was knighted and appointed principal painter to the King.

For the first time since Holbein, English painting had as its leader an artist whose genius had gained him a European reputation and whose technique was of impeccable modernity; as a man, he displayed courtly manners and a considerable intellect, and was acquainted with many of the great men of Europe. Accordingly, the English aristocracy were careful not to treat him as a mere craftsman, as had hitherto been the custom with painters. Van Dyck's gifts were patently of a different order from those of Mytens or Johnson.

Van Dyck had principally been brought over to paint the royal family, and they it was who inspired his finest works. These include the group of the King and Queen and their two children (Buckingham Palace), the King with groom and horse (Louvre), and perhaps most magnificent of all, the equestrian portrait of the King set against an Italianate landscape (National Gallery). The latter was obviously inspired by Titian's painting of the Emperor Charles V on horseback and reflects a renewed interest on Van Dyck's part in the Venetian school; this may have been because he now had access to Charles I's collection of Titians, one of the finest extant.

The most controversial aspect of Van Dyck's royal portraits is the way in which he idealized his sitters. It is certainly instructive to compare the awkward, almost snub-nosed little Charles I of Mytens and Honthorst with Van Dyck's usual rendering of a tall and elegant cavalier with a saintly air. As for his portraits of Henrietta Maria, Sophia of Bavaria, who first met the Queen in 1641, was surprised to find that she '. . . who looked so fine in painting, was a small woman raised up on her chair, with long skinny arms and teeth like defence works projecting from her mouth . . .'

Whatever modern taste might think of these 'modifications' by Van Dyck, it was undoubtedly he who crystallized the theory of English portraiture right down to the nineteenth century: the careful painter must stress those aspects of a sitter's personality which conform to society's concepts of the noble, brave, compassionate, and so on. Waller approvingly called Van Dyck's studio a 'beauty shop'. Certainly, the English nobility who sat for Van Dyck were given a far more elegant image of themselves than the four-square, rather pedestrian efforts of Mytens. Van Dyck's mastery of the sinuous curves of the baroque style meant that their poses were always fluent and varied, and his knowledge of the external trappings of society meant that the sitters are always immediately assignable to a particular class, whether as an English duke, an Antwerp burgher, or an Italian prince. Their faces are likewise rendered with scrupulous care, but most of them wear the remote, almost uncommunicative expression that has become part of the Van Dyck legend; all this may have been a response to the age they lived in, as well as a reflection of the painter's temperament. However, Van Dyck was quite capable of doing justice to strong and positive personalities, as in the portrait of the Marchioness of Hertford (Syon House), and also of showing warm sympathy with sitters who happened to be close friends, as in his many paintings of Strafford.

In his six-and-a-half years in England Van Dyck executed a vast number of private and royal commissions. His usual studio method was to paint the sitter's face, make notes of his costume and draperies, and hand the painting over to an assistant for completion; however, he would give it a final going-over himself, to give the brushwork his personal 'feel'. A painter of the rich and famous, he lived an extravagant and luxurious life himself, and the precarious state of his finances was not helped by his royal pension being invariably in arrears. Van Dyck was attractive to women, and this proved troublesome too; when in 1640 he agreed at the King's instigation to marry the well-connected Mary Ruthven, his long-standing mistress, Margaret Lemon, tried to cut his right hand off.

In 1640 Rubens died and Van Dyck, realizing he was now leader of the Flemish school, rushed back to Antwerp in an attempt to take over the dead painter's outstanding (and lucrative) commissions. He was balked, so he tried to secure the commission for the decoration of the Louvre. But, as had happened with Charles I's Whitehall scheme, Van Dyck was destined never to accomplish a large-scale decorative painting. He returned to London and died, disappointed and prematurely aged, on 9 December 1641. He was buried in Old St. Paul's Cathedral, but his monument was destroyed in the Great Fire. However, perhaps his best memorials are his paintings – and those of Reynolds, Gainsborough, and Lawrence, whose portraits are unthinkable without the precedent of Van Dyck.

Sir Lionel H. Cust, *Anthony Van Dyck* (1900).
Gustav Glück, *Van Dyck* (Berlin and Stuttgart, 1931).
Michael Jaffe, *Van Dyck's Antwerp Sketchbook* (1966).
Marie Mauguoy-Hendrickx, *L'Iconografie d'Antoine van Dyck* (Brussels, 1956).

Portrait: oil, half-length, copy of a self-portrait, *c.* 1621: N.P.G.

Vane, Sir Henry (1589–1655), the elder, courtier and politician instrumental in the overthrow of Strafford (see Wentworth, Thomas).

He was born on 18 February 1589, eldest son of Henry Vane or Fane, a gentleman of Hadlow, Kent. He entered Brasenose College, Oxford, in 1604, and Gray's Inn in 1606. Vane was ambitious, filled with a sense of his own importance. A natural schemer, he chose the court as the suitable place to enrich himself and launched upon a swiftly successful career with the assistance of Sir Thomas Overbury (q.v.). King James I knighted him in 1611 and in 1612 he bought his first court office. The following years saw him purchase a series of positions and win election to Parliament for numerous different constituencies.

In 1617 Vane was appointed cofferer to the Prince of Wales, a post that he retained when his master became Charles I in 1625. He won the trust of the prince, through whose favour he gained great wealth and was appointed to two diplomatic missions, both unsuccessful, and a number of offices, including the comptrollership of the royal household (1629). Vane acquitted himself well in his court posts, but when in 1630, through his close relationship with Charles, he was made privy councillor and moved into political affairs, he displayed consistent mediocrity.

In the late 1630s the King's unwarranted reliance upon Vane's advice increased, but this did not bring Charles to follow his comptroller's counsels of moderation towards the Scots and his opposition to the war against them in 1639. Accordingly, when the expedition proved a disaster, Vane was selected in 1640 as one of the peace negotiators with the Scots. That same year, in opposition to Strafford, the Queen and the Marquis of Hamilton (see Hamilton, James) won for Vane a secretaryship of state, a post for which he later admitted that he was not suited. In this capacity he represented the government in the Short Parliament, where he offered the end of ship money in exchange for a vote of twelve subsidies – a proposal that Pym (q.v.) correctly interpreted as a sign of the government's weakness. The Commons demanded instead that their grievances be discussed first, and Charles dissolved Parliament in May, largely on Vane's advice.

When the Long Parliament assembled, Vane escaped attack since in fact he was one of the royal ministers least responsible for hated measures and because of the close association of his son, Sir Henry Vane the younger (q.v.), with the opposition leaders. The brunt of the assault was directed against the Earl of Strafford (see Wentworth, Thomas). The latter had in 1640 chosen Baron Raby as a secondary title for himself, although Raby Castle belonged to Vane; for this affront, Vane never forgave Strafford. When the Long Parliament impeached the earl in April 1641, Vane was its most important witness, testifying that at a Privy Council meeting in May of the previous year Strafford had advised Charles to employ his Irish army against the English opposition. Although Strafford's conviction could not be secured by impeachment, a bill of attainder was successfully brought against him; its passage was greatly facilitated by a copy of Vane's notes of this Council meeting, produced by Pym with the assistance of the younger Vane.

Vane was not dismissed immediately by the King, since he needed to find a replacement, and in August Charles took his secretary of state with him to Scotland in an abortive attempt to settle with the Covenanters behind Parliament's back. But in December Charles stripped Vane of all his offices; the latter promptly joined the parliamentary opposition, which attempted to reward him with posts at its disposal. In 1644 he was chosen a member of the Committee of Both Kingdoms, the Parliamentarian executive, but he was not of the first rank among its leaders and played no significant role in the formulation of policy. He remained in the Long Parliament after Pride's Purge and the trial of Charles and was elected to Cromwell's first parliament in 1653. He died in about May 1655.

Portrait: oil on panel, half-length, after M. van Miereveldt: N.P.G.

Vane, Sir Henry (1613–62), the younger; Puritan statesman, diplomat, and mystic.

Baptized on 26 May 1613, at Debden, near Newport in Essex, the son of Sir Henry Vane the elder (q.v.), Henry Vane was educated at Westminster School, Magdalen Hall, Oxford, and the University of Leiden. At the age of fifteen, young Henry Vane, who had been noted for his recklessness and high spirits, suddenly became a Puritan, a transformation that was to affect his whole career. In 1631, after leaving university, he was sent to Vienna by his father as part of an English embassy. Prospects of advancement and a promising court career were open to him by virtue of his father's position and influence, but his Puritan conscience was deeply disturbed by the Laudian tendencies in the church, and in 1635 he went to Massachusetts, where his social standing and religious enthusiasm won him a warm welcome. Despite his youth, he was elected governor in 1636 and filled the post with success for a year, but the treacherous waters of ecclesiastical politics led him into isolation and defeat in 1637. Later that year, he returned to England.

In January 1639 Vane obtained a joint treasurership of the navy through his father's influence, and proceeded to fit out ships against the Scots and otherwise

431

serve the King loyally. The next year he was elected to both the Short and the Long Parliaments and knighted. But his loyalty to the court was greatly weakened in September when, while looking through his father's notes of Privy Council meetings, he discovered a memorandum of Strafford's plans to use Irish troops against 'this kingdom'. He passed a copy of his memo to Pym (q.v.), who later used it to great effect in securing Strafford's attainder.

In spite of the fact that he held office in the government, Vane soon proved himself a supporter of ecclesiastical reform in the Long Parliament, co-operating with Oliver Cromwell and Oliver St. John (qq.v.) in pressing for the extirpation of the episcopacy. In consequence of this and of the fall of his father, he was dismissed by the King from his post in the navy office in December 1641.

The younger Vane quickly established himself as one of the leaders in the Parliamentary opposition to Charles. Once the Civil War had broken out, Parliament appointed him treasurer of the navy. He belonged to the 'war party' in the Commons and was accordingly sent to Scotland in 1643 to conclude an alliance with the Covenanters. The Scots made adherence to the Solemn League and Covenant the price of their help, but Vane was clever enough to obtain a modification of one clause, so that the door was left open to religious independence in this otherwise Presbyterian document.

The death of Pym in December brought Vane and St. John to the fore. They persuaded Parliament to establish the Committee of Both Kingdoms in 1644, which served as the Parliamentarian executive and on which they naturally had seats. Vane used his powerful position to oppose religious conformity, obtaining a Commons resolution on behalf of toleration and using his influence in New England for toleration there. But most of his effort went into the prosecution of the war, and he was instrumental in establishing the New Model Army and obtaining passage of the Self-Denying Ordinance. In these matters Vane found an ally in Cromwell, and this co-operation continued after the first stage of the war was over. He sided with the Army as the breach between it and the majority of Presbyterians in Parliament widened, and soon the opposition of the Presbyterians was joined by the hatred of the Levellers, for Vane was too much the gentleman and oligarch to support their egalitarian visions. In the context of the late 1640s, he was one of the moderates who sought a settlement based on the three traditional elements of King, Lords, and Commons that would be acceptable both to the Army and to Parliament. He took part in the negotiations with Charles that brought about the abortive Treaty of Newport (December 1648) and, although disagreeing with parts of it, was willing to give it his support.

Although Vane was not excluded from the Commons by Pride's Purge, he refused to attend the sessions of the Rump or participate in the trial of Charles. After the King's execution he re-emerged and gradually resumed his relationship with Cromwell, serving the Commonwealth with great loyalty and ability both in Parliament and in the Council of State. He was especially active in naval, foreign, and colonial affairs.

Vane saw the Rump as the sole body empowered to speak for the people and opposed Cromwell's expulsion of it in 1653. He retired to Belleau, Lincolnshire, where he engaged in religious speculation. In 1656 he was briefly imprisoned after writing a pamphlet hostile to the Protectorate, but waited until the Protector's death before re-entering politics. He was elected to Richard Cromwell's Parliament, in which he spoke out in defence of parliamentary sovereignty, opposing all moves to restore the Stuarts; he also expressed his hostility to the semi-monarchical position of the Protector and the upper chamber. Vane helped bring about the recall of the Rump in May 1659, and was immediately elected to the Council of State. For the next few months he was very active, trying to assert civilian control over the Army but still seeking the co-operation of the officers. When Fleetwood and Lambert (qq.v.) expelled the Rump in October, Vane remained at first only in his naval post, but afterwards resumed his co-operation with the generals. The restoration of the Rump in the following year brought about his downfall. He was expelled from Parliament and, at the Restoration, arrested and jailed.

Vane was one of the handful exempted by Parliament from the general pardon, but it was agreed that a petition be sent to the King requesting that any capital sentence he should receive would be commuted. In 1662 he was brought to trial. With eloquence and sincerity, he defended his past conduct, basing his actions on the concept of parliamentary sovereignty, thereby sealing his fate. The court had desired a performance of humility, and convicted him of treason. Charles II refused to commute his sentence, and on 14 June 1662, Sir Henry Vane was executed on Tower Hill.

Vane was never understood by his contemporaries and, by the end of his life, was thoroughly distrusted. His highly mystical religion is not very comprehensible, although his belief in toleration is more easily grasped. As a politician and diplomat, he was subtle and highly effective. Like John Locke

(q.v.), he believed in a social compact between ruler and ruled, seeing sovereignty as the prerogative of the people, by which he probably understood the propertied classes.

J. H. Adamson, *Sir Harry Vane: His Life and Times* (1973).
J. K. Hosmer, *The Life of Young Sir Henry Vane* (1888).
Margaret Judson, *The Political Thought of Sir Henry Vane the Younger* (Philadelphia, 1969).
V. Rowe, *Sir Henry Vane the Younger* (1970).
J. Willock, *Life of Sir Henry Vane the Younger* (1913).

Vaughan, Henry (1622–95), poet.

Born on 17 April 1622 at Newton-by-Usk, Breconshire, Vaughan was the son of Thomas Vaughan, a country gentleman from an ancient Brecon family (but described by his nephew John Aubrey (q.v.) as 'a coxcomb'). After early schooling by the rector of Llangattock, in 1638 Vaughan entered Jesus College, Oxford, but left at his father's request two years later to study law in London. While there he probably moved in the same social circles as the Cavalier poets. On the outbreak of civil war in 1642 he was summoned home, but he may have served as a surgeon with the Royalist army at Rowton Heath. By 1647 he was practising medicine at Newton-by-Usk, where he remained for the rest of his life.

Vaughan's earliest collection, *Poems* (1646), reflects his brief London sojourn in its rather shallow imitations of the fashionable Metaphysical style of Habington. *Olor Iscanus* ('The Swan of Usk'), written before 1648 and including translations from classical authors, shows a deepening sensibility, especially in the translations of Boethius and the elegies on friends killed in battle. It was not published until 1651, and then by Vaughan's father, prefaced with a vehement retraction by the poet of his 'idle verse'. The reason for this was the prior publication (1650) of his *Silex Scintillans*

('Sparkling Flint'), a collection of vision-ary sacred poems which powerfully con-firm that Vaughan had experienced a religious conversion. This seems to have been a gradual process, brought on by the country's civil and religious unrest, Vaughan's deeper study of the Bible, his safe recovery from a serious illness, and his brother William's death in 1648. Vaughan himself attributes it to 'the blessed man, Mr. George Herbert, whose holy life and verse gained many pious Converts . . . of whom I am the least.'

The debt is genuine, for Vaughan's poems in fact frequently borrow themes, stanza forms, and even whole phrases from Herbert. Vaughan is often inferior to his mentor, both in his structures and his handling of the colloquial tone. He can often begin a poem with startling immediacy, only to allow it to deterior-ate into diffuseness and syntactical awkwardness. In fact, the originality of Vaughan's writing lies chiefly in the in-tensity and sincerity of his religious vision. Vaughan is orthodox in religion, and his fundamental poetic preoccupa-tion is in fact with sin and redemption: Fallen Man, instead of pursuing the melancholy delusions catalogued in *The World*, should seek regeneration by con-templating joyful nature and unspoilt infancy, since they are closer to God, who is 'thy life, thy Cure'.

However, Vaughan draws his sym-bols with such freshness that this strong moral strain in his poems never detracts from their simple sense of the wonder of life. In contrast, his translations, of which the best are the meditative *Mount of Olives* (1652) and the life of St. Paulinus of Nola (1654), are rather ponderous, and disfigured by the oblique rhetoric popular at the time. Vaughan also trans-lated two mystical German medical treatises, *Hermetical Physick* (1655) and *The Chemist's Key* (1657), probably at the instigation of his twin brother Thomas, a noted alchemist.

Vaughan, stated Anthony à Wood, 'was esteemed by scholars an ingenious person but proud and humorous.' He was married twice, first to Catherine Wise, who gave him three daughters and a son, and when she died he married her sister Elizabeth, who also gave him three daughters and a son. Still a country doctor, his magnificent poetry largely ignored by his contemporaries, Henry Vaughan died on 23 April 1695, and was buried in the churchyard of his home town.

E. K. Chambers (ed.), *Poems of Henry Vaughan, Silurist* (2 vols.; 1896, 1905).
A. B. Grossart (ed.), *Complete Works* (4 vols.; 1870–71).
L. C. Martin (ed.), *Works* (2 vols.; 1957, 2nd ed.).
F. E. Hutchinson, *Henry Vaughan: a Life and Interpretation* (1947).

Verrio, Antonio (1630–1707), decora-tive painter.

Verrio was born at Lecce in southern Italy, and received his early training as an artist in Naples. He arrived in England probably in 1671, having been sent for by Charles II to help re-establish the tapestry works at Mortlake that had fallen into disuse during the Civil War. Verrio's reputation had been established by his work as a painter of historical scenes in France; an altarpiece for the Carmelite church in Toulouse is one of his best surviving works from this period. The Mortlake project did not in fact advance beyond the planning stage, Charles II preferring to employ Verrio's decorative talents on the ceilings at Windsor Castle, but a number of com-missions for the country nobility soon enabled Verrio to establish himself sec-urely in England.

In 1674 Verrio was appointed 'chief and first painter to the King', succeeding

Lely (q.v.) as court painter. Charles II provided Verrio with apartments at Windsor Castle and a house in the Mall as well as paying generously for all his work, and after Charles's death Verrio was retained in this favoured position by James II. Under William III Verrio concentrated on various commissions for the nobility rather than for the King – notably for the Duke of Devonshire at Chatsworth in Derbyshire and for the Earl of Exeter at Burghley House in Lincolnshire – but he was persuaded by the Earl of Exeter to accept a royal commission for a series of decorative paintings at Hampton Court. Verrio's work at Burghley House has usually been acclaimed as his finest, especially the work in the Heaven Room with its feigned architectural structure through which gods and goddesses tumble and, according to Pope, 'sprawl'. Most critics, however, have discovered little of original merit in any of Verrio's surviving work, and undoubtedly his contemporary success was chiefly due to his ability to satisfy the taste for extravagant and gaudy splendour made fashionable by Louis XIV's reconstruction work at the Palace of Versailles.

Verrio's work at Hampton Court continued into the reign of Queen Anne, but soon after her accession his eyesight became badly impaired and the progress of his work was slowed. Verrio died at Hampton Court in 1707; the popularity of his work did not long survive him, the fashion for French influences having declined. The fact that he is remembered at all is chiefly owing to some satirical references to his work in the poetry of Pope.

Portrait: self-portrait, oil, half-length, *c.* 1700: N.P.G.

Verulam, Baron (1561–1626), see Bacon, Francis, in *Lives of the Tudor Age.*

Villiers, Barbara (1641–1709), Duchess of Cleveland and Countess of Castlemaine; mistress of Charles II.

Barbara Villiers was born in the autumn of 1641, the daughter of William Villiers, 2nd Viscount Grandison, who was killed during the Civil War at the siege of Bristol (1643), fighting for the Royalist cause. She was the granddaughter of Sir Edward Villiers, the half-brother of George Villiers, 1st Duke of Buckingham.

In April 1659 Barbara Villiers married one Roger Palmer. Her association with the King began soon afterwards, probably in the spring of 1660. In February 1661 she gave birth to a daughter, whom Charles acknowledged as his own. Barbara's husband was created Earl of Castlemaine the same year. She maintained her position as royal favourite for the first seven years of Charles's reign, although her affairs with other men were rumoured as early as 1662. Quarrels about other lovers reportedly ended with Charles asking pardon and heaping lavish gifts upon her. In 1662 Charles

forced her upon his Queen, Catherine of Braganza, as a lady in waiting.

Despite her position, Lady Castlemaine's political influence was small, although in 1667 she had a considerable share in the downfall of Clarendon: prompted largely by personal dislike, she candidly expressed her desire to see this minister's head on a stake.

Lady Castlemaine's financial as well as her sexual greed was enormous and, although her income was large, it hardly matched her expenditure. As her income increased, it was rapidly spent as new paramours were added to her pension list. In 1668 she retaliated against Charles's weakness for actresses such as Nell Gwynne by forming a liaison with the actor Charles Hart. She favoured an ill-assorted series of lovers, including John Churchill, later Duke of Marlborough, by whom she had a daughter, and the dramatist William Wycherley. In 1670 she was created Baroness Nonsuch, Countess of Southampton, and Duchess of Cleveland, and received further extensive money presents and other grants from the King. She had borne Charles at least five children, and presents that he bestowed on her, being in the nature of a final payment, signalled his emancipation from his infatuation with her. By 1674 she had been entirely supplanted in his affections by Louise de Kéroualle (q.v.).

In 1677 Lady Castlemaine, now Duchess of Cleveland, went to Paris, where she lived for a time with the English ambassador, Ralph Montagu (q.v.). Upon finding that he preferred her eldest daughter to her, she communicated this news to the King, along with a full account of Montagu's low estimation of him. Montagu hurried back to England in an attempt to save his reputation, but found himself disgraced. In an attempt to retrieve his position, Montagu denounced the chief minister, Danby (see Osborne, Thomas), and managed to bring about his impeachment. In this way Lady Cleveland indirectly brought about the fall of the government.

Shortly before Charles died in 1685, she returned to England. On the death of her long-suffering husband in 1705 she married Major General Robert Fielding. The marriage was stormy and short-lived: Fielding was briefly committed to Newgate for mistreating her, and within a year the discovery that he was already married led to the annulment of their marriage. Lady Cleveland's remaining years were spent at Chiswick, where she died in October 1709.

M. Gilmour, *The Great Lady: a Biography of Barbara Villiers, Mistress of Charles II* (1944).

G. S. Steinman, *A Memoir of Barbara, Duchess of Cleveland* (1874).

Portrait: oil, half-length, by Lely, c. 1666: Hampton Court.

Villiers, George (1592–1628), 1st Duke of Buckingham; court favourite, politician, and military leader during the reigns of James I and Charles I.

Villiers was born in August 1592, at Brooksby, Leicestershire, a younger son of Sir George Villiers, the county sheriff, by his second marriage. His father died while he was still a boy and his mother, having ambitions for her handsome son, had him educated for a place at court, sending him first to a school at Billesdon. Then, in 1610, when he was eighteen, he was sent to France, thus coming into contact with Sir John Eliot (q.v.), who later came under his patronage but eventually became his political opponent.

After his return from France, Villiers was brought to the attention of the King during a royal hunting trip in Nottinghamshire (August 1614). James I, now finding the demands of government weighing heavily upon him since the death of Salisbury in 1612, took a liking to the young man, whose cultured attitudes and ebullient manner impressed and cheered him. However, Villiers's appointment as cupbearer to the King late in 1614 aroused the hostility of Robert Carr (q.v.), Earl of Somerset, who saw in this new situation a threat to his own position at court. Carr's reported sullenness at this time with the King may be seen as a symptom of his premonitions of his imminent downfall; the revelation of his complicity in the murder of Sir Thomas Overbury (q.v.) in 1615 served only to seal his fate.

Villiers's advancement under James following the displacement of Carr was rapid. In 1615 he became gentleman of the bedchamber and received a knighthood; in 1616 he was appointed master of the horse, became a Knight of the Garter, and was created Viscount Villiers and Baron Whaddon, receiving also an enormous grant and estate; and then in 1617 he was given an earldom, becoming Marquis of Buckingham a year after that. Throughout this period he appears to have been greatly influenced by the lord chancellor, Lord Verulam (see Bacon, Francis, in *Lives of the Tudor Age*), a man far more experienced in statecraft than the young Villiers. Villiers, however, had the more power by virtue of being closer to the King.

Now thoroughly established as James's favourite and almost the richest nobleman in England, Villiers took steps to advance his family as well as himself, forcing an heiress to marry his backward brother John and withholding the promotion of Cranfield (q.v.) until the latter consented to marry one of his impoverished cousins.

Appointed by the King as lord high admiral in 1619, Buckingham began to play a major part in the administration and showed an active interest in international politics. The popular indignation over the treatment of Protestants in continental Europe, and in particular the expulsion from Bohemia by a Catholic force that had Spanish support of Frederick, the Elector Palatine and James's son-in-law, led Buckingham at first to encourage James in a hostile policy towards Spain. But a change of heart came over the favourite, possibly due in part to his marriage in 1620 to Katherine Manners, outwardly a conformist to the established religion of England but in actual fact a Roman Catholic; it may also have been due to anger directed against Holland over Dutch treatment of English sailors in the East Indies. Undoubtedly, however, the strongest single factor in bringing about this reversal of his original hostile attitude towards Spain was his association with Gondomar, the Spanish ambassador.

Diego Sarmiento de Acuna Gondomar was undoubtedly one of the most brilliant as well as the most cunning of the diplomats of his time. As ambassador to England in the two periods 1613–18 and 1620–22, he came to exercise considerable influence at court, to the point where he more or less controlled British foreign policy.

Certainly, his machinations on this occasion were effective enough. When Parliament was convened in 1621, it expressed patriotic fury over the fact that Frederick V of Bohemia had received no help; attacks were also launched on Buckingham over the numerous monopolies from which his relatives had derived large profits. Buckingham was compelled to admit the implication of his family and dependants in unfair practices and proceeded to disown them. In the impeachment for accepting bribes of Francis Bacon that now followed,

Buckingham's own position was too weak for him to protect the lord chancellor. At first he did what he could and provided some protection, but eventually he defected to the side of Bacon's opponents.

Gondomar's influence was at this time quite overwhelming and Buckingham almost became a Catholic as a result of it. He was dissuaded from this course by Bishop Laud (q.v.), who in 1622 had been called in by James over the controversy of the conversion to Romanism of Buckingham's mother. Gondomar left England in May 1622.

Buckingham now considered the possibility of an alliance with Spain consolidated by a royal marriage. There seems little doubt that the scheme had been agreed with if not suggested by the ambassador before his departure. Buckingham thought it politically sound: an alliance with the Spaniards could only facilitate James's attempts to mediate with the Catholic Holy Roman Emperor for his son-in-law Frederick in Bohemia, and a marriage between the Prince of Wales and the Infanta Maria seemed the ideal way of cementing such an alliance. In 1623 then, Buckingham and Charles went to Madrid. The treaty negotiations, however, turned out to be a charade, since neither side was prepared to make significant concessions; they broke down acrimoniously when it became clear that the Spanish court would not make Charles become a Roman Catholic. In its turn, Spain refused to intercede for Frederick against the Habsburgs. Humiliated and infuriated by this waste of time and effort, Buckingham and Charles returned home in September 1623, resolved upon war with Spain.

The question of an Anglo-Spanish alliance had been unpopular in England and the termination of the bargaining in Madrid was greeted with joy. At the decision to go to war with Spain, English Protestantism moulded itself into a national pride and patriotism of considerable force against the Romanists.

James had meanwhile made his favourite 1st Duke of Buckingham of the second creation (1623). But the old King was fast declining into senility. In the face of an alliance between his son and favourite on one side and his Puritan Parliament on the other, James was prevailed upon in 1624 to declare war on the Spaniards. The opposition of James's financial minister Cranfield (q.v.) was removed when Buckingham and Charles agreed to impeach him. However, they now found themselves embarking on a war without sufficient funds to pursue it. Buckingham sought an alliance against Spain with the French, the terms of which immediately alienated the Commons. Louis XIII agreed to the marriage of Charles to his sister Henrietta Maria, but in return he wrung considerable concessions from Buckingham for English Catholics.

The death of James in 1625 made little difference to Buckingham's position at court. He already enjoyed intimate relations with Charles and from now on was effectively head of his administration. After Charles's coronation Buckingham went to France to urge the full implementation of the terms of the alliance. But the rebellion of the Huguenots of La Rochelle prompted Louis to demand the already promised English assistance in suppressing it. Buckingham agreed to put English ships at Louis's disposal and Charles's marriage to Henrietta Maria went ahead.

Parliament's reaction was predictable. It demanded the full enforcement of the restrictions upon Catholics in England and clamoured for a full explanation of Charles's foreign policy, since it suspected that unfavourable treatment of Protestants abroad was involved. All this Charles refused, and Parliament was dissolved.

Buckingham had now got his royal master into an impossible position. They were supposedly engaged in an expensive Continental war, but had no funds with which to pursue it. The only sure source of funds, Parliament, had no confidence in Buckingham, was opposed to any alliance with any Catholic monarch, and refused to vote a penny for war supplies.

In spite of his great energy and febrile scheming, there can be no doubt about Buckingham's incompetence as an administrator and politician, and his next actions show this well. In the autumn of 1625 he sent an expedition against Cadiz, for the funding of which he pawned the Crown Jewels in The Hague. In the face of hostile public opinion he had also proceeded to repudiate his treaty with France and reintroduced the anti-Catholic laws. The English navy also began to seize French ships, on the pretext that they were carrying Spanish supplies. Buckingham had failed to calculate in advance the likely effect of his actions. The expedition to Cadiz was a total failure; Parliament still refused to vote any funds; and the French were infuriated by such perfidiousness.

Buckingham was attacked in the parliament of February 1626 and his former friend Sir John Eliot headed an appeal for his impeachment and arraignment on criminal charges. Charles's intervention saved him, however, and he subsequently gained an acquittal in the Star Chamber.

War eventually did break out between England and France and in 1627 Buckingham himself led a military expedition to the relief of the Protestants at La Rochelle, who were under siege by the French. Attacking the French position on the Ile de Rhé, Buckingham laid siege to it. But by a combination of bad luck and bad management his siege became a blockade, which the French succeeded in breaking to reinforce their garrison on the island. Buckingham was eventually obliged to retire with heavy losses and no possibility of reinforcements from home. He got back to England with less than half his men.

Thanks to Buckingham, England was now at war with France as well as Spain, had not a single powerful European ally, had failed to accomplish a single one of her foreign policy objectives, and had no funds with which to prosecute the wars. In 1628 the Commons forced through the Petition of Right and again called for Buckingham's dismissal and arraignment. Charles remained true to his favourite and once more prorogued Parliament. Meanwhile Buckingham, who if nothing else was a man of considerable resilience, was preparing another expedition against France. He was disheartened when he went to Portsmouth in August, however, by the languid attitude of his officers at the prospect of another battle. In the case of one of these officers, John Felton, this attitude was inflamed to hatred by the fact that he had incurred permanent injury in the previous year's exploit and had not received any pay. Thus, taking advantage of the rising tide of public opinion against the royal favourite, he decided to act in redress of his personal grievance. On the morning of 23 August 1628, Felton stabbed Buckingham to death. His death removed the immediate obstacle to understanding and co-operation between Charles I and his parliament, but had little long-term effect since the King turned out to be every bit as pig-headed and politically inept as his favourite had been.

Philippe Erlanger, *George Villiers, Duke of Buckingham* (English translation 1953).

M. A. Gibb, *Buckingham, 1592–1628* (1935).

Philip Lindsay, *For King or Parliament* (1949).

R. H. Tawney, *Business and Politics Under James I* (1958).

Hugh Ross Williamson, *George Villiers, First Duke of Buckingham* (1940).

Villiers, George (1628–87), 2nd Duke of Buckingham; courtier, politician, and playwright; friend and companion of Charles II.

Born 30 January 1628, at Wallingford House, Westminster, George Villiers was the elder surviving son of the 1st Duke of Buckingham (also George Villiers, q.v.).

After the assassination of his father, the 2nd Duke of Buckingham was brought up together with his younger brother Francis in the royal family, with the future Charles II and James II. The two boys were sent to Trinity College, Cambridge, and received their M.A.s in March 1642. They ran off to join the Royalist army early in the Civil War and served under Prince Rupert at

Lichfield Close in April 1643. As a result, Parliament promptly sequestered their estates. Their relatives and guardians had them sent off to the Continent, where they spent four years on the Grand Tour, passing much of their time at the splendid, debauched court of Florence, where they were treated like princes.

In 1647 Parliament restored the Villiers estates and the two brothers returned to England, where they were soon embroiled in Royalist plots. They fought in the Second Civil War, but were immediately involved in defeat. Buckingham escaped to Holland, but his brother Francis was killed. Parliament again confiscated Buckingham's lands, but he remained well off compared with most of the exiles, since a servant had smuggled jewels and pictures to him. He entered Charles II's court and Council, in which he supported a conciliatory policy towards Argyll (see Campbell, Archibald, 8th Earl) and the Covenanters and earned the enmity of Edward Hyde (q.v.).

Buckingham accompanied Charles in 1650 to Scotland, where he received command of the English Royalists, a position that proved to be without substance when the invasion of England actually took place. He fought with Charles at Worcester, and, like his royal master, managed to escape.

Buckingham's continual intriguing and quarrelling accomplished his isolation at the exiled court, alienating even Charles. Accordingly, he turned to England and, although unable to obtain a pardon, returned to his homeland, where he proceeded to woo and marry Mary Fairfax, only daughter of General Thomas Fairfax (q.v.), to whom Parliament had assigned his estates. His father-in-law's influence was sufficient to save his neck but not his freedom.

Buckingham was released after Cromwell's death. The Restoration ensured the return to him of his vast estates and the favour of Charles. As one of the richest men in England, and an intelligent and witty figure, he gained prominence at court and in the Privy Council, to which he was appointed in 1662. He indulged in his love of intrigue at the expense of his old enemy Hyde, now Lord Clarendon, whose downfall in 1667 he contributed to with Arlington (see Bennet, Henry) and his cousin Lady Castlemaine (see Villiers, Barbara), who was also Charles II's mistress. All the while he indulged his every whim, achieving notoriety as the greatest rake in England after Rochester (see Wilmot, John). On one occasion he was arrested for punching a fellow member of the House of Lords during a debate; on another for 'casting the King's horoscope'. Nevertheless, he managed to retain the King's favour.

Although he possessed no high office, Buckingham became one of the leading members of the Cabal, Charles's group of advisers. But he lost ground to Arlington after 1670, despite his fervour on behalf of Charles's French alliance, for the King knew he could not be trusted with the scheme to restore Catholicism in England; however, Buckingham's religious scepticism could be relied upon to win his support for the Declaration of Indulgence (1672), a keystone to the royal plans. Accordingly, he was sent to France to partake in the sham negotiations that led to war with the Netherlands, but made no mention of Catholicism. He was treated with great respect by Louis XIV, who gave a pension of 10,000 livres a year to Buckingham's mistress, Lady Shrewsbury.

The success of French arms against Holland alarmed Buckingham, who urged a separate peace with the United Netherlands. He was sent with Arling-

ton (see Bennet, Henry) to negotiate with the Dutch in June 1673, but their mission proved unsuccessful. The country was growing suspicious of Charles's designs, and when Parliament reassembled in January 1674, it turned its anger on Buckingham, blaming him for the King's arbitrary government, the French alliance, and the advancement of popery. In reply, he attempted, unsuccessfully, to impeach Arlington and made disparaging remarks about Charles. The Commons requested Charles to remove Buckingham from the royal presence, which he promptly did, dismissing him from all his offices.

Buckingham retired to the country, where he wrote letters and composed poems. As a writer, his greatest triumph was already behind him: his play, *The Rehearsal*, an amusing satire on heroic drama in general and Dryden in particular, had been first performed in 1671 and had proved immensely popular. More dramatic works followed, although none enjoyed the same success. He was also active as a patron of writers and of science.

Buckingham still retained a considerable personal following, which he put at the disposal of Shaftesbury (see Cooper, Anthony Ashley) when he returned to Parliament in 1675. In this alliance he helped to thwart the Non-resisting Bill of Danby (see Osborne, Thomas), which would have compelled all office-holders to swear an oath denying them the right to try to alter the government or to oppose the King. Buckingham thus associated himself with the country opposition. He continued in this camp, seeking without success the relief of Dissenters.

When Parliament reassembled in 1677, it was still essentially the old Cavalier Parliament of 1661. Shaftesbury, Buckingham, and Wharton proceeded to declare in the Lords that the previous prorogation, lasting more than a year, had the force of a dissolution. For this assertion, they were clapped into the Tower of London. Buckingham's release is traditionally attributed to the good offices of Nell Gwynne (q.v.). Although he roistered with Charles again, and took money from Louis XIV, he continued to co-operate with Shaftesbury, and pounced on the opportunities offered by the Popish Plot (see Oates, Titus) to prosecute his enemies. In the election of January 1679 he supported Whig candidates, but when the critical Exclusion Bill reached the Lords in 1680, he absented himself, apparently not being prepared to vote to exclude James from succession to the throne, while by no means being a supporter of the Catholic heir.

As Shaftesbury grew more extreme, Buckingham withdrew from politics. His health and fortune were both undermined by a life of debauchery, and he retired to Yorkshire, where he lived the life of a poor country squire. At the accession of James II, he penned a pamphlet arguing for religious toleration that caused a brief flurry. He died at Kirkby Moorside, Yorkshire, on 16 April 1687, and lies buried in Westminster Abbey.

Buckingham was in many ways the ultimate Restoration aristocrat. Handsome, witty, and unprincipled, he fascinated his contemporaries, but achieved little. To Dryden he was Zimri,

> A man so various that he seemed to be
> Not one, but all mankind's epitome;
>
> Stiff in opinions, always in the wrong,
> Was everything by starts and nothing long;
>
> But in the course of one revolving moon
> Was chymist, statesman, fiddler, and buffoon.

Lady Burghclere, *George Villiers, 2nd Duke of Buckingham* (1903).

Hester W. Chapman, *Great Villiers* (1949).

M. C. Lee, *The Cabal* (Urbana, Ill., 1965).

J. H. Wilson, *The Rake and His Times: George Villiers, 2nd Duke of Buckingham* (New York, 1954).

Portraits: oil, quarter-length, by Daniel Mytens, *c.* 1620–22: Hampton Court; oil, quarter-length, by Lely, *c.* 1675: N.P.G.; oil, full-length, by unknown artist: N.P.G.

Waller, Edmund (1606–87), poet and political figure.

Born at Coleshill, now in Buckinghamshire, on 3 March 1606, Waller was educated at Eton and King's College, Cambridge. He studied law for a time at Lincoln's Inn, and it is possible that he served as Member for Amersham in James I's parliament of 1621. With a brief interval during Charles I's parliament of 1626, he continued to sit in the Commons for over 21 years.

Waller came of a wealthy, well-established family and had inherited an estate at Beaconsfield while still a child. In 1631 he increased his fortune by marrying Anne Banks, rich heiress of a London merchant. His wife died in 1634 and he turned his affections to Lady Dorothea Sidney, the 'Sacharissa' addressed in some of his finest poems. His love, however, was unrequited, and the girl married someone else in 1639.

Waller's political activities until this time had inclined him toward the party of John Pym (q.v.). He was a cousin of John Hampden and more distantly related to Oliver Cromwell. But his family was at heart Royalist, and in the parliament of 1640 he himself took a more moderate position alongside Falkland and Hyde (q.v.). So far did this change of allegiance take him that in 1643 he was involved in a conspiracy to restore Charles I's authority in London. The plot was discovered, and Waller was arrested in May. In fear of his life, and acting with supine and abject cowardice, he recanted and betrayed his associates, escaping himself with a fine of £10,000 and the imposition of banishment.

Waller's years of exile were spent in France, Switzerland, and Italy. He spent some time with John Evelyn (q.v.), settling in Paris, where he showed hospitality to Royalists in exile. In 1652 Parliament allowed him to return home, and he lived quietly at Beaconsfield for the rest of the Interregnum. In 1655 he wrote his laudatory poem to Cromwell entitled *A Panegyric to My Lord Protector*, full of extravagant classical allusions.

In 1659, however, he felt able to write a second poem *On the Death of the Late Usurper, O.C.*, and at the Restoration he followed the example of Dryden (q.v.) and composed yet another poem *To the King, upon his Majesty's Happy Return*. When challenged by Charles II about the inferiority of this latter poem to the earlier *Panegyric*, Waller replied, 'Poets, Sire, succeed better in fiction than in truth.'

Waller re-entered Parliament in 1661, attending there until his death. He exhibited tolerance and a moderate standpoint in his politics, especially concerning religion. His second wife, one Mary Bracey of Thame, whom he had married just before his banishment, died in 1677 and Waller withdrew more and more to his Beaconsfield home. He died there on 21 October 1687.

The first edition of Waller's poems is dated 1645 and includes one of his loveliest poems, *Go, lovely Rose*, set to music by Henry Lawes (q.v.). It begins:

Go, lovely Rose,
Tell her that wastes her time and me

> That now she knows
> When I resemble her to thee
> How sweet and fair she seems
> to be.

His later works include *Instructions to a Painter* (1665), *Divine Poems* (1685), and a posthumous publication, *The Second Part of Mr. Waller's Poems*.

Popular enough during the 18th century, Waller's poetry no longer appeals to contemporary taste. Its artificiality seems too apparent. He is remembered chiefly today as the forerunner of the Augustans. 'Mr. Waller's reformed our numbers,' wrote Dryden, and the extent of Waller's reform was to approach English versification along neoclassical lines. Sentence inversion and a consequent avoidance of ordinary speech accent, together with a formal and elegant diction, rank as Waller's most important contributions to the techniques of English verse. The symmetry and balance of the heroic couplet are the tools that were tempered if not forged by him and were later used with great effect by Dryden and Pope.

G. Thorn-Drury (ed.), *The Poems of Edmund Waller* (2 vols.; 1905).
A. W. Allison, *Towards an Augustan Poetic* (1962).
F. W. Bateson, 'A word for Waller', *English Poetry* (1950).
R. L. Sharp, *From Donne to Dryden* (1940).
R. Skelton, *Cavalier Poets* (1960).

Waller, Sir William (?1597–1668), Parliamentarian general in the Civil War.

Waller was the son of Sir Thomas Waller, lieutenant of Dover, and was educated at Magdalen Hall, Oxford, and later admitted to Gray's Inn. He married Jane, daughter and heiress of Sir Richard Reynell of Devon, and subsequently twice re-married.

He acquired early military experience in the Venetian army and in the English expedition in the Palatinate, where he began a lifelong friendship with Sir Ralph Hopton (q.v.). His religious faith was sincerely Puritan, and in Parliament he was numbered among the opponents to the court policies.

At the outbreak of the Civil War he took command of a regiment of horse, which fought on the left wing of the Parliamentary line at Edgehill. This wing was broken by Prince Rupert's charge, and Waller had his horse killed under him. His reputation had already been firmly established by his capture of Portsmouth in September 1642 while on detached service, and he added to it after Edgehill by taking Farnham Castle, Winchester, Arundel Castle, and Chichester. As a result, he was designated the major general of the Parliamentary forces in the Severn area, with Bristol as his base and astride the road from South Wales, the Royalists' best recruiting area.

His first stroke was to destroy Lord Herbert's small but well-equipped army of Welshmen threatening Gloucester. Moving rapidly, Waller took Malmesbury by assault (21 March), crossed the Severn by boats, and surprised Herbert at Higham (24 March), securing about 1,000 prisoners. He then continued into Monmouthshire to seize Monmouth, Chepstow, and Ross-on-Wye. Prince Maurice (q.v.) was sent against him from Oxford and endeavoured to cut his line of retreat to Gloucester, but Waller broke through with some confused skirmishing at Little Dean.

Soon afterwards he met his first defeat, north of Tewkesbury at Ripple Field (13 April 1643). Prince Maurice had some advantage of numbers, and Waller had resolved to withdraw from the field when his force was struck by a well-timed charge by Maurice's cavalry, which routed the Parliamentarians completely, although not with excessive casualties. Maurice returned to Oxford, and Waller once more resumed his activity with the capture of Hereford (25 April).

The march of the Royalist Western Army through Devon and Somerset next demanded his attention. He concentrated at Bath to threaten their progress, being severely handicapped by lack of reliable infantry. The Royalist commanders, among whom were numbered Hopton and Prince Maurice, attempted to turn his position by a flank march east of Bath, but he outmanœuvred them by night marches and thereby brought about the Battle of Lansdown (5 July) on ground of his own choosing. Although he gave it up by an orderly withdrawal, again by night, the Western Army was almost ruined in the process of dislodging him.

The Royalists retreated to Devizes where Waller, who had been following closely but was unable to trust his infantry in an open battle, blockaded the town. A relief force of Royalist cavalry under Lord Wilmot was sent from Oxford, which attacked Waller on Roundway Down (13 July), broke his cavalry, and destroyed his infantry. Although he escaped to Bristol with the remnants of his army, he was unable to protect the city or prevent the subsequent conquest of almost all of the West Country by the Royalists.

Confidence in him was undiminished, however, and in November 1643 he was given command of fresh forces to be raised in the southern counties, augmented by troops of the City. The Parliamentarian commander, the Earl of Essex (see Devereux, Robert), exhibited some jealousy over this development and eventually was allowed to retain a nominal authority over Waller, as hitherto. At the same time the Royalist

council of war had decided upon a drive through the south towards London. This Waller checked by the storm of Alton (13 December) and the capture of Arundel Castle (6 January 1644), and on 29 March brought the main Royalist army under Hopton and the Earl of Forth to battle at Cheriton, an undistinguished battle in which the Royalists were defeated by their own lack of organization and numerical inferiority, but which nevertheless ended their hopes in that quarter decisively.

In May, the two armies of Essex and Waller were directed upon the King's capital at Oxford, the Royalists wisely declining battle and withdrawing their field army along their line of communications to Worcester. For a time the two commanders followed, but Essex's inability to co-operate with Waller and his lack of strategic sense induced him to part company and take his own force into the West Country, leaving Waller to march and countermarch in the wake of the King's army alone. With the morale of his soldiers deteriorating rapidly, he eventually was offered an opportunity to strike at the Royalists marching across his front at Cropredy Bridge (29 June 1644), but was repulsed, the total disintegration of his disaffected regiments taking place during the retirement southwards which followed.

In September he was sent with a force of cavalry to prevent the King's return from the southwest, where he had taken his army after Cropredy to defeat Essex. Waller was unable to fulfil his task for lack of strength, but in falling back before the advancing Royalists he was able to make a junction with the armies of Essex and the Earl of Manchester, and shared the command at the second Battle of Newbury (27 October 1644), himself leading (and probably initiating) a vital flank march by night around the north of the Royalist positions, which put the balance of victory on the Parliamentary side.

Waller's last military act took place in February 1645. Ordered to relieve Taunton, he could get no further than Devizes, his own men being mutinous through lack of pay, Essex's cavalry refusing to serve in his command, and that of Cromwell being persuaded to do so only by the presence of their own leader. The Self-Denying Ordinance passed by Parliament later that year rendered its members ineligible for army commands, and Waller laid down his without regret.

Waller had not been a hired sword, but a firm believer in the cause which he served; his endeavours on its behalf were now made in the House of Commons, where he became one of the leaders of the Presbyterian faction. As such, this brought him into increasing conflict with the Independents, whose instrument the New Model Army had become. Thus he came to be regarded by the Army as one of its principal enemies, and a campaign of calumny was mounted against him. He withdrew from the Commons, and in August 1647 he retired to France, returning to England the following summer to resume his place in Parliament in support of the proposed treaty with the King. He was arrested by the Army with other M.P.s in Pride's Purge (6 December 1648), but unlike the others was not released, spending three years imprisoned without any kind of trial and being released without compensation to make what he could of his ruined estates.

He was arrested again in March 1658 and examined by Cromwell himself on suspicion of plotting the overthrow of the Protectorate. Nothing was found to incriminate him, although he was in fact involved in dealings with Royalist agents to promote a rising in favour of Charles II. He was arrested again in August 1659 and was confined in the Tower until he obtained his freedom in October by means of a writ of Habeas Corpus. By now the restoration of legally constituted government was of greater importance to him than the establishment of a Presbyterian form of church, and he was prepared to sacrifice the chances of the latter for the former in any settlement that might be reached. Readmitted to Parliament with others by the action of Monck (q.v.), Waller was elected to the last Council of State of the Commonwealth and in the 1660 Convention Parliament was a member for Westminster, his known Presbyterian sympathies being important in reconciling the doubters among those of like mind. With the Restoration accomplished, he retired from public life without any sign of royal favour for his services at the last. He spent his last eight years in obscurity, dying on 19 September 1668.

J. Adair, *Roundhead General* (1969).
J. Adair, *Cheriton* (1973).
Margaret R. Toynbee and P. Young, *Cropredy Bridge* (1970).

Portrait: oil, half-length, by unknown artist: N.P.G.

Walpole, Sir Robert (1676–1745), 1st Earl of Orford of the second creation; Whig politician and statesman, see *Lives of the Georgian Age*.

Walter, Sir John (1566–1630), judge and M.P.

Born at Ludlow, Shropshire, Walter was the son of a distinguished member of the bar, Edmund Walter. He matriculated from Brasenose College, Oxford, in 1579, was created M.A. in 1613, was called to the bar in 1590, and was elected bencher of the Inner Temple in 1605. From the time of his admittance to the Inner Temple (1582), he began to acquire a high reputation for scholarship and was elected autumn reader in 1607. The year previous he had been selected to assist the Privy Council and the exchequer barons in their deliberations on the privilege of the court, and to defend in the House of Lords the royal prerogative of alnage (the fees charged for the official inspection and measurement of woollen cloth).

Walter established a flourishing law practice in the chancery and exchequer courts. In 1613 he was appointed the Prince of Wales's attorney general and was made a trustee of the prince's revenues as well. A knighthood was conferred upon him at Greenwich in May 1619. He became M.P. for East Looe, Cornwall, on 13 December 1620, and kept his seat in the next general election.

Throughout his career, Walter was generally a sound and moderate legal practitioner and a judge of integrity. A High Churchman (he obtained an indulgence from the Bishop of London in 1626 to eat meat on fast days), he steered a somewhat erratic legal course in deliberations on the controversial questions of royal prerogative and parliamentary privilege. On the impeachment of Edward Floyd in May 1621, he uncharacteristically proposed that the barrister should be whipped and his goods sequestered.

In 1625 Walter was made King's serjeant and also became chief baron of the exchequer. At the beginning of the reign of Charles I, he helped draft the prohibitions against plays, interludes, sport on Sundays, and bull and bear baitings. He generally supported the royal prerogative in money matters: he refused to inquire into the validity of the claims of tax farmers, and in 1628, when merchants resisted payment of the tonnage and poundage levy, his sentences were severe. However, in a minor case in the same year he pronounced legal judgment that words themselves could not amount to treason.

After the dissolution of Parliament in 1629, Walter deliberated with the other common law chiefs on whether M.P.s' privilege covered them in cases of defamation of privy councillors and allowed them to resist adjournment of the Commons forcibly. The judges' verdict, such as it was, was evasive and couched in more or less incomprehensible legal jargon. The King submitted the same question to the entire bench of common law and again received evasive legal replies, but did establish that the Star Chamber could proceed against the nine M.P.s who had resisted the adjournment. Walter dissented from the common law bench's opinion, and the King suggested to the attorney general that the chief exchequer baron should resign. Walter declined, and the King did not issue a writ against him, but on 22 October 1630, inhibited him from sitting in court. Although he did not sit again, Walter held his position until his death on 18 November. He was buried at Wolvercote, Oxfordshire.

Walter, Lucy (?1630–58), mistress of Charles II and mother of James, Duke of Monmouth (q.v.).

Lucy Walter was born in Roch Castle, Pembrokeshire, the daughter of a Welsh Royalist. In 1644 the castle was destroyed by Parliamentary forces and the family fled to The Hague. Colonel Robert Sidney (later Earl of Leicester) became her lover soon afterwards. During the summer of 1648 she caught Charles II's attention and became his mistress. She is often said to have been his first mistress, although there is some doubt about this.

Lucy spent the summer of 1649 with Charles in Paris, and the diarist John Evelyn (q.v.), who travelled with her from Paris to St. Germain, describes her as being 'a brown, beautiful, bold but insipid creature'. Charles's brother James thought she had not much wit but a great deal of cunning, and praised her looks. In April 1649 she bore Charles a son, who became the Duke of Monmouth.

In June 1650 Charles went to Scotland, leaving Lucy at The Hague. While he was away she took Henry Bennet (q.v.), later the Earl of Arlington, as her lover, and on his return Charles abandoned her. She was persuaded to return to England in 1656 by some of the King's friends, but Cromwell's agents reported her as a suspected spy and after temporary imprisonment in the Tower she was deported. She returned to Paris and in the autumn of 1658 died there, probably of venereal disease.

Until her death, Lucy embarrassed Charles by claiming to be his lawful wife, and this claim was revived during the Exclusion crisis of 1678–81. It was asserted that a marriage contract was preserved in a black box belonging to Sir Gilbert Gerard, the son-in-law of a bishop who had known Lucy in Paris. However, Sir Gilbert appeared before the Privy Council and stated that he knew nothing of the marriage contract. Charles himself issued three declarations in 1680 denying that a marriage had taken place and there is little doubt that Lucy's claim was untrue.

Lord George Scott, *Lucy Walter, Wife or Mistress* (1947).

Portrait: miniature, by Nicholas Dixon: Duke of Buccleuch and Queensberry Collection.

Walton, Izaak (1593–1683), author and biographer.

Born in Stafford on 9 August 1593, Walton was the son of an alehouse-keeper. Although in later life he was the friend of a number of prominent churchmen and other learned literary men, Walton himself received little formal education and it seems that writing, to which he turned in middle age, was never easy for him. As a youth he was apprenticed to his brother-in-law in London and was soon in business for himself as a draper, with a shop in Fleet Street. He was admitted as a freeman to the Ironmongers' Company – which does not imply that he was ever involved in that trade – and served in certain offices in the parish of St. Dunstan-in-the-West. Here he became acquainted with John Donne (q.v.), the subject of his first biography, who was vicar of St. Dunstan from 1624. He was married twice, on both occasions to women who were related to distinguished churchmen and who must have shared his deeply committed Anglican and Royalist views. Rachel Floud, his first wife, was a grand-grandniece of Archbishop Cranmer. Anne Ken, whom he married after the death of his first wife, was the half-sister of Thomas Ken, hymn-writer and Bishop of Bath and Wells. Of the large number of children borne by both his wives, only two by his second wife survived – a son, Isaac, and a daughter, Anne, who married Dr. Hawkins, a prebendary of Winchester Cathedral. It was with his daughter and son-in-law that he spent the last years of his long life. He died at Winchester and was buried in the cathedral.

Walton was successful at his business and by 1650 seems to have retired from London. He had already written the *Life of Dr. Donne* (published 1640). Originally, Sir Henry Wotton (q.v.) had intended to write a life of Donne and had asked Walton to provide him with material on his subject. Wotton, however, died in 1639 and Walton undertook the task which his friend had not lived to complete. The biography was rapidly written and printed as a preface to a collection of Donne's sermons in 1640. Short and simply written, intimate, lively, and interspersed with anecdotes, it was the first of the series of biographies for which Walton was most admired by his contemporaries. In 1651 he published *The Life of Sir Henry Wotton*, in 1665 *The Life of Mr. Richard Hooker*, in 1670 *The Life of Mr. George Herbert*, and in 1678 *The Life of Dr. Richard Sanderson*. The *Lives*, some of which Walton conscientiously revised a number of times for accuracy, were first collected in one volume in 1670 and appeared in several revised editions thereafter.

The *Compleat Angler, or the Contemplative Man's Recreation* (1653; fifth edition, with a continuation by Charles Cotton, 1676) was not received with the same esteem as the *Lives* during Walton's own lifetime; indeed, it was not until long after his death that the book, which commends the quiet and rural pleasures in which he spent the last forty years of his life, came to be regarded as his masterpiece. As well as being an instructive manual on angling, the book celebrates the countryside and pastoral life in a pleasant, discursive, old-fashioned spirit that readers since the late 18th and early 19th centuries have found irresistible. Beginning in the form of a dialogue between Piscator (fisherman), the author, Auceps (a falconer), and Venator (hunter), the book opens with each character presenting the case for his own pastime. Piscator soon becomes the dominant voice and proceeds to teach Venator about the various aspects of angling for all kinds of freshwater fish, with comments on the preparation of fishing lines and flies, and on ponds and rivers. The setting along the River Lea near London is described and songs and verses intervene between the discourses on fishing. In the second part, Walton's friend Charles Cotton made good a deficiency in Walton's original dialogue by elaborating on the description of fly-fishing, a subject that Walton, an expert angler, says that he has knowledge of only at second hand. In this continuation, Piscator and Viator (traveller, soon revealed to be Venator of the first section) discuss fishing for trout and grayling and the preparation of artificial flies against the picturesque setting of the River Dove between Derbyshire and Staffordshire.

Geoffrey Keynes (ed.), *The Compleat Walton* (1929).
M. Bottrall, *Izaak Walton* (1955).
R. B. Marston, *Walton and Some Earlier Writers on Fish and Fishing* (1894).
S. Martin (pseudonym for J. S. Walton), *Izaak Walton and his Friends* (1904, rev. ed.).
D. Novarr, *The Making of Walton's Lives* (Ithaca, N.Y., 1958).

Portrait: oil, half-length, by J. Huysmans, *c.* 1675: N.P.G.

449

Warwick, 2nd Earl of (1587–1658), see Rich, Robert.

Warwick, Sir Philip (1609–83), Royalist politician and historian of the Civil War.

Born in Westminster on 24 December 1609, the son of Thomas Warwick, organist of Westminster Abbey and the Chapel Royal, Warwick was educated at Eton and Westminster Abbey, where he was a chorister for a short time.

Philip Warwick travelled on the Continent after his schooling, before returning to London to become secretary to Lord George Goring (q.v.), who in 1636 obtained for him the post of secretary to the lord treasurer of England, Bishop William Juxon (q.v.). Warwick progressed to becoming clerk of the signet (1638) and was admitted to the bar at Gray's Inn.

He is famed for his memoirs of the early years of the Long Parliament, of which he was a member. A staunch supporter of the court, Warwick was one of the small number of M.P.s who voted against Strafford's attainder (see Wentworth, Thomas), and in 1642 he faithfully followed Charles I to Oxford, where he sat in the Royalist 'Anti-Parliament' that was summoned. As a result in 1644 he was expelled from the Long Parliament.

Before this date Warwick had already taken up arms for the King as a volunteer, fighting in the royal guard at Edgehill (1642). The King sent him on important missions to the Marquis of Newcastle and others during later stages of the war. When Charles was a prisoner of the New Model Army in 1647–48, Warwick attended him as secretary. The King had perfect trust in him, and he admired and loved the King greatly. After Charles's execution in 1649, Parliament forced him to compound for his estates.

Although highly regarded in Royalist circles, Warwick appears not to have engaged in plots during the Commonwealth; nevertheless, he was imprisoned once, and in 1660 he began to work actively and with considerable effect, especially among members of the House of Lords, towards achieving the return of the Stuarts. A grateful Charles II rewarded him with a knighthood, and in 1661 he was appointed secretary and *de facto* deputy to the lord high treasurer, the Earl of Southampton. This post he held for seven years, filling it with industry and integrity and making the professional acquaintance of Pepys (q.v.), with whom he formed a close friendship. When Southampton died in 1667, Warwick lost his Treasury post, but received a sinecure as a reward for his services.

In 1661 also he was elected to the long-serving Cavalier Parliament, in which he exerted little influence and loyally supported the ministry on most issues. Warwick died on 15 January 1683.

His writings – two books – were both published posthumously. The more famous, the *Memoirs*, which appeared in 1701, was written between 1675 and 1677 from sketchy notes and from memory, but it is a significant source for the history of the Civil War, since it includes invaluable characterizations of Charles I, leading Royalists, and others, an account of the early years of the Long Parliament, and a record of the deeds and words of Charles in captivity. Although not to be compared with Clarendon's work in merit, Warwick's *Memoirs* stand out for their relatively moderate and unbiased writing.

Sir Walter Scott (ed.), *Memoirs of the Reign of Charles I . . . with a continuation to the Happy Restoration of Charles II* (1813).

Webster, John (?1580–?1625), Jacobean dramatist.

Born in London, the son of a tailor, Webster was possibly admitted to the Middle Temple in 1598. Virtually nothing is known of his life. He appears to have started his literary career as a hack with the actor-manager Philip Henslowe (see *Lives of the Tudor Age*), collaborating with dramatists such as Thomas Middleton, and Dekker (qq.v.). With Dekker, he worked on the citizen comedies *Westward Ho!* and *Northward Ho!* (1603–04; published 1607). He also worked with Dekker, Heywood, and Chettel on *The Famous History of Sir Thomas Wyatt* (probably produced 1602 under the title of *Lady Jane*; printed 1607), and on other plays that have not survived, including *Caesar's Fall* with Middleton, Drayton, and others. Other lost works include *A Late Murder of the Son Upon the Mother* (with Ford, q.v.), while the Dedication of *The Devil's Law Case* (1623) refers to yet another lost play, probably called *Guise*. Various other works, including *A Cure for a Cuckold* (?1625) and *Appius and Virginia* (?1626) have been attributed without certainty to Webster. Among minor works, he wrote an elegy upon the death of Prince Henry (*A Monumental Column*; printed 1613), the city pageant *Monuments of Honour* (1624), and he contributed a number of 'New Characters' to the sixth edition of the *Characters* of Sir Thomas Overbury (q.v.).

Gildon's *Lives and Characters of the English Dramatic Poets* (1698) states questionably that Webster was clerk of St. Andrew's, Holborn, a theory supported by Charles Lamb among others and made attractive by the abundance of references in Webster's own plays to death, tombs, and charnel houses. What seems certain is that he was made a freeman of the Merchant Taylors' Company in 1604 – which does not mean he ever pursued that profession – and in the same year wrote the Induction to Middleton's *The Malcontent*. Among the few clues we have to Webster's likely character is his own address 'To the Reader' in *The White Devil*, in which he defends himself against the charge of being a slow worker by quoting a classical analogy in which Euripides scores over a similar gibe made by Alcestides. The hint of slowness, and also of a crabbed, crotchety, and somewhat pedantic manner, is taken up in a contemporary verse attack on 'Websterio' (a reference to the Italianate setting of Webster's tragedies) by one Henry Fitzjeffrey of Lincoln's Inn in *Certain Elegies done by Sundry Excellent Wits*.

Such a picture of the dramatist is not difficult to accept, given the characteristics of the three plays published under his name that have survived, *The White Devil* (1612), *The Duchess of Malfi* (1623), and *The Devil's Law Case* (1623). Of these, the latter is a tragi-comedy of an inferior sort and Webster's reputation as one of the greatest, if most greatly flawed, of the Jacobean dramatists rests on two plays alone.

These two plays are remarkably similar in tone and character. On one level, they are examples of the Senecan revenge tradition that was introduced into the popular Elizabethan theatre by Kyd with his *Spanish Tragedy* and developed with Shakespeare's *Hamlet*, Marston's *The Malcontent*, and Tourneur's *Revenger's Tragedy*. The main characteristics of the revenge tradition, apart from the solemn duty of revenge itself, are a certain predilection for supernatural stage tricks, Gothic 'horrors', and above all, violent language, furious quarrels, and inhuman deeds. Add to these a special obsession with imagery of decay and dissolution, of corrupt sexuality and power, and a magnificent poetry that seems to catch fire with its cadences, and you have the essential Webster, most essential perhaps in the language of that other creation of the Italian Renaissance, the Machiavellian tool who chafes constantly at his fate, the malcontent who sins and is conscious of sinning and yet stoically continues in his doomed path:

> We endure the strokes like anvils or hard steel,
> Till pain itself make us no pain to feel.

Such a figure is Flamineo in *The White Devil*, to whom these lines belong, and Bosola in *The Duchess of Malfi*, both of them cynical schemers who still retain some moral sense and also a sense of disgust at their own – as well as the world's – wickedness. Disgust, indeed, plays a large part in the psychology of many of Webster's most memorable characters, whether it is the world-weariness of the Cardinal in *The Duchess of Malfi* or the violent mad imaginings of his brother Ferdinand, whose temper is matched by his language:

> I would have their bodies
> Burnt in a coal-pit with the vantage stopped,
> That their cursed smoke might not ascend to heaven.

Such language, together with grotesque stage effects such as the gift of a dead hand by Ferdinand to his sister the Duchess, does not appeal to all. 'Tussaud laureate' was how Bernard Shaw summed up Webster, and William Archer criticized him thus: 'Ramshackle looseness of structure and barbarous violence of effect . . . hideous cacophonies, neither verse nor prose .. Bedlam-broke-loose ... poor Webster.' Of these criticisms, perhaps the one least reducible to personal taste is that of poor structure; certainly, the fifth act of Webster's plays is invariably an anti-

climax, and in *The Duchess of Malfi* it is not easy to adjust to the transition from the end of Act II, where the Duchess's brothers have just learned of her secret marriage and the birth of her child, to the beginning of Act III, where we learn that she has had two more children. Even admitting these faults, however, one should remember that dramatists of Webster's time composed essentially scene by scene, and that such gaps or faults in structure may be overriden by the successive swift strokes of action and the heightened poetic language that was Webster's great gift to the Jacobean theatre:

> Whether we fall by ambition, blood, or lust,
> Like diamonds we are cut with our own dust.

J. R. Brown (ed.), *The White Devil* and *The Duchess of Malfi* (Revels Plays; 1964, new. ed.).

F. L. Lucas (ed.), *The Works of John Webster* (4 vols.; 1927).

Travis Bogard, *The Tragic Satire of John Webster* (Berkeley, 1955).

Rupert Brooke, *John Webster and the Elizabethan Drama* (1916).

R. W. Dent, *John Webster's Borrowing* (Berkeley, 1960).

C. Leech, *John Webster: A Critical Study* (1951).

Peter B. Murray, *Study of John Webster* (The Hague, 1970).

Elmer E. Stoll, *John Webster* (Boston, Mass., 1905).

Webster, John (1610–82), Puritan preacher and writer.

Born on 3 February 1610 at Thornton in Yorkshire, Webster was ordained in 1632 and two years later became curate of Kildwick in Yorkshire. There are references in his own writings to studying at Cambridge, but there is no evidence in the university records to support this claim.

During the Civil War Webster served as chaplain and surgeon in the Parliamentarian army; by 1648 he had left the established church, and after the war ended he achieved a wide reputation for his Nonconformist sermons at Mitton, also in Yorkshire, where he was installed by the new government. Webster's opinions on contemporary university education excited particular attention, and to define his own position as clearly as possible he published in 1654 his *Academiarum Examen*, in which, he claimed, he was not attacking the universities themselves, 'but only the corruptions that time and negligence hath introduced there.' The Bishop of Salisbury published a reply, and during the ensuing controversy Webster's books were taken from him by the authorities. For the remainder of his life Webster appears to have abandoned the ministry and to have devoted his time to the study of metallurgy and medicine.

In 1677 Webster published his most important book, *The Displaying of Supposed Witchcraft*, in which he attacked the credulity of several prominent members of the church. Five years later, on 18 June 1682, Webster died at Clitheroe. He had an active intelligence and is notable in a century of superstition and bigotry for his open-mindedness and objectivity.

Weelkes, Thomas (?1570–1623), organist and composer, see *Lives of the Tudor Age*.

Wentworth, Thomas (1593–1641), 1st Earl of Strafford; statesman and minister under Charles I.

Born in London on 13 April 1593, son of William Wentworth, a rich landowner from Wentworth-Woodhouse near Rotherham in Yorkshire, where the family had been established for several generations, Thomas Wentworth was educated at St. John's College, Cambridge, and entered the Inner

Temple in 1607. Four years later he was knighted and married Lady Margaret Clifford, daughter of the Earl of Cumberland, whose family, though impoverished, still exercised great influence in the northern counties.

In 1614 Wentworth returned from a visit to France, undertaken as part of his education, and sat for Yorkshire in the 'Addled Parliament'. He appears to have taken no active part in the debates, and during the period between this session and James's third parliament of 1621 he concerned himself with local politics. In 1615 he became *custos rotulorum* (keeper of the rolls) in Yorkshire, keeping out his powerful neighbour Sir John Savile from that position and only vacating it in 1626, when he was dismissed.

The sway that Wentworth exercised in the North seems to have released him from the necessity of court patronage. Yet, being a constitutionalist, and favouring the smooth running of the government without interference from religious considerations, he took up a moderate position in the session of 1621.

Again representing Yorkshire, he supported the King's determination to resist the Puritans' clamour for war with Spain, but opposed the King's denial of freedom of discussion to the Commons.

In James's last parliament (1624) Wentworth again took little part, but he must have been unsympathetic to the policy of aggression that Buckingham (see Villiers, George, 1st Duke) and Charles were pushing through. His relations with the royal court were by no means improved by his second marriage. Following the death of his first wife in 1622, Wentworth wed Arabella, the daughter of John Holles, Earl of Clare, a man out of favour with the court, in February 1625.

In June of the same year, Charles I summoned his first parliament. Wentworth, while having no wish to antagonize the King, nevertheless stood with those who opposed Buckingham's policy of war with Spain and later also with France. After the dissolution, the court resorted to the device of appointing Wentworth sheriff of Yorkshire in order to keep him out of the second parliament. His disapproval of the expensive policy that the court was pursuing led him to withhold any support for the raising of money without parliamentary consent. This was probably a contributory factor in his dismissal from the offices of Justice of the Peace and *custos rotulorum* in 1626. In 1627 Wentworth refused to contribute to the forced loan levied by Charles for the purposes of financing the war effort. As a consequence, he was imprisoned.

In the parliament of 1628 Wentworth joined the general outcry against the illegal fund-raising and imprisonment carried out by the King. As early as January, he was preparing a Parliament proposal to lay before Charles. The proposal was, however, too moderate for the more militant members of the Commons, and Eliot and Coke (qq.v.) took the initiative to draw up the instrument that later became known as the Petition of Right. Out of respect for the constitution, Wentworth was probably anxious not to offend too greatly the royal prerogative. It is possible that the court realized this, or perhaps the King, having lost his minister Buckingham through assassination, was concerned to make up for his past ill-treatment of Wentworth and hoped to turn his opposition into alliance. However that may be, in July 1628 Wentworth was offered a barony, which he accepted. At the end of the same year he became Viscount Wentworth and Lord President of the North, and in 1629 he was appointed to the Privy Council. Though consistent with his attitude of loyalty to the crown and constitution, his change of allegiance seemed remarkable to his contemporaries. It must be noted that during this period Wentworth at no time supported any drastic alteration in the power of the executive, nor was he interested in allowing the religious climate to influence measures to be taken in the national interest. Put off by the rising tide of Puritanism and the extremism associated with it, he now moved away from the Parliamentarians, who labelled his defection as apostasy.

As lord president of the north, Wentworth was in virtual control of the whole of England north of the Humber. He was able to implement some of the policies that he was later to pursue in Ireland, putting down all defiance of his authority as the representative of the King, whose power he was assiduous in maintaining. The assassination of Buckingham and the rise of Wentworth led to a period of more responsible policies; some of the benevolence and paternal indulgence that characterized the early years of Charles's government is due possibly to Wentworth's influence in the Privy Council. But some of his energetic ruthlessness was also apparent in his repression of the King's opponents. He was also a man of personal ambition eager for power and the fruit of power. Yet here again he had a vision of good and just government, as his measures for closer supervision of the Justices of the Peace and more effective implementation of the poor law both demonstrate.

At the end of 1631 Wentworth's second wife died; within a year he secretly married Elizabeth Rhodes, daughter of Sir Godfrey Rhodes, a neighbouring squire.

In January 1632 Wentworth was named lord deputy of Ireland and took up his appointment in July 1633. At once he set to work making firm the authority of the King. He broke the hold of the English landlords and did much to help the native Irish poor. He improved methods of agriculture, increased the productivity of the land and utilization of resources, and stimulated the spread of industry. He took advantage of the recent peace made with Spain to set up favourable trading relations between that country and Ireland. He cleared the sea of pirates, personally taking over the administration of customs, and enormously increased the revenue. He recovered much church property misappropriated by unscrupulous landlords. He reformed Trinity College, Dublin, and founded the first theatre in that city. Finally, and perhaps crucially, he raised a small army in Ireland.

Yet all these achievements were obtained by arbitrary and brutal means. Ruthlessly repressing all opponents, he enforced his will by frequent recourse to the prerogative Court of Council Chamber. The summary manner in which he ousted inefficient English

officials was remarkable, however worthy their replacements might be. An example of his arbitrariness was his treatment of Lord Mountnorris, the vice-treasurer. In order to take over the administration of customs, Wentworth had to remove Mountnorris; this he achieved in 1635 by having him convicted of treason and then pardoned before the sentence of death was carried out. Undoubtedly, Wentworth was a despot. His government was referred to by both himself and Laud (q.v.), with whom he regularly corresponded, as the policy of 'thorough'. Inevitably, however, he alienated both the English, whose authority he had undermined, and the Irish also. For in his rule he contrived not only to extend English settlement – he moved into Connaught, despite a promise made by Charles not to do so – but also attempted to impose English Protestantism upon the nation. Laud encouraged him to imitate those reforms that he himself was endeavouring to introduce in the English Church. Not surprisingly, such measures antagonized both the Catholics and the Puritans.

Wentworth was recalled to England in 1639 as adviser to Charles, following the disaster of the First Bishops' War against Scotland. Seeing the Scots as rebels, Wentworth counselled the recall of Parliament; he felt certain that with careful handling they could be prevailed upon to grant subsidies for a war against rebels. He went so far as to tell Charles that the Irish Parliament would definitely do so.

In January 1640 Wentworth was created Earl of Strafford. Two months later he returned to Ireland and fulfilled his promise to the King by obtaining from the largely Catholic Parliament a generous grant to fight the Presbyterian Scots. The English Parliament was, however, unco-operative; they wanted nothing short of peace with Scotland. Upon his return to England in April, Strafford suggested that Charles should accept less than he had asked for. Yet this too availed nothing and on 9 May 1640, Parliament was dissolved, Strafford voting for its dismissal much against his better judgment.

During the summer of 1640, Strafford, urging Charles either to pursue his original design against the Scots or leave them alone, supported various schemes for raising money, such as debasing the coinage or seeking a loan from Spain by the offer of an alliance. He also reminded Charles, 'You have an army in Ireland you may employ here to reduce this kingdom.' By 'this kingdom' he meant Scotland, but the phrase was ambiguous and the ambiguity was exploited by his opponents.

After the outbreak of the Second Bishops' War, Strafford took command. But he fell very ill, and following the catastrophe of Newburn and the loss of the northern counties, Charles was constrained to give up the fight and call his last parliament.

The Long Parliament assembled on 3 November 1640. Strafford was recalled to London by Charles and arrived there on 9 November. The King promised Strafford that he 'should not suffer in his person, honour, or fortune.' Yet Strafford, now the main target for attack, was about to face impeachment in the Commons. He tried to prevail upon Charles to forestall this by accusing John Pym (q.v.) and his associates of having had treasonable communications with the Scots. Pym was forewarned, however, and commenced proceedings against Strafford before he could take his seat in the Lords. He was committed to the Tower, and at the end of January 1641 detailed charges were

brought against him accusing him of trying to subvert the laws of the kingdom. His trial began in March. Strafford made an able and reasoned answer to his accusers, whose case was weak and circumstantial. His judges, the members of the House of Lords, were not unimpressed, and the trial was going very much in his favour. The possibility that the impeachment might fail caused Pym to introduce a bill of attainder in Parliament, by which Strafford could be summarily done away with. The bill was forced through both houses amid popular rioting.

Strafford's fate hung on Charles's signature to this document. At the introduction of the bill of attainder, the King had reiterated his promise to protect Strafford and rumours that he had a scheme to free his minister led to the riots just mentioned. He delayed putting his signature to the bill as long as he could, but with the situation becoming increasingly volatile, Strafford himself offered Charles a means of cooling it down. Writing to the King to release him from his promise, Strafford said: 'I do most humbly beseech you, for the prevention of such massacres as may happen by your refusal, to pass the bill.' Charles eventually signed the bill of attainder on 10 May 1641, and two days later Strafford was executed amid general rejoicing.

A man of severe, ruthless methods and greedy ambition, Strafford nevertheless had a vision of good responsible government. An upholder of the King's power against that of the people, Strafford made many enemies, yet he also made firm friends. In the last analysis, his readiness to die in order to reconcile Charles with his subjects, and the dignity with which he met his fate, show him to be a patriot and a man of great personal loyalty.

Earl of Birkenhead, *Strafford* (1938).

H. Kearney, *Strafford in Ireland, 1633–41* (1959).

W. Knowler (ed.), *The Earl of Strafford's Letters and Despatches* (1739–40).

C. V. Wedgwood, *Thomas Wentworth, First Earl of Strafford: A Revaluation* (1961).

Portraits: oil on panel, after Van Dyck: V. & A.; oil, three-quarter length, after Van Dyck, *c.* 1633: N.P.G.

Wharton, Thomas (1648–1715), 1st Marquis of Wharton; politician under William III and Queen Anne and member of the Whig Junto.

Thomas Wharton was born in August 1648, the third and eldest surviving son of Philip, 4th Baron Wharton, by his second wife, Jane. He received a strict Puritan upbringing and seems to have spent most of his adult life compensating for it. He acquired the title 'the greatest rake in England' as a young man and maintained a good claim to retaining it until his death. In 1673 he married Anne, daughter of Sir Henry Lee. The main attraction was probably Anne's £10,000 dowry and income of £2,500 a year, rather than her personal qualities. There were no children of the marriage.

Wharton rapidly acquired a reputation as a judge of horses and spent a great deal of time at Newmarket, apparently owning a number of racehorses.

He entered Parliament in 1673 as Member for Wendover. He retained this seat until 1679, when he became Member for Buckinghamshire. He displayed little active interest in politics, however, until 1679–80, when he supported the Exclusion Bill. In 1685 he was one of the small minority who voted against settling a revenue on James II for life. In 1688 he corresponded with William of Orange and in November joined him at Exeter. However, his greatest blow against James and his court was his composition of the anti-Jacobite song *Lilliburlero*, which, set to music by Purcell, became a tremendous success. Wharton is said to have boasted later that he 'had sung a king out of three kingdoms.'

In 1689 Wharton voted for the motion declaring the throne vacant, and shortly after William and Mary's proclamation he was declared a privy councillor and comptroller of the household. On his father's death in 1696 Wharton succeeded to the barony and an annual income of £6,000. By 1697 he was emerging as a prominent Whig and clearly hoped for further political advancement. He was at first disappointed in this respect, but did receive the lucrative post of warden of the royal forests south of the Trent. In the same year he was appointed lord lieutenant of Oxfordshire and in an excess of Whig zeal removed five heads of Oxford colleges from the commission of the peace and put in twenty-four new justices. His favour stood high at court and in 1698 King William was his guest and stood godfather to his son by his second marriage. In 1702 he was made lord lieutenant of his own county of Buckinghamshire.

Wharton was dismissed from all his posts upon the accession of Queen Anne, who is said to have disliked him personally and regarded him as an enemy of the Church, but this setback served only to further stimulate Wharton's commitment to Whig principles. In 1702–04 he attacked the Occasional Conformity Bill, a measure by which the Tories intended to weaken the political power of those Dissenters who attended just sufficient Church of England services to enable them to retain their positions. In 1703 he increased his personal popularity in Buckinghamshire by his support for Matthew Ashby, a burgess in Aylesbury who was being denied the right to exercise his franchise by the mayor and returning officer of that town. In 1705 Wharton spent over £12,000 in promoting the return of a Whig parliament, and though he did not receive an official government post he became closely associated with the policies of the Whig Junto of Halifax (see Montagu, Charles), Orford (see Russell, Edward), Somers (q.v.), and Sunderland (see Spencer, Robert).

In 1706, despite Queen Anne's continued disfavour, Wharton was named as a commissioner for the negotiations of the treaty of union with Scotland, and was then created Viscount Winchendon and Earl of Wharton. The passionate speeches which Wharton delivered in the House of Lords embarrassed some of his colleagues as well as his enemies, and many were relieved when in 1708 he left England to take up his new appointment as lord lieutenant of Ireland. Joseph Addison (see *Lives of the Georgian Age*) acted as Wharton's secretary in Ireland. Wharton's policy in Ireland, chiefly characterized by consistent attempts to suppress Roman Catholicism, won him the support of the Irish Parliament and the enmity of many of the more High Church leaders, the latter being especially angered by the tactlessness of several of Wharton's personal appointments. In 1710 Wharton was recalled to England, probably because the Whig leaders were now missing his abilities as a party manager, but ironically Wharton's vehement support for the impeachment of Henry Sacheverell (q.v.) did the Whig cause far more harm than good.

After the defeat of the Whig party in 1710, there was some discussion as to whether any kind of alliance should be formed with the Tories. Wharton took matters firmly into his own hands and persuaded his fellow Whigs to refuse to compromise. They threw themselves into opposition with fervour, and under Wharton's direction fostered every element of discontent and opposition to the Tory government. He vigorously opposed the Schism Bill in 1714 and seized every opportunity to attack the Treaty of Utrecht.

During Anne's last illness he was prominent among the Whig leaders who reasserted their right, even though they were in Opposition, to sit in the Privy Council, from which they ensured the peaceful proclamation of George I.

In February 1715 George created him Marquis of Wharton and Marquis of Catherlough in the Irish peerage. He did not live to enjoy his honours for long: in March he became ill and he died at his house in Dover Street, London, in April 1715. He was survived by his second wife, Lucy, an heiress of great fortune, whom he had married in 1692, and their three children, Philip, 2nd Marquis and 1st Duke of Wharton, Jane, and Lucy.

Wharton can be regarded in some respects as a precursor of Walpole. He was a skilful party organizer and honestly believed that no Tory could be a true Englishman, but must, at heart, be a Jacobite. His successes at elections were always overwhelming, but this is easy to understand: he spared no expense in getting his electors drunk on good ale, and it is said that he knew all the electors' children by name.

John Carswell, *The Old Cause* (1954).

Portrait: oil, half-length, by Kneller, *c*. 1710: N.P.G.

Whitelocke, Bulstrode (1605–75), Parliamentarian lawyer and politician.

Born on 6 August 1605, in London, the son of Sir James Whitelocke, a judge, Bulstrode Whitelocke was educated at Merchant Taylors' School and St. John's College, Oxford.

Bulstrode Whitelocke was called to

the bar of the Middle Temple in 1626, where he directed his energies both into the social life of the Inns of Court, with his friend Edward Hyde (q.v.), and to his legal career, which was much helped by his father's influence and, perhaps, by his election to the parliament of 1626. He was of sufficiently high social standing to make the acquaintance of Cardinal Richelieu while travelling in France in 1634.

By defending popular causes, such as the civil jurisdiction against the ecclesiastical, Whitelocke prospered and won popularity in the 1630s. He was elected to the Long Parliament, where, as chairman of the Commons' prosecuting committee, he played a prominent role in the destruction of Strafford (see Wentworth, Thomas). He played a similar role in other great issues of the day, such as the act preventing the dissolution of the Long Parliament and the Grand Remonstrance. Although he was considered by all to be a moderate, he sided with Parliament at the outbreak of the Civil War but took little part in the fighting. His activity was more political – the abortive peace negotiations with Charles I and the counselling of Essex and Fairfax.

After the first stage of the Civil War, when Parliament quarrelled with the Army, Whitelocke opposed the attempts by the extreme Presbyterians to disband the troops. He remained aloof from the ensuing conflict, turning again to the law. In March 1648 he was appointed one of the commissioners of the Great Seal, a post he held repeatedly until 1660. In this capacity he encouraged moderate reform of the law, replacing Latin and Medieval French by the English language in legal proceedings and improving procedure in many other ways.

After the second stage of the Civil War, Whitelocke attempted but failed to find a compromise over the fate of the King between the Army and Parliament. He found himself called upon to draw up charges against King Charles, but refused to take any part in the trial of the King. However, later he agreed to serve on the first Commonwealth Council of State. His conservatism came repeatedly to the fore: he opposed the abolition of the House of Lords, and in 1651, after Parliament's defeat of Charles II at Worcester, advised the victorious Cromwell to restore the Stuarts. Things came to a head in April 1653 when Whitelocke opposed the dissolution of the Rump Parliament and was singled out by Cromwell as one of his opponents. But by September relations between the two had been restored, and Whitelocke was dispatched as ambassador to Sweden, where he negotiated a treaty of alliance with great finesse.

Although Whitelocke, as a lawyer, opposed the reform of chancery proceedings initiated by Cromwell, he remained in government posts and exercised considerable influence in the realms of trade, foreign affairs, and finance. In 1657 he was one of the leaders among those who wished Cromwell to take the throne, and received a seat in the new upper chamber, where, after the death of the Lord Protector, he also upheld the rule of Richard Cromwell and opposed the dissolution of Parliament, which the Army sought. When the younger Cromwell fell and the Rump was restored, Whitelocke was immediately elected to the Council of State (May 1659). At the expulsion of the Rump (October), he was taken onto the new governing committee set up by the Army leaders, and co-operated with them. Distrustful of Monck, he sought in vain to persuade Fleetwood to restore Charles II, and when Monck triumphed and reinstated the Long Parliament, Whitelocke was forced to retire to the country, since he was associated with the defeated Army leaders.

Whitelocke was not persecuted after the Restoration, for, as his friend Clarendon wrote, he was thought never to have acted out of malice and had indeed given aid to the defeated Royalist rebels of 1659. He was allowed to retire to Wiltshire, and died on 28 July 1675, at Chilton Park, Berkshire.

Whitelocke was a profuse author on the subjects of history, politics, theology, and commerce. His best-known work is his account of the Civil War and Commonwealth, compiled after the Restoration and now deemed to be highly unreliable in many parts. However, his description of his Swedish embassy of 1653–54 is a valuable document because of his perceptive descriptions of the great people of the court.

Memorials of the English Affairs from the Beginning of the Reign of Charles I to the Happy Restoration of Charles II (reprinted in 4 vols.; 1853).
R. H. Whitelocke, *Memoirs, Biographical and Historical, of Bulstrode Whitelocke* (1860).

Portraits: oil, quarter-length, by unknown artist, *c.* 1650: N.P.G.; oil, half-length, by unknown artist, 1634: N.P.G.

Wilbye, John (1574–1638), musician and composer of madrigals.

Born at Diss in Norfolk, the son of a prosperous tanner and farmer, Wilbye was baptized on 7 March 1574. His father died while the boy was quite young, and left him a lute. Little else is known of his early life except that he came to the attention of the music-loving Cornwallis family, and in 1595 when Elizabeth Cornwallis married Sir Thomas Kytson of Hengrave Hall, Bury St. Edmunds, she took the young man with her as resident musician. He never married, and remained in the family's service for the rest of his life, even after

Sir Thomas Kytson's death in January 1602.

In 1613 Wilbye leased a sheep farm from the Kytsons and later came to own property in Diss, Bury St. Edmunds, and Palgrave. In 1628 Sir Thomas Kytson's widow died and Wilbye accompanied her youngest daughter, Lady Rivers, who was separated from her husband, to Colchester, where he continued as resident musician. The exact date of his death is unknown, but his will was probated in November 1638.

Wilbye's instrumental works have survived in only a fragmentary state and are too insubstantial to allow a proper judgment of them. His sacred works are few and unimportant. The great achievement for which he has come to be best known consists of the two sets of madrigals published in 1598 and 1609. These pieces, sixty-four in number, together with a contribution to Thomas Morley's *Triumphs of Oriana*, represent what are still justly regarded as the finest works in the literature of the madrigal. He was a perfectionist in style, and obtained great effect through the grouping of voices. Through the editions published by Edmund H. Fellowes from 1913 to 1924 they have become firm favourites in the repertoire of modern madrigal choirs.

Wildman, Sir John (?1621–93), political agitator.

Born about 1621 and educated at Cambridge University, Wildman probably saw action during the Civil War under Sir Thomas Fairfax, but it was not until 1647 that he first came into prominence.

In the autumn of that year Wildman was actively involved with a dissident section of the New Model Army who opposed any compromise between their officers and the King. These dissenters were influenced by the ideas of political democracy propounded by the Levellers, of which group Wildman became a member. In October 1647 he acted as spokesman for the dissidents at a meeting of the officers' council at Putney, and was one of the architects of the 'Agreement of the People', which was discussed at the meeting. In a pamphlet entitled *Putney Projects*, he made an attack on Oliver Cromwell, and he was also probably the author of the rank-and-file manifesto embodied in the pamphlet *The case of the Army stated*.

In January 1648 the authorities, acting on information received, moved against Wildman and John Lilburne (q.v.), another prominent Leveller. Both men were, however, released in the following August, and set about redrafting the 'Agreement of the People', the first draft of which had failed to find acceptance at Putney. Wildman had been very much to the fore in urging the Levellers' appeal to natural rights. The movement advocated the abolition of the monarchy and of the House of Lords, the investment of all power in the Commons, and a wider suffrage. The Army commanders at Putney had rejected the demands of the dissidents on the grounds that political democracy led to economic democracy, which was the overthrow of property. The changes that the generals now wished to make to the new proposals were totally unacceptable to most of the Levellers, including Lilburne. Wildman, however, seems to have been satisfied with them. At all events, he gave up the struggle and from 1649 became involved in property speculation, buying and selling land appropriated from Royalists and the church. He obtained considerable wealth and prestige and bought an estate at Shrivenham, Berkshire. In 1654 he was elected M.P. for Scarborough.

Cromwell's inauguration as Lord Protector in 1653 was an outrage to men of republican persuasion like Wildman. There is some evidence that he was refused permission to take his seat in Parliament in 1654 for failing to give the required undertaking not to try to alter the government. His career as a conspirator and agitator now began in earnest. Intriguing with both Levellers and Royalists, he hoped to engineer a combined uprising to overthrow Cromwell. His plans were abortive, and on 10 February 1655, he was committed to prison. A petition by his business associates secured his release in 1656 and he immediately recommenced his plotting, continuing right up to Cromwell's death in 1658. After the forced dissolution of the Rump Parliament in 1659, he was involved in drawing up a form of government for the council of the officers. But again he plotted, this time with Parliament against the Army. He assisted in gaining Windsor Castle for the Parliamentary forces. For this action and for his hostility to Cromwell during the Protectorate, he escaped punishment at the Restoration.

Wildman now held a position at the post office, where in 1661 he was the centre of a scandal in which he was accused of malpractice involving alleged interference with letters. Also suspected of plots to overthrow the monarchy in favour of a republic, he was arrested in November 1661 and imprisoned for the next six years. His detention was welcomed by Clarendon (see Hyde, Edward), who had not trusted him during the years of exile. While Clarendon controlled the administration, Wildman had no hope of release, but upon Clarendon's fall in 1667 he was set free, and in July 1670 he was given leave to go abroad for his health in company with his family.

Wildman had developed a friendship

with George Villiers (q.v.), 2nd Duke of Buckingham. It had been rumoured that he was to get a seat on a Parliamentary commission through the interest of Buckingham in 1667, although nothing came of this. Throughout his travels abroad, he kept in close touch with Buckingham and became a trustee of his estate in 1675.

Back in England in or before 1680, Wildman began to intrigue again, this time against the prospect of a Catholic monarchy. He played a significant part in the conspiracies that followed the parliament of 1681, including, no doubt, the Rye House Plot, in which a group of Exclusionists planned the assassination of Charles II and his brother James. Wildman was arrested and placed in the Tower on 26 June 1683. How he got away with his life and liberty is not known. Nevertheless, he was released on 18 February 1684.

At liberty again, Wildman embarked on more intrigue. After the succession of James II in 1685, he gave secret support to the Duke of Monmouth (q.v.), but because of disagreements over how to manage the uprising and also because Monmouth had failed to tell the people what he would do for them in the event of his success, Wildman withdrew at the eleventh hour and took no part in the rebellion. His original complicity was known, however, and in June 1685 he was compelled to flee to Holland to escape arrest.

He remained there, probably at Amsterdam, for the rest of James's short reign, and returned to England with William of Orange in 1688. In 1689 he sat for Wootton Basset in the Convention Parliament and was made postmaster general and freeman of London. Suspected of using his position to discredit William III's supporters and of intriguing with the Jacobites, he was

dismissed in 1691. Yet despite this latest piece of plotting, William awarded him a knighthood in 1692.

Wildman's whole life had been devoted to sedition and agitation. Whether he was serious in wishing to see a republic with sovereignty invested in the people rather than just the men of property or the monarch is not easy to say. He himself had thought of the 'Agreement of the People' as laying 'the foundation of freedom for all manner of people'. But he was too wilful to lead a united democratic movement with properly formed objectives. Playing off one side against another to gain advantage availed him nothing, and in the end he succeeded in being, in Sir William Coventry's phrase, 'a false fellow to everybody.' He died on 2 June 1693, and was buried at Shrivenham.

M. Ashley, *John Wildman* (1947).

William III (1650–1702), King of England, Scotland, and Ireland (1688–1702), ruling jointly with his wife, Mary II, during her lifetime.

Born in the stadholder's apartments in the Old Palace at The Hague on 4 November 1650, posthumous and only son of William II, Prince of Orange, and his wife Mary, eldest daughter of Charles I. William of Orange was born in most inauspicious circumstances. His father had died eight days before of smallpox, his mother's confinement being brought on early as a result of the grief and shock. William's father died in the midst of schemes to redeem a failed coup d'état designed to increase the authority of the stadholderate. The States General of Holland, led by John de Witt and his brother Cornelius, seized the opportunity of an infant Prince of Orange to weaken the power of the house of Orange. They were helped by factious differences inside the family, especially as seen in the fight between the formidable Princess Dowager Amalia (William's grandmother) and the Elector Frederick William of Brandenburg (his uncle) for the child's guardianship. An uneasy compromise was reached, leaving William's mother in charge.

In 1654 Oliver Cromwell concluded a peace treaty with Holland on condition that the Prince of Orange or his descendants should never hold the offices of stadholder or captain general of the union. This was revoked in 1660 with the Restoration of the English monarchy.

In 1664 William's mother died, and the States of Holland assumed the supervision of his education. At this point Charles II intervened. As William's uncle, he felt he had a right to a say in the boy's upbringing, especially since William was a possible heir to the English throne through his mother. An unseemly squabble resulted, which Charles lost. De Witt now took a personal interest in William's education, particularly his political instruction. William appears to have been good at languages: he spoke Dutch, English, French, and German with equal ease and fluency, and understood Spanish, Italian, and Latin. He seems to have been a dour, reserved child with little interest in amusements except for hunting. He was already exhibiting the impenetrable self-control and graveness of manner which characterized him throughout his life. His health was weak and his body frail. He was very small and thin in stature, and suffered from asthma.

In 1671 de Witt admitted William to the Council of State, but insisted on a perpetual edict abolishing the office of stadholder in Holland and separating it for ever from the captain generalcy. This was an obvious plan to ensure that the house of Orange did not regain the

ascendancy. However, France was proving an increasing threat to the Low Countries, and pressure came from all sides for William's appointment to the traditional role of the Prince of Orange, namely that of captain general. De Witt was forced to agree, and William was appointed in February 1672 both captain general and admiral general.

On 12 June a French army five times as large as the Dutch forces crossed the Rhine. William was forced into retreat, but retained firm discipline and good order. De Witt's reputation was smashed, as he had earlier disbanded half the army, and the country looked to William as a leader against the threat from Louis XIV. The perpetual edict was abolished, and in June 1672 William became stadholder. He was still only twenty-two. The de Witt brothers were assassinated and, although William was in no way implicated, this event certainly eased his situation. De Witt's successor, Fagel, supported William absolutely, and the house of Orange regained its former ascendancy.

William refused to surrender to Louis XIV and concluded an alliance with Brandenburg and the Empire. In 1673 Spain joined the alliance. William meanwhile rebuilt his army and in 1673 captured Naarden, a key fortress, and moved into Cologne. Faced by the possibility of encirclement, the French withdrew from the Low Countries. In 1674 England concluded a separate peace treaty with William, and France's attempt to seize the Low Countries was temporarily repulsed.

Throughout 1674 the war continued and was mainly favourable to France. At the Battle of Senef in August, both William and the French general Condé claimed victory. However, William managed to hold his position in the face of attempted French encroachments. In the same year William succeeded in making the stadholderate hereditary in the house of Orange. He now had firm control in Holland.

In 1675 William contracted smallpox and was nursed by his faithful friend Bentinck (q.v.), who remained his close adviser almost to the end of William's life. In 1676 and 1677 the war with France continued, but William, despite his great personal bravery, was unable to make any impression on the French forces. He suffered a defeat at St. Omer in April 1677, but this was more than offset by his diplomatic victory in obtaining an English marriage for himself.

The possibility of a marriage between William and Mary, eldest daughter of the Duke of York, had been talked of for some years, and in the autumn of 1677 William went to England. He received Charles II's approval and on 4 November married Mary, took her back to Holland, and became involved in international politics again. In August 1678 he concluded the peace of Nijmegen with France. The Empire and Spain pressed on with the war, but their losses only demonstrated to the people of the United Provinces the wisdom of William's policy. His reputation as a leader grew, and he became the natural choice to lead any further European alliance against France. In 1681 he achieved an alliance between the United Provinces, Sweden, the Empire, and Spain for the maintenance of existing treaties. In 1682 France occupied the principality of Holland, but William had domestic troubles and was unable to raise the support necessary to repel the invading forces; in 1684 France annexed Luxembourg.

Meanwhile William was becoming, by virtue of his birth and his marriage, an important figure in English politics. In 1685 Charles II died and was succeeded by his brother, Mary's father, as James II. James was becoming increasingly unpopular at home because of his overt Roman Catholicism, but William was scrupulous not to interfere in his father-in-law's affairs. Although both the Argyll and Monmouth expeditions against James left from Amsterdam, William tried to prevent them sailing. He went so far as to send the three Scottish regiments in his service to James's assistance, closely followed by his three English regiments, even offering to command the latter himself. Good relations subsisted between England and the Netherlands until Louis XIV's revocation of the Edict of Nantes (1685). William – a Calvinist – gave shelter to the Huguenots. This marked the beginnings of disagreement, and when James intensified Roman Catholic appointments in England, William became a focus for Protestant hopes.

In the summer of 1688 Edward Russell (later Earl of Orford) arrived in Holland to sound William out, and he agreed to undertake an armed expedition to England provided that he received an invitation from a certain number of responsible and powerful Englishmen. He very soon received such an invitation, and with the support of the new Elector of Brandenburg, Frederick III, and the grudging agreement of the States of Holland, set out for England, arriving at Brixham in Devon on 5 November. Bentinck accompanied him, and Marshal Schomberg was second-in-command. James II fled the country and William met with no resistance. When James was arrested and brought back by a group of zealous Protestant fisherman, William connived at a second escape by him.

William refused to accept the crown by right of conquest and summoned a Convention Parliament. There was a move to make Mary sole monarch, but William made it clear that he was 'not prepared to become his wife's gentleman-usher.' Halifax's proposal to put William on the throne as sole monarch met with little support, and, influenced by Danby, Halifax, Shrewsbury and others, both Houses made a resolution to ask William and Mary to rule jointly. The Declaration of Right was drawn up by a committee. The Glorious Revolution was seen by Parliament and the classes it represented as a conservative issue, restoring rights and privileges to Parliament which had been ignored or usurped by James. The Declaration of Right listed Parliament's grievances against James, and settled the succession after Mary to go to her issue, then to Anne and her issue, then to the issue of William. Mary arrived from Holland in February 1689, the crown was formally offered to William and Mary jointly on 13 February, and on 11 April they had a joint coronation, Compton (q.v.), the Bishop of London, officiating. The Scottish Convention met in March and proclaimed William and Mary joint

sovereigns, but William was blamed for neglecting Ireland, where James had established a parliament.

England now declared war on France. William laid the foundation of the future Grand Alliance by agreeing, as King of England, to a treaty between the Empire and the United Provinces. A secret clause undertook to support the Emperor's claim to the Spanish succession.

After raising sufficient revenue from Parliament William left for Ireland, leaving Mary to conduct the government in his absence. He met joint French and Irish forces at the Boyne where William, showing his habitual personal courage, led his men into battle and put James to flight (14 July). The victory at the Boyne had stopped James using Ireland as a 'stepping stone' to England, and the English conquest was completed by the capitulation of Limerick (1691).

William's energies were now chiefly directed towards raising funds to continue the Continental wars. In 1691–92 he was involved in a winter campaign in Europe, and in 1692 he was forced to dismiss Marlborough (see Churchill, John) because of the latter's involvement with Jacobites. In the same year, William's orders for severe treatment of any Highland rebels, particularly the troublesom MacDonalds, led to the Massacre of Glencoe (see Macdonald, Alexander). Also in that year Louis XIV equipped a powerful fleet to invade England, which was resoundingly defeated at La Hogue. William was not so successful on land, however. There was a series of failures, but the French suffered too many casualties to press home their advantage. William fell back on Brussels and returned to England.

The two years' campaign had led only to the retention of the status quo, and in England many Tories were beginning to grow weary of the war, which the

Whigs and merchants saw advantages in continuing. In 1693 further loans were raised through the new institution of the Bank of England, the bill establishing the Bank of England receiving royal assent in 1694. The administration was now almost entirely Whig, and William returned to the Continental war – with inconclusive results. In December 1694 Mary died of smallpox. William effected a reconciliation with Anne and showed consistent kindness to Anne's son and his own heir, the Duke of Gloucester, until the child's death in 1700. Rumours of his remarriage were at first rife, but were apparently without foundation and soon died out.

In 1696 an election was due, according to the provisions of the Triennial Act, and William visited various parts of the country. A decided Whig majority was returned. William's opening speech to Parliament showed his determination to continue with the war, although he was forced to make concessions, especially in respect of Irish land grants made by James, which were now revoked. By this time, however, both England and France had suffered great financial losses from the war and William was inclined towards peace. In 1697 the Peace of Ryswyk was signed by England, France, the United Provinces, and Spain. England secured an undertaking from France not to assist enemies of William – in effect, a recognition of William as king. James, however, remained ensconced at St. Germain. The treaty also provided for the safety of the Empire's frontier and an advantageous commercial treaty was arranged for the United Provinces with France.

William was accorded a hero's welcome in England. But disagreements broke out between the King and Parliament as to the retention of a standing army. William employed delaying tactics, meanwhile negotiating with Louis XIV for a settlement over the Spanish succession. Parliament became increasingly hostile to William and he was again forced to compromise. His desire for union with Scotland was thwarted, the whole Darien disaster was brought up (see Paterson, William), he was forced to agree to a bill voiding his Irish land settlements, and perhaps most insulting, an address was carried against the employment of any foreigner in the service of the state (except Anne's husband, Prince George of Denmark). William prorogued Parliament to avoid receiving this address.

The year 1700 brought two deaths which were vitally important to European succession. Anne's only surviving child, the Duke of Gloucester, died and the succession was settled on the Electress Sophia of Hanover; and Charles II of Spain eventually died, willing the entire Spanish empire to the younger son of the French Dauphin. Not surprisingly, Louis XIV accepted this will. In 1701 Parliament met again. It was mainly Tory, as is evidenced by Harley (q.v.) being the Speaker. Parliament was divided as to whether to go into another war with France. Harley proposed that this matter should be left to William to decide and after much inconclusive argument this was how the matter rested. The Act of Settlement was passed and William prorogued Parliament.

William immediately embarked for the Continent, leaving Marlborough, now restored to favour, to follow with an army, and set about forming what came to be known as the Grand Alliance. Scarcely had negotiations been concluded before he heard of the death of James II and the recognition by Louis XIV of James's son, the Old Pretender (see James Francis Edward Stuart in *Lives of the Georgian Age*).

Support for William in England increased. On 30 December 1700, William opened his last parliament and put the treaties of the Grand Alliance before both Houses. He was voted an army of 70,000 men, and the Security Bill was passed – all officeholders, whether in Church or state, had to swear allegiance to William and abjure the Pretender.

William's frail health had been bad throughout the winter and he had consulted many eminent physicians, sometimes by post. He was riding at Hampton Court when his favourite horse, Sorrel, stumbled on a molehill and threw him. He broke his collarbone, but it was not a serious injury and he was taken back to Kensington Palace to recover. However, he suffered with pain and fever and died on 8 March 1702. His death was apparently due to pleurisy following the accident and inflammation of one lung.

The most important factor in William's life was his determination to check French expansion in Europe. His aim was to save the United Provinces from being overrun by France and he devoted all his efforts to this cause with a single-minded consistency and determination. To further this end, he ensured that he had the military leadership of a united Europe. He took the English throne to bring England into the alliance and put it on a firmer footing, and he allowed Parliament to get away with extreme provocations as long as he had financial support for his army. It is true that Holland became less important after William left, but he ensured its independence, freedom, and prosperity. In England, his reign was of immense constitutional importance. The power of Parliament grew, and the balance between the crown and Parliament steadied. By inclination William was a soldier, and regarded as a great one by his contemporaries. He was not a fortunate general, but he conducted his campaigns with great circumspection, determination, and dash. Although the brilliant military victories went to Marlborough, it was William who created the Dutch and English armies and left England in a position of great military strength at the core of a powerful European alliance.

Stephen B. Baxter, *William III* (1966).

Marjorie Bowen, *William, Prince of Orange* (1928).

E. L. Ellis, 'William III and the Politicians', *Britain after the Glorious Revolution 1689–1714*, ed. G. Holmes (1969).

G. J. Renier, *William of Orange* (1932).

Nesca A. Robb, *William of Orange* (2 vols.; 1962–66).

Portraits: oil, three-quarter length, by W. Wissing, 1685: Hampton Court; oil, full-length, by Kneller, 1691: Windsor Castle; oil, half-length, after C. Johnson: N.P.G.; oil, three-quarter length, after Lely, 1677: N.P.G.; engraving, full-length, by unknown nineteenth-century artist.

Williams, Roger (?1603–83), founder of Rhode Island and apostle of religious liberty.

Born in London, the son of James Williams, a merchant, Roger Williams was educated at Charterhouse and Pembroke College, Cambridge, and was a protégé of the famous jurist, Sir Edward Coke (q.v.), who furthered his education. Williams was awarded his B.A. in 1627 and took holy orders before the end of 1628, when he was appointed chaplain to a Puritan family in Essex. There he fell in love with a cousin of his employer's wife, but his suit was refused by the girl's mother. In response he wrote an angry letter acknowledging the rejection but questioning whether the proud mother would ever enjoy the fruits of paradise.

Nevertheless, by 1630 Williams had found himself a wife. That year he sailed to New England to join the new colony on Massachusetts Bay, where he was to be received as a 'godly minister'. But when he arrived in 1631 he quickly became disillusioned with the theocratic society he saw around him. In contradiction to the settlement's establishment he declared that the civil authority had no right to enforce any religious creed.

Williams spent the next two years in the neighbouring colony of Plymouth, returning in 1633 to take up the post of assistant to the minister of Salem, with whom he attacked the conferences of clergymen, alleging that their meetings subverted the liberties of the congregations. When his minister died, in August 1634, Williams was elected his successor, despite the opposition of the general court, which he did nothing to mollify by attacking the appropriation of Indian land. He continued to be a thorn in the side of the local rulers, and in October 1635 the general council banished him from its territory.

Before leaving, Williams attempted to collect followers with whom he could settle on Narragansett Bay, but when the authorities received word of his efforts they set out to frustrate his plans, and he was forced to flee alone.

He spent the winter in the wilderness and survived only through the friendship of the Indians. In the spring, with a few companions from Massachusetts, he founded Providence. From the first, the new colony separated Church and state and maintained religious freedom. Land was bought from the Indians, with whom close relations were maintained. This benefited both the hostile Massachusetts colonists, for whom Williams negotiated when they were engaged in wars with the Indians, and the native peoples themselves, whom Williams respected and tried to defend from the greed and land hunger of the other settlers.

Unlike so many other Puritans, Williams did not try to convert the Indians. This was probably due to his own religious scruples; he was never a conventional Puritan and for a while declared himself a Baptist before becoming in 1639 a Seeker, one of those who rejected all the Churches, sects, and ministries in their search for God. This endeared him even less to the theocracy of Massachusetts and, despite his good offices during their troubles with the Indians, these stern Puritans spared no opportunity to harass Providence and its associated settlements. In fact, they sought a patent for the land around Narragansett Bay. To foil their designs, Williams was sent by his fellow Rhode Islanders to England in 1642, where – with the aid of Sir Henry Vane the Younger (q.v.), a Seeker who had personally experienced the intolerance of Massachusetts – he obtained from Parliament a patent for the land around his colonies two years later.

While in England, Williams entered into the great pamphleteering battles of the day. His most significant contribution to the controversies that were raging was *The Bloody Tenent of Persecution* (1644), in which he defended religious liberty for all mankind, including Muslims and heathens. But his struggles for the survival of Rhode Island were not yet ended. A faction in the settlement attempted to split them into two separate colonies, and Williams had to spend the years 1651–54 in England again, where he succeeded in getting the colony reunited by the Commonwealth government. While in England he published more tracts and made the acquaintance of Hugh Peter and John Milton.

Williams served three terms as president of the colony (1654–57), during which time he allowed Jews and Quakers to settle, although he disagreed violently with Quakerism. When George Fox (q.v.) visited Rhode Island in 1672,

Williams challenged him to a debate, but was forced to settle for a public disputation with two of Fox's assistants, from which both parties emerged declaring themselves winners.

A shadow was cast over the last years of his life by King Philip's War (1675–76), in which the colony fought the Indians. Roger Williams died in the first quarter of 1683.

O. E. Winslow, *Master Roger Williams* (New York, 1957).

Willis, Thomas (1621–75), English physician and anatomist; known for his extensive work on the anatomy of the brain.

Willis was born at Great Bedwin, Wiltshire, on 27 January 1621, and educated at Christ Church, Oxford. After obtaining his B.A. (1639) and M.A. (1642) degrees from Oxford, Willis temporarily bore arms for the King. After a short period of military service, he resumed his studies and obtained an M.B. degree (1646). In 1660 he was appointed Sedleian professor of natural philosophy, and in the same year obtained his M.D. degree. Willis was a founding member of the Royal Society, and in 1664 was elected an honorary fellow of the Royal College of Physicians. Two years later he moved to London and established a medical practice. In this he was apparently richly rewarded, for it has been reported that 'in a very short time he became so noted and so infinitely resorted to for his practice, that never any physician before went before him, or got more money yearly than he.'

In 1664 Willis published the results of his anatomical studies of the brain (*Cerebri anatome*, 'Anatomy of the Cerebrum'), to which Christopher Wren contributed several drawings. In this great work, Willis clarified the previous classification of the cranial nerves and named the spinal accessory nerve. He also described the roughly polygonal meeting of arteries at the base of the brain (known today as the 'circle of Willis'). He was able to observe this ring of vessels by injecting *aqua crocata* (a preservative) into prepared specimens, which rendered the vessels firm.

In addition to his anatomical research, Willis was one of the first physicians to mention the diagnostic signs of sweetness of breath and urine in persons suffering from diabetes mellitus, and was the first to describe myasthenia gravis and puerperal fever.

He died in London on 11 November 1675, after a career that was successful both financially and academically.

C. Singer and E. A. Underwood, *Short History of Medicine* (1962).

Wilmot, John (1647–80), 2nd Earl of Rochester; poet, wit, courtier, and rake.

Born on 10 April 1647, at Ditchley, Oxfordshire, Wilmot was the eldest son of Henry Wilmot, a Royalist general who helped Charles II escape after his defeat at Worcester (1651) and in return was created 1st Earl of Rochester (1652). John succeeded to the title in 1658, when its chief value was as a guarantee of the exiled monarch's goodwill.

After private tuition from Francis Giffard, a clergyman, young Rochester attended Burford Grammar School, where he was considered 'an extraordinary Proficient at his Book'. All this changed when in 1660 he went up to Wadham College, Oxford; despite the presence there of the brilliant group of scholars that eventually became the nucleus of the Royal Society, Rochester preferred to allow himself to be debauched by Dr. Robert Whitehall, a hard-drinking fellow of Merton. White-

hall would disguise the thirteen-year-old earl in an M.A.'s gown and take him around the taverns. He also apparently taught him to write verse, for Rochester published a precociously accomplished poem on Charles II's Restoration. His father's loyal actions now meant substantial rewards for Rochester; when he was only fourteen, Edward Hyde procured for him an M.A. The King gave him a pension of £500 a year and in late 1661 sent him on the Grand Tour, supervised by Andrew Balfour, a learned Scottish divine who was 'to bring him back to love learning and study'. After extensive travels in France and Italy, Rochester in 1664 returned to England and presented himself at court, where his 'easy and obliging' manner won him instant popularity.

Rochester soon fell in with the 'merry gang', a group of much older men that included the Duke of Buckingham, the Earl of Dorset, and Sir George Etherege, whose 'cursed bawdy talk' appalled Pepys. They were great pranksters; on one occasion Buckingham and Roches-

ter, posing as innkeepers, took charge of a tavern on the Newmarket Road and seduced all the local girls. In the spring of 1665 Rochester paid court to Elizabeth Malet, the beautiful grand-daughter and heiress of Lord Hawley, and when she rejected him he hired an armed gang to abduct her to Uxbridge. For this he was thrown into the Tower, but was soon freed and promptly volunteered for the navy. He took part in Teddiman's bold attack on the Dutch East India fleet in Bergen harbour, showing 'as brave and as resolute a courage as was possible'. The following spring, during the fierce Four Days' Battle in the English Channel, Rochester braved Dutch gunfire to ferry despatches in a small boat.

Surprisingly, in January 1667 Elizabeth Malet finally agreed to marry Rochester, who had just been made a gentleman of the royal bedchamber at £1,000 a year. From now on the earl led an extraordinary double life. His letters demonstrate his genuine affection for Elizabeth, and he was to prove a devoted father to their four children. Otherwise, he was 'prince of all the devils of the Town', and once claimed that he had been drunk for five years continuously. His rakishness appears to have sprung, not from a frivolous disposition, but from an energetic determination to pursue immorality and defy Puritan conventions.

Charles II greatly enjoyed Rochester's scurrilous and witty talk, and used him as a spy in his more sordid amatory adventures; the earl would dress up as a footman or a palace guard and listen at ladies' chambers. In return, Rochester's more outrageous deeds were frequently forgiven; in January 1669 he boxed the actor Tom Killigrew's ears at a state banquet for the Dutch ambassador, and the following July he started a brawl at the Paris Opera. Ultimately, though, Rochester's position at court was precarious, since he could never resist turning his acid tongue on the ministers, the royal mistresses, and even Charles himself, of whom he said, 'He never said a foolish thing and never did a wise one.' For this he was sent away in disgrace at least once a year, invariably to be soon recalled. Even exile did not dampen Rochester's spirits; during one banishment, he spread rumours about the King's love-life amongst respectable City society, and during another he posed as a quack and sold patent medicines to gullible housewives on Tower Hill.

However, there was a more serious side to Rochester. He would laughingly relate how he 'used to retire to the country for a month or two to write libels', but these periods of rural peace were in fact spent in serious literary effort. Although he took many mistresses, usually from among the serving-maids of court ladies, he was considerate to them; he took great pains to train Elizabeth Barry for the stage, where she had a very successful career.

From 1670 on, Rochester revealed himself as a shrewd, if rather savage, literary critic, especially in his 'imitation' of Horace's tenth Satire. He also took under his wing such promising writers as Dryden and Otway. But his patronage was fickle; he quarrelled bitterly with Mulgrave, Dryden's other patron, even fighting an inconclusive duel with him, and he abruptly abandoned Otway when the playwright made advances to Elizabeth Barry. The character of Count Rosidore in Nathaniel Lee's *Princess of Cleves* (1681) is flatteringly modelled on Rochester.

But being both a court favourite and a member of the 'merry gang' still took up much of Rochester's time. In 1674

Charles II generously made him keeper of Woodstock Park, and in 1676 Rochester took part in a drunken battle with some Epsom watchmen, in which one of his friends was killed. In 1679 Rochester fell seriously ill, probably with venereal disease, and during convalescence he read Bishop Burnet's *History of the Reformation*, much to the surprise of his rakish friends. He later had long talks about religion with Burnet, and when in 1680 he realized he was dying, he urgently summoned the good bishop to Woodstock Park. Burnet spent four days at Rochester's bedside, hearing the 'profane' earl's dying repentance, and later wrote a best-selling book about it. John Wilmot, 2nd Earl of Rochester, died on 26 July 1680, and was buried in an unmarked grave at Spelsbury, Oxon.

In late 1680 appeared Rochester's *Poems on Several Occasions*, under a spurious Antwerp imprint. The collection is of a consistently high literary standard, and such lyrics as 'Absent from thee I languish still' and 'An age in her embraces past' are among the finest of their time. The satires *The Maim'd Debauchee* and *Tunbridge Wells* are full of caustic observations and brilliantly reproduced dialogue, expressing Rochester's fundamental disgust at the mediocrity of contemporary English society, with its dandies, cuckolds, and 'fantasticks'. His most disturbing poem is *A Satire Against Mankind*, where he marries his own disillusionment to the philosophy of Hobbes and La Rochefoucauld to produce a philosophy of outright libertinism, placing honest natural impulses above rational behaviour. Rochester was probably the most brilliant member of Charles II's court, but disappointed idealism produced in him a profoundly amoral cynicism which ultimately destroyed him.

J. Hayward (ed.), *The Collected Works* (1926).

V. de Sola Pinto (ed.), *Poems by John Wilmot, Earl of Rochester* (Muses' Library; 1964, rev. ed.).

Poems on Several Occasions by the Right Honourable, the Earl of Rochester – a facsimile of the original 1680 edition with an introduction by J. Thorpe (Princeton, N.J., 1950).

J. H. Wilson (ed.), *The Rochester-Savile Letters 1671–1680* (Columbia, Ohio, 1941).

E. B. Chancellor, *The Lives of the Rakes* (6 vols.; 1924–25).

Graham Greene, *Lord Rochester's Monkey* (1974).

Charles Norman, *Rake Rochester* (1954).

V. de Sola Pinto, *Enthusiast in Wit: a Portrait of John Wilmot, Earl of Rochester, 1647–1680* (1962).

Johannes Prinz, *John Wilmot, Earl of Rochester* (Leipzig, 1927).

C. W. S. Williams, *Rochester* (1935).

Portraits: oil, three-quarter length, after J. Huysmans, 1665–70: N.P.G.; oil, by Lely: V. & A.

Wimbledon, Viscount (1572–1638),
see Cecil, Edward.

Winchilsea, Countess of (1666–1720),
see Finch, Anne.

Winchilsea, 6th Earl of (1647–1730),
see Finch, Daniel.

Windebank, Sir Francis (1582–1646),
secretary of state to Charles I and one of his most intimate advisers during the period of government without parliaments (1629–40).

Born in 1582, the son of Sir Thomas Windebank of Hougham, Lincolnshire, Windebank was educated at St. John's College, Oxford, which he entered in 1599 through the good offices of William Laud (q.v.) and from which he obtained his B.A. in 1602, the same year that he entered the Middle Temple.

After travelling on the Continent (1605–08), Windebank held a number of minor positions in public life, eventually becoming in 1624 clerk of the signet. In 1632, the year of his knighthood, Charles appointed him secretary of state, a post that he shared with Sir John Coke.

In this appointment, Windebank acted for Charles in many secret negotiations. Sympathetic both to Roman Catholicism and to Spain, he co-operated with others who held similar views in assisting the King to maintain veiled political relations with the Spaniards. In December 1634 he had secret talks with the papal agent, Gregorio Panzani, and discussed with him the feasibility of a union between the Anglican and Roman Catholic Churches, suggesting that the Puritans might be paralysed into submission by sending their leaders off to war in the Netherlands. In 1635 Windebank, as Treasury commissioner, became involved in shielding a number of people guilty of corruption, and thus incurred the anger of Laud. In the following year he suffered a period of disfavour after the unauthorized appropriation of Spanish funds to pay Spanish troops in the Netherlands. In 1638 he urged Charles to make war on the Scots.

With the resumption of parliamentary sessions in 1640, Windebank sat as M.P. for Oxford University (in the Short Parliament) and Corfe (in the Long Parliament). In December 1640 the Commons discovered that he had sent letters of favour to recusant clergymen and to Jesuits. To escape the wrath of Parliament, he fled to France, where he remained an exile until his death in Paris on 1 September 1646.

Hardly an attractive character, Windebank had been elevated to the heights of office by reason of religious and political inclinations rather than ability. Though far below his contemporaries in aptitude, he undoubtedly possessed some sincerity. Shortly before his death he was received into the Roman Catholic communion.

Winstanley, Gerrard (1609–?60), revolutionary theorist and leader of the Digger movement.

Born in Wigan, Winstanley was presumably educated at a grammar school. In his youth he listened to sermons and was involved with the Anabaptists, the representatives of Christian communism in 17th-century Europe. He set up as a cloth merchant in London, but was ruined by the Civil War and withdrew to the country to live with friends in the Thames Valley, where he was put in charge of the cattle.

In 1648 Winstanley began his short but fruitful career as a pamphleteer, writing in vigorous simple prose. In that year he wrote four pamphlets on religious themes. His thought is dominated by mysticism, but of a peculiar type. In his first pamphlet he rejects the belief that souls can be eternally damned, and in later works denies the existence of heaven or hell. His thoughts on the after-life are agnostic, and he rejects the entire Christian theology of the resurrection, ascension, and salvation. In fact, the historical Christ is insignificant in his thinking. He becomes pantheistic, and views God as Reason, the order of the universe. For Winstanley, as for the Quakers, this all-pervading truth is revealed by an inner light, the Voice of God. Study and scholarship are secondary if not outright negative in effecting this revelation.

From this inner voice and his radical perception of the universe developed Winstanley's communism, first expressed in *The New Law of Righteousness* (1649). By this time, he was involved in practising his beliefs. On 1 April 1649, in a small party led by William Everard, he began to cultivate the common lands on St. George's Hill, near Walton-on-Thames, Surrey. Winstanley soon assumed the leadership of this group,

known as Diggers, which refused to recognize private property in land and believed that it was beginning a peaceful revolution that would win converts by reason; soon, all England would be cultivated by the people for themselves. Converts spread the word in other parts, and before long this community had swollen to fifty members, others springing up in nearby counties. This initial success was perhaps aided by the extremely high price of food at this time. But the landlords were not passive in the face of this threat. They destroyed the crops of the Diggers, using mob violence, and by March 1650 the Commonwealth troops had finished the dispersal of the St. George's Hill community.

Winstanley now produced a stream of pamphlets addressed to the City, the Army, and Parliament, describing the actions and principles of the Diggers, who called themselves the True Levellers. In 1652 he wrote his last, most mature work, *The Law of Freedom in a Platform*, which he dedicated to Cromwell. In this he sketches a communist society and the logical and mystical justification for it. For Winstanley, as for the ordinary Levellers, the Civil War had been fought against the 'Norman power' of the King, lawyers, clergy, and especially gentry, whom he describes as the descendants of the Norman invaders exploiting the peasantry, children of the Anglo-Saxons. Now that victory has been achieved, he says, its fruits are to be enjoyed by the abolition of money and of private ownership in land.

In Winstanley's eyes, the only just society was one based on co-operation. To him, contemporary Christian religion, no matter how radical, served to maintain the class society, and presented men with heaven and hell-fire as distractions from their earthly needs. In the place of sermons and services, he suggested lectures on history, the constitution, and science.

Like the Fifth Monarchists, Winstanley was firmly convinced of the imminent Second Coming. But for him Christ was 'the spreading power of light' – the Reason of his communism peacefully conquering the world and bringing to an end all war and government.

After 1652, this remarkable man all but passes from view. In 1660 he was reported to be living in Cobham and was probably well off. There is no record of his death.

G. H. Sabine (ed.), *Works* (Ithaca, N.Y., 1941).
L. D. Hamilton, *Selections from the Works of Gerrard Winstanley* (1944).
L. H. Berens, *The Digger Movement* (1906).
E. Bernstein, *Cromwell and Communism* (1930).
D. W. Petegorsky, *Left-Wing Democracy in the English Civil War* (1949).

Winthrop, John (1588–1649), governor of Massachusetts.

Born on 12 January 1588, at Edwardstone, Suffolk, the son of Adam Winthrop, a lawyer and landowner, Winthrop was educated at Trinity College, Cambridge, from 1602 to 1605.

John Winthrop underwent a religious experience during his studies in Cambridge, which were cut short when, at the age of seventeen, he married and settled on his wife's estate. His religion became a Puritanism plagued by guilt and morbidity, and only developed into a calmer piety, through which he could give rein to his gentleness and kindness, after he had married his third wife in 1618.

In 1613 Winthrop had entered Gray's Inn and had begun a thriving legal practice. Once he resolved his religious problems, he spread his energies into other fields, becoming active in local affairs and gaining recognition as a natural leader among the Puritan gentry. But in 1629, when Charles I dissolved Parliament, arresting Eliot and beginning eleven years of personal rule, Winthrop saw a catastrophic future for England. His gloomy outlook was probably compounded by the death of his mother and the bad state of his financial affairs. After a brief sojourn in Rotterdam, where he had fled to escape religious persecution, he turned his gaze to the colonies, and when the newly formed Massachusetts Bay Company agreed to transfer its general court and charter to New England, he pledged himself, along with other Puritan gentlemen, to emigrate with his family. On those terms he was elected governor, and in 1630 he sailed across the Atlantic, where his expedition increased the size of the nascent Salem colony sevenfold.

Upon arrival, Winthrop drew up a Church covenant and settled on the peninsula that was soon to house Boston. As governor, he won a reputation for justice, competence, and honesty. In 1631, with his concurrence, the general court took the momentous step of tying participation in political life to membership in one of the recognized Puritan congregations, thus cementing the basis of the Massachusetts theocracy. In the same year Winthrop's son John (1606–76) joined him in the colony: he was to be one of his father's most valued assistants and another of the leading men of the Puritan settlement.

Winthrop remained a magistrate for all 18 years until his death, often serving as governor and dedicating both his energies and money to the growing colony. During this long career he underwent another transformation that left him a narrower and more intolerant Puritan. In 1636 he was officially rebuked for leniency as a magistrate, a reprimand in which the clergy played a large part.

Henceforth, he was unable to withstand pressures from the ministers and displayed a harder attitude towards religious dissent, such as the Antinomiarism of Anne Hutchinson (1637).

As governor, Winthrop could also act more constructively. In 1638 it was his skill that preserved the colony's charter from the demands of the commissioners for plantations. And in 1643 a limited confederacy of New England settlements, long sought by him, was finally achieved. The last years of his life he spent as governor, and he died on 26 March 1649, leaving behind in his journal one of the most valuable sources of colonial history.

James K. Hosmer (ed.), *Winthrop's Journal: History of New England, 1630–1649* (2 vols.; New York, 1908).

Edmund S. Morgan, *The Puritan Dilemma: the Story of John Winthrop* (Boston, Mass., 1958).

Wood, Anthony (1632–95), self-styled 'Anthony à Wood', antiquary and historian of the city and university of Oxford.

Wood was born in Merton Street, Oxford, on 17 December 1632. At the age of eight he was sent to New College School, transferring later to Thame Grammar School. Wood's father died in 1643 and, after the move to Thame, his education was further disrupted by the Civil War, during which Oxford became Charles I's capital. His elder brother Edward, who was a student at Trinity College, now became his tutor. His mother wanted him to take a trade, but this, as he tells us, was something 'which he could never endure to hear of.' Instead, he took on a university education, entering Merton College, just across the road from his home, in 1647, and becoming postmaster there.

Wood was a lazy and unenterprising student, preferring music, ploughing, and bellringing to his academic studies. It was five years before he was examined for the degree of B.A. He was then allowed access to the Bodleian Library and proceeded to take an M.A. in 1655. In the same year his brother died and Wood was led to undertake the pious act of editing some sermons left by him.

A sense of purpose was at last injected into Wood's life by the appearance in 1656 of *Antiquities of Warwickshire* by William Dugdale. The book impressed Wood greatly, and he resolved to produce a similar work for his home county of Oxfordshire. In the event, he devoted his researches to the city of Oxford and its university and colleges. He was given free access to records and manuscripts, including university registers and (in 1660) the archive collection of the antiquary Brian Twyne. He systematically copied monumental inscriptions from the city and the surrounding district, and engaged assiduously in historical studies.

The result of his labours was a history of the University and Colleges of Oxford, which through the patronage of John Fell, the Dean of Christ Church, was brought to the recently founded press of the Sheldonian Theatre. Fell (who later became Bishop of Oxford and was the subject of Thomas Brown's parody-translation of one of Martial's epigrams, beginning 'I do not love thee, Dr. Fell') had Wood's work translated into Latin; it appeared in 1674 under the title *Historia et Antiquitates Universitatis Oxoniensis* (History and Antiquities of Oxford University).

During the period spent compiling his history, Wood seems to have developed into an unpleasant character. Full of his own importance in carrying out his monumental task, he frequently quarrelled with his associates, his family, and his patrons. Becoming more and more estranged, he was made to feel further isolated and suspicious by the onset of deafness, which sharpened both his temper and his prejudices.

Early in his historical researches he received much help from various scholars and laymen in Oxford and also gained assistance in London, where he was allowed to inspect archives kept in the Tower and in the library of Sir Robert Cotton. In the 1660s, however, he took to the life of a recluse, living like a hermit in a garret at his home in Merton Street, with occasional visits to the Bodleian and trips elsewhere in Oxford necessitated by his researches.

After the appearance of the *Historia et Antiquitates*, Wood embarked, with financial help from Ralph Sheldon and aid in research from such people as John Aubrey (q.v.), upon the compilation of a biographical dictionary of writers and ecclesiastics associated with Oxford. The resulting work, published in 1691–92, was *Athenae Oxonienses*. This work, which chronicles the lives of Oxford worthies in the period 1500–1690, is seriously marred by the incursions of Wood's own petulant character. His temper had by no means improved and the book betrays his spiteful prejudices and exhibits his uncharitable tendency to fail to make allowances for the testimony of disaffected correspondents. Nowhere does he adequately acknowledge his debt to his patrons and contributors; to Aubrey he seems especially ungrateful, and his peevishness annoyed Sheldon.

The publication of the *Athenae Oxonienses* occasioned a legal battle. Henry Hyde, 2nd Earl of Clarendon, brought a libel case for defamation of his father (see Hyde, Edward), whom Wood, on information supplied by Aubrey, had accused of corruption during his time as lord chancellor. Wood was convicted in

1693 and expelled from the university, an event which served to embitter him even more than before. Yet he continued his researches in the teeth of attacks from such men as Burnet (q.v.), compiling material for an appendix to the *Athenae*. After a short illness, he died on 29 November 1695, and was buried in the chapel of St. John the Baptist, Merton College, this being the only recognition accorded him by the University.

Wood's researches were extensive, and the amount of collected material was so enormous that he added to his biographies in the *Athenae Oxonienses* the *Fasti*, or annals, of the university for the same period. His manuscripts and papers, including diaries (for 1657–95) and an autobiography, were bequeathed to the library of the Ashmolean Museum.

As a writer, Wood suffered some adverse criticism during his lifetime. As Thomas Barlow, Bishop of Lincoln, observed, in the *Historia et Antiquitates*, 'not only the Latin but the history itself is in many things ridiculously false.' Undoubtedly the translation was full of gross errors, and Wood's original English version is faulty and lacks literary style. Yet his works in general, including the whole mass of material left unpublished at his death, constitute an extremely valuable detailed source of information concerning life in Oxford University in the 17th century.

In 1761 William Huddersford, keeper of the Ashmolean, published a catalogue of the Wood bequest. The English version of the *Historia et Antiquitates*, edited by John Gutch, appeared as *The History and Antiquities of the Colleges and Halls in the University of Oxford, with a continuation* (2 vols.; 1786–90) and *The History and Antiquities of the University of Oxford* (3 vols.; 1792–96). The *Athenae Oxonienses* appeared in a scholarly edition by

P. Bliss (4 vols.; 1813–20). To these must be added Andrew Clark's superb editions for the Oxford Historical Society, both of the *Survey of the Antiquities of the City of Oxford . . .* (3 vols.; 1889–99), and of Wood's diaries and autobiography, under the title *The Life and Times of Anthony Wood, Antiquary of Oxford, 1632–1695, described by himself* (5 vols.; 1891–1900).

Wotton, Sir Henry (1568–1639), poet, diplomat, and schoolmaster.

Born on 30 March 1568, on his father's estates at Boughton Malherbe, Kent, Wotton was educated at Winchester and New College, Oxford, where he acquired a B.A. in 1588 and where he struck up a lifelong friendship with John Donne.

After leaving Oxford he set out on a protracted tour of Europe, and in the event spent most of the next thirty-six years of his life abroad. In 1594, while he was in France, he became an agent for the ambitious Earl of Essex (see Devereux, Robert, 2nd Earl, in *Lives of the Tudor Age*), supplying the earl with information about the activities of foreign courts. He also wrote a survey of the politics of contemporary Europe, *The State of Christendom*, which was not published until eighteen years after his death. Wotton was in London at the time of Essex's fall, but left hastily to take up residence in Italy, at first in Venice and later in Florence. It was, apparently, the discovery in Florence of a supposed plot to poison James VI of Scotland, heir to the English throne, that brought Wotton back to the British Isles in 1602. Travelling under an assumed name via Sweden, he brought warning of the supposed plot and a collection of Italian antidotes to poison to the King in Stirling. He was warmly received, and a year later, after James

had set up court in London, Wotton again returned to Britain, on this occasion to receive a knighthood and to be made ambassador to Venice, a post that he held intermittently for nearly twenty years (1604–12, 1616–19, and 1621–24). Between assignments, he served for a spell as M.P. for Appleby (1614–16), and was employed in negotiations over several complex European squabbles. On the death of Lord Salisbury (see Cecil, Robert, in *Lives of the Tudor Age*) in 1612 he had held some hopes of higher preferment, but these were dashed, at least in part because of a reputation for being an incorrigible liar, a reputation probably founded on an indiscretion committed eight years before, when he had facetiously defined an ambassador as 'a good man sent abroad to lie for his country'. The solemn and credulous Scots King was gravely offended by Wotton's 'merriment' on finding out about it eight years after the event.

While at court, Wotton had been greatly smitten with the beauty of the King's daughter, Elizabeth (q.v.). He wrote one of his best-known poems in praise of her (*You meaner Beauties of the Night*) and remained devoted to her until his death: he even attempted to use his diplomatic influence, without any perceptible effect, on her behalf just before her husband lost the throne of Bohemia and the Palatinate.

Throughout his life Wotton was beset by money troubles and, when early in 1624 he returned home for good, he found himself in desperate need of employment. Hoping for a job as court architect, he published a tract expressing his views on the subject, *The Elements of Architecture*, which is clearly influenced by his thorough knowledge of Venice. Fortunately, he was successful in applying for a more suitable job, namely the provostship of Eton. In addition, in 1630

477

he was granted a pension of £500 p.a. to write a history of England.

Wotton remained at Eton for the rest of his life and by all accounts was a conscientious schoolmaster, though he never finished his history of England, nor indeed any of the other literary works upon which he embarked. He died at Eton in December 1639 and was buried in the college chapel.

His papers, collected in 1651 as *Reliquiae Wottonianae*, provide some useful insights into the politics, diplomacy, art, and science of the period by an inquisitive and perceptive observer, while as a poet, though not of major importance, he is noticeable for an ability to write in several different styles. He has a dry sense of humour, and in the much-praised *Character of a Happy Life* he demonstrates skill in dressing up a platitude; but perhaps his best poems are those written on a particular event – his sickness, a general plague, or the fall of a great earl:

> No man marks the narrow space
> 'Twixt a prison and a smile.

J. Hannah (ed.), *Poems by Henry Wotton and Others* (1845).
F. Hard (ed.), *The Elements of Architecture* (1968).
Logan Pearsall Smith, *The Life and Letters of Henry Wotton* (2 vols.; 1907).

Portraits: oil, full-length, by unknown artist: N.P.G.; oil, by unknown artist: Eton College, Bucks.; oil, by Cornelius Johnson: Bodleian Library, Oxford.

Wray, John (1628–1705), see Ray, John.

Wren, Sir Christopher (1632–1723), architect, mathematician, and astronomer.

Wren was born on 20 October 1632 at East Knoyle, Wiltshire, son of the Rev. Christopher Wren, then the local rector but later Dean of Windsor. In 1642 the nine-year-old Christopher, delicate and small for his age, was sent to Westminster School to study under the celebrated Dr. Busby. But the Civil War soon brought ruin to his orthodox Anglican family: Parliamentary troops sacked his father's Windsor deanery, and his uncle Matthew, Bishop of Ely, was imprisoned in the Tower. The Wrens eventually took refuge with a relative, William Holder, an Oxfordshire vicar and a skilled mathematician, who taught Christopher arithmetic, geometry, and astronomy, and so introduced him to the practical scientific experiments that were to engross him until his early thirties.

Wren entered Wadham College, Oxford, in 1649 and joined a group of gifted scientists which included the physicist Robert Boyle (q.v.) and the astronomer Rooke. 'Invincibly armed against the enchantments of enthusiasm', they had spurned the troubled politics of the times to pursue the 'new experimental learning'. Wren's chief interest at this time was astronomy, and he made original use of geometry to solve some of its traditional problems, particularly comets, eclipses, and Saturn's rings. In addition, he built working anatomical models for the surgeon Scarburgh, investigated blood transfusion, and collaborated with Boyle in designing a barometer.

In 1653 Wren took his M.A. and was immediately elected a fellow of All Souls. In 1657 he succeeded Rooke as professor of astronomy at Gresham College, London, where his rooms became the meeting-place of an 'experimental philosophical club' made up of the prominent scientists of the time. Wren returned to Oxford in 1661, to receive his doctorate and the post of Savilian professor of astronomy. The informal club of his Gresham days had just been officially chartered as the Royal Society.

Though only 29, Wren was now one of the most famous scientists in the country, and was described by Isaac Barrow as 'a miracle, nay, even something superhuman'.

The common factor behind Wren's apparently diffuse researches was his intense interest in the practical application of science, as demonstrated by his gift for devising models with which to put his theories to the test. Architectural design is a logical progression from model-making; hence Wren's appointment in 1663, at the King's instigation, to the commission for repairing old St. Paul's caused little comment: in the seventeenth century, architecture was not yet considered as a distinct profession, but rather as an extension of mathematics.

Wren's influential family was responsible for his first architectural commission: in 1663 his uncle Matthew, once again Bishop of Ely after eighteen years in the Tower, asked him to design a new chapel for Pembroke College, Cambridge. The result, a somewhat unimaginative reworking of a Serlio design with the addition of some motifs designed by Inigo Jones (q.v.), nevertheless displays impressive competence for a first attempt at architecture. In 1664 Archbishop Sheldon asked Wren to design a theatre to house academic ceremonies at Oxford. Wren's response, the Sheldonian Theatre, typically combines the engineer's and scholar's approach. For the exterior, he closely followed Vitruvius's description of the theatre of Marcellus, but added a roof in deference to the English climate. Within, he wished to avoid supporting columns, so he asked his friend Wallis, Oxford professor of geometry, to design a concealed wooden truss to sustain this roof.

In 1665–66 Wren made his sole trip abroad, to Paris. There he met Bernini and the leading French architects, Mansart and Le Vau, and also viewed the Louvre and Louis XIV's building projects at Versailles and Fontainebleau. The French design books Wren brought home with him thereafter inspired a more cosmopolitan strain in his work.

On 27 August 1666, the ecclesiastical authorities accepted Wren's emergency scheme to prevent the decayed old St. Paul's Cathedral from collapsing by rather awkwardly placing over its crossing a dome similar to that of St. Peter's, Rome. Unfortunately, six days later the cathedral, together with much of the remainder of the City of London, was devastated by fire. Adaptable as ever, on 12 September, only four days after the flames died down, Wren put before the King a plan for the complete reconstruction of the City. But London's commercial life could not spare the time needed to build Wren's spacious avenues and piazzas, so the city grew up again on its medieval street-plan.

However, some kind of overall coordination was obviously required, so

Wren, Roger Pratt, and Hugh May were commissioned to survey the entire City, and their recommendations were embodied in the 1667 Rebuilding Act, which made brick construction thereafter compulsory and also stipulated minimum wall thicknesses and floor heights. In 1668 Wren reached the summit of his official career when, thanks to royal favour, he was appointed surveyor general against stiff competition. An immense task confronted him: of London's public buildings, St. Paul's Cathedral, the Royal Exchange, the Guildhall, forty-five companies' halls, and over fifty churches had to be rebuilt. Wren is credited with at least thirty-six of the companies' halls, but it is the fifty-one London churches he designed that best demonstrate his strengths and weaknesses as an architect.

There were few domestic precedents for the suitable ground plan for a classical church, so Wren adopted the simple but flexible shape of the Roman basilica as described by Vitruvius. St. Magnus Martyr exemplifies its unadorned basic form, without galleries or transepts. Unfortunately, the sites Wren had to build on were frequently so irregularly shaped that he usually had to elaborate his basilica, for example into a Greek cross as at St. Mary Athill or into the strange polygon of St. Benet Fink. At St. Clement Danes and St. James Piccadilly, Wren developed the galleried nave to produce in effect a two-storey basilica; he himself considered this 'the ideal town church'. The grand St. Stephen Walbrook, built for the wealthy Grocers' Company, is Wren's first attempt to reconcile a dome with an aisled nave, and a foretaste of his problems with St. Paul's.

Wren's towers and spires are equally ingenious, ranging from the pastiche Perpendicular of St. Mary Alderman-bury, through St. Mary-le-Bow's Gothic motifs on a classical framework, to the straightforward baroque of St. Vedast. Interiors were the responsibility of individual parishes, but fortunately most of the craftsmen employed were competent practitioners of the then current Anglo-Dutch woodworking style. External detail on the churches is often crude, but this is hardly noticeable in their usual hemmed-in sites. Wren simply had no time to supervise every stonemason, possibly because he was continually assailed by parishes trying to extract more money from him. The churches were financed by taxing all coal coming into London, and Wren had considerable say in how the proceeds were distributed. To have designed fifty churches was a gigantic achievement, yet the many failures amongst them suggest that Wren still approached architecture with the empirical and intellectual approach of the geometrician, rather than with an assured overall aesthetic.

In 1669, soon after the fire-damaged ruins of old St. Paul's had finally collapsed, Dean Sancroft invited designs for a new cathedral, to be a credit to 'the City and the Nation'. Wren's first offering was a modest structure, distinguished mainly by its rectangular choir with a domed vestibule, reminiscent of the Temple church. Although this was duly approved by the King, Wren, obviously inspired by the great domed churches of Italy and France, went on to produce the drastically revised Great Model of 1673. This centrally planned church, on a Greek cross groundplan but with a western extension, had a domed crossing supported on eight columns. Opinion was divided: the 'connoisseurs and critics' considered the design intellectually satisfying, but Dean Sancroft and the churchgoing public, mindful of the processional element in Anglican worship, demanded a long nave leading up to the choir. Despite such controversy Wren was knighted in 1673. He duly reverted to a medieval groundplan with his 1675 Warrant Design, a bizarre Gothic paraphrase having a slender dome with a spire on top. This proved to be the final and authorized version, but during construction it was modified beyond recognition. Wren exercised great ingenuity in designing the dome: to harmonize its internal and external appearance, he devised three superimposed domes, with massive screen walls to conceal the flying buttresses needed to support them. Building dragged on for decades, and in 1697, when the dome and entire west front were still unfinished, Wren was put on half pay to hurry him up.

However dissatisfied Wren may have felt at this treatment, he could at least console himself with having been president of the Royal Society (1681–83) and designer of some ambitious secular buildings for the Crown. Chelsea Hospital, begun in 1682, is in essence simply a barracks arranged around three sides of a courtyard, but Wren's gigantic Doric order unifying the composition foreshadows Vanbrugh, and the shape of Chelsea set the style for hospital and almshouse design for decades. In 1689 Queen Mary decided to rebuild completely Wolsey's long-neglected Hampton Court palace, so Wren submitted a design centred around two courtyards, with massive corner pavilions and restless silhouette recalling Le Vau's work at the Louvre. But this was rejected and instead Wren, obviously under constraint, rebuilt only a portion of the palace, with a uniform skyline and mechanical fenestration producing a monotonous flatness reminiscent of Mansart's Versailles. For Mary's projected Greenwich Hospital (1694), Wren offered another inventive scheme, for receding and ever-narrowing courtyards, with a domed building to close the vista, but once again it was rejected, in favour of a compromise arrangement that framed Inigo Jones's elegant but relatively small Queen's House.

Amidst all this activity Wren found time to be M.P. for Plympton (1685–87) and Weymouth (1701–02). His private life seems to have been relatively uneventful. In 1669 he married Faith Coghill of Bletchingdon, where he had spent much of his youth, and after her death in 1675 he was married again (1677) to Jane Fitzwilliam, who bore him a son and a daughter. From the 1690s on, the ageing architect was assisted in his surveyorship by Vanbrugh, Hawksmoor (qq.v.), and others, giving rise to some stylistic inconsistencies in his later buildings, and in 1718 the 85-year-old Wren was dismissed as a result of court intrigues.

Sir Christopher Wren died on 23 February 1723, and was buried in his own St. Paul's Cathedral, with the famous epitaph *Si monumentum requiris, circumspice* ('If you seek a monument, look about you'). His dispassionate and intellectual style, placing order and clarity of conception above applied ornament and extravagant asymmetry, and his intelligent reworking of French and Italian prototypes were chiefly responsible for the classical style of architecture taking firm root in Britain.

A. T. Bolton and H. D. Hendry (eds.), *Wren Society Publications* (1924–43).

E. J. Enthoven, *The Life and Works of Sir Christopher Wren* (1903), being in part a reprint of the *Parentalia: or Memoirs of the Family of the Wrens* (1750), by Wren's son, also Christopher Wren.

E. F. Sekler, *Wren and His Place in European Architecture* (1956).

Sir John N. Summerson, *Sir Christopher Wren* (1953, reprinted 1965).

G. F. Webb, *Wren* (1937).

Portraits: oil, three-quarter length, by Kneller, 1711: N.P.G.; ivory, by D. Le Marchand, *c.* 1723: N.P.G.

Wycherley, William (?1640–1716), playwright and poet.

Born at Clive, Shropshire, the family seat since 1410, Wycherley was the eldest son of Daniel Wycherley, a Treasury official who later became steward to the Marquis of Winchester. Nothing is known of Wycherley's early years, but at the age of fifteen he was sent to live in western France, probably at Saintonge. There he managed to charm Voltaire's friend, Madame de Montausier, who called him her 'little Huguenot' until he became converted to Catholicism. In 1659 Wycherley took up residence at the Queen's College, Oxford, but left soon after, having in the mean time been persuaded to revert to Protestantism. He was already enrolled in the Inner Temple, but for Wycherley law and scholarship quickly paled before the prospect of a London socialite's life. Over forty years later he boasted to Pope that he had written two of his best plays before he was 21; since both

are obviously the work of a mature talent, this was probably an old man's vanity.

Wycherley's first play, *Love in a Wood*, was staged in the spring of 1671, and its extravagantly satirical characterization, in particular the hypocritical Alderman Gripe and the husband-hungry Lady Flippant, brought it immediate popularity. The witty dialogue and plentiful innuendo were much appreciated at court. One day in Pall Mall the Duchess of Cleveland (see Villiers, Barbara), Charles II's mistress, recognized Wycherley and hailed him with a coarse allusion to *Love in a Wood*. Thereafter the playwright cultivated this slight acquaintance to the point where they apparently became lovers; the duchess is said to have often stolen out of the palace disguised as a peasant girl to visit Wycherley's chambers at the Temple. The Duke of Buckingham (see Villiers, George, 2nd Duke) was so disarmed by Wycherley that in 1672 he made him a lieutenant in his infantry regiment.

Wycherley's next play, *The Gentleman Dancing Master*, first performed in early 1672, was 'liked but indifferently' and only ran for six days. Its central idea, that of a young girl disguising her lover as a dancing teacher to outwit her suspicious father, was adapted from Calderon's *El Maestro de Danzar*, but Wycherley's comedy of errors has an individual lightheartedness and lack of cynicism that makes it one of his most attractive plays.

In contrast, *The Country Wife*, produced in 1673, was as coarse and sardonic as it was lively, though Steele later pointed out that the rakish Horner did no more than practise the morality of his time. Once again the plot, concerning the jealous Pinchwife's attempts to shield his gullible young wife from the wicked world, was borrowed, this time from Molière's *L'École des Femmes*.

The Plain Dealer, first seen at Lincoln's Inn in 1674, was described by Dryden as 'one of the most bold, most general, and most useful satires which has ever been presented in the English theatre.' Molière provided the play's basic inspiration but, as Voltaire remarked, Wycherley's mocking tone is very different from the French playwright's warmhearted comedy. Certainly, the chief characters, especially the 'honest surly' sea captain, Manly, are fierce caricatures, but the subplot, dealing with the litigious exploits of widow Blackacre, is in a more kindly vein.

This was Wycherley's last play, for in 1678 he fell seriously ill, and although Charles II gave him £500 and sent him off to Montpelier to convalesce, the dramatist never fully recovered. However, in the following year the King offered Wycherley the job of tutor to his son the Duke of Richmond, at the enormous salary of £1,500 a year. Wycherley was about to accept, when he had another lucky encounter. One day in a Tunbridge Wells bookshop he overheard Laetitia, Countess of Drogheda and a rich young widow, asking for a copy of *The Plain Dealer*. He introduced himself, and after some sedulous wooing finally persuaded her to marry him in 1680. The court disapproved of this *mésalliance*, so Wycherley kept away, only to find himself accused of ingratitude.

Laetitia was so jealous that whenever Wycherley crossed the street from their house to drink at the Cock Tavern opposite she insisted that he leave a window open so that she could check that he was not consorting with other women. She died in 1681, leaving her husband a considerable fortune, but legal expenses were so enormous that Wycherley was thrown into the debtors' jail. Since neither his father nor his publisher would help him, he remained in distress for seven years, until James II, impressed by *The Plain Dealer*, paid his debts and gave him a £200 pension.

Wycherley now retired to his birthplace at Clive, 'a humble hermit', though he often visited London to meet Dryden (q.v.) and other writers at Will's coffeehouse. His father's death in 1697 only created more problems, for Wycherley was not allowed to raise money on the estate. However, he carried on writing and is credited with the anonymous *A Vindication of the Stage* (1698), which defended Congreve (q.v.) against Jeremy Collier's attack.

In his old age Wycherley had taken to writing poetry, and in 1704 published *Miscellany Poems*. They did not help him financially, since the printer went bankrupt, but they inspired his extraordinary friendship with the sixteen-year-old Alexander Pope (see *Lives of the Georgian Age*), whom he nicknamed 'my little infallible'. Wycherley corresponded frequently with the confident young writer, permitting him to edit his later poems drastically before publication. But by about 1711 the friendship had cooled, mainly because Wycherley disliked Pope's proposal that his poetry should be recast as prose, and also because of satirical references to himself in Pope's *Essay on Criticism*. In 1735 Pope published their correspondence, skilfully edited to emphasize his own precocity; he claimed they had become estranged because he found Wycherley 'not grave enough or consistent enough'.

Wycherley's mind was certainly failing; he read Montaigne or Seneca at night, and next morning would write a mediocre poem incorporating these authors' thoughts. But Wycherley played one last joke. His nephew was his sole heir, but Wycherley disapproved of his 'ill-carriage' and resolved to deprive him of the inheritance by re-marrying as soon as it became obvious he was dying. Hence, on 20 December 1715, the senile dramatist married the young and virtuous Elizabeth Jackson and died at his London house eleven days later.

Montague Summers (ed.), *The Complete Works of William Wycherley* (4 vols.; 1924).

W. Connely, *Brawny Wycherley* (New York, 1930).

C. Perromat, *William Wycherley: sa vie, son oeuvre* (Paris, 1921).

Portrait: oil, quarter-length, after Lely (?), *c.* 1668: N.P.G.

Y

Yeardley, Sir George (?1580–1627), English governor of Virginia (1618–21 and 1626–27).

George Yeardley was the son of Ralph Yeardley, a merchant taylor of London. He served as an officer of the English army in the Low Countries, and in June 1609 he sailed for Virginia as captain of the guard for the new colonists. They were shipwrecked in the Bermudas and eventually reached Virginia in May, 1610. Yeardley was appointed to the council of the colony in 1611, and in April 1616 became acting governor for Sir Thomas Dale, who was returning to England. Yeardley seems to have made a firm impression on the colony during his short tenure of the post. He relaxed some of the severities of government practised by Dale, and under him the colony apparently began to prosper. However, in May 1617 Yeardley was replaced as governor, and the following year he returned to England.

As a result of his success as deputy, Yeardley was commissioned as governor of Virginia in November, 1618. On the 24th of that month, he was knighted at Newmarket by James I. Yeardley reached Jamestown in April 1619, and soon began to implement the instructions of the Virginia Company to set up a system of land division and to call an assembly of planters once a year. A small assembly – the first colonial representative assembly – met in a church at Jamestown on 30 July 1619. The following year a Dutch ship landed twenty Negro slaves in Virginia, the first brought into the English colonies.

In 1621 Yeardley asked that he might be relieved, so that he could devote his time to private business affairs. He was replaced by Sir Francis Wyatt, but remained a member of the council. When Virginia was made a crown colony in 1625, Yeardley was sent to England to request the King to allow Virginia to keep her representative government. He returned in April 1626 to Jamestown with a commission as royal governor to succeed Wyatt. Yeardley remained in office until his death in 1627, when the colonists of Virginia wrote a glowing letter to the Privy Council in praise of his virtues.

Nora Miller, *George Yeardley, Governor of Virginia* (Richmond, Va., 1959).

York, Duchess of (1637–71), see Hyde, Anne.

York, Duke of (1633–1701), see James II.

INDEX

Where more than one reference is given, **bold type** indicates a main entry

CLASSIFIED INDEX

MEDICINE
Arbuthnot, John
Bastwick, John
Browne, Sir Thomas
Harvey, William
Radcliffe, John
Sydenham, Thomas
Willis, Thomas

MERCHANTS
Cokayne, Sir William
Courten, Sir William
Cranfield, Lionel, 1st Earl of Middlesex

MUSICIANS
Blow, John
Byrd, William
Clarke, Jeremiah
Gibbons, Christopher
Gibbons, Orlando
Humfrey, Pelham
Lawes, Henry
Lawes, William
Locke, Matthew
Purcell, Henry
Tomkins, Thomas
Tudway, Thomas
Wilbye, John

NATURALISTS
Ray, John
Willughby, Francis

PHILOSOPHERS
Digby, Sir Kenelm
Herbert, Edward, Baron Herbert of Cher-
  bury
Hobbes, Thomas
Locke, John

POLITICIANS
Argyll, Archibald Campbell, 1st Duke of
Arlington, 1st Earl of
Ashley, 1st Baron, of Wimborne
Bacon, Francis, Baron Verulam
Baltimore, Cecilius Calvert, 2nd Baron
Baltimore, George Calvert, 1st Baron
Bennet, Henry, 1st Earl of Arlington
Bentinck, William, 1st Earl of Portland
Berry-Godfrey, Sir Edmund
Bolingbroke, 1st Viscount
Boyle, Richard, 1st Earl of Cork
Boyle, Roger, 1st Baron Broghill and 1st
  Earl of Orrery

Breadalbane, 1st Earl of
Bristol, George Digby, 2nd Earl of
Buckingham, 1st Duke of
Buckingham, 2nd Duke of
Calvert, George, 1st Baron Baltimore
Campbell, Archibald, 1st Duke of Argyll
Campbell, John, 1st Earl of Breadalbane
Carlisle, Charles Howard, 3rd Earl of
Cary, Lucius, 2nd Viscount Falkland
Cecil, Robert, 1st Earl of Salisbury
Churchill, John, 1st Duke of Marlborough
Clarendon, 1st Earl of
Clifford, Thomas, 1st Baron Clifford of
  Chudleigh
Colepeper, John, 1st Baron Colepeper
Cooper, Anthony Ashley, 1st Earl of Shaftes-
  bury
Cromwell, Oliver
Cromwell, Richard
Danby, 1st Earl of
De Witt, John
Digby, George, 2nd Earl of Bristol
Douglas, James, 4th Earl of Morton
Eliot, Sir John
Fiennes, Nathaniel
Fiennes, William, 1st Viscount Saye and Sele
Finch, Daniel, 2nd Earl of Nottingham and
  6th Earl of Winchilsea
Finch, Heneage, 1st Earl of Nottingham
Finch, Sir John, Baron Finch of Fordwich
Godfrey, Sir Edmund Berry
Godolphin, Sidney, 1st Earl of Godolphin
Halifax, 1st Marquis of
Hamilton, James, 3rd Marquis and 1st Duke
  of Hamilton
Hampden, John
Harley, Robert, 1st Earl of Oxford
Hesilrige, Sir Arthur
Holles, Denzil, 1st Baron Holles
Howard, Charles, 3rd Earl of Carlisle
Hyde, Edward, 1st Earl of Clarendon
Inchiquin, Murrough O'Brien, 1st Earl of
Ireton, Henry
Lauderdale, John Maitland, 2nd Earl and 1st
  Duke of
Leeds, 1st Duke of
Ludlow, Edmund
Maitland, John, 2nd Earl and 1st Duke of
  Lauderdale
Middleton, Charles, 2nd Earl of Middleton
Mompesson, Sir Giles
Montagu, Charles, 1st Earl of Halifax